Planning the Twentieth-Century American City

Planning the Twentieth-Century American City

Edited by

MARY CORBIN SIES and

CHRISTOPHER SILVER

The Johns Hopkins University Press

Baltimore and London

Published in cooperation with the Center for American Places,
Santa Fe, New Mexico, and Harrisonburg, Virginia

© 1996 The Johns Hopkins University Press
All rights reserved. Published 1996
Printed in the United States of America on acid-free paper
9 8 7 6 5 4 3 2

The Johns Hopkins University Press
2715 North Charles Street
Baltimore, Maryland 21218-4363
www.press.jhu.edu

Library of Congress Cataloging-in-Publication Data

Planning the twentieth-century American city / edited by Mary Corbin Sies and
    Christopher Silver.
        p.   cm.
    Includes bibliographical references and index.
    ISBN 0-8018-5163-7 (acid-free paper).—ISBN 0-8018-5164-5 (pbk.: acid-free
paper)
    1. City planning—United States—History—20th century. I. Sies, Mary Corbin.
II. Silver, Christopher, 1951–
HT167.P557   1996
307.1´216´09730904—dc20   95-22859

A catalog record for this book is available from the British Library.

Contents

Contents

Contents

Contents

Contents

Preface and Acknowledgments

In the mid-1980s planning history and urban history experienced a dynamic convergence. Heralded in 1985 by a special symposium in the *Journal of the American Planning Association*, this creative fusion of interests and methodologies sparked a decade of study of the planning and shaping of America's urban places. From this exchange has come a more interdisciplinary approach to history and a more instrumental history itself. Scholars sharing and applying techniques, insights, and problematics from neighboring fields or disciplines have altered the basic definitions of planning and contributed to a greater understanding of both the planning process and its impact on specific neighborhoods, regions, or communities. Daniel Schaffer's edited volume *Two Centuries of American Planning*, published in 1988 by the Johns Hopkins University Press, presented the first intellectual products of the coalescence between urban and planning history. The present anthology showcases the more complex and contextually grounded research that has issued from this marriage.

Planning the Twentieth-Century American City should be of interest to a diverse audience: all those students, scholars, planners, and citizens concerned with the social, economic, and spatial dimensions of modern metropolitan America. It should provide useful food for thought for political, urban, planning, and architectural historians; urban geographers; urban studies scholars; historic preservationists; and urban policy makers. Above all, it is intended to meet the needs of planning students and practitioners. As a result, the discussions move well beyond the institutional framework of twentieth-century planning to the contexts in which the planning process unfolds in a given urban place. In other words, the studies here constitute a practical history of planning that can inform the decisions of practitioners and policy makers alike. The chapters that follow investigate planning systematically in order to understand it and how it has affected and sometimes failed the nation's cities in changing ways throughout the twentieth century.

One result of these inquiries is that the definition of planning has had to be expanded, for the authors have found that professional planning did not follow a straight and single path in its evolution, nor does it encompass only the activities of professional planners. Rather, planning includes a broad range of actors and actions that have historically shaped urban development. This realization, a positive consequence of the collaboration between urban and planning historians, is at the heart of this book. Thus the authors investigate a wide range of cities, planners, and intellectual and popular influences to find out how planning and development operated. They furnish several new case studies of the social, economic, bureaucratic, and political factors that influenced planning in a given locale. They also examine the effects of specific values, assumptions, and planning or urban policy discourses on the development of the twentieth-century built environment. In addition, several essays begin the long overdue task of assessing the impact of major twentieth-century planning initiatives on the nation's neighborhoods, downtowns, and metropolitan regions.

Preface and Acknowledgments

The twenty essays in this volume are organized into four parts, preceded by an introduction that surveys the historiography of planning history from its inception during the 1960s to the present time. These divisions group the chapters roughly chronologically and by themes. Each chapter opens with a brief introduction that summarizes its principal argument and the significance of its contribution, and sets the piece within its appropriate historiographical context. A concluding chapter brings the anthology up to the present time by focusing on the new American metropolis of the post-1970s era and delineating the planning assumptions that have guided its development.

The editors incurred a number of debts as they brought the essays in this anthology together. Four chapters of this volume are reprinted from other works through the kind permission of Sage Publications, Inc., which originally published "Home Building and Industrial Decentralization in Los Angeles: The Roots of the Postwar Urban Region," by Greg Hise, in the *Journal of Urban History* 19(2), Feb. 1993; Pennsylvania State University Press, which published Carl Abbott's "Five Downtown Strategies: Policy Discourse and Downtown Planning since 1945" in the *Journal of Policy History* 5(1), 1993; the *Journal of the American Planning Association,* which originally featured Thomas Hanchett's "Federal Incentives and the Growth of Local Planning, 1941–1948" in its volume 60(2), Spring 1994; and the University of California Press, Journals Division, which published "World War II and Urban California: City Planning and the Transformation Hypothesis," by Roger Lotchin, in the *Pacific Historical Review* 62(2), May 1993. We also wish to thank urban historian Mark H. Rose and planning historian Laurence C. Gerckens for reading the entire manuscript; their comments and criticisms enabled us to improve its quality tremendously. To our editor George F. Thompson, at the Center for American Places in Harrisonburg, Virginia, we offer sincere thanks for his patience and judicious good sense in guiding the book from its conception through the manuscript preparation and production processes.

Preface and Acknowledgments

Mary Corbin Sies wishes to acknowledge the assistance of the National Endowment for the Humanities and the Winterthur Museum, Library, and Gardens for a fellowship that enabled her to complete a large part of the editing of this volume. She is also grateful to R. Gordon Kelly, former chair of the Department of American Studies, and Robert W. Griffith, former dean of the College of Arts and Humanities, at the University of Maryland, College Park, for their support for this project, and to her graduate assistant Gilda Anroman and to Christopher Stark for their assistance during its final stages.

Christopher Silver received unflagging support from his faculty and administrative colleagues at Virginia Commonwealth University (VCU) when book production demands superseded competing academic duties.

We both wish to express our deep gratitude to Virginia "Jenny" Brandt and Cindy Ann Mills Baumgartner at VCU, who mastered the challenge of merging twenty manuscripts produced with nearly a dozen different softwares into a file suitable for production. Special thanks also go to Mary Beth Taliaferro from Academic Campus Computing Services for timely assistance to Jenny and Cindy when the machine refused to cooperate.

Both of us also owe a special debt to the members of two organizations largely responsible for pushing planning and urban history much closer together: the Society for American City and Regional Planning History and the Urban History Association.

The History of Planning History

MARY CORBIN SIES

CHRISTOPHER SILVER

Planning history emerged as a recognized field of study only quite recently but since the 1960s has produced layer upon layer of knowledge about city and regional planners, designs, the planning process, its institutional loci, and its broader social, political, cultural, and intellectual contexts. Some of the contributions, like map overlays, provide a single perspective on a complex landscape. Others integrate information from several perspectives to provide startling new insights. Thus an appropriate place to begin this volume on the history of city planning in the United States is to review briefly that body of literature: it will show at a glance the many separate paths that planning ideas and experience and the histories written about them have taken.

As scholars have grappled with the challenge of mapping the history of planning thought and practice, they have changed their very definitions of the phenomena that qualify as planning activities. At different times, "planning" has meant the design of comprehensive plans and discrete urban spaces, or the creation of enabling legislation, or the conduct of social research, or the practice of a wide array of community development functions. At the same time, the cast of characters known as "planners" has expanded to include not only individuals belonging to the planning profession, narrowly defined, but all those public officials and private citizens, men and women, who create the urban landscape and shoulder the many responsibilities this entails, from zoning and transportation to settlement house work, subdivision development, and historic preservation.

Planning historians have also increased their purview and their understanding of the contextual circumstances—social, racial, cultural, economic, and political—that have influenced both planning and plan implementation in a given locality. This broadening has led many scholars to adopt interdisciplinary approaches to their work that are in tune with the complexities of planning and therefore have great potential for informing contemporary planning practice. Indeed, one of the purposes of this volume is to demonstrate that planning history has much to offer in the way of useful lessons for contemporary and future planners, policy makers, and residents of the nation's urban places. The rest of this chapter provides a roughly chronological review of planning history as it has pursued the dynamic interdisciplinary scholarship for which it is known today.

Planning Historians' Initial Concept of Planning

According to the first planning historians, the modern planning movement began at the turn of the twentieth century. Mel Scott, author of the first standard planning history text, *American City Planning since 1890* (1969), noted that as early as 1900 a wide array of intellectuals, social reformers, business leaders, professionals, and officials at all levels of government consciously embraced the idea of "planning," in the belief that it was necessary to safeguard the country's social system. How that novel concept was to be defined, however, was hotly contested. Consequently, the modern planning movement had no coherent identity in the earliest years of the century. In 1917 the movement achieved formal recognition with the formation of the American City Planning Institute. Its fifty-two charter members, each of whom had at least two years of city planning experience, included fourteen landscape architects, thirteen engineers, five architects, four real estate figures, and a larger contingent of academics and civic reformers. All were intent upon advancing the practice of city planning, although it was still undefined and evolving in various directions. As Scott generously observed, "Collectively they provided the new institute with a richness of experience certain to contribute to a breadth of understanding of urban problems and opportunities. But the very diversity of their backgrounds also indicated that this would be a professional organization in which consensus might be difficult to achieve."[1]

By the 1920s, most adherents of the nascent movement had decided that the central purpose of planning was to guide and manage efficiently the processes of metropolitan development. In both city and suburbs, planners focused their attention on the design or redesign of the physical landscape. A handful of intellectuals and social activists, like Walter Lippmann, Charles Zeublin, and Mary Kingsbury Simkhovitch, defined planning quite differently: they saw it as a process of establishing and implementing economic and social priorities at the national and even international levels.[2] Nevertheless, the mainstream of planning thought in the early twentieth century concentrated almost exclusively on the spatial dimensions of urbanization. Underlying this focus was a widely shared environmental determinism rooted in the reform tradition of the Progressive Era. Early-twentieth-century planners believed that through proper design of the metropolitan environment it would be possible to alleviate a wide range of social, economic, and political problems. Influencing the spatial city offered a common cause to those persons who advocated intervention in the urban development process through planning, even though they may have supported distinctive types of spatial solutions with conflicting objectives and decidedly different consequences.

Planning History as Celebration of Planning's Pioneers

Many of the scholars who began to write the history of American city planning in the 1960s shared the reform ideals and accepted a good deal of the environmental determinism of the early twentieth- century planners. They focused their research on the "master planners," especially those whose ideas were firmly rooted in the Progressive reform tradition. Thus the first historical studies were biographical in nature, concentrating on the lives and times of a handful of leading practitioners and their plan making or plan conceptualizing, as demonstrated by the sketches of Henry Wright and John Nolen, two of "city planning's truly great men," that appeared in the November 1960 issue of the *Journal of the American Institute of Planners* (*JAIP*). Both articles, and the whole series of comparable sketches that followed, celebrated the reform ideals and design achievements of the pioneers of American city planning. Most of those planning pioneers had built their reputations on their work as consultants to civic groups and to a prominent urban elite. While serving in this capacity, they experimented with new urban forms and designed spatial alternatives to the much maligned industrial metropolis.[3]

The historical sketches published during the 1960s occasionally featured a British figure such as Ebenezer Howard or Sir Raymond Unwin, whose Garden City and new town concepts helped shape British reform efforts and eventually American planning.[4] In its November 1972 issue, the *JAIP* launched a new historical biography series that became a regular feature. Over the next few years, the journal published carefully crafted biographical sketches of a select group of both theorists and practitioners: Patrick Geddes, the urban theorist; Rexford Tugwell, America's greenbelt advocate; Benjamin Marsh, congestion fighter and organizer of the first national planning conclave in 1909; Charles Dyer Norton, promoter of the Regional Plan of New York; Harland Bartholomew, the prolific professional consultant and America's first public planner; Walter Burley Griffin, the expatriate planner of Canberra; Lewis Mumford, the holistic thinker; Benton MacKaye, the park planner; and E. A. Gutkind, the outsider.[5] In 1978 *JAIP* finally acknowledged that the planning pioneers included women as well as men, a point that Eugenie L. Birch established in "Woman-Made America: The Case of Early Public Housing Policy."[6]

The journal commissioned articles on these particular individuals because planning historians judged their reform ideas seminal to the development of the best of the mainstream American planning movement. These discussions of pioneering planners and their reform ideals and design achievements were addressed primarily to members of a rather young profession seeking a clearer understanding of its founders and its ideological origins. Although narrowly framed and often one-dimensional, these early planning "histories" were important for their canonizing function. Dominating planning history for more than a decade, they laid the ideological groundwork for what later became "a systematic study of institutionalized planning."[7]

The American Planner: Biographies and Reflections (1983), edited by Donald Krueckeberg, reprinted some of the biographical essays from *JAIP* and supplemented the discontinued biographical series with additional sketches, expanding the definition of figures central to planning history in the process. He included a discussion of women in planning by Eugenie Birch and chapters on zoning experts Edward Bassett and Alfred Bettman; housing planners Edith Elmer Wood, Coleman Woodbury, and Charles Abrams; and planning consultant Ladislas Segoe. Krueckeberg's volume concentrated on planning figures whose careers spanned the first half of the twentieth century, a "special" period in which "a new profession devoted to the unified and comprehensive planning of cities and regions [endeavored] to satisfy human needs with both beauty and efficiency."[8] What made the early years of the American planning movement special, Michael Brooks recently agreed, was the crucial work of the first generations of planners who established "the underlying values of the profession"; they "reminded us of the critical responsibilities we bear for the well-being of all who reside in the communities we purport to serve."[9]

The American Planner canonized key figures who "played a direct role in the development of the planning profession" while broadening the range of recognized planning activities and acknowledging the plurality of professional interests among the planning pioneers. Krueckeberg offered his collection of biographies, published at the close of a period in which the planning profession had grown from several hundred persons after World War II to nearly 25,000 by 1980, for the explicit purpose of helping members of a more diverse profession (re)discover their shared ideals and training. Writing in direct response to the rapid growth and magnitude of change in the profession and the mood of shattered optimism characterizing urban life in the late twentieth century, Krueckeberg foresaw a coming period of redirection for the profession and held out the pioneer planners' ideals and experiences as a springboard for reflecting on what its nature might be. Planning history, as he approached it, would serve to "restore our memories, review our commitments, and to extend our sense of company."[10]

Planning History as the Chronicle of Institutionalized Planning

With Mel Scott's *American City Planning since 1890,* a massive commissioned history published in 1969 to commemorate the fiftieth anniversary of the founding of the American Institute of Planners, planning history received its first systematic study of institutionalized planning. Defining planning as the "development of the planning function in modern government," Scott reified the conceptual framework first developed by planning's historical biographers. Building on the initial portraits of the planning pioneers, he traced the origins of modern planning in the United States and its institutions to the reform ideals of the progressive movement. While cognizant of the many shortcomings of the planning movement over the ensuing years, Scott treated all practitioners as direct ideological descendants of those early reformers, or implied they should have been. Thus parts of *American City Planning* take on a heroic tone, the fundamental idea being that "entire cities and metropolitan regions can be developed and renewed by a continuous process of decision-making based on long-range planning."[11] Throughout the 653 pages of text, the author emphasized the evolution of master planning by providing extended discussions of Burnham's plans for Washington, Cleveland, San Francisco, and Chicago, and of plan making through the City Functional Era, the New Deal, and into the post–World War II period. In other words, the formulation and implementation of comprehensive plans in the nation's largest metropolitan areas formed the central plot in Scott's history, and he relied upon an impressive array of original plans and interviews with planners to flesh out the details of his narrative.

It is difficult to overemphasize the importance of *American City Planning* in the historiography of planning history; it remained the standard text on the subject, a source of indoctrination and inspiration for students in schools of planning, well into the 1980s.[12] With his authoritative study, Scott greatly broadened the subject matter of planning history and gave it an important place in the history of the nation, arguing that "the planning function in society touches almost all interests, affects almost all aspects of our lives, and holds enormous potential for improving our institutions and our environment." Scott recognized that city planning was closely intertwined with "highly complex social, economic, and political forces," although his investigation of those forces was highly selective. As a commissioned work for the American Institute of Planners, *American City Planning* concentrated on showcasing many of the institute's most prominent figures. But Scott also included those "persons outside the profession—financiers, industrialists, merchants, members of other professions, writers, professors of political science, economics, sociology, and law, legislators, mayors, governors, and presidents—[who] have influenced the development of planning perhaps as much as the recognized practitioners and their cohorts, the professors of city and regional planning in our universities."[13]

American City Planning thus achieved two milestones in planning historiography: it greatly expanded historians' definition of persons contributing to the planning process, and it synthesized an impressive if highly selected amount of data on institutionalized planning that would come to represent the standard account. What Scott left out of the work, however, was almost as significant as what he included. For his case studies of city planning, he relied exclusively on the major American metropolises, especially Boston, Chicago, Los Angeles, New York, Philadelphia, St. Louis, and Washington, D.C. Planning in small towns and cities, indeed in whole regions, received no mention at all. Except for a passage on the Atlanta Region Metropolitan Planning Commission and a few brief comments on Dallas, Scott overlooked virtually the entire urban South and Southwest. Although he carefully examined efforts since the 1920s to initiate regional planning, he omitted the striking phenomenon of residential suburbanization from his survey.

The most serious intellectual shortcoming of *American City Planning*, however, was Scott's failure to distance himself from the profession sufficiently to assess critically its fundamental values and motives; he was unable to penetrate the rhetoric of reform that planners drew upon to legitimize their actions. A related and telling deficiency was the lack of attention to the differential impacts of institutionalized planning on the diverse array of districts, neighborhoods, and communities in the modern metropolis. For example, Scott studiously avoided considering the racial implications of twentieth-century planning. Since the early 1970s numerous scholars have worked steadily to redress this oversight in the planning history literature. Christopher Silver and Marc Weiss have documented the racial basis of early zoning. Silver, Howard Gillette, and others have pointed out the racial and ethnic exclusion objectives of Clarence Perry's neighborhood unit plan and the community planning process that it spawned over the next four decades.[14] In "Zoning and the American Dream," Weiss has demonstrated that when the Supreme Court embraced zoning in the *Euclid* v. *Ambler* case in 1926, it was clearly concerned with issues of social segregation as well as issues of land use.[15] In quite a range of studies, several historians have investigated the powerful impact that significant federal and local planning initiatives—like highways, housing, urban renewal, and downtown development—have had on urban minority communities.[16]

The Call to Expand the Scope of Planning History

Those scholars who studied the racial implications of planning decisions broadened the conceptual base of planning history considerably by explaining some of the contextual factors that shaped key planning decisions. Following their lead, planner/educator David A. Johnson and planning historian Daniel Schaffer organized a special symposium, published in the *Journal of the American Planning Association* (*JAPA*) in 1985, to define a new planning history. Entitled "Learning from the Past—The History of Planning," the forum championed a more *instrumental* planning history, one more critical, more methodologically adventuresome, more cognizant of the external circumstances within which planners made and implemented their decisions and urban citizens responded to the outcome. In short, it was a planning history more useful to those engaged in planning practice. Noting the "multidisciplinary international movement" that planning history had become, Johnson and Schaffer asked symposium participants to address the question, "How usable is planning's past to planning's present—and future?" The discussions illustrated two premises: that "history is often an effective tool in formulating planning policy," and "that the past—or at least selective segments of the past—is always with us in the here and now." As Seymour Mandelbaum put it in his contribution, history is an "'intellectual battleground' where images of the past count not only because they serve as justification for current policies, but also because they help to set the agenda within which the debate takes place."[17]

While cautioning about the dangers of historicism, Johnson and Schaffer urged planning historians to relate their research to present-day practices in order to understand those of the past, and vice versa, and to move beyond the chronicle of institutional development that Scott's history provides. An effective historical analysis, they argued, can "uncover and understand those truly historic moments" when the choices of planners and policy makers "made a difference in the shape and functioning of cities and regions." Historians can best study those "critical junctures" systematically and on several levels at once: by analyzing the decision-making process, the issues raised, the contextual circumstances, and the underlying values shaping the planning profession and the institutions it has served.[18]

The promotion of urban deconcentration during the early twentieth century as a solution to various social ills caused by congestion and the lack of proper housing for the expanding urban population was just such a "critical juncture" in planning history. In the early 1980s scholars investigating deconcentration and the suburbanization process began producing more conceptually sophisticated histories of the kind Johnson and Schaffer advocated, for a time moving planning history from an urban to a suburban focus. The new suburban histories fell into two broad categories. One treated the history of suburban development from the perspective of its place within the larger geopolitical development of American cities.[19] The second category—generally case studies—concentrated on the suburbs themselves and analyzed their designs and community-building processes from the inside out.[20]

Studies from the first category—like Sam Bass Warner's *Streetcar Suburbs*, Kenneth T. Jackson's *Crabgrass Frontier*, and Edel, Sclar, and Luria's *Shaky Palaces*—have clarified greatly the forces shaping urban and suburban growth: notably, regional population growth, new transportation and production technologies, class conflict, and racial discrimination. Histories from the second category—Henry C. Binford's *The First Suburbs*, Robert Fishman's *Bourgeois Utopias*, and Michael H. Ebner's *Creating Chicago's North Shore*, for example—have brought to light important social, cultural, and ideological influences that guide local decisions on suburban form and lifestyle. At the same time, these works have expanded the historian's conception of the term "planning" itself. In the development of suburbia, "the term *planned* suburb does not imply necessarily that for each . . . community there existed a formal and written plan. Many . . . suburbs possessed no formal plan but were nonetheless products of deliberate and systematic decisions made on the part of an identifiable set of key citizens to guide design and development."[21]

Throughout the 1980s urban historians also produced an impressive array of books and articles documenting the critical role that planning decisions played in metropolitan development. Like their counterparts studying suburban history, urbanists challenged the very definition of "planning." Their research demonstrated that professional planners were not always doing the planning, and even when they were involved, the planning was characteristically piecemeal rather than comprehensive. Edward K. Muller and John F. Bauman suggested that scholars look beyond officialdom to understand fully how cities were planned in the twentieth century. The Olmsted firm, they pointed out, served the private "landscape needs of the urban-industrial elite" by introducing striking new community forms that have survived in the face of rapid change during the latter part of this century. Records in the Frederick Law Olmsted papers document the firm's pervasive influence on private subdivision planning throughout urban America.[22] Mary Corbin Sies's research on planned, exclusive suburbs, as well as Ann Durkin Keating's *Building Chicago* and Weiss's *The Rise of the Community Builders*, published during the late 1980s, established the importance of private initiatives in planning history.[23]

The growing involvement of urban and suburban historians in planning history helped bring about both the innovations in methodology that Johnson and Schaffer called for and a more critical assessment of the role of the planner and planning. Seymour Mandelbaum noted that urban historians, in contrast to planners, were "not likely to accept a narrative of urban development that exaggerates the role of professionals, regardless of its salutary influence on the morale of novice planners." As long as planning historians focused their research on the creation of master plans, the actions of heroic planners, and the influence of official planning organizations on the urban development process, planning history would maintain only a "peripheral niche" in urban history.[24]

Planning History Joins Urban History

Johnson and Schaffer's view—that planning history should concentrate less on eternal verities and more on contemporary practice—represented a wholesale shift in approach if not in purpose. *Two Centuries of American Planning* (1988), edited by Daniel Schaffer, signified the completion of this transformation; its contributors set forth more systematically than ever before the history of urban planning as an extension of urban history. In so doing, they suggested that planning history had to provide an understanding of the metropolitan structure that had evolved in the nineteenth and twentieth centuries if it was to inform professional practice successfully. Thus Schaffer's anthology, prepared for the most part by leading urban historians, shifted planning history more squarely into urban history's purview.

Professional planning as defined in Krueckeberg's biographical or Scott's institutional accounts seemed all but forgotten. Instead, interest groups, private individuals, politics, and public policy initiatives spearheaded planned urban change. Of the scores of professional planners discussed in Scott's *American City Planning,* for example, only Frederick Law Olmsted and his stepson John C. received prominent treatment in Schaffer's compilation. Among its contributors, William H. Wilson discussed not only John Olmsted's planning of Seattle's park system but also the influence of various planning movements on Olmsted's plans and the recasting of those plans through the political process so that they could be implemented. Wilson and other contributors replaced planning as an activity of independent actors with planning as a complex political process filled with compromises and incremental accomplishments.[25]

The urban historians who contributed to *Two Centuries of American Planning* also cast a more critical eye on the planning process, as Mandelbaum had predicted they would. In his introduction, Schaffer linked the recent intellectual vitality of planning history to the contemporary crisis in the planning profession; practitioners were turning to their past for insights and answers. Noting the loss of public confidence the profession had suffered during the 1980s, Schaffer argued that planning had become a metaphor for the problems of government and the contradictions in American life. "Each metropolis exists as a visible reminder of the nation's economic successes and failures. In the process each reveals the limits of planning, and more significantly of government, either to guide our prosperity or to overcome our poverty."[26]

Implicated in these contradictions, Schaffer suggested, were two centuries of a serious conflict in purpose at the heart of the planning profession. "At one level, it is concerned with economic growth—setting the stage for private development and individual prosperity. On another level, it focuses on issues of reform and equity . . . so as to ensure a greater level of equality rather than more vigorous competition." In strong contrast to planning historians writing in the 1960s and 1970s, who emphasized the profession's indebtedness to Progressive reform ideals, the contributors to Schaffer's volume argued that private economic development had become the dominant concern.[27] By promoting a more self-reflexive and instrumental planning history, they joined the many practitioners who in the late 1980s had begun calling for a new planning vision that would enable the nation to balance the desire for economic growth with the need for social equity.

In their widely ranging pursuit of a more usable past, the urban historians achieved another interpretive landmark: they pushed the origins of modern planning well back into the nine-teenth century, demonstrating convincingly that progressive reform ideas represented merely a new synthesis of well-established reform currents. At the same time, they continued to reconceptualize both the planning process and its cast of characters. In *The New Urban Landscape* (1986), David Schuyler demonstrated not only that Fred-erick Law Olmsted was practicing "comprehensive planning" in the mid-nineteenth century but that he and some of his contemporaries had developed a multifaceted vision of urban form—a vision that was not just an aesthetic but "involved a statement of political and social ideology." As David Hammack, one of Schaffer's authors, pointed out, real estate attorneys, developers, manufacturers, and merchants had all made important contributions to the planning and building of the actual urban landscape during the nineteenth century. "All of these men promoted comprehensive planning," Hammack wrote, "even though none was trained as a professional planner or claimed the title of landscape architect." Moreover, their "planning" had greater impact on the urban environment than did the impressive formal designs of gardens, parks, or streetscapes prepared by landscape architects like Olmsted, who were canonized as pioneer planners. Most of the latter's best plans were either never implemented or were realized only in piecemeal fashion, so they had little influence except on fellow design professionals.[28]

In a pivotal essay in *Introduction to Planning History in the United States* (1983), edited by Donald Krueckeberg, Jon Peterson cited further evidence of urban planning's early origins. Peterson noted that the invention and widespread application of the water carriage sewer system during the mid–nineteenth century facilitated the building of a comprehensive urban infrastructure. Sanitary reform-ers of the time also promoted the sanitary survey, a primitive form of urban planning that "entailed the systematic mapping and re-cording of sanitary conditions on every parcel of land . . . [and] was among the first efforts to collect detailed data on an entire city for the purpose of formulating and implementing plans for the com-mon good." The sanitary survey, in turn, fostered what Peterson called "townsite consciousness," the practice of thinking through the major physical aspects of the city—circulation system, land uses, community facilities, utilities, and visual amenities—as part of one comprehensive plan. Sanitary surveys and townsite consciousness provided additional examples of planning before there were professional planners; they also indicated the broad and ambitious range of concerns that planning encompassed in the mid–nineteenth century.[29]

Planning History as Interdisciplinary History

Stanley K. Schultz pushed the origins of modern planning back even further in *Constructing Urban Culture: American Cities and City Planning, 1800–1920* (1989), but his scholarship was more noteworthy for its broad-ranging perspectives—cultural, legal, technological, physical, social, and moral—which allowed him to produce a complex and richly textured interpretation. Drawing from sources generally overlooked in planning history research—literary tracts, legal tracts, articles and surveys produced by urban sanitarians, and records of city engineers—Schultz argued that the nineteenth century gave birth to a new urban culture based on new attitudes toward "the relationship between the physical environment and bodily, mental, and moral health." This culture embodied what were to become the fundamental premises of twentieth-century planning practice, especially the conceptualization of the ideal city form as a middle landscape that blended urban densities with a harmonious natural setting.

An important part of the evolving urban culture was a new legal landscape, one of the bulwarks of modern city planning. A new body of laws granted municipal corporations limited rights to take or to regulate private property for public benefit through eminent domain, police power, and, eventually, zoning. Another facet of the new urban culture was the moral environmentalism of sanitarians—Peterson's nascent planners—who stressed cleanliness, beauty, and technological and scientific solutions to urban physical and social problems. According to Schultz, the expanding profession of municipal engineers contributed comprehensive planning schemes that combined all of these concerns, laying the foundation for modern municipal administration both before and after the initiation of formal city planning. Thus, progressive reform and the City Beautiful movement formed not the beginning, but the culmination of a century of planning thought and organizational development that established the basic structure of modern city planning.[30]

Constructing Urban Culture showcased the broadened scope and interdisciplinary character of the scholarship produced by the marriage of urban and planning history during the mid-1980s. The explosion of multidisciplinary studies stimulated by that union was most evident in *American Urbanism: A Historiographic Review* (1987), a collection of bibliographic essays edited by Howard Gillette and Zane L. Miller. It contained fourteen essays that surveyed the urban and planning history literature from the multiple perspectives that typified the new scholarship on the city. Some were topical essays: Andrea Tuttle Kornbluh discussed race and ethnicity, Jon Teaford urban rule, and Leonard Wallock work and labor. Others were thematic essays: Alan Marcus treated cities as social systems, Joel A. Tarr and Josef W. Konvitz focused on the development of urban infrastructure, and Patricia Mooney Melvin looked at neighborhood-city relationships. The volume also contained disciplinary essays on urban culture by Howard Gillette, urban geography by Edward K. Muller, urban planning by Eugenie Birch, and urban architecture by Richard Longstreth.[31] Subsequent review essays in a variety of academic journals reported on the multidisciplinary contributions of still other fields related to planning history: among these were "Reconsidering the Suburbs: An Exploration of Suburban Historiography," by Margaret S. Marsh (1988); "Real Estate History: An Overview and Research Agenda," by Marc A. Weiss (1989); and "Technology and the City," by Josef W. Konvitz, Mark H. Rose, and Joel A. Tarr (1990).[32]

Many of the studies cited in these bibliographic essays provided a single new perspective, much like a transparent overlay, over the growing base of knowledge about planning history and metropolitan development and spatial patterns. The multidisciplinary nature and sheer volume of these overlays also tended sometimes to obscure the picture and threatened to eclipse urban and planning history as identifiable fields. In "Rethinking American Urban History: New Directions for the Posturban Era" (1990), Howard Gillette once again surveyed urban and planning history scholarship, warning of the dangers of fragmentation and insularity among urbanists: he called for greater synthesis, "more comparative studies, and . . . the interdisciplinary collaboration needed to advance the fuller perspective we all strive for."[33] Many of the more successful attempts to integrate the knowledge derived from interdisciplinary research have taken the form of penetrating case studies: Carl Abbott's work on Portland; Christopher Silver's *Twentieth-Century Richmond;* and Mary Corbin Sies's research on the planned, exclusive suburbs of Short Hills in New Jersey, St. Martin's in Philadelphia, Kenilworth in Illinois, and Lake of the Isles in Minneapolis.[34] The collaborative effort of literary specialist William Sharpe and social historian Leonard Wallock has produced a growing body of interdisciplinary scholarship probing the ways in which cultural values and social assertions have framed and constrained various perceptions and experiences of the city.[35]

Revisions: The Intellectual and Cultural Roots of American Planning

In fact, among the richest harvests to result from the interdisciplinary scholarship of the late 1980s are analyses of the cultural assumptions and intellectual roots of American city planning. The best of these works have generated careful and far-reaching revisionist interpretations of several planning pioneers and movements, most notably Frederick Law Olmsted, the City Beautiful movement, and Ebenezer Howard and his Garden City scheme. In *The New Urban Landscape* (1986), David Schuyler shows that Olmsted's naturalistic landscape designing supplied modern city planning with a coherent scheme for ordering urban spaces. His analysis establishes firmly that several key modern urban design concepts predate the Progressive Era; Schuyler traces their origins back to the rural (and urban) cemetery movement of the 1830s, a subject that has drawn increasing attention from planning history scholars.[36]

Rural cemeteries, according to Schuyler, integrated scenery, landscape design, architecture, sculpture, and ideology into a single spatial package that provided a model for a new *urban* form, "one that introduced nature as a means of countering the overcivilization of the city." Concurrently, landscape designers like Andrew Jackson Downing were being commissioned to plan public grounds that "would stand as an antidote to conditions of life within cities." Olmsted reconstituted these separate approaches to fabricating urban spaces into a comprehensive "process of creating a new, more openly built urban environment"; he did so not simply through the development of individual parks, but with entire spatial systems that included parks, parkways, and residential suburbs.[37] In other words, Olmsted defined and practiced a form of comprehensive planning that embodied the assumptions of the new urban culture and formed a crucial precedent for twentieth-century planning practice. In a similar study, Irving D. Fisher, writing in 1986, considered Olmsted the seminal urban theorist of the nineteenth century, who blended art and science "to produce a comprehensive plan for the metropolis."[38]

In another interdisciplinary work of revision, urban historian William H. Wilson questioned the long-held view that the City Beautiful movement was an intellectually shallow attempt to impose European classicism on ugly American cities. Mel Scott, for example, dismissed the movement, arguing that "in most cities it had produced few noteworthy changes"; eventually it was transformed into "something more realistic and practical," by which he meant the City Practical movement, the approach that in his view represented the more praiseworthy values of the mainstream of the twentieth-century planning profession.[39] In his prize-winning book, Wilson refuted Scott's claim that the City Beautiful was an elitist fad of the pre–World War I era, arguing instead that it was the logical extension and refinement of Olmsted Sr.'s legacy and of the new city culture that evolved during the nineteenth century.

The penetrating insights of Wilson's *The City Beautiful Movement* (1989) were a direct result of his multilayered, interdisciplinary research. He pointed out, first, that the City Beautiful was not just concerned with aesthetics; it "was a political movement" that forged "a politics of accommodation" between planning professionals, city officials, and enlightened citizens. City Beautiful proponents helped create planning, park, and beautification groups that in turn promoted urban planning and secured the necessary voter approval for public financing of expensive civic improvement efforts. Second, although the City Beautiful planners favored the neoclassical architectural tradition, their vision of an improved urban environment was centered on the tenets of "comprehensiveness, utility, and functionalism." It also included a heavy dose of Olmsted's naturalistic aesthetics.[40]

Wilson's other significant contribution was his shift of emphasis from the big cities to smaller urban places where, in fact, many City Beautiful initiatives were actually carried out. Perhaps planning historians have downplayed the City Beautiful's success because they have overlooked places like Seattle, Denver, Kansas City, Dallas, and Harrisburg (Pennsylvania), where the movement helped implement some of the primary objectives of the nineteenth-century urban reform agenda. Possibly, too, scholars scrutinizing only the formal aspects of City Beautiful planning have failed to recognize the movement's complexity—"its development into a cultural, aesthetic, political, and environmental movement." Daniel Bluestone's *Constructing Chicago* (1991) supports Wilson's suspicion that the poor reputation of the City Beautiful has more to do with the modernist bias of the twentieth-century planning and architectural professions. In a study of architectural expression as it was conceived in its social, cultural, and economic contexts, Bluestone shows how the building of Chicago respected "notions of aesthetics, civility, and moral order" deeply embedded in nineteenth-century urban culture.[41]

As part of the effort to reassess planning's intellectual origins, urban and planning historians have been devoting increasing attention to the Garden City reform scheme of Ebenezer Howard, much as the neoclassical town planning movement has rediscovered the virtues of plans designed by John Nolen and others.[42] Peter Hall, in his heavily biographical "intellectual history of urban planning," *Cities of Tomorrow* (1988), fostered the Howard revival by declaring that he was "the most important single character" in twentieth-century planning thought. Howard's supporters as well as his critics, Hall charged, "have, at one time or another, been wrong about almost everything he stood for." Their most egregious error was to classify Howard as a physical planner instead of a social visionary. Like the other planning theorists Hall discussed, Howard offered a radical social vision not merely of an alternative built form, but of an alternative society, neither capitalistic nor bureaucratic-socialistic—a society based on voluntary cooperation among men and women, working and living in small, self-governing commonwealths.[43] Although planning historians have long celebrated Howard's influence on twentieth-century planning, Hall continued, the standard histories have eviscerated the intellectual substance of his ideas.

Stanley Buder went a step further and placed Howard's alternative social vision under close scrutiny in the hope of better understanding its nineteenth-century sources and assessing more accurately its salience for planning problems of the twenty-first century. Buder contributed another layer to historians' knowledge by focusing on the cultural and social origins of planning ideas. In *Visionaries and Planners* (1990), he argued "that Howard's garden city joined together two very different types of late nineteenth-century experimental communities"—the utopian cooperative and the model industrial village—"creating a tension never fully resolved." Although distinctive as a planning model, key elements of the Garden City were commonplace ideas among London reformers in the 1880s. The Garden City was not the romantic, antimodern, and antiurban ideal that many have believed it to be; what Howard offered was a middle landscape, a new form of dispersed residential settlement that did not sacrifice the advantages of urban density or urban life.

Buder notes wistfully—and here he is in agreement with Hall—that Garden City proponents abandoned the communitarian dimension of Howard's new urban scheme in their effort to translate the paper version of the plan into actual built communities in Britain and the United States. In the contest between a visionary ideal community and bureaucratically sponsored stewardship, the sense of limitation won out over the sense of possibility.[44] In a contrasting and more upbeat interpretation, British historian Dennis Hardy reiterated Peter Hall's assertion that Howard's ideas were central to twentieth-century planning, and on a very practical level. He documented that Garden City proponents became the most important political pressure group not only for Garden City and garden suburb ideas but for urban and town planning in general throughout the United Kingdom.[45]

Revisions: Planning, Politics, and Power

A second set of thought-provoking interdisciplinary histories written during the mid-1980s examined the relationship between planning, economy, and polity in American cities. The most controversial studies challenged directly the reform ideology claimed by and for the mainstream of the twentieth-century planning profession. One such critique, *Dreaming the Rational City: The Myth of American City Planning* (1983), by M. Christine Boyer, provided a tendentious reappraisal of planning ideology and practice. Although Boyer framed her research as a postmodern analysis of the "structures of planning thought," her true subject was power. She drew from the insights provided by French poststructuralist thinker Michel Foucault, who argued that societies were governed by a "disciplinary order," which he defined as an "integrated [political] system not meant to be seen but infused across an apparatus of observation, recording and tracking." She likened city planning to "a disciplinary mechanism watching over and regulating urban development in order to create the correct and ideal spatial [and social] order."[46]

By scrutinizing the language of planners over time, Boyer uncovered an overarching quest to impose "disciplinary order and ceremonial harmony" over the unregulated social and physical changes in the sprawling turn-of-the-century industrial metropolis. Planners, she argued, engineered the transformation of the nineteenth-century city from a place of disorder but a place with human scale to the contemporary megacity of glass and steel boxes that organizes but alienates human beings. Although *Dreaming the Rational City* is a controversial and curiously disembodied analysis of the development of the planning profession, its trenchant criticism of planners' motives directly challenged the central tenets of Krueckeberg's and Scott's planner-as-reformer thesis. Boyer argued persuasively, as have a handful of other planning historians, that an important objective (and not just a consequence) of planning is to expand the state's role so as to enhance the stability of urban land values and support capital productivity.[47]

Instead of a Foucauldian framework, Richard E. Foglesong combined a carefully theorized Marxist framework with "concrete historical research" in his equally controversial study, *Planning the Capitalist City* (1986). His central purpose was to investigate the role of planners and planning advocates in the development of planning, including those "whose interests they represented, and [to show] how their efforts contributed to the maintenance of the existing political economy." Unlike Boyer, who studied only the writings of planners, Foglesong examined both the ideas and the works of some of the key individuals who helped planning become "a legitimate function of local government." During the nineteenth century, he pointed out, the notion of land as a public resource characteristic of town planning in precapitalist colonial America gave way to the concept of land as a valuable private economic commodity. Planning subsequently developed "from a recognition of the need for some kind of collective control, organized through the state, to overcome the irrationality and inefficiency of the [urban] built environment wrought by the market system." According to Foglesong, reform efforts like Benjamin Marsh's campaign against population congestion, the Garden City movement, and the building of company towns were doomed to fail as a basis for city planning because they did not adequately support the economic interests of the dominant groups in urban society.[48] Mainstream planning ideology—the City Practical approach—succeeded where other efforts failed because it organized planning "in the form of elite-dominated local planning commissions insulated from institutions of popular control."[49]

Although Foglesong's use of Marxist theoretical constructs yields predictable conclusions, his analysis nonetheless illuminates the prevailing power relations in some early-twentieth-century cities. Several other studies of planning and its relationship to urban power have arrived at different conclusions, however. Blaine Brownell explored this theme in his assessment of a commercial-civic elite in Southern cities and their use of political influence to advance a self-serving view of the New South city during the 1920s.[50] Judd Kahn's study of earthquake-devastated San Francisco also revealed how politics intruded upon an opportunity to implement Daniel Burnham's comprehensive plan.[51] In separate case studies, Christopher Silver and Carl Abbott demonstrated the myriad ways in which politics, dominant economic interests, and planning intertwined in Richmond and Portland, respectively.[52] In their view, successful city planning took into account politics and, indeed, became an extension of it.

Despite the growing body of information on the relationship between planning and politics, the nature and uniformity of that relationship from city to city are far from clear. Whereas some scholars, like David Goldfield in "Urban Growth in the Old South," see a unified business elite directing public improvements to benefit their own economic interests, others, like David C. Hammack in *Power and Society: Greater New York at the Turn of the Century* (1982), find that several social groups possessing conflicting aims and values are competing for decision-making power.[53] Christine Meisner Rosen's comparative study of Baltimore, Boston, and Chicago in the late nineteenth century looked at the relationship between power and environmental reforms in the aftermath of the great fires that destroyed large sections of all three cities. Although Rosen's major purpose in *The Limits of Power: Great Fires and the Process of City Growth in America* (1986) was to examine planning as a process of instigating physical change, she also identified the sources of political power that directly affected that process. She refuted the notion that a handful of business elites monopolized power in those three cities; instead, she concluded that neighborhoods, individual property owners, and organized interest groups shared power. The result was a kind of negative power, since power was used to limit "in practical and complex ways society's ability to take action to solve problems."[54]

The tendency of competing interests to create "negative power" may explain why city planning proponents in the early twentieth century thought it was important to promote a single, definable public interest. Without a political and policy consensus, cities were unable to respond to crises adequately, let alone anticipate future needs through effective planning. At the same time, as Joel Schwartz has demonstrated in *The New York Approach: Robert Moses, Urban Liberals, and Redevelopment of the Inner City* (1993), a strong consensus of urban interest groups could wreak as much havoc on the urban social environment as a lack of consensus and the absence of planning. Schwartz documents the collusion between liberal/leftist New York and Robert Moses in support of Moses' redevelopment efforts in New York City and concludes that neither pluralism nor global capitalist forces determined the course of planning during Moses' period of leadership in public housing and redevelopment. For an unsettling variety of purely local reasons, liberal "New Yorkers who were otherwise considered his most rabid critics" endorsed Moses' ruthless slum clearance and housing policy programs.[55]

New Contributions to American Planning History

The many questions about planning, politics, and power that remain unanswered indicate just how much work still needs to be done. At the same time, it should be pointed out, with some pride, that a vast territory has already been explored, covering everything from the pioneer planners and master plans, to the institutionalization of the planning function in official government agencies, the impact of planning on changing urban form, private planning initiatives, planning's social context and social impact, its reigning cultural and intellectual assumptions, and the ideals not realized and paths not followed. Furthermore, planning historians have borrowed profitably the methods and insights of neighboring disciplines in order to broaden the scope and perspectives of their own activities. The result is a body of scholarship of greater use to planners and policy makers and to all thoughtful persons concerned about the nation's cities.

The research completed since the mid-1980s demonstrates, to quote Seymour Mandelbaum, that strong connections do exist "between the construction of pasts and the construction of futures."[56] Two important observations linking twentieth-century planning practice to its past have emerged from the historiographical review in this chapter. First, the profession's core beliefs derive not from the progressive movement but from assumptions underlying the upper-middle-class urban culture that developed over the course of the nineteenth century. As Schuyler, Schultz, Sies, and others have shown, the central assumptions of the new urban culture have been codified and transmitted in the form of landscape ideals, lifestyle ideals, bodies of laws, environmental and technological tenets, and standards for professional practice.[57] Second, for this reason, planners and policy makers have frequently justified and sometimes based their design solutions on assumptions that are outdated and dramatically out of sync with the social, environmental, demographic, economic, and regulatory circumstances of contemporary urban life. Both observations can, at times, apply just as aptly to the work of planning historians.

There is still much to learn about the way planners conceptualize and rationalize their ideas, the way metropolitan areas actually get built, and the historical and contextual circumstances that constrain all of those processes. These are the fundamental issues addressed by the contributors to this collection. They follow three main lines of inquiry. First, they analyze a wider range of geographic locations, individual "planners," and intellectual and popular influences. Second, they provide several new and detailed case studies of the factors shaping planning and the plan implementation or building processes and their impacts in a given locale. And third, they pay special attention to the effects of values, assumptions, and policy discourses on the twentieth-century built environment. Their efforts produce some startling insights, model significant methodological innovations, and provide important revisions of American planning history.

Exploring the Breadth of Planning History

One important imperative of this collection is to expand the geographic breadth of planning history. Far too much research has drawn from too few metropolitan areas to conclude that the issues confronting planners in those locations represent national trends. The authors of this volume have therefore taken into account the planning process in smaller American cities, as well as in cities of the previously neglected South and West. Research on Chicago, Los Angeles, St. Louis, Detroit, and New York shares center stage with studies of Charlotte, North Carolina; Birmingham, Alabama; Columbus, Ohio; Dallas, Texas; San Diego, California; and Savannah, Georgia.

In addition to expanding the geographic coverage, several chapters enlarge the cast of characters that historians recognize as having played significant roles in the shaping of American cities during the twentieth century. Six essays profile the achievements of planning pioneers who have received only minimal attention to date. Jon Peterson analyzes the career of Frederick Law Olmsted Jr., shifting the focus of Olmsted scholarship from father to son. He shows how Olmsted Jr. transformed the visionary qualities of his father's planning into practical professional concerns more suited to an era when planning became a complex and continual process, involving too broad a range of specialties for any one person to master. Susan Wirka and Joan Draper document the central roles that settlement house workers played in the early city planning movements in New York and Chicago, respectively; they focus on Florence Kelley, Mary Kingsbury Simkhovitch, Lillian Wald, Mary McDowell, J. Frank Foster, and Charles Zeublin.

Michael Lang illuminates planning pioneer Frederick Lee Ackerman's immense contributions to the design of the Emergency Fleet Corporation's planned industrial communities during World War I. Ackerman, with the assistance of Electus Litchfield and a young Henry Wright, applied British Garden City ideas and a socialist reform agenda to the development of worker housing in the United States. Robert Ireland profiles the career of one of the nation's first regionalist thinkers, Joseph Hyde Pratt. A planner and environmentalist previously unknown to historians, Pratt prepared the ground for the better-known regionalists, like Howard Odum and Rupert Vance, three decades later. June Manning Thomas critically evaluates Detroit's longtime and influential planning director Charles Blessing and his magnificent but unrealized vision for the city's redevelopment during the 1950s and 1960s. In addition, John Hancock, the leading expert on John Nolen, offers a fresh look at this well-studied planning pioneer, by reviewing Nolen's role in establishing city planning as an ongoing public process through his efforts to implement his 1908 and 1926 plans for San Diego.

A set of companion essays focuses on the contributions of nonprofessionals to the shaping of planning discourses and metropolitan form. In a revision of the scholarship on zoning practices, Patricia Burgess documents the importance of private community and neighborhood developers in determining land uses in metropolitan Columbus, Ohio. Robert Fairbanks examines how a shift in the popular understanding of comprehensive planning influenced the implementation of the Trinity River Reclamation Project in Dallas during the 1920s and 1930s, and Hancock notes the influence of realtors and political leaders in setting the terms framing public debates concerning planning initiatives in San Diego. Greg Hise shows how "a series of uncoordinated but mutually reinforcing decisions and actions taken by manufacturers, federal housing personnel, land developers, and homeowners" produced the peripheral urbanism so characteristic of post–World War II Los Angeles and other cities. In a study of historic preservation in Savannah, Robert Hodder chronicles how a series of citizen coalitions introduced alternative perspectives on urban revitalization during the heyday of slum clearance and urban renewal.

Several of the articles on lesser-known planners also elucidate their subjects' contributions to the profession's intellectual foundations, indicating the breadth of ideas from which planners have drawn in their commitment to better-designed and more humane cities. Wirka coins the term "City Social" to describe the planning perspective advanced by female reformers involved in the settlement house movement; she outlines their achievements as founders of the modern field of social planning. In his study of Yorkship Garden Village, Lang probes what he argues is one of the most radical expressions of housing and planning reform ideas in the early twentieth century—a successful adaptation of the British Garden City to a federally sponsored industrial community. Ireland identifies civil engineer Joseph Hyde Pratt's carefully articulated concepts of regionalism and conservation as the basis for regional planning and infrastructure improvements in early-twentieth-century North Carolina. Draper argues persuasively that park planning in Chicago's South Park District from 1902 to 1905 represented an early attempt to rationalize the planning process by applying social science methods to it well in advance of the better-known work of the Chicago School in the 1920s. In a critical analysis of the range of professional perspectives offered concerning the design of freeways in inner cities, Cliff Ellis outlines the characteristic worldview of highway engineers that formed the basis for crucial freeway planning doctrines in the 1930s and 1940s.

Case Studies of Planning, Plan Implementation, and Planning's Impact

The authors of the case studies in this volume recognize that planning has in practice been a far more complicated undertaking than historians often depict. Although much previous scholarship has treated the design of the plan as the essence of planning, most of the following chapters depict plan making as simply the first step in the planning process, as a means, not an end. Several contributors shed considerable light on urban metropolitan growth and design by examining the larger social and political contexts in which planning occurs and by reconstructing the arduous process of implementation. Still others undertake the difficult task of assessing the differential effects of planning as well. In his case study of San Diego, John Hancock answers Catherine Bauer's query, "Planning is politics, but are planners politicians?" in the affirmative with respect to John Nolen's efforts to see his own plans implemented in that city. Hancock delineates the roles played by Nolen, the city government, politicians, public opinion, and Nolen's plans of 1908 and 1926 themselves, in successfully guiding planned and integrated development in one of the nation's booming cities during the pre–World War II era.

In another case study, Robert Fairbanks outlines the long and complex effort to reclaim the Trinity River Bottom for urban development and argues that comprehensive planning in Dallas was not determined by a unitary business elite, as previous urban and planning history literature has revealed to be the case in other cities. In a study questioning planning's impact, June Manning Thomas explains why Charles Blessing's brilliant planning ideas failed to win support among Detroiters: Blessing lacked the political skills needed to sell his vision to the public. Focusing on the impact of civic improvement efforts, Eric Sandweiss reconstructs how and why planning in early-twentieth-century St. Louis failed to transform the city's cultural landscape or social geography. He demonstrates how civic reformers and planners, including Harland Bartholomew, employed the rhetoric of civic improvement to cloak parochial social and economic interests.

This anthology also turns needed attention to the role and impact of the federal government in local planning. For example, Thomas Hanchett shows how federal incentives from 1938 to 1948 transformed the staunchly antiplanning southern metropolis of Charlotte, North Carolina, into a thoroughly planned urban center. Charles Connerly explores a similar theme involving another politically conservative southern city, Birmingham, Alabama. He chronicles the influence of federal urban policy on citizen participation in Birmingham's planning process, focusing especially on the Workable Program, Community Action, and Model Cities initiatives. Unlike Charlotte, however, where none of the federal programs required the involvement of citizens from all parts of the community, Birmingham by 1974 boasted one of the first successful citizen participation programs in the nation. Connerly traces out in detail the history of Birmingham's planning process, which now features democratic representation and serious opportunity for minority citizens to influence public policy.

Two other selections contribute to the growing body of scholarship focusing on race and the federal policy and local planning nexus. June Thomas analyzes the shift in planning philosophy from an emphasis on physical design to social planning that occurred in Detroit in the 1960s and 1970s as growing racial conflict and socio-economic problems made good design seem like an irrelevant and impractical goal. Robert Hodder narrates the succession of efforts between 1955 and 1973 of citizen coalitions in Savannah to use historic preservation as a means of social reform. Ethnically mixed and African American neighborhood groups successfully adapted federal preservation guidelines and opportunities to serve their needs for community building and neighborhood improvement. At the same time, they were able to promote an expanded preservation ethic and local interpretive programs informed by their own per-spectives. Although the verdict is still out on whether and how federal influence can help to implement more equitable planning policies, these case studies firmly establish the government's central role in the major planning initiatives of the twentieth century.

Another group of chapters takes up the little-studied but im-portant subtopic of the federal government's role in public and private planning during wartime. Michael Lang's discussion of Yorkship Village probes the interrelationships between the federally sponsored industrial community's core group of architects, plan-ners, and housers and the larger continuum of radical planning thought and practice from which they drew their inspiration. Roger Lotchin's overview of planning in several California cities during and immediately after World War II explores the connections be-tween planning practice and changing urban form. He argues that the pell-mell urbanization associated with the war effort, the re-newed emphasis on planning stimulated by the defense emergency, and the dual focus on decentralization and redevelopment set the tone for postwar metropolitan planning all over the United States. Greg Hise draws similar conclusions from his research on private planning initiatives in greater Los Angeles just before and during World War II. He argues that "peripheral urbanism"—the new urban form that Joel Garreau has labeled "Edge Cities"—grew from a process of planned urban expansion driven by the establishment of decentralized industrial growth poles supporting defense industries. These modern "spread cities" were the first expressions of a massive urban restructuring that developed as a direct response to the defense emergency and industrial reorganization precipitated by World War II.

Analyses of Values, Assumptions, and Policy Discourses

In addition, several chapters offer important perspectives on the values, underlying assumptions, and policy discourses that have shaped—or failed to shape—twentieth-century planning practice. In the Chicago Small Parks, Joan Draper uncovers and analyzes the roots of the City Functional movement in one of the earliest attempts to rationalize the planning process through the application of social scientific research methods. Jon Peterson argues that Olmsted Jr.'s process-oriented and bureaucratic approach to planning signified a break with nineteenth-century planning traditions and anticipated a way of thinking that would come to characterize the profession in the late twentieth century. Susan Wirka, Michael Lang, and Robert Hodder all bring to light alternative ideas to twentieth-century planning's mainstream. In a sharp refutation of the heroic narrative of the reform ideology of the planning pioneers, Eric Sandweiss reveals Harland Bartholomew's construction of a professional rationale to sell to the public a civic beautification scheme that could only preserve the existing urban order. In another interesting reversal, Patricia Burgess's study of zoning practices in metropolitan Columbus finds little basis for the planning truism that zoning is an effective means of land-use control.

Finally, three essays offer overviews of the policy discourses related to urban revitalization and address controversies central to contemporary metropolitan planning. Cliff Ellis turns to postmodern linguistic theories to elucidate the professional assumptions underlying the design of urban transportation networks. He demonstrates that the separate worldviews of each group of professionals—highway engineers, city planners, architects, and land-scape architects—severely constrained the design solutions they proposed, to the detriment of many urban neighborhoods. Carl Abbott examines the continually changing framework of images and assumptions that has shaped the post–World War II redevelopment of central business districts in major American cities. As planners and policy makers embrace each decade's particular design paradigm, he contends, they find themselves struggling to implement ideas "at right angles" to the planning and building of the previous decade. Elliott Sclar and Tony Schuman assess the contradictory pulls of ideology and circumstances on town planning in the United States, from the Garden City movement to the contemporary New Town–In Town. They point to the contemporary profession's implicit assumption that private investment creates economic value but also assert the historic inability of the private sector to plan comprehensively or merge housing development with social equity.

Conclusion

As the following chapters demonstrate, planning history can best inform planning practice when it captures the past in its full measure of complexity and applies a systematic analysis to understanding the past. Planning historians must continue to hone their skills in interdisciplinary scholarship and expand their purview if they are to understand planning as a practice with social, political, economic, cultural, and moral as well as formal, functional, and artistic components. As the blurring of boundaries between planning and urban history continues, however, scholars must be careful not to lose sight of the plans and the physical components of the metropolitan built environment in their zeal to comprehend the contextual circumstances that conditioned their design. They must follow interdisciplinary, not just multidisciplinary, paths in order to recognize and capture the dynamic relationship between planners, design, the physical metropolis, use patterns, cultural values, and the larger circumstances in which these phenomena interact.

Some of the chapters note that a gap exists between cities as perceived by citizens or planners and the actual cities as they appear to have existed at a particular time. At times, a similar gap exists between the histories historians perceive and the actual circumstances of a given time. As this volume makes clear, scholars and planners need to become more aware of the assumptions that drive their points of view. And both need to beware, as Seymour Mandelbaum has warned, of two kinds of determinism: a "radical historicism" that assumes history unfolds according to a set of immutable laws and a "conservative historicism" that assumes a society can only change in accordance with its essential nature.[58] The studies presented in this anthology offer a wealth of ideas for interpreting more precisely the planning of the twentieth-century American city in the hope that they will encourage renewed efforts to bring about healthier cities in the future.

FOUNDATIONS OF TWENTIETH-CENTURY PLANNING

CHAPTER 1

Frederick Law Olmsted Sr. and Frederick Law Olmsted Jr.

The Visionary and the Professional

JON A. PETERSON

The question of when the modern planning movement began and whether planning ideas and practice changed appreciably from the nineteenth to the twentieth centuries has recently become the subject of some controversy. Stanley K. Schultz, in Constructing Urban Culture *(Philadelphia: Temple University Press, 1989), David Schuyler, in* The New Urban Landscape *(Baltimore: The Johns Hopkins University Press, 1986), and others have analyzed certain nineteenth-century cultural values and assumptions and shown how they have shaped the mainstream of twentieth-century planning practice. In this chapter, Jon Peterson points out important discontinuities between Gilded Age and Progressive Era planning practice, as reflected in the ideas and designs of Frederick Law Olmsted Sr. and his lesser-known but still illustrious son, Frederick Law Olmsted Jr.*

In Peterson's view, Olmsted junior approached planning in a "professional" way, whereas Olmsted senior, the "practical visionary," sought to mold urban society according to a set of deeply held values about nature, morality, public health, and public taste. Drawing from letters, reports, and published plans, Peterson delineates crucial differences between the practices of Olmsted senior and junior through a comparison of their concepts of comprehensive planning. Olmsted senior advocated the comprehensive planning of discrete areas of the city, in contrast to subsequent planners, like Daniel H. Burnham, for whom comprehensive planning meant the application of rational planning to an entire city through the vehicle of a master plan. Olmsted junior departed from both of these conceptions, rejecting the master plan as unworkable, and redefining planning as an ongoing process and standard function of local government.

Unlike his father, whose nineteenth-century view of planning embodied a concrete vision of the future, Olmsted junior stressed procedure and the continuous application of expertise to oversee and coordinate discrete changes in the city. Through his criticism of City Beautiful planning, he laid the groundwork for the "more bureaucratic, pluralist, fluid, and hence modern conception" of planning articulated by Robert A. Walker in his classic, The Planning Function in Urban Government *(Chicago: University of Chicago Press, 1941). By scrutinizing changes in the definition of comprehensive planning, Peterson cautions planning historians that they must pay closer attention to the meaning of one of their central terms.*

Readers wishing additional information on Frederick Law Olmsted Sr.'s vision of comprehensive planning may refer to Schuyler's The New Urban Landscape *or Irving D. Fisher's* Frederick Law Olmsted and the City Planning Movement in the United States *(Ann Arbor: UMI Research Press, 1986). For more background on Olmsted junior and his achievements, see Edward Clark Whiting and William Lyman Phillips, "Frederick Law Olmsted, 1870–1957,"* Landscape Architecture *48 (April): 145–57; the unpublished master's thesis of Susan Klaus, "'Intelligent and Comprehensive Planning of a Common Sense Kind': Frederick Law Olmsted, Junior, and the Emergence of Comprehensive Planning in America, 1900–1920" (George Washington University, 1988); and*

Frederick Law Olmsted Sr. and Frederick Law Olmsted Jr.

Peterson's "The Mall, The McMillan Plan, and the Origins of American City Planning," in Richard Longstreth, ed., The Mall in Washington, 1791–1991 *(Washington: National Gallery of Art, 1991).* EDITORS

The urban planning ideas that emerged during the Progressive Era of American history can be differentiated from those of the Gilded Age by comparing the views of two celebrated landscape architects, Frederick Law Olmsted Jr. and his illustrious father. Each is remembered today as an urban planner, and each was a major figure in his own time. The two periods are usually distinguished on the basis of taste and urban form: the mid to late nineteenth century is associated with the romanticism and naturalistic designs of Andrew Jackson Downing, Frederick Law Olmsted, and Horace William Shaler Cleveland, whereas the early twentieth century is associated with the neoclassicism and City Beautiful schemes of McKim, Mead, and White; Daniel H. Burnham; Arnold Brunner; and other architects.[1] The Olmsted legacy points to other differences as well.

Many planning historians consider the senior Olmsted a farsighted advocate of "comprehensive planning" for cities and thus an advocate of precisely the concept that Progressive Era planners would embrace as their core ideal.[2] This claim to continuity and modernity, made explicitly by Irving Fisher, for example, and implicitly by David Schuyler, bears close examination.[3] The father and son, in fact, differed enough in their approaches to the shaping of cities and in what they meant by comprehensive planning to demonstrate that Progressive Era thinking took off in new directions even as it built on the past.

The first Frederick Law Olmsted, the most renowned planner of the second half of the nineteenth century, may best be described as a practical visionary (figures 1.1 and 1.2). Deeply concerned about the onset of urbanization in the northeastern United States, he sought first in New York's Central Park and then in park systems throughout the nation to upgrade the quality of urban life by drawing on his most fundamental ideas about aesthetic taste, family values, public health, and civilized behavior. In this effort, he saw

FIGURE 1.1. Frederick Law Olmsted senior, architect-in-chief and co-designer of Central Park, New York City, about age 38 (c. 1860). Courtesy: National Park Service, Frederick Law Olmsted National Historic Site, Brookline, Massachusetts.

nature as his primary resource. And he consistently used it to achieve a higher-quality urbanism not only in Central Park but in his design of fashionable suburban communities like Riverside and in urban park systems such as those in Buffalo and Boston. From a late-twentieth-century vantage, the senior Olmsted stands out as a reformer who clearly defined the directions he wanted urban society to take and who, by dint of intellect, administrative ability, and personal authority, found ways to realize some of his vision on the ground.[4]

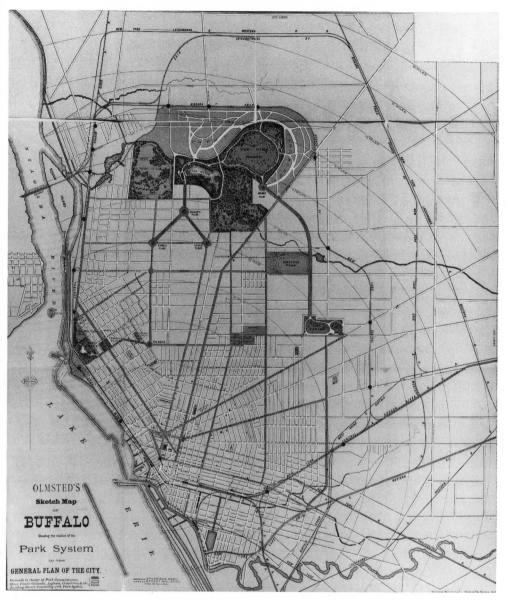

FIGURE 1.2. The Buffalo, New York, park system by Frederick Law Olmsted senior (1868 plan, 1876 illustration). The first park system built as planned in the United States. Courtesy: Avery Architectural and Fine Arts Library, Columbia University in the City of New York.

FIGURE 1.3. Frederick Law Olmsted Jr., copartner of Olmsted Brothers and chairman of the National Conference on City Planning, about age 40 (c. 1910). Courtesy: National Park Service, Frederick Law Olmsted National Historic Site, Brookline, Massachusetts.

His son, by contrast, was more of a professional, albeit a farsighted one (figures 1.3 and 1.4). Born in 1870, raised in New York City and Brookline, Massachusetts, Frederick Law Olmsted Jr. grew up enjoying advantages not available to the father: he attended the best private and public schools, had personal knowledge of great public undertakings, and gained early entry to the intellectual and cultural circles of late-nineteenth-century America.[5] But it all came at a price. Although christened Henry Perkins at birth, he was renamed Frederick Law at age four to bear his father's mantle.[6] Any impulse toward independence was overwhelmed by his

Frederick Law Olmsted Sr. and Frederick Law Olmsted Jr.

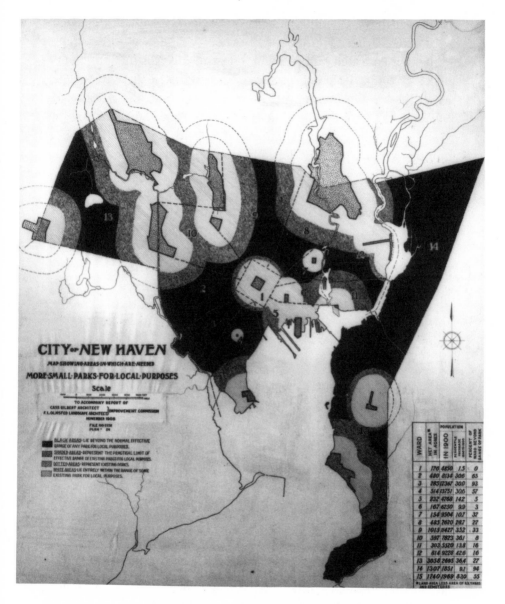

FIGURE 1.4. Small park usage and needs in New Haven, Connecticut, 1908. A graphic study by Frederick Law Olmsted Jr., for the 1910 city plan. Courtesy: National Park Service, Frederick Law Olmsted National Historic Site, Brookline, Massachusetts.

father's zeal to make him his successor. Entering Harvard College at age twenty, Olmsted junior already knew what he was meant to be: a liberally educated landscape architect of high distinction. Under his father's eye, he prepared himself accordingly. While in college, he spent the summer of 1891 helping Chicago architect Daniel H. Burnham prepare for the Chicago World's Fair, and the following year he traveled with his father in England and France for five months, visiting parks and estates that his father considered to be landmarks.[7]

Olmsted senior struggled until his mid-forties to define his professional identity, shifting from scientific farming to journalism and then to landscaping. In contrast, Olmsted junior plunged into his career and achieved prominence at a young age. Soon after graduation from college in 1894, he joined his father for thirteen months in a demanding apprenticeship at the immense Biltmore estate of George Vanderbilt, then under construction in Asheville, North Carolina, taking over full responsibility for its landscaping in 1895, after his father's health failed.[8] Two years later, he and his half brother, John Charles Olmsted, formed Olmsted Brothers.[9] Working out of Fairsted, the grovelike home and office compound established by their father in the Boston suburb of Brookline, they upheld the Olmsted name as the standard bearer of American landscape design throughout the Progressive Era and beyond. It is little wonder that Olmsted junior, with his liberal training, keen intelligence, and consummate professionalism, would become, at age thirty, a member of the U.S. Senate Park (McMillan) Commission for the replanning of Washington, D.C., in 1901 and in that capacity would design a state-of-the-art park system for the nation's capital.[10]

From 1897 to 1909, the junior Olmsted fulfilled his professional role through constructive, farsighted actions rather than a new social vision. In 1899 he helped found the American Society of Landscape Architects, the first professional organization in his field. He also created and taught the first course and, later, the first curriculum on landscape architecture in the United States, at Harvard University.[11] Next, he focused his analytical skills on the legal basis for regulating outdoor advertising, an issue never explored by his father and one that foreshadowed his later interest in the legal basis of planning.[12] Perhaps more significant, he began responding to requests from local groups for plans directed at urban betterment, especially civic centers and citywide improvements. At the same time, he attended to the firm's customary work since his father's day: the planning of parks and park systems, the laying out of suburban and institutional sites, and the designing of private estates and gardens.

From 1910 through World War I, Olmsted junior became the acknowledged leader of the American planning movement, serving as chairman of the National Conference on City Planning, the first national organization to give the movement a sense of direction. During those years he did not seek to amplify his father's vision of the urban future. Instead, he drew on a family-nurtured sense of high professionalism by encouraging leaders of the new movement to deepen their expertise, advance their understanding of the legal underpinnings of their field, and build organizational mechanisms by which to foster cooperative relationships with each other.

Even more important, he applied his probing and skeptical mind to determining what planning was all about. The conclusions he reached set him apart from both his father and the very movement he led. Rejecting visionary impulses, especially those prevalent among City Beautiful enthusiasts like Daniel H. Burnham, who believed that planning should produce a completed or nearly completed design for a city, he came to see planning as a dynamic and continuing process.[13]

The visionary quality of the senior Olmsted's outlook had its roots in the social transformation of the northeastern United States. During his lifetime (1822–1903) the region moved from an agrarian, small-town, merchant-maritime way of life toward a faster-paced commercial and urban existence. Unlike the son, who grew up in and around big cities, the senior Olmsted personally experienced this transformation, and much of his thinking was a response to it.[14] Indeed, he shared with the cultural elite of his era the exhilaration and anxiety that the transformation inspired.

Because Olmsted senior possessed the rare ability to respond in boldly creative ways to the perceived needs of his generation, his vision of the urban future assumed striking and innovative forms. Whether planning parks, park systems, or residential subdivisions, his goal was to develop cities that were more spacious, more healthful, more verdant, and at the same time more conducive to mutually beneficial human association as well as to family privacy.[15] In this way he sought to counteract the congestive and socially coarsening tendencies that accompanied city growth in the United States during the second half of the nineteenth century. Although his vision is difficult to sum up in a word or two—Laura Wood Roper describes it as "communicativeness," Charles Eliot Beveridge as the "more openly built city," and David Schuyler as the "naturalistic city"—Olmsted senior clearly had a compelling sense of the general direction in which he hoped to move urban life.[16]

Unlike his son, Olmsted senior never advocated planning as an end in itself or an abstract public value. Nor did he analyze it as a process in its own right. Rather, planning was a necessary means to the realization of his social and aesthetic objectives. Citywide park systems, for example, called for designs on a citywide scale, but he was concerned less with the methodology of devising such arrangements than with their ultimate physical appearance and whether their scale and function fit societal needs.[17]

It is important to remember that city planning was not an organized movement at this time. Any large-scale shaping of the urban physical environment that was attempted during the second half of the nineteenth century for already built cities generally took the form of limited-purpose endeavors. These included plans for water supply, sewerage, institutional sites, residential subdivisions, and rapid transit, as well as for the citywide park systems devised by the senior Olmsted.[18]

All such planning, no matter how broadly conceived, addressed the needs of a city in limited ways. It was usually concerned with developing a restricted physical area, such as the site of a college campus, or with meeting a specific functional need, for example, for a system of pleasure grounds. The senior Olmsted firmly believed that all such schemes should be thoroughly studied and prepared in all respects. When he urged that their planning be "comprehensive," he meant that the schemes should be fully worked out in all their essential and anticipated features.[19] This approach was applied in his planning of outlying districts, such as the Twenty-third and Twenty-fourth wards of New York (the Bronx and lower Westchester area), Staten Island, and the south side of Buffalo.[20]

Never, however, did the senior Olmsted suggest that planning should address all the major physical needs of an entire, existing city—center and periphery—all at once. Indeed, almost no one in the post–Civil War generation urged this idea.[21] To advocate so grand a view for already built cities would have implied, among other things, a more far-reaching conception of the public interest, a greater willingness to concentrate public authority, and a fuller devotion to abstract ideas of order and rationality than was typical of Olmsted and his peers. It would also have entailed a commitment to the reshaping of the central city, which Olmsted already regarded as irrevocably fixed in brick and mortar by prior decisions.[22] And it would have meant that the planner had to have even broader talents than those possessed by the senior Olmsted or that planning had to become the task of teams of diversified experts.

Olmsted junior belonged to a generation that contemplated planning in almost precisely these terms. The America they faced at the beginning of the twentieth century was a place of booming prosperity, big public improvements, great business mergers, titanic railroad empires, and a new assertiveness on the world stage. Consequently, a whole army of practical and theoretical reformers had begun redefining the public interest in far more sweeping ways than had Olmsted senior's generation. Although Progressive Era reformers generally resisted calling for a statist social order, they hoped that their pleas for a more activated and broadened definition of public life, especially in the civic context, would result in the general uplift of American society.[23]

For those imbued with this new sense of public interest, the old concept of comprehensive planning took on new meaning. The Chicago World's Fair of 1893 and especially the U.S. Senate Park Commission (McMillan) Plan for Washington, D.C., issued in 1902, pointed toward the cooperative use of expertise to frame general, citywide, all-purpose physical plans that provided for virtually all the major environmental needs of existing cities.[24] Comprehensive planning now meant more than the farsighted and thorough working out of a specific agenda. It became something more responsive to hopes for upgrading the whole social order, especially the urban order. It was this new, enlarged sense of planning that the junior Olmsted both shared and sought to recast.

As the new movement got under way, its earliest practitioners traveled about the nation advising civic groups and public officials on how to develop their cities along these more broadly imagined lines. Nearly all their reports proposed visible public improvements, especially parks and parkways, playgrounds, public building groups, boulevards and street openings, railroad terminals, and street furnishings.[25] Because these advisers were by training or outlook design oriented, their schemes could usually be depicted on paper as visions of the future city. By giving concrete form to the public interest in this way, they hoped that client groups would embrace their advice and, in time, carry out their ideas. No one upheld these schemes as final or beyond change, but they came as close to end-state conceptions as practical men ever get.

Like others drawn to comprehensive planning, Olmsted junior initially accepted commissions from civic groups and furnished his share of advice. In the years before World War I, he submitted planning reports for places as diverse as Utica, New York; Boulder, Colorado; Pittsburgh, Pennsylvania; and Newport, Rhode Island.[26] These reports and the public addresses he gave as chairman of the National Conference on City Planning indicate, however, that his idea of the new planning was strikingly different from that of most people in the movement. In this divergence one detects the living legacy of the senior Olmsted, manifested as critical intelligence coming to terms with a new era of American history.

In an essay entitled "How to Organize a City Planning Campaign," probably written in 1913, Olmsted junior analyzed the new planning ideal by dividing its supporters into two groups.[27] The first he called the "central" group, which comprised those who conceived of planning as a centralized endeavor in which a single expert or group of experts formulated a scheme intended to shape the future development of an entire urban area for the foreseeable future. This group, he suggested, viewed a plan as if it were a city charter that offered a framework for all subsequent action. Implicit in such thinking, he believed, was the idea of the plan as the work of a "single master mind."

Such thinking did in fact represent the major thrust of the American city planning movement from its City Beautiful beginnings at the opening of the twentieth century through its City Practical phase and beyond to World War II. During that span, those who subscribed to prevailing ideas kept faith with the notion that cities should appoint planning commissions and that these commissions should, at least in principle, obtain for their city a comprehensive plan, or as it came to be known in the 1920s, a master plan; this plan, in turn, was to control all major lines of physical development.[28]

Olmsted questioned this idea long before it earned its reputation as an ineffectual civic ritual. Local private and governmental groups in the United States had begun asking "experts" to frame general plans from 1904–5 onward. As early as December 1908, Olmsted noted the pitfalls. In a long letter to John Ihlder, secretary to the Comprehensive City Planning Commission of Grand Rapids, Michigan, and later a noted housing reformer, Olmsted remarked that "a report based upon a comparatively superficial examination by an outside expert can hardly be more than a lot of dreams." An ad hoc commission that operated independently of a city's administrative departments is, he argued, "apt to accomplish very little in the long run—to make but a flash in the pan."[29]

One year later he sharpened his critique in a letter to Philadelphia civic reformer Andrew Wright Crawford: "City Planning will never give the best results until it is regarded not as a spasmodic and dramatic thing to be done in a 'once-for-all' manner, but as a continuous process of annually revised forecasting and planning, keeping pace with the city's growth and always far enough in advance thereof to give intelligent guidance and control."[30] Nearly two years would pass before he made any of these views public.[31]

Meanwhile, as he personally responded to civic groups that requested general plans, he wrestled with the big-plan formula in a variety of ways. As early as 1907, in a scheme for Utica, New York, he openly declared that "the future of a live city cannot be clearly forecast, not [sic] can any man pass wise judgment on all the best means of meeting its future needs."[32] Such heresy exposed the pretense to rationality underlying orthodox comprehensive planning. His solution was to suggest a limited number of projects for Utica, resisting the dominant practice of generating all manner of proposals.

Still more revealing of Olmsted's skepticism about big once-for-all schemes was the comprehensive plan that he and two other experts proposed to the Pittsburgh Civic Commission in 1909. Instead of working out a general plan in all its details, they sketched a twelve-point program that reflected the extraordinary breadth of the Progressive Era planning ideal in that it included virtually all aspects of the physical city from water supply to street systems, open space, and private buildings. It even listed smoke control.[33] But it was left to the commission to decide what elements of the program to pursue. In short, Pittsburgh would undertake real planning only for special-purpose objectives. And that is what it did. In 1910 Olmsted submitted a detailed major thoroughfare plan, while other experts separately addressed such matters as electric and steam railroads, sewerage, and a new building code.[34]

Olmsted's uneasiness about one-shot, overall plans was also evident in the general report that he and two other experts framed for the Rochester Civic Improvement Committee of Rochester, New

York in 1911. It was a sketchy affair running thirty-nine pages, printed on slick paper with numerous diagrams and photographs.[35] When Olmsted learned that it would be issued as *A City Plan for Rochester,* he attempted, unsuccessfully, to change the title, offering even to cover the cost. "I do not really regard a report of that sort as a city plan," he told Arnold Brunner, one of his collaborators. Better titles would be either "Studies for a City Plan" or "Report on a City Plan."[36]

By 1913, Olmsted's views had matured, and in his essay that year, he identified himself with a second school of planners, which he labeled the "departmental" group. This group objected to the "central" school's form of comprehensive planning on the grounds that human intelligence was too limited and the city too complex, too dynamic, and too pluralist to be controlled by means of an end-state plan. Although he shared the orthodox idea of the city as an organic, interconnected entity, he insisted that no individual or small group could, at a given point in time, grasp all the interconnections, let alone make complete and long-term provision for them all at once.[37]

There is a distinctly modern quality to Olmsted junior's outlook, especially his sense of the limits of human intelligence, his recognition of the dynamic nature of social reality, and his revolt against planning formalism.[38] Given such a mentality, he backed off from any suggestion that planning should produce a definite vision of the future. Here he departed fundamentally from his father, who had sought to move society in clearly defined directions. Nonetheless, Olmsted junior still drew on his father's capacity for independent judgment grounded in a keen sense of social reality, although he reached very different conclusions about the nature of that reality and people's ability to grasp it.

As a result, Olmsted junior found himself upholding the new planning ideal but questioning the form it was then taking in the United States. In his view planning should not be the production of a centralized, end-state vision, but a continuing process and ongoing function of local government.[39] Its goals lay less in achieving some forecasted end result than in ensuring that all specific improvement projects undertaken by a city be harmonized and be responsive to ever changing definitions of need.

To suggest how planning might work when conceived as a process, Olmsted imagined a new kind of government agency, the City Plan Office. It would have three oversight functions. First, as "custodian of the city plan," it would maintain an archive recording "the entire physical environment" of its city. Files would be kept on everything from the smallest underground conduit to the largest terrain features, "including every piece of land and every building and improvement thereon, both public and private" as well as all past, present, and proposed schemes "deemed worthy of really serious consideration." Second, as "interpreter of the city plan," the office would evaluate all new ideas in light of accepted schemes and physical realities. Finally, as "amendor of the city plan," the office would initiate changes whenever conflicts among the lines of activity developed or unmet needs became apparent.[40]

A comprehensive plan, so conceived, would not take the form of a single, splashy report. It would be a "patchwork general plan," representing a "self-consistent" yet evolving body of officially accepted ideas, never completed, but always controlling a given city's physical environment. Breaking dramatically with the design traditions then dominant in the new field of city planning, Olmsted argued in 1913 that the City Plan Office should keep itself "free to the utmost possible degree from the burden of designing the several parts of the plan." These parts would be better done by departmental "specialists acting under the criticism, control, and creative stimulus of a competent central authority."[41] Here, then, planning stressed not design but procedure, the continuous application of expertise, and the notion that most of the actual changes in the physical city would be made incrementally, as they had long been made, by many different individuals and agencies, only now with a higher degree of ongoing coordination.

In effect, Olmsted junior voiced an early and trenchant critique of the orthodox ideal of American city planning. Crystallized within the City Beautiful movement, the ideal had expressed a kind of philosophical idealism that conceived of a rational, unitary plan framed by an all-knowing expert as the embodiment of the public interest. In its place Olmsted proposed a more bureaucratic, pluralist, fluid, and hence modern conception of comprehensive planning. But it was also a harder one to implement. Remarkably, Olmsted's critique had anticipated by thirty years Robert A. Walker's now classic *The Planning Function in Urban Government* (1941), which also saw planning as "a continuous process" and argued for a more administratively based form of intervention.[42]

These views had at least three important consequences where the Olmsted legacy was concerned. First, Olmsted junior rejected his father's dream of pushing urban society in a clearly prescribed direction. At no point did the son set forth in some compelling way his preferred future. Second, it meant that Olmsted had to be seen as a conservative planner, more so than his father and even his contemporaries. Skeptical of the visionary, he proffered a view of planning more hospitable to the accommodation and harmonizing of existing city-building forces than to the fundamental reshaping of the metropolis. A city that worked better at achieving whatever it was seeking to become seemed to sum up his views on the subject (see figures 1.2 and 1.4).

Finally, although Olmsted junior was willing to exercise leadership within the new planning movement, he never sought to become a commanding figure. Because he regarded planning as a complex and ongoing process, he realized that the field must be peopled by a great variety of experts working cooperatively.[43] He even grasped the point, not too well understood by urban planners since his day, that there could be no such thing as a true profession within the planning field. The requisite skills were too complex and covered too wide a range of specialties for any single person to master them.[44]

As a result, Olmsted junior concentrated on upgrading and deepening planning expertise of many sorts. He pushed hard for improved subdivision design, found ways to advance common knowledge of the legal basis for planning, gave close study to problems of street-intersection layout and small-park usage, and took special interest in legally mandated building-setback requirements.[45] None of this is as exciting as his father's vision of a more openly built city, but it is the stuff from which an amorphous field of public endeavor was given a more solid foundation and brought to a higher state of professionalism. Olmsted continued to associate himself with planning throughout the 1920s, but he gave up formulating orthodox comprehensive plans. It became his objective to strengthen the process of planning, not to fix its overall mission. He was, in short, not a visionary but a statesmanlike professional who, for all his doubts, served his cause well.

CHAPTER 2

The City Social Movement

Progressive Women Reformers and Early Social Planning

SUSAN MARIE WIRKA

The common assumption that "there were, alas, almost no founding mothers" of modern city planning (Peter Hall, Cities of Tomorrow, *p. 7) is corrected in this chapter by Susan Wirka, who firmly establishes the central role several women played in the initial organization of the planning movement in the United States. Wirka argues that between the City Beautiful and City Practical streams of planning in the early twentieth century, there was a third current: what she terms the City Social, a movement "primarily concerned with the social and economic injustices underlying urban problems." Among its leading proponents were Mary Kingsbury Simkhovitch, Florence Kelley, Lillian Wald, and a group of progressive reformers involved in the settlement house movement in New York City.*

Foundations of Twentieth-Century Planning

In two articles, "Woman-Made America: The Case of Early Public Housing Policy," and "From Civic Worker to City Planner: Women and Planning, 1890–1980" (in Krueckeberg, ed., The American Planner, *New York: Methuen, 1983), Eugenie Birch evaluated female participation in twentieth-century planning and concluded that women "had little direct impact" on the rise of the profession. Through fresh research in Simkhovitch's writings and the contemporary published record, however, Wirka has discovered that women were important participants in the earliest activities of the city planning movement. Kelley, Simkhovitch, Wald, and others worked with the Committee on Congestion of Population to organize events that led to the first meeting of the National City Planning Conference held in Washington, D.C., in 1909. Scholars like Birch and Marlene Stein Wortman, in "Domesticating the Nineteenth Century American City" (in Jack Salzman, ed.,* Prospects 3, 1977), *have long recognized the involvement of women in Progressive reform efforts aimed at alleviating overcrowded housing and harsh working conditions for urban dwellers. As Wirka demonstrates, these particular women reformers went on to develop and promote a conception of city planning based on their reform experiences and their conviction that social and physical planning should not be separated from one another.*

Simkhovitch, in particular, advocated an approach to planning that corrected what she considered to be grave biases in City Beautiful and City Practical planning as they were evolving during the early twentieth century. Central to her alternative vision—the City Social—were neighborhood self-determination, community organization, and the integration of social services with design- and policy-based planning. Wirka delineates the City Social ideas set forth at the National City Planning Conference and documents their marginalization during subsequent years. Her contribution brings to light an important stream of planning history and an all-but-forgotten group of planning thinkers; thus it provides a useful framework for analyzing urban social issues today.

For background on the City Beautiful and City Functional movements of the early twentieth century, readers should consult the standard account, Mel Scott's American City Planning since 1890 *(Berkeley: University of California Press, 1969). William H. Wilson's more recent*

The City Social Movement

The City Beautiful Movement *(Baltimore: The Johns Hopkins University Press, 1989) challenges Scott's and Wirka's depiction of that movement as devoid of social content. For the standard account of the work of the Committee on Congestion of Population—one that focuses on Benjamin Marsh and plays down the contributions of women—see Harvey Kantor's* "Benjamin C. Marsh and the Fight over Population Congestion," Journal of the American Institute of Planners *(Nov. 1974): 422–29. Jon Peterson provides an overview of the role of women in civic improvement efforts in "The City Beautiful Movement" (in Krueckeberg, ed.,* Introduction to Planning History in the United States, *New Brunswick, N.J.: Rutgers University Press, 1983, 40–57). For a related study on late-nineteenth-century domestic reform alternatives championed by women, see Dolores Hayden's* The Grand Domestic Revolution *(Cambridge: MIT Press, 1981).* EDITORS

By 1900 the compounding effects of industrialization and urbanization had created unparalleled problems in cities throughout the United States. Overcrowded housing, unsafe working conditions, and public health risks were still important issues on the urban agenda, despite decades of improvements in housing reform, labor relations, and sanitation. Competing ideologies, which arose within the emergent planning movement over the next two decades, responded to these conditions in different ways and vied to define the direction urban planning would take.

According to planning historians, the precursors to contemporary urban planning were the City Beautiful movement, which stressed the aesthetics of urban form, and the City Practical movement, which stressed the efficiency of city management and fiscal policy. Although both are undoubtedly important movements in the history of planning, a third movement, which I have termed the "City Social," also contributed to the formative stages of planning. This movement was primarily concerned with the social and economic injustices underlying urban problems. Among its leading advocates were progressive women reformers involved in the settlement house movement. By failing to recognize explicitly the signif-

FIGURE 2.1. Florence Kelley, c. 1920. Courtesy: Nicholas Kelley Papers, Rare Books and Manuscripts Division, The New York Public Library, Astor, Lenox, and Tilden Foundations.

icance of this third movement, planning historians have long ignored the role of women in planning, particularly in the early development of social planning.

Two women in particular—Florence Kelley (figure 2.1) and Mary Kingsbury Simkhovitch (figure 2.2)—spearheaded the City Social movement. Simkhovitch and Kelley became interested in housing issues, public health, and industrial abuse as a result of their hands-on experience in the settlement house movement. Simkhovitch was a leader in that movement, founding and directing her own settlement house in New York City, while Kelley made settlement houses "home bases" from which she conducted her research and work. In New York, in particular, Simkhovitch and Kelley were part of an expanding network of progressive women reformers who sought to make social welfare issues key concerns of the emerging planning movement.

Under the auspices of the New York Committee on Congestion of Population, Simkhovitch and Kelley helped organize the first national planning conference in the United States. Along with Lillian D. Wald, head of the Henry Street Settlement, Simkhovitch, then director of Greenwich House, and Kelley, Secretary of the National Consumers' League, played an important role in articulating the agenda and goals of the first National Conference on City Planning (NCCP) in 1909.[1] The theme of the first NCCP was "using planning to deal with social problems," and Simkhovitch was the only woman to speak at that conference.[2] Her experience as a progressive reformer led her to advocate a physical *and social* ap-

FIGURE 2.2.   Mary Kingsbury Simkhovitch, c. 1930. Courtesy: Tamiment Institute Library, New York University, New York.

proach to urban planning. That is to say, she argued for links between housing and social services in neighborhood planning and presented both short- and long-term planning strategies for creating more livable urban environments through neighborhood regeneration.

Florence Kelley was a principal organizer of the Committee on Congestion of Population (CCP), which quickly provided a forum for discussing the need for city planning throughout the United States. As active members of the CCP, Simkhovitch and Kelley were among a small but growing group of progressive reformers—many of them women—who believed unhealthy and unsanitary housing conditions were a direct consequence of the seemingly uncontrollable processes of urbanization and industrialization. Another of their concerns was how overcrowded housing and working conditions related to population densities in early-twentieth-century American cities.

Through their experience in urban and social reform movements, most notably the settlement house movement, Simkhovitch and Kelley came to believe that planning should address the social aspects of urban problems. This idea formed the backbone of the City Social movement and led it to focus on the interplay between the physical environment and social conditions of life. Thus the movement placed particular emphasis on social services such as child care, health care, education, and recreation. The vision of planning put forward by Simkhovitch and Kelley and the role of women in the development of early initiatives in social planning are the subjects of this chapter.

The Settlement House Movement as Backdrop

Through its pragmatic approach to reform, the settlement house movement enabled young men and women to bring their sociological talents and perspectives to bear on the social problems of the industrial city. Founded in 1886, the movement was named for its workers who lived (or "settled") in the communities where they worked and thereby had firsthand experience of these problems. Despite the movement's efforts to improve the lot of urban workers, many scholars have criticized it for pacifying, rather than empowering, the settlement communities. Although this is a valid criticism of the mainstream movement, its more radical, primarily socialist, wing—which included Simkhovitch, Kelley, and Wald—did organize impoverished immigrant communities and help them press for better living and working conditions. In moving beyond the mainstream charity approach toward a demand for social change, this branch of the settlement house movement took the first steps toward social planning in the United States.

Mary Kingsbury Simkhovitch (1867–1951) and Florence Kelley (1859–1932) came from remarkably similar backgrounds in terms of factors that influenced their social awareness and motivation toward progressive reform. Each was raised in an extended family of ardent abolitionists and was exposed from an early age to arguments about social justice. Each had strong role models in their fathers. Colonel Issac Franklin Kingsbury was devoted to public service. He served in both the Customs House and the Massachusetts state legislature before becoming the city clerk of Newton, a suburb of Boston. William Darrah Kelley served nearly thirty continuous years as a member of the U.S. House of Representatives, always representing the Fourth Congressional District of Pennsylvania.

As progressive reformers, Simkhovitch and Kelley came of age during a time when middle-class women were attending college in record numbers and creating "female professions" as channels for their newly earned educations. In 1882 Kelley graduated from Cornell University with a bachelor's degree in politics. After being denied admission to the University of Pennsylvania law school, she attended the University of Zurich, Switzerland, where she studied law and government and "converted" to socialism. Simkhovitch received her bachelor's degree in economics from Boston University in 1890 before completing a graduate program in economic history and political science at Radcliffe College. Following a familiar pattern among middle-class women, Simkhovitch also went abroad to expand her educational and social opportunities. In 1893 she traveled to Berlin on a scholarship from the Women's Educational and Industrial Union. There she studied history and sociology, while also exploring her interest in socialism. Like many middle-class women reformers, Simkhovitch and Kelley were drawn to settlement work as a way to put educational and political theory into practice.

Both Simkhovitch and Kelley met their future husbands in Europe; however, each would experience the institution of marriage quite differently. Mary Kingsbury married Vladimir G. Simkhovitch, a Russian Jew, in 1899. Vladimir shared her interests in economics, social reform, and socialism. Throughout Mary's settlement career, Vladimir continued to support her work through his salary and his position as an economics professor at Columbia University. He helped open and maintain many important social networks that were crucial to Simkhovitch's successful settlement career. They raised two children, often combining child care with settlement responsibilities. In 1883, Florence Kelley married Lazare Wischnewetzky, also a Russian Jew, who was a medical student and a socialist. They had three children between 1884 and 1887. Burdened by debt and estrangement, however, their marriage deteriorated after seven years; by 1891 the Wischnewetzkys were separated. Then a single mother of three, Florence moved to Chicago where she got a divorce, took back her family name, joined Jane Addams's Hull House, and began looking for paid employment. Obviously, Simkhovitch and Kelley did not depend equally on the personal, social, and the economic relationships afforded by marriage.

Simkhovitch exhibited an extreme settlement philosophy based on the principles of collective effort and cooperation. Perhaps her most important historical contribution was to the democratization of the movement. In fact, she often referred to settlement workers as "passionate democrats," encouraging them to contribute "a helping hand to the social movements and activities which make for a more democratic society."[3] Acting on the theory that the revival of cities could be achieved through a participatory process, Simkhovitch formed the Cooperative Social Settlement Society in 1901 and founded Greenwich House, the first cooperative social settlement in New York City, a year later. Through both the settlement society and Greenwich House, she worked to demonstrate that politically every neighborhood could act on its behalf, that the settlement's role was to facilitate and protect the neighborhood's interests, and that a strong settlement program was essential to achieve that end. "The activities settlements conduct," as she later wrote, "are wholly secondary, no matter how useful or fascinating, to their primary purpose of energizing their neighborhoods to develop a common consciousness of need and a common effort to meet those needs, in other words, as we say nowadays, a plan."[4] In fact, Simkhovitch came to see the work of settlements and the idea of planning as one and the same endeavor.

Planning meant community organization, and community organization meant the "conservation of all the resourcefulness that exists in humanity for the benefit of all."[5] Simkhovitch perceived settlements to be natural vehicles for community organization, to articulate the neighborhood's needs. She believed that every city neighborhood had three basic needs: social services, a center to provide such services, and local community involvement. Settlement workers determined the need for such services through social survey work based on sociological and economic research. On a practical level, settlement houses became the primary providers of social services for neighborhood residents. In essence, Simkhovitch's Greenwich House functioned as a social planning agency as it coordinated the provision of child care, health care, and recreational and educational services to the Greenwich Village community. Greenwich House also conducted a series of groundbreaking social investigations into urban industrial conditions, sponsored a number of permanent educational committees, and published numerous studies on housing, health, and education.

The Committee on Congestion of Population

Eventually, Simkhovitch expanded her horizons to urban social issues beyond the settlement community. One such opportunity to do so arose when she became chair of the Committee on Congestion of Population in New York City, which promoted housing reform as a means of alleviating overcrowded urban conditions. Under the influential leadership of Florence Kelley, a small group of "alert social-minded citizens" organized the CCP early in the winter of 1907.[6] Five of the committee's original members (Simkhovitch, Benjamin C. Marsh, Carola Woerishoffer, Edward Bassett, and George B. Ford) were members of Greenwich House; much of the "Committee's work," as Simkhovitch explained, "therefore, largely centered in the Greenwich House membership."[7]

According to Simkhovitch, "Mrs. Florence Kelley, then living on Henry Street, was largely responsible for the formation of the Committee."[8] Although Kelley was not primarily identified as a leader in the settlement house movement, she did have vast knowledge and experience in settlement methods because of her involvement with Jane Addams's Hull House in Chicago and Lillian Wald's Henry Street Settlement in New York City. By the time Simkhovitch and Kelley began working together on the congestion committee, New York City had an active network of progressive women reformers. It was a distinctly female support network that "enable[d] politically and professionally active women to function independently and intensively."[9] The network was a natural extension of women's collective work on urban social issues as well as a result of their shared generational experience as educated women.

Florence Kelley was someone "who had probably the largest single share in shaping the social history of the United States during the first thirty years of this century."[10] She was a sociologist at heart, and she dedicated her life to understanding urban industrial conditions, particularly as they affected the lives of women and children. Key reform issues for Kelley included child labor, infant and maternal mortality, occupational diseases, and industrial accidents. Perhaps her most significant work was done in the minimum wage campaign and the movement for a shorter working day for women.

During her years at Hull House (1891–99), Kelley was an adviser to working women seeking employment. Through her interaction with the women of Chicago, she learned that the problem of tenement piecework—the practice of taking unfinished garments home to finish—was invading neighborhoods and keeping children away from school. In order to fully understand the scope of the issue, Kelley conducted a survey of housing conditions, sweatshops, and tenement piecework in Chicago for the U.S. Commission of Commerce and Labor. Kelley became the chief factory inspector for the state of Illinois in 1893; as such, she was instrumental in passing legislation that instituted the eight-hour work day and prohibited the employment of children under the age of fourteen in factories.

In 1899 Kelley moved to the Henry Street Settlement on New York's Lower East Side where she lived for the next twenty-seven years.[11] That same year she was appointed general secretary of the National Consumers' League. In the absence of unions in the predominantly female garment worker industry, the league developed its own label to identify garments produced in factories that had reformed their labor practices, for example, by not sending piecework home. Kelley worked through the league to improve working conditions for women by harnessing the "boycott" power of the consumer at the national level.

After moving to New York, Kelley sought Lillian Wald's help in a crusade against abusive child labor practices. In 1902 Kelley and Wald were both appointed to the New York Child Labor Committee, which investigated the need for legislation to protect child workers. Their collective efforts called attention to the problem nationwide; later, both women helped establish and served on the first National Child Labor Committee. In 1912 Julia Lathrop joined Kelley and Wald to establish the Children's Bureau, and the three then went on to introduce a bill to Congress demanding the "public protection of maternity and infancy" to combat high rates of infant and maternal mortality exacerbated by industrial life.

Kelley felt that none of the popular reforms would improve living, working, and health conditions for immigrant families unless something was also done about overcrowding in the inner city. Kelley therefore initiated discussions about the "different phases of the dominating influence of congestion on the community life of New York." She consistently drew connections between housing conditions, industrial conditions, and opportunities for health and recreation, while also pointing out the "sinister" side effects of congestion: the rise in the death rate from tuberculosis; the failure of the general death rate to fall below 16 per 1,000 in New York, compared with 12 per 1,000 in the large working-class areas of London; and the rapid increase in population density in the tenement districts of New York.[12]

Much of the work of urban and social reformers over the previous twenty-five years would, she feared, be invalidated by the tacit acceptance of population overcrowding as inevitable. This concern, along with her belief that poverty needed to be addressed as a systemic force—not as a class affair—fueled her desire to form the CCP. In thinking about the problems of congestion and overcrowded housing conditions, Kelley was "struck by an elementary idea." Instead of assuming that people who are poor must be crowded, was it not the crowding that kept people poor?[13] To Kelley and her immediate colleagues on the congestion committee, poverty associated with overcrowded conditions in the city had to be tackled as a societal problem, not as a problem of individual moral character. By the turn of the century, population congestion was widely recognized as "one of a few basic causes of modern city problems."[14]

The CCP defined overcrowded housing conditions as more than two persons living in one room. It attributed this overcrowding to the economic advantages resulting from the concentration of people in a centralized area, which created a larger and more stable market, an abundant and varied supply of cheap labor, and a more efficient means of transportation. At the same time, the CCP warned, congestion should not be confused with concentration or the normal growth of cities. Congestion was "due to unregulated concentration and social neglect . . . rather than the normal operation of economic and social forces." People lived in unsanitary tenement districts, the CCP argued, because such districts were allowed to exist. Likewise, factories were abnormally crowded "in particular blocks and sections because there [was] no rational system of regulating their location."[15]

The Congestion Exhibit

Since the CCP was dedicated to studying the relationship between abject poverty and overcrowding, its main function was to "collect data on the population question and to present it to the public in hopes of arousing concern."[16] The committee's first order of business was a public education campaign "to put on an exhibit showing the terrible conditions, hoping to lead the city authorities to more basic action than any tenement-house legislation or social action attempted up to then."[17] A precursor to the first national planning conference, the Exhibit of Congestion of Population (figures 2.3 and 2.4) in New York was held from 9 to 28 March 1908 at the American Museum of Natural History and proved to be a resounding success.

With its theme that "Every City Needs a City Plan Now," the official objective of the exhibit was "to make clear the conditions, causes and evils of the massing of people in New York and in limited areas; the present methods of dealing with the problems involved; and the methods, legislative and other, which should be adopted to remedy such congestion."[18] As chair of the CCP, Simkhovitch headed the general delegation that was responsible for developing the congestion exhibit; she also spoke at the opening session. The exhibit emphasized the "relation of housing to a proper city plan" as well as the relationship between good health and good housing.[19] It also depicted the extent to which population congestion in New York City had increased housing and transportation difficulties.

The exhibit was an important aspect of the CCP's anticongestion campaign; the committee believed it was the most effective way

Foundations of Twentieth-Century Planning

to increase public awareness of the congestion problem and to sell the idea of planning. The ramifications of the congestion exhibit were widely felt as the exhibit traveled throughout the state of New York. Following the exhibit, the CCP persuaded then Governor Charles E. Hughes to create a commission on the distribution of population "to study methods of securing a more efficient placement of people."[20] New York City soon followed suit when Mayor William J. Gaynor set up the City Commission on Congestion of Population to study the city's overcrowded housing conditions and congestion. Among the city commission's chief recommendations were public ownership of transportation, regulation of construction to ensure better living conditions, and higher taxation of land values.

As a result of the congestion exhibit's overwhelming success and positive public reception, the committee was able to secure the

FIGURE 2.3. A section of the Exhibit of Congestion of Population in New York, held at the American Museum of Natural History, New York, 9 to 28 March 1908. From *Charities and the Commons* 20, no. 1 (1908): 29.

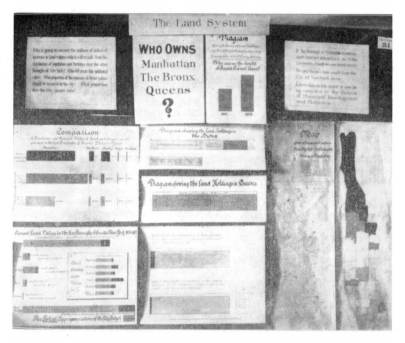

FIGURE 2.4.   A side wall of the congestion exhibit detailing the system of land ownership in Manhattan, the Bronx, and Queens. From *Charities and the Commons* 20, no. 1 (1908): 31.

first New York zoning ordinance designed to reduce density in the inner city. All of these efforts helped the CCP begin developing a national program for city planning. As Simkhovitch explained, "We held an exhibit in New York which pictured graphically what overcrowding meant in New York's tenements. This was the beginning of city planning and zoning and the organization of a national body devoted to planning."[21] Through the exhibit, the CCP suggested that better housing conditions in New York City depended on more parks, playgrounds, and schools and advocated a far-sighted approach to city planning that included improved tenement house laws and public transportation systems. To the committee, these were the essential ingredients for alleviating overcrowding and congestion in New York City.

First National Conference on City Planning

The organizers of the congestion committee felt that it was vital to bring their concerns to a larger audience; hence, a natural extension of their work was to call and organize the first National Conference on City Planning and the Problems of Congestion, held in Washington, D.C., on 21 and 22 May 1909. This meeting brought together the nation's leaders in urban affairs for the first time to discuss a variety of social issues facing American cities at the turn of the century.

The primary objective of the Washington conference was to validate the study of city planning from "hygienic, economic and social" perspectives.[22] This was consistent with the goals of earlier sanitary reform movements that had pressed for a variety of social services to deal with the uncoordinated and unregulated processes of urban expansion. Concerned more with economics than aesthetics, conference participants called for an urban planning process based on sociological research: "a type of research alien to the City Beautiful leaders."[23] Many of the speakers were critical of the growing City Beautiful orientation in planning. One speaker even turned the logic of the City Beautiful around, declaring that "city planning for social and economic ends will logically result in a genuinely and completely beautiful city."[24]

The challenge at this first conference on congestion was What should the United States provide its citizens? The answer, conference participants responded, was to focus planning efforts on "housing, schools, parks, playgrounds, hospitals, transportation facilities, and cultural institutions . . . industrial plants, stores, and offices . . . governmental services . . . the physical environments of towns, cities, and entire metropolitan areas."[25] The 1909 conference program reflected the interests of many groups concerned about the status and future of city planning: municipal art societies, civic improvement clubs, conservationists, settlement house leaders, social workers, public health officials, civil engineers, architects, and landscape architects. Their representatives had clearly come to the conference to address "the multifaceted problems of housing, transportation, recreation, and planning in the cities."[26]

Simkhovitch's Address at Planning Conference

The only woman to address the conferees was Mary Simkhovitch. She argued that better and cheaper transit facilities and regional planning were needed to remedy the congestion facing turn-of-the-century industrial cities. She therefore urged that a national commission be appointed to study and report on the entire subject of city planning and the possibility of an "educational campaign to bring about a city plan for every city and growing community in the United States."[27]

Simkhovitch's experience in the New York settlement house movement gave her a unique perspective on the relationship between urban industrial conditions and the problems experienced by immigrant communities living in industrial cities. In her address, Simkhovitch identified many urban social problems that adversely affected the quality of life for thousands of New York City immigrants. Through the convincing use of statistics, she described the harsh consequences of congestion "in terms of disease and death, the demoralizing effect of noise, and lack of privacy."[28] Population density and distribution were, she said, key elements of the "congestion problem," always making strong connections between overcrowded housing and working conditions *and* urban poverty and industrial abuse.

Congestion, Simkhovitch continued, had come to mean "a conglomeration of pale faces, filthy streets, noise, poverty, disease." But such an image was not the real root of the problem: "We mean by congestion simply overcrowding, and we have to ask ourselves how far congestion is itself an evil and how far it accentuates other coexistent evils." In other words, overcrowding intensified poverty and disease, death and infant mortality rates, but was not "accountable" for them.[29] If overcrowded conditions were relieved through sound population densities and distribution, however, some of the stress caused by congestion could be removed from the already stressful daily existence of working-class immigrant families.

Simkhovitch also described the many social and economic causes of congestion. In concert, they "trapped" people into believing there were no feasible alternatives to unhealthy and dangerous living and working conditions. High rents, for example, forced "a large number of people to live in a small space" and industrial conditions made it "desirable for people to live near their work."[30] They would be able to escape from this trap, she argued, if they had adequate, affordable, and rapid public transit to take them from where they lived to where they worked.

What complicated the issue, however, was that the practical benefits of city life formed "a very conspicuous cause of overcrowding." Being located near the local school, church, butcher, grocery store, dry goods shop, 5-cent theater, and park meant a great deal to New York City's poor. With all these conveniences, Simkhovitch asked, who would not want to live in the city? "The reason the poor like to live in New York is because it is interesting, convenient, and meets their social needs. They live there for the reason that I do; I like it."[31] With those few words, Simkhovitch "cut through the assumption held by many at the conference, that if given the chance the poor would move out of the city."[32]

Indeed, Simkhovitch was opposed to the wanton removal of people from the inner city to the outer suburbs. Instead, a sensible approach that she called "conscious suburbanization" needed to be adopted if population dispersal to the suburbs was going to be used to address the congestion problem. In Simkhovitch's view, the "less congested surroundings" of suburban communities would offer a dismal solution if they did not have "the same social advantages which the city affords."[33] Relocating people to empty suburbs as a way to decongest cities was not an option for her; rather, suburbs needed to be equipped with services that would support the working families living there, services such as child care, health care, recreation, and education. Thus settlement houses—as community centers—provided the basic organizational means of helping inner-city and suburban neighborhoods work effectively.

The City Social: Another Movement in Planning

Simkhovitch's commitment to the integrity and vitality of neighborhoods led her to question the growing trend in the planning movement of treating physical and social issues as if they were unconnected. She strongly felt that planning should not be a purely academic pursuit divorced from reality, as it was becoming in the case of conventional planning, which increasingly focused on the aesthetics of urban form and design, as characterized by the City Beautiful movement, and the efficiency of city management and fiscal policy, as characterized by the City Practical movement. Simkhovitch disagreed with the top-down approach associated with the narrow concept of planning relegated entirely to private individuals and business interests.

Simkhovitch was deeply concerned about what she considered to be the dispassionate nature of the City Beautiful and City Practical movements. Neighborhood self-determination and community organization, notions rarely found in those movements, were central to Simkhovitch's vision of planning: "no matter how good a plan looks from the point of view of a sound economy, it is not a good plan unless the people like it."[34] Since urban social issues were all interrelated, it was vital to link housing and social services in neighborhood planning: "parks, playgrounds, schools, churches, shopping centers, residences, and good transit facilities all hang together."[35]

Settlement houses were at the core of Simkhovitch's vision of planning because they were institutions centrally involved with the development of local neighborhoods at the turn of the century. In both their philosophy and methodology, settlements were well equipped for what she termed the mission of neighborhood planning; she saw settlement work and planning as an integrated enterprise and thus stressed community organizing and neighborhood planning in settlement work. The settlement's aim, she asserted, was "to organize and plan for a local area." Likewise, she felt that the activities of the settlement house itself should play a part in local planning efforts. The function of the settlement house was to bring about "a *conscious plan* shared by the neighbors themselves which will make the neighborhood a good place in which to live and work."[36]

Conclusion

Mary Simkhovitch's vision of planning differed substantially from the one that eventually dominated the planning movement. Her experience in the settlement house movement and the congestion committee led her to plead for "neighborhood planning as the necessary groundwork for a realistic city plan—but a planning not only from a civic, but also from a social point of view."[37] In a sense, she became a spokesperson for the City Social ideology. For her, planning meant attending to both the social and physical conditions in the urban environment. This perspective was by and large absent from the City Beautiful and City Practical movements.

Planning historians have remarked that 1909 represented a brief association between planners and progressive reformers during a time of intensive municipal reform. Within a couple of years, the NCCP was dominated by "landscape architects, civil engineers, architects and lawyers," owing to the growing tensions between housing reformers and those planners allied with the City Beautiful and City Practical movements.[38] Progressive housing reformers rejected the notion that planning should be defined as the physical layout of the city from a purely aesthetic standpoint, in other words, that it should concentrate on form over function. Grandiose civic center plans were useless if the city was not planned so as "to make of it from all points of view an ideal place in which to live."[39]

In response to this trend, members of the CCP, including Simkhovitch, organized the National Housing Association and began holding separate conferences in 1911. Following this split, the planning movement's agenda shifted largely to aesthetic and physical concerns. For progressive reformers, it became increasingly clear that the organized planning movement would not become the arena in which they could address social problems. Consequently, many reformers—especially women—joined the growing ranks of the social work profession in order to continue addressing social welfare issues.

With the exodus of women who defined the basic tenets of the City Social movement, planning lost an important force in its history—namely the contribution of women to the development of social planning. Yet progressive women reformers have not been adequately recognized for their key role in helping define the direction of planning during an era of competing ideologies. Not only have women been left out of most planning history literature, but their vision of planning—linking housing and social services to neighborhood planning—has been altogether ignored by traditional planning historiography. Restoring women like Simkhovitch and Kelley to their rightful place in planning history means expanding the boundaries of that history to include other social movements, particularly the settlement house movement, which regarded social welfare issues as being inseparable from the urban industrial environment.

CHAPTER 3

Fenced-Off Corners and Wider Settings

The Logic of Civic Improvement in Early-Twentieth-Century St. Louis

ERIC SANDWEISS

*Many planners and planning historians have characterized civic improve-
ment campaigns undertaken during the early twentieth century as monolithic efforts aimed at restructuring the physical and political landscape of
the city. Readers will find such a portrayal in two standard histories,
Scott's* American City Planning since 1890 *and* The American City
*(Cambridge: MIT Press, 1979), by Giorgio Ciucci et al. In a more recent
interpretation,* Dreaming the Rational City *(Cambridge: MIT Press,
1983), M. Christine Boyer contends that early-twentieth-century city planning was the calculated response of endangered capitalists acting to safeguard their own interests from a restive populace and the inherent
contradictions of their own past investments. In this chapter, Eric
Sandweiss demonstrates that civic improvement in St. Louis did not*

conform to either model. The municipal reform and beautification campaigns waged in the city between 1895 and 1925 were neither harbingers of change nor centrally orchestrated efforts to preserve the economic and political status quo. At various times, Sandweiss argues, planners and politicians in St. Louis promoted changing and contradictory goals; eventually the city fathers acknowledged that civic improvement had failed to eliminate the city's long-term social problems and rationalized those limits in urban planning's name.

Sandweiss has constructed his case study of the process of civic improvement in St. Louis from a rich cache of primary sources: records of the city's Civic Improvement League; the papers of John H. Gundlach, George Kessler, and Harland Bartholomew; and contemporary newspaper reports from the Missouri Republican *and the* St. Louis Post-Dispatch. *Those sources depict powerful sectional interests and the conflict-fraught process through which urban planning measures were implemented over a thirty-year period. In particular, Sandweiss reconstructs planning pioneer Harland Bartholomew's efforts to mediate sectional differences by constructing a professional rationale that made "the preservation of a familiar urban order seem like a path of bold reform." In this manner—employing civic improvement rhetoric to cloak parochial interests—planners and reformers in St. Louis were able to see their planning ideas realized in urban form.*

Hence, the planning process revealed in "Fenced Off Corners and Wider Settings" does not conform to the heroic narrative depicted in early histories of the planning pioneers. Sandweiss emphasizes instead the process, with all its particularities and complexity, by which the residents of St. Louis implemented and justified their city planning decisions and explains why those decisions failed to transform the city's social geography. Although Sandweiss concludes, along with Richard E. Foglesong in Planning the Capitalist City *(Princeton: Princeton University Press, 1986), that planners functioned ultimately to "legitimate the interests of capital," he demonstrates that in St. Louis those interests were not the monolithic forces Foglesong theorizes; businessmen who profited from planning at one time found their economic interests jeopardized by later decisions. In its elucidation of the process of planning, Sandweiss's discussion joins a growing body of important planning histories. Readers should see also Stanley K. Schultz's* Constructing Urban Culture *(Philadelphia: Temple University Press, 1989) and Jon C. Teaford's* The Unheralded Triumph *(Baltimore: The Johns Hopkins University Press, 1984). For a very different perspective on Harland Bartholomew—one that lauds his achievements and their impact—readers should refer to Norman J. Johnston's "Harland Bartholomew," in Krueckeberg's edited collection,* The American Planner. EDITORS

In 1910, on the first day of spring, 21 March, two quite different public gatherings took place on the south side of St. Louis. The first was a somber event: in front of a dark brick home on south Thirteenth Street, a line of men and women stood waiting to pay their final respects to the city's former mayor, Henry Ziegenhein. A few blocks north, the tolling of church bells gave way to the more spirited strains of "My Country 'Tis of Thee." The music came from a children's choir standing on the broad front steps of a new brick-and-granite building, overlooking a cleared plot of land. The choir's performance was followed by a series of enthusiastic speeches, which culminated in the announcement that the Soulard Branch of the St. Louis Public Library was now officially open.[1]

More than a few city blocks separated the two events that took place in south St. Louis on that March afternoon. Between the career of Henry Ziegenhein and the planning of the Soulard Civic Center—of which the library was the first stage—there lay two quite different notions of how to plan the American urban landscape. The first view treated the city's component parts as inevitable competitors in a political marketplace, each vying for its share of the public improvements that made private development possible; together, those competing parts defined the broader city that comprised them. The second notion began with a vision for a more predictable urban whole, a grand system that, once defined, would determine the character of the city's component parts.

The second view is the one that has come to be associated with the practice and ideology of American city planning. Until recently, the city planning movement of the early twentieth century was regarded by its detractors and supporters alike as having brought about a fundamental change in the management of the urban landscape.[2] But in at least one American city, St. Louis, the Progressive Era planners—like the neighborhood-based advocates to whom they were often opposed—accepted that the city would always be split into disparate and unequally served parts. Their achievements rested more in the ways in which they rationalized and maintained those inequities than in the ways they changed them.

In other words, city planning in St. Louis was neither as revolutionary in its conception nor as effective in its realization as has usually been assumed.[3] In the early twentieth century, the movement in St. Louis and elsewhere was rarely a well-oiled machine. It often suffered from internal dissension and shortsighted reasoning. Indeed, the same certainty of logic that encouraged both contemporary political successes and later historical credulity was also responsible for the movement's failings.

City planning was one among several improvised responses to the disparities of the urban landscape in 1900. By examining the movement's genesis in one city, one can better appreciate the circumstances that enabled planners and reformers to lay claim to a fundamentally new understanding of how to reshape the city. That genesis should also make clear some of the practical limits that kept them from realizing their claim. The St. Louis example extends the more balanced, process-oriented assessments of historians like Jon C. Teaford and Stanley K. Schultz, who consider city planning to be something less than a leviathan force.[4]

The sources of the conflicts that came to a head in St. Louis in the early twentieth century were as old as the city itself. They stemmed from the consistent failure of an ideal shared by the colonial overseers of the eighteenth century and the Americans who succeeded them after the Louisiana Purchase of 1803: the ideal of coordinated public improvements, spread equitably across the city's constantly expanding area. Evidence of that ideal is scattered throughout St. Louis's early history. The limited townscape of the

French and Spanish settlement, founded in 1764, was meant to be a well-maintained collection of central houselots, surrounding fields, and communal pasturage; although property was not distributed equally, it was nevertheless to be maintained in a uniform manner by all of the town's residents. After the annexation of the Louisiana Territory, the new American government sought to lend this initial order a more democratic cast, passing municipal ordinances that enforced citywide compliance with public improvement plans, even as it allowed greater liberties in the actual disposition of private property.

Further opportunities for establishing order in the context of a free land market came as the city expanded its borders through the course of the nineteenth century: in the 1830s, for instance, the government subdivided and platted the 2,000-acre expanse of the old town common, the only extensive property in the city actually remaining in public ownership. This land was parceled into even, 40-acre squares divided by an orthogonal street grid whose scale dwarfed that of the colonial village. Four decades later, the city's landmark home rule charter called for an even wider imposition of landscape order: it established a uniform street plan to be adhered to not just in the common but in all developments, public or private, thenceforth into the future. Each of these moves suggests that city officials had faith in their power to impose a systematic, citywide framework on the private development process.[5]

Through this century of governmental experimentation, legislators consistently saw that faith dashed to pieces. The widening gap between citywide authority and localized autonomy was obvious by the end of the 1800s. The industrial metropolis that Henry Ziegenhein inherited on his election in 1897 was, like all large American cities of the time, an uncertain patchwork of spacious boulevards and unpaved alleys, of new homes with neat front yards and decaying lean-tos clustered around shared outhouses. Such uneven development, though sparsely documented in the historical record, had become progressively more pronounced from the earliest days of settlement. In fact, any pretense of the intended sociospatial order of colonial rule had been abandoned even before Louisiana was turned over to American authority.[6] By the time that American officials began to deal with public improvements, they found that unchecked private development in the colonial period had all but obscured even the actual paths of the city's streets. In 1823 members of a survey commission, appointed simply to find out just where those streets were, had despairingly reported that the old streets were so obscured by obstructions and haphazard development that new streets ought to be established around them and the original survey abandoned. The common, that urban tabula rasa optimistically redrawn in the image of the American grid, proved nearly impossible to sell and develop until it was broken down into individual houselots twenty years later; and the idea of enforcing a new street plan in the 1870s was quickly scrapped in favor of a policy of declaring that unregulated private developments, as they were dedicated, were to constitute the official plan.[7] Piecemeal private development remained the rule, rather than the exception, throughout the century.

Uncoordinated development brought increasing differences not just in the private spaces through which the city's residents moved, but in the quality of the public landscape. Not surprisingly, those differences also reflected the widening gap between St. Louis's social classes. Because the government had never found a way to provide public improvements without resorting to special assessments or case-by-case deliberations, neighborhoods of greater wealth and political clout (particularly along the central corridor that ran west from downtown to the fashionable West End) had captured the lion's share of such improvements.[8] On the north and south sides of the city, poorer residents lived in neighborhoods hampered by poorly improved streets, inadequate transportation, and outdated public services. In the public mind, class inequities came to be tied to spatial inequities; to note social differences was to note spatial differences. When the Socialist Labor Party formed a St. Louis organization in 1893, it included within its platform a demand that "in the matter of public services and improvements, the municipal government shall give the same attention to the districts inhabited by working men and small businessmen as to the grand west end boulevard districts inhabited by the 'better class.'"[9] Those underserved districts were, it went without saying, on the north and south sides of the city, beyond the central corridor.

Choosing Sides: The Sectional Politics of Turn-of-the-Century Reform

There were at least two ways of conceptualizing a solution to the uncoordinated regional polarization of St. Louis's landscape. The first was illustrated by Henry Ziegenhein's victory in the 1897 mayoral election. Ziegenhein won the election by exploiting sectional resentment. He tapped a wellspring of distrust against downtown and the central corridor and campaigned successfully as a candidate for the working people of the city's poorer quarters. "My friends," he told the audience at a Republican Party rally on the eve of the 1898 presidential election, "if you travel over that portion of the city where I hail from, South St. Louis, you would think it is the healthiest place on God's earth. North St. Louis needn't take a back seat either," he continued, "and we can make up for the West End."[10] If the mayor's appeal seemed radical to some, it was in another sense deeply conservative: he inflamed sectional neighborhood loyalties, but he did so in the name of obtaining for his constituents traditional privileges and liberties—especially well-improved streets—that had long been promised rhetorically to all St. Louisans, though delivered to few.[11] His was a vision of a city made up of parts defined from within, by their own residents. The competing claims made by those parts, long ignored, could now be fairly mediated by the political process, which promised to people like Ziegenhein and his neighbors a measure of opportunity that had long been lacking.

Ziegenhein, an outsider to the city's power elite, was unsuccessful in translating his vision into lasting political power. The man who defeated him in 1901, Rolla Wells, was a Democrat whose actual position differed surprisingly little from Ziegenhein's, but whose rhetoric fit more neatly the mood of the West End community that had traditionally held sway over the electoral process. Among his efforts, Wells pushed a central parkway designed to expedite traffic from the West End to downtown, as well as a new city charter that would have eliminated the ward-based House of Delegates and left the Board of Aldermen (the members of which were elected on a citywide basis) as the city's only elected legislative body. Wells and his allies defended this change in terms that suggested the enduring power of Ziegenhein's sectional rhetoric, even as they sought to cast it in the worst possible light. Charter advocates stressed the abolition of the earlier bicameral system as the triumph of the entirety over the part, explaining that currently the "people as a whole have no recourse against boss domination in local districts," and promising that the day would soon come when "no fenced-off corner of the city . . . can force an unworthy man upon the community."[12]

But the rhetoric that equated the "whole" with "the community," and opposed both terms to the narrow interests of the "fenced-off corner," had itself a localized bias. This became apparent on the day of the election, when the charter was defeated by a margin of more than two to one. Only the three wards of the West End voted in favor of change.[13] Support for Wells was as sectionally based as had been support for his predecessor, but it had been defined in less parochial terms.

Evidently, then, the residents of the city's fenced-off corners did not feel that their interests were adequately represented by those downtown and West End voices that claimed to represent "the people as a whole." Their collective voice spoke loudly enough to forestall the new charter that Mayor Wells and his supporters had backed, as well as to defeat other elements of their improvement agenda. But the 1911 charter fight proved to be a temporary setback rather than a crushing defeat in a larger campaign to centralize the management of the increasingly heterogeneous city in the hands of a more select, more powerful group of civic leaders. It was, too, the start of a new explanation of the relation of the part to the whole in an undeniably uneven urban landscape. This explanation accompanied a growing conviction that planners and civic reformers were uniquely equipped to reshape the city in a fundamental way.

From "Municipal Beauty" to "Neighborhood Feeling"

The drive to centralize control of the urban landscape had already been brought to the fore by a volunteer group called the Civic Improvement League, which was formed in 1901. The league's goals were, at first, simple and uncontroversial: to "cultivate a taste for municipal beauty" and to "work up steadily a sentiment among the people" for civic improvement. Its members—most of whom lived in the West End—hoped to set an example that would prove irresistible—to make the benefits of civic beauty obvious and therefore widely desired.[14]

But in St. Louis, as elsewhere, advocates of the City Beautiful (including the architect Henry Wright, landscape architect George Kessler, and attorney Roger Baldwin, all Civic Improvement League activists) soon saw that their aesthetic plans depended on quite practical changes in the way that the city was run. Rechristening their organization with the more matter-of-fact title of the Civic League, they published their comprehensive City Plan for St. Louis in 1907. The plan proposed an alternative to the "riot of conflicting and selfish interests" that had characterized the city in previous years (a thinly veiled reference to the personal-interest politics of the Ziegenhein administration) and argued that the "city, after all, is a great business establishment," which needed to be equipped with the kind of centralized decision-making authority that the executives of a modern corporation might enjoy.[15] In effect, it replaced the paradigm suggested by Ziegenhein's success—of an urban landscape susceptible to the vagaries of competing local interests—with a hierarchical system that translated centralized civic power clearly into civic space. Despite their apparent conviction that this shift represented a fundamentally new direction, the plan's authors offered little in the way of real spatial change. They proposed not to reorient the center–periphery split so embedded in the city's past, but to legitimize it. The case of public building ensembles offers one clear example of that effort.

At the symbolic and physical head of the new city, as conceived in the plan, was the public buildings group, just west of downtown, featuring a new "executive building"—home to a constitutionally strengthened mayor—that would overshadow the existing city hall, the dark refuge of ward-heelers like Ziegenhein (figure 3.1). The hierarchy of power and space that originated in the mayor's office would reach outward from the public buildings group by means of a handful of "civic centers" planned for the city's ethnic neighborhoods on the north and south sides of town. These areas were, according to the league's Civic Centers Committee, filled with "poor, self-respecting, law-abiding [and] ambitious" men and women, eager to receive instruction in the ways of American life. The new civic centers would, the committee wrote, "give to the immigrant—ignorant of our customs and institutions—a personal contact with the higher forms which the government exercises toward him." The committee's plan cleared out the densest blocks of areas like the Soulard neighborhood (Ziegenhein's home turf) in order to provide residents with a school, library, bath house, model tenement, settlement house, and police and fire stations surrounding a newly created park. More than simply an opportunity to provide improved facilities and open space, it was intended as an object lesson in modern civics, a tool for "develop[ing] a neighborhood feeling" in the people who lived around it.[16]

The 1907 plan, particularly the civic center proposal, was a powerful reminder of the rift that divided those who criticized existing conditions in the city. To a politician like Henry Ziegenhein, "neighborhood feeling" might have accurately described a sense of

FIGURE 3.1. Public Buildings Group, proposed in 1902 and reprinted in the 1907 *City Plan for St. Louis*. Courtesy: Missouri Historical Society, St. Louis.

pride based in the relative powerlessness of an area like south St. Louis. That pride was provoked and, in part, defined by an accompanying resentment of the "nonneighborhood," or downtown-based, feeling that had grown more pronounced in St. Louis toward the close of the nineteenth century.[17]

Civic reformers, on the other hand, wished to see the city as a collection of parts defined by their relation to a clearly understood whole. To them, neighborhood feeling implied an immediate identification with institutions and standards that originated downtown and were disseminated in uniform fashion throughout the city. Like their opponents, Mayor Wells's backers presumed the necessity of a firm connection between individual citizens and the larger public interest. They differed in believing that that connection was impeded, rather than aided, by the intervention of neighborhood-based delegates and their self-interested cronies. In place of the city of "fenced-off corners" that they feared, they proposed to place a new fence around the entire city, one that would hold in check the basic divisions in the landscape as they had developed up to that point. When the principal realized element of the Soulard Civic Center plan—the branch library—was finally opened on 21 March 1910, Henry Ziegenhein was no longer in any condition to fight their pending victory. The Civic League and its allies, on the other hand, had just begun to test their strength. The presentation of the city plan signaled their increasing ability to offer new ways of explaining and controlling a familiar city.

Selling Civic Improvement: 1911–1915

The success of civic improvement did not, however, follow an entirely smooth, upward curve. Through the rhetorical veneer of the 1907 plan, the rough edges of a fragmented city continued to reveal themselves. Speaking as individuals, Civic League members did not hesitate to express their frustration with what Henry Wright termed the "lamentable lack of tangible results" arising from the plan.[18] Chief among the perceived symptoms of civic improvement's slow progress was the persistence of St. Louis's deep-rooted sectionalism. Executive Board member George Markham admitted that by and large the league's efforts to enlist grass-roots support from the city's neighborhoods had failed. Existing neighborhood groups, he wrote, "are not united and most of them know little of the efforts of the Civic League." George Kessler—originally brought from Kansas City to consult on the design of the 1904 Louisiana Purchase Exposition and now officially employed as the city's consulting landscape architect—seconded the lament, complaining that St. Louis remained no more than "a group of segregated villages." In 1911, in a rare show of public candor, the league's president suggested that part of the responsibility for these shortcomings lay with the reformers themselves. "The fact must be admitted," he wrote, "that the Civic League has always been an organization of the well-to-do and well-educated men and women of the community and has not enlisted the interest and cooperation of all sectors of the city and men and women in all walks of life."[19]

Civic improvement advocates in St. Louis still lacked two things in their drive to reconceive the order of the city: legal power and philosophical conviction. Both would come, ironically, through the dissolution of the Civic League and its faith in the persuasive power of a positive civic attitude. Perhaps because of its continued public affiliation with the narrow class interests that had proven vulnerable in the 1911 charter election, the Civic League began to lose its status as a leading voice of reform. In that same year, the league faded further into the background, as its members helped to establish a city plan commission with the legal authority to bridge the gap between advocacy and public policy. The commission included both citizens and public officials, and exercised legislated control over city planning decisions once left either to the private sector or to the scattered departments of municipal government.

To serve as engineer, and effective head, of the city plan commission, Henry Wright recruited the young Harland Bartholomew, at the time an associate in the planning firm of George Ford and the author of a new city plan for Newark. Bartholomew, who arrived in St. Louis in 1915, enjoyed statutory authority and set about redressing the second great lack in the existing reform program, a compelling but realistic rationale. Under Bartholomew's guidance, the intractable problem of sectional difference within the city went from being the bane of modern planners to becoming the necessary ingredient for planning's success. He accomplished this change by convincingly defining the planner's job as one of applying innovative means to implement conservative, realistic goals.

Bartholomew began by courting the hearts and minds of those whose sentiments were most influential: the city's business and civic leaders. In the terms they best understood, he informed them that "cities are nothing more than great business institutions." He wrote that the city's prosperity could only be ensured if the "*welfare of the group*" were placed above the "*rights of the individual.*"[20] Although this rhetoric echoed the bottom-line practicality of the 1907 plan, it became in Bartholomew's hands more contrived and self-conscious, in keeping with the professionalized detachment that he and the plan commission had brought to the improvement process. Like others entering the fledgling profession of city planning, they saw themselves not as the actual keepers of the "great business institutions" but as the ones best equipped to reason with people in a way that might benefit the entire city. As Mayo Fesler, formerly of the Civic League and later a key player in the Cleveland planning scene, counseled plan commission chairman and longtime activist John Gundlach, "You must avoid going too fast with them. . . . You ought to have a conservative . . . in the saddle; then the highbrows would not become suspicious."[21]

"Conservatism" is in fact the word that best characterizes Bartholomew's tone in the thirteen volumes (spaced across a period of as many years) that made up his new city plan. Bartholomew continued to treat the landscape as a collection of necessarily disparate pieces, even as he developed a new and more compelling picture of the encompassing whole that comprised them. To create this picture, he developed a persuasive logic that made the preservation of a familiar urban order seem like a path of bold reform.

The most striking and fundamental example of the new articulation of the urban landscape was found in *The Zone Plan*, issued in 1919.[22] Like earlier planning documents, *The Zone Plan* was written in such a way as to excuse and justify its provisions to precisely that group that actually stood to benefit most, the city's better-off residents. Early in the text, Bartholomew reminded his readers that the general goal of city planning was not "to make cities merely beautiful" but to make them profitable as well. John Gundlach contributed an essay, appended to the report, testifying pointedly to the "economic advantages of use segregation."[23]

Furthermore, there was little question in the structure of the report as to whose "economic advantage" was most carefully considered. Bartholomew began by justifying zoning as a solution not simply to problems such as overcrowding and poor sanitation, which afflicted poor districts, but as an antidote to the "wholesale shifting of neighborhoods with consequent deterioration and depreciation of property value." Later in the report, this general statement was developed into the more specific assertion that "no city has suffered more through decline of property values *in the former good residential districts* . . . than has St. Louis."[24] The property-value question, which was key to the zoning law, applied especially to the rapidly changing central corridor, where initially higher land values had created the greatest pressure for speculative investment and for more intensive land uses. Those tendencies had helped lead, in turn, to blight, desertion, and the eventual collapse of property investments. Restrictive zoning was meant to lock in land values through time, by alleviating the kind of rapid succession of land uses that had resulted from the very success enjoyed by the central corridor. Zoning gave legal status to the neighborhood-level distinctiveness that had already evolved through a development process largely controlled by private initiative.[25] More effectively than earlier planning efforts, the zone plan marshaled central authority to formalize existing differences between the parts of the city.

That practical effect was shored up by Bartholomew's developing philosophical outlook. In earlier works, he had described urban growth as "an artificial, not a natural process," one that therefore demanded artificially imposed control in order to stay on a proper course.[26] But the new use-districts, as Bartholomew explained them in the zoning report, were described in quite different terms: they represented "merely the perpetuation and regulation of the majority of present tendencies" and were designed to "let present growth adjust itself to its most natural functions." In fact, "first residential" districts, the most restrictive category, were confined to streets already limited by private deed restriction to single-family homes. (Such restrictions could hardly be considered natural, but they did constitute one aspect of "present growth.") "Second residential," commercial, industrial, and unrestricted zones all corresponded to areas within the city already characterized by the mixture of uses encouraged in each category. The planner's job, then, was not to impose artificial order on the structure of the city but rather to "promote the natural processes and so to curb the artificial processes of growth that the city may become a place of safety . . . where healthy living conditions obtain."[27] By emphasizing and praising the natural or organic aspects of urban growth, Bartholomew stressed the role of the city planner as conservator, rather than innovator, and positioned himself firmly in favor of the status quo of extant growth patterns and social divisions within St. Louis. Although those patterns and divisions had originally evolved apart from the guiding hand of public regulation, they were now redefined and conserved in terms that sprang from the government alone. The symbolic (and largely ineffectual) unification of the city envisioned in earlier plans such as the civic centers scheme now acquired a new solidity at both the practical and philosophical levels. The old, factional city was wrapped together within a new, encompassing package of regulations and civic ideals, then sealed with an explanation of its past and future development that was almost biological in its certainty.

"Failing to Note the Wider Setting": Planning Confronts Its Limits

This emphasis on the city's "most natural functions" may have made the reform agenda in St. Louis more credible, but it also left

Bartholomew and his associates vulnerable to at least two problems: first, a historical naïveté that had practical consequences for their recommendations, and second, the possibility that others could appropriate those same claims to make a case for opposing views. The evolutionary paradigm expressed in the zone plan was used to justify a number of additional aspects of the new city plan that focused more on public improvements than private uses. Among them was the study that Bartholomew later recalled as his proudest accomplishment: his *Major Street Plan for St. Louis.*[28] As in the *Zone Plan,* the engineer posited the existence of a natural pattern of urban growth that, if understood and adhered to, would rationalize traffic circulation even as it protected property values. But instead of focusing on ways of clearly setting off the component parts of the city, the street plan began the accompanying task of tying them together. In developing the systematic, citywide approach that characterized the major street plan, Bartholomew attempted to transcend the old case-by-case, bottom-line approach to street improvement.

Just as in the use-districts, however, the traces of that earlier process cast sharp shadows across the supposedly forward-thinking plan. The abstract, weblike system that Bartholomew showed underlying the existing system, and that he proposed to perfect in his new plan, appeared on paper to represent a major step toward Kessler's earlier expressed goal of using street improvements to "eliminate the terms North St. Louis and South St. Louis":[29] it seemed not to favor any section of the city over another, and to offer a seamless, undifferentiated network of connections emanating from the downtown waterfront (figure 3.2).

In practice, however, the street plan did display familiar, localized biases. These leanings were at once more entrenched and less obvious than they had been in the past, thanks to Bartholomew's evolutionary faith that that which existed was that which was meant to be. As in the zoning study, the empirical grounding of the *Major Street Plan* carried with it an implicit assumption that most existing conditions in the city had come about for good reason and,

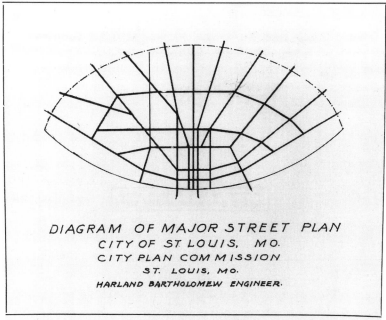

DIAGRAM OF MAJOR STREET PLAN
CITY OF ST LOUIS, MO.
CITY PLAN COMMISSION
ST. LOUIS, MO.
HARLAND BARTHOLOMEW ENGINEER.

Plan No. 7.—The basis of an excellent major street plan already exists in St. Louis. Certain widenings, extensions and connections are needed to complete the system. Each of the lines in the diagram represents an existing street.

FIGURE 3.2. Diagram of the Major Street Plan in St. Louis was prepared by Harland Bartholomew and his City Plan Commission staff in 1917. Courtesy: Missouri Historical Society, St. Louis.

further, that they should be encouraged to continue after their "natural" inclination. This historical judgment had specific policy implications. Bartholomew's data indicated that the south side, with a greater population than either the central corridor or the north side, was nevertheless home to a far smaller percentage of the total automotive traffic headed downtown.[30] Taken together, these statistics might have indicated any of several things, including perhaps the poor street connections that continued to limit traffic between downtown and south St. Louis. But to the commission, they seemed more than anything else irrefutable evidence of the continued priority of road improvements through the heavily traveled central corridor. If those streets saw more traffic, the commissioners reasoned, then that was where heavier traffic must be anticipated. A year later, when the commission updated the status of its original recommendations, the practical effects of this interpretation became clear. In spite of their expressed desire to "benefit every section of the city rather than to provide for a few pretentious thoroughfares" and in spite of their stated intention to pay particularly close attention to circulation "north and south from the business district," Bartholomew and the commission focused their early efforts almost exclusively on the same area that had seen the greatest public attention in years past: the east-west streets of the central corridor.[31] Their conviction that the landscape had taken its form by means of an impersonal, evolutionary process, rather than by a series of conscious and unconscious (but in either case not inevitable) decisions, led them to interpret their data selectively and to speak of their solutions as appropriate and inevitable. In the generation that followed, this interpretation would ensure that the southern portion of the city remained poorly connected to the center and that its overall development remained slower. In the generation after that, the street plan provided the basis for interstate highway planning. At that point, the impact of the early traffic studies became more deleterious, as a range of neighborhoods in the center and periphery alike were shattered by the ultimate response to a study that had been conducted to assist them in meeting their "natural" needs.

Further downtown, where much of the plan commission's attention focused in the years after World War I, the self-justifying rhetoric of planning collided against itself in a more immediately apparent way. Bartholomew had helped to engineer an unprecedented $87 million bond issue in 1923. The bonds at last allocated money to complete a public buildings ensemble in the vicinity of City Hall—this was the oldest, most dearly held aspect of the civic reform agenda. Among the buildings scheduled for the site was a new courthouse to take the place of the old one, eight blocks to the east. Supporters of the new site defended it as a logical response to the natural westward movement of business and civic functions.

The problem was that the old site was in the heart of a still-thriving downtown; landowners there saw the relocation as a step toward the desertion of downtown and the destruction of their property values. Among those objecting to the move was John Gundlach, chairman of the plan commission and long Bartholomew's ally. Now Gundlach turned the farsighted pretensions of city planning against his old colleague, arguing that Bartholomew and others were "so absorbed by the bewitching glamour of this new found jewel of civic improvement that they fail[ed] to note the wider setting of which the plaza [was] but a part." The new public buildings group, fulfillment of a twenty-year-old promise of civic progress, would, he now wrote, "stamp St. Louis as an overgrown county-seat town."[32]

Behind Gundlach's principled but ultimately unsuccessful protest lay a simple concern for the fate of downtown property investments, a concern not too different from the earlier objections of North and South Siders that Gundlach and others like him had for years dismissed as shortsighted and petty. The courthouse issue brought home the fact that civic improvement—even though it attempted to accommodate the interests of the entire city—inevitably served some areas at the expense of others. One person's necessary improvement was another's "bewitching glamour." Such divisions of opinion were inevitable, but never before the 1920s had they split the well-forged chain of professionals, business people, and social reformers that supported city planning. It was at that point that a Civic League veteran like Gundlach could find himself using the rhetoric of the progressive urban vision to dispute an agenda that other adherents of that vision had set forth; and it was then that a Gundlach could perceive that some planning decisions might actually divide, rather than unite, the interests of different sections of the city. When the plan commission's decisions jeopardized downtown property values or encouraged expressways that inevitably carried more people away from the city than into it, the potential detriment of "improvement," which had in any case never been demonstrably more widespread or positive in its impact than earlier, less focused approaches to ordering the urban landscape, finally became apparent for all to see.

The chinks that appeared in the armor of civic improvement in the 1920s should come as no surprise: planning before the depression was rarely the overpowering, comprehensive overhaul of the city that either its supporters or detractors have claimed. The plans of the Civic League and the city plan commission were largely premised on existing spatial divisions and existing inequities in the improvement of the urban landscape. In a sense, they *had* to be. Once accepted, however, their creators built an elaborate system of justification—and encouraged a sense of inevitability—around circumstances that were just as likely the result of neglect or accident. More radical in a way, if less successful, had been the brief, failed attempt of Henry Ziegenhein and his supporters to apply the free-wheeling democratic processes of nineteenth-century government to the realities of the twentieth-century city. That attempt had been labeled selfish and parochial, and in fact it was. So, too, was the high-minded rhetoric of progressive planning. In either case, one group in an increasingly stratified city sought to ensure that the improvement of the landscape reflected its own interests. And in either case, they did so in the name of larger principles of justice, efficiency, or necessity. Whether one defined those principles primarily in relation to an extant urban whole, or in relation to its component parts, depended on where one stood in the city.

Civic improvement was one among several potential approaches to addressing the crises of turn-of-the-century St. Louis. The "disciplinary control" that has been said to underlie the City Beautiful movement is evident less in any sweeping reorientation of urban space than in the planners' skill at justifying the various historical circumstances that together helped to make American cities look as they did at the turn of the century.[33] The controlling hand of civic improvement, which grew out of the City Beautiful movement, eventually found itself opposed not only to the city's poor and outcast but also to some of the same men and women who had first articulated the dream of a rational city in St. Louis. The

Fenced-Off Corners and Wider Settings

Soulard Civic Center, like a few pieces of the street plan and a reduced version of the public buildings group, would live on. Without a sustainable rationale for reworking the social and spatial order of the city, however, they would not have a major impact on the conduct of daily life, either in the "wider setting" of the metropolis or in the "fenced-off corners" and "segregated villages" that stubbornly assert themselves to this day.

CHAPTER 4

The Art and Science of Park Planning in the United States

Chicago's Small Parks, 1902 to 1905

JOAN E. DRAPER

In American City Planning since 1890, *planning historian Mel Scott argued that the City Beautiful gave way to the City Functional movement, a more professional approach to city planning that emerged after World War I. City Functional proponents defined planning as "a systematic method of solving urban problems" based on the gathering and scientific analysis of appropriate factual information (Scott, p. 122). In the small parks constructed in the South Park District of Chicago between 1902 and 1905, Joan Draper has discovered one of the earliest attempts to rationalize the planning process through the application of social scientific research methods. Her research documents the work of several lesser-known figures in planning history—Mary McDowell, J. Frank Foster, Charles Zueblin, and Dwight Perkins—and provides insight into the historical origins of City Functional planning.*

The Art and Science of Park Planning

Using contemporary newspaper articles, published reports, and the records of the Special Park Commission, housed at the Chicago Historical Society, Draper reconstructs the design of the Chicago small parks and documents the decision-making processes that brought them into being. While noting that the commissioners hired Olmsted Brothers to provide the landscape designs and Burnham & Co. to design the field houses, Draper demonstrates that McDowell, Foster, Zueblin, and Perkins were most responsible for developing the standard for play-park site design adopted by the South Park District. By basing their model on data generated by a systematic social survey of conditions in the city, these individuals placed recreational planning on a scientific foundation, setting an important early precedent for City Functional planning. When completed in 1905, the ten small "play-parks" in Chicago's South Park District collectively represented the state of the art in recreational design and planning in the United States.

Draper's findings are important because they reveal that the Chicago small parks were constructed by an early date and that their designs were widely publicized across the country as the products of a thoroughly rationalized planning process. Of special significance, however, is the fact these designs reflected all three main concerns of early-twentieth-century planning thought: aesthetics, social melioration, and technical efficiency. Of these three, the pursuit of social reform obtained through environmental means was the central impetus for the design of the parks for Foster, McDowell, Zueblin, and Perkins. But while advocating greater professionalism in planning, these individuals—unlike many of the later City Functional planners—saw no conflict between science and the aesthetics of the City Beautiful movement.

For an overview of positive environmental reform efforts in the early twentieth century, readers should consult Paul Boyer's Urban Masses and Moral Order in America, 1820–1920 *(Cambridge: Harvard University Press, 1978). Dominick Cavallo's* Muscles and Morals *(Philadelphia: University of Pennsylvania Press, 1980) is the best source on the Playground movement. On the history of park design with special emphasis on Chicago, see Galen Cranz,* The Politics of Park Design *(Cambridge: MIT Press, 1982). Both Michael P. McCarthy and Daniel Bluestone offer fresh insights into the Chicago business establishment's sponsorship of*

reform and beautification efforts. See McCarthy, "Politics and the Parks,"
Journal of the Illinois State Historical Society *65 (1972): 158–72;
and Bluestone,* Constructing Chicago *(New Haven: Yale University
Press, 1991).* EDITORS

On a sultry June evening in 1907, thousands of spectators
gathered at Chicago's Ogden Park to watch children and
adults from various ethnic neighborhoods perform games, gymnastic exercises, and traditional folk dances. The festival took place on
a broad playing field only recently turfed and planted with spindly
trees. This lively display was the culmination of the first annual
meeting of the Playground Association of America, which had
drawn two hundred prominent visitors to Chicago. For these men
and women, who were leaders of the playground movement, the
60-acre park was as much an attraction as were the displays of
Indian-club twirling and Swedish wooden-shoe dancing. This park
was one of ten small parks completed in 1905 by the South Park
District of Chicago. Collectively they represented the state of the art
in recreational design and planning in the United States. President
Theodore Roosevelt, an honorary member of the Playground Association, had urged that official delegations be sent to Chicago to
"gain inspiration" and to see "one of the most notable civic achievements in any American city."[1]

The historical origins of the small-parks design type in Chicago
and the park planning process there provide insight into the development of professional planning practices and norms in the United
States. The attempts in 1902 and 1903 to rationalize the land-use
planning process through the application of social science research
methods paved the way for practices of the 1920s and for the
so-called science of city planning of the early twentieth century. At
the same time, Chicago park planners of those early years saw no
conflict between their attempts to systematize the planning practice
and the prevailing aesthetic idealism of the City Beautiful movement.[2]

The distinctive feature of small parks at the turn of the century
was that they combined the playground with certain aspects of the

large pastoral park, such as Central Park in New York, and the neighborhood recreation and civic center. They contained not only lawns, flowering shrubs, and groves of trees but also playing fields, sandboxes, swings and slides, gymnasia, showers, swimming pools, clubrooms, restaurants, libraries, and assembly halls. These facilities operated year-round, offering structured recreational, cultural, and social programs for people of all ages. Though they varied in design, the parks were similarly conceived landscapes (figures 4.1 and 4.2). The ten small parks completed in Chicago by 1905 were among fourteen of a group planned for the South Park District, one of four park districts in the city at the time; the others were the Lincoln Park District, the West Park District, and the Special Park District. The South Park District was the richest, since it included the Loop— the central business district—in its taxation area. Its leaders also put the most effort into expansion after the Illinois state legislature lifted a ban on the acquisition of new parks in Chicago in 1903.

The South Park commissioners hired the long-established firm of Olmsted Brothers of Brookline, Massachusetts, to design the small parks landscapes and the Chicago architectural firm of Burnham and Company to do the field houses. The field houses were designed by Edward Bennett, a young graduate of the Ecole des Beaux-Arts in Paris who had recently been recruited from New York by Daniel Burnham.[3] The field houses were the first designs Bennett made for his new employer. Representatives of both the Burnham and Olmsted firms had worked together before on major commissions, including the 1893 World's Columbian Exposition in Chicago and subsequently the Senate Park Commission Plan for Washington, D.C.[4] The two firms were also working on designs for Chicago's Grant Park in the Loop.

The South District's new parks were to be quite different from Chicago's existing "pleasure grounds," which had been completed over the years since 1869 and included Washington and Jackson parks, also designed by the Olmsted firm.[5] In contrast, the ten new parks of 1903–5 were to be smaller and were intended to be neighborhood recreation centers in some of the city's most congested

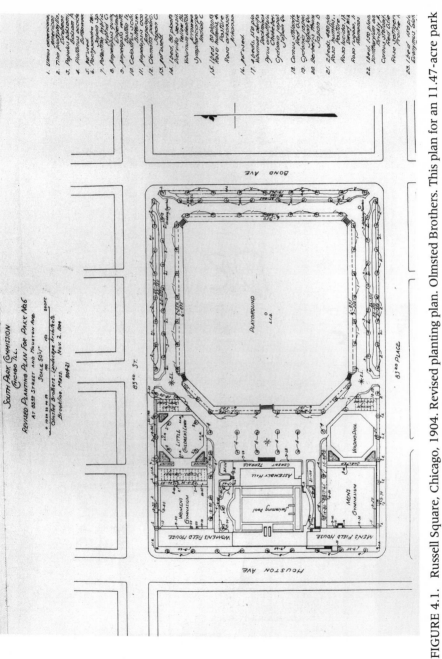

FIGURE 4.1. Russell Square, Chicago, 1904. Revised planting plan. Olmsted Brothers. This plan for an 11.47-acre park is similar to the other smaller parks among the fourteen new parks. The field houses and assembly hall building were designed by Edward Bennett for Burnham and Co. Courtesy: Chicago Park District Special Collections.

The Art and Science of Park Planning

FIGURE 4.2. Davis Square, Chicago, c. 1905. A settlement house kindergarten class, probably from the University of Chicago Settlement, in the sand court in front of the field house. Courtesy: Chicago Historical Society.

tenement areas rather than large parks serving the city's entire population. Two additional parks planned in 1903, but not completed until 1913, followed the original Olmsted and Burnham schema, making a total of twelve neighborhood parks in this group. These first small parks ranged in size from 7.41 acres (Hardin Square) to 60.6 acres (Sherman Park). The small-park schema developed by John Charles Olmsted had been worked out for a plot of approximately 10 acres; Armour Square with 10 acres and Davis Square at 8.29 acres are typical examples. This schema later became recognized in landscape and planning handbooks as a standard. The planning literature referred to the type as a "play-park," a more descriptive term coined for use in zoning codes by legal expert Edward Bassett.[6]

The planning and design of the first Chicago small parks were influenced by all three ideological threads of early-twentieth-century American planning: aesthetic idealism, social melioration, and technical efficiency. The search for the "science of city planning" that dominated planning practice in the 1910–20 period was already evident in Chicago's planning activities from 1903 on: a conscious attempt was made to apply the research methods of social science to the process of park location and to effect social control through site design. At the same time, beauty mattered. The park designs reflected the same yearning for beauty, monumentality, and order that had been inspired by the 1893 Chicago World's Fair. Like the architects and patrons of the fair, the designers and advocates of Chicago's small parks believed in aesthetic idealism, that classical order in civic architecture could help forge social cohesiveness and move civilization to a higher plane: "The effect of a good building, in which an untrained boy studies or plays, is far more insidious than is that of some imposing, but remote public monuments. . . . Such surroundings cannot fail in the long run to make for a higher standard of public or private taste."[7]

With their use of classical detail, symmetry, axiality, and a formal landscape setting, the designs of the small-parks buildings came to resemble that of an ideal civic center of the City Beautiful era. Although the field houses have no domes or free-standing colonnades, the ten buildings—nine of which are off-white, rough-cast concrete structures with green tile roofs—clearly reflect the conventions of classical architecture and Beaux-Arts urban design. Each of Bennett's buildings has a decidedly public and official character, looking more like a library or city hall than a sports facility and neighborhood social hall. Pilasters and cornices molded in concrete articulate these symmetrical buildings. Each field house dominates its setting by virtue of its hierarchical placement, at the focus of an axis defined by flanking structures. The U.S. Capitol building stands in such a relationship to the buildings on the Mall in Washington, D.C. The 1902 Senate Park Commission Plan by Burnham and Frederick Law Olmsted Jr. strengthened the hierarchical motif. Emulating the nation's capitol, the ideal city hall would stand in the same relationship to other public buildings in a contemporary civic center plan. The 1909 *Plan of Chicago* by French architect Fernand Janin shows an arrangement similar to that between Bennett's field house and gymnasium buildings at Sherman Park, except that a swimming pool replaces the plaza.[8]

Officials of Chicago's South Park District had originally favored picturesque landscape designs, while the Olmsted firm recommended the decidedly formal style.[9] The final site plans show a compromise. The lines of the landscaping were softened, but the architecture and its placement on the site remained formal.[10] South Park District President Henry Foreman, obviously won over to the designers' point of view, proudly remarked that the new small parks "reflected in miniature the architectural beauty of the White City."[11] He was not alone in believing that "proper" architecture could have salutary effects on the residents of tenement neighborhoods. As one St. Louisan declared of his city's proposed neighborhood civic center, "It would foster civic pride and its influence extend to every home in the district. . . . It is in relation to the immigrant that the neighborhood center would perform one of its most important functions."[12] Henry Foreman also helped bear out the prediction of World's Columbian Exposition Director Franklin Head, who proclaimed in 1893, "The appreciation of the use and value of beauty and of the arts which make gentle and embellish life, has, by the object lesson of the Fair, been far more widely diffused among our people than ever before. . . . The result of this must be a vast improvement in domestic and public architecture."[13]

Nevertheless, Chicago's small-parks agenda was primarily the result of a move to achieve social reform through environmental means. Its instigators certainly collaborated amicably and fruitfully with Edward Bennett and John Charles Olmsted, but for different ends. These reformers initiated the small-parks project and defined the content of the designer's program. They also introduced the idea that decisions about the shape and location of parks should be based on a rational analysis of social science data. In this respect, the social reformers were more professionally farsighted than the "planning professionals" Olmsted and Bennett. Bennett, of course, was at this time young and inexperienced, just beginning his planning apprenticeship with his mentor, Burnham. Olmsted's role here was not unprofessional; it was merely limited—by the firm's contract with the South Park District—to providing landscape design services. His correspondence with district officials contains little of a conceptual or theoretical nature, and his firm did not participate in the selection of park sites.

The evidence also suggests that Olmsted Brothers had not intended this commission to produce a national standard for the design of play-park sites, but that was the result nonetheless. John Charles Olmsted had advised the Chicago South Park Commission "against the adoption of a uniform list of accommodations to be provided in these playgrounds," and he thought "it undesirable to make these playgrounds substantially all alike." Furthermore, he felt that "a strong effort should be made . . . to discover some sensible reasons for making the plan of each playground unique."[14] Although each of the parks is different, owing to the variation in lot size and facilities provided, a general standard was developed, not only for Chicago but also for the country. Adaptations of this Chicago play-park type appeared almost immediately in other cities: two notable examples are the 1905 San Francisco Plan by Daniel Burnham and Edward Bennett, and the 1907 St. Louis City Plan, which contained several illustrations of Chicago's small parks.[15] The widely disseminated 1909 *Plan of Chicago* included a site plan of the largest of the new parks, Sherman Park, along with photographs of two others. Illustrations of "typical examples" from Chicago's South Side, usually Davis Square or Armour Square, soon appeared in books about park design aimed at professionals. One example is *American Playgrounds,* edited by Everett B. Mero; this 1909 publication contains a whole chapter on the park system in south Chicago.[16] Another is *Playground Technique and Playcraft* by Arthur Leland and Lorna Higbee Leland, first published in 1909 and reissued in 1913; it illustrates Armour Square.[17] Many more plans and photographs of Chicago's small play-parks appeared in popular magazines and periodicals on landscape architecture and planning.[18]

The Chicago play-park site design apparently satisfied the desire of the landscape architects and planners to set standards for their professions according to recognized criteria, even though that had not been John Charles Olmsted's stated aim. Like recreation workers, landscape architects and planners of the first decade of the century were attempting to professionalize their practices. In this regard, the aims of environmental designers paralleled those of the new recreation professionals. Later, in the 1920s, planners pursued the same goal when they developed expertise in coping with automobile traffic.[19] Thus social science and the recreation movement underwent two kinds of changes in this era. First, professionalism replaced the reforming psychology of social science associations; academics and expert professionals took over from morally driven reformers. Second, professionalism pronounced ordinary citizens unfit to manage their own lives and their own communities. The parks and recreation profession and its national organizations furthered this dependence, declaring city streets and vacant lots unfit for play. Hence, the myth arose that the only wholesome play environment was one that had lush lawns and hired supervisors.[20] The landscape architects and planners pursued these goals, as well as their own professional development.

But where, exactly, did this model come from? The original Chicago play-parks were, in fact, elaborate versions of earlier prototypes designed for other American cities by Olmsted Brothers. These prototypes all combined the playground with the landscaped park and various neighborhood-center facilities. Earlier models included the Olmsteds' 1889 Charlesbank Playground in Boston and Central Park in Louisville of about 1900.[21] The origin of these professionally designed landscapes, however, was a physically modest concept applied in the first American playgrounds established in the 1880s and 1890s in Boston, New York, Philadelphia, Baltimore, and Chicago. An example is Chicago's Hull House Playground, which Jane Addams opened in 1894. The first concern of the creators of these early playgrounds was not aesthetic quality, and they were able to provide far fewer facilities than in the play-parks of 1903. The impetus to build these first playgrounds had come from the newly organized Playground movement, which saw a need for "sand gardens," play equipment, and playing fields for urban children who had no family yards or access to country fields. The campaign to build playgrounds was one of many Progressive Era initiatives, which included child labor legislation, welfare and public health programs, tenement house regulations, and social settlements. Playground movement leaders such as Joseph Lee of Boston and Dr. Luther Gulick of New York agreed that urban working-class children, especially the offspring of immigrants, needed to be rescued from the unsafe and socially and morally destructive conditions in city streets, tenements, saloons, and penny arcades. These recreation specialists considered organized and supervised play to be a vital medium for developing cognitive skills, moral virtues, and social values, as well as healthy bodies. The ultimate purpose of the playground, they believed, was to help shape a cohesive, stable, modern society out of a disparate and disruptive population. In short, the playground was to be an environmental agent of social reform and social control.[22]

Many Chicagoans were active in the Playground movement, including members of the civic elite and the professional, philanthropic, and academic communities.[23] The academics in particular helped build the scientific foundation of recreation planning in Chicago and elsewhere. Four individuals, in addition to designers John Charles Olmsted and Edward Bennett, deserve recognition for advancing the cause of the model small park in South Chicago and for putting its design and planning on a more scientific basis: Mary McDowell, J. Frank Foster, Charles Zueblin, and Dwight Perkins.

Mary McDowell had been head resident since 1894 of the University of Chicago Settlement. She lived and worked in the Packinghouse area of south Chicago, in the vicinity of the Union Stockyards. Davis Square was located near her house. Of all the settlement house directors in Chicago, McDowell seems to have been the most forceful and consistent in goading Chicago park boards into action. Significantly, she had been to Boston to observe early playgrounds there. In 1907 she became a founding member of the Playground Association of America. In the 1890s she had ridden herd on Chicago's Special Park Commission, a woefully underfunded body established by the city council to build playgrounds. The commission began its rudimentary playground-building work in 1899. It stemmed from a parks survey made by the Municipal Science Club, but not published. The club had been spurred on by New York reformer Jacob Riis, who gave a rousing speech about parks at Hull House. In 1902 and 1903 McDowell put her weight behind the new, expanded small parks of the South Park District. In her mind, these parks were the municipal equivalent of the settlement house, though on a grander scale.[24]

Another important figure was J. Frank Foster, the long-time superintendent of the South Parks. He was of humble origins but rose steadily through the ranks. He was obviously well connected with the local Playground movement and had looked at playground and park planning in other cities. Although Henry G. Foreman, president of the South Park Commission's Board, had led the financial and political campaign in support of enlarging the South Park System, it was Foster who conceptualized the new parks. He drew up two complete prototype plans for a 10-acre park and presented them to John Charles Olmsted when the landscape architect was contacted about the commission in 1903. Olmsted's copies of Foster's schemes are preserved in the Olmsted Archives at Brookline, Massachusetts, which also contain a letter from Olmsted to the board president criticizing Foster's plans for their lack of order and waste of space.[25] Nevertheless, the finished park plans closely resemble one of Foster's diagrams. Olmsted had merely regularized Foster's scheme, which, significantly, consisted of a combination of elements from earlier Olmsted park plans that Foster had studied over the years in various Playground movement publications.

Typically, the Chicago small park is rectangular; its dimensions were determined by the existing plat plan, since land had to be purchased in already developed neighborhoods and the buildings cleared from the site. The field house was symmetrically placed at one end of the rectangular plot. To one side of the building was the men's outdoor gymnasium, which usually included a running track and elaborate gymnastic equipment. On the other side was the outdoor gymnasium for women and children, often equipped with a wading pool. Pictures of Davis Square after it opened in 1904 show a swimming pool between the field house and the street. The large, tree-ringed playing field was opposite the pool, along the central axis of the park and the field house. Other parks repeated the general schema, with variations. All parks were originally fenced all around with iron pickets. Similar fencing was used within park grounds to keep men, women, and children apart for the convenience of the professionally trained recreation directors and to preserve propriety. Accounts of park programs explain how the supervised recreational and educational programs made use of the highly structured spaces. As these documents underscore, park officials and recreation directors were intent on controlling and molding the social behavior of residents in immigrant neighborhoods.[26] Old photographs of the small parks in the National Park Service's Olmsted Archives reveal a plethora of directive signs posted at gates (figure 4.3), and the policemen frequently appearing in these images seem to reinforce the controlling nature of the physical environment.

Charles Zueblin, who also played an important role in the creation of Chicago's small parks, was a sociologist and urban reform activist. After training as a minister at Yale and in Germany, he moved to Chicago in 1891, living first at Hull House. He founded the Northwestern University Settlement in Chicago in 1892, while he was on the faculty of Northwestern University.[27] In 1894 Zueblin joined the new Department of Sociology at the University of Chicago, where he remained until 1908. Zueblin taught primarily in the extension department and was not a leading scholar in the field of sociology. He focused on municipal improvement as applied sociology. Zueblin led a number of civic and philanthropic organiza-

FIGURE 4.3. Bessemer Park, Chicago, 1904. View of the field house and the entrance to the children's playground and the gymnasium. Courtesy: National Park Service, Frederick Law Olmsted National Historic Site, Brookline, Massachusetts.

tions. He was elected president of the American League for Civic Improvement in 1901, shortly after the founding of this activist organization for municipal improvement.[28] He also authored numerous articles, a chapter in the *Hull House Maps and Papers,* and four books, which attest to his reformist zeal.[29] After being forced to resign from the university faculty for speaking publicly against business interests, he became a freelance journalist and lecturer.

Zueblin had a special interest in parks. He served as a member of the Municipal Science Club, a business and professional organization. This group's study of parks and recreation in Chicago around 1898 prompted the creation of Chicago's Special Park Commission the next year. Zueblin was a founding member of the commission, along with nine aldermen, the architect Dwight Perkins, the landscape architect Ossian Simmonds, Graham Taylor of Chicago Commons Settlement, the president of the Art Institute of Chicago, a physician, and representatives of the three other park commissions. The Special Park Commission had three tasks—to study park and playground needs in Chicago, to present a plan for a metropolitan park system, and to establish playgrounds wherever possible—and Zueblin played a key role in achieving each of them. The commission ultimately accomplished these aims, but its appropriations before 1910 were woefully small. Consequently, it acted more as a policy and planning body than as a modern parks and recreation department. What playgrounds it could provide used land and equipment scrounged from any and every source. The small, ill-equipped playgrounds built by the Special Park Commission were located wherever a scrap of land could be leased or begged.[30] The city's ad hoc approach to design and planning continued the earlier practices of settlement houses, which were eager to provide any bit of open space for children in crowded neighborhoods.

Zueblin and his colleagues on the commission worked to professionalize and to systematize these methods, however. Several documents reveal how the idea of rationalizing park location planning developed in Chicago. In 1898, as a result of the Municipal Science Club's study of parks, Zueblin published an extensive article on the subject in the *American Journal of Sociology*.[31] In the article he not only described the few existing playgrounds, but printed maps of their location and began to correlate this spatial information with population figures. He noted, for example, that "between six and seven hundred thousand people live more than a mile from any large park" and that in the eleven wards with the most existing parks, there were 234 people to an acre of park space, whereas in twenty-three other wards the figure was 4,720 people per park acre.

Zueblin's approach, though rudimentary in comparison with later park planning practices, reflects the influence of Hull House, which pioneered the mapping of social information, as well as the tenor of the sociology department at the University of Chicago around 1900. His senior colleagues, Albion Small and Charles Henderson, also worked to link scholarship and activism and through empirical studies of social welfare problems, attempted to uncover their causes and thus find the means to resolve them.[32] These founding fathers of Chicago sociology, like their colleagues elsewhere in the United States, were "eager to create a scientific description of society and driven by a conviction that science not only liberated by giving understanding, but provided the practical tools with which to realize the just and virtuous [democratic] society."[33]

Driven by such convictions, as well as being inspired by English precedents, American sociologists and social reformers began conducting social surveys of Chicago neighborhoods in which they perceived pathological conditions. In 1894, for example, Charles Henderson of the University of Chicago's sociology faculty published a small book, *A Catechism for Social Observation*, describing simple techniques for use by untrained investigators.[34] The Hull House survey undertaken by Jane Addams and her colleagues in 1895 describes conditions in her West Side neighborhood. This famous early survey used the mapping technique, although it came to be regarded as piecemeal and unsystematic by academic sociologists.[35] Similarly, the City Homes Association, in its 1901 study *Tenement Conditions in Chicago*, focused on only a few target areas of moderate deterioration and social disorder, mostly on the west side of Chicago.[36] At the same time, other social scientists ventured into areas of the urban "social laboratory" that constituted some of Chicago's most notorious slums on the South Side: Steeltown and Packingtown, or "Back of the Yards," the setting for Upton Sinclair's muckraking novel, *The Jungle*.[37]

Using data collected by sociologists and social reformers in various Chicago neighborhoods, as well as its own data, the Special Park Commission assessed conditions in each of the three geographical regions of the city, as delimited by the Chicago River and by park district boundaries established in 1869. Condition reports, one for each region, noted that population density was as high as 360 persons per acre in spots, and that the South Side stockyards area had 500 saloons but only 26 schoolyards. Impressionistic data about poor housing and environmental conditions were mixed with statistics. Large-scale maps were made to illustrate concentrations of juvenile delinquency and other social problems (figure 4.4). In addition to the reports on existing conditions, the Special Park Commission produced three "Reports on Sites and Needs," one for each of Chicago's park districts.[38] These reports referred to actual sites by street address in the neighborhoods most in need of open space and recreational facilities. Their significance lies in their attempt to be systematic and objective in fixing park locations. The determination of sites and needs was based on "studies of density of population, bad housing, remoteness from parks, excessive mortality, destitution of open spaces and recreation grounds, juvenile criminality and delinquency."[39]

The methodology was crude, especially in comparison with the confidently proscribed formulas of the 1920s handbooks on planning and recreation.[40] For example, the Special Park Commission reports of 1902–3 failed to differentiate clearly between playgrounds and small parks, whereas only a few years later park planners clearly defined a hierarchy of park types.[41] Nor did these early reports attempt to relate park size to the estimated number of potential users within a half-mile, the presumed optimum walking distance. By recommending a standard of 1 park acre for every two hundred inhabitants, the Special Park Commission did prepare the groundwork for the norms established in the 1920s. In 1902 the ratio of park acre to population for the city as a whole was 1 to 787, while the South Side was somewhat better served with a ratio of 1 to 515, although it was still deficient. The Special Park Commission's suggested ideal small-park size—10 acres—would later be revised upward to 20.[42]

What happened as a result of the reports? Only the South Park Commission acted immediately; the West and Lincoln Park districts responded more slowly and less generously. Enabling acts first had to be passed by the state legislature in 1899, 1901, and 1903 to allow new land to be purchased and additions of more than 10 acres

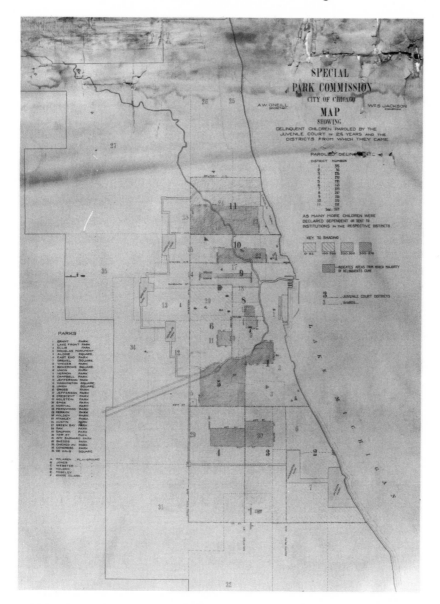

FIGURE 4.4. Special Park Commission map showing the number of delinquent children paroled by the juvenile court in 2½ years and the districts from which they came, c. 1902–3. Courtesy: Chicago Park District Special Collections.

to be made. In a 1902 referendum South District voters approved the use of their tax dollars to pay the interest on bonds to be sold for park construction. The district's commissioners then went to work to enlarge their park system.[43] This district had the financial resources, as well as the committed leadership of Henry Foreman— board president, banker, and one of the founders of the Chicago stockyards. The commissioners began their program of developing neighborhood parks with the 34-acre McKinley Park, built in 1902 on the site of a racetrack turned unsightly cabbage patch; this park gave Foster a chance to try out the new schema combining landscaping, playgrounds, a field house, and a pool, but it was not located according to the Special Park Commission recommendations, nor was it designed by the Olmsted and Burnham firms, who were hired in 1904. Once on the job, they jointly began work on designs for fourteen more small parks and for Grant Park along the lakefront in downtown Chicago.

The professionals had no role in the selection of small-park sites, however; that task was performed in 1903 by the South Park Board of Commissioners, a body appointed by the Supreme Court of Illinois. The board followed the recommendations in the Special Park Commission report closely. Seven of the fourteen new parks were located exactly as the report had suggested. Three sites, however, were chosen in response to requests from local residents or politicians. For example, the location of Bessemer Park, built on 22.99 acres at Muskegon and 89th streets in south Chicago, was suggested by Alderman Patrick H. Moynihan, and several others, including representatives of the South Chicago and Calumet Improvement Association. Fuller Park, initially a 10.5-acre site near the Union Stockyards, was moved twice, first when the site authorized by the commission proved too expensive, and again when property owners and members of the Patrons and Parents Club of the local school objected to the new location.[44] All new parks exceeded the recommended sizes. Twelve of the parks were to be recreation centers adjacent to schools, also as suggested. Four of the parks were in the stockyards area, four were in south Chicago, and three were in or near Bridgeport, another dense, working-class neighborhood by the river. Three new parks were in middle-class areas. By 1905 the city had spent nearly $3 million completing ten small parks with field houses, and by 1907 expenditures by the South Park Board for small parks totaled $6.5 million.[45]

None of the early reports was ever published, so they had only an indirect influence on park plans, although they did form the basis of a comprehensive 1904 plan for metropolitan parks, also produced by the Special Park Commission. This plan was primarily the work of architect Dwight Perkins and landscape architect Jens Jensen, but Zueblin and others made many contributions.[46] Perkins was a multi-talented architect who combined professional practice with public service. Trained at the Massachusetts Institute of Technology, Perkins apprenticed with Henry Hobson Richardson in Brookline, Massachusetts, and with Daniel Burnham and John Root in Chicago between 1888 and 1893. His own best-known buildings from subsequent years are the schools designed in the Prairie style during his tenure as architect for the Chicago Board of Education (1905–10) and buildings for the Lincoln Park District, including the Refectory (1908) and Lion House (1912). Perkins also had strong ties to settlement house workers, through his mother's association with Jane Addams. He designed new buildings for the University of Chicago Settlement and the Northwestern University Settlement in 1900. Thus his involvement with the Municipal Science Club and the Special Park Commission forms part of a lifelong commitment to environmental reform.[47]

The 1904 Metropolitan Park Plan (figure 4.5) formulated for the entire Chicago region was in keeping with City Beautiful ideology: professional planners should be the managers of the entire urban environment and parks and other "municipal improvements" had the potential to mold to positive ends people's attitudes and behaviors.[48] A comparison of population and park acreage in several large cities showed that between 1870 and 1900 Chicago had dropped from second to nineteenth place in terms of inhabitants per acre of parks. In the period from 1900 to 1904, however, the total acreage in Chicago's four park systems increased from 2,000 to

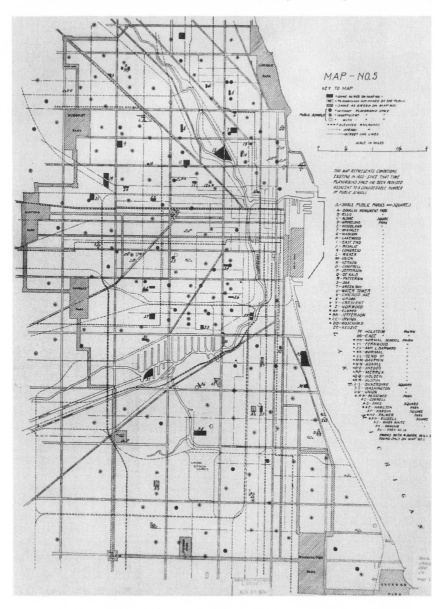

FIGURE 4.5. Existing parks and playgrounds, Chicago, 1902. Map from the Metropolitan Park Plan by Dwight Perkins, issued by the Special Park Commission in 1904. Courtesy: Map Section, University Library, University of Illinois at Chicago.

3,174. The plan called for a single metropolitan system and an increase in its size and extent. Not only did it recommend a substantial expansion of the neighborhood play-parks (thirty-eight recommendations for the crowded inner wards), but it also made detailed proposals for the purchase of lands for an outer park system in the suburbs. Perkins's report paralleled the work of the Outer Belt Park Commission established in 1903 by the president of the Cook County Board of Commissioners, Henry G. Foreman, who served simultaneously as president of the South Park Commission. Daniel Burnham was also a member of the Outer Belt group, along with representatives of the other Chicago park commissions.

The 1904 plan, in turn, became the basis of the comprehensive scheme for park system development and expansion presented in the 1909 *Plan of Chicago* by Daniel Burnham and Edward Bennett. Both documents contained recommendations for creating a whole hierarchy of park types, from the neighborhood small park to the suburban forest preserve on the city's Outer Belt. The primary difference between the 1904 and 1909 park plans was that Burnham and Bennett suggested a much more extensive park development along the north and south shores of Lake Michigan.

As this history of Chicago's small parks makes clear, there were indeed early attempts to rationalize the planning process through the application of social science research methods, although the trend did not take a firm hold until the 1920s, in the heyday of the City Functional movement.[49] Most of the 1903–4 play-parks had been sited in a relatively systematic manner, their locations closely corresponding to recommendations in a citywide survey of social and physical conditions. Social survey techniques were being applied to park siting, and the fundamental organization of each park plot was based on functional criteria concerned with social control through recreation. Nevertheless, these goals did not prevent Bennett and Olmsted from producing beautiful parks that reconciled formal and naturalistic qualities. In 1904 artistic and scientifically derived park-planning principles were fluid and not in conflict with one another.

CHAPTER 5

The Design of Yorkship Garden Village

Product of the Progressive Planning, Architecture, and Housing Reform Movements

MICHAEL H. LANG

Peter Hall, in Cities of Tomorrow, *elucidated some of the "magnificent vision[s] of the possibilities of urban civilization" that in his view formed the intellectual foundations of twentieth-century planning. He aimed to "strip away the layers of historical topsoil that have buried and obscured" these original visions, and then "understand the nature of their transplantation" as they were later adapted to alien sociopolitical circumstances, sometimes with disastrous consequences. In "The Design of Yorkship Garden Village," Michael H. Lang performs a similar set of operations, but his research is especially noteworthy because Yorkship Village was and remains a successful realization of a remarkably progressive planning vision. Located in Camden, New Jersey, Yorkship Village was a planned industrial community built by the federal government to house wage workers in the shipbuilding and munitions industries. The garden village was designed and influenced by a number of prominent housing and planning reformers who passionately envisioned better living conditions for wage workers in America's industrial cities. Lang carefully analyzes the design of Yorkship Village, both its sources and inspirations, and introduces the work of several lesser-known individuals who contributed to the community's design or management, particularly Frederick Ackerman, Electus Litchfield, Frederick Law Olmsted Jr., Charles Whitaker, and the very young Henry Wright.*

Lang delves into the mostly British sources and precedents that formed the genesis for Yorkship Garden Village: these included suburban limited-dividend housing estates such as Hampstead Garden Suburb; the London County Council cottage-housing projects; and Ebenezer Howard's garden city ideas, particularly as applied in the work of Parker and Unwin. A rare instance of federally financed and administered progressive planning, Yorkship Village broke new ground in several ways. It featured a central green and innovative street plan, houses designed to meet reformer Lawrence Veiller's housing standards, innovations in land tenure, and one of the first successful experiments with the neighborhood-unit plan. Lang argues that this planned industrial village was perhaps the best American expression of the progressive architecture, planning, and housing reform movement of the twentieth century. Despite its location in a severely depressed industrial city, Yorkship Village constitutes a more successful adaptation of progressive planning ideals than other more famous and better-studied communities like Sunnyside, Radburn, and Reston.

The history of Yorkship Village is an important chapter in twentieth-century planning history because it forms a key link between the Garden City movement in Britain, Progressive Era housing and planning reform, and the formation of the Regional Planning Association of America in the 1920s. Lang bases his analysis on the published writings of the principal figures involved in Yorkship Garden Village's planning: Whitaker, Ackerman, Litchfield, Henry Wright, and Olmsted junior, through his position as chief of design of the U.S. Housing Corporation. For information on other working-class planning alternatives, readers should consult John Garner's "S. S. Beman and the Building of Pullman," in Garner, ed., The

Midwest in American Architecture *(Urbana: University of Illinois Press, 1991), Richard Candee's* Atlantic Heights: A World War I Shipbuilder's Community *(Portsmouth: P. E. Randall, 1985), and Stanley Buder's* Visionaries and Planners *(New York: Oxford University Press, 1990). On the British precedents for Yorkship Village, see Susan Beattie,* A Revolution in London Housing *(London: Architectural Press, 1980), Mark Swenarton,* Homes Fit for Heroes *(London: Heinemann, 1981), and Stephen V. Ward, ed.,* The Garden City *(London: E. & F. N. Spons, 1992). The best introduction to Progressive Era planning and housing reform is Roy Lubove's* The Progressives and the Slums *(Pittsburgh: University of Pittsburgh Press, 1962).* EDITORS

> Thorough sanitary and remedial action in the houses that we have; and then the building of more, strongly, beautifully, and in groups of limited extent, kept in proportion to their streams and walled around, so that there be no festering and wretched suburb anywhere, but clean and busy street within and open country without, with a belt of beautiful garden and orchard round the walls, so that from any part of the city perfectly fresh air and grass and sight of far horizon might be reachable in a few minutes' walk. That is the final aim.
> —JOHN RUSKIN, *SESAME AND LILIES*

The community of Yorkship Village, now known as Fairview, is one of the best achievements of the progressive architecture, housing, and planning reform movement that flourished at the turn of the century. At its height, this movement broke new ground in relating planning practice to progressive concepts of urban design, political economy, and community development, as determined by the needs of the working classes. This movement was profoundly Anglo-American. It drew, for example, from John Ruskin's and William Morris's concept of community-based social justice as expressed in Morris's utopian novel *News from Nowhere* (1890). Its physical realization was influenced by Henrietta Barnett's and

Ebenezer Howard's progressive garden suburb/city concept in general, and the "free" vernacular architectural design philosophy of British architect Philip Webb in particular. In the United States, the housing and planning reform movement was also influenced by the more standardized bureaucratic tendencies of Fabian socialism as exemplified by Raymond Unwin and his simplified public (council) housing designs.

Like their counterparts in England, from whom they borrowed both ideas and inspiration, the American reformers were passionately dedicated to improving the squalid living conditions of the wage worker in America's industrial society, either through the regulation of private development or through direct governmental provision of housing. They were clearly interested in all aspects of housing and planning, but their supreme accomplishment was the singularly successful adaptation of the Garden City concept to the American industrial city, as exemplified by Yorkship Village. Although Ruskin's description in *Sesame and Lilies* remains the single best statement on the aesthetic aims of the Garden City movement, a further elaboration of this concept by the Garden City Association should also be noted: "A Garden City is a town designed for healthy living and industry; of a size that makes possible a full measure of social life, but not larger; surrounded by a rural belt; the whole of the land being in public ownership or held in trust for the community."[1] The first practical demonstration of these principles was carried out in England at Ebenezer Howard's Garden City of Letchworth, designed by Raymond Unwin and Barry Parker (1904).

Context

Yorkship Village is located in Camden, New Jersey, a depressed industrial city with a population of about 83,000 situated across the Delaware River from Philadelphia. In general, the New Jersey economy has made the transition from an industrial manufacturing base to one characterized by service- and technology-related industries.

Nevertheless, Camden City, with its overwhelmingly Black and Hispanic population, has become the poorest city in New Jersey and one of the poorest in the country in the 1990s. Per capita income stands at just $5,731. Initially, a blue-collar industrial center, Camden today reports that some 33 percent of its inhabitants are below the poverty line. The city suffers from the second highest reported crime rate in the state, and its school district is under the threat of a state takeover owing to the low achievement rate of its students. The city's main street, once a bustling commercial strip, now consists of a long array of vacant stores, and locals have very few of the services that most people elsewhere take for granted.

Much of the physical appearance of the city is extremely bleak. No new private housing has been built in the city for decades; the existing housing stock is old and in poor condition. Many of Camden's neighborhoods appear only partly inhabited. Median house values are about $15,800. One or two neighborhoods have experienced some limited renovation and gentrification, but at present this applies to only a handful of buildings. Although some limited revitalization efforts have been realized, these constitute small islands of subsidized prosperity in a sea of continued decline.[2]

Genesis of Yorkship Village

Yorkship Village was built in 1918 on the 225-acre Coopers Farm at the southern edge of Camden to house workers at the nearby New York Shipbuilding Company. Started during World War I by the federal government through the U.S. Shipping Board's Emergency Fleet Corporation (EFC), it was one of many similar garden villages developed by the Corporation to ease the critical shortage of housing for war industry workers in various cities. A companion program of emergency housing was established under the U.S. Housing Corporation (USHC) (figures 5.1 and 5.2).[3]

The Design of Yorkship Garden Village

FIGURE 5.1. Yorkship Village under construction looking north from village center, 1918. Courtesy: National Archives.

Different architects and planners were selected for each project. Yorkship Village was designed by Electus Litchfield, Pliny Rodgers, Henry Wright, and others under the direction of Frederick L. Ackerman, who had been appointed the chief of design of the Fleet Corporation's housing division (Frederick Law Olmsted Jr. was his double at the USHC).

With the possible exception of a few of the best company towns, these wartime communities far surpassed anything then available to the working classes in the private housing market. Indeed, they surpassed most of what was then available to the middle classes as well. Although all the communities built by the USHC and the EFC conformed by and large to Garden City prin-

FIGURE 5.2. Yorkship Village under construction looking toward village center, 1918. Courtesy: National Archives.

ciples, Yorkship Village can claim to be the best expression of the intentions of these planning and housing reformers.[4]

The list of notable housing and planning reformers directly involved with these wartime communities includes the architects Frederick L. Ackerman, Henry Wright, and Robert D. Kohn, as well as Frederick Law Olmsted Jr. and John Nolen, who were land planners. Many of these individuals would later become associated with the Regional Planning Association of America. Also important were those housing reformers, architects, and land planners who, while not directly involved in the EFC or the USHC, formed a community of interests that influenced the work of these agencies. In this Anglo-American group were Charles Whitaker, the editor of the *Journal of the American Institute of Architects*, the British architects

Philip Webb, William R. Lethaby, and Raymond Unwin (who was both an architect and land planner), as well as the American housing reformers Lawrence Veiller and Edith Wood.

An important influence, too, was the progressive philosophy of the social reformers, particularly the British art critic John Ruskin and his disciple, William Morris, the Arts and Crafts designer and ardent socialist. Morris and Ruskin combined their social criticism with architectural and design theories based on a new appreciation of the aesthetics of craftsmanship. Working in this context, Lethaby and Webb (the architect of Morris's Red House) developed a modern architecture, often called English Free Architecture, that was a creative synthesis: it was both modern and yet oriented to vernacular designs based on an appreciation of the diversity of picturesque styles found in local villages.[5]

Urban Design Principles

Trained in the European aesthetic tradition, the planning team for Yorkship Village was familiar with seventeenth-century European picturesque and romantic influences in the fine arts, landscape architecture, and land planning. Based in part on adaptations of Chinese and Japanese garden design concepts, these traditions informed the work of important design theorists such as Uvedale Price, Payne Knight in Britain, and Andrew Jackson Downing in the United States.[6] Their theories emphasized irregular lines, rough-textured surfaces, vistas, architectural surprise, and the artistic application of water so as to produce an evocative composition that appeared to be at once naturalistic and picturesque. Such principles, while initially applied by the British landscape architects Lancelot "Capability" Brown and Humphry Repton to the design of large country estates for the aristocracy, were soon extended to include the design of entire tenant villages on these estates. A number of villages were designed in this manner, such as Milton Abbas (1773) and Blaise Hamlet (1811).[7] These villages were to have a significant impact on the design of model industrial communities and garden cities.

The notion of erecting model villages for the working classes developed through related experience with planned company towns, philanthropic housing experiments, and early public housing. By the turn of the century, well-known examples of most of these experimental efforts existed both in the United States and abroad, among them the well-planned company towns of Port Sunlight (1898) and New Earswick (1902) in Great Britain and Echota, New York (1892), and Pullman, Illinois (1881), in the United States.[8]

Also known to the Yorkship team was the pioneering work in Germany of Camillo Sitte, whose study of the design principles inherent in successful medieval town centers, *City Building According to Artistic Principles* (1889), emphasized the enclosure, focal point, irregularity, and street vistas in town planning. British land planners and architects such as Raymond Unwin were quick to see the importance of such compositional elements in town planning; indeed, Unwin relied heavily on Sitte's work in his own book, *Town Planning in Practice: An Introduction to the Art of Designing Cities and Suburbs,* published in 1909.

Unwin's design concepts influenced the development of suburban limited-dividend housing estates such as Brentham Garden Suburb (1901) and Henrietta Barnett's Hampstead Garden Suburb (1907). Both developments received widespread publicity and approval in progressive circles. Although most of these developments consisted of attached or row housing, the application of a picturesque-cottage architectural style along with creative site planning produced a result entirely unlike typical terraced housing. Instead of monotonous parallel rows of similar dwellings, the units had varied roof slopes and distinctive architectural details and were grouped with varied setbacks and relationships to the street. A comprehensive architectural and physical plan provided a curvilinear street system, public open spaces, and enclosed street vistas. There was a real sense of unity to the developments; they felt like small-scale, semirural villages, yet were built to a rather high density.

Anglo-American Linkage

Although these developments formed an important contextual background, British wartime housing programs, which preceded the development of Yorkship Village by several years, had a more immediate impact. Charles Whitaker, editor of the *Journal of the American Institute of Architects*, provided the link between the American architects and planners and the British program for war housing. An ardent activist who was educated in Europe, Whitaker openly encouraged progressive architects, planners, and housing experts to submit articles dealing with housing reform, town planning, and land tenure issues. In an effort to influence national housing policy, Whitaker sent architect Frederick L. Ackerman to England in 1917 to study the wartime communities that the British government was building for industrial workers.

By this time Britain already had a head start in building government-supported garden villages for the working classes. In 1913 the London County Council (LCC) had embarked on the construction of a series of cottage-housing projects designed along garden village lines. Although it is not known whether he did so, Ackerman would have been able to visit the Old Oak Estate, the Norbury Estate, and the White Hart Lane Estate during his visit to London.[9] All were villages produced as a result of pressure by newly ascendant socialists and other progressives in the LCC who were anxious to improve housing conditions for the working classes. Inspired by the aesthetic and social philosophy of Ruskin and Morris and the architectural theories of their colleagues, Lethaby and Webb, a group of young architects jumped at the chance to work for the LCC, where they were given the opportunity to create a new standard of community housing for the working classes. All of these garden villages, while built at rather high densities, were quite successful. Some were provided with shops and community facilities and were well designed, in view of the economic and political pressures arrayed against them.[10]

While in London, Ackerman met with Raymond Unwin, the supervising architect for the central government's new garden village housing program, which had been established in 1915 to house the workers attracted to the increasing number of war-related jobs in munitions industries. Unwin's prewar success as the architect for Letchworth and Hampstead Garden suburb helped him persuade the British government to build complete village communities rather than temporary barracks. He was responsible for the effective yet simplified design of the influential World War I garden villages at Gretna and Eastriggs in Scotland that were to have an enduring impact on British housing and planning policy in the postwar era and beyond.

On this visit, Ackerman also saw Well Hall, another influential wartime housing community (1915), designed by Frank Baines, Unwin's counterpart in a separate government wartime housing program. In the 1890s Baines had apprenticed with Charles R. Ashbee, founder of the Guild of the Handicraft and one of the pillars of the Arts and Crafts movement. His training under Ashbee exposed him to the teachings of Ruskin and Morris, as well as the architectural theories of Webb and Lethaby. Unwin's links to Fabian socialism and its centralizing tendencies led him to develop a simplified design for his wartime garden villages, an approach he developed more fully after the war for council housing. Baines's work, on the other hand, was heavily influenced by Ruskin's aesthetic approach, with its emphasis on responding to indigenous contexts and needs. The result was spectacular. Indeed, Well Hall has been called an architectural tour de force. It succeeded in providing the visitor with an ever-changing panorama of architectural styles and street vistas in what appeared to be a low-density English village, but was in fact, a large public housing project of 1,600 units. On one street, for instance, he designed a continuous row of some twenty attached units with such varied setbacks, creative designs, and imaginative use of building materials that they appeared to be a collection of detached houses. Based as it was on the design principles of continuity, enclosure, contrast, and surprise, his approach ensured that the estate looked "as if it had grown and not merely been dropped there."[11] The use of varying building materials and methods, as well as the reliance on a creative mixture of vernacular architectural patterns, clearly drew on the work of Webb and Lethaby. This village is perhaps the best example of the extension of English Free Architecture to the design of a whole village for the working classes. Unfortunately, after the war it was Unwin's standardized cottage approach that, for reasons of economy and politics, carried the day with the British government and led to the spread of the successful, if uninspired, council estates known to all in Britain.[12]

Upon Ackerman's return, Whitaker used his influence to ensure that the resultant laudatory report—complete with plans and data on Well Hall, Gretna, and Eastriggs—was presented to Congress, which was holding hearings on war industry production problems. At these hearings, Whitaker and Ackerman were successful in convincing Congress of the link between increased industrial production and the provision of community-based housing for war industry workers. Recognizing the inability of the private sector to produce housing during the war, Congress reluctantly authorized the wartime housing program.[13]

Although the British architects and planners often provided the inspiration for these American garden village developments, it remained the task of American architects and planners to interpret and adapt British design experience to fit the American context. Of all the planning reformers attracted to work with the American emergency housing program of World War I, Ackerman was, perhaps, the most singular. Historian Roy Lubove, an authority on the Progressive movement, cites him as an active participant in many of the early meetings concerned with housing and city planning reform. He was, almost certainly, the most radical member of the group of progressive architects, planners, and housing reformers who share the credit for the wartime housing program. A disciple of the radical economist Thorstein Veblen, Ackerman publicly supported the moral, aesthetic, and social values of sound housing, good comprehensive planning, and landscape design. He also advocated the novel forms of tenancy (public, cooperative, and limited dividend) employed by the British. Lubove credits Ackerman (among others) with leading a revolt against the purely regulatory approach to housing reform championed by Lawrence Veiller and with favoring instead direct government provision of planned communities of public housing. These interests would also come to be adopted by many reform-minded American housers and planners, but few pursued them with Ackerman's intensity.[14]

Chief of Design for Yorkship Village

As chief of design, Ackerman was largely responsible for the design orientation of the Emergency Fleet Corporation's housing projects. He used this opportunity to pursue what he felt to be the correct approach to community development. After the war, Ackerman described the program as follows:

> [While] designed and constructed under the handicap of tremendous speed . . . they will mark a milestone in our progress, and this great enterprise will awaken an interest in the development of our surroundings which will react upon America no less powerfully than did the Columbian Exposition of 1893. But the reaction will be of another sort; for instead of focusing our concept of town planning upon the magnificent, the planning of a community will come to be conceived in more rational and more humble terms. The benefits to be derived from orderliness of arrangement and forehand planning will be measured in terms of better conditions of living.[15]

The layout of Yorkship Village shows how Ackerman and Litchfield adapted design principles gleaned from British company towns, garden cities, limited-dividend housing, and early council-housing estates. The focal point of the plan was the village green (see figure 5.3). It was meant to be a functioning center of village life,

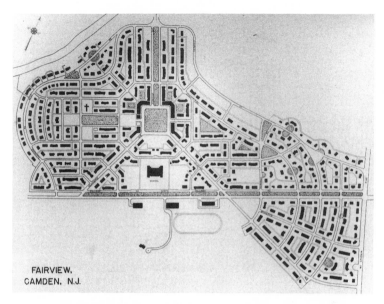

FIGURE 5.3. Yorkship Village site plan. From National Resources Committee, Research Committee on Urbanism (1939).

not just decorative open space. As such, it exemplified the belief of American landscape architect Frederick Law Olmsted Sr. in the importance of nurturing neighborly communication, or what might be called community spirit, as the central function of a comprehensive urban design. As Litchfield pointed out, Yorkship Village "was to afford the physical plant where the worker might quietly and in comfort discuss among his fellows the problems which affect him, thus developing a cooperation, a unity, and a community of spirit between himself and his fellow workers."[16]

Designing Yorkship Village

The village green was surrounded on two sides by attractive low-rise apartment houses that provided a strong sense of enclosure. Churches, the library, public meeting hall, and the school were located off the central green, but on the several greenswards that radiated outward from it. This diversity of land uses and functions ensured that the village green would serve as a community focal point throughout the day and into the night. Today, people work, shop, and socialize in and around this organic urban space. Yorkship Village is a close-knit community; indeed, in many respects it could function as a textbook example of Jane Jacobs's "eyes of the street" concept (although she was no great fan of garden cities).[17] This concept suggested that active street life would attract observers from the community and thereby provide a natural security system.

The village green was also the central focus of the street plan. It was surrounded by a series of concentric curvilinear roads in addition to radial roads and footpaths that extended out from it. The effect of this street system was to discourage through traffic so prevalent in communities with streets based on the grid system. The provision of footpaths segregated from vehicular traffic ensured that the village was completely accessible by walking. Terminal vistas and tree-shaded views from the footpaths were provided by the astute placing of larger buildings. The overall community design clearly downplayed the car while it supported the pedestrian and the free movement of children. Although some automobile garages have been added, they were generally tucked away out of sight. These design features show that the community functioned as a primer for the planning of Radburn, New Jersey, which was to follow some years later. Indeed, Henry Wright, who was on Acker-man's staff at the EFC, went on to plan Radburn, along with Clarence Stein.[18]

The nongrid layout adopted in Fairview allowed the planners to express their creativity in regard to site planning. Blocks of land of various size accommodated a variety of housing types that were mixed throughout the community. Varied setbacks, groupings, and placements of houses on their lots all provided visual stimulation within a unified village plan. A community of some 1,400 homes, Fairview was typified by quite modest two- and three-story row, twin, and triplex housing units, but single-family housing, as well as

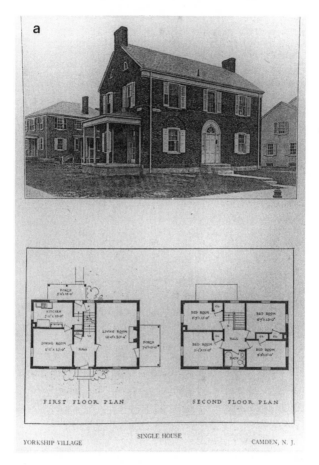

FIGURE 5.4a. Typical single house and floor plan. From U.S. Shipping Board Emergency Fleet Corporation (1920).

apartments, were also provided (figures 5.4a and 5.4b). Although the housing was modest, the EFC and the USHC adopted the housing standards promulgated by Lawrence Veiller, the prominent housing reformer. These standards have been summarized by Lubove as follows:

> No row or group homes more than two rooms deep (in order to insure adequate light and ventilation); twenty feet of space

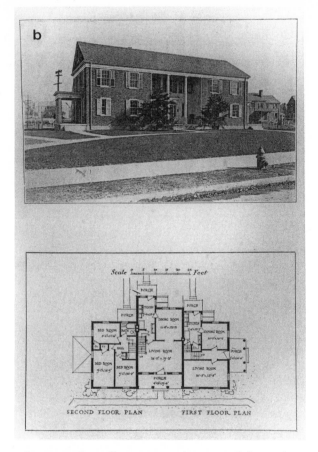

FIGURE 5.4b. Typical small apartment house and floor plan. From U.S. Shipping Board Emergency Fleet Corporation (1920).

between adjacent buildings, or an absolute minimum of sixteen feet; no basement living quarters; no privies or cellar water closets; no private alleys for access to row or group homes; a window in every room, opening directly to the outside; a rear yard depth of not less than the height of the building, or in no case less than twenty feet; a minimum distance of fifty feet between the backs of houses.[19]

The architecture of Fairview is essentially neo-Georgian vernacular and is reminiscent of planned colonial villages such as nearby New Castle, Delaware. The attention to detail and the high quality of the original buildings is still evident today. Red-brick construction, porches, windows with mullions and shutters, slate roofs, and architectural ornamentation—all were of the highest standard. As such, this architectural style demonstrates the influence of both the Free vernacular approach championed by Webb and the more simplified approach espoused by Unwin (figures 5.5 and 5.6).

Although the need to build with haste due to the exigencies of the war precluded extensive efforts to fathom the particular desires of the residents, it can be said that, to an unusual degree, the designers were motivated by a desire to meet or exceed the needs and wishes of the people who would occupy their community. The

FIGURE 5.5. Streetscape showing use of short row. Photograph: Michael H. Lang.

FIGURE 5.6. Streetscape showing use of varied setbacks. Photograph: Michael H. Lang.

standard of accommodation reflected an astute sensitivity to the domestic needs and aspirations of the future occupants. Similarly, the design approach reflected a deep understanding of the desire of the aspiring working class for an architecture evocative of traditional societal norms as reflected in the small cottage. It was unfortunate that many of the later attempts to provide low-cost housing, such as Sunnyside Gardens (1924), also designed by Ackerman and then under the sway of the emerging Bauhaus philosophy, produced a high-density, rectilinear series of apartment blocks that failed to reflect his earlier broad cultural and design sensitivity.

Neighborhood Unit

In planning Yorkship Village, the designers recognized that the local school plays an important role in the life of a community. Accordingly, it was given a central location, placed just behind the village green. This placement ensured easy accessibility from all parts of the village. This design feature met the main requirement of the so-called neighborhood-unit concept associated with Clarence Perry, but actually pioneered by Jacob Riis, Lillian Wald, Florence Kelley, and Mary Simkhovitch in New York and St. Louis in the early part of the century.[20] These reformers saw the need for urban design to support functional social relationships at the community level. They proposed that "a public school, parochial school, branch library, park and playground, public bath, model tenement, settlement house, church, police station, fire engine house, and homes of athletic and social organizations be grouped around a common center."[21] To this, Perry added specific buffers such as roads or green-belts to delineate clearly one neighborhood from another. The plan for Yorkship Village combined most of these elements in a harmonious design.[22]

The sensitive distribution of open space was another striking feature of Yorkship Village, and it was here that the influence of Frederick Law Olmsted Sr. was most evident. Yorkship Village was planned with a keen eye toward preserving natural areas and allowing the surrounding greensward to extend throughout the village. The feel of a small rural village was achieved in part by the high densities and clustering of housing on small lots, while the provision of well-planted public open space, allotment gardens, and playing fields afforded extensive green vistas. In addition to the allocation of internal open space, Yorkship Village was surrounded on three sides by parks or protected watershed areas. The fourth side abutted a major thoroughfare, which provided a means of contact with the city as well as a buffer to it. In short, the village's open space was apportioned so that it would function both as a buffer and as a means of bringing residents into contact with nature. While there has been some encroachment, and some inappropriate infill development, Yorkship Village appears today much the same as when it was built: a bucolic country village near the city.[23]

Innovations in Land Tenure

In addition to achieving a good urban design, Ackerman and Litchfield also pointed out the relevance of new forms of housing tenure. Ackerman's initial conception for land ownership in Yorkship Village was similar to Howard's for his garden cities. Specifically, Ackerman favored cooperative or public ownership that would have allowed the community to maintain rents reflective of the initial working-class nature of the community while capturing any increase in equity for the benefit of the community.[24]

Yorkship Village Today

Yorkship Village has been a success in many ways, but, given the trend toward federal antiurban fiscal and land-use policies in the United States, its most notable achievement has been its ability to resist being affected by the decline of Camden and the availability of nearby affordable suburban housing. Although some small sections have remained stable, most of Camden's other neighborhoods have experienced a severe decline in property values. This observation holds true even for those neighborhoods that were initially more affluent than Yorkship Village. In contrast, Yorkship Village has consistently experienced an appreciating market for its housing units and the highest resale level in the city. Today, it is a strong middle- and working-class community with few of the physical signs of decline and neglect so visible in other Camden neighborhoods. It has a strong local preservation committee that has been able to secure federal historic designation for the village and is currently seeking local designation (figure 5.7).[25]

Critical Reaction

Ironically, instead of receiving high praise for their work, the staff of the Housing Corporation and the Emergency Fleet Corporation were admonished by Congress for building to such a high standard

FIGURE 5.7. A portion of Yorkship Square showing mix of residential and commercial uses. Photograph: Michael H. Lang.

that it reflected badly on the product of the prevailing private housing industry. As part of the political compromise that secured congressional support for the wartime federal building program, it had been stipulated that after the war the program would be terminated and all the completed communities would be sold off to private buyers. Despite their best efforts, the architects and planners were unable to get Congress to reverse this position. In a sorry chapter in the history of government housing policy, scores of tenants who had built America's warships were displaced in 1921 when they were not able to meet the prices paid by local realtors and housing speculators.[26]

Yorkship Village: Its Place in Planning History

Lubove and others see the housing program of the EFC and the USHC as constituting a direct link between the early progressive housing and planning reform movement and the formation of the influential Regional Planning Association of America in the 1920s. This latter group was formed by many of the housers, planners, and architects who had worked in the wartime industrial housing program. Ackerman, Kohn, and Wright were joined by Lewis Mumford, Clarence Stein, Edith Wood, Catherine Bauer, Benton Mackaye, and others to form what was to become the main force in America advocating progressive principles of regional community planning and land tenure. It was this group that embarked on the notable experiments in community development at Sunnyside Gardens, New York, and Radburn, New Jersey, in the 1920s. The link between these projects and Yorkship Village is a strong one.[27] It can be argued, however, that the importance of Yorkship Village has often been overlooked in favor of the more upscale derivations of the Garden City concept such as Radburn and Reston, Virginia. Ironically, Yorkship Village can claim to be a more successful application of progressive Garden City principles than its more famous relations, and this accomplishment is all the more striking when one considers the negative environmental context with which it has had to contend.

Yorkship Village and some of the other communities built by the U.S. Housing Corporation and the Emergency Fleet Corporation were unique in that they aimed to provide the working classes with a comprehensive community that equaled or surpassed what the more wealthy could obtain. Litchfield, echoing Ruskin, stressed this in his many public remarks:

> We did not expect to create a new Utopia—the realization of the fond dream of the philosophers of all ages—but we did hope to produce a community providing the opportunity for those things which are so often denied to the worker and which we will all agree are really essential for the development of a true American citizenship. . . . it was to be a place where the worker and his family could be healthy, happy and con-

tented; a place where the harassing strain of ill health and mounting doctor's bills might in great measure be eliminated; a place where the toil and drudgery of housekeeping should be reduced to its ultimate limit, and where in exchange there should be offered to the mother and her growing children new opportunities for education and development.[28]

In the final estimate, Yorkship Village continues to stand as a product of the best and brightest minds in the progressive housing, architecture, and planning reform movement. Major reformers like John Ruskin, William Morris, Henrietta Barnett, and Ebenezer Howard saw architects and land planners as having a special duty to provide the working classes with a truly civilized community environment, while ensuring that it remained available for people of similar means in the future. Yorkship Village was initially planned as a cooperative housing community for the working class. Instead, it is part of the private speculative market in real estate that prevails in this country. Although Yorkship Village has not undergone gentrification, it has become priced out of the reach of most of Camden's poorer citizens.

Planners who wish to revitalize the inner city or offer an alternative to continued suburban sprawl would do well to study the history and design of Yorkship Village. Clearly, Yorkship Village has shown that good comprehensive urban design and planning can produce lasting communities of a truly urban character and scale of which its inhabitants can be proud. Equally important is the fact that the success of Yorkship Village has demonstrated that good planning and successful project implementation can emanate from a central governmental authority.[29]

At the same time, it should be recognized that Yorkship Village was a costly community to build and the federal government lost money on it when it precipitously auctioned it off.[30] The New Towns program in Britain and other countries, as well as the failed New Communities Program in the United States, provide clear evidence

that well-conceived, government-sponsored, community development, while ultimately profitable, requires a long-term financial
commitment. When the country finally begins to address seriously
the needs of its urban areas and the rebuilding of the abandoned
sections of its cities, it would be wise to consider the lessons of
Yorkship Village.

CHAPTER 6

Conservation, Resource Management, and Regional Planning

The Pioneering Role of Joseph Hyde Pratt

ROBERT E. IRELAND

The concept of regional planning in the South owes much of its substance and credibility to the work of University of North Carolina professors Rupert Vance and Howard Odum in the 1930s. Vance's Human Geography of the South *(Chapel Hill: University of North Carolina Press, 1935) and Odum's classic statement of regionalism,* Southern Regions of the United States *(Chapel Hill: University of North Carolina Press, 1936) provided the underpinnings for thinking about environmental and socioeconomic problems from a southern regional perspective. But three decades before their arrival in Chapel Hill, another University of North Carolina (UNC) professor had already established a regional rationale for several important planning initiatives: a highway system, forest and fishing reserves, drainage and land reclamation projects, hydroelectric power, and regional resource development. Robert E. Ireland outlines the public*

Foundations of Twentieth-Century Planning

service career of pioneer planner Joseph Hyde Pratt, the first modern regional planner in North Carolina.

Pratt's career, spanning the late 1890s to the 1930s, provides considerable insight into the growing professionalism and some of the intellectual foundations of twentieth-century planning. Relying primarily on Pratt's published writings, Ireland reconstructs Pratt's development of the concepts of regionalism and conservation as the basis for regional planning and infrastructure improvements in the southern Appalachian region. He demonstrates how Pratt's sense of professionalism derived from his identification with the Progressive movement; he advocated a style of regional planning based on rational thinking, nonpartisan politics, and scientific expertise. A friend of Gifford Pinchot's, Pratt based his regionalism on physiographic data and pushed for a vision of planning and conservation that reached beyond political boundaries. Although partial to the use of voluntary professional associations to formulate policy and administer the management of resources, Pratt gradually came to recognize the need for state and federal resource regulation.

Thus Ireland uses the course of Pratt's career to illustrate changing patterns of policy and management in the evolving role of the professional regional planner during the early twentieth century. Pratt's ideas bridged the parochial New South campaigns in the late-nineteenth-century and the early-twentieth-century regional resource conservation initiatives favored for a time by Pinchot, and the industrial resource exploitation of the 1920s and 1930s. For an overview of the development of regional planning, readers should consult chapter 4 of Mel Scott's American City Planning since 1890 *(1969). Carl Abbott provides a thoughtful commentary on recent scholarly attempts to come to terms with the definitions of regions in his bibliographic essay, "Frontiers and Sections: Cities and Regions in American Growth," in Gillette and Miller, eds.,* American Urbanism *(Westport: Greenwood, 1987). On the Progressive conservation movement, see Samuel Hays,* Conservation and the Gospel of Efficiency *(Cambridge: Harvard University Press, 1959). For information on one of the nation's most noteworthy examples of regional planning, see Edwin C. Hargrove and Paul K. Conklin, eds.,* TVA *(Urbana: University of Illinois Press, 1983).* EDITORS

Conservation, Resource Management, and Regional Planning

In 1938 Howard Odum offered to a generation of students of regional planning a host of definitions of the terms *region, regionalism, and regional planning.* Citing some twenty-eight differing
concepts of "region," he noted that the basis of what constitutes a
region might well be determined by its physical contours, its political history, its economic characteristics, its cultural parameters, or
one of a hundred other features deemed similar. Odum proposed six
criteria for the designation of a region, criteria that, incidentally,
were to cause ceaseless controversy among planners who felt his
societal areas were far too broadly defined to have any meaningful
use. Still, at the heart of Odum's notion of region was a geographic
construct borrowed from professional geographers and geologists.[1]

The concept of a geographic region had been gradually forming
in the Southeast for some time. Indeed, it was another University of
North Carolina professor, Joseph Hyde Pratt (figure 6.1), who initiated
the use of a uniform geographic designation for the region more than
twenty years before Odum's arrival on the Chapel Hill campus. Unlike
Odum, Pratt eschewed the role of theoretician, preferring instead to
concentrate on the collection of data, identification of problems, and
the provision of solutions. In this respect, Pratt deserves attention for
several reasons. First, he was an important figure in the classification
of regions to be employed by planners in the early years. He also was
an active advocate of the voluntary, professional association method of
resource management and policy formulation. Thus an examination
of the remarkable career of Joseph Hyde Pratt also makes it possible to
assess the influence of the changing of resource management in the
evolving role of the professional regional planner.

Defining the Region: The Powell Construct, 1879–1910

Joseph Hyde Pratt received his doctorate in geology from the Shef-
field School of Yale University in 1896 and for the next ten years

FIGURE 6.1. Portrait of Joseph Hyde Pratt. Courtesy: North Carolina Collection, University of North Carolina Library at Chapel Hill.

served as an agent for John Wesley Powell's U.S. Geological Survey. The Powell concept of physiographic regions was to become a guiding principle for Pratt, as soon became apparent not only in the terminology he employed to describe the Appalachian Mountains, central piedmont, and coastal plains of North Carolina, but also in his early maps of those regions. What is more important, Pratt also began to conceive of these areas as regions in the functional sense.

Pratt came to North Carolina in 1897 to serve as a mining engineer and soon thereafter was appointed state mineralogist. He then followed in the footsteps of Joseph A. Holmes, becoming state geologist and professor of economic geology at the University of North Carolina. By 1905 Pratt also had become the chief spokesman for the North Carolina Good Roads Association and director of the North Carolina Geological and Economic Survey, both based in Chapel Hill. Through these multiple roles, he worked to create a regionally planned road system in the early 1900s.

From the outset of his tenure as the state's chief road consultant, Pratt discovered the deep distrust of the predominantly rural populace to legislative measures that called for state authority in road building. Localism was more than an attitude to be reckoned with: it was an implacable barrier to progress, even on the state level. Hoping to salvage something in the way of improved roads, Pratt urged the use of local and state convict labor and the issuance of county bonds to finance a county-by-county highway system.[2] Although he was beginning to understand the political realities of North Carolina road building, Pratt also believed that highways did not end at state lines and that roads were meant to tap the commercial and industrial potential of an entire region.

Thus in 1909 Pratt organized and presided over the Southern Appalachian Good Roads Conference in Asheville, North Carolina. Here, Pratt planned an extensive publicity campaign to be carried out in six states, selected on the basis of geographic, rather than political factors. Pratt reasoned that the southern Appalachian Mountains presented a formidable barrier to road builders that required engineering expertise not commonly available in the area. Therefore the creation of a transmountain transportation system would demand a much higher degree of cooperation and planning than individual states might provide. He hoped that the use of a regional designation based on physiographic features would bring together individuals whose perception of transportation problems had, until this time, been focused on local or state levels.

Indeed, the 1909 Asheville conference was in many ways a precursor of regional planning sessions to come, for though it served no official legislative capacity, the conference established a point of view that was essential to rational development. By stressing roads in the development of tourism, forestry, and education, Pratt sought to overcome localism and provincialism with the appeal to a uniform set of economic and cultural needs. He also hoped to create a spirit of cooperation necessary for such a plan to succeed. And by attempting to coordinate and plan a system of regional highways, Pratt, the progressive social engineer, was setting the stage for future generations of professionally trained public officials who labored to persuade local and state authorities to accept more exacting engineering standards and more efficient methods of construction.

The experience of Pratt and an emerging cadre of professional engineers in the South was not unlike that of early planners elsewhere in the nation. The dawning of the auto age had forced many cities to reexamine their own structure and form, for "during the progressive era, highway planning made up a visual and physical component of urban revitalization and social reform."[3] Clearly, the demand for roads was creating a demand for planning. Pratt was well aware of these national trends, and sought to persuade largely rural North Carolina that a state highway commission, staffed by competent professional engineers, was needed to plan and develop highways that extended beyond the reach of city planners. But Pratt was unable to translate his agenda for progress into a state mandate for change. Lacking state support for a commission with the power to plan and build state and regional highways, he even resorted to a legislative charter in his own name to create the Crest of the Blue Ridge Highway, designed to span the six states of the region. Ultimately, Pratt's initial plan for a transmountain highway became a casualty of World War I and was not revived until financed by the Civilian Conservation Corps in the 1930s, when it was renamed the Blue Ridge Parkway.[4]

From Highways to Forest Reserves

While he labored on his regional plan for a transmountain road system, Pratt was also using a physiographic pattern on another of his projects, the Southern Appalachian Forest Reserve. The concept of a national forest reserve was first conceived in 1892 by the fertile minds of Joseph A. Holmes (then North Carolina state geologist) and Gifford Pinchot (then serving as a private forester for the Vanderbilt holdings in North Carolina and adjacent states). The largest single tract of land, the Pisgah Forest, was owned by Vanderbilt and had been originally managed by landscape architect Frederick Law Olmsted. According to Pinchot, the idea was the natural outgrowth of a need to preserve and protect the dwindling forest of the region. Recognizing that the only way to ensure such protection and use of scientific forest management was through the intervention of the federal government, Holmes and Pinchot hatched their plan for a national forest reserve. There in the forester's little stone house at Biltmore Estate, Holmes and Pinchot were to share their vision of a regional forest reserve with young Pratt, during his first annual trip to western North Carolina as a mineralogist in search of specimens.[5]

Pratt and Pinchot became fast friends, bonded in part by their both having been Yale men, both with family connections in Hartford, Connecticut, and both imbued with an abundance of personal and professional energy. In the years that followed, Pratt was to lead the legislative campaign in North Carolina that made possible the acquisition of hundreds of thousands of acres of forest to be included in the proposed forest reserve. In addition, Pratt recognized the potential for creating vast national parks in the mountain region of the Southeast. During the prewar decade, he was named to serve on the Appalachian Regional Forest Reserve Commission, as well as the Forest Experimentation Board, both of which continued to shape his view of the role and function of the regional planner. Conservation became a major concern for the Connecticut Yankee in North Carolina and continued to consume much of his professional attention. In 1909, for example, he wrote innovative legislation that created drainage districts throughout the South.

It is important to note, however, that his efforts on behalf of drainage, like those devoted to the cause of forestry and highway development, were predicated on physiographic boundaries, not political structures. Pratt was, from the beginning, ever seeking effective means of resource management. Therefore, even when his domain was established by statute, as it was in his capacity as state director of fisheries and state geologist, his interests quite naturally followed certain physical features beyond those of his official mandate. Refusing to limit his expertise to the state level, he sought a broader context in which to operate. Thus he was named to the National Forestry Association board of directors, served as a member of the American Association of State Highway Officials, and was elected president of the National Fisheries Association Board, all of which promised a more comprehensive approach to resource management.

In some instances, Pratt took upon himself the task of creating boards of governance and management, usually composed of professionals, educators, and scientists. Insofar as his boards actually planned for their various entities, they did so without government authority. Yet they, like Pratt himself, were considered the legitimate agents of planning in a nation where businessmen and their associations also ruled.[6]

Defining the Planner: From Association to Commission, 1917–1927

The impact of World War I was significant for Pratt and his approach to regional planning. Not only was his vigorous leadership style hampered by a war-related back injury, but he also returned to a rather inhospitable political world. A Wilsonian Democrat, who had dined privately with the president in 1912, Pratt now found himself with few political allies. Equally important, from the standpoint of his concept of regional planning, was his experience in wartime Europe. While serving in a planning capacity in France, Colonel Pratt was exposed to the details of European state forestry, which convinced him of the need for scientific management and state regulation in America.

In 1922 Pratt brought his message to the Southern Forestry Congress in Jackson, Mississippi. Federal legislation is necessary, he warned the association of forest industry leaders, "in order that the regulations passed may be uniform for the several forested regions."[7] The congress remained unimpressed and unmoved by his logic. Indeed, the Southern Forestry Congress was soon to run upon the shoals of indifference and apathy, forcing Pratt to weld his own replacement organization in 1923. Fearing the loss of what he assumed to be a valuable mechanism for investigation, publicity, and planning, Pratt rechartered the Southern Forestry Congress in his Chapel Hill living room. In each of the succeeding congresses Pratt attempted to effect a gathering of state foresters, industry spokesmen, and representatives of various federal agencies in order to share their common concerns and plans for more effective legislation.

Yet what Pratt seemed unable to grasp was the changing nature of regional planning. Government agencies, commissions, and bureaus were already well advanced in their management and planning capacities; in fact, by the mid-1920s a large number of overlapping administrative units were competing for authority to carry out their plans. Pratt might well have learned the lesson that Pinchot had gleaned from his efforts to work with the Inland Waterways Commission. Pinchot had discovered that that agency's single greatest problem was how to achieve a unified system of planning amid the commission's almost constant struggles for departmental autonomy and jurisdiction.[8]

Having lost his place in this politically sponsored elite of scientific managers, Pratt was unable to duplicate their function in a private organization. He could no longer anticipate, as he had with the Southern Appalachian Good Roads Association Conference fifteen years before, that plans generated by such an organization would lead to the development of government action. Moreover, planning was moving from the geophysical boundaries envisioned by geologists, foresters, and others trained in scientific methodology to the much less precise definitions proposed by those seeking a political and cultural base for their study of regions. Coincidental with these conceptual changes was a movement away from organization within the private sector to that of the officially sanctioned government body.

Not only was Pratt sadly out of step with these recent efforts at resource planning, but he seems also to have badly misread the ability and desire of voluntary organizations to come to grips with conservation issues. As historical hindsight reveals, the conservationist impulse of the Roosevelt years had moved from the political arena to the administrative realm under William Taft and Woodrow Wilson, to become a low-priority function of the Harding and Coolidge administrations (attested to, in part, by the Elk Hills and Teapot Dome scandals).[9] Perhaps an even more telling commentary on the changing role of government planners is suggested by the later career of Pratt's conservationist ally, Gifford Pinchot.

Pinchot had become the nation's foremost advocate of conservation measures during Theodore Roosevelt's 1904–8 presidential term. He was to run afoul of Roosevelt's successor, Taft, however, and in a much-publicized controversy with Secretary of the Interior Richard Ballinger was relieved of his duties as chief of the Forestry Division of the Department of Agriculture. Anticipating the lack of a governmental base of operation during the Wilson years, Pinchot turned his attention to the National Conservation Association. Like Pratt, Pinchot was using a nineteenth-century organizational framework to build a basis of public support. But unlike the North Carolina conservationist, Pinchot could see that the national appetite for conservation dogma had been satiated and that such an organization suffered from its lack of a political legitimacy. The National Conservation Association drifted out of existence in 1923. Meanwhile, election to the governorship of Pennsylvania in 1920 provided Pinchot with a politically respectable forum from which to operate. As governor, Pinchot chose to modify his rampant conservationism to the more specific topic of hydroelectric power development and control.

It was Pinchot's renewed interest in waterpower, in fact, that led to Pratt's last major effort in the field of resource planning. In

April of 1924 Pinchot invited Pratt to attend a private meeting in Harrisburg concerning Muscle Shoals and the Giant Power Survey, a state-sponsored agency with quasi-planning authority. Behind the Giant Power Survey was Pinchot's desire to promote the pooling of hydroelectric power by the state prior to its distribution to private companies. Pratt, who was later to serve as an expert witness at U.S. Senate hearings on the Muscle Shoals power project, eagerly embraced the topic and later offered an address on the subject, entitled "Operations of the Inter-connected Power System of the South," to the American Society of Civil Engineers in Atlanta.

From Forest Reserves to Hydroelectric Power

With characteristic fervor, Pratt sought to approach the problem of regional waterpower planning in the same manner that he had confronted the issues of highway building, forest conservation, and drainage planning. By June of 1924, Pratt was ready to assemble the first Southern Appalachian Waterpower Conference, which was to meet in Chattanooga, Tennessee. No doubt, Pratt's inclusion on Pinchot's Giant Power Survey Board and his service as American delegate to the World Power Conference in London fueled his assurance that, under his leadership, the Southern Appalachian Waterpower Conference would serve as a means of meeting the needs of hydroelectric planning in the region. Yet, unlike the Giant Power Survey, which would compile a report for existing planning groups within the structure of the government to act upon, and then expire, Pratt's conference was to discuss and suggest policy on an indefinite basis. That it was to become moribund six years later was only partly attributable to the effects of the depression.

In fact, as the Southern Appalachian Waterpower Conference was to demonstrate, the role of the progressive engineer, so important to early regional planning efforts, had been dramatically transformed. No longer were Pratt and other engineers called upon to devise methods of design or construction for a geophysically defined area. Once a potent mechanism for change, the voluntary conference and association now seemed to exist without a clearly defined purpose. No specific plan of action was called for in these meetings, and none was proposed, even by Pratt. The conference had become an information exchange, and Pratt had become a facilitator of that exchange. It had become an academic performance, with little relevance to the real world of regional planning.

Even in the 1927 Southern Appalachian Power Conference, which counted among its speakers Secretary of Commerce Herbert Hoover and Secretary of the Interior Hubert Work, the task of planning was not addressed. Voluntary associations such as those supporting the Forestry Congress and Southern Appalachian Power Conference were, in reality, no longer interested in the details of regional planning. They were what has been called "an integrated, scientifically administered system of cooperative private management with the indirect support of the federal government," exhibiting considerable political leverage, but without the power to determine exactly how to achieve change.[10]

The real work of planning was being carried out by professional planners, whose experience as urban developers and designers had been established shortly after World War I, and who now were expanding their scope to metropolitan regions. Reflecting the influence of British planner Patrick Geddes, the Regional Planning Association in America (RPAA) was formed in 1923 and soon featured expansive intellectuals such as Clarence Stein, Lewis Mumford, and Benton MacKaye.[11] In addition, the focus of regional planning was undergoing considerable modification. Although regionalization was first perceived by American urban planners as metropolitan or municipal in scope, a shifting emphasis to sociological and cultural characteristics was broadening the definition of regions. Ironically, much of the "new" regionalism resulting from these changes was attributable to the influence of Pratt's colleague at the University of North Carolina, Howard Odum. During the next decade Odum, who had arrived at UNC in 1920 with degrees in psychology and sociology, and who had worked with the Philadelphia Bureau of Municipal Research, set about to redefine the South in regional terms. Pratt, on sick leave from his teaching duties, was seldom on campus, however, and does not appear to have had any professional ties with Odum during this period. By 1931 Odum's preeminence as a regionalist was reflected not only through a popular, pace-setting text, but in his selection by President Hoover to set up a paradigm program in social research.[12]

Professional engineers like Pratt, on the other hand, who had come to the need for planning from a perspective shaped by the existence of scientific, geographic, and physical factors, were giving way to the new breed of planner. A governing principle in Pratt's planning philosophy had always been the primacy of the physiographic region as a means of developing and managing resources. And like the generation before him, Pratt had also relied on the voluntary private association to transform his findings into legislation, frequently based on political regions. His experience in World War I, however, had strengthened a belief that the federal government alone could provide the authority to remedy what were essentially regional problems. What had originally been perceived as a resource problem, defined in terms of its physical boundaries, was increasingly seen as a political issue requiring the cooperation of existing political units and subdivisions. But Pratt was neither a political scientist nor a sociologist; his expertise lay in the fields of geology, forestry, and resource management. No longer a state official nor university faculty member in 1934, Pratt hoped that his concept of regional planning might at last be put to use in the recently created Tennessee Valley Authority (TVA).

The TVA was perhaps the best illustration of a regional approach to a major project based on both a geophysical and a geopolitical perception. In many respects the TVA represented the intersection of the old and new methods of regional planning. Certainly, by the time of the New Deal, both brands of planners had come to the conclusion that a managed environment as well as a managed economy was necessary. The avenues to planning had converged on the sprawling Tennessee River Basin, and armed with the authority and material resources of the federal government, the planners who met there erected a new form of investigation and creativity.[13] Pratt was not destined to be a part of that living definition of regionalism. His letter of inquiry to the TVA and extensive résumé were unceremoniously and symbolically placed in a file.

Meanwhile, a combination of RPAA planning goals and objectives and those formulated by Odum and the southern regionalists were to become realities under the TVA. And from the confluence of those concepts was born yet another definition of regional planning, which in turn would give way to succeeding generations of theory and practice. Pratt and Odum were perfect mirrors of their age, each approaching in their own way the thorny issues of how to organize public and private resources to best solve the problems of a specific geographic and political area.

Pratt had assumed the uncomfortable role of the atavistic conservationist, reminding his audience of the days of Teddy Roosevelt, when the state was just beginning to consider the possibility of regional planning. Indeed, as Albert Lepawsky noted in his 1949 study of state planning in the South, "Any attempt to understand state planning and development in the South and the nation today, and any attempt to gauge the emerging future trends in these American governmental functions, requires some review of [the] conservation and development ideas expressed by Theodore Roosevelt in 1910."[14] Pratt was a conveyor of progressive ideas that had found new voices and new forms by the 1930s. And while Odum was in the process of becoming one of the nation's foremost spokesmen for the new regionalism, Pratt the pioneering regionalist and Wilsonian Democrat was denied the opportunity to contribute to the new generation of regional planning as embodied in the New Deal's TVA.

THE ORGANIZATION AND PROCESS OF PLANNING

CHAPTER 7

"Smokestacks and Geraniums"

Planning and Politics in San Diego

JOHN HANCOCK

Like Eric Sandweiss, John Hancock focuses on the process by which citizens established planning as a central municipal function in the early twentieth century. His case study is San Diego, a western boomtown that has received considerably less attention from planning historians than St. Louis. Hancock turns the traditional approach to planning history on its head by asserting that planning must be judged not by the quality of the master plan but by what actually gets built. The latter criterion, he argues, is "a test preeminently political." To understand the politics of planning, Hancock analyzes what planners proposed and the components eventually realized and then deduces from that comparison the vitality and purposes of city planning in San Diego. He considers in turn several distinct contexts of the planning process: the principal groups involved, the terms on which they conducted the debate, the leadership of strong individuals, the quality of John Nolen's San Diego plans of 1908 and 1926, the city's changing demographics, and changes in the form of its municipal government. Hancock builds his case study from an examination of an array of primary sources: census statistics; local histories; contemporary newspaper accounts; Nolen's diaries, papers, and comprehensive plans; and reports, surveys, and documents from the city of San Diego.

In San Diego, planning was sponsored by a relatively homogeneous set of interests: affluent reformers, the business community, and the navy, the city's largest developer. The city's boomtown status, booster spirit, and function as a military port shaped the "smokestacks-versus-geraniums" terms by which city planning initiatives were debated. Thus in San Diego the form of the local government had negligible impact on the adoption of city planning. The key factors influencing the institutionalization of planning there were Nolen's 1908 and 1926 plans, as well as Nolen's and businessman George Marston's skillful political presentation of both plans to the citizens of San Diego. Nolen's plans galvanized the supporters of both smokestacks and geraniums, provided a clear vision for the city's future, and established planning as an ongoing public process.

Hancock's observations about the politics of planning in San Diego contrast interestingly with Sandweiss's comments on the same phenomenon in St. Louis; in both cases, planning mirrored "the conservative influence of its major patrons," but in ways peculiar to the particularities of local politics. For other contrasting treatments, readers should consult David C. Hammack's Power and Society *(New York: Russell Sage Foundation, 1982) and Carl Abbott's case study of another less-studied western city,* Portland *(Lincoln: University of Nebraska Press, 1983). The discussion in this chapter also confirms that in San Diego planning became a formal municipal function by gradual, conservative increments, rather than all at one time on a citywide scale. Hancock's portrait of planning by a limited circle of individuals and balkanized agencies accords with Barry Cullingworth's views in* The Political Culture of Planning *(New York: Routledge, 1993). Both studies raise questions about whether a planning process so constituted can serve the diverse constituents of a twentieth-century city.*

For more on John Nolen, his career, and his planning ideas and achievements, the best sources are Hancock's unpublished dissertation,

"John Nolen and the American City Planning Movement" (University of Pennsylvania, 1964), and "John Nolen," in Krueckeberg, ed., The American Planner, *as well as Nolen's own writings,* Replanning Small Cities *(New York: B. W. Huebsch, 1912) and* New Towns for Old *(Boston: Marshall Jones, 1927). For additional information on the impact of the military presence on San Diego planning, see Martin Gordon, "The Marines Have Landed and San Diego Is Well in Hand,"* Journal of the West *20 (Oct. 1981): 43–50, and Roger Lotchin's comments in chapter 13 of this volume.* EDITORS

The highest test of planning is not what is planned but what gets done—a test preeminently political. In Edward Banfield and James Wilson's famed definition, city politics is the art "of managing conflict in matters of public importance."[1] Conflicts continually arise over city planning. Planners recommend actions they believe have public importance; politicians and voters decide whether to carry them out. The political history of city planning can reveal a good deal about its public uses and appeal in the United States. This chapter considers the establishment of city planning in modern San Diego, California, particularly the impact of two plans made by an outside consultant under changing political conditions that heralded city planning's institutionalization there.

The Setting

City boosting is an art in San Diego. To everyone willing to listen, promoters have proclaimed it "Harbor of the Sun," "Our Italy," "Plymouth Rock of the Golden West," "America's Finest City," and other fancies.[2] Their common purpose is to make San Diego the region's dominant economy and culture. To promote growth, they turned to city planning early in this century.

Their enthusiasm is understandable. San Diego is the urban center of a beautiful, varied natural region facing the Pacific Ocean above Mexico. The city's beaches, cliffs, long bay, canyons, mesas, and prevailing Mediterranean climate, and the mountains and deserts beyond have long attracted health seekers, outdoor enthusiasts, and retirees.[3]

Much of the city's attractive setting is human made, the result of careful planning. Indeed, "San Diego is, in its natural form, a desert."[4] San Diegans imported precious freshwater and most of the trees, other plants, and crops one sees there today. They deepened the harbor and dredged tidelands to create miles of new shoreland, set aside 60 percent of their superb ocean beaches for public use, transformed a marsh into one of the world's largest marine parks, and continue to alter nature in positive and negative ways today.

Four successively dominant cultures have shaped the city. Kumeyaay Indians developed villages, irrigation, and farming in and around San Diego c. 950 B.C. Next, the Spanish arrived on 16 July 1769 (commemorated as the state birthday). They gave the area its present name and built a presidio and mission, the first European settlement above Baja California. In 1834 the new Mexican government gave it two crucial legacies: status as a "pueblo" (municipality), and 48,557 acres of public land. After Americans seized it in 1846, the new state legislature upheld the legacies by making San Diego California's first city and county and giving it more public land than any other city in the state and perhaps the nation.

Americans gave San Diego growth mania, gridiron streets, and city planning. They acquired Indian and Mexican land by purchase, chicanery, and theft. And then they divided it into small lots for sale and touted the city's growth potential. It boomed after 1869 when Alonzo Horton persuaded the city to sell him 1,000 acres of pueblo land at 27½¢ per acre, which he sold off in what became today's downtown. In the next twenty years, other speculators laid out uniform additions (80-foot-wide streets and blocks measuring 200 × 300 feet, with twelve 50 × 100-foot lots per block) across the city and in twenty new towns from the Mexican border to Oceanside 70 miles north.[5] The platting frenzy extended the grid across steep hills and arid canyons miles beyond the built-up area, thereby "entailing great unnecessary expense and destruction of rare opportunities to secure significant beauty."[6] So much land was platted by 1888 that the city added few new streets until 1925. When the land boom suddenly collapsed in 1889, San Diego's population plunged from an estimated 40,000 residents in 1888 to 16,159 in 1890.[7] More serious for its future, the city had sold more than a third of its vast public lands.

Adversity seems to have been good for public planning in San Diego. Voters adopted a new, more democratic city charter in 1889. They replaced "trustees" with a mayor and bicameral council (a board of nine aldermen and a common council consisting of eighteen persons, two per ward); created police, fire, health, public works, and other services; and prohibited further sale of pueblo land until 1930. In the next fifteen years the city finished building a modern public infrastructure—paved and lighted streets, trolley lines, landscaped parks, sewers, water, gas and electric utilities—that fixed patterns and directions of growth for decades to come.

Although extensive public works in hard times signified unquenched optimism about the city's future, municipal reformers wrought a more narrow way to guide it when growth resumed. A 1905 charter amendment created a unicameral city council, reduced it from twenty-seven to nine members (one per ward), and provided initiative, referendum, and recall—the first citizen review in California.[8] While streamlining governance, the amended form was less democratic than the old one: the people had fewer representatives, and decisions involved a thinner mix with fewer men (and no women) in power.

The city's economic elite solidly supported the urban growth process. The most powerful wealthy individual, John D. Spreckels, owned more land and buildings than anyone else in the region plus several banks, the two largest daily newspapers, the city streetcar system, and the county water company. He opposed municipal regulation of land and public service companies but usually joined other rich local magnates like sporting goods king A. G. Spalding, newspaper tycoon E. W. Scripps (who won a council seat in 1905), and his daughter, philanthropist Ellen B. Scripps, to support large-scale plans to stimulate growth.[9]

The 1905 municipal reforms were led by another wealthy businessman, George Marston, the leading city planning advocate in the first half of this century and one of the most illustrious citizens in San Diego history. Marston came from Wisconsin in 1870, built the region's largest department store, and got involved in civic affairs and politics. A self-described "independent," he was a councilman in 1887–89 and first commissioner of parks in 1905, founded the local Progressive Party, twice ran for mayor, and voted Socialist in the 1932 presidential race. He founded the first civic improvement, park, and social service boards; was a founding trustee of Pomona College; and gave much land and money to the city, county, and state for parks and playgrounds. Liberal, pragmatic, and generous, Marston spent his wealth and long life trying to make San Diego an exceptional place to live. In 1902 he hired New Yorker Samuel Parsons to landscape the 1,400-acre City Park, one of the nation's largest urban parks. Marston took a giant step toward city planning five years later when, on Parsons's recommendation, he hired John Nolen of Cambridge, Massachusetts, to make a city plan. City planning became a leading political issue in San Diego as soon as the "Eastern Man" arrived on 7 September 1907.[10]

Impacts of the First Nolen Plan

Sixteen months later Nolen presented his recommendations in a published report, *San Diego: A Comprehensive Plan for Its Improvement*, summarized in a supplement to the *San Diego Union* on New Year's Day 1909. His stated aim was *not* to provide "final . . . plans that can be executed without further study or revision . . . or . . . carried out at once. Primarily, they are intended to awaken and form public opinion and furnish a goal toward which all future development should tend." Emphasizing the public value of natural resources in great cities, it was less a comprehensive plan than an essay on how to systematically obtain, develop, and link three types of public land use: *central meeting place* (bayfront civic center–plaza–esplanade); *traffic* (multivehicle on varied street forms); and *open space* (neighborhood playgrounds to regional wilderness parks). After assessing the city's cultural and natural resources, Nolen made ten specific recommendations. None directly addressed economic development, but he stressed the need for a long-range "comprehensive and practical plan" rooted in local history and natural conditions. Correctly foreseeing great growth in the next generation, Nolen posed the essential planning issue as a question of what San Diego, a town of 30,000 people, should become: not an ordinary but "an important, perhaps a great city" center of a vast region (figures 7.1 and 7.2).[11]

The next year, Marston progressives led another successful reform to streamline decision making and to enhance city adoption

FIGURE 7.1. The San Diego bayfront in 1908. The Santa Fe Railroad Station is visible on the left, the Court House on the right. From Nolen (1908), p. 277.

FIGURE 7.2. John Nolen's vision of San Diego's refurbished waterfront in his 1908 plan. The waterfront was to include an esplanade, an art and pleasure center, and a paseo linking the bay to City Park. From Nolen (1908), p. 216.

of Nolen's plan. A 1909 amendment further reduced the council from nine partisan to five nonpartisan members elected at large as commissioners (one also as mayor)—California's first commission government.[12] The commissioners made laws and policy and directed departments, making them both legislators and administrators and the mayor a figurehead, thus short-circuiting democratic checks and balances.

The commission did not adopt Nolen's plan but took up some minor recommendations. Between 1909 and 1914 it widened and renamed major streets and City Park to reflect local history and nature, and it imposed limited commercial, industrial, and subdivision controls. Voters passed bond issues for sewers, playgrounds, parks, a city forest, and water system and harbor dredging. Meanwhile reformers joined other leaders and New York architect Bertram Goodhue to plan a Panama–California Exposition (1915–16) in Balboa Park to celebrate the city and the opening of the Panama Canal.[13]

These modest planning gains cannot be attributed to modified commission government, however. Most commissioners elected in those years were not Civic Association candidates, and their views of development differed sharply from Nolen's. They favored un-restricted industry on the bayfront and refused a Civic Association request for a public vote on a bond issue to develop the central bayfront for the civic, social, and recreational uses urged by Nolen. Instead they asked voters to approve a bond issue to build two long warehouse piers at the foot of Broadway. Nolen, brought back by Marston a month before the 1911 election, supported "practical, well-considered businesslike improvement of . . . [the] great bay, especially for commercial purposes," but urged voters to reject the proposal because city planning

> should be from not business or other interests alone but of the whole people . . . settled with regard to the permanent welfare of the city. Not the San Diego of 1911 or even of 1915, but of the long years thereafter. . . . The present issue is not a question of one man's plans against another. It is a question of different methods and policies. . . . I have come here simply because I want to do all I can to keep San Diego from what appears to be a grave mistake. This city stands on the threshold of an almost unbelievable future.[14]

With women voting for the first time, voters turned out in record (double the usual) numbers for "the most sensational, the most spectacular, and the most vigorously fought political battle in the history of San Diego." Comprehensive planning was soundly defeated: the bond issue passed by a two-to-one margin. The commissioners, thus emboldened, then ignored attempts by the Women's Club to tear down and replace waterfront and other shacks with modern low-cost houses; and to prohibit prostitution, gambling, and other illicit activity. An outside socioeconomic survey team studying San Diego in 1914 concluded that "up to the present time, the energy of the community has directed itself along com-mercial lines, developing the opportunities of the real estate boomer and his moneyed patron."[15]

Progressives misread the potential impact of municipal reform on city planning in pre–World War I San Diego for several reasons. First, they underestimated the continuity of change with the past. They assumed a commission would improve management and adopt the Nolen plan; but in fact little changed. Commission government did not lessen partisan politics or adopt the plan; and it actually reinforced San Diego's historical lack of a strong leader, dominant party, and common interests beyond growth.

Second, the reformers' concept of urban democracy was fundamentally flawed. They assumed American municipal government worked better if its "politics" were diminished. Like most urban reformers in the twentieth-century Progressive Era—when upheaval in all areas of life accompanied the rise of the United States as an industrial urban nation and world power—San Diego reformers wanted to minimize public turmoil and maximize administrative efficiency by making government an apolitical institution run by expert "civil servants" and a few nonpartisan elected representatives.[16] The reformers put more faith in management than in democratic decisions by a growing, diverse, unevenly informed citizenry. By eliminating wards, reducing the number of elected officials, and increasing the number and authority of bureaucrats and hand-picked citizen advisory boards, they deliberately obscured the pluralistic give-and-take of democracy. Far from making it more democratic, reformers made San Diego government more awesome, remote, and difficult for ordinary citizens to control.

Third, progressives perhaps did not grasp that voters distrusted centralized power even while wanting efficient administration and some city planning. Dissatisfaction was evident just six years later, in 1915, when voters scrapped the commission to get a bit more balance between democracy and efficiency. Citizen-initiated amendments restored mayor–city council government (six members at large including a separately elected mayor); gave the mayor control of departments; and created a civil service and manager of operations for public works. In 1916, after the state legislature enabled

California cities to appoint city planning commissions, make long-range plans, and regulate land subdivisions (1915), the new council ordained San Diego's first city planning commission.

The modest 1915 changes still did not basically alter political behavior or improve prospects for city planning. Elections continued to be free-for-alls, political power and leadership remained diffused, and the central conflict was still over the kind and means of planned growth. Between 1901 and 1921 one businessman after another, regardless of party, was elected mayor, commissioner, or councilman on the strength of promises to bring economic growth to the city. In that span only one mayor was reelected (during explosive wartime growth) to a second two-year term. Councils after 1915 did not fund and the mayor did not appoint anyone to the planning commission for seven years (1923).[17] Yet the 1908 Nolen plan continued to be a leading issue in San Diego, and Nolen returned regularly to champion planning.

The battle over city planning before World War I came to a climax in two mayoralty elections involving Marston. In 1913 Spalding, Scripps, and other influential progressives induced him to run as a pro-planning, nonpartisan candidate. His opponent, realtor Charles F. O'Neall, favored acquiring commerce and industry over public parks and recreation—payrolls first, civic beauty second, as he put it. Marston campaigned for harbor improvements, a new dry dock, a great navy center, railroad to Arizona, and other projects, arguing the city could be both beautiful and prosperous. The opposition waged a vicious campaign via anonymous pamphlets accusing Marston of using the Nolen plan to buy the mayor's job and to promote friends' real estate schemes. He was also accused of being a "Custodian of the People's Pleasanunce [sic], a lover of trees and an outspoken foe of 'Brutal Commercialism,'" and there were other inferences that he was an unprincipled dreamer who did not need to make a living. Marston lost by 668 votes.[18]

He ran again in 1917, in the most famous mayoralty campaign in San Diego's history. Again planned growth was the key issue.

The Organization and Process of Planning

This time civic leaders entered the fray with experience in making it happen. Their six-year planning of the Panama–California Exposition had paid off in shared knowledge and promotion of San Diego as a city with great prospects. The fair attracted several million visitors and several thousand new residents. At the same time, unable to attract factories, local leaders closed ranks to elect Democrat William Kettner, head of the Chamber of Commerce, to Congress in 1912. They worked closely with him, the navy, and Marine Corps to bring *military* industry to San Diego. Because he did not view this effort as smokestack growth, Marston supported it. As he wrote to a friend, "Eventually San Diego is destined to become a great naval station with a training school on North Island, and a harbor as a haven where our fighting craft can repair and replenish."[19]

The backgrounds of the 1917 contestants differed as sharply as their views of the city. Soft-spoken philanthropist and reformer Marston was opposed by promoter par excellence Louis Wilde, flamboyant, Iowa-born banker and resident since 1903. He pushed silkworm, real estate, and wildcat oil schemes; founded two banks; built the city's most famous hotel (the U.S. Grant); and billed himself the "Smokestack Candidate" and his opponent "Geranium George."

Marston campaigned on a platform advocating compatibility of city planning, energy conservation, and building and pollution controls with industrial development. He argued that in order for San Diego to fulfill its destiny as a great city it needed both "manufacturing and business that fits with our natural conditions" and a "comprehensive city plan . . . without prejudice" to any group in the city. In his campaign newspaper, the *Daily Smokestack*, Wilde argued unabashedly for many large factories to stimulate the economy and employment and said city planning was a cosmetic to beautify the city at the cost of its economic prosperity. Wilde's campaign song expressed his views:

> Oh we love to have the tourists come,
> in our sunshine to bask,
> But we need some smokestacks:
> Give us work: a chance is all we ask.

Although supported by Scripps, Spalding, Spreckels, and all daily papers, Marston lost again, by a margin six times larger than in 1913—it was a resounding defeat. In his words, "Smokestacks won. The forces for commercialism and rapid superficial growth defeated the people who stood for more conservative and sensible methods of building the city."[20] San Diegans have used "Smokestacks versus Geraniums" ever since to characterize the politics of local planning.

Why the two losses? Marston's strengths as civic leader were weaknesses as a politician. "I am not a good mixer," he wrote to Spalding, "and I think this is one reason that makes it hard for people to elect me. Notwithstanding my real sympathy for the laboring man and the real vital interests of the community, my way of getting at it is more or less misunderstood." His views on city planning appealed more to upper-middle-class than to working-class voters, for good reason. Abhorrence of sprawl and call for slow, comprehensive planned expansion were not enough to convince listeners who did not have his privileges "that his vision would mean economic prosperity for them as well as a beautiful environment," as Gregg Hennessey notes. Moreover, improving physical environs was an easier and more conservative task than improving social and economic life. Marston was more comfortable, and effective, quietly working behind the lines with others of like belief and class, giving money and unflagging support to civic causes, than he was out front trying to lead people with diverse interests.[21]

Three days after the election, the United States entered World War I. All thoughts of comprehensive city planning faded temporarily as San Diego expanded into a temporary armed camp for army, navy, and air training, hospitals, ship berthing and repair—a condition civic leaders helped make permanent in the 1920s. "It was now a military city and would so remain."[22] By 1919 six agencies were doing the physical planning—City Public Works Department, Harbor and Park Commissions, State Highway Department, Navy Bureau of Yards and Docks (base construction), and Army Corps of Engineers (dredging)—each with a special task, some overlap, and

The Organization and Process of Planning

FIGURE 7.3. San Diego's central waterfront at the foot of Broadway, c. 1925. Balboa Park is at left center. From Nolen (1926), p. 23.

little coordination except with the Chamber of Commerce, which supported most planning projects in the region.

Attracting the navy was costly in land removed from local use, but produced cooperative planning on a grand scale, dramatic growth and economic benefits, and the city's formal adoption of planning long advocated by reformers. The civic and military coalition made San Diego the naval center of the West Coast almost overnight. Between 1916 and 1926 the city and private citizens gave or sold more than 5,000 acres (40%) of bayfront land, 18 acres of Balboa Park, and thousands of acres in northern valleys to the Navy, which built ten major installations. The pattern for success began in 1916 when, with crushing approval (40,288 to 305), voters gave 500 acres of tidelands to the Marine Corps to build an expeditionary base just 3 miles north of downtown, and a business-man sold 270 acres adjacent to the Marine Corps at below market price. Bertram Goodhue's base plan helped popularize Spanish co-lonial architecture in the city, and his proposal to border the parade ground with a public esplanade at Bayside was a remarkable joint military-civilian use in twentieth-century American cities. Nolen improved the idea in 1926, but it was never implemented as recom-mended by the two famed designers. Nevertheless, the coalition's overall achievement in bringing the navy to the city during the interwar period was phenomenal.[23]

This great change fostered a boom from which came the basic form of today's city between 1920 and 1930, the decade of most

FIGURE 7.4. San Diego Harbor, c. 1925, showing downtown, reclamation of tidelands, construction of several naval and marine bases, North Island–Coronado, Point Loma, and north. From Nolen (1926), p. 22.

sustained growth. The city's population doubled (the county's nearly did) and sprawled east, south, and unevenly north, partly by annexation (for example, east San Diego in 1923 expanded its population by a third). Society was heterogeneous and mobile, with few unifying traditions or well-defined lines except money and race. There was lots of room for the eighteen new neighborhoods—each with a distinct business center and socioeconomic identity—in the nearly 100-square-mile city. Meanwhile, downtown's high-rise skyline was built (essentially unchanged until the 1960s); streetcar lines and other infrastructure were extended; trucks and automobiles crowded newly paved city streets, two of them new (north-south and east-west) national highways. In short, San Diego began to spread over a huge area beyond the bay. By then (1930) a third of the city's economy came from military expenditure (payroll, supplies, construction). The naval presence also lured industry, particularly airplane manufacturers, which became the city's second largest employer in 1935, after the military, followed by tourism and agriculture (figures 7.3 and 7.4).[24]

Second Nolen Plan: A New Era of City Planning in San Diego

The pressures and promises of this dramatic growth tipped the political balance and led the city to adopt public planning in the early 1920s. Pro-city planning "geraniums" finally won the mayor's office in 1921 and held it (two mayors, both engineers) through 1931. After passing a zoning ordinance in January 1923, the council reorganized and funded the moribund city planning commission in June as an operating board to make zoning and planning recommendations to the council. They appointed three regular ("blue-ribbon") citizen members and three ex-officio city ones (mayor as council representative, city attorney, manager of operations); and added a professional planner to the staff. As he did in other cities, Nolen got the city to hire a young man from his Cambridge office,

Kenneth Gardner. While an inside planner was advantageous to Nolen, his prime purpose in those pioneering days was to get planning under way as a regular municipal function.[25]

With behind-the-scenes help from Marston and Nolen, the campaign for a second comprehensive city plan for San Diego began on 5 April 1924, when the planning commission hosted a luncheon in the Civic Auditorium for local leaders to meet with planners from all over the United States en route to their fifteenth national conference in Los Angeles. Nolen and Edward Bassett, preeminent national authority on zoning and planning law, discussed municipal planning. Two months later the council authorized $10,000 for Nolen to make a comprehensive plan for the city planning commission, cosponsored by the Park and Harbor Commissions. In March 1925 the council created the post of planning engineer and appointed Gardner to it. Now, Nolen's backers were not only Marston, the Civic Association, and Chamber of Commerce but also the city and many public and private organizations (such as the Playground Commission, Board of Education, American Legion, and Labor Council), all of which wrote to him about specific issues they wanted addressed. Public interest in city planning was never higher.[26]

Nolen skillfully orchestrated presentation of the finished plan to build a wide base of public support. After eighteen months of study and getting responses to three preliminary plans, he returned to review the second Nolen plan with city officials on 5 February 1926. He made a well-publicized multistage report to a mass public audience on 8 February and addressed special interest groups over the next week. After he returned to Cambridge, Gardner and members of the city planning commission, council, Chamber of Commerce, and other organizations made dozens of speeches at public meetings in the city and county to explain and promote the plan. The County Board of Supervisors liked it, as did all the daily newspapers (they featured it as an ongoing public interest story) and a dozen weeklies. The plan was discussed at the largest meeting on record of the Realty Board, which, along with Marston and the

Chamber of Commerce, agreed to pay the city's cost of printing it. There was no significant opposition to the plan.[27]

The 1926 plan was metropolitan and regional in outlook and, as in 1908, oriented to the bayfront and natural environment. Again, Nolen addressed three interrelated major functions: waterfront, parks and recreation, transportation and streets. He made eighteen linked recommendations for what he called "Regional Planning for a Metropolitan District," which "cannot exactly be defined, but it would seem that it should include, under some properly organized commission, not only San Diego, but [everything south to the border] . . . and perhaps some of the more distant places to the east of the present city boundaries" (figure 7.5).[28]

The plan mirrored several changes in local concerns since 1908. Nolen gave special attention to integrating military and civilian activities, notably in a proposed 200-foot-wide, 11-mile-long Harbor Drive from the south city limits north to the tip of Point Loma. The drive was carefully aligned with twelve existing and proposed streets, parks, and six major activity zones along the waterfront—industry, commerce, civic center, airport, military bases, recreation island, and yacht basin—all to be built on the tidelands in a "city beautiful" necklace around the bay.[29]

The plan had weaknesses as well as strengths. Nolen barely considered water supply and housing, the growing city's two greatest needs. He also ignored north San Diego County beyond Torrey Pines, the area of greatest residential growth after World War II. Not perceived as a shortcoming by anyone then but significant ten years later was his recommendation that a municipal airport be built on tidelands next to the Marine Base. Like many people then, Nolen was more entranced by the romance than the potential growth of airplane travel. Thinking of airplanes as swift, tiny passenger ships, he believed an over-water approach was the most calming and safe entrance to a city center, as did colleagues in the days before mass air travel and turbopropeller and jet aircraft became huge land eaters and noisy polluters. Nolen always tried to eliminate grade-level train traffic in cities but he saw no difficulty with near-down-

"Smokestacks and Geraniums"

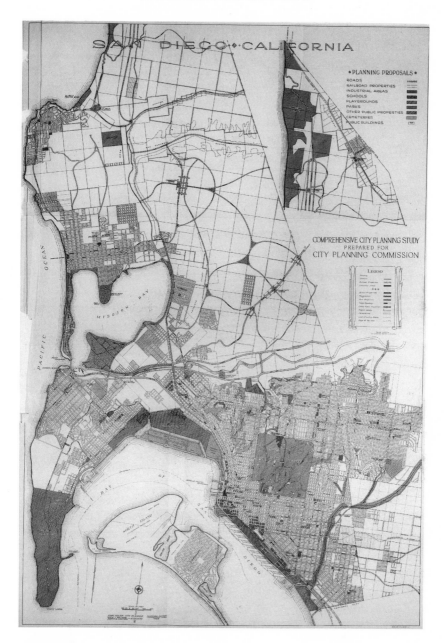

FIGURE 7.5. John Nolen's comprehensive city plan proposals for San Diego, 1926. From Nolen (1926), facing p. 34.

town airports, and indeed lauded "the advantages in convenience of location, close to the heart of the city." Today's airline pilots regard vastly expanded, often foggy Lindbergh Field as one of the most unsafe airports in the world.[30]

The City Council swiftly adopted the 1926 plan as its "guide-line" for future development, gave the city planning commission design control over public buildings and spaces as well, and implemented most of it piecemeal over several decades. Like the 1908 plan, it is one of the few American city plans still known and referenced by San Diegans generations later. It has a remarkable longevity of image appeal for a modern American city plan.

Most of the eighteen major recommendations and many lesser ones were realized, if not always as Nolen intended. The first success came that fall when voters, with a plea by Nolen, rejected by two to one a measure to put the new San Diego State College campus in Balboa Park. The next year they narrowly approved the Civic Center tidelands site. The county voted strongly for it, but the city divided evenly, with a heavy "no" vote on the south side, where Nolen envisioned future residential development but supported the Harbor Commission's "industrial" designation of the waterfront and proposed few public amenities for adjacent low- to moderate-income neighborhoods. In 1928 voters approved a $650,000 bond issue to construct the airport, dedicated as Lindbergh Field later that year. A new street plan was adopted in 1930, as were a new building code and an enlarged inspection department to prevent shoddy construction. By then, state law required cities to have a master plan and provided broad power and scope for planning and zoning. However, all planning projects in San Diego were halted between the crash of 1929 and the beginning of President Franklin Roosevelt's New Deal recovery programs in 1933–34.[31]

In the interim deepening depression, San Diego's restless voters made the most important reform in municipal government. After rejecting a city manager charter in 1929, opponents from new outlying neighborhoods agreed to support a revision if it added council representation of their areas. A large majority of voters approved the new city charter of 1931, which is still in force today. It provided for a city manager, a new mayor–city council of seven members (six by district, one citywide to also serve in the mostly ceremonial role of mayor); and a planning commission enlarged to seven regular members (four appointed by the city manager and three by council), two ex officio (city attorney, engineer), and staff. The city manager directed it and most other operations.

Thus once more reformers tried to centralize policy and operations, this time in one person, the city manager. The new government got off to a rocky start, however, when the council refused to acknowledge the city manager's broad power and overruled the planning commission's recommendations for zoning exceptions more frequently during this period (1932–35) than at any other time in the 1930s. After going through four city managers in less than three years, the charter reformers organized a Civic Affairs Conference to support pro-charter aspirants to the city council. By 1937 all council members except the mayor had conference backing. In contrast to their predecessors, whose backgrounds were primarily in real estate, the seven pro-charter councilmen who served between 1935 and 1938 were affluent professionals (an architect, a chartered public accountant, two military officers) and business executives.[32]

The 1931 charter did not alter the course of city planning in San Diego, however. By then it was well established and had broad political support, even when Nolen's guidelines were not followed to the letter. Opposition could be costly to one's political future. In 1935, for example, a new city manager experienced fierce opposition when he proposed to build a security complex (police headquarters, courtrooms, jail) on a site designated for a park, rather than in the civic center where Nolen proposed putting all the government buildings. Several councilmen went along, but strong opposition came from the Harbor Commission, which owned the land, and the mayor, a congressman, banker, the Chamber of Commerce, and others who formed the Citizens' Nolen Plan Committee to support the Civic Center site. It took the manager (who consistently ignored his planning engineer) three years to win public approval and then only after he moved the site to a Nolen-approved tidelands location and approved a Spanish colonial design to harmonize with the Civic Center rising ten blocks north. A year later (spring 1939) the pro-planning mayor was reelected with two new council candidates that he put up and an independent. As a result, the conference lost its council majority and the city manager was forced to resign. While Nolen plan supporters lost the opportunity to put all new public buildings in a "city beautiful" group on the central bayfront, the main structure—the Civic Center (County Administration Building today)—was built on the site designated and the city continued to implement the Nolen plan, regardless of who was city manager or on the council.[33]

Thanks to New Deal emergency funds, work on most major elements of the plan resumed in the midst of the depression and was completed before World War II. In January 1936, Glen Rick, the new planning engineer, reported that all six harbor and waterfront proposals, five of the six major highway recommendations, and two of the six main recreation and park proposals had been carried out or were under construction. The last four, completed after 1945, established the region's unique network of seashore, urban, mountain, and desert parks. Rick also prepared a "Long-Term Program of Capital Expenditures" for the projects and made a plan to deal with natural catastrophe. In 1939–40 the National Resources Planning Board studied San Diego and four other cities (Cincinnati, Milwaukee, New York, Richmond) "with a reputation for orderly programming of public works" to devise a model methodology for using a long-range plan and budget to select and finance capital projects and demonstrate it in other cities. Pleased with San Diego's progress, Nolen told Marston during his last visit in 1936, "Someone has said that the city and regional planner should have a biological sense of time. However, as compared to other cities, San Diego has moved rapidly."[34]

John Nolen did not live to see all the changes nor the vast urbanization of San Diego County that he anticipated long ago. He died 18 February 1937, thirty years after first visiting the area. San

"Smokestacks and Geraniums"

FIGURE 7.6. John Nolen, c. 1936. From *Steel and Garnet* (1936).

Diegans' high respect for his work was apparent in a newspaper obituary calling him "probably the world's foremost city planner, to whose genius San Diego paid tribute when it adopted the Nolen plan as a guide to development in 1926" (figure 7.6).[35]

Learning from San Diego

By the standard of sheer growth, San Diego has surpassed the wildest dreams of its early boosters and planners. It has grown dramatically in every decade since 1900 and has been transformed from a sleepy town of 17,000 residents to a bustling metropolis of more than 1.1 million people today. The fastest-growing California city in this century, it is the sixth largest city in the United States and the center of an urban region of 3.5 million people (the county, city, and Tijuana, Mexico), the most populous bi-national region in North America. No longer just a resort, retirement, and "navy town," San Diego has diversified socially and economically as it continues to grow.[36]

What light does San Diego shed on the history of American city planning before World War II? It affirms the literature insofar as it shows that formal municipal planning was established by conservative, gradual changes rather than all at once and on a grand scale.[37] Unlike many cities, however, San Diego found rapid, steady (in this case, military-related) growth impelling it to empower public planning relatively early in the century.

American city planning mirrors the conservative influence of its major patrons. In San Diego various organized groups (realtors, big business, Chamber of Commerce, progressives, women's club, navy, and so on) exerted influence on planning. But they were culturally limited groups not representative of the city's growing socioeconomic diversity as a whole. Planning's greatest promoters were efficiency- and control-minded reformers composed of educated, affluent men and women, followed by the city's biggest boosters: the business community and its single-minded largest developer, the navy. They occasionally fused effective coalitions for planning, but only temporarily. So did the six autocratic public agencies with separate but overlapping planning tasks. Although they occasionally worked together, they had no legal mandate or strong informal pressure to coordinate their work. As a British scholar recently observed, "The most striking feature of the American planning process is that it lacks the features of a 'system' . . . There is . . . a multiplicity of local systems with a wide range of differing policies."[38] There is an implicit political system here—democracy. However, planning by limited interest groups and undemocratic balkanized agencies raises questions about how well they serve a diverse urban society and environment.

The San Diego case is particularly important because it suggests the *form* of local government is not the crucial factor in city planning's adoption, as reformers thought it would be. San Diegans have tried five different government structures since 1889, hoping to strike a balance between democratic and central management. Planning gained strength in each structure. More notable was an intertwining of real estate and political occupations among elected officials, especially when planning finally was adopted. Between 1925 and 1932 five of the seven councilmen who served full terms came from real estate fields (the others from labor unions). They have been called "opportunists."[39]

Another point to note is that exceptional individuals are major players in the politics of planning. Two of them—John Nolen and George Marston—stand out in San Diego. Nolen translated their shared liberal ideals and dream of beauty, nature, and community well-being in the future city into two grand plans. Marston fostered them, led the political fight, and generously helped implement planning with his wealth and energy for more than fifty years, an amazing record of commitment. The two champions did not always carry the day, of course. It took fifteen years (1908–23) to get municipal planning adopted, and some key proposals have never been taken up.

Nolen's plans stand out for their visionary impact. They are thin documents by today's standards, concepts not working plans, and, like his sponsors, not informed by income, race, gender, and other societal data. Yet no other plans have so stirred local imaginations, perhaps because they are the only citywide-cum-regional visions ever made for San Diego. Since then, voters have rejected at least one general plan (1965) and adopted two others (1967, 1979); but it is hard to find residents today, even civic leaders, who can identify one of the plans, much less be enthusiastic about it.[40] In contrast, Nolen's 1926 work was the city's master plan guide for more than forty years, and his 1908 bayfront ideas keep resurfacing. To Raymond Starr, "The [1908] drawings suggest plans that would have made San Diego one of the most spectacularly beautiful cities in the world." Richard Pourade found "many people in San Diego who had been nurtured on the idea of the 'City

Beautiful' as it had been so inspiringly described long before by . . . Nolen." His plans were a major theme in the last three books of Pourade's seven-volume history, which ends on the dream of "a new generation of San Diegans, with a new concept of the 'City Beautiful.'" Nolen and Marston's work is recalled today in third-generation San Diegan Roger Showley's *Union-Tribune* urban planning and design column, "Smokestacks & Geraniums."[41]

Marston, Nolen, and many first-generation twentieth-century San Diegans helped establish city planning as an ongoing public process for transforming dreams of an urban region in which all people can live well among one another into general plans, zoning and building codes, urban design and environmental guidelines. Their answer to the question, "Can citywide planning help promote desirable growth?" was "Yes"; but they disagreed on what it was. "Geraniums or smokestacks" remains the leading issue in San Diego politics and is a persistent theme in American history. It surfaces today as "environment versus jobs," "managed versus unlimited growth" and other contemporary versions of ageless American ideas of progress. The appropriate mix, and the city planning needed to achieve it, undergo continual redefinition in San Diego, and in the United States.

CHAPTER 8

Planning, Public Works, and Politics

The Trinity River Reclamation Project in Dallas

ROBERT B. FAIRBANKS

In Portland *(Lincoln: University of Nebraska Press, 1983) and* Twentieth-Century Richmond *(Knoxville: University of Tennessee Press,
1984), Carl Abbott and Christopher Silver, respectively, portrayed city planning as an enterprise dominated by a business elite who set and carried
out their own urban improvement priorities. In chapters 3 and 7 of this
anthology, Eric Sandweiss and John Hancock depicted strong sectional interests and differences in philosophy among the community of businessmen
and politicians who shaped the implementation of planning in St. Louis
and San Diego, respectively. Robert B. Fairbanks provides another perspective on the politics of planning in his case study of the Trinity River Reclamation Project in the little-studied sunbelt city of Dallas. He argues that in
addition to planners and a fragmented business community, the voting
public—with their changing assumptions about the nature of the*

city—influenced the scope of planning there. The broader political discourse in Dallas formed the critical context in which planning initiatives could or would not be accomplished.

From 1912 until 1946, the Trinity River Reclamation Project stood at the center of a prolonged controversy over planning priorities in the city of Dallas. Fairbanks demonstrates that beginning in the 1920s a broad shift occurred in the city's political discourse, from a piecemeal to a comprehensive conception of planning and from a sectional to a unified view of the city. He narrates the evolution of this public discourse and its impact on the long process to reclaim the Trinity River bottoms for urban development. To build his case study, he draws from the minutes and reports of the city planning commission, contemporary newspaper accounts, the records of key committees and improvement districts, George Kessler's A City Plan for Dallas *(Dallas: Dallas Park Board, 1912), and the George Dealey Papers in the Dallas Historical Society. He concludes that planning in Dallas had a tremendous impact on politics; during the 1920s and 1930s it was the central tool used by civic and public leaders to foster civic loyalty and stem the perceived growing fragmentation of the city's body politic. The progress of the Trinity River project waxed and waned with the public's perception of its promotion of sectional or citywide interests.*

"Planning, Public Works, and Politics" cautions scholars that they must attend to the voting public's changing perspectives on the scope and definition of "comprehensive" planning. Fairbanks also suggests the need for planning historians to understand better the role of the public and of popular discourse in determining what planning initiatives get implemented in a particular locale. For a fuller treatment of the fundamental shift that Fairbanks argues took place nationwide during the 1920s in people's perception of cities, see his Making Better Citizens *(Urbana: University of Illinois Press, 1988). William H. Wilson offers a strongly contrasting interpretation of planning in early-twentieth-century Dallas in* The City Beautiful Movement *(Baltimore: The Johns Hopkins University Press, 1989); he considers the Dallas commitment to comprehensive planning largely rhetorical, whereas Fairbanks believes rhetoric was a key factor in shaping the city's built environment. For a contrasting treatment of the politics of planning in New York City during the interwar and im-*

mediate post–World War II eras, see David Johnson's "Regional Planning for the Great American Metropolis," in Schaffer, ed., Two Centuries of American Planning *(Baltimore: The Johns Hopkins University Press, 1988). See also Joel Schwartz's* The New York Approach *(Columbus: Ohio State University Press, 1993) for a biting commentary that challenges Fairbanks's observations on the role of civic leaders and popular rhetoric in the implementation of planning projects.* EDITORS

On 24 July 1928 more than a thousand people gathered into the south end of the Trinity River bottoms adjacent to downtown Dallas and watched a huge excavating machine claw the first clump of earth for a Trinity River levee—a massive flood control and land reclamation project for their city. The action initiated a $21 million project to relocate the channels of the Trinity River 3½ miles from its current course and remove more than 220 million cubic yards of earth in the process. The 35-foot-high levees, 135 feet wide at the base and stretching for about 12½ miles, would eventually salvage more than 10,000 acres of smelly, overgrown river bottoms, and drastically alter the geography of Dallas.[1]

Although such a project had been discussed for at least eighteen years, its final undertaking was closely linked to the new emphasis on comprehensive planning that emerged in Dallas during the 1920s, and to a discourse that reflected a new way of thinking about and acting toward the city.[2] That discourse characterized the city as a social system inextricably linked and requiring comprehensive and coordinated treatment and assumed the public interest could best be served by strategies focusing on the city as a whole rather than strategies fostered for specific interest groups, geographic sections, or class concerns. Indeed, local civic leaders became alarmed at what they perceived to be a growing fragmentation within the civic body and turned not only to comprehensive planning, but to governmental reform to stem this trend in the "new" city of the twentieth century. Just as the city had turned to comprehensive planning in the 1920s, civic leaders initiated a campaign for the city-manager-at-large council form of government in the late 1920s and secured such a government in 1930.

The new emphasis on comprehensive and coordinated treatment of the city in no way resulted in a consensus about the specific planning agenda, however, as efforts to determine and implement planning priorities occupied much of city government's business in the 1920s and 1930s. The controversy that surrounded the reclamation project in Dallas during this time delayed its final completion because some in Dallas feared it promoted selfish agendas rather than serving the city as a whole. In addition, final completion of the reclamation project stalled during the 1930s because of the city's limited financial resources and the growing demand for improved city services. Only when the federal government intervened in the 1940s was the vision of a massive industrial section on reclaimed river bottoms realized.

Piecemeal Planning, 1912–1919

Early planning efforts in Dallas were piecemeal rather than comprehensive. In 1899, when this north Texas city had a population of about forty-two thousand, civic leaders organized the Cleaner Dallas League to help plan and promote a better physical environment, particularly in regard to surface sanitation. Three years later they created the Civic Improvement League as another planning vehicle. That civic body promoted park planning. Yet it was not until the next decade, in 1910, after a period of spectacular growth that left the city's infrastructure underdeveloped, that Dallas broadened its definition of city planning. Led by newspaperman George B. Dealey of the *Dallas Morning News*, a man planner John Nolen would later call "the father of planning in the southwest," city leaders organized the Dallas City Plan and Improvement League. On 23 May 1910 that group employed George Kessler to develop a city plan for Dallas.[3]

The city published Kessler's forty-page *City Plan for Dallas* in February of 1912. It contained broad proposed improvements, including a belt railroad system, a passenger station, a freight terminal, a civic center, grade crossings, street openings, parks, parkways and boulevards, playgrounds, and levees. Although most of Kessler's attention focused on the development of streets and parkways to make the center more accessible, the initial item discussed was a proposal to straighten and levee the Trinity River. Such an undertaking would accomplish several goals. First, it would promote flood protection, a very real concern for the city after the devastating flood of 1908. Second, it would better link the Dallas community of Oak Cliff, on the west side of the Trinity, with the rest of Dallas, located on the east side of the river. Third, the levees would reclaim the Trinity bottoms and give the city valuable additional land next to the downtown.[4]

As historian William Wilson has observed, "the Plan was comprehensive in the sense that it addressed city wide problems and offered city wide solutions—but rarely paused to explain how they might be related."[5] Nor did Kessler offer any way to carry the plans out through a coordinated program. Even though the city now had a type of "comprehensive" plan, officials carried it out in a piecemeal fashion. The city's initial zoning ordinances also reflected this piecemeal approach to planning. Instead of zoning the entire city, Dallas commissioners passed a law in 1915 forbidding the placement of business establishments in residential areas. The ordinance provided a citywide solution to one problem but did not attempt to tie the solution of zoning to other land-use problems or to designate land uses for the entire city. A racial zoning ordinance passed the following year followed this pattern too.[6] Early zoning in Dallas, as well as the Kessler plan, reflected a certain perception of the city. Planners approached the city as a system of differentiated parts, problems, and functions that were connected but could be treated separately. After World War I new notions about the city influenced the nature of planning in Dallas and gave a boost to those promoting the Trinity Reclamation Project.

In 1919 planning in Dallas appeared in transition. Some efforts continued the piecemeal approach to planning but others seemed more comprehensive. Newspaperman George Dealey, long associated with planning in Dallas, promoted still another planning organization after World War I. He had seen the demise of the Dallas City Plan and Improvement League and the city's lack of success in implementing all of the Kessler plan. Worried in particular about the deterioration of the West End, the home of his newspaper, Dealey joined with others to form the Dallas Property Owners Association (DPOA) to undertake "intensive city planning in one section."

The twenty participants at the first meeting of the DPOA were particularly interested in better accommodating their end of downtown to the automobile through street openings such as the Lamar Street extension; they also urged the reclamation project for the Trinity River bottoms, adjacent to their part of town (figure 8.1).

FIGURE 8.1. The old Trinity River channel and the West End of downtown Dallas in 1926. Courtesy: Texas/Dallas History and Archives Division, Dallas Public Library, Dallas, Texas.

Indeed, the overall goal of this association was to prevent the further change and deterioration of what had been the original site of Dallas. According to one association member, the DPOA was Dallas's version of the Fifth Avenue Association of New York City, an organization formed to combat encroachment of industries and commerce in that city's retail district. Not by accident, members of the association elected Charles L. Sanger as their first president; he was the nephew of department store magnate Alex Sanger. Sanger's department store was also located in the deteriorating West End. The DPOA helped persuade George Kessler to revise his 1912 plan, particularly in regard to the West End. Kessler paid much attention to accommodating the automobile better and to improving his proposed reclamation project.[7]

Shortly after organizers formed the DPOA, uptown businessmen created their own organization, the Central Improvement Association. Headed by Realtor Clayton Browne, this group promoted Kessler plan improvements for the uptown (east) section of the city's core. It, too, was very interested in making its area more accessible to the automobile by street widenings and the extension of Harwood and St. Paul streets into the East End. Some members of this organization opposed public financing for the reclamation of the Trinity River bottoms area because they felt it disproportionately helped the West End. The two groups accomplished little but did manage to stir up sectional animosity and sectional prejudices. Other improvement organizations also embraced piecemeal planning at this time. For instance, the Pacific Avenue Improvement Association played a critical role in having the Texas and Pacific Railroad remove its tracks from that downtown street, another recommendation of Kessler's *City Plan.*[8]

These groups, then, reflected a certain type of approach to "comprehensive" planning that suggested the city was made up of discrete parts, connected together yet individually treatable. That approach to "comprehensive" planning would in the 1920s give way to a new one suggesting the city's problems and parts were so inextricably linked that only systemwide solutions would suffice.

The Metropolitan Development Association (MDA) became one of the first manifestations of this view in Dallas.

Comprehensive Planning and the Citywide Solution, 1919–1929

The Chamber of Commerce created the MDA in 1919 "to obviate any appearance of diversity as between sections of the city in the consumption of the [Kessler] plan." Toward this end, the MDA attempted to refocus attention from the individual city section to the comprehensive whole. To achieve this goal, it provided an umbrella organization for the city's thirty-eight improvement associations, published a planning periodical entitled *Dallas Metropolitan,* and hired Kessler as consultant to help update and improve the city's plan and develop a comprehensive zoning ordinance for the city. It also employed E. A. Wood, Kessler's planning representative, as resident engineer. Finally, the MDA worked with others interested in planning to create Dallas's first city plan commission in February 1919.[9]

The new commission not only seemed interested in providing systemwide solutions to the city's planning needs, but it also expanded the number of elements associated with planning in Dallas to include treatment for blighted areas, health and sanitation measures, and water works developments. When E. A. Wood, who worked both for the MDA and for the City Plan Commission, sketched out the topics that he thought should be covered by a city plan in 1922, he included seventeen elements. Some, such as zoning, flood prevention, and street development, had appeared earlier. But the Wood outline also included a number of topics not discussed in the earlier Kessler plan: treatment for blighted areas, health and sanitation measures, and water works development. Wood also called for cooperation "between city and county officials in county or regional planning," suggesting a new definition of the planning unit.[10] During the 1920s Dallas planning promoters came to realize that the corporate city marked an artificial unit, and emphasized the need to plan for the metropolitan community.

Changes in the Dallas Property Owners Association also reflected the new type of comprehensive planning emerging in Dallas. Despite the appearance of the MDA as a citywide planning organization in 1919, the DPOA remained independent and continued to promote a planning agenda specifically designed to improve the fortunes of the West End of downtown Dallas. Agreeing with Kessler that the Trinity River Reclamation Project was the city's most important one, it proceeded vigorously to support that initiative. Problems with funding the levee, however, thwarted all efforts to erect it. Kessler proposed that since the reclamation project would benefit the entire city, it should be paid for by the entire city. Others disagreed and wanted only nearby property owners to pay the cost. In response, the DPOA helped create Reclamation District No. 10 in April 1920 to help straighten the Trinity River and reclaim adjacent land. That group, composed of a number of downtown property owners, stalled, however, when the high cost of the project became known.[11]

The DPOA's inability to rally adequate support for the reclamation project forced it to rethink its role as a sectional planning association. Concerned that the city needed a broadly based planning organization to educate citizens to the city's planning needs, members of the DPOA dissolved the association and created a new organization in March 1924, about a year after Kessler's death. John Surratt, secretary of the DPOA and cofounder of the Texas Town and City Planning Association, played a leading role in this reorganization, which was to create a "real honest to goodness city wide organization." He argued that the organization's two most important priorities, the reclamation project and the development of the Lamar Street traffic way, were citywide projects in scope and should be promoted by a citywide organization. "There never was a greater fallacy," he declared, "than the idea that the development of one section would hurt another section of Dallas."[12]

The Organization and Process of Planning

Following Surratt's recommendation, the DPOA established the Committee for County and City-Wide Association, which concluded that Surratt was right and urged formation of a new group to promote "scientific city planning for Greater Dallas." With a strong endorsement from Dealey and the *News,* supporters formed the Kessler Plan Association to promote the implementation of the entire Kessler plan. The new planning organization pursued this goal several ways. First, it sought to educate the Dallas public on the need for citywide planning by preparing pamphlets, giving lantern slide shows, and publishing a grade school text in 1927 entitled *Our City—Dallas: A Community Civics.* Written by former Dallas School Superintendent Justin F. Kimball, the book stressed the need for planning and enumerated the successes of the Kessler plan. The association also helped organize and coordinate neighborhood improvement leagues and street development committees to promote action on local problems and to provide input for citywide planning needs. In addition, the Kessler Plan Association attempted to educate state legislators on the need for better statewide planning legislation.[13]

Although the DPOA formed an important core of the new Kessler Plan Association, special efforts were made to ensure that the new planning group really became an inclusive group. The association's Board of Directors reflected the city's geographic and political composition. DPOA leaders also held public meetings to solicit input from the general membership on what to emphasize. At the first meeting, called by President Charles Sanger, the membership agreed that traffic congestion deserved special attention. Since better roadways promised a way of alleviating congestion and more effectively connecting the city, street and roadway development became a priority of the citywide planning association. Rapid, haphazard growth had created a geographically fragmented city; if Dallas was to be united, neighborhoods needed access to the downtown core, as well as to each other. And since civic leaders viewed geographic unity as a prerequisite for civic unity, a priority continually emphasized during this era, street thoroughfares seemed important. Planning in Dallas was clearly a tool to promote civic unity and a sense of community, as well as orderly geographic development. The Kessler Plan Association's commitment to comprehensive planning was tied to two strategies; publicity and participation. First it tried to educate the public on the interdependence of the whole city. Second, it provided a forum that allowed various neighborhoods in the city to bring their concerns about planning to civic leaders. This underscored the point that comprehensive planning would be for the city as a whole, and not dominated by special, parochial interests.[14]

This different approach to citywide comprehensive planning continued throughout the 1920s. Infused with new enthusiasm for planning and recognizing the city's inadequate infrastructure, the City Plan Commission appointed a committee to recommend a program of future public improvements for Dallas and to develop adequate financial and legal machinery to see it carried out. Dubbed the Ulrickson Committee, after its chair, C. E. Ulrickson, the committee devised a comprehensive and budgeted program of civic improvements for Dallas to embrace all the city's needs for the next nine years. The committee modeled it after a St. Louis general program for public improvement that had been developed in 1923. The five-man civic committee, composed of one lawyer and four businessmen, proposed a $23.9 million public works program based on the Kessler plan. In all, it recommended fifteen major projects, including better sewers, a municipal airport, a fine arts institute, improved library facilities, hospitals, schools, parks, and, of course, streets.[15] Emphasizing planners' preoccupation with better connecting the city's parts, the report called for eighty street projects, observing that the streets of Dallas were "the veins and arteries through which the life of the city must flow."[16]

The report did not set a specific timetable for the development of each project but called for the formation of a fifteen-person citizens' committee made up of representative civic leaders to oversee the entire program and to recommend the sequence of expenditures to the city commissioners.[17] Although not exactly a city plan, the report helped Dallas plan for the future. Moreover, it urged additional planning through the development of comprehensive surveys and plans to coordinate the committee's recommendations.[18] The city council cooperated with the planners and called for a 15 December public referendum to approve the fifteen separate bond issues proposed by the Ulrickson Committee, as well as the thirty-four amendments to the city charter to allow the program to be effectively carried out. The publicity for this election emphasized the comprehensive nature of the package being offered for city approval. One *News* editorial noted: "This is not a city of sections but one community, every citizen of which ought to be deeply wishful for the development of every part of the city." The efforts and rhetoric of the plan's promoters apparently worked, as every bond issue and every amendment passed on election day.[19]

Shortly after voters approved the bond package, the Chamber of Commerce's Master Plan Committee urged the creation of a master plan not only for Dallas but for additional territory at least 5 miles beyond the city limits. The Chamber of Commerce argued that such a plan would better coordinate the Ulrickson recommendations and complement the city's efforts to develop a comprehensive zoning ordinance. The City Plan Commission agreed and urged the city council to employ Harland Bartholomew of St. Louis to develop the plan. The council, however, had other ideas and hired former city engineer E. A. Wood as master planner and supervisory engineer for Dallas. His proposal shows how far planning had come in Dallas since the Kessler plan. He believed a good plan would address all of the following topics: Black housing, density of population, and vacant areas, as well as railroads, schools, water and sewer service, streets, civic art, and land valuation. He also advocated preparing a master plan for street development, one of the city's most pressing needs.[20]

At the very time the Ulrickson Committee developed its program, property owners of the Trinity River bottoms fashioned a strategy for building a levee and reclaiming those bottoms (figure 8.2). After reviewing engineering reports about the cost of

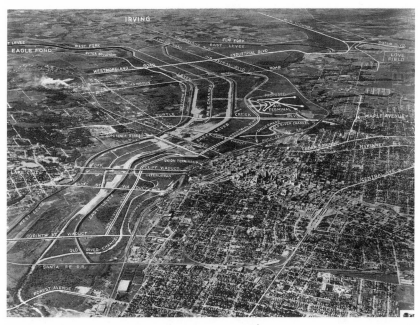

FIGURE 8.2. Proposed changes for the Trinity River bottoms by the Dallas Levee Improvement District. Courtesy: Texas/Dallas History and Archives Division, Dallas Public Library, Dallas, Texas.

reclaiming the Trinity River bottoms, a group of thirteen hundred property owners in 1926 asked the County Commissioners Court of Dallas to create the City and County of Dallas Levee Improvement District. Under the laws of Texas, this body could sell bonds to help finance improvement of the river bottoms. The owners of the property, led by John J. Simmons, manufacturer and longtime civic leader, and Leslie Stemmons, president of the Southwestern Land and Loan Association and the Atlas Metal Works, agreed to improve the bottoms after working out a comprehensive improvement program with the city, county, railroads, and utilities to shoulder some of the improvement costs. The city agreed to provide $3.27 million for water mains, sewers, and underpasses, while county officials committed $3.34 million for providing underpasses and viaducts for the area. The railroads and utilities promised another $5.41 million of improvements for the area. In return, the district agreed to spend $9 million to build the levee, refill the soggy bottoms, and share the costs for storm sewers and roads. Estimates of the final cost for the project exceeded $21 million (figure 8.3).[21]

Despite earlier resistance to heavy public financial subsidy of the reclamation project, both the city bond proposals included in the Ulrickson program and the county bond election held the same year passed by impressive majorities. Part of the success of the reclamation program was its close association with the larger planning efforts for the city as a whole and the special efforts of the Kessler Plan Association. It led an impressive educational effort to sell the reclamation program as an essential part of the original Kessler plan. In one pamphlet the association announced the citywide benefits of carrying out the Kessler plan. "It will give every section of Greater Dallas wide and ample traffic ways," the pamphlet observed, "relieving traffic congestion, guarding against the shrinkage of values and reviving blighted areas." The pamphlet concluded by promising that the plan would make "Greater Dallas a unified City, with every section accessible to every other section, with wide thoroughfares for the main flow of traffic in every direction."[22] That last reference was a particularly telling reason for the city to support the straightening, leveeing, and reclamation of the Trinity River since five new viaducts included in that project would better link Dallas to its isolated and cantankerous appendage, Oak Cliff. In the very first issue of the *Kessler Plan Salesman,* published in 1926 by the Kessler Plan Association, a feature article underscored the importance of that project to all of Dallas. Other Kessler publicity for the reclamation would follow. John Surratt, executive secretary of the Kessler Plan Association, wrote national planning figure Edward Bassett after the successful Ulrickson bond election and bragged that his association had played a critical role in educating many previously hostile civic leaders to the worth of the reclamation project for the city as a whole.[23]

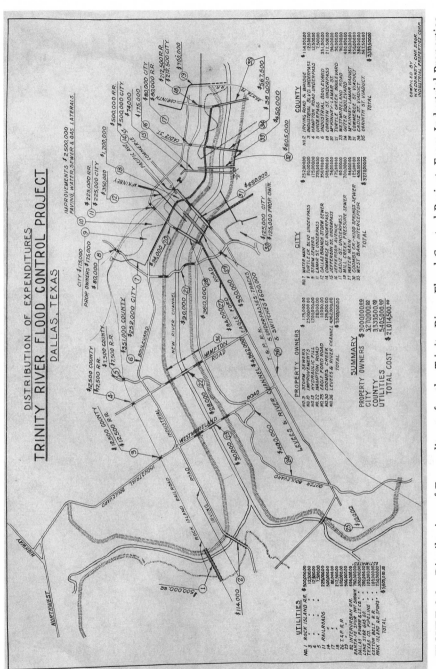

FIGURE 8.3. Distribution of Expenditures for the Trinity River Flood Control Project. From Industrial Properties Corporation (1931).

The relationship between leaders of the Kessler Plan Association and the levee district would change drastically during the next several years, however, as the former group really became a city-wide organization.[24] By 1927, that group sought to expand its membership to twenty thousand and recruited not only city dwellers but county residents to promote good planning for Greater Dallas. Even more important, it continued to work closely with the city's numerous improvement leagues. Such actions altered the leadership's priorities and created tension over the nature of comprehensive planning for the city. The reclamation project would be in the center of that controversy.

Battle over the Bottoms, 1929–1935

Although the reclamation program had been sold to the public as a better way to link downtown Dallas with Oak Cliff, protect the city from flooding, and open up new land for industrial development, many remained concerned about what they viewed as a huge public subsidy for a private real estate venture. Shortly after the county court organized the reclamation district, Leslie A. Stemmons and John J. Stemmons established the Industrial Properties Corporation to develop the Trinity bottoms. That group, which owned or controlled nearly 75 percent of the land in the district, planned it as a massive industrial development. Estimates that the reclaimed property would be worth $52 million raised the question of how much the city should be helping private developers. Other business transactions undertaken by the property owners also raised concerns about the reclamation district's business practices. For instance, the district offered its bonds without competitive bidding and gave the excavating contract for the levee to an in-house firm. In addition, Leslie Stemmons and John J. Stemmons constantly pressured city officials to give their project top priority in regard to bond money.[25] Such action ran counter to the notion publicized by both the Ulrickson Committee and the Kessler Plan Association that the gigantic bond program operated for the city as a whole and threatened to undo the consensus that the Kessler Plan Association had tried to create for comprehensive planning.

One of the first public signs of discord occurred during the April 1929 elections for city commissioners. One nonpartisan slate, the United Dallas Association, charged that the powerful levee district had pressured city officials to commit more funds to the levee district than approved by the voters. Such charges brought an angry response from Simmons and a statement from city hall repudiating the claims. But action by the district would soon alienate substantial numbers of Dallas civic leaders and threaten the entire reclamation project.[26]

By 1930, Dallas felt the impact of the Great Depression. A loss of city income led Mayor J. Waddy Tate to announce that he would have to raise taxes if he sold all the Ulrickson bonds for sewer development of the Trinity River bottoms demanded by the levee district. Such an announcement created an outrage in the community since many wanted retrenchment rather than tax increases. The levee supporters responded that they needed the $1.1 million for a pressure sewer to allow for the completion of their reclamation effort. After meeting with the levee officials, Tate reaffirmed his support of a tax increase and promised that he had the necessary support of other city commissioners to get one.[27]

That announcement set off a protest movement that helped delay completion of the reclamation project for more than fifteen years. A 7 June meeting brought out a crowd of between eight hundred and one thousand protesters against the tax, including downtown theater owner Karl Hoblitzelle and Kessler Plan Association president, Dr. E. H. Cary. They applauded when Rosser J. Cooke observed that the reclamation project was a private undertaking and not deserving of more public money. The protesters also created a committee to fight the tax increase, a committee that included Hoblitzelle and Cary. When John J. Stemmons attempted to explain why the district needed the money immediately, the crowd walked out on him.[28]

The insistence that more money be spent on the district irritated those who remembered that the $3.5 million drainage bond had been passed for the city as a whole. The city suffered from horrible drainage problems and neighborhoods flooded badly during rainy season; in some instances residents drowned.[29] Some wondered why the first bonds were going to the unpopulated levee district rather than built-up sections of the city. For instance, attorney J. Hart Willis asked when sewers would be provided for "those of us who live on Turtle Creek Boulevard in East Dallas and in other parts of the city [that] have suffered for years from flooding."[30]

In order to counter the charges of selfish interest, the levee district volunteered to provide the city with two gifts of land from the reclaimed Trinity River bottoms. First, it offered 3,300 acres for a city park. Proposing that this could be the Central Park of Dallas, the levee district detailed how valuable such a park would be for the city's downtown workers. It also promised generous acreage for the city to develop a new airport next to the central business district. The city declined both offers, citing the high costs of upkeep involved in maintaining the district's present facilities.[31]

The levee district's actions did little to soften the charge of special interest from some critics. For instance, in an editorial titled "Will the Taxpayers Be Bluffed?" the *Dallas Times Herald* pointed out that the Ulrickson Committee had recommended that no sewer money be spent until consulting engineers developed a citywide plan. Others, such as Dr. E. H. Cary, Karl Hoblitzelle, and Kessler Plan Association Secretary John Surratt, also took up this theme and petitioned the commissioners to consider all parts of the Ulrickson plan, and the work to be "done in all sections of Dallas." The immediate crisis passed in regard to the proposed tax hike as the mayor and commissioners decided to service the bonds through cutbacks in the city government. But the controversy over the propriety of providing bond money to the levee district immediately did not.[32]

Several days after the commissioners' decision to sell the Ulrickson bonds for that year, Hoblitzelle, Surratt, and future mayor

Tom Bradford met with others and formed the Dallas City and County Taxpayers League. That organization called for the "co-ordinated development of Dallas" and observed that "we are not fighting development of the levee district but are opposing the efforts to place that undertaking paramount to other sections of Dallas."[33] Many affiliated with the Kessler Plan Association, which had campaigned for the reclamation plan as part of a broader, comprehensive package of improvements, now argued the reclamation program was unfairly being singled out for special attention while other populated areas in south and east Dallas, in desperate need of sewers, were being ignored. In this view, advocates of the levee were willing to sacrifice the needs of the larger city for their own special interests.

Supporters of the reclamation project viewed the situation differently and argued that theirs was a critical program for the city as a whole. W. L. Prehn, general manager of Southwestern Bell Telephone, took such a line when he reminded the citizens of Dallas that the reclamation project would create five new viaducts better connecting Oak Cliff to the rest of the city. That would help bind "these two sections together," Prehn went on, "[so] as to eliminate any sectional or factional feeling." J. L. Lancaster, president of the Texas and Pacific Railroad, also supported the reclamation project, calling it "the most important development in the city since its founding."[34] George Dealey, the city's leading planning advocate, threw the weight of the *News* behind the reclamation project and lobbied incessantly with city officials on behalf of it. Opponents of the project pointed out, however, that Dealey owned 15½ acres of the river bottoms and would clearly personally benefit from the reclamation.[35]

By 1930 bad feelings about the reclamation project had polarized the city. One side viewed the excessive preoccupation with it as damaging to the development of the rest of the city, while supporters saw the project as the key to more rapid development of Dallas as a whole and felt that opponents were motivated by their own selfish agendas. Close friends and business associates split and "bitter and irreconcilable enmities developed" between good friends. The city's Critic Club, a forum where important civic issues were discussed, also suffered heavily from these tensions.[36]

Hoblitzelle, Cary, and Surratt joined with Finance Commissioner John C. Harris to demand that the city develop a comprehensive plan for its sewer system before spending more money on piecemeal development. The Committee on Supervision of Expenditures concurred. As a result, the local commissioners, now led by independent-minded Mayor J. Waddy Tate, secured an engineer to develop one. But since the commissioners refused to employ an engineer recommended by the Kessler Plan Association and hired a less-qualified man to undertake the survey and plan, controversy continued.[37] In addition, the city announced it would release some money for drainage sewers in the reclamation area before the engineer completed a sewer plan. This infuriated Karl Hoblitzelle, who secured a temporary injunction to halt that action.[38]

The debate over priorities within the Ulrickson program took place at a time when Dallas leaders were also attempting to restructure city government. Dallas had been governed by a city commission form of government since 1907. In many ways, that government reflected the shortcomings characteristic of early Dallas planning efforts. Although the five commissioners were elected at large and were supposedly concerned with governing the city as a whole, the structure of government encouraged piecemeal rather than a comprehensive approach to solving the city's problems. By the 1920s the government was racked by petty squabbles and seemed to lack adequate coordination to govern Dallas as a whole. During the same time that efforts were being made to bring more coordinated and comprehensive planning to Dallas, the *News* joined in by campaigning for a city-manager-at-large council form of government. Just as civic leaders pushed comprehensive planning to overcome fragmentation and sectional conflict, leaders of the government reform movement attacked the politics of special interests and viewed the city-manager-at-large council as the best way to eliminate fragmentation and promote the interests of the city as a whole. Suspending the good-government movement until after the Ulrickson bond issue passed, reformers secured the city manager form of government in 1930. The Citizens Charter Association (CCA), which had led the campaign for voter approval of the city manager system, filed a slate of candidates for the first election in 1931. All nine won and shortly afterward appointed John Edy, former president of the International City Managers Association, as city manager.[39]

When the CCA officials took office, the levee project was dumped in their lap. The new city council, which had been elected by a citywide constituency, along with John Edy, proceeded cautiously but gradually antagonized the levee district supporters. First, City Manager Edy named O. H. Koch public works engineer for the city. Koch had earlier been identified with the group fighting the actions of the levee district group. The council's next concern was to get the best sewer plan possible for the entire city, and it employed the services of W. W. Horner of St. Louis to develop a general plan for the city's drainage. Until it had Horner's plan, the council refused to provide more money for the levee district.[40]

Horner's finished plan, however, brought new optimism that appeased both sides. It recommended eight new sewer lines, including one for the levee district's hydraulic fill area. He also proposed a sewer system for the reclamation area that would allow the district to close its levee walls, without having the city build the expensive pressurized sewer for the reclaimed area. The city finally had the comprehensive citywide sewer plan that had been called for by the Ulrickson plan. The new mayor, Charles E. Turner, greeted Horner's findings with the comment that the conflict had been resolved. Those wanting a more comprehensive plan and an orderly development of the city's sewers had gotten their wish, while those who had emphasized the reclamation project were seemingly given what they had wanted, a chance to start development in the reclamation area. Turner concluded that the plan would "benefit the entire city of Dallas and with the adoption of a definite policy of this sort, serving the entire community, there should be a new unity of thought and effort for the city's development."[41] After the council

approved Horner's plan, the *Dallas Times Herald* editorialized that
"the new city council [had] demonstrated that its purpose is to
promote the growth of Dallas as a whole, giving each section its fair
sense of bond money. Plainly its object is to prevent factional controversy and bring all groups into a unit in developing Greater
Dallas."[42]

The initial response from the district also seemed positive.
However, L. A. Stemmons, bitter over what he saw as a reneging of
the deal cut in 1927, continued to push city officials to immediately
give the district everything it had promised in the original deal. He
and other district supporters emphasized that the city had a moral
obligation to fulfill its commitment of 1927, even if the Ulrickson
report was just a recommendation. But Horner, the developer of the
drainage plan, responded that there was something wrong with the
city providing thousands of dollars for sewer development in an
unpopulated area while much of populated Dallas lacked adequate
drainage facilities. Kessler Plan Association Secretary John Surratt
reminded Stemmons that the city was neither legally nor morally
bound by the Ulrickson report.[43]

Matters were complicated further by the depression's continued impact on the city's budget. Although the Ulrickson report had
originally anticipated the selling of $3 million worth of bonds in
1932, Edy cut that to $1.2 million. This created new tensions
between the residents of east and south Dallas and those of the
levee district. The Kessler Plan Association, now speaking for those
people rather than the West End interests, continued to protest
about allotting the bond money to the levee district. Surratt, secretary of the association, invited officers of various improvement
leagues to his office and heard them emphasize the dire needs of
their neighborhoods. South Dallas neighborhoods, for instance, had
storm sewers constantly overflowing; some backed up to their bath-
rooms. Surratt thought that these conditions needed top priority
since Ulrickson bond money was "supposed to take care of all of
Dallas, and not just one set of people."[44] The opinions of people like
Surratt and Koch carried extra weight with the public because they

had no significant property interests in either the east or west end of town.

The demands of the levee district intensified after 1 October 1931, when the district defaulted on its loans.[45] Angered by this development and the city's unwillingness to build the drainage sewer in the reclaimed area, the district backed out of its agreement to the Horner plan, and John Simmons, one of the project's leaders, unsuccessfully sued the city for breach of contract.[46] Although Simmons lost the suit, the city finally completed its commitment to the levee district as outlined by Horner in March 1935.[47] By then, however, the depression as well as the erosion of the levees stalled efforts to develop the area as an industrial district, and it remained unoccupied until after World War II.

The debate over the drainage system for the levees helped undermine the political reform instigated by the *News*. George Dealey, frustrated by City Manager John Edy's unwillingness to directly intervene for the reclamation district, withdrew his support from the Citizens Charter Association in 1933 and 1935. The *News's* lack of endorsements in 1935 help explain the defeat of this good-government group.[48]

Completing the Trinity River Reclamation Project, 1935–1946

Only after the Army Corps of Engineers, authorized by a Congressional Act in the 1940s, committed more than $8 million to strengthen the levees and to develop the pumping plants and pressure sewers for the area, did the last chapter in Trinity River bottoms reclamation begin. On 1 September 1946 the Industrial Properties Corporation finally opened its property for sale, an undertaking that would usher in major development for the former swampy bottoms.[49]

Despite the bitterness and rancor connected with the reclamation project, Dallas leaders did not forsake the idea of comprehensive planning, nor did they abandon their vision of the metropolitan area as an inextricably connected unit. Indeed, in the midst of the debate itself, leaders from both factions called for a new, truly comprehensive plan. For instance, Dealey wrote in 1930: "If Mr. Kessler were alive today, he would unquestionably urge . . . yet another plan for Dallas; a new city plan extending into the county as a regional plan, coordinating the needs of the present with the probable needs of the immediate future, and unifying the whole metropolitan area in a great scheme for continuing development by plan."[50] Planning, then, continued to be a valuable tool used by civic and public leaders not only to unite the area geographically into one but also to produce social unity by better educating the area's different neighborhoods and districts about their connection to the whole. Planning not only offered a valuable economic tool but provided a means to produce civic loyalty, a chief concern of the era.

In some ways, Dallas's planning experiences in the 1920s and early 1930s left an indelible mark on the city's future planning and politics. The paralysis brought on by the reclamation controversy and the need to coordinate effective leadership to help the city win the right to host the state's centennial celebration in 1936 are most responsible for the formation of the Dallas Citizens Council, made up of the city's one hundred most powerful businessmen. This group settled differences behind closed doors, not in the newspapers, and only acted on issues it could reach a consensus on. This, of course, limited the type of issues the group could tackle, but made it very effective in what it chose to pursue. One issue it supported was comprehensive planning. Largely because of its efforts, Dallas employed Harland Bartholomew in 1943 to write a new comprehensive plan for Dallas. His three-year effort produced a fourteen-volume plan that on paper truly embraced comprehensive planning for the city as a whole. Yet volumes tackling controversial issues such as housing for Blacks and neighborhood revitalization were never realized because of the intense political controversy they evoked, while volumes on thoroughfares and park development were more nearly realized.

The DCC also revitalized the Citizens Charter Association (CAA) in 1939. With the massive financial support of DCC members, and benefiting from a rhetoric that emphasized working for the city as a whole, the CCA completely dominated local politics and government for the next twenty years. Both the DCC and the CCA, sensitive to the discourse about the metropolis that emphasized it as a special kind of place needing comprehensive treatment, sold its programs in this context. Even more important, it portrayed groups opposing its plans as parochial or promoters of special interests, something that spelled political doom in Dallas during the 1940s and early 1950s.[51]

Conclusion

The Dallas experience with comprehensive planning during the 1920s and 1930s represents a different type of approach to planning than was practiced at the turn of the century. In the main, it was a response to the failure of earlier "comprehensive" efforts undertaken to unify a city some feared was seriously fragmenting into sectional and special interests. As a result, the new movement attempted to rally the city's civic leaders, dominated by the business elite, to a citywide vision. Its activities in the 1920s also suggest new assumptions about the nature of the city.

As this chapter has demonstrated, the new planning movement was not entirely successful in unifying the city, since competing strategies for and interpretations of the city as a whole continued to mobilize differing factions of the city's business leadership and its general citizenry. A discourse that emphasized a systems approach to planning for the city as a whole, rather than a piecemeal approach, first aided reclamation supporters, then later thwarted their designs for an industrial district in central Dallas. The public perception of special interest had a chilling affect on the Dallas reclamation project, even though it had been included in the city's first comprehensive plan. By the 1940s, however, with the city's economy booming and the federal government contributing huge financial aid, a consensus emerged not only for the reclamation project, but for other planning priorities, too, as long as they focused on economic rather than social problems.

The Dallas experience also adds to the growing body of literature on the role of business leaders and planners in the process of developing plans. Three groups played a critical role in influencing planning and its implementation in Dallas: planners and planning advocates, businessmen, and the voting public and their elected officials. Each brought different priorities to planning, whether it was professional norms, political awareness, economic interests, or neighborhood interests. Their actions helped shape and restrict the actions of the others. The planning process will not be completely understood, however, until more attention is given to the context in which all these participants operated. In Dallas, that context was not only linked to real events but was shaped by ideas about the nature of planning and the city. Those perceptions influenced not only how planners and politicians responded to real problems, but also how the public responded to the development and implementation of planning functions. That response was critical, because the success of planning ultimately depends on popular support.

CHAPTER 9

Of Swimming Pools and "Slums"

Zoning and Residential
Development in Post–World War II
Columbus, Ohio

PATRICIA BURGESS

During the twentieth century zoning has become one of the most widely used weapons in the planning profession's arsenal to regulate private land use. Zoning's proponents have advocated it to control density in residential areas, to protect them from noisome or undesirable intrusions, and to direct growth and development, usually as part of a comprehensive planning scheme. But how well does zoning actually serve these purposes? Patricia Burgess has put zoning to the test by examining the role it played in land-use decisions in the city and suburbs of greater Columbus, Ohio, between 1922 and 1970. She has examined city ordinances, reports of the Columbus City Planning Commission, and officially recorded subdivision plats, but the most important component of her research is an analysis of the practices in granting zoning variances over time.

The Organization and Process of Planning

In Columbus and seven of its adjacent suburbs, zoning did not function as an effective means of land-use control. Zoning appeals boards routinely granted zoning variances, with the result that developers directed growth while cities exercised only an occasional veto. In low-income areas, zoning did not prevent deterioration or the introduction of mixed land uses, nor could it direct growth throughout the metropolis in a unified manner because of "jurisdictional fragmentation" between Columbus and its suburbs. Although developers consistently voiced their support for zoning ordinances, they routinely applied for zoning variances whenever they found it in their interests to do so. To protect those interests, developers employed deed restrictions rather than depend on zoning by itself.

Burgess's study, reported in full in her book Planning for the Private Interest *(Columbus: Ohio State University Press, 1994), is important because it calls into question the efficacy of zoning as a planning tool. In Columbus and its surrounds private interests directed development; once that direction was established, zoning could then function in a more limited role to protect it. Moreover, in metropolitan Columbus, zoning actions "follow[ed] the economic values of land"; they served to protect wealthy areas but failed to afford full protection to low-income neighborhoods when developers could profit by introducing higher densities and mixed land-uses. Burgess's work has profound implications for scholars' and planners' understanding of the contributions of nonplanners and private community builders to the shaping of metropolitan urban form.*

Readers wishing to know more about zoning and the history of its uses in the United States can consult a growing body of literature. Two standard overviews are S. J. Makielski Jr., The Politics of Zoning *(New York: Columbia University Press, 1966), and Seymour I. Toll,* Zoned American *(New York: Grossman Publishers, 1969). See also two important biographies of "the pioneers of planning law": "From the Autobiography of Edward M. Bassett," introduced by Donald Krueckeberg, and Laurence C. Gerckens's "Bettman of Cincinnati," both in Krueckeberg, ed.,* The American Planner *(New York: Methuen, 1983). For a recent collection of critical essays, readers are referred to Charles M. Haar and Jerold S. Kayden, eds.,* Zoning and the American Dream *(Washington, D.C.: American Planning Association Press, 1989). On the uses of zoning,*

Of Swimming Pools and "Slums"

deed restrictions, and lending practices of the Federal Housing Administration (FHA) to enforce racial exclusion, see Christopher Silver, "The Racial Origins of Zoning," Planning Perspectives *6 (1991): 189–205; Mary Corbin Sies, "Paradise Retained,"* Proceedings of the Third Conference on American Planning History *(Hilliard, Ohio: Society for American City and Regional Planning History, 1990); and Kenneth T. Jackson, "Federal Subsidy and the Suburban Dream," chap. 11 of* Crabgrass Frontier *(New York: Oxford University Press, 1985).* EDITORS

On 17 April 1961 the Board of Zoning Appeals of Upper Arlington, Ohio, granted a homeowner's request for a variance from the city's zoning ordinance provisions for rear yard areas. The variance allowed the homeowner to add an enclosed attached swimming pool to his home. Two years later the same body approved another homeowner's request—this time to exceed the allowable height for fences so the owner could construct a 10-foot-high backstop around a tennis court in his backyard.

Somehow it is difficult to believe that those who first supported zoning in the United States and who later promoted its spread anticipated that people seeking residential swimming pools and tennis courts would benefit from zoning practice. Yet fifty-five years after New York City adopted the nation's first comprehensive zoning code, that is exactly what happened. Zoning actions followed the economic value of land. They protected the neighborhoods of middle- or upper-income residents, but lower-income neighborhoods were subject to changes that offered the potential of greater profit.

First brought to national attention in the United States in 1909, adopted by a major city in 1916, and legitimated by the U.S. Supreme Court in 1926, zoning spread widely and quickly. During these same years the rationale for its use expanded. Initially justified to prevent overcrowding in residential districts and protect them from incongruous intrusions, zoning grew to be thought of as a part of comprehensive planning to direct growth and development.

In the 1910s, and even more so in the booming 1920s, U.S. cities of all sizes adopted zoning to protect existing neighborhoods and to plan for future growth. Then, the Great Depression and World War II all but halted new development. The years following the war thus provide the first real opportunity to examine and evaluate zoning in a growth environment similar to the one that stimulated its spread.

The metropolitan area of Columbus, Ohio, which includes suburban Upper Arlington, is a good location for such a study. In form it was like many other metropolitan areas where separately incorporated suburbs adjoined a major city of several thousand people. But Columbus had an advantage over many older industrial cities in that its suburbs did not completely surround it. Moreover, an annexation policy practiced in the 1950s made certain that the city could continue to grow and capture at least some of the new outlying development brought on by the postwar boom. Thus zoning in the Columbus metropolitan area in the twenty-five years after World War II provides an interesting case study of how both the city and the suburbs used zoning and to what effect.

This discussion focuses on zoning's impact on residential areas, since they were the primary concern of zoning's earliest supporters. Applications of zoning had unexpected consequences, however: several municipalities in the same region practiced zoning independently of one another and for their own purposes. At the same time, the use of restrictive deed covenants by residential developers also had a substantial effect on land-use patterns. Whereas in earlier decades residential developers had shaped metropolitan residential patterns, using restrictive covenants to designate whole neighborhoods for upper- or upper-middle-income (generally White) residency, after World War II they varied their use of restrictions in response to the zoning provisions of the city in which their development was to be located. Furthermore, although zoning and deed restrictions had no legal relationship, they worked in a reciprocal manner to protect and maintain upper- and upper-middle-income neighborhoods of single-family homes while allowing areas occupied by renters or lower-income persons to deteriorate.

Of Swimming Pools and "Slums"

The Hopes for Zoning

Zoning was a logical outgrowth of both building codes and nuisance law. Building codes set standards for construction, governing building height or floor area and lot coverage, as well as other things. Nuisance laws prohibited certain property uses, such as tanneries or slaughterhouses, from residential areas or even from whole cities. Zoning codes combined the two principles, dividing an entire city into districts, or "zones," and designating the permitted uses, building height, and lot size or coverage for all properties in each district.[1]

Zoning received national attention in the United States at the first National Conference on City Planning (NCCP), held in 1909. There Benjamin Marsh, Frederick Law Olmsted Jr., and other participants described overcrowding and deterioration in urban tenements and slum districts and told how German cities used municipal laws to address similar conditions.[2] Those attending the NCCP in subsequent years echoed their statements: they sought laws to control population density by limiting the number and size of dwellings allowed in a given area. They also sought to prevent deterioration by prohibiting incongruous, potentially harmful, uses from residential areas. Zoning could do both.[3]

Zoning's first purpose, then, was to protect residential areas. Moreover, poor and working-class areas roused the early zoning proponents' greatest concern, for these areas were the most overcrowded and deteriorated.

In gaining its legal justification—the police power—zoning acquired its second purpose. The police power gave a city authority to provide for its citizens' health, safety, morals, and welfare. Legal authorities feared that a zoning ordinance protecting only certain neighborhoods would not gain court approval; however, one that was part of a comprehensive planning process would. As an element of planning, then, zoning could direct residential, commercial, or industrial development to areas where it would be most beneficial and least harmful to the city. Zoning and planning were joined in the model enabling acts that the U.S. Department of Commerce developed and promulgated in the 1920s and that formed the basis for most states' enabling legislation.[4]

The enabling acts and the U.S. Supreme Court's legitimation of zoning in the 1926 *Euclid* v. *Ambler* decision set two primary purposes for zoning: to protect residential areas and to direct growth and development.[5] Cities large and small hastened to adopt zoning in order to obtain its benefits. By 1930 more than five hundred cities in thirty-nine states had zoning ordinances and more than 80 percent of the U.S. urban population lived in zoned municipalities.[6] Zoning entered the literature and theory of city planning as well, though always tied to comprehensive planning.[7]

Business interests also supported zoning, which aided its spread. Individual businesses might oppose the specific provisions of a local zoning ordinance as it applied to them, but once they discovered that zoning could stabilize property values or even cause them to increase, they encouraged adoption. Financial institutions realized zoning made land attractive for long-term investment rather than short-term speculation.[8] Merchants, like those on New York's Fifth Avenue, realized that zoning could keep industrial uses out of exclusive retail districts.[9] Most supportive were suburban developers and real estate interests. Zoning could stabilize land prices and thus prevent the ruinous competition of speculation. It could also function much like the deed restrictions developers used to establish and ensure the desirability of upper- and upper-middle-income neighborhoods. So realtors and developers encouraged their cities to adopt zoning ordinances.[10]

Although zoning was the norm in many communities, by the 1930s and 1940s the Great Depression and World War II limited development and turned property owners' attention to other issues. Then, with the war's end, came economic prosperity and large-scale suburbanization.[11] Zoning was in place to direct the growth process.

By the 1950s and 1960s, however, questions were being raised about zoning. Some planners viewed it primarily as a technical device and argued over the level of standards that should be set for different land-use categories or about how and by whom elements of the zoning process ought to be handled.[12] Others were concerned about the relationship between zoning and planning, which often seemed tenuous at best and reversed at worst. The zoning ordinance, noted one planner, was "all too frequently better served in the breach than in the observance."[13] Moreover, contended some, it had lost its early concern for protecting low-income and working-class neighborhoods and come to emphasize the "economic values of land"—serving either land's income-producing potential or the upper-income suburb.[14] Maybe zoning was no longer an appropriate planning tool; the assumptions about urban growth and development that had underlain New York's pioneering 1916 ordinance were no longer valid.[15] Jane Jacobs's 1961 book *The Death and Life of Great American Cities* went so far as to blame city planners' excessive application of rigid land-use controls for separating urban residents by race and class and for destroying diverse and lively urban environments. Then, in 1964, planner and planning educator John Reps issued a "requiem" for zoning, which he characterized as a once-lusty "infant" now preserved "well into senility."[16]

The preceding discussion provides a framework for measuring the functions and impact of zoning in postwar Columbus, Ohio. As already mentioned, early zoning proponents believed zoning should do two things: protect residential areas from overcrowding and deterioration and direct new growth and development. Business interests wanted zoning to stabilize property values and protect exclusive neighborhoods. Moreover, by the postwar era, when zoning codes ostensibly governed urban land-use practices in much of the United States, both the efficacy and appropriateness of zoning were in question.

Zoning the Growing Metropolis

By midcentury, the Columbus, Ohio, metropolitan area exhibited a common pattern. Scattered around a central city were several separately incorporated suburban municipalities.[17] There were also several zoning codes simultaneously governing land use in various parts of the metropolitan area. The city of Columbus had a zoning ordinance, first adopted in 1923, but each suburb also had a zoning ordinance. Each municipality's code governed land use only within its corporate limits.[18]

Columbus also had an advantage not enjoyed by many older industrial cities in the East and Midwest. Because its suburbs did not completely surround the city, it could grow by annexing outlying land. Some of the suburbs, however, could not; other suburbs or the city itself hemmed them in. Consequently, those suburbs that could not expand experienced little new development in the postwar era, whereas the city and the growing suburbs spread out with new subdivisions. Theoretically, both Columbus and the suburbs could use their zoning codes to direct and control new growth and development. (Figure 9.1 illustrates the metropolitan area in 1970.)[19]

The city of Columbus first adopted zoning in 1923. Although the original ordinance had been occasionally amended for clarity and specificity, it was still in effect at the war's end. In 1954 the city replaced the original code with a new one, greatly increasing the number and type of residential and apartment districts but retaining the ordinance's basic structure. Although the new code raised the minimum development standards for some types of single-family or apartment development, the least restrictive minimums still applied to others. Also in 1954 the city adopted an unofficial policy of granting water and sewer extensions only for developments that would annex to the city or one of its designated service districts.[20] Since such development would then be subject to the city's zoning code, the city could control and direct it.

However, the city did not exercise these functions. Throughout the postwar period the general practice of the city of Columbus was to zone all newly annexed land for the most restrictive (that is, largest minimum lot size or floor-area requirements) single-family housing. This low-density single-family zoning even applied to land bordering major arterials, which might be expected to develop for commercial purposes. Making no provision for office buildings,

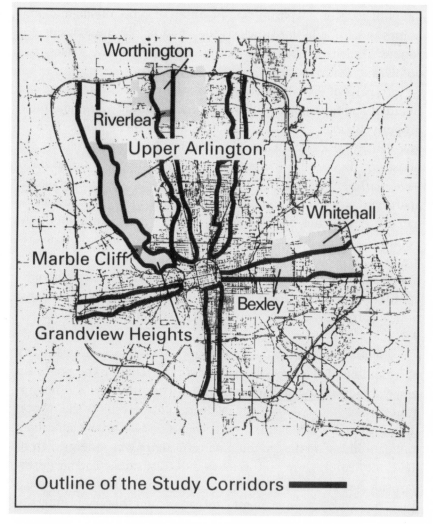

Outline of the Study Corridors ▬▬▬

FIGURE 9.1. The Columbus, Ohio, metropolitan area. From Burgess (1994).

shopping centers, or apartment complexes in outlying areas, the city's practice for the next twenty-five years was to wait instead for developers to submit proposals for whatever use they thought profitable. If a proposal was approved, the city then rezoned the land to match the proposed development. Thus developers decided where new offices, stores, apartments, or different types of single-family homes would be built—much as they had before the existence of zoning. The city essentially exercised only a veto power over proposals, and that not often.

In parts of the city already developed, the city council and the Board of Zoning Adjustment (BZA) were equally accommodating to property owners. Not far from downtown, the council rezoned low-density residential parcels so that landlords could convert old houses or duplexes into apartments or tear them down and build new apartment buildings. The council also rezoned residential and apartment parcels for commercial use. Meanwhile, the BZA granted variances from the building setback or lot area requirements to permit the construction of larger buildings containing more apartments than the code allowed or stores closer to the street. Rather than seeking a rezoning from the council, some property owners approached the BZA for a variance to initiate, expand, or alter a nonconforming use. They were rarely disappointed (figures 9.2 and 9.3).

Table 9.1 presents a brief overview of zoning actions by the city of Columbus. The effect on the city was as follows. The policy on newly annexed land affected primarily the northeast side. (Previous annexations had extended the city out to or beyond its suburbs on the north and east sides; the northwest side was totally suburban; and continuing a long-standing pattern, there was little growth or development pressure on the south and west sides.) The far northeast side became an unplanned collage of single-family tract housing, small and large apartment complexes, and shopping centers of various sizes. Meanwhile, just beyond the city's core, once-fine turn-of-the-century single-family homes on the north and east sides, now serving a rental market, were subdivided or replaced by large apartment buildings. Other parts of the city just beyond the core, where low- and moderate-income households lived in modest one- or two-family homes or older apartments, were subject to commercial intrusions or expanding institutions. In older but stable middle-income areas more than three miles from the city's center,

Of Swimming Pools and "Slums"

TABLE 9.1. Zoning Actions in Columbus, 1946–1970

Decisions by council	Approval rate (%)	Decisions by BZA	Approval rate (%)	Total decisions	Total approval (%)
542	72.5	683	79.1	1225	76.2

Distribution of requests by section of the city (%)

North	25.4
Northeast	13.7
East	23.9
South	18.8
West	18.1

Distance from city center of changes to commercial use (%)

Less than 3 miles[a]	59.3
3–6 miles	28.4
More than 6 miles	12.4

Most requested changes (70.6% of total requests)

Change	Percent of total requests	Percent of change type granted
Setback variance for building	16.3	83.4
Lot size or area variance	20.6	74.9
Use change[b]	33.7	79.0

SOURCE: Author's research in public records.

[a]Excluding core.

[b]Change use category if by council; initiate, expand, or alter nonconforming use if by Board of Zoning Adjustment.

zoning changes generally applied only to land or buildings along the major streets. Thus, neighborhoods where people owned and occupied their own homes changed little while land use in older rental areas became increasingly dense and intense; any new development was up for grabs.

Zoning in the suburbs was quite different. The four that experienced little growth used zoning primarily to maintain the status quo. Riverlea, the smallest with a population of about five hundred,

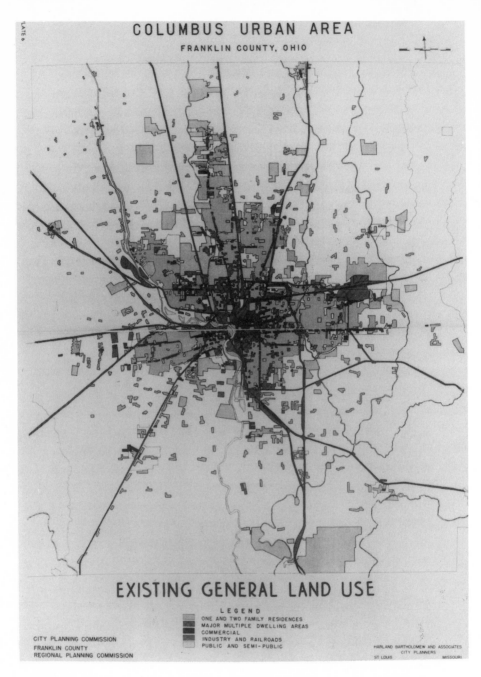

COLUMBUS URBAN AREA

FRANKLIN COUNTY, OHIO

EXISTING GENERAL LAND USE

LEGEND

ONE AND TWO FAMILY RESIDENCES
MAJOR MULTIPLE DWELLING AREAS
COMMERCIAL
INDUSTRY AND RAILROADS
PUBLIC AND SEMI-PUBLIC

CITY PLANNING COMMISSION
FRANKLIN COUNTY
REGIONAL PLANNING COMMISSION

HARLAND BARTHOLOMEW AND ASSOCIATES
CITY PLANNERS
ST LOUIS   MISSOURI

FIGURES 9.2 and 9.3. Despite considerable difference between existing land uses and designated zoning noted by consultant Harland Bartholomew, when the city of Columbus revised its zoning code it did not realign

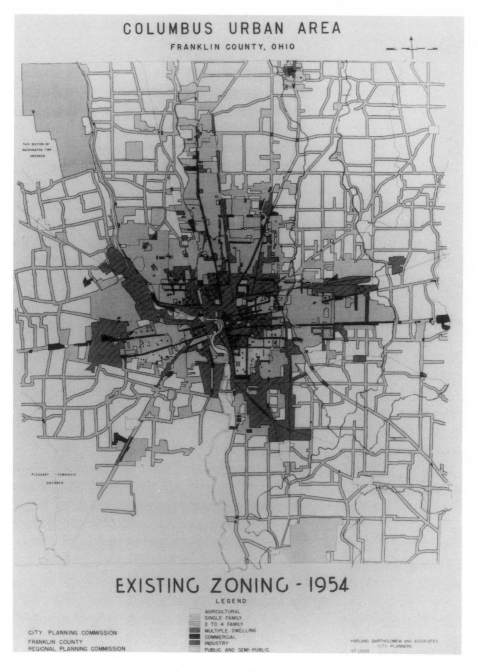

COLUMBUS URBAN AREA

FRANKLIN COUNTY, OHIO

EXISTING ZONING - 1954

LEGEND

AGRICULTURAL
SINGLE FAMILY
2 TO 4 FAMILY
MULTIPLE DWELLING
COMMERCIAL
INDUSTRY
PUBLIC AND SEMI-PUBLIC

CITY PLANNING COMMISSION
FRANKLIN COUNTY
REGIONAL PLANNING COMMISSION

HARLAND BARTHOLOMEW AND ASSOCIATES
CITY PLANNERS
ST LOUIS

zoning districts to stabilize low- and moderate-income residential areas in order to make zoning a more meaningful planning device. From Harland Bartholomew and Associates (1954, 1957).

was wholly residential and primarily an upper- or upper-middle-income community. No one suggested change. Though almost as small, Marble Cliff had a few commercial establishments where it adjoined Grandview Heights or Upper Arlington. The small commercial district was not permitted to expand, and the only undeveloped tract became a very low-density, high-priced condominium complex, consistent with the rest of Marble Cliff.

Grandview Heights, whose area and population grew only slightly between 1950 and 1970, contained a blend of middle- and upper-middle-income housing, some small commercial areas, and an industrial tract that bordered a rail line and predated the zoning code. In the years after World War II, neither commercial nor industrial areas expanded. The small amount of new housing was consistent with the suburb's middle-class standards, with one exception. In the mid-1960s a developer sought rezoning to construct a luxury, high-rise apartment block fronting a major street on the edge of town. Despite much public opposition, the request was granted and the high-rise built.

During the same twenty years, Bexley's population grew by 20 percent (12,378 to 14,888), but its area did not expand at all. Like Marble Cliff, it was an old upper- and upper-middle-income community with limited commercial uses. The one attempt to change the zoning code and allow apartments on the upper floors of commercial structures failed. New single-family homes had to meet the community's fairly high standards. Apartments, which buffered single-family districts from commercial uses or from neighboring Columbus, were subject to strict case-by-case review. With little growth and not much change, then, four suburbs had only to preserve their characters and protect their residents' property values. They did both well.

The three suburbs that grew faced a greater challenge (see table 9.2). Worthington and Upper Arlington both annexed much new land and grew in population (from 2,141 to 15,526 and from 9,024 to 38,727, respectively). Although each had some commercial uses (and Worthington an industrial area), both were primarily

Of Swimming Pools and "Slums"

TABLE 9.2. Zoning Actions in Growth Suburbs, 1946–1970

Action	Upper Arlington	Worthington	Whitehall
Percentage submitted to Council	10.3	43.2	60.8
Approval rate	75.0	55.0	94.0
Percentage submitted to Board of Zoning Adjustment	89.7	56.8	39.2
Approval rate	80.0	77.0	74.0
Percentage of change requested			
Setback	53	20	18
Nonconforming use	4	1	25
Special permit	9	3	12
Fence	11	18	—
Lot area	5	1	10

SOURCE: Author's research in public records.

developed as single-family residential communities. As they annexed new territory, both zoned some new land—along arterials or at major intersections—for additional commercial uses to serve their growing populations, but neither permitted commercial intrusions into existing residential areas. Worthington also provided for some expansion of its industrial district, which, like Grandview's, paralleled a rail line. Both communities raised the lowest minimum development standards for single-family and apartment districts so that new housing would be of at least a middle- or upper-middle-income level. Few property owners asked to initiate a nonconforming use and, in contrast to conditions in Columbus, the setback and lot area variances were not of a nature to increase density. Rather, some homeowners sought to allow porches or decks, room or garage additions, fireplace chimneys, or bay windows to encroach into the setback so they could remodel older homes built on narrow lots. Others, like the two in Upper Arlington, wanted their own tennis courts or in-ground swimming pools in the backyard.

Whitehall also grew in both area and population (from 4,877 to 25,269). It contained a wider range of income groups and housing types, commercial uses along major streets (rather than a commercial district), and an industrial area. The industrial area was not expanded, but rezonings or use variances allowed commercial intrusions into residential areas and apartment construction in single-family neighborhoods. Although additional residential categories were created, setting higher minimum standards for some types of development, the lowest minimums were never raised. Lot area variances allowed property owners to split existing parcels, producing two lots that were both smaller than the code minimum. Businesses requested, and were granted, permission to place their signs in or extend the front of their structures into the front setback to have greater visibility than adjacent establishments. Like their counterparts in Columbus, Whitehall zoning officials generally acceded to developers' and property owners' wishes. Meanwhile deed restrictions protected upper-middle-income neighborhoods from change whereas in modest ones such restrictions were nonexistent or had expired.

All in all, six suburbs used zoning effectively; Whitehall did not. Although one might criticize their overwhelmingly upper- or upper-middle-income characters on social equity grounds, that is a matter of local standards, not process. Given how little construction actually took place, it would have been difficult for either Riverlea or Marble Cliff to zone for economic diversity, but Grandview, Bexley, Worthington, and Upper Arlington could have allowed for stable low- or moderate-income areas by setting different standards and consistently adhering to them. And given Whitehall officials' willingness to permit changes to some aspects of the zoning code, higher standards there would probably not have turned Whitehall into an exclusive community.

It is also worth noting that the suburbs were overwhelmingly White, although none practiced explicit racial zoning. Rather, because minorities had disproportionately lower incomes than Whites, high minimum development standards probably kept minority residents from moving in. Probably of greater importance, though, was real estate developers' use of racially restrictive deed covenants, a widespread practice from 1910 until 1948, when the U.S. Supreme Court declared them not legally enforceable.

The Developers' Response

Clearly, zoning in central Ohio in the decades after World War II did not work as early proponents had hoped. It did not protect residential areas uniformly—or at all, in some cases. Nor did it direct growth and development in the metropolitan area as a whole. Instead of there being a single agency responsible for comprehensive planning for the whole region, each of eight municipalities (one central city and seven suburbs) designed its own zoning code according to its own needs. It then administered that code, effectively or otherwise.

Still, although there was no unified comprehensive plan or zoning code to guide the process, real estate developers did alter their practices in response to zoning. In the late nineteenth century, those developing exclusive upper-income residential areas began to insert restrictive covenants into the deeds. They might prohibit future subdivision of the lot, mandate construction of only one single-family house, specify building materials or a minimum size or cost, or even require that they review and approve building plans. The practice spread so that some type of restriction was the norm for new developments by 1920. It also became common for developers to exclude members of some racial or ethnic groups from ownership or occupancy.[21] By promising future purchasers that their neighborhoods would not decline, developers could ask a higher price for their lots. While increasing their use of deed restrictions, developers also encouraged public adoption of zoning codes. A developer could not control what happened on the 20, 40, or 100 acres adjoining his subdivision, but the city could.[22] Moreover, zoning codes and deed restrictions had no legal relationship, for the former were ordinances passed by local governments, while the latter were part of a contract between two private individuals (the seller and the buyer of the property).

By the postwar era, not only was zoning commonplace, but aggressive annexation policies brought much more undeveloped land under city or suburban municipal control than previously. With much of the land they were platting by then subject to zoning, developers might logically be expected to stop applying restrictive deed covenants to new developments. They did not, however. Where they had once used restrictive covenants to appeal to upscale purchasers, they now varied their application of covenants, targeting some subdivisions for upper- or upper-middle-income residents and other subdivisions for moderate-income homebuyers, as examination of postwar platting in metropolitan Columbus shows (see table 9.3).[23]

Despite the presence of zoning, developers of two-thirds of the subdivisions platted after World War II imposed some sort of restrictive deed covenant.[24] In four areas they developed much as they always had, using restrictions to ensure middle- to upper-income development. These areas were in the suburbs of Worthington and Upper Arlington and on the east and northwest sides of Columbus, where the city was reaching out to surround its suburbs. In those areas developers kept the lot sizes large for low density, and the floor-area or construction-cost minimums comfortably high (by pre-1970 standards).[25] Given that Worthington and Upper Arlington both raised their lowest minimum zoning standards, the levels developers specified in those suburbs make sense (figure 9.4). The far northwest subdivisions were not yet in Columbus when platted, but they adjoined Upper Arlington, so subdividers there restricted them accordingly. Since the subdivisions on the far east side adjoined polyglot Whitehall, the high level of their restrictions seems curious at first glance. Closer examination reveals that the nearest Whitehall neighborhood was Whitehall's most exclusive, which had been platted alongside Big Walnut Creek and the Columbus Country Club. So, in areas whose upper-middle-income or exclusive character was already established, new development was consistent. Still, many developers did not trust zoning—even in the suburbs—to provide the only protection.

TABLE 9.3. Restricted Subdivision Platting

Location	Total platted	Number restricted	Number requiring single family	Number with race restriction	Mean lots/acre	Mean setback (ft.)	Mean minimum construction cost	Mean minimum floor area (sq. ft.)
East	5	5	5	0	1.2	36.5	—	1,610
Upper Arlington	37	30	30	9	1.7	40.0	14,192	1,500
Worthington	16	13	5	2	2.3	48.8	16,250	1,322
Northwest	5	4	4	0	1.3	40.0	—	1,025
Northeast	17	13	12	0	4.7	25.0	10,143	933
Whitehall	22	9	9	1[a]	4.1	30.3	6,833	799
South	3	2	2	0	4.6	25.0	6,000	720

SOURCE: Author's research in public records.
NOTE: None were platted on the west side or in Riverlea; subdivisions platted in Bexley, Marble Cliff, and Grandview Heights were all subject to fairly rigorous municipal development controls.
[a] Only one subdivision contained an explicit race restriction. Another allowed the residents' association to exercise a first right of purchase (which theoretically could have been used to prevent minority entry into the neighborhood) but did not require it.

FIGURE 9.4. More than half a century after its founding, Upper Arlington, Ohio, still exhibited the exclusive character developer King Thompson's prospectus had promised. From "The Country Club District," Special Collections, Ohio State University Engineering Library.

A few developers in Worthington and Upper Arlington also tried to control for race. Despite the 1948 U.S. Supreme Court ruling that racial covenants were not legally enforceable, some developers continued to insert them.[26] One developer, King Thompson in Upper Arlington, provided for racial unity in another manner. He made membership in a community association and payment of an annual membership fee a condition of purchase. Since prospective homebuyers had to apply for membership and be voted into the association by those who were already members, residents of an area could block entrance of anyone they deemed undesirable for any reason, racial or otherwise.

Subdivisions platted in the other three areas were as consistent with nearby development as the ones in Worthington, Upper Arlington, and the far northwest and east sides, as developers there used restrictions to target homebuyers of more moderate means. Lot density was two or three times greater, and the construction-cost or floor-area minimums much lower (they were comparable to the modest tract houses on Long Island's Levittown).[27] Efforts to attract upper-income people to these areas would likely have been futile, and only one subdivision contained a race restriction. Proximity to the landfill, sewage treatment plant, and women's jail had long made the south side undesirable for exclusive residential development. On the northeast side, developers had once tried to use restrictions to create upper-middle-income neighborhoods, but the depression and war intervened before construction occurred on lots platted before the 1930s. Restrictions that would once have been comfortably middle class provided for a much lower level of development—or had expired altogether—by the 1950s.[28] The modest dwellings actually built set the tone for new subdivisions. And then there is the case of Whitehall. Along with its exclusive neighborhood and country club (which was actually outside the municipal corporation limit), Whitehall also contained, in the late 1940s and 1950s, working farms and truck gardens, small homes, and some apartments. Rather than try to pull the wealthy to a mixed community and have to compete with Worthington and Upper Arlington, developers aimed lower. But though they were targeting a lower-income group than their counterparts elsewhere in the metropolitan area, developers in Whitehall and Columbus's northeast and south sides still wanted to provide some protection to prospective buyers. Zoning practices there indicated that they could not rely on municipal officials.

Instead of using deed restrictions to appeal only to upper-income buyers as they had previously, developers after World War II varied the standards in their restrictions. Thus they might appeal to different income groups in different places. But they did not abandon restrictions altogether, for despite zoning's widespread existence, it provided unreliable protection in some places.

Zoning and Development:
The Reciprocal Relationship

Zoning practices in Columbus and its suburbs had two distinct impacts on the social and spatial structure of the metropolitan area. First, they altered the way real estate developers used restrictive deed covenants. Second, although there was no legal relationship between them, zoning and deed restrictions together provided differing levels of protection to different types of residential areas. In doing so, zoning lived up in part to the hopes of both its earliest proponents and its supporters in the real estate industry. It also justified some—but not all—of the criticisms raised against it in the 1950s and 1960s.

Zoning was not so much separated from planning, as 1950s critics charged, as substituted for it. Contrary to the ideals expressed in the standard enabling acts, neither Columbus nor any of its suburbs adopted a comprehensive plan before passing a zoning ordinance. Only two of the municipalities discussed here—both suburbs—had comprehensive plans by 1970. Instead, in most communities, the zoning ordinance itself essentially served as a less than comprehensive land-use plan. Moreover, in Columbus and Whitehall, it was subject to frequent revision at property owners' or developers' requests.

Zoning had been tied to planning, which was intended to promote the public health, safety, morals, and welfare, to gain its legitimacy. But whether the tie was explicit or implicit (as it was in central Ohio), planning proved to be a more effective guide for zoning practice in upper-income residential suburbs than in mixed areas like those just beyond the central city of Columbus or in Whitehall. Indeed, the economic value of land seemed to guide zoning more than the residential, consumer, and employment needs of the citizenry as a whole. Neighborhoods where middle- or upper-income people owned and occupied their own homes were protected and stable, but income-producing properties where residents rented were subject to changes that held the promise of greater profit. Thus zoning promoted the well-being of some parts of "the public" better than others.

Zoning did not necessarily prevent diversity of land use, at least not in low- and moderate-income areas. Jane Jacobs (1961) contends that since it separated land uses, zoning produced homogeneous areas of only single-family homes or apartments or businesses, thus robbing those areas of diversity and vitality. In older parts of Columbus, near the city center, as well as in Whitehall, however, city council or BZA actions allowed apartments in single-family neighborhoods and shops and other commercial uses in residential areas. But the resulting diversity did not produce "vitality" so much as it encouraged disinvestment and deterioration in areas where low- and moderate-income households rented modest homes and apartments.

The issue of how zoning separated people by race and class is an equally complex matter. When reformist planners and attorneys touted zoning at the planning conferences in the 1910s and 1920s they did not openly suggest that race or class separation was one of its purported benefits. However, at least some early supporters recognized that by separating land uses—particularly apartments (which are more often rented by low- and moderate-income households) from single-family homes (more often owned and occupied by upper- and upper-middle-income households)—zoning would also separate different types of people. Both planning consultant Robert Whitten and attorney Edward Bassett expressed concern in the 1920s about the use of zoning for such exclusionary purposes and doubted its legitimacy.[29] That is one reason why zoning was tied to planning to establish its legal basis. Real estate developers supporting zoning, on the other hand, clearly knew of its exclusionary potential. They counted on it. Separating land *users* through zoning, much as developers separated them through deed restrictions, would stabilize or increase property values.

In many cities, including Baltimore, Chicago, Richmond, Atlanta, and Louisville, racial zoning was practiced for a while.[30] In central Ohio, however, racial zoning was not necessary. Until 1948 developers' use of racially restrictive deed covenants determined what new housing was available to non-Whites; after 1948 FHA lending practices accomplished the same thing.[31] In addition, both before and after World War II high development standards in exclusive areas priced many minorities out of the market. Zoning did not so much cause racial segregation as maintain it.

If zoning only partly merits the criticisms leveled at it in the 1950s, it also only partly lived up to the hopes of its supporters. One of those hopes had been to prevent the deterioration of residential areas by limiting population density and preventing harmful intrusions. In this respect zoning served middle- and upper-income neighborhoods quite well. But while zoning probably prevented the most harmful intrusions (such as industrial uses) into working-class areas, zoning changes allowed some incompatible uses to intrude into low- and moderate-income neighborhoods. Zoning changes also allowed greater residential density, as older single-family homes and duplexes in low- and moderate-income neighborhoods were converted to, or replaced by, apartments. Consequently, those areas deteriorated, though perhaps not as much as they might have had there been no zoning at all.

The other public purpose of zoning was to direct new growth and development according to a comprehensive plan for the metropolitan region. But there was no single comprehensive plan. Nor could there be, for the region was jurisdictionally fragmented. Even in the 1910s and 1920s, when city planners actively promoted zoning for its ability to direct regional growth and development, the conditions preventing that possibility solidified. There was zoning in the region, but it was not regional zoning. A large city and seven of its suburbs practiced zoning independently of one another, and there was no supramunicipal agency to impose a larger vision.

Nor did zoning function quite as its early business supporters had hoped. If it had, they would not have continued applying deed restrictions to their developments; municipal controls would have provided the desired level of protection. Columbus developers apparently did not believe they could rely on local authorities to set or maintain the "right" standards. So they continued to restrict some developments for exclusive occupancy.

Zoning did alter their practice, however, as the functional relationship between the two forms of land-use control changed. When one examines the postwar residential development process and compares it to preceding eras, one can see that zoning and development formed a reciprocal relationship. Early in the twentieth century developers established some of the suburbs and bequeathed to them a degree of exclusivity. The restrictions they imposed there and on other upper- or upper-middle-income subdivisions—that were outside the corporate boundaries when platted and not subject to municipal controls—also established those areas as desirable. When the city and suburbs adopted zoning, it had merely to protect existing exclusivity. Thus, in essence, zoning followed the developers' lead. But the differential application of zoning throughout the metropolitan area caused developers to alter their practices after World War II. Where zoning was consistent with an already high standard of development, as in Worthington and Upper Arlington, developers platted new subdivisions at an equally high—or even higher—standard. But where zoning practice was unreliable or standards low, as on the northeast side or in Whitehall, developers scaled down their efforts. In this way, they were responding to zoning practice rather than shaping it. Although zoning did not guide and direct development quite as early proponents had anticipated, it did alter development practices. Development patterns initially guided zoning, which in turn later guided development practice.

At the same time, both zoning and development practice, the latter through the use of restrictive covenants, provided differing levels of protection to different types of residential areas. After World War II both zoning and deed restrictions prevented potentially harmful land-use changes in neighborhoods where middle- and upper-income families owned and occupied their own homes. Where low- and moderate-income families lived, however, deed restrictions had often expired by the 1950s—if they had ever existed. Meanwhile zoning, as practiced in Columbus's and Whitehall's low- and moderate-income areas, allowed intrusions of incompatible use and increased density, thus lessening residential quality.

There is no reason to believe that the Columbus, Ohio, metropolitan area was an anomaly with respect to zoning and development. During the postwar era it looked like many others. It had a commercial downtown that would soon lose retail establishments to suburban shopping centers. Surrounding downtown were decaying areas in which commercial and some industrial uses were scattered among low-rent housing. Beyond those areas were stable middle-income neighborhoods and exclusive suburbs.

Moreover, those questioning zoning at the national planning conferences might well have been speaking of zoning in Columbus, though they came from cities all over the country. NCCP president John Nolen had noted in 1927 that there were almost three times as many cities with zoning ordinances as with comprehensive plans. By 1941 the ratio of zoning ordinances to comprehensive plans had increased to ten to one.[32] Although no one recorded a count in the 1950s, the lack of comprehensive plans in Columbus and its suburbs was probably the norm. Throughout the 1950s, planners commented on the excessive amount of spot zoning, special permits, variances, and nonconforming uses and complained that preventing working-class neighborhoods from becoming slums had taken a back seat to protecting property owners' investments.[33] Certainly that was the case in central Ohio.

Although zoning in postwar metropolitan areas did not live up to its earliest supporters' hopes, it did affect residential environments. Zoning actions allowed older neighborhoods near the city's core that were unprotected by deed restrictions to become increasingly undesirable, encouraging the departure of those whose income or race gave them other housing options. In middle-income and exclusive areas, meanwhile, zoning added a public layer of property value protection to the private layer created by developers' deed restrictions. For their part, developers noted the differential application of zoning and altered their practices accordingly. Early proponents had expected zoning to protect residential areas and direct development. Instead, it allowed some neighborhoods to have swimming pools while others became slums.

CHAPTER 10

Homebuilding and Industrial Decentralization in Los Angeles

The Roots of the Post–World War II Urban Region

GREG HISE

Planning historians characteristically think of Los Angeles as the quintessential twentieth-century spread city, but few have analyzed the "nature and timing of the city-building process underlying our contemporary metropolitan landscape." Those historians who have offered causal explanations for decentralized development in Los Angeles usually posit transportation as the primary stimulus for the city's distinctive form. Two good examples of the technological determinism argument are Robert M. Fogelson's The Fragmented Metropolis *(Berkeley: University of California Press, 1967) and Scott L. Bottles's* Los Angeles and the Automobile *(Berkeley: University of California Press, 1987). Greg Hise approaches the question of how Los Angeles developed from an entirely different angle. He focuses on large-scale homebuilders and their land development decisions and emphasizes the role of industry and the importance of the workplace–residence link. Industrial and housing policy associated with the World War II defense emergency spurred the city's massive postwar urban expansion.*

Hise argues that what he calls "peripheral urbanism" grew from a process of planned urban expansion driven by the establishment of "decentralized industrial growth poles" where new facilities for the defense industries were located just before World War II. This wave of urban restructuring between 1935 and 1947 produced a series of new urban communities—many of them "scientifically planned" developments that packaged modern housing with schools, recreation, health care facilities, churches, and commercial centers—all in close proximity to the aircraft industry's newest plants. Hise examined a wide range of primary sources: the records of regional planning commissions, bank reports, U.S. Federal Housing Administration annual reports, population and manufacturing censuses, contemporary newspaper accounts, aerial photography collections, and the papers of several principal developers of the new "edge" cities. From this material, he has developed case studies of several planned communities—Westside Village, Toluca Wood, Westchester, Fontana, and Panorama City—and analyzed the broader factors forming the context for their development.

Understanding these new decentralized regional cities of the World War II era is crucial because they formed the basis for postwar homebuilding and for the technoburbs so characteristic of post-1970 metropolitan development. Peripheral urbanism was not the product of unplanned sprawl. Rather, these communities set the pace for the metropolitan spatial transformation that occurred throughout the nation during the postwar period. For a history of community builders like Fritz Burns, president of Kaiser Homes, see Marc A. Weiss's The Rise of the Community Builders *(New York: Columbia University Press, 1987). Two of the best-known studies of spread cities are Robert Fishman's* Bourgeois Utopias *(New York: Basic Books, 1987) and journalist Joel Garreau's* Edge City *(New York: Doubleday, 1988). On Los Angeles, see E. W. Soja, "Taking*

Los Angeles Apart," Environment and Planning D: Society and Space *(Feb. 1986): 255–72; Rob Kling, Spencer Olin, and Mark Poster, eds.,* Postsuburban California *(Berkeley: University of California Press, 1991); and Mike Davis,* City of Quartz *(New York: Vintage, 1992). For an argument that challenges Hise's contention that peripheral urbanism differed substantially from traditional suburbs, consult William Sharpe and Leonard Wallock's "Bold New City or Built-Up 'Burb?" and the discussion that follows in the* American Quarterly 46 *(Mar. 1994): 1–61.* EDITORS

> Enough has been said to demonstrate that the old "town" and "city" will soon be . . . terms as obsolete as "mail coach." For these new areas that will grow out of them we want a term. . . . We may, for our present purposes, call these coming town provinces "urban regions."
> —H. G. WELLS

After solving a "People Are Funny" radio riddle, Mrs. Ward George and her family left their home in Lebanon, Oregon, to start a new life in Panorama City, California. Their prize dwelling was the first unit in a planned community designed and constructed by Kaiser Community Homes. Located in the San Fernando Valley, 15 miles from downtown Los Angeles, the house came equipped with a Kaiser hydraulic dishwasher, Kaiser garbage disposal, and a two-car garage for their 1948 Kaiser-Frazer sedan (figure 10.1). The sponsors also offered the winning contestant a "responsible job" in southern California; Mrs. George would join the personnel department at Lockheed's Burbank facility. When, in a carefully choreographed pageant, Fritz Burns (president of Kaiser Homes) and Art Linkletter presented the Georges the key to homeownership, the couple completed the transition promised to all American wage-earners in the postwar period.[1]

In Oregon, the Georges had lived in a town of 2,700 inhabitants. Lebanon's residents depended on Corvallis (population 8,400

FIGURE 10.1. Mr. and Mrs. Ward George in the doorway of their prizewinning dwelling in Panorama City, California (1949). Note Kaiser-Frazer sedan. Courtesy: The Examiner Collection, Department of Special Collections, University of Southern California.

in 1940), a regional center 40 miles away, for governance, civic institutions, and health care. According to the 1940 Census of Housing, Lebanon had 863 dwellings; enumerators found 35 percent of these lacked a private bath or required major repair. Their house, built to local standards, did not have running water. Mortgage financing for home purchase, if available, was most likely short-term with balloon payments at both ends.[2]

In contrast, at Panorama City the newcomers entered a 2,000-unit self-contained community. Corporate officers from Kaiser's Housing Division had "scientifically planned" this "City in Itself" as a complete community, a place for "living, work, and play." Here they integrated "modern" housing with schools, recreation, health care facilities, churches, and a commercial center. Just as important for the Kaiser land agents who purchased this property was the site's proximity to regional industries such as General Motors, Anhauser-Busch, Schlitz, and Rocketdyne. At Panorama City, wage-earning homebuyers capitalized on the sophisticated system of insurance and loan guarantees the Federal Housing Administration (FHA) and Veterans Administration offered.[3]

The Georges' saga offers an anecdotal entrée to the central concern of this chapter: What was the nature and timing of the city-building process underlying this country's contemporary metropolitan landscape? Most studies of American urban expansion follow the railway, streetcar, and automobile out from the city to a suburb. Their itinerary can be cataloged briefly: a romantic nineteenth-century cottage suburb, the Garden City movement, Radburn, the Resettlement Administration Greenbelts, and Levittown, the paradigm of postwar suburbanization. Beginning in the late 1930s, however, Angelenos from a broad income spectrum purchased single-family dwellings in large-scale, planned communities plotted in relation to decentralizing industry. Their experience challenges the received planning and urban history.[4]

Suburbanization as Urbanization

Framing the question this way does not imply that peripheral growth was a new phenomenon. There has always been development at the edge of American cities. Urban residents relegated noxious or hazardous land uses to the urban fringe to ensure safety, and activities that consumed space in excess of what could be controlled in the core gravitated to the city's edge.[5] However, both the traditional residential suburb and the industrial satellite were specialized segments within a center-dominated metropolis. The Chicago school sociologists and Homer Hoyt captured this paradigm in concentric-zone theory and the sectoral model of urban growth.[6] Neither proved elastic enough to encompass the postwar spatial order. Urban geographers were the first to define a theoretical corrective. James Vance, for example, provided a prescient alternative. His analysis of retail trade centers and regional perspective suggested the San Francisco Bay area was composed of a number of "internally-functioning urban realms" within a "non-centric city."[7]

Los Angeles (defined to include Orange, Riverside, and San Bernardino counties) is often portrayed as the prototypical urbanized region. To date, the majority of accounts, whether written by urban historians, geographers, or sociologists, fail to explain how this decentralized pattern developed. Causal explanations rely overwhelmingly on the transportation thesis. Most histories cast the interurban railways and the automobiles that supplanted them as the primary agents of urban form. Technological determinists posit personal mobility as the vehicle that freed workers and their families to live in isolated neighborhoods of their choice. In this view, the auto and federally funded highway projects opened up the urban fringe to leap-frogging residential suburbanization, and the metropolitan region was the inevitable product of sprawl projected along transit routes.[8]

As an antidote to the technological determinists, this study began with the homebuilders. An analysis of land development and locational decision making led to industry, which revealed the continued importance of the workplace–residence link. These findings suggest, first, that the emergence of Los Angeles as a fully urbanized region occurred around a set of decentralized industrial growth poles; second, that defense-related industrial and housing policy accelerated this emergent pattern of decentralization; and third, that historians should look here to uncover the roots of the "technoburb," a "postsuburban spatial form," and the "spread" or "edge" city.[9]

The Workplace–Residence Link

In his summary for the planning committee of the 1931 President's Conference on Home Building and Home Ownership, Secretary of

Commerce Robert P. Lamont wrote: "Home building . . . include[s] not only the construction of houses, but the layout of subdivisions and the relationships between home neighborhoods, the location of business and industrial centers, and the whole problem of industrial decentralization."[10] Here Lamont spelled out the central elements of the complete community. Projects by developers Fritz B. Burns and Fred W. Marlow in Mar Vista (Westside Village), North Hollywood (Toluca Wood), and Westchester ("Homes at Wholesale") demonstrate that before World War II, Los Angeles homebuilders had adopted and perfected the planning principles and construction practices essential for mass-housing and community building. And, following Lamont's dictum, Burns and Marlow sited these new neighborhoods near the manufacturing facilities of Douglas, Lockheed, and North American Aviation respectively, three of the region's "Big Six" aircraft firms.

Airframe production came to be concentrated in southern California during the 1930s. When the U.S. Department of Commerce surveyed the nation's businesses for the 1939 *Census of Manufactures,* it found that among the key 139 industrial sectors the aircraft industry had recorded the greatest interregional shift. Over the preceding decade (1929–39), the West Coast's share of national output increased from 14 to 40 percent. Industry leaders and an earlier generation of business historians attributed this solely to topography and California's temperate climate.[11] The critical variables were, in fact, the engineering advances developed by innovators such as Douglas, a skilled nonunion labor force, and the presence of support institutions such as the California Institute of Technology.[12]

Industrial expansion spurred regional employment. The number of wage-earners employed in aircraft and parts increased 50 percent in 1937. After modest growth in 1938, the ranks of nonsalaried workers grew 122 percent in 1939, 80 percent in 1940, and 110 percent in 1941. Initially, increased labor demands were met locally through sectoral shifts in employment, the absorption of the previously unemployed, and new wage-earners entering the work force. Eventually the inmigration of additional workers became mandatory. In 1941, new workers were being added to the industrial payroll at the rate of 13,000 a month. By 1944, one-quarter of Los Angeles County residents had arrived during the preceding four years.[13] Increased production in the 1935–41 period has been attributed primarily to additional work shifts and improved production efficiency. However, greater floor space, achieved either by physical expansion or leasing, was essential.[14]

The ascent and speed of the industry's trajectory can be gauged from developments at North American. In November 1935, 75 employees relocated from Baltimore into temporary quarters in Inglewood. In January 1936, 175 workers entered a new 158,678-square-foot assembly plant. Between September 1939 and December 1941, the company increased monthly output from 70 to 325 units, added 14,000 employees to its work force, and expanded floor space from 425,000 to more than 1 million square feet. In addition, by 1940 the company had upward of a thousand firms under subcontract and had begun construction of a branch plant at Hensley Field, Dallas.[15]

The work force was changing qualitatively as well. Before 1935, aircraft manufacturing and assembly was essentially craft based. Vultee introduced the first powered-conveyor assembly in 1942. In the interim, a production system dominated by point assembly had been transformed into an integrated-line assembly system. Production engineers reconfigured specialized tasks so that lower-paid wage-earners could accomplish them following a minimum of training. In just three years (1940–43), wage-earners employed in aircraft and parts classified as either "operatives and kindred workers" or "laborers" rose from slightly less than one-third to more than two-thirds of the labor force.[16]

Until 1940, contracts called for one to three planes on average. Management routinely scheduled concurrent production on ten different models, and various aircraft crowded the assembly floor. Military orders for multiple units of a single aircraft supported the adoption of continuous-flow principles, which reduced production time dramatically and cut costs almost in half.[17] To meet production deadlines, prime contractors such as North American and Douglas relied on feeder plants and ancillary industry. These included shops that manufactured metal castings and forgings, wood patterns, coil springs, electrical supplies, radio and communication equipment, and safety instruments. Between 1939 and 1941 the Los Angeles Chamber of Commerce reported on more than fifty firms that either began initial business operations, moved to the Los Angeles region, or expanded to new production facilities within the county. Their locational decision making reinforced the emerging pattern of peripheral clustering.[18]

FHA Incentives

Homebuilders anticipated an influx of defense workers drawn by these employment centers and selected sites in close proximity to new production facilities for the plotting and construction of new communities. In May 1938 analysts at Security First National Bank called building "the brightest spot in the current industrial picture." They noted the concentration on small homes and inexpensive lots, "reflecting the new FHA program." Throughout this period the bank placed housing reports, rather than the aircraft industry's take-off, on the front pages of its *Monthly Summary of Business Conditions*. As an index to the strength of this recovery, it is important to note that from 1936—when FHA *Annual Reports* first published data on mortgages insured by states—to 1941, California averaged 19 percent of the national total.[19]

As Security Bank's reports suggest, Federal Housing Administration policy amendments provided the supply-side stimuli for increased housing starts. In February 1938 the FHA initiated a new class of mortgage guarantees targeted precisely toward small homes. Title I, Class 3 loans were restricted to purchases with principal under $2,500. The FHA designed this program to entice builders toward the burgeoning market of factory workers such as those entering the aircraft industry. A second inducement, Section 203, extended the percentage of the home mortgage available from 80 percent of appraised value to 90 percent and extended the repayment period to a maximum of twenty-five years on owner-occupied homes valued under $5,400.[20]

Following the extension of FHA guarantees, private sector residential construction in the Los Angeles metropolitan region attained levels surpassed only during the boom of 1923.[21] More important, the southern California FHA office received 1,793 Class 3 applications, one-fifth of the national total.[22] This homebuilding wave crested in the spring and summer of 1941 when authorizations for family units averaged 4,550 a month. Between 1 April 1940 and 1 May 1942, Los Angeles builders constructed 95,000 family units countywide.[23]

The 1939 FHA *Annual Report* included the most extensive data on housing and homebuyers from the 1935–50 era. That year, 31 percent of the new, single-family dwellings approved for mortgage insurance in Los Angeles were valued below $4,000. By contrast, of the largest twenty metropolitan areas in the country, only in St. Louis did more than 10 percent of FHA-insured dwellings fall within that price range.[24] In short, Los Angeles and southern California were in the forefront of a national recovery and, specifically, were in the lead in the provision of low-cost homes for wage-earners previously locked out of homeownership.

A set of discrete but mutually reinforcing factors converged at this moment, allowing for what Marc Weiss has termed the "rise of the community builders." As Security Bank noted in its *Monthly Summary*, "Large-scale housing projects, the subject of much interest in recent years, are at present becoming reality in the Los Angeles metropolitan area." Typical of FHA-insured projects were Wyvernwood (at 1,100 units the largest housing project in southern California) and Thousand Gardens (later renamed Baldwin Hills).[25] Then in July 1940 the bank reported: "There continues to be considerable activity in private mass construction of relatively inexpensive homes selling, for the most part, from $2,500 to $3,000. A large majority of these houses are being built . . . within close proximity to industrial plants, principally aircraft factories." That same month, wage-earners employed at a Los Angeles County aircraft production facility earned $1,656 a year. Their $138 monthly income qualified them for a house purchase of up to $3,500, assuming a twenty-year mortgage. These workers fell within an income group ($1,500–$1,999) that accounted for one-quarter of the region's FHA-insured home sales.[26]

Community Building in Los Angeles

Westside Village, a 788-unit community development begun in 1939 by Fritz B. Burns, illustrates the trend. Burns came to Los Angeles a real estate salesman and capitalized on the 1920s boom. After the downturn, he recapitalized through oil and gas holdings to return in the vanguard of real estate and land development. Then in the late 1930s he made the transition from land packaging and lot sales to community builder. As the developers of a 788-unit project, Burns and his partner Fred W. Marlow (Marlow-Burns) were almost without peers. Less than one-tenth of 1 percent of Los Angeles builders completed 100 or more units that year.[27]

For this project, Burns selected a site approximately 2 miles from Clover Field, Douglas Aircraft's parent facility in Santa Monica. Print ads highlighted the workplace–residence link. In an aerial perspective, the Douglas plant was given visual prominence while the distance between the new homes and potential employment was artfully reduced.[28]

Westside Village showcased many elements central for later community developments. Here site planners incorporated formal strategies promoted by the FHA, such as distinguishing between major and minor streets, and surveying lots with proportions of 1:2 and 1:3 where property lines were drawn at right angles or radial to the street. On these 5,400- to 6,000-square-foot lots, Burns placed two-bedroom, 885-square-foot dwellings. He used a single-floor plan throughout, alternating the garage location and roof massing, and adding covered porches and trellises to enliven an otherwise homogeneous tract. Homeowners were encouraged to enhance this formal variety. Burns offered residents building material for fences, trees, shrubs, and perennials at volume prices. The inclusion of a neighborhood center attests to the fact that Burns and his associates conceived of this development as a discrete community.[29]

In 1939 Westside Village houses sold for $2,990 complete. The buyer needed $150.00 down; monthly payments were $29.90. Burns kept the final cost low by leaving sitework, such as driveway paving, and finish work, including exterior painting, to the homebuyer. Burns was, in essence, selling an entire project rather than a single house. Westside Village is notable because it offered working-class families a community package.[30]

It was at Westside Village that this particular group of real estate entrepreneurs made the transition from land developers and lot speculators to community builders. Burns held the property title, hired J. Paul Campbell as his builder, and financed the construction. And it was here that Marlow-Burns first applied the principles of mass-building. They organized a staging area along National Boulevard where suppliers delivered materials that work-men precut and preassembled for eventual trucking throughout the construction site.[31] The site itself became a continuous produc-tion process. Specialized teams of laborers and craftsmen moved sequentially through the project grading and grubbing, preparing and pouring foundations, framing and sheathing the building envelope, and applying finish materials. A full decade before Levittown, manu-facturing practices developed for quantity production in the factory were being applied to the on-site assembly of housing. This transfor-mation in homebuilding was the product of a twenty-year debate concerning the standardization of unit design, industrial organiza-tion, and rationalized production. Horizontal building operations, and the added degree of management and coordination it required, were essential for mass-housing and the low-cost manufacture of multiple units.[32]

Similar factors informed development at Toluca Wood, a 400-unit project built on open acreage straddling the North Hollywood–Burbank line. Marlow-Burns began construction in May 1941; the development was substantially complete a year later. Here the identical dwellings sold for $3,690, including house, garage, lot, and improvements. According to the sales brochure, "Standardized floor plans and large-scale operations made possible many luxury features usually associated with residences costing many hundreds of dollars more." The brochure also touted the homes' location—"Within a three mile circle are the great Vega and Lockheed Aircraft plants and scores of allied industries"—while claiming that homebuyers were "representative of scores of diversified industries throughout the great San Fernando Valley."[33]

An aerial photograph of the Lockheed facility published in *Los Angeles: Preface to a Master Plan*, illustrated North Hollywood's low-density land-use pattern. The caption cited the number of autos as indicative of the "need for convenient housing facilities; the space available for such housing is clearly evident." In 1940, census enumerators reported that three-quarters of the homes in this sparsely settled tract were built after 1930. Between 1940 and 1946, 29,000 new residents (75+ percent) moved to this section of the metropolitan region.[34]

Congress passed Title VI of the Housing Act in March 1941. This provided homebuilders additional incentives for concentrating on the small-home market. Title VI was restricted to 146 industrial areas where the Defense Housing Coordinator forecasted critical shortages. The stated objective was to stimulate private construction proximate to defense manufacturing. Under Title VI, homebuilders in critical housing areas could apply for direct guaranteed loans up to 90 percent of a project's appraised value. These loans reduced developers' up-front costs and assigned risk to the federal government. Only defense workers employed in certified industries earning less than $3,000 a year were eligible for these units, which had to be purchased or rented for under $50.00 a month. During the first year, California accounted for more than one-quarter of the Title VI loans guaranteed nationwide.[35]

A contraction in home construction began in August 1941. The business community attributed the drop-off to material shortages associated with the defense buildup. Then, on 22 September 1941, the Priorities Division of the Office of Production Management initiated restrictions on critical building materials for defense housing. In April 1942 the War Production Board banned nonessential construction. But these regulations and material allocations actually encouraged the operations of builders like Fritz Burns. They focused the industry toward authorized work, which, in addition to war production plants, included "small homes for war workers." In effect, the building materials priority system sustained the volume of low-cost private residential construction in areas where there was a critical need for defense housing. In Los Angeles, the programs solidified and further stimulated an existing pattern of peripheral development and a particular configuration in the homebuilding industry. Both had been established in the late 1930s.[36]

Building Up the Homefront

Marlow-Burns participated in the premier example of wartime nodal development, Westchester in southeast Los Angeles (figure 10.2). In just three years, four sets of developers converted a 5-square-mile parcel owned and master-planned by Security Bank into a complete community for 10,000 residents housed in 3,230 units.[37] The bank's development plan centered on a commercial district along Sepulveda Boulevard from Manchester Avenue south to Ninety-sixth Street. Security Bank sold 3,000 acres to community builders with restrictions against commercial development in lieu of a percentage holding in their business center. The Burns organization marketed their tract as "Homes at Wholesale" and built more than a thousand houses. Two-bedroom dwellings sold for $3,650 to $3,990. Title VI restricted sales to workers in designated defense industries.[38] The National Housing Agency reinforced this advanta-

FIGURE 10.2. Oblique aerial of Westchester taken from the southwest looking toward Los Angeles City Hall (1945). "Homes at Wholesale" is right of center. Courtesy: The Examiner Collection, Department of Special Collections, University of Southern California.

geous market position in July 1942, when they restricted residential building in Los Angeles County to the area south of Manchester and Firestone boulevards.[39]

"Homes at Wholesale" formed the southeastern quadrant defined by the intersection of Sepulveda Boulevard and Manchester. The Board of Education constructed a primary school on property Marlow-Burns deeded to the city.[40] Real estate advertisements highlighted the proximity to Los Angeles Municipal Airport and the cluster of ancillary industries extending along Century Boulevard at the northern boundary of the airfield. A map in the *Los Angeles Herald-Express* noted "substantial business enterprises employing many thousands of workers" and identified twelve "important plants and allied projects."[41]

Westside Village, Toluca Wood, Westchester, and other war-time developments in Los Angeles were not intended as suburbs if that term is taken to mean an economically inert bedroom community populated predominantly by middle- and upper-income White families. The social homogeneity of these "good residential neighborhoods" was mirrored in a low-density and functionally exclusive land-use pattern zoned to prohibit incompatible or noxious uses that might diminish property values.[42] Nor were Lakewood Village, Lynnwood Park, and Murray Woodlands the less expensive spin-offs of middle- and upper-class neighborhoods of good address. These developments were planned as communities for "balanced living," affordable for workers and their families.[43]

What were the salient features that set a Westchester apart from the traditional suburb? Although it contained quiet, curved streets fronting rows of single-family housing occupied by home-owning families, Westchester was not planned as a commuter shed for workers destined for the urban core. And even though the developers sited their "modern" dwellings on lots ample enough for side and rear yards, the land-use density was greater here than in the traditional suburb.[44]

Homogeneity of income and occupation, a central tenet for the traditional suburb, did not hold here, either. Data on class of workers from the 1940 census reveal a high degree of heterogeneity in Westchester. Semi-skilled and skilled workers predominated, but there was a statistically significant number of laborers, managers, and professionals. The census classified approximately one-quarter of the residents employed outside their homes as operatives and laborers, another quarter as professionals, one-fifth as craftsmen, and just under one-fifth as proprietors and managers. These percentages remained consistent into 1950 despite an increase of 3,900 percent in the number employed.[45] Community builders presented this diversity as a selling point. Ads for Lakewood Village, a 2,500-unit project adjacent to Douglas's new Long Beach facility, promoted it as a "fifteen-million dollar community of individualized homes for defense workers and executives."[46]

Note, too, that these communities subverted the principal raison d'être of the traditional suburb: upper-class flight from the industrial city. These case studies demonstrate that homebuilders recognized and capitalized on the workplace–residence link. It was essential to the whole enterprise of satellite development. The aircraft industry provided the economic foundation, the manufacturing base, and the people that necessitated and sustained community building, and that in turn accelerated an emerging pattern of regional metropolitan growth.

Planning the Postwar Urban Region

While the preceding examples illustrate the working-out on the ground of a community development strategy and the expanded scale of building operations, it was a transitional moment, and it is instructive to look elsewhere for examples of the complete communities Burns and other large-scale builders intended. A case in point is Fontana. Wartime practice at its Fontana steel mill alerted the Henry J. Kaiser Company to mass-housing and the advantageous coupling of homebuilding and community services. At Fontana, the company planned an 800-unit community to house a quarter of its work force. Seventy percent of these workers took home under $36.00 a week. Housing was in short supply, and turnover at the plant reached 17 percent in 1944.[47] On a 280-acre tract, Kaiser proposed to build one-, two-, and three-bedroom houses. Although these dwellings would have been only slightly less expensive than comparable FHA homes in the area, the Kaiser proposal offered medical services and community facilities.

The community plan placed the housing around a central core with a recreation center, school, and Kaiser-Permanente clinic. A commercial center with an 8,000-square-foot market, 13,000-square-feet of shops, and a 400-person theater fronted Foothill Boulevard. An east-west arterial and north-south collector divided the site into four quadrants. Internal pedestrian paths linked the resultant superblocks. A system of alternating courts and cul-de-sacs limited interior auto access for privacy and safety. Except for the compromised siting of a neighborhood park adjacent to the commercial center, the formal principles Kaiser engineers employed represent a literal adaptation of FHA planning standards.[48]

The policies and practices traced to this point came together in the large-scale community projects Kaiser Homes developed after the war. California's population grew 53 percent during the 1940s. From 1940 to 1946 Los Angeles alone gained 301,410 new residents, a growth rate of 20 percent, equal to that of the entire preceding decade. Pent-up housing demand and projections from the California Reconstruction and Reemployment Commission led Kaiser housing analysts to predict 200,000 new units a year as the minimum required to meet the expected shortfall. In response to this "crisis," Henry J. Kaiser envisioned a homebuilding program based on "industrial methods" that would "create a new home market among the majority of U.S. families who do not now own their homes."[49]

Burns and Kaiser were equal partners in this venture. In addition to the 3,000 acres of developable property he held in Los Angeles, Burns brought to the organization his years of experience in land development and more recent experience as a community builder. The Kaiser Corporation offered access to capital; the control, production, and handling of raw materials; expertise in fabrication and quantity production; testing labs for research into building materials and new product development; and public confidence in the "miracle man" of wartime production. Kaiser Homes stated that its objective as a "national home-building enterprise" was to create communities "founded on the belief that home, health, [and] recreation . . . can be formed into a unit of living." In his statement to the California State Housing Committee, Kaiser promised that "eventually our community developments will include hospitals, recreation facilities, theaters, child welfare centers, and all the conveniences and necessities of modern family living."[50]

Following the war, the Los Angeles Regional Planning Commission reported that the "area of greatest growth [was] occurring at . . . a radius of fifteen miles from the Civic Center."[51] Within the 15-mile circle, sections such as the 212-square-mile San Fernando Valley—which contained almost half the incorporated land area in the city—were still predominantly agricultural. A 1943 Los Angeles Master Plan document stated that the "valley should be planned as a self-contained unit, that is, industry and commerce should be introduced to supplement the agricultural economy and supply employment for present and future residents."[52] A 1944 zoning plan had these recommendations: the recognition of eighteen communities as nodes for urbanization; the creation of residences, light industry, and a small amount of agricultural zones around urban centers; and the establishment of balanced relationships between residential neighborhoods, commerce, and industry. According to Director of Planning Charles Bennett and Milton Breivogel (the principal planner), if "adopted and followed" the land-use plan would "result in the form of a community known among planners as the 'regional city' in which [would] be found a number of well-planned and moderately sized communities of reasonable density, separated by agricultural areas." To encourage their objectives, the commission published a series of "Special Studies"; one featured a "planned community" at the Panorama Ranch, a 397-acre dairy farm owned and operated by the Pellissier family.[53]

Kaiser Homes developed Panorama City on the vestiges of the Panorama Ranch. In 1946 when Burns was negotiating the land purchase, General Motors had begun construction of its new Chevrolet assembly plant in the southwest corner of the property. Schlitz operated a brewery adjacent to the Southern Pacific rail line south of the site. The Bank of America described the "surrounding district[s]" as "raw acreage and scattered small farms." Their appraisers defined the proposed project's assets as a "self-contained community [in close] proximity to employment." In other words, Panorama City epitomized the convergence of a planning ideal, the decentralized regional city, with the production emphasis and community building expertise of a corporation such as Kaiser Homes.[54]

An aerial view taken from the south illustrates all the attributes of a complete community. Roscoe Boulevard bisects the site on an east-west axis and serves as a collector for the main arterial of the valley, Van Nuys Boulevard. Along Roscoe, in the center of the image, is St. Genevieve and, to the east, the church's school site. Directly north is a community recreation center and primary school. South and east, one block below Roscoe, is the public high school. Kaiser and Burns developed a linear commercial district with department stores, supermarkets, and theater, along the business frontage on Van Nuys Boulevard. Just south of Roscoe in the bend of Woodman Boulevard (the project's eastern boundary) is a vacant site that now houses a Kaiser-Permanente Medical Center. Readily apparent in the southwest corner of the site is the GM plant.

Occupational diversity—a factor that distinguished these developments from the traditional suburb—characterized Panorama City as well. The 1950 census reveals the heterogeneity of residents. Wage-earners were divided evenly between operatives and laborers, and craftsmen and kindred workers. Taken together, these two classifications constituted one-half of the work force. Another one-quarter of the residents enumerated were professionals and managers.[55] This was not happenstance. Kaiser and Burns explicitly programmed in a degree of heterogeneity. Writing as the southern California representative for the California Reconstruction and Reemployment Commission's report on postwar housing, Burns spelled out the requirements for "modern neighborhoods" in "satellite cities." The attributes included open space, community facilities, superblock planning, and jobs within walking distance "if possible." While suggesting that individual homes should display a "certain congruity" of design, Burns argued for variety in unit prices "to provide a varied community atmosphere and to prevent un-American economic and social stratification." However, there were strict limits to the social mixing community builders advocated. Kaiser restricted his dream of homeownership for all to the industrious working classes, and Burns and Marlow supported restrictive covenants designed to exclude people of color from purchasing homes in their developments.[56]

Conclusion

In every other respect, Panorama City was a far cry from the gridded, single-lot sales, and small-time contractor approach to neighborhood building that characterized residential construction up to the 1930s. The significance of Kaiser Community Homes was the way corporate officers, engineers, and field personnel thought about housing. The home was conceived as the spatial core of an entire package programmed to include recreation, health care, religion, education, and consumption. This package was scientifically analyzed, rationally produced and managed, and organized to be reproducible on open tracts throughout the country. Rarely achieved, this nonetheless became an ideal for postwar homebuilding.[57]

These case studies are of value, however, beyond their clarification of the historical record. Although the immediate pre- and postwar urban expansion is now all but indistinguishable within the confines of greater Los Angeles, a historical analysis reveals that these communities were not the result of unfettered growth and unmitigated sprawl. They were planned through a series of uncoordinated but mutually reinforcing decisions and the actions taken by manufacturers, federal housing personnel, planners, land developers, and homebuilders. This history is important because the spatial transformation in Los Angeles, and the new social geography that came in its wake, have parallels in other metropolitan areas that were restructured by the defense emergency, such as San Diego, Wichita, Kansas City, and Dallas. By extension, a comprehensive analysis of the forces that drove regional development in this period becomes mandatory for interpreting the contemporary metropolitan landscape. It is, for example, essential for conceptualizing development affiliated with high technology in Orange County, the Silicon Valley, and similar techno-

poles throughout the country that are undergoing rapid urbanization around specialized industry.

A majority of urban historians continue to view the urban
expansion after World War II as being continuous with that of the
corporate industrial city, that is, as urbanization anchored in a
dominant central core. In this view, regional growth is tied to jobs in
the center or service and back-room employment that trickles out to
the urban fringe. A history of the community building process in
Westside Village, Westchester, and Panorama City can serve as a
corrective. To conceive of Los Angeles as a "suburban metropolis" in
the traditional sense of the term is only a half-truth.[58] Westchester
and Panorama City developed within a metropolitan region comprised of dispersed and discrete clusters. They were not the sprawling in-fill of isolated residential neighborhoods projected along mass
or private transit routes. These nodal developments were dynamic
hubs of manufacturing and job creation, the foundation necessary
for operative builders' experiments in communities of balanced
living.

CHAPTER 11

Professional Conflict over Urban Form

The Case of Urban Freeways, 1930 to 1970

CLIFF ELLIS

Specialists in the history of urban freeway construction have uncovered several issues that have shaped transportation infrastructure systems in U.S. cities: debates over costs versus benefits, the relationship between cities and suburbs, the impact of freeways on urban form, and professional conflicts between highway designers with different kinds of expertise. These issues have been articulated in Mark S. Foster's From Streetcar to Superhighway *(Philadelphia: Temple University Press, 1981), Mark H. Rose's* Interstate *(Knoxville: University of Tennessee Press, 1990), and Paul Barrett's* The Automobile and Urban Transit *(Philadelphia: Temple University Press, 1983). In this chapter, Cliff Ellis examines more closely the issue of professional expertise; he presents a pointed analysis of the distinctive worldviews that highway engineers, urban planners, architects, and landscape architects applied to the design of freeways for inner cities. Ellis argues that the perspectives characteristic of the training for each group of professionals have determined the freeway design solutions each group has proposed.*

The fundamental principles that would guide freeway planning doctrines were forged by highway engineers during the 1930s and 1940s and were codified thereafter. Strongly influenced by an engineering worldview and by the rural and suburban location of most highway construction, these ideas broke down in the inner cities, where strikingly different spatial and social conditions prevailed. Community protests eventually forced highway officials to reevaluate their plans, and "conflict flared between engineers, planners, architects, and landscape architects as each profession struggled to recast urban freeway planning to incorporate neglected aesthetic and social considerations." Ellis draws from state highway division reports and U.S. Bureau of Public Roads publications as well as published reports and official policy statements from professional associations to analyze the ways in which a characteristic professional worldview has shaped the design perspective of each group. Various participants viewed freeways, in turn, as "traffic conduits, urban architecture, land-use boundaries, economic stimuli, redevelopment catalysts, and tools of social policy."

The clash of professional worldviews forms an important part of the history of American city planning. The disparities in perspective among the principal professions responsible for the design of American cities belie the possibility of genuine comprehensive planning. Professional training and the conventions of standard practice, Ellis suggests, too often "congeal into blinkered views of urban life." The result is a fractured planning process and a series of bad design decisions, evident, for example, in the urban decay left behind by inner-city freeway construction during the 1950s and 1960s.

For two of the most trenchant critiques of inner-city redevelopment and freeway construction, readers should consult Jane Jacobs, The Death and Life of Great American Cities *(New York: Random House, 1961), and Lewis Mumford,* The City in History *(New York: Harcourt, Brace & World, 1961). For recent scholarship on issues of race, urban redevelopment, and urban form, see John F. Bauman,* Public Housing, Race, and Renewal *(Philadelphia: Temple University Press, 1987), and Raymond*

The Organization and Process of Planning

A. Mohl, "Race and Space in the Modern City," in Arnold Hirsch and Raymond Mohl, eds., Urban Policy in Twentieth-Century America *(New Brunswick: Rutgers University Press, 1993). For more on the occupational worldviews of specific professions, see Mark Foster's book cited above; "Architecture vs. Planning," a special issue of* Center: A Journal for Architecture in America *6 (1990); Louis Ward Kemp, "Aesthetes and Engineers: The Occupational Ideology of Highway Design,"* Technology and Culture *27 (Oct. 1986): 759–97; and Bruce Seely,* Building the American Highway System *(Philadelphia: Temple University Press, 1987).* EDITORS

C ities are shaped by many actors, and inevitably experts collide over issues of power, prestige, money, and style. The freeway-building era in the United States brought an array of professional conflicts to the surface, as diverse groups struggled to influence the reshaping of American cities for high-speed motor vehicle travel. Urban freeway policy emerged from heated political battles over costs and benefits, impacts on urban form, and professional expertise. Although technical analysis and arcane methodologies were marshaled to justify the motorization of American cities, the battleground was also one of ideas and images. The city of the future was rendered differently by different actors, as they struggled to influence the insertion of freeways into the congested fabric of America's central cities. This clash of professional worldviews forms an important part of the history of American city planning in the twentieth century.[1]

Crucial freeway-planning doctrines were forged between 1920 and 1945. These doctrines gained widespread support during the 1950s as cities were aggressively rebuilt to accommodate the automobile. Freeways were scaled up to handle ever-increasing flows of vehicles.[2] Freeway-planning ideas, strongly influenced by rural and suburban precedents, eventually broke down in the inner city, however, where strikingly different architectural and social conditions obtained. Community protests eventually forced a reevaluation of freeway plans in many large cities. During the 1960s, the design professions generated an outpouring of reports, books, and articles on urban freeway issues. Although imaginative proposals did emerge from this ferment, and post-1970 freeways ran a much more complex gauntlet of reviews, most urban freeway mileage was completed as planned. Both the "joys of automobility" and the sorrows of congestion and sprawl became embedded in the nation's urban fabric.[3]

Professional Worldviews

Urban freeways were designed and built primarily by highway engineers, but city planners, landscape architects, and architects took part in the debates over freeway design. The involved professionals used different ideas and images to advance their goals: intellectual tools acquired through education, professional socialization, and daily practice. Professional worldviews shaped the styles of research, the generation of alternatives, and the presentation of proposals to the wider public.[4]

Professions amass intellectual capital, which is appropriated and modified by each generation of practitioners. Although professions harbor diverse individuals, typical approaches to problem solving congeal into standard practice. In order to enhance their legitimacy, professions project auras of scientific rigor, nuts-and-bolts competence, or, in the design fields, of aesthetic subtlety, intellectual complexity, and personal panache. Professional worldviews, with their associated images of good city form, are hard to dislodge since they are bound up with the struggle for social prestige, intellectual legitimacy, and market share.[5] These worldviews influence policy making in powerful, if not obvious, ways. The debates over urban freeway policy illustrate this point with unusual clarity.

Inventing Urban Freeways

Images of a "city of freeways" evolved over many decades as automobile use expanded. Traffic congestion was already a serious prob-

FIGURE 11.1. Threading an elevated highway through the central city.
From Whitten (1930).

lem in the 1920s. City planners and traffic engineers attacked the
problem with rationalized thoroughfare plans, traffic control de-
vices, and proposals to expand existing streets. It quickly became
evident, though, that a "leap" toward a new scale of speed and
capacity was desirable, rather than expensive tinkering with
streetgrids laid down many decades before (figure 11.1).[6]

Municipal engineers in Chicago and Detroit produced plans for
express highways as early as the 1920s.[7] The celebrated *Regional
Plan of New York and Its Environs* portrayed a complete highway
network for the New York region. The first true limited-access
parkway in the United States was the Bronx River Parkway in
Westchester County, New York, completed in 1923. On a more
visionary plane, modernist architects drafted compelling images of
new urban landscapes configured around high-speed arterials.[8]
These early designs made the public conscious of alternatives, inch-
ing the idea of urban freeways steadily toward acceptability.

Robert Moses' parkways of the 1920s and early 1930s served as crucial exemplars of parkway design and would soon show up as models in the federal documents launching the interstate highway system.[9] His early works successfully combined landscape architecture and highway engineering. Located in rural areas, these early parkways were intentionally rustic. As Moses advanced into the built-up parts of the city, his roads lost much of their bucolic flavor, but he was still hailed as the harbinger of a new urbanism—clean, efficient, and strong. A 1941 *Architectural Forum* article on the Gowanus Parkway in Brooklyn intoned: "Like a Roman road the highway cuts through the dreary city . . . and sweeps across its incongruous confusion and decay. There is a new scale to this structure that is truly contemporary, and next to it the incongruous disorder of our environment is shown up as hopelessly indefensible. Sweeping through the old city and over it—it is the first real taste of the coming urbanism."[10] But the Gowanus foreshadowed a troubling metamorphosis, as promised "parkways" gradually became stripped-down traffic conduits.[11]

Precedents for freeway construction in dense urban areas existed: the building of the railroads, Haussmann's great boulevards in Paris, and the construction of rapid transit lines. The technical lore of railroad building had permeated civil engineering, but was not accompanied by a concern for the aesthetic and social impacts of urban construction.[12] Haussmann's boulevards were admired by most American planners; clearance of insalubrious zones and their replacement with new arterials seemed a positive good, worth the costs in disruption and displacement of residents. Rapid transit construction had established the difficulty of running linear transportation corridors through built-up areas, and the blighting effects of elevated structures had become evident. But with technical innovations and sufficient funds it seemed that these obstacles could be overcome; highways and autos would be more compatible with the city than noisy, clanking railroads.[13] Photographs and renderings of freeway plans from the 1930s show the freeways as noble urban artifacts, flowing smoothly through the jumbled land uses of the city center, with streamlined autos speeding along uncongested pavements.

Freeways promised a clear technological solution for traffic congestion, could be combined with slum clearance, created jobs, and responded to public preferences for the automobile.[14] Newly constructed turnpikes and parkways in Pennsylvania, Connecticut, and elsewhere established the viability of the limited-access highway. Landscape architects contributed their design skills to many early parkways, demonstrating that utility and beauty could be combined. Los Angeles produced an extensive parkway plan in 1939, and the first segment of the Arroyo Seco Parkway was opened to traffic in 1940. In the realm of speculation, Norman Bel Geddes's Futurama exhibit at the 1939 New York World's Fair publicized the notion of urban freeways, although hard-nosed pragmatists such as Moses considered it a mere "work of the imagination."[15] Americans also cast an eye toward Europe, where the German *Autobahnen* and Italian *autostrade* reinforced the notion that the time for limited-access roads had arrived.

The federal government entered the urban freeway debates forcefully only during the 1930s. The two crucial federal highway planning reports were *Toll Roads and Free Roads* in 1939 and *Interregional Highways* in 1944.[16] These documents provided blueprints for the insertion of freeways into the old industrial city. They were urban planning documents of the first importance.

Toll Roads and Free Roads, researched and written by highway engineers at the Bureau of Public Roads (BPR), was submitted to Congress in 1939. The bureau seized the initiative in highway politics with two proposals: a plan to construct a 26,700-mile non-toll interregional highway system, and the idea of moving *urban* highways into a prominent place on the bureau's agenda, in a departure from historic policy. *Toll Roads* presaged elements of the booming "edge cities" and troubled urban cores that are all too familiar today. The authors viewed the inner city largely as an obstacle to smooth traffic flow, one that could only be rectified by new urban freeways and "a radical revision of the city plan." *Toll*

FIGURE 11.2.   Proposed design for a depressed express highway in a city.
From U.S. Bureau of Public Roads (1939).

Roads showed that urban bypass routes were no solution, since most
traffic within urban areas was moving from one destination to
another *within* the metropolis. The report also endorsed an early
version of the radial-concentric freeway pattern that would become
standard during the following decades (figure 11.2).

The *Interregional Highways* report, also written largely by BPR
engineers under the supervision of the National Interregional Highway Committee, was released in January 1944. The committee
included well-known city planner Harland Bartholomew, National
Resources Planning Board chairman Frederic A. Delano, and New
York City Planning Commission chairman Rexford Tugwell. Other
members were Thomas H. MacDonald, head of the Bureau of Public
Roads; G. Donald Kennedy, Michigan highway commissioner and
president of the American Association of State Highway Officials;
former Alabama governor Bibb Graves, and California highway
engineer Charles H. Purcell. In spite of the presence of Bartholo-

mew, Tugwell, and Delano, three notable representatives of the planning profession, the philosophy of the Bureau of Public Roads dominated the study. Traffic service came first.[17]

The report proposed a freeway system of 33,920 miles, of which 4,470 miles were to fall within city limits. This mileage would be augmented by an additional 5,000 miles of circumferential or distributing routes required in the larger cities, for a total freeway mileage of about 39,000 miles.[18]

Expanding on the basic themes of Toll Roads, Interregional Highways presented a concentric-ring model of urban spatial structure, similar to that used to justify urban renewal. The race and class segregation of the mid-twentieth-century capitalist city, with its corresponding gradients of environmental quality, was construed as the result of normal competition over urban space. According to this model, as cities age, two rings of deteriorating tissue emerge around the central business district: an inner slum area of "mixed land uses and run-down buildings," awaiting engulfment by the central business district; and an even larger ring of "blighted" residential property. Healthy residential areas lie outside this frontier.[19]

Both the penetrating radials and the inner belts around the central business district would cut through these inner rings. Many planners and highway engineers argued that freeways would help to cure blight and revitalize the city center by removing traffic from surface streets and razing corridors of dilapidated structures. Mixed-use areas with shops, light industry, and single-room-occupancy (SRO) housing were prime candidates for removal.[20] Residents of these districts were almost invisible in highway-planning documents. In addition, stream valleys, urban parks, and "wedges of undeveloped land" between existing radial highways were targeted as freeway corridors, since no expensive clearance of buildings would be required. Although the committee recommended that a metropolitan authority be formed to resolve conflicts between municipalities, and to "avoid obvious mistakes in the location of the interregional routes," a powerful authority of this type was not mandated in subsequent interstate legislation.[21]

These fundamental principles, codified during the 1940s, shaped urban freeway planning for the next three decades. The Federal Aid Highway Act of 1944 designated a National System of Interstate Highways, not to exceed 40,000 miles. This mileage included routes *through* American cities, although specific locations were not provided. In 1947, the Bureau of Public Roads and the state highway departments reached agreement on 37,681 miles of interstate highways, including 2,882 urban miles. Designation of 2,319 miles of additional urban circumferential and distributing routes was deferred until further studies could be performed. These culminated in the *General Location of National System of Interstate Highways* of 1955, known as the "Yellow Book."[22] Adequate funding for the interstate highway system was not secured until the passage of the Federal Aid Highway Act of 1956.[23]

Constructing Urban Freeways

During the late 1940s and early 1950s most city planners favored new networks of urban arterials, although they often proposed more modestly scaled "expressways" with four to six lanes and speed limits near 45 miles per hour. Urban planners also suggested that mass transit (rail or express bus) rights-of-way be provided within the new freeway corridors, and that freeways be more closely integrated with urban renewal schemes.[24] However, transit corridor sharing, a concept alien to the state highway departments, was defeated with only a few exceptions. In cities where central-city growth coalitions were strong enough to force the issue, freeways were integrated with redevelopment. Here, a new freeway would often weave through a complex of civic buildings, sports facilities, housing projects, or landscaped areas, as in the plans for the waterfronts in Cincinnati and Pittsburgh.

The schemes of local planners and municipal engineers for more modestly scaled expressways were gradually replaced by the more ambitious designs of state highway engineers. This shift began in California during the 1940s, where "the metropolitan freeway replaced the urban parkway as the focal technology of regional highway plans," and "freeways were first scaled-up to serve commute traffic in massed volumes."[25] Concurrently, fissures between planners and engineers began to widen. In 1950 Walter Blucher of the American Society of Planning Officials argued that no amount of freeway building would ever solve the traffic problem: "I helped spend a great many millions of dollars for street widenings in the city of Detroit. I helped invent the super-highway . . . but I cannot say that there is less congestion upon the public streets, less turmoil at terminals or fewer accidents than when we started this tremendous program of acquiring additional right-of-way for the movement of automobiles."[26] But the highway community was eager to build, and although engineers espoused respect for city plans, they had limited patience for the complexities of the city planning process, or for visionary planning schemes. As Robert Moses had stated back in 1943: "We do not believe in revolution. The city is not going to be torn up and rebuilt on a decentralized satellite or other academic theory. Therefore, we do not have to wait for the painting of the new, big, over-all picture constantly referred to by the revolutionary planners."[27]

Also during this period, highway engineering's scientific aura was strengthened by the expansion of quantitative analytic techniques: origin-destination studies, computerized transportation models, cost-benefit analysis, and land value studies—all tending to affirm the necessity of extensive new highway building.[28] When combined with a newly emphasized "national defense" rationale, the argument for urban freeways was formidable.[29] In comparison, social and urban design analyses appeared "soft" and subjective.

During the crucial decade of the 1950s, especially after the passage of the Interstate Highway Act, highway engineers embraced their task with energy and authority. They developed a carefully codified set of urban freeway-planning concepts and images.[30] Engineers valued their image as apolitical experts, even as they proved to be shrewd political actors. Their analyses reduced the city to its functional essentials in order to simplify action. Compared with the other involved professions, engineers used a more abstract conception of space as a plane on which traffic movements occurred in predictable patterns. In order to make use of computer models, engineers made simplifying assumptions about land uses and trip generation, projecting existing trends into the future. Their texts dryly cataloged the rules for successful technical performance, purged of ambiguities. Aggregate statistics, computer models, and aerial views of projects emphasized the big metropolitan picture rather than the detail of urban neighborhoods and streets. Their vision was bold, but narrow. Asked to build an enormous network of highways in a short time, engineers sought to standardize the production of highway mileage, not convert it into an unwieldy urban design project requiring careful molding of each urban segment to fit local needs. An internally coherent profession, highway engineering was not weakened by major disputes over the wisdom of highway construction.

City planners were still struggling for professional legitimacy, and they lacked support from powerful private constituencies, except where their interests overlapped with those of the real estate industry.[31] The profession was also divided into segments: traditional land-use planning, social science, and urban design. These were almost subprofessions, with different standards, methods, and audiences. Land-use planners portrayed urban space as a two-dimensional array of land uses and associated activities, or as the legal space of zoning districts defining allowable height, bulk, density, and use. Social science–oriented planners viewed the city through the lens of statistics, mathematical relationships, and demographic data, searching for variables to explain patterns of urban economic and social change. Urban designers inherited the cognitive training, language, and skills of architecture and landscape architecture, viewing the city as an array of three-dimensional forms, textures, and activities laden with symbolic meanings.

These divisions, exacerbated by the planning profession's aversion to strategic political action, made entrepreneurial activity difficult. Planning's mosaic of viewpoints never coalesced into a sophisticated policy on the form of central cities. City planners saw the conscious shaping of the urban environment as their domain, but had no powerful theory of good city form.[32] Hobbled by their lack of consensus, small numbers, and underdeveloped political skills, planners had little chance of strongly influencing urban freeway policy.

Architects also staked a claim to the design of cities. Historically, they had generated the most compelling and vivid images of urban design. Twentieth-century architects generated bold schemes for reconfigured urban centers, with transportation channels ingeniously built into the architectural forms.[33] Architects framed urban problems in terms of volumes, spaces, symbolic references, cultural meanings, and social needs, searching for specific, buildable solutions. Architects might have provided the missing aesthetic dimension in freeway planning, correcting for the austerity of the engineers. But architecture's center of gravity was the aesthetics of the individual building, not the evolution of urban systems.[34] Architects were outside the freeway policy network, and had limited skills at bureaucratic competition over utilitarian structures such as freeways, traditionally the property of engineers.[35] In addition, the profession was riven by its own internal debates over the proper building styles, public spaces, and transportation networks for the modern city.

Although landscape architects had produced pioneering designs during the parkway era, they played a more limited role in the post–World War II era, mainly as designers of landscape plans for the freeway environs. Thus marginalized, the full array of their design talents was not brought to bear on the problem of integrating freeways into the urban context. During the 1960s, however, they would stake a renewed claim on the design of regional infrastructure.[36]

The 1960s: Protest and Transformation

The freeway revolts began as soon as the urban freeway-building program accelerated during the mid-1950s. The first urban freeway segments were often built in industrial, low-income, and minority areas, where land values were lower, the rationale of "slum clearance" could be invoked, and opposition was weaker.[37] When the freeway builders moved into stable, middle-class neighborhoods, however, local groups organized to stop construction. The San Francisco revolt, which erupted in 1955, became the most famous. In 1959, after a lengthy battle, the San Francisco Board of Supervisors passed a resolution opposing most of the remaining planned freeways; by 1965 most further construction was halted.[38] Other well-known battlegrounds included Boston, Philadelphia, San Antonio, Richmond, New Orleans, and Washington, D.C.

By the early 1960s, a powerful critique of urban freeways was beginning to coalesce. Prominent urbanists such as Jane Jacobs and Lewis Mumford unleashed critical fusillades at the highway builders. Jacobs explained how "big projects" can devastate the fragile ecology of the city and warned against the creation of new "border vacuums": barriers, such as freeways, that created strips of dead space by cutting off normal foot traffic.[39] Mumford argued that central cities would be destroyed as livable public spaces if freeways were thrust into the center, disgorging rivers of cars: "In the act of making the core of the metropolis accessible, the planners of congestion have already almost made it uninhabitable."[40] For Mumford, the highway engineers were repeating the mistakes of the railroad builders, usurpers of precious downtown and waterfront land, and of the transit companies, which had defaced urban streets with noisy, unsightly elevated structures.[41]

A growing number of architects and city planners echoed these critiques, arguing that "expressway blight" was damaging the urban fabric.[42] Freeways were called "brutally paved and walled gashes" and "wild beasts."[43] Damage-control operations appeared in the form of joint conferences between the highway planners and the design professions: the Sagamore Conference of 1958, the Hershey Conference of 1962, and the Williamsburg Conference of 1965.[44] At best, however, these conferences produced uneasy truces.

The early 1960s also witnessed an extraordinary resurgence of urban design research, which bore directly upon the urban freeway debates. In particular, the work of Kevin Lynch at the Massachusetts Institute of Technology began to lay the foundations for a more systematic approach to urban design, one more capable of influencing public policy.[45] Transportation-planning publications began to feature more articles on the aesthetic and social aspects of freeway planning, although these new perspectives did not percolate immediately into daily practice.[46]

Eventually, some highway authorities conceded that interdisciplinary design teams should be used to plan freeways in sensitive urban areas.[47] In San Francisco, landscape architect Lawrence Halprin was hired by the State Division of Highways to generate less intrusive freeway designs for that city.[48] Across the nation, more elaborate freeway alternatives began to appear in planning documents: tunnels, cantilevers, covered cuts, joint-use projects, and lavish landscaping. The trouble was, many of these proposals were doomed beforehand by their astronomical expense and questionable technical feasibility; furthermore, they tended to deflect attention away from a more thorough rethinking of the proper role of freeways in the city. As Louis Ward Kemp has noted, planners' hopes for a dramatic improvement in urban freeway planning "went largely unfulfilled as engineers exercised their power to reduce planning techniques to a limited program of landscaping palliatives and tools for predicting traffic demands."[49]

The freeway revolts spawned legislation mandating a more inclusive highway-planning process, involving more actors and encompassing a wider range of impacts on both urban neighborhoods and the natural environment.[50] Citizens and local governments gained new legal tools to challenge unpopular freeway segments.[51] Freeways that were captured in the new regulatory net underwent more detailed scrutiny, and many became tangled in extended litigation. Some cities chose to delete freeway segments from their plans. Although highway engineers were dismayed by this change in public sentiment, there was no going back to the freewheeling era of urban highway construction. Disruptions caused by the first round of urban freeways had provoked countervailing forces. After 1970, highway builders would face a more daunting array of critical interest groups, armed with more sophisticated arguments for alternative transportation systems.[52]

Freeways and the Search for Good City Form

Freeway planning was originally conceived as an apolitical, technical process. It proved to be politically explosive, value laden, and fraught with aesthetic dimensions. The convergence of design professionals in the arena of urban freeway planning yielded what has been called "planless planning," the symptom of a larger "failure of democratic institutions to make reasoned choices about technology."[53] In an example of "technological barn-door closure," more appropriate transportation alternatives were considered only after an irrevocable commitment was made to a new urban form.[54]

The new freeway landscapes that appeared after World War II were "planned" in one sense. Large public bureaucracies and private developers projected needs, drew up design documents, arranged funding, and constructed infrastructure and buildings. Professional engineers, planners, and designers were involved at every step. But this was not comprehensive planning infused with a concern for social equity, environmental quality, urban aesthetics, and the preservation of urban culture.

Highway building was centralized, single-minded, and dominated by the engineering profession. In contrast, responsibility for "city design" was dispersed, ambiguous, and subject to conflicting claims from engineers, planners, developers, architects, landscape architects, politicians, and other actors. Advocates of urban freeways made their case tirelessly in important venues. Opponents lacked the resources and entrepreneurial vigor to respond effectively and were armed with few compelling images of a more compact, transit-rich urban form.

None of the involved professions fully grasped the transformation of the city that would be launched by urban freeway construction. Like the automobile, "The new means did not simply take people more swiftly to the same old ends; the means altered the ends. The process of going deflected one from former goals."[55] The expanded "gateways" into the central business district, once touted as the catalysts of downtown revitalization, made an exodus from the center possible. A new land-use structure, following gradients of accessibility, race, and income, emerged along the suburban radials and beltways, deflating the economic dominance of the center. Lower-income groups were left behind in the decaying inner ring, already battered by urban renewal and housing policies.[56] The promise of fair and thoroughgoing urban revitalization faded, as America's central cities developed into disturbing patchworks of devastation and affluence.[57]

Professional worldviews played an important role in shaping this troubling outcome. These worldviews—as embodied in methodologies, recurring solutions, standards, and habitual ways of framing a problem—can congeal into blinkered views of urban life: "Representations were not simply the way the planners presented a world, intimately known, in order to achieve some particular effect on an audience; the planners to a substantial degree experienced the city through their own representations of it."[58] Professional worldviews are not transparent lenses, but refracting prisms. They enable people to act, but also prevent them from seeing avenues for action.

Various groups have viewed freeways as traffic conduits, urban architecture, land-use boundaries, economic stimuli, redevelopment catalysts, and tools of social policy. Could any profession distill these diverse perspectives into a coherent policy, or must the complexity of comprehensive, long-range planning lead to stalemate and the defeat of all large infrastructure projects?

Urban planning has, at times, laid claim to the comprehensive view. Yet planning's eclectic methods and broad perspective have weakened its impact in rough battles over urban policy, where nuanced thought, concern for neglected social groups, and long-term perspectives are often liabilities in confrontations with single-minded technicians and growth coalitions.[59] Compounding this, Americans have never embraced self-conscious, theoretically sophisticated urban design. Most of their urban landscapes have been mass-produced without elaborate theories of metropolitan form.[60] Developers rarely agonize over the long-term, regional impacts of development. They focus on the internal features of individual projects, given their general location within stable, middle- or upper-class sectors of the metropolitan area. Within the complex apparatus of this growth machine, the exacting strictures of urban design are just sand in the gears.[61]

The era of urban freeway building exposed persistent weaknesses in the urban development process. Today, despite some fragile bridges, the different professions responsible for shaping the built environment still speak different languages. At times they work at cross purposes. Urban design is often eclipsed by the single-minded concern with traffic movement, two-dimensional land-use planning, or architectural showmanship. Engineers are pressured to achieve functional efficiency, planners to referee land-use conflicts, and architects and landscape architects to satisfy their immediate clients. The professions responsible for the built environment lack a coherent theory of good city form, although there is an extensive literature on the design of urban fragments. In the absence of such a theory, the vacuum will be filled with one-sided urban landscapes that fall far short of what a city should be.

SECTION 3

THE FEDERAL PRESENCE IN PLANNING

CHAPTER 12

Roots of the "Renaissance"

Federal Incentives to Urban Planning, 1941 to 1948

THOMAS W. HANCHETT

Mel Scott's comprehensive history of planning, American City Planning since 1890 *(Berkeley: University of California Press, 1969), regards the World War II era as one that witnessed a "nationwide renaissance in city planning." John F. Bauman's "Visions of a Post-War City," in Donald A. Krueckeberg, ed.,* Introduction to Planning History in the United States *(New Brunswick, N.J.: Rutgers University Center for Urban Policy Research, 1983), shows that this renaissance offered two contrasting objectives for planning the postwar city: one focusing on the needs of urban slum dwellers and the other concentrating on redeveloping the commercial core. This latter perspective, pressed by downtown business interests, won*

Reprinted from *Journal of the American Planning Association* 60 (1994): 197–208 by permission of the *Journal of the American Planning Association.*

out in the struggle to shape an urban renewal program in the 1949 federal housing act. The lucrative federal financial incentives of the urban renewal program succeeded in persuading conservative local governments to expand their planning function during the 1940s.

Thomas Hanchett's study of the conservative New South city of Charlotte, North Carolina, demonstrates this point. Although city leaders enthusiastically embraced planning in the pre–World War I era, the interwar decades saw that enthusiasm wane. Subsequently, North Carolina's local planning boards multiplied from twelve in the 1930s to more than one hundred by the late 1940s, as a host of federal programs, most of them related to the war effort, broke down local resistance to planning. The crowning jewel of Charlotte's new planning initiatives, the city's 1949 master plan, revealed a critical shortcoming in the planning renaissance, however. Like so many plans of its vintage, it represented a simple project list and failed to provide a unified vision to guide the city's future development. The most serious omission, Hanchett points out, was attention to the city's growing social concerns.

For an assessment of the pre-1940s city planning movement in the South, see Blaine A. Brownell, "The Commercial-Civic Elite and City Planning in Atlanta, Memphis, and New Orleans in the 1920s," Journal of Southern History 41 *(Aug. 1975): 339–68, and Christopher Silver, "Urban Planning in the New South,"* Journal of Planning Literature 2 *(Autumn 1987): 371–83. Other case studies of local planning that provide a useful counterpoint to Charlotte include Carl Abbott,* Portland *(Lincoln: University of Nebraska Press, 1983); John F. Bauman,* Public Housing, Race, and Renewal *(Philadelphia: Temple University Press, 1987); Robert Fairbanks,* Making Better Citizens *(Urbana: University of Illinois Press, 1988); Christopher Silver,* Twentieth-Century Richmond *(Knoxville: University of Tennessee Press, 1984); and Margaret Ripley Wolfe,* Kingsport, Tennessee *(Lexington: University Press of Kentucky, 1987).* EDITORS

One of the most active, but least examined, periods in the development of American planning is the 1940s. During the early and middle years of the World War II decade, a remarkable enthusiasm for urban planning swept the United States. "It is probably no exaggeration to say that next to war production, city planning was the most popular homefront activity during the year [1944]," announced the *Municipal Year Book.* "Hundreds of new planning agencies were set up in cities and towns all over the country."[1] The planning boom continued past the war's end, reaching something of a high point around 1946—"undoubtedly," according to the *Year Book,* "the best year city planning has ever known in this country."[2] Such contemporary observations have been corroborated by historians such as Carl Abbott, Christopher Silver, Kay Haire Huggins, and Mel Scott.[3] In Scott's words, the period beginning about 1942 constituted "a nationwide renaissance in city planning."[4]

Scholars have assumed that this renaissance resulted from functional necessities and local political currents. They argue that cities felt the need to plan in order to meet the considerable requirements of the war effort, which drew thousands of new factory workers into some urban centers.[5] City administrators also feared the specter of a postwar depression such as had followed World War I, if they did not plan a smooth transition to peacetime production.[6] Some historians also describe a "neoprogressive resurgence" at the local level in American cities during these years, which created a political climate more conducive to activist government.[7]

These explanations are consonant with the widely accepted notion that the federal government did little for city planning in the years between the New Deal and the Wagner-Ellender-Taft Housing Act of 1949. Mel Scott, Phillip Funigiello, and others portray the mid-1940s as a nadir of federal support for urban planning.[8] Looking largely at the actions of Congress, they stress the discontinuation of the National Resources Planning Board (NRPB), the New Deal agency that had held forth the promise of nationally centralized planning. They also emphasize the many defeats suffered by the planning legislation that would eventually emerge after 1949 as urban renewal. About the only influence that Washington exercised over urban planning in the 1940s, they suggest, was through the how-to publications distributed by the short-lived NRPB.

Although functional needs and local political climate undoubtedly did contribute to the planning renaissance, close examination will show that federal incentives in fact played a key role. During the early and mid-1940s, a host of programs instituted by Washington quietly prodded localities to plan.[9] Some of the programs, particularly Federal Housing Administration (FHA) mortgage insurance and Federal Highway Act funding for urban roads, are familiar, though their impact on city planning is not well known. Other war-era programs, such as the Lanham Act with its grants for community facilities, and the War Mobilization and Reconversion Act with its financial assistance to local planning bodies, are less familiar. Seemingly unrelated federal activities, from the rationing of building materials to the regulation of airline routes, also had the effect of encouraging cities to draw up planning documents. Together, the roster of programs forged new local coalitions in favor of municipal involvement in urban development. Because business leaders, civic boosters, and real estate developers realized that such actions would bring federal largess, they pushed city governments to step up planning and zoning work. This national phenomenon, and its workings in one particular municipality, the city of Charlotte, North Carolina, are the subject of this chapter.

World War II as a Spur to Local Planning

Many of the federal incentives to urban planning in the 1940s came as part of the effort to gear the country up for World War II. The Lanham Act stands as a prime example. Congress passed the Lanham Act in 1940 initially as a military housing measure, to fund the building of federally owned housing at military bases and at key industrial sites. In June of 1941, however, President Franklin Delano Roosevelt signed an amendment to the Lanham Act allocating $150 million to construct "community facilities" for defense workers.[10] These public works grants could be used anywhere that war-related activities were taking place—which meant nearly everywhere in the United States.

Roots of the "Renaissance"

Between 1941 and 1946, the Lanham Act funded some four thousand public works projects in cities and towns throughout the country. These included 1,149 schools, 905 water and sewer facilities, 874 hospitals, 776 recreation facilities, 160 fire and police stations, 90 child care facilities, and 86 street and highway projects.[11] Some, typically those facilities that served federal installations, were constructed entirely with federal money. In more than half of the projects, though, the local government made a contribution. In those cases, which accounted for 61 percent of the grants, the municipality received title to the completed project.[12]

Mayors welcomed the Lanham Act as the best thing since the New Deal's public works grants, but they found that the application process carried more stringent requirements. The Public Works Administration (PWA) and Works Progress Administration (WPA) of the 1930s had represented Washington's first serious forays into funding local projects. The primary goal of both the PWA and WPA was to do some economic "pump-priming" and put people to work. Consequently federal officials approved almost any project if it spent money and promised high employment. With the Lanham Act, grant rules became stiffer. Mayors now needed to prepare planning documents to demonstrate that their localities urgently required particular public works, and they had to show how the facilities would serve industries and workers.

To help municipalities meet these requirements, Congress eventually added a sister program explicitly designed to underwrite planning. The War Mobilization and Reconversion Act signed in 1944 authorized loans to help states and cities draw up public works plans. Such plans would assist with wartime grant projects and also aid in the transition back to a civilian economy, according to an agency report. "By putting the plans into operation 'when the extra-ordinary private demands [for construction] begin to run out,'" the report explained, "it should be possible to contribute substantially to the stabilization of the construction industry, an important sector of the American economy, and provide much useful employment at a time when it may be badly needed."[13]

During its short life, the Reconversion Act underwrote planning in thousands of communities. Over a period of a little more than three years, staffers approved a whopping 7,338 "applications for repayable planning advances," making more than $61 million in loans to states and cities.[14] The loans proved so popular with local governments that the Federal Works Agency began to hope that the program might continue even after economic recovery from World War II was complete. Congress, however, held with its original intent and terminated funding in 1947.[15]

At the same time that the Lanham Act and Reconversion Act promoted planning of "community facilities," another war-related program quietly encouraged planning for both public works and housing. In April 1942 the U.S. War Production Board added building materials to its list of rationed items, along with gasoline, tires, and consumer foodstuffs. Conservation Order L-41 put virtually all civilian construction, public and private, under federal control. As one government report stated dramatically, "Decisions to build houses or not to build houses became war decisions."[16]

A consortium of federal agencies carried out the program for rationing building materials, and it explicitly made local planning a main requirement for getting supplies. The War Production Board decided what fractions of the nation's building materials stock could be devoted to particular uses. Once those basic figures were set, the National Housing Agency (NHA) and the Federal Housing Administration took over the task of specifying which communities would get what. The NHA and FHA officials based their decisions on planning documents submitted by local governments. "The important thing at this stage of the game," emphasized the NHA's 1943 annual report, "is to get the localities to . . . lay plans now for getting better housing for better living through better neighborhoods, and to encourage them to think of total housing need in an area so that the parts of their local goals will fit together and make sense."[17]

Rationed building materials went largely for federally owned defense projects at first, but permitted uses gradually expanded over the course of the war. As pressing demands were filled, supplies became available for local public works. Mayors found they could win allocations if they submitted documents demonstrating that a city school or sewer plant would serve war workers. By the last months of the war, scarcities eased to such an extent that the NHA began to release supplies "to meet housing needs that [had] piled up in congested areas and which were impeding war production."[18] Developers' ears perked up. Since nearly all urban areas had some military manufacturing, virtually every city in the country could qualify. In all, the NHA authorized more than thirty thousand units of this civilian "H-2" housing during 1944 and 1945. The allocations were parceled out in small amounts—two hundred houses to this community, five hundred to that one—encouraging hundreds of communities to submit the necessary planning documents.[19]

Nondefense Incentives to Local Planning in the 1940s

Complementing these various wartime initiatives were a number of nondefense programs that offered additional incentives for local planning. Two Washington agencies, the Public Roads Administration and the new Civil Aeronautics Board, focused on urban transportation. The FHA, meanwhile, implemented regulations that encouraged cities to draw up land-use plans and corollary documents including subdivision regulations and zoning ordinances.

For American cities, perhaps the most important transportation initiative from Washington in the 1940s was the Federal Aid Highway Act of 1944.[20] This legislation would subsequently be overshadowed by the Highway Act of 1956, which created America's interstate expressway system. The 1944 act, though smaller, nonetheless stands as a landmark in urban transportation. Federal money had been flowing for highway construction since 1916, and planning dollars had been available to states since 1935. But for cities, the 1944 act represented a "new departure in Federal high-

FIGURE 12.1. Charlotte, North Carolina, was one of fifty cities that received urban planning assistance under the Federal Highway Act of 1944.
One result of the federal help was a new six-lane "cross-town boulevard,"
opened in 1949 as Independence Boulevard. Photograph c. 1960. Courtesy: Robinson-Spangler Carolina Room, The Public Library of Charlotte &
Mecklenburg County.

way legislation," in the words of officials at the Public Roads Administration. Over a three-year period it earmarked $125 million specif-
ically for urban roads, making possible "for the first time with
federal aid the correction of highway defects in the cities which now
constitute the most troublesome traffic bottlenecks" (figure 12.1).[21]

The 1944 act specifically set aside money for planning. "Comprehensive surveys of traffic needs in urban areas, hitherto an
almost untouched area, have been inaugurated," an agency report
announced.[22] Much of the actual work was carried out in Washington, but when possible the feds sought to bolster local planning
agencies, making it a policy to "delegate to cities and counties the
planning and design work on federal-aid jobs wherever adequate

staff is available."[23] During its first two years, the program helped initiate or conduct surveys in fifty metropolitan areas all over the United States, ranging from such big cities as St. Louis and Denver to small communities including Ottumwa, Iowa, and Charlotte, North Carolina.[24]

Even as Washington inaugurated aid to urban highway planning, another federal program was having the effect of encouraging planning for air transportation. Across the nation, the construction of urban airports had received a boost from the PWA grant program of the late 1930s. To cope with the mushrooming number of airfields, the newly created Civil Aeronautics Board (CAB) set up an elaborate hearing process to award airline routes.[25] Beginning in 1938, an airline company seeking a route had to submit briefs to the CAB demonstrating service needs and estimating the number of passengers likely to board at each stop.

Mayors who desired additional air service for their cities discovered that chances improved if they filed supporting documents with the Civil Aeronautics Board in the airlines' behalf. One such filing in 1944 included data on "population, industrial trends, manufacturing output, banks and bank clearings, wholesale and retail sales, railway and bus transportation, rainfall, highway facilities, distribution center, hotel registration and dozens of other sets of facts and figures, including present air transport services."[26] The preparation of such reports not only involved cities in air transportation planning, but also made mayors assemble the sort of data, maps, and charts that would form the foundation of a full-scale city plan.

Along with promoting the planning of highways and airports, federal incentives pushed local governments to take on land-use issues. The chief agency in this effort was the Federal Housing Administration. Founded in 1934 as part of the New Deal, the FHA sought to aid the American housing industry by underwriting mortgage insurance for homebuyers. Historians have long recognized that FHA mortgage policy spurred the rapid suburbanization that reshaped American cities beginning in the late 1940s. Recently, historians have begun to document other far-reaching side effects of FHA policies, from the "red-lining" of America's inner cities to the growing dominance of large-scale "community builders" over the housing industry.[27] The agency, it is becoming clear, also exercised considerable influence over urban planning and land-use regulation.

The *FHA Underwriting Manual,* first published in the late 1930s, stated that the administration would use eight criteria in deciding whether to back mortgages in a particular neighborhood:

1. relative economic stability (weighted 40 percent)
2. protection from adverse influences (20 percent)
3. freedom from special hazards (5 percent)
4. adequacy of civic, social, and commercial centers (5 percent)
5. adequacy of transportation (10 percent)
6. sufficiency of utilities and conveniences (5 percent)
7. level of taxes and special assessments (5 percent)
8. appeal (10 percent)[28]

The most insurable communities were those in which local laws and planning procedures helped guarantee "relative economic stability," "protection from adverse influences," "adequacy of transportation," and the rest. The administration's 1938 *Circular No. 5: SUBDIVISION STANDARDS for the Insurance of Mortgages on Properties Located in Undeveloped Subdivisions,* for example, specifically included zoning and subdivision regulations among its "Minimum Requirements."[29] Although technically it could not mandate local ordinances, the FHA emphasized that its loan evaluators would "insist upon the observance of rational principles of development in those areas in which insured mortgages are desired."[30]

A pair of defense-related events in 1942 and 1944 sharply increased the impact of these FHA "recommendations." The fact that the FHA played a key role in administering building materials rationing starting in 1942 meant that most of America's residential construction came under its purview for the duration of the war. Between 1942 and 1945, well over half of the new houses in the country were built with FHA-insured mortgages.[31] Real estate men began in earnest to press municipalities to set up planning boards and enact the necessary laws.

The pressure was stepped up in 1944. In that year, the Veterans Administration (VA) instituted its generous mortgage-insurance plan, which allowed returning GIs to borrow the entire price of a house (up to $2,000) with no down payment. Though administered separately, the VA effort was closely tied to the FHA program. Nearly a fifth of the 2.1 million loans insured during the first five years of the VA effort were second mortgages supplementing an FHA first mortgage.[32] With tens of thousands of potential VA/FHA sales at stake, builders all over the United States lobbied their local elected officials to put planning and zoning and subdivision regulations swiftly into place.

One City's Experience

Before this roster of federal incentives set the stage for the American planning "renaissance" of the 1940s, the community of Charlotte, North Carolina, had shied away from anything resembling a city plan. The Queen City was one of a number of "New South" railroad towns that had blossomed in the Dixie upcountry following the Civil War. Charlotte grew as a wholesale and banking hub for the burgeoning Southern textile belt, a manufacturing region that covered the Carolina piedmont and extended into Virginia and Georgia. By 1940 the town ranked as the largest urban place in North and South Carolina, with 100,899 people.[33] Like many midsized cities, especially in the South, Charlotte proudly maintained a tradition of minimal local government. Throughout the early decades of the twentieth century, civic leaders and real estate men alike actively opposed the notion that municipal government should be involved in planning.

That opposition came notwithstanding the fact that Charlotte had been an early leader in the South in the practice of neighborhood design. During the 1910s two local developers hired the famed Olmsted Brothers and their noted Boston competitor John Nolen to plan the elegant naturalistic Dilworth and Myers Park suburbs. Nolen's protégé, Earle Sumner Draper, stayed on in Charlotte to become the first professionally trained planner resident in the Southeast.[34] Although Charlotte's businessmen liked the seclusion of winding residential avenues, they showed a strong antipathy to schemes that involved public expenditure or regulation. In 1917 one influential citizen managed to talk the Chamber of Commerce into hiring John Nolen to conduct a "Civic Survey" of existing conditions, but the chamber subsequently refused to pay Nolen to expand that preliminary document into a city plan.[35] In 1930 an eager-beaver city manager tried again, bringing New Jersey consultant Herbert Swan to town to draw up a zoning map and master plan. Citizens rose up in arms, with some of the loudest objections coming from suburban developers. F. C. Abbott, "dean of Charlotte's real estate dealers," attacked zoning as "a serious damage to all property owners," and another leading developer threatened to seek a restraining order. Zoning opponents showed similar anger toward planning, applauding a public hearing speaker who declared, "These people down here are opposed to the government being grandmother to the citizens of Charlotte."[36] The city council not only shelved Swan's work before it was completed but fired the city manager for good measure.

As the 1930s drew to a close, Charlotte had no city plan or planning office. There were no zoning regulations, and no governmental involvement in housing. Local officials were so reluctant to take a hand in development that the city possessed only the most rudimentary of building codes, regulating little more than basic fire safety, and exerting no control over such things as subdivision creation, street layout, or even plumbing in existing buildings.

The first stirrings of change in Charlotte came in the late 1930s and early 1940s, as a result of initiatives begun under the New Deal. The Wagner-Steagall Act—passed by Congress in 1937 as America's first major federal housing legislation—offered loans to cities to build public housing. In Charlotte, the local Business and Professional Women's Club directed an exposé of slum conditions, which succeeded in convincing city fathers to construct two Wagner-Steagall housing projects in 1940.[37] The effort had two important side effects. For one thing, Charlotte conducted its first survey of housing conditions and discovered that nearly one-fifth of the city's housing stock was seriously substandard.[38] For another, the newspaper photos and survey figures began to impress Charlotte voters with the need for a more activist government. In 1941 a candidate named Herbert Baxter jumped into the mayor's race promising energetic progressive leadership, a marked contrast to his opponent's traditional minimal-government platform. The contest itself showed that change was in the air; normally Charlotte's political "kingmakers" anointed a candidate who ran unopposed. Baxter lost the election by a narrow margin, but soon events at the national level would tip things in his favor.[39]

In December 1941 the United States entered World War II. For a handful of Southern cities—particularly the naval centers of Norfolk and Mobile—the conflict meant hard times on the homefront as municipalities struggled to cope with the deluge of newcomers who poured in seeking work in defense plants.[40] To most towns, though, including Charlotte, the war was more an economic blessing than a curse. The feds enlarged Charlotte's municipal airport as Morris Field, a small airbase. An abandoned Ford Motor Company plant became a bustling Army Quartermaster Depot. United States Rubber built a large facility south of town to assemble shells for navy guns.[41] The three installations, plus the defense contracts secured by local manufacturers, never overwhelmed Charlotte's ability to provide services and housing. The population grew by 33 percent during the decade of the 1940s, a respectable rate of increase but one that actually fell below the city's average growth rate of 49 percent per decade during the twentieth century.

Although the war did not put much of a strain on the town, it did add momentum to the growing desire for activist—"neoprogressive"—

government. As the feds instituted new regulations and grant programs aimed at retooling the nation's economy for war work, business leaders in cities across the United States discovered that an energetic mayor could work wonders with Washington. In Charlotte, Herbert H. Baxter fit that job description perfectly. President of the posh Myers Park Country Club and a dealer in construction supplies, he enjoyed the respect of the city's conservative elite. But he was also a man with an innate enthusiasm for change, whose favorite expression became "Let's stick the needle in them and get things moving."[42] In 1943, with the national war effort in full swing, Baxter ran for mayor again and captured the election "on the promise that he would do everything possible to lead a progressive government at city hall and . . . initiate measures that [would] put Charlotte in the position at the end of the war to begin a program of improvement and expansion."[43]

In office, Mayor Baxter aggressively sought out new Washington programs and worked hard to get Charlotteans to do what was required to take advantage of them. Among Baxter's earliest actions in office was to spur the city to draw up public works plans and send them to Washington as a means of procuring rationed construction supplies to update the Charlotte sewerage disposal system and construct a new incinerator.[44] Subsequently Baxter helped win Reconversion Act money to prepare plans for new sewer lines and a disposal plant.[45] With an eye toward the Lanham Act, the mayor talked the Board of Aldermen into commissioning studies of the city's needs for new libraries and parks.[46] Baxter devoted considerable energy to getting federal rationing officials to release construction materials under the H-2 civilian housing program. The mayor secured the assistance of the U.S. Census Bureau, which conducted a careful survey of Charlotte's existing housing; Baxter then carried the study to Washington, where he lobbied successfully to win H-2 permits for 235 new houses.[47] To bring more airline service to Charlotte, Baxter assisted in the filing of briefs with the Civil Aeronautics Board.[48] When the Federal Highway Act passed in 1944, Baxter worked with state officials to ensure that Charlotte would

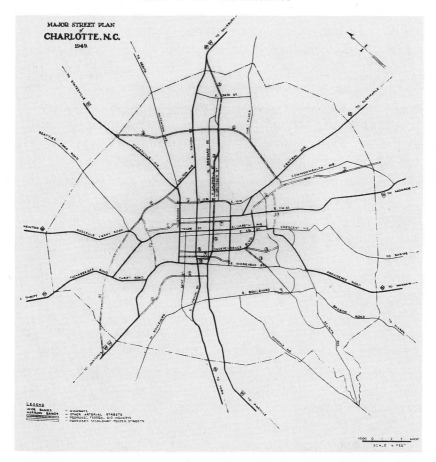

FIGURE 12.2. As a result of new federal incentives, Charlotte drew up its first thoroughfare plan in 1946: "To Support Bid for U.S. Funds," a newspaper headline explained. The street scheme was subsequently included in the city's first comprehensive planning document: *A Masterplan Outline for Charlotte* (1949). Courtesy: Robinson-Spangler Carolina Room, The Public Library of Charlotte & Mecklenburg County.

receive planning and construction assistance. One of the fruits was a joint city-state study of Charlotte traffic patterns, the town's first such effort.[49] Soon after, the city hired a local engineer to draw up Charlotte's first thoroughfare plan, "To Support Bid for U.S. Funds," a newspaper headline explained (figure 12.2).[50]

Because they realized that such documents could bring federal dollars, Charlotte business leaders and civic boosters began looking favorably on the notion of municipal planning. In 1943 the Charlotte Chamber of Commerce formed a committee to consider the matter, and the following spring it issued a report calling for a "postwar planning" effort in the city.[51] "Unless Charlotte takes such action," the report cautioned, "this city may find itself at a disadvantage [alongside competing cities] when the war is ended and the period of postwar development begins."[52] The chamber report focused largely on projects that were becoming eligible for federal dollars—public works, transportation, parks, schools, libraries, and health facilities. "We can hold our own . . . without assistance," said the chamber, acknowledging the position of many business conservatives. But, the report argued, if "the Federal Government should appropriate funds for all and sundry projects, let us have plans for worthwhile projects ready."[53]

Initially, the Chamber of Commerce assumed that it, not the city, would handle this planning. In the past, chambers had acted as planning bodies in many municipalities, and indeed it had been the Charlotte chamber that had sponsored the aborted John Nolen planning effort back in 1917.[54] The notion fit well into Charlotte's tradition of minimalist government. But with the welter of new federal programs requiring attention, and with the lure of federal planning funds available to municipalities through the Reconversion Act, even conservative businessmen began to concede that a private agency could not do the job. Late in 1944 the chamber committee submitted a second report, recommending that a city-sponsored body take over the task. On 20 December 1944 Mayor Herbert Baxter appointed the first Charlotte Planning Commission.[55]

Once created, the planning commission picked up support from an unexpected quarter: Charlotte's real estate men. Two circumstances brought these former opponents into the fold. One was the developers' desire to get the city into compliance with FHA/VA underwriting regulations. The other was the announcement that Mayor Baxter might soon apply for a second round of federal public housing. Developers feared public housing as unfair competition with their lucrative rental market; planning might offer strategies to stave off that threat to private enterprise. In February 1945 the Charlotte Real Estate Board put forth its own proposal to eradicate substandard dwellings. "These slum conditions were caused by lack of planning in the past," they asserted, executing a blithe about-face from their position of the 1930s.[56] The solution to slums was not public housing. Rather, the city planning commission should create a "standard house ordinance" mandating indoor plumbing, electric lights, and the like, and it should regulate the lay-out of new subdivisions to prevent bad conditions in the future.[57]

Mayor Baxter welcomed the powerful real estate men into his planning coalition. He dropped the public housing proposal and appointed a realtor and a prominent contractor to round out the new Charlotte Planning Commission.[58] The body settled into its work, taking over the execution of Baxter's library, park, and transportation initiatives. In accordance with the 1944 Chamber of Commerce report, the commission also worked to establish recreation centers for returning servicemen and build a YMCA for the city's Black population. The bulk of the commission's time, though, turned out to be taken up with housing and land-use matters—things that the chamber report had never mentioned.

Indeed, the notable achievements of the Charlotte Planning Commission during its first three years all sprang from FHA requirements. In 1945 the commission created a "standard house" ordinance for the city. Despite the talk about ending slum conditions, it covered only new construction, helping to guarantee "freedom from adverse influences" in the suburban neighborhoods where developers sought FHA and VA mortgages.[59] In 1946 the commission approved a subdivision ordinance, which fulfilled FHA recommendations by establishing minimum street widths and lot sizes in new developments and setting up a review process to ensure compliance.[60] In 1947 the planning commission fulfilled another major FHA requirement when it wrote Charlotte's first zoning ordinance.[61] The accomplishments showed the influence of the Real

Estate Board and, even more so, the power of federal incentives in shaping urban planning.

By the end of the 1940s Charlotte could boast most of the hallmarks of progressive planning. The city had a zoning board and a subdivision ordinance. It at last possessed a building code that mandated not just fire-safe but habitable dwellings. A busy planning commission was about to hire a professional director, and work was under way on *A Master Plan Outline for Charlotte,* the town's first comprehensive plan.[62] The document clearly showed the effects of incentives offered by Washington during the decade. Sections on sewer and water needs came out of work begun in order to get rationed building materials and continued under the Reconversion Act. Pages on parks and libraries were drawn from the studies inspired by the Lanham Act. The influence of the Civil Aeronautics Board was evident in sketches for airport improvements, while the 1944 Highway Act and the FHA's mandate for suburban "adequacy of transportation" shaped the maps depicting a comprehensive thoroughfare system. In barely ten years' time, a city that had once shunned planning had come to embrace the notion that local government should take an active role in guiding development.

A Boom in Municipal Planning

A similar enthusiasm for planning took hold simultaneously in hundreds of localities across the United States. At the start of the 1940s most of the nation's larger cities claimed to have planning and zoning bodies, but many of these were in name only. After a period of popularity in the 1920s, many citizen planning groups had ceased to function. Those towns claiming to have a planner on staff often simply added such duties to the job description of an already busy engineer or building inspector. Kenneth Schellie, director of the Indiana Economic Council, summarized the situation in his home state, and by extension in many others: "City planning and zoning acts have been on the state law books since 1921; the county planning enabling act since 1935, and yet it is difficult, if not impossible to point to any municipality or county which has made any real progress in planning action."[63] Indeed, a survey published in 1942 by the International City Managers Association showed that fully half the cities in the United States had spent nothing on city planning during the previous year.[64] Even in America's largest metropolitan centers, outlay for planning was often minimal—San Francisco's department, for instance, consisted of just three people at the dawn of the decade, one of them a stenographer.[65]

This lethargy dissolved as Washington's planning incentives kicked in. The American Society of Planning Officials (ASPO) devoted its 1944 conference to the outpouring of activity in postwar planning. Profiles of twenty-four communities, ranging from New York City to Waukegan, Illinois, conveyed an air of excitement. "The war," said Frank O'Malley, director of the Boston City Planning Board, "has made planning socially acceptable."[66] Alfred Bettman, chair of the Cincinnati Planning Commission, marveled at his city council's turnabout after twenty-five years of meager funds: "Participating in the present burst of enthusiasm for what is called postwar planning, the council has appropriated $100,000 directly to the planning commission, with the promise that the appropriation will be repeated when more is needed."[67] Likewise, reported another speaker, in Toledo and surrounding Lucas County, Ohio, local planning budgets had jumped from $10,000 to $45,000. Communities that did not already have planning agencies now launched them. At the 1944 ASPO conference, Philadelphia's Robert Mitchell announced that his city was creating a new central planning office, which would soon employ thirty-four people. From Kansas, John Picton noted that "with greatly increased appropriation for planning activities in Kansas City we have assembled staff and made a start toward preparing a masterplan."[68]

The wave of enthusiasm continued through the years immediately after the war, as more and more communities moved to create planning departments or pump resources into existing ones. At ASPO's 1948 conference, for instance, Russell VanNest Black rose to report that in New Jersey, "four years ago none of the State's cities with a population of 100,000 or more had an active planning board. Now all are engaged in intensive planning programs, or are about to do so."[69] Across the country, in California, thirty-one agencies sprang up in 1947 and 1948 alone, mostly in towns and counties previously considered too small to warrant a planning office.[70] At the opposite end of the population scale, San Francisco experienced a similar "awakening." By 1948 the annual planning budget there had increased from barely $15,000 to "$126,000 for the general program, $16,000 for zoning revision, and $140,000 for the transportation plan," and the three-person office had mushroomed into a staff of twenty-six.[71] Zoning work, in particular, emerged as a major focus all over America in these years. During the half-decade following announcement of the VA mortgage program in 1944, fully 50 percent of American cities with over 10,000 population wrote new zoning ordinances.[72]

The buzz of activity heralded a new era for the planning profession. During the 1940s the day-to-day work of local planning shifted away from citizen boards, chambers of commerce, and consultants. Henceforth, most planning would be done by full-time professional planners on local government payroll. Membership in the American Society of Planning Officials rose steadily through the decade, nearly doubling in the 1940–45 period alone.[73] Perhaps the most impressive evidence of the new municipal commitment to planning came in city budgets. Back in 1936 only 39 cities had spent as much as $5,000 a year on planning, the minimum needed to support one full-time professional and a stenographer. That number climbed gradually to 57 cities in 1941, then zoomed to 110 by 1948.[74] Growth was most impressive in medium-size towns. In 1941 barely one-third of cities with 100,000 to 250,000 in population budgeted as much as $5,000 for planning. Seven years later the proportion was up to two-thirds. Overall, the total amount of money that all American towns with a population of more than 25,000 spent on planning rose from $1.2 million in 1941 to $3.8 million in 1948, an increase of 323 percent.[75]

An Incomplete Coalition

The quantity of planning activity jumped dramatically during the 1940s as localities rushed to fund planning agencies. But what of quality? What effect did this era of federal incentives have on the plans that municipalities produced?

Historians, as well as commentators in the period, have found much to criticize in the planning work of the decade.[76] Charlotte's 1949 master plan provided a case in point. For all its handsome drawings, it was more a project list than a unified plan. It said nothing about such matters as public transportation or creating decent housing for the poor. The document offered no overarching vision of the city's future, of how Charlotte might become a better place for all its citizens to live. Such shortcomings were typical of planning work nationwide during the 1940s. Most urban plans of the decade were "narrow in conception and results," a "pragmatic postwar planning with active business participation . . . rather than planning for social betterment."[77]

The reason for the weaknesses as well as the strengths that characterized American urban planning in the 1940s can be found in the federal incentives that spurred this period of growth. The new programs lured mayors, boosters, businessmen, and real estate developers to the planning table by offering juicy possibilities for economic gain. Responding to the incentives, local movers and shakers forged coalitions that proved extremely effective in making planning a municipal priority. Washington's actions, in short, were geared precisely toward "active business participation."

The incentives put the planning focus on new highways, suburban subdivisions, and public works, not on broader "social betterment." Federal programs contained little if anything that encouraged businessmen to consider the interests of citizens who stood outside the economic power structure. In Charlotte, Black Bishop Buford G. Gordon angrily noted the imbalance soon after the city planning commission began its work: "It is evident, from the published proposals and from the organizational structure of those sponsoring the post-war plannings for Charlotte, that the post-war world will be the conservation and extension of the exact pattern, only enlarged, of the present world order, with its . . . undemocratic customs and traditions."[78]

Such criticisms would grow louder during the era of urban renewal and interstate highway construction in the 1950s and 1960s. The narrow planning coalitions assembled during the 1940s in America's towns and cities stood ready to control the local use of this gushing stream of federal dollars. Only much later, in response to the destruction often wrought by these mammoth plans, would Washington take steps to mandate full "citizen participation" in planning—which entailed public hearings and consultation with affected residents.[79] In many respects, the requirements for citizen participation that came in the 1960s and 1970s would finally complete the transformation of local planning begun a generation earlier by the federal incentives of the 1940s.

CHAPTER 13

World War II and Urban California

City Planning and the Transformation Hypothesis

ROGER W. LOTCHIN

In World War II and the West *(Lincoln: University of Nebraska Press, 1990) and* The American West Transformed *(Bloomington: Indiana University Press, 1985), historian Gerald D. Nash argued that the war played a powerful role in the transformation of the western United States. Roger W. Lotchin tests this hypothesis by examining the history of wartime planning in several California cities to determine "the relationship of war to urban society as a whole." To examine this question, Lotchin consulted census data, city master plans, the reports and records of planning commissions and associations and chambers of commerce, federal government documents, and contemporary published reports of planning initiatives for the*

Reprinted from *Pacific Historical Review* 62 (May 1993), pp. 143–71. Copyright © 1993 by the Pacific Coast Branch of the American Historical Association.

cities of greater San Diego, Los Angeles, and San Francisco. He disputes the contention that World War II produced "a revolution, transformation, second Gold Rush, or cataclysmic change" for California city planning; the war's effects were complex and ambiguous.

"In general," Lotchin argues, "the debits to city planning [occurred] during the war itself, while the credits were banked for the future." During the conflict, both the war effort and planning took an "improvisational" form. California's municipalities were unable to gauge or to plan for population shifts stimulated by the national emergency, and planning offices were short-staffed and rushed for time. As a result, many bad decisions were made and major planning initiatives like the Reber plan in San Francisco were sidetracked or postponed. On the positive side, the war stimulated a host of transportation and infrastructure improvements needed for the defense emergency, and cities with master plans saw some of their plan's components implemented out of wartime need. The federal government tied wartime domestic spending to the preparation of plans, and the explosive growth in metropolises hosting defense industries underscored the need for planning and stimulated planning thought.

Lotchin demonstrates that postwar planning in California contrasted in important ways with the planning efforts of cities in the rest of the country. Some of the latter are chronicled in Carl Abbott's The New Urban America (Chapel Hill: University of North Carolina Press, 1981); John F. Bauman, "Visions of a Postwar City," in Krueckeberg, ed., Introduction to Planning History in the United States (1983); and Christopher Silver, "The Ordeal of City Planning in Postwar Richmond, Virginia," Journal of Urban History 10 (1983): 33–60. Rather than focusing on the provision of jobs or the prevention of postwar depression, California's cities moved quickly to protect their wartime winnings of industry and population, practicing a mode of urban planning that was booster-driven. In its dual emphasis on decentralization and redevelopment, however—problems that pitted center cities against both their own suburbs and other cities— California planning may well have set the tone for the rest of the country.

For further reading on the impact of World War II on city planning, the best sources are Gerald D. Nash, "Planning for the Postwar City," Arizona and the West 27 (1985): 99–111, and Martin Schiesl, "City Plan-

ning and the Federal Government in World War II," California History
59 (1980): 127–43. For a detailed account of some of the ways in which cities have transformed their military assets into civilian ones, see Roger
Lotchin's book, Fortress California, 1910–1961 *(New York: Oxford University Press, 1992).* EDITORS

In recent years, the topic of war and society has made considerable strides though few urban historians have yet discovered this interesting subfield. Somewhat surprisingly, however, the field of war and society has witnessed considerable debate. John U. Nef gave the classic modern voice to the argument that war is not essential to societies in his 1952 book *War and Human Progress.*[1] On the contrary, the impact of war would seem to be overwhelmingly negative. One has only to read of the street fighting in Stalingrad in 1942–43 to get a glimpse of the dire physical destruction that war can wreak on cities.

Yet some scholars do link war and human progress. William McNeill is perhaps the most notable among them. In *The Pursuit of Power: Technology, Armed Force, and Society since A.D. 1000,* McNeill repeatedly emphasizes the beneficence of military influences on western societies. Although he speaks of the moral "ambivalence" of war, in case after case he found the origins of modern, and generally useful, practices, techniques, and technologies in the art of war. Sociologists posited this view even earlier.[2]

War and Progress: A Theory

A vigorous American proponent of this view is Gerald Nash, who argues that World War II profoundly transformed the West, although it was but one of several forces involved in the West's development. The war, Nash says, played the crucial role of an initiator. It triggered monumental changes in western geography, stimulated cities, crystallized culture, and reversed the transit of civilization. Some historians have called the war a "Second Gold Rush"; others have referred to it as a revolution, an unprecedented change, a "great and cataclysmic" change, a disruption, and an upheaval. Looking at the effects of the conflict on his own city, the postwar mayor of San Diego agreed that the conflict had brought a "hurricane of change."[3]

War and urbanization are both hyperdeveloped in the American West, and therefore their relationship begs for analysis. A bit of this analysis has occurred of late, but much of it is fragmentary in nature, rather than devoted to uncovering the relationship of war to urban society as a whole. To sharpen the point still more, war and urbanism have been two of the most important continuities in human history. Both have survived what are considered epochal changes in human culture. We need no reminder of the prevalence of wars, but there also seems to be an "iron law of urbanization" working in the history of Western civilization. In other words, war has been a major continuity in history, but so has urbanization.

Thus one would do well to consider the history of city planning in California during World War II in this larger context of the literature of war and human progress.[4] The California experience suggests that the war benefited city planning somewhat, but that it did not create for city planning a revolution, transformation, second Gold Rush, or cataclysmic change. Yet neither did war badly damage the profession, as it did the physical structures and social life of great cities like Hiroshima, Tokyo, London, Dresden, and Stalingrad. In general, it had a mixed effect, with the debits to city planning occurring during the war itself, while the credits were banked for the future.

Limited Planning in Wartime California

In some ways, World War II greatly discouraged planning of any kind. Although city planners are usually meticulous about population matters, especially those regarding density, they were completely overwhelmed by the population explosion that hit California's cities in the 1940s. San Diego's population increased by 64 percent, from roughly 203,341 to 334,387, San Francisco's from 634,536 to 775,357, and Los Angeles' from 1.5 million to 2.0 million. The greatest population change occurred in the suburbs at the periphery of California's cities. Suburban counties like Solano, Marin, and Contra Costa registered the largest percentage gains; the suburb of Richmond, for example, grew from 23,642 to 99,545 in the 1940s.[5] Thus the greatest population change occurred precisely where the planning expertise and experience were thinnest.[6] In addition, metropolitan governmental fragmentation limited the influence that the bigger cities could have on the suburban planning process.[7]

This change was not just large. It was also rapid, unpredictable, and antithetical to a planning process. New military bases, headquarters, housing, shipyards, and airplane factories had to be carved out of an urban landscape on demand (figure 13.1). Shipbuilders constructed extensive yards in nine months or less, which was far faster than it would ordinarily have taken to formulate plans and secure their approval. Since the military effort itself was spontaneous and improvisational, planning activities for cities were bound to be the same. Zoning variances and building code relaxations were resented by planners, but had to be accepted.[8] Even a representative of the CIO and member of the California Housing and Planning Association like Paul Pinsky observed that "war housing is solely a production problem. . . . Considerations of architecture (flat roofs vs. pitched, etc.) or postwar planning should be of little or no concern."[9] It is little wonder that the decisions made often created more problems than they solved. In San Diego, the government built 17,000 public housing units where there were "no sewers, no utilities, no shopping district[s], no schools, and no transportation."[10] Richmond, Vallejo, and San Francisco were given equally difficult assignments and could do as little about them. Some of this building occurred even before the war. As one Bay area civil defense official put it, "Whole new towns are springing up, a thousand

FIGURE 13.1. Instant war housing under construction, 1942. Courtesy: Whittington Collection, Huntington Library, San Marino, California.

houses at a clip, where yesterday were empty fields, and where still today there are no provision for sewers, playgrounds, fire and police protection, hospital facilities, and all the other local services."[11] In general, the war displaced social housing with temporary war housing, often poorly built and badly sited (figure 13.2).

It was difficult for local governments to plan anything during the war because city workers were already laboring under extra burdens. Governments lost many experienced workers either to the draft or to the higher-wage defense industries. As the Los Angeles County Regional Planning Commission put it, "The inability to secure a full quota of experienced planning personnel to replace our previous losses has definitely retarded this year's [1944–45] program."[12] Few cities in Los Angeles County passed even the most

FIGURE 13.2. Wartime homemaking. A "war-wife" in front of her war-constructed house. Courtesy: Whittington Collection, Huntington Library, San Marino, California.

fundamental planning legislation, such as basic zoning, basic planning, or land subdivision ordinances between 1942 and 1945. Hardly any zoning and planning ordinances were even revised. In most cases, land subdivision ordinances did not exist, and only two were passed by the forty-five cities of Los Angeles County in World War II.[13] As table 13.1 indicates, Los Angeles City had the same experience.

Between 1941 and mid-1945 planning legislation came to a virtual halt; it issued in volume in 1940–41 and again in mid-1945 through 1946, but virtually ceased in between. The progress of planning legislation in Long Beach was essentially the same. Besides conscripting planners, engineers, architects, draftsmen, and others with planning skills, the war loaded everyone else down with extra

TABLE 13.1. Progress Chart: City of Los Angeles Master Plan Summary—
31 December 1946

Plan	Date of adoption	Adopted by	Status
Traffic Arteries	10-9-34	City Planning Commission	Being revised
Administrative Center	12-23-40	City Planning Commission	Officially adopted
(Civic Center)	1-2-41	Regional Planning Commission	(being revised by
	1-30-41	City Council	the Civic Center
	1-30-41	County Board of Supervisors	Authority)
Original Zoning Ordinance	11-30-21	City Council	Officially adopted
Comprehensive Zoning	7-31-45	City Planning Commission	
Ordinance	6-1-46	City Council	Officially adopted
Parks and Recreation			In process of study
Shoreline Development	8-5-41	City Planning Commission	Officially adopted
	12-29-41	City Council	
Santa Monica Bay Development	8-30-45	Regional Planning Commission	
	9-4-45	City Planning Commission	Officially adopted
	9-4-45	County Board of Supervisors	
	10-16-45	City Council	
Parkways	6-23-41	City Planning Commission	Sent to Council 8-4-41
Housing			In process of study
Community Redevelopment			In process of study
Mass Transit			In process of study
Airports	10-23-40	Regional Planning Commission	Revised 9-10-45
Municipal Airport	8-15-44	City Planning Commission	
	11-6-45	City Council	Officially adopted

burdens. The understaffed police and fire departments, for example, also had to function as civil defense personnel, and this new role reduced the spare moments that might otherwise have been devoted to planning where future police and fire stations must be located or preparing reports and compiling data that a master planner might have required. Because of the rationing of building materials, all projects but war-related private subdivisions and public works were suspended. Throttling these normal additions to the cities' physical layout eliminated one more task that planners would ordinarily share. The scarcities even affected supplies and materials; the Los Angeles County Regional Planning Commission was not even able to complete and publish its reports.[14]

And with large areas of land turned over to military activities, planners found their area of influence greatly diminished. Even though the war effort had not been directed from Washington by a central plan, city planning suffered from the marked backlash against what planning there was. Although the war encouraged a spirit of sacrifice and community feeling on the local level, it also created numerous frustrations. Everyone—the business community, city officials, and ordinary citizens—constantly complained about the government at every level of activity and this only complicated the life of government workers all the more. When Mayor Fletcher Bowron of Los Angeles demanded a relaxation of tire and gas rationing because his city was horizontal and therefore people had to drive longer distances, San Franciscans demanded the same exemption because *their* city was vertical and cars therefore burned more gas climbing the hills. (They apparently did not subtract the lesser amount burned while coasting down the other side.) The Los Angeles Chamber of Commerce criticized the "long-haired" social planners for trying to impose their utopian blueprints on the western arsenals of democracy. Although city planners had little say in these decisions, they got the blame nonetheless. Thus, although not as well known, a marked backlash arose against planning alongside the cries for postwar planning.

The war also postponed consideration of the largest and perhaps the most original plan yet conceived for San Francisco Bay. As David Long has shown, from the early 1930s John Reber had evolved a plan for the entire Bay area. The "Reber Plan" called for a balance between centralization and decentralization and was striking in both its scope and its originality. The concept was certainly controversial and eventually ran afoul of both Bay area environmentalists and city boosters, but it was nonetheless an important moment in Bay area and American city planning history.[15]

Yet this setback and the others that affected planning in these years did not represent a transformation, or a cataclysmic change, or a revolution. City planning was a small enterprise in 1941 and it remained so in 1945. Nonetheless, the influence of war was not one-directional. As William McNeill warns us, history can be ambiguous, and it was in the case of California city planning.

War and the Planning Rationale

Although the war made planning difficult in the short term, it reemphasized the great need for it. As Martin Schiesl has written, planners and city officials "shared the conviction of other big city administrations that the changes brought by the war offered a better opportunity than had existed before for integrating social and economic factors into the planning process."[16] Mel Scott, historian and member of the California Housing and Planning Association, described the war's impact as chaotic. Both the pell-mell urbanization of the war effort and war-induced visions of the future drove planners and others to think seriously about postwar planning.

The war also forced cities to experiment with planning techniques that would be of some use in the future. Among the latter were both long-lasting major gains and minor ones that did not outlast the war. In order to relieve war-related traffic problems and to get people off the streets in time for the nightly dim-outs, for example, cities staggered shopping, work, and school hours. The traffic gridlock typical of urban California today suggests that these hours should have remained staggered. In San Francisco, the war helped resolve a transportation problem. For years "The City" had talked about merging the failing private transit system with the more robust Municipal Line. Still, no progress occurred until the war: the merger finally took place in 1944. Vallejo also took over its private transit in 1944.[17]

The war also improved the transportation system of Los Angeles and brought it several airports, two of which came to the city as a direct result of the war. The military recycled both to the city as war surplus. San Diego received an even greater windfall. The war vastly increased the navy's demand for freshwater, but San Diego had not yet built its pipeline to the southern California Metropolitan Water District's aqueduct mouth at Riverside. The water crisis forced the navy to help finance the project in the form of an interest-free loan for the aqueduct. It is easy to see the planning importance of a guaranteed major water supply to a desert city like San Diego.[18]

Despite the pressures of the war, cities were making their first efforts at planning all over the United States. So were some California governments, which created planning boards and commissions.[19] The federal government stimulated planning by tying its wartime urban domestic spending to the preparation of plans.[20] The Bay area also witnessed some large-scale, if local and transient, planning. When the Marinship yard was built in nine months in Sausalito, just outside San Francisco, it triggered a need for nearby housing, schools, and shopping areas. Partly built by the Bechtel Corporation and run by the Marin County Housing Authority, Marin City, with its 6,000 inhabitants, materialized to meet these needs. Marin City was "outstanding among war-born developments, both in planning and in community facilities."[21] A number of the other war-housing projects were poorly sited, but otherwise well planned, and cities eventually put in the infrastructure and amenities omitted in the haste of initial construction.[22]

Unfortunately, Marinship vanished right after the war, and Marin City became an African American ghetto. In contrast, San

Diego witnessed a large-scale planning achievement that did last. Ever since 1913, San Diego had been ardently courting the navy, and its campaign finally paid off. In 1917, it created one of the first city planning commissions in the state. In 1908 John Nolen devised a first plan and came back with another in 1926. The second Nolen plan "served as the master plan for San Diego's physical development for the next eighteen years."[23] By 1930, the county had its own planning agency and the San Diego Harbor Commission had begun planning its port development as well, usually in concert with the navy.[24] As a San Diego master plan, the Nolen plan "formed the basis" for a 1938 ten-year capital improvements list. Shortly thereafter, "military necessity, war industry necessity, and the press of population made most of the projects on the 1938 public works list immediate requirements in San Diego," one postwar study explained. For example, "when the Federal Government announced it would build a waterfront highway to aid Navy traffic, the city produced, ready-made, its already formulated plans for a Harbor Drive and Harbor Drive was tailored to the city's own specifications."[25] By the war's end, master plans were springing up everywhere: San Francisco, San Diego, Los Angeles, Los Angeles County, Oakland, and Vallejo.[26]

Postwar Planning in California

Perhaps the greatest windfall for the future came at the expense of the immediate war years. Until the nineteenth century, European cities surrounded themselves with walls. The American nation-state also reserved large metropolitan areas for fortifications, bases, and factories. By the end of World War II federal reservations devoted in large part to the military ranged from 18 percent in San Francisco County to 40 percent in San Diego County.[27] This military presence kept land off the market and therefore preserved much of it as open space for later public use. These reservations were sometimes created before World War II and sometimes during it, but in either case, that conflict helped keep them out of private hands and often enlarged them. This unintended and ironic benefit of militarism has already created a large park in San Francisco out of the former Presidio.[28] Thanks to the presence of Forts Barry, Baker, and Cronkhite, it also established what amounts to a greenbelt separating the urbanized southern part of the Marin County peninsula from San Francisco.[29] Perhaps not all of these lands will revert to civilian or public control; yet the government has already recycled the Presidio, which is currently being incorporated into the national park system after various planners finish looking at it.[30]

The precious land of the Presidio, with its trees, rolling hills, bayside location, and view of the Golden Gate, had long been eyed by businessmen, anxious to create what 1940s planners called "speculative values" by turning the area into another luxury housing site. Diagonally across the city to the southeast, the nearly 1 square mile of the former Hunter's Point Naval Shipyard is about to revert directly to the city. With the current military reductions, cities up and down the California coast are planning how to recycle similar ironic assets to civilian purposes.[31] It should perhaps be emphasized that these are magnificent and rare open-space resources that long-established cities seldom have an opportunity to acquire without resorting to the torch or the wrecking ball. Chicago has a kind of greenbelt in its lakefront and forest preserves, but it is hardly part of the standard American urban environment.

The planning stimulated by the war throughout the country has been called a renaissance of city planning.[32] By 1944 and 1945, when victory seemed certain, planners and other citizens began thinking of the metropolitan implications of peace. Providing jobs, preventing another depression, and coping with war-enhanced forces of decentralization seemed to be the main postwar planning agendas. Slums, downtown blight, veteran reemployment, urban redevelopment, suburbia, and the business cycle were all important to urban California, but not overwhelmingly so. California postwar planning differed in several ways.[33]

Having contributed to winning the war, urban California now girded itself to protect its winnings. First and foremost, cities made postwar plans to keep their winnings rather than to provide jobs or prevent depression. Second, although state planning sought to consolidate and augment the gains of war, the means differed from city to city. Third, some of their postwar planning aims were uniquely military. Fourth, professional planners seem to have played a more important role there than anywhere else. Fifth, urban California's plans, although often crafted by civic-commercial elites, were community plans that included diverse groups and reached compromises rather than hegemonic solutions. Furthermore, California planning did not seem to exemplify the extreme division between the style promoted by Robert Moses and that of "liberal" planners, which existed in other places.

On occasion, city leaders suspected the worst from postwar conditions. For example, the representative of the Alhambra (outside Los Angeles) Chamber of Commerce feared a glut of some 500,000 workers in postwar southern California. Mayor Fletcher Bowron, normally the unflappable optimist and booster, also worried sometimes. Unlike Detroit, which would benefit from renewed automobile demand, his region could not expect peace to bring a comparable market to the airframe industry.[34] Still, Bowron's career as mayor reflected the booster rather than the pessimist approach, especially with the military, which he continually wooed. The San Francisco City and County Citizens' Post-War Planning Committee spoke for the optimists when it noted: "We do not subscribe to the theory that there need be any long or widespread business recession in this community." In explaining their choice of airport modernization as the number one postwar planning task, the committee noted the fiercely competitive relations between cities for basic industry. "Competition among American cities for the aviation industry already is becoming very keen," observed the committee. "New York has expended more than $50,000,000 on La Guardia Field and has begun work on Idlewylde Airport which ultimately will cost $100,000,000." Worse yet, they argued, "Los Angeles voters recently approved by a majority of more than six to one a $12,500,000 bond issue" for its Mines Field airport.[35] Every city that could afford an airport felt the same way.

The same rivalry that underlay a decentralizing issue like an airport drove centralizing issues. The idea of redeveloping San Francisco dated back to at least 1943, when the city delegation introduced a bill in the state legislature to allow rehabilitation of cities. Temporarily held up by Los Angeles representatives, the bill provided "the legal machinery by which the blighted areas of the community may be reconstructed under a master plan for the making of a greater San Francisco," explained the central business district's *Downtowner*. A greater San Francisco was expected to rid the city of the war-affected Fillmore district, which would have been a standard exercise in "Negro removal" and poor White removal, plus the creation of a world trade center. This huge trade district would house representatives of foreign interests and include a free-trade zone that would allow the manufacture and reexport of overseas goods duty-free. Thought was even given to building a monumental auditorium that could seat 20,000 persons to facilitate world trade. Some officials felt that such a center would help San Francisco become the permanent seat of the United Nations, then meeting in the San Francisco Opera House.[36]

Although Oakland did not aspire to become capital of the world, it, too, hoped for the best from the future. The fear of unemployment did not dominate its postwar plan, and, although it mentioned decentralization, the subject of redevelopment remained latent. The Oakland Postwar Planning Committee instead considered redevelopment to eliminate blight and provide parking spaces downtown, but it agreed only to investigate the possibility. Growth was the central agenda. As the committee put it, "With the expansion of our highways and freeways and other planned civic improvements, Oakland is purchasing in advance the industrial expansion and growth which make this the leading center of the New Industrial West."[37]

Perhaps the urban imperial flame burned most brightly in San Diego and San Bernardino. The California Senate Interim Committee on Economic Planning voiced the fears and aspirations of many cities in 1942 when it observed that "California is at the cross-roads in her economic program. She will either become a great industrial empire or she will become a *ghost state—a casualty of the war.*" Although San Diego's public and private postwar plans stressed the need to create new jobs, that aim was clearly subordinate to the movement for a "Greater San Diego." After all, the labor force and market created by the war could have been allowed to go back to Arkansas, Oklahoma, Louisiana, and other places; and the city could have reduced its scale of operation to prewar levels and comfortably digested its martial windfall.

Not only did the city want to keep its payrolls, it wanted to increase them. San Diego's "future has been re-cast," argued the committee; "we are on the threshold of a development within our city and county heretofore undreamed of." Unless the city planned now to keep its winnings, "these payrolls may be lost to San Diego forever. The competition for the retention or bringing in of supplementary industry will be most keen."[38] San Bernardino County, whose population had jumped 22 percent between 1940 and 1944, from 161,108 to 197,000, described this and the accompanying industrial buildup simply as "war winnings," and it was the task of postwar planning to hang onto them.[39]

Although war winnings motivated all the towns, some had uniquely military postwar plans. The goal of San Diego's postwar planning could be easily summarized: to retain the navy and to achieve economic diversification. The mayor called San Diego a victim of a "hurricane of change" brought on by the war, but there was enough tantalizing military wreckage littering the beach to convince the city that it did not need to break its ties with its military patron. As one San Diegan put it, "No expansion, whether recreational or industrial, should be planned without due regard to the needs of the navy."[40] Yet everyone knew, too, that overdependence on the navy was the source of the need for diversification.

Thus the plan included sections on stimulating agriculture, tourism, trade, and transportation.

Vallejo leaders agreed with San Diego about the navy's importance, and in any case had even less choice in the matter. The great metropolitan areas did not share the postwar problems of their expanded suburbs. Vallejo's postwar study revealed that the city possessed a flour mill, a meat packing plant, the Navy Yard at Mare Island, and no other industry. Consequently, the navy played an important role in the postwar plans of this largely working-class town. Yet the city saw the war as a way of moving beyond its near monocultural military dependence. Its efforts to cope with the war are somewhat reminiscent of the discussion of eastern planners about redevelopment, housing for the poor, land assemblage, and decentralization, but both the tone and the tactics were predicated on the war. The conflict opened new vistas, but it also created major problems for Vallejo. When the conflict ended, Vallejo was beset by numerous problems that it attributed to its overdependence on the navy. Not only did that service subject the city's economy to a boom and bust cycle, based on military conflict or preparations for it, but war housing co-opted eligible residential and industrial sites. The war had decimated city services like education. By its overdependence on the navy, the city had nothing else to turn to when peacetime forced a cutback at the Navy Yard. To make matters worse, the federal property used by the navy could not be taxed. Therefore, between the Navy Yard and the temporary war housing erected to house yard workers, the city lost both a large portion of its tax base and eligible land that could be used for permanent housing or civilian business.

In the postwar plan, housing was not treated as a right for the poor, but as a way to raise the tax base and keep what was left of the navy at the Carquinez Strait. If the temporary structures could be cleared, then new, taxable housing could be built that would allow the city to provide a level of services high enough to keep Navy Yard officers and enlisted men in Vallejo. Since 1900, Vallejo had criticized naval personnel for preferring to live in San Francisco rather than in Vallejo. The opening of Hunter's Point Naval Shipyard in World War II had also badly frightened this single-industry town. "Vallejo must also remember that the majority of the Navy officers and enlisted men would prefer to be headquartered at Hunter's Point, near San Francisco, because Vallejo lacks attractive residential and recreational facilities," admitted the town's master plan. Given that inclination, the navy might just decide that it did not need a second yard at the inconvenient and poorly situated Carquinez Strait town. Hence, the plan emphasized raising the tax base and providing homes that would secure the loyalty of the navy and the patronage of naval officers and the current commuters to the city.[41]

Vallejo wanted to rehabilitate its downtown, but not just by helping the central business district. It also favored downtown industrialization. There was a good deal of unused land at the waterfront, and the plan proposed that this space be used for industrial diversification.[42] Residents had a third strategy for coping with center-city problems. The war had produced a large migration of workers to the yard, and these camp followers were often bivouacked outside the city limits, which caused more physical problems and further restricted the tax base. If they were taken into the city limits through annexation, their housing would generate taxes in Vallejo, where the tax base was already narrow and the rates high. Even in Mare Island–Vallejo, the urge to become an imperial city was very great. As the plan noted, "It was always conceded that the San Francisco Bay Area, by virtue of its strategic location and basic facilities, could and should be the heart of this great western industrial and agricultural empire. The impact of the war has literally catapulted this region right into the very center of that future."

For Vallejo, its population increase opened up new horizons: "From a small town, Vallejo has suddenly expanded into a teeming industrial city of approximately 90,000 people," argued the plan, and even "another 40,000 if present commuters could find housing accommodations for themselves and their families in Vallejo."[43]

> For the first time since it was founded, Vallejo has a local
> population of sufficient size to justify the expansion and diver-
> sification of all of its business and industrial potentialities.
> Viewed constructively, this new population is the greatest ad-
> junct to its natural assets that it is possible to have. If it is held
> for the operation of new commercial and industrial enterprises,
> Vallejo will take its place among the most progressive and
> prosperous communities in all of northern California.[44]

But the navy was a vital component in this scheme. Long scorned
by its larger neighbors and sensitive to its own weaker position
relative to them, Vallejo now saw the opportunity to be a player in
the Darwinian competition among cities. Meanwhile Los Angeles,
San Francisco, and Oakland also courted the navy and the army, but
they did not plan their postwar existence so completely around
either.[45]

Despite their primary commitment to boosterism, California
cities differed widely as to means. San Diego and Vallejo sought to
retain the navy, but also to diversify away from its quasi-monocul-
tural economic base. Oakland, San Francisco, and Los Angeles
stressed transportation. Far from fearing the consequences of decentralization, Richmond sought to cope with the consequences of
overcentralization by ousting the federal government from its valuable city land and receiving compensation for its war sacrifices. San
Diego's plan stressed beauty as well, but Richmond was too fatigued
by war to care about aesthetics. Instead of being hurt by decentralization away from the central city, Los Angeles County sought to
benefit from it. To this end, it hoped to mold land use and industrial,
recreation, transportation, and other patterns in advance of settlement, rather than after the population had fled.[46]

Another significant feature of the California experience is that
professional planners played an important role in postwar planning.[47] Although most of the cities opted for what Carl Abbott has
called the "ad hoc blue ribbon citizens committee of civic-
commercial elites" to formulate their final postwar plans, planners

played an important role in these committees. For example, the San Diego postwar plan was hammered out by the professional staffs of the city planning commission and a special planning staff hired to deal with postwar problems. In addition, the city hired the Philadelphia firm of Day and Zimmermann to plan for jobs in the postwar years. Their report, in turn, became the basis for an evolving master plan, itself the product of previous city planning commission studies in 1942 and 1943.[48]

San Francisco's planning commission was heavily involved in the postwar planning process. Every detail of the public works element of the final San Francisco plan was requested from the city departments, evaluated by the planning commission, and judged by the blue ribbon panel. Of course, the city government had the final voice in the process.[49] Of the twenty-two items on the final list on which the city planning commission had submitted a recommendation, the commercial-civic elite committee accepted half. In nearly every case where the two disagreed, the ad hoc committee accepted higher rather than lower financial estimates on city projects, including those for the schools, recreation, fire, police, and health departments and the public library. The committee also virtually doubled the planning commission's recommendation for the De Young Museum and the Palace of the Legion of Honor and vastly increased the appropriations for the criminal justice system, most of which were not to be spent simply on jails.[50] Oakland and the East Bay allowed enough professional planning input to convince even a skeptic like Mel Scott that "responsible citizens had come to value city planning as the most effective means of insuring a well organized city." Los Angeles City and County followed suit. They planned early and often.[51]

Although it is true that not every interest was represented, booster planning also resembled community planning. The civic-commercial elites usually led these efforts, but they consulted widely. Often their efforts were both initiated and ratified through the democratic process. Issues that pitted one city against another tended to encourage consensus, and city leaders worked at maintaining that sentiment. For example, the San Francisco postwar planning committee consulted widely before hammering out its own program. It sought advice from each of the city departments, double-checked their recommendations against those of the city planning commission, and conferred widely in the general community. Of the people singled out for special recognition in the consultation process, fourteen of thirty-seven were either elected or bureaucratic representatives of the city government (including both the planning commission and its director). Two were union men, including George Wilson, president of the San Francisco Congress of International Organizations (CIO) Council; two were representatives of the California League of Cities; two were from the San Francisco Housing and Planning Association; and one was a representative of the San Francisco Municipal Conference. Among the remaining sixteen, the committee conferred with several big businesses like Southern Pacific, Pacific Gas and Electric, and Pacific Telephone and Telegraph, but most often it sought the advice of newspapers, which made up four of the sixteen remaining participants. The committee also sought information from many community publications, including that of the Communist Party.[52] The planning process of Oakland was less broadly based, but generated popular support nonetheless. As the author of the study of Oakland at war indicates, the Left-Labor coalition, which represented Blacks, labor, migrants, and the working class in general, and incidentally included the CIO and communists, accepted the Oakland postwar public works planning program. It went even further, demanding more rapid implementation than the civic elites thought practical.[53]

The San Francisco committee recommended some $177 million worth of public improvements, which would command wide community support, including that of city planners. For example, the committee urged $20 million be allocated to its number-one priority, airport modernization. California city boosters had long discussed the economic importance of airports and expected aviation eventually to trigger another transportation revolution, comparable to that started by the automobile. They hoped to gain both transportation efficiency and economic multipliers from the airport district itself. It would create construction, house airline regional operations, feature extensive repair and overhaul, lure military and national guard units, and create an extensive payroll. These factors would in turn stimulate demand for many products and services in the surrounding communities.

Oakland, Los Angeles, and San Diego boosters also included airport modernization in their postwar plans, and both San Francisco and Los Angeles electorates ratified these decisions shortly after the war by passing bond referenda to finance airport modernization. All this would appeal to aviation, construction, and other unions; to contractors, building suppliers, engineers, insurers, and truckers; to newspapers, brokers, and bankers; to planners who favored public works to counteract the swings of the construction business cycles; to federal bureaucrats and politicians; to local city builders; and to boosters in San Mateo County, where the airport was physically located. Unlike redevelopment, this recommendation was not designed to save the downtown region, but rather to make the metropolis polycentric.

It would be a mistake to think that the war was of epochal importance in generating the specifics of these plans. The war did put the spotlight on the airport question, but even that issue had been around since the 1920s, and other public works items—like the Los Angeles freeway system, the San Diego drive for road and rail connections to Arizona, the Oakland Eastshore Freeway, San Francisco's plan for transit rehabilitation, the San Diego quest for water, and most of the other specific projects—also dated from an earlier time. Nor did the war transform planning thought in general. The war produced nothing comparable to the Garden City, New Towns, zoning, public housing, or comprehensive planning concepts of earlier eras. Catherine Bauer perhaps represented the frontiers of California planning thought, but she did not advance beyond these city planning novas of earlier years.[54] To the extent that the war induced a renaissance in planning thought, it stimulated a burst of familiar ideas.[55] In neither a programmatic nor a conceptual sense did the war establish the planning agenda for the future.[56]

To an extent, California cities reflected the same division of planning opinion symbolized by Robert Moses on one side of the spectrum and liberal planners on the other. The California Housing and Planning Association represented the liberal side of the familiar argument. The membership of that group included liberals like Melvyn Douglas, Helen Gahagan, Mel Scott, John F. Shelley, Catherine Bauer, William Wurster, John Anson Ford, Robert W. Kenney, Dr. Harry Girvetz, and labor leaders (besides Shelley) C. J. Haggerty of the American Federation of Labor and Paul G. Pinsky of the CIO.[57] They rejected several parts of the booster agenda. Catherine Bauer, Mel Scott, and others viewed competitive city planning as destructive and counterproductive. The liberals also saw housing as a tool for achieving social justice rather than progress and growth. In addition, they favored rehabilitation of neighborhoods, feared for the fate of those dispossessed by redevelopment, and urged the creation of new towns.[58] They approved of redevelopment, but some harbored a healthy skepticism about the motives behind it. Catherine Bauer, for example, interpreted redevelopment as a subsidy for downtown property owners whose properties were no longer profitable. In general, liberal planners opposed the speculative values of downtown overdevelopment.[59]

Both sides fretted about the consequences of decentralization. Liberals favored federal aid and participation in the postwar replanning process, but not just to help businessmen. Boosters were more ambivalent, favoring federal participation only when it meant subsidies with few strings attached. The Los Angeles Chamber of Commerce, in particular, clearly did not want to accept any Washington planning agendas that did not coincide with their own.[60]

Despite these differences, the two groups agreed on a surprisingly large agenda. Both favored redevelopment, and "rebuilding the slum and blighted areas of our cities after the war" was one of the principal goals of the California Housing and Planning Association.[61] Sometimes the reformers led on this issue. Despite its studies, Los Angeles had not approved a redevelopment plan by the end of 1946, San Francisco had budgeted only a small sum for it, and the Oakland postwar planners allotted redevelopment an even lower priority and *no* money. Long Beach did not even mention a redevelopment plan in its list of accomplishments for 1944–46 or among its future goals.[62] In contrast, the San Francisco section of the California Planning and Housing Association favored redevelopment strongly and for not very liberal reasons.[63] One of the few civic committees ever to balance the sexes, the six-person subcommittee recommended the destruction of the supposedly blighted Fillmore neighborhood, which was home to some 9,000 Black and 27,000 White war workers. In fact, the association was already helping remove Fillmore residents on health grounds, knowing full well that they could not find alternative housing in this arsenal of democracy. Instead of favoring the construction of more temporary housing in "The City," committee members urged San Franciscans to march into the factories in greater numbers to replace the ousted Blacks and poor Whites.[64]

Beyond this redevelopment consensus, both favored measures to create jobs, agreed on the necessity of master planning, and felt that cities could not plan simply for themselves without looking at the broader regional contexts in which they operated.[65] Scott criticized the war effort for its lack of regionalism, but the San Francisco Chamber of Commerce, newspapers, the Downtown Association, Los Angeles' Mayor Bowron, the *Los Angeles Times,* and others had long assumed the economic unity of their metropolitan areas. Regional planning per se was more of a liberal item, but both ends of the spectrum recognized the regionalism of urban development. Strikingly enough, both groups agreed on the need for municipal public works after the war. And the public works idea came straight from the National Resources Planning Board, the supposed liberal bugaboo of the business community.[66]

Moreover, both sides agreed on the necessity of using city planners to shape their cities for the postwar era. City and county planners in both Los Angeles and San Diego fashioned the postwar planning responses of their areas. L. Deming Tilton, director of planning of the city and county of San Francisco, may have best exemplified the mix between planner and booster. A representative of the National Planning Resources Board before becoming head of San Francisco planning, Tilton favored both the city efficient and a Greater San Francisco.[67] Even such a bona fide planning and housing liberal as Catherine Bauer of the University of California at Berkeley recognized the great war winnings that southern and western cities had collected. She subscribed to the popular notion that the prewar South and West were colonial economies. Bauer argued that "a better balanced economy is needed in both regions, and the war has done much to further such a balance, temporarily at least." She felt that "the national interest therefore requires that the new industrial activity in the South and West shall not only continue but must expand still further after the war."[68] The Los Angeles Chamber of Commerce could not have put it any better. And Bauer saw planning as a tool to preserve these war winnings. "The defense worker immigration can be absorbed in time to the great ultimate advantage of the West if we take strong measures to tide over the bad period of adjustment following the war," she argued. "We must take bold and even ruthless measures."[69]

Conclusion

World War II exerted an ambiguous rather than a cataclysmic influence on California city planning. War did not transform this aspect of urban society. It slowed down short-range planning to cope with the war, and then stimulated planning thought and created planning assets that might be used in the future. But this could hardly be described as a revolution. Indeed, planning had not been revolutionized by the 1960s, much less the 1940s.[70] Finally, one might ask if these findings are relevant to the larger context of postwar planning history. Were Greater San Francisco, Greater Los Angeles,

Greater San Diego, and Greater Vallejo metaphors for postwar planning elsewhere in the United States, or was the booster approach just another supposed California aberration? Historians have not yet reached a consensus on the major issues of postwar planning. Neither had contemporaries. Yet decentralization and redevelopment seem to have been the principal issues in eastern big-city, postwar planning.[71]

These issues bear more than a little resemblance to the planning style of the California imperial city. After all, both decentralization and redevelopment (recentralization), and even preservation and rehabilitation, were matters that pitted center cities against their own suburbs and other cities. California planners may not have been so eccentric after all. Perhaps they simply were more frank about their behavior or perhaps ahead of their time. "Planning is politics," explained Catherine Bauer in 1944, "but are planners politicians?" she queried dubiously. Perhaps they were better politicians than her skepticism implied. The war did not transform the planning aspect of urban society, but, depending on the outcome of further research about eastern cities, it may well be that urban California booster planners had set the pace for the rest of the country.[72]

CHAPTER 14

Federal Urban Policy and the Birth of Democratic Planning in Birmingham, Alabama, 1949 to 1974

CHARLES E. CONNERLY

*The influence of federal policy on local planning initiatives has been dealt
with in several important works in twentieth-century urban history, most
notably Mark I. Gelfand,* A Nation of Cities *(New York: Oxford University Press, 1975), Philip Funigiello,* The Challenge of Urban Liberalism
*(Knoxville: University of Tennessee Press, 1978), and Roger W. Lotchin,
ed.,* The Martial Metropolis *(New York: Praeger, 1984). Urbanization
in the Sunbelt offers a particularly compelling example of federal influence
on urban development since the early 1940s, as Carl Abbott demonstrates
in* The New Urban America *(Chapel Hill: University of North Carolina
Press, 1981 [1987]). Birmingham, Alabama, the subject of this chapter, is
atypical of the Sunbelt pattern, however, because it declined economically
and demographically while the rest of the cities in the region expanded.*

Yet, as argued in Christopher Silver, Twentieth-Century Richmond *(Knoxville: University of Tennessee Press, 1984), urban decline was exacerbated by federal programs that served to widen the urban-suburban split, although local development values as much as a national urban agenda undermined revitalization efforts.*

Charles Connerly's selection examines local planning values by paying particular attention to the emergence of citizen participation in a southern city made famous by its unrelenting opposition to the Civil Rights movement. Birmingham, Alabama, with one of the worst records in race relations in the South through the 1960s, became a pioneer in citizen-driven planning by the 1970s. Federal policy, most importantly through the Workable Program requirement of the Housing Act of 1954, provided both the carrot and the stick to engender minority participation in Birmingham planning.

Connerly contends that there was an initial cautiousness among Black leaders in Birmingham about demanding a role in local planning, owing in large part to the legacy of intimidation by anti–civil rights activists. The Model Cities Program and the federal Office of Economic Opportunity opened the door of change. By 1975 Birmingham boasted a nationally recognized citizen-participation program, the Birmingham Citizen Participation Program, that provided direct election of citizen representatives from all neighborhoods to a group that determined significant local funding and policy decisions.

Readers seeking further discussion of the Model Cities Program should consult Charles Haar, Between the Idea and the Reality *(Boston: Little, Brown, 1975). Connerly's chapter also adds an important minority perspective to the emergence of neighborhood planning. For a comprehensive study of neighborhood planning, see William M. Rohe and Lauren B. Gates,* Planning with Neighborhoods *(Chapel Hill: University of North Carolina Press, 1985). For case studies of neighborhood planning and federal initiatives in other southern cities, see Clarence N. Stone,* Economic Growth and Neighborhood Discontent *(Chapel Hill: University of North Carolina Press, 1976), and Christopher Silver, "The Changing Face of Neighborhoods in Memphis and Richmond, 1940–1985," in Randall M. Miller and George E. Pozzetta, eds.,* Shades of the Sunbelt *(Westport, Conn: Greenwood, 1988), 93–126.* EDITORS

Federal Urban Policy and Planning in Birmingham, Alabama

When political leaders in Birmingham, Alabama, adopted a citywide citizen-participation program in 1974, the city was in the forefront of community-based planning. It was among a handful of Community Development Block Grant (CDBG) jurisdictions to feature a participation program in which all citizen representatives were elected. According to a 1977 U.S. Department of Housing and Urban Development (HUD) report, of 558 entitlement jurisdictions, only ten cities, including Birmingham, had such a program.[1] More recently, a national citizen-participation study selected Birmingham's program as among the top five such programs in the nation.[2]

Birmingham, of course, is well known for its role in the Civil Rights movement. In 1956, an NAACP official proclaimed that Birmingham was "the worst city for race relations in the South." It was selected for major demonstrations in 1963 because civil rights leaders felt that the city's violent opposition to the rights of Black Americans would focus favorable attention on the Civil Rights movement.[3] Given the events of 1963, it is hard to imagine that just eleven years later, the city would lead nearly all U.S. cities in the development of a strong citizen-participation program.[4] This chapter considers how this rapid transformation took place. It also examines the impact of federal urban policy on citizen participation in Birmingham and the degree to which federal programs such as urban renewal, the War on Poverty, and Model Cities encouraged citizen participation.

The role played by the Workable Program in stimulating citizen participation in Birmingham is of particular interest. Although this program required all cities receiving assistance for urban renewal, public housing, and selected privately developed affordable housing projects to develop a work program that included citizen participation, relatively little research has been done on the program's impact, and the few conclusions reached about its impacts have been negative.[5] Gelfand barely mentions the Workable Program, but concludes that its enforcement by the federal government was "a well-known farce."[6] Rohe and Gates claim that the Workable

Program was "lax" in enforcing the citizen-participation requirements under the program.[7]

Citizen Participation before the Workable Program

When urban renewal planning in Birmingham began in 1949, the city's Black residents had almost no say in the governance and planning of their community. At that time, the city's emerging Civil Rights movement focused primarily on putting an end to racial zoning in Birmingham. This was accomplished when Black residents moved into areas designated for White occupancy and mounted a legal challenge that culminated in a 1951 Supreme Court decision invalidating Birmingham's racial zoning ordinance.[8]

The city's initial participation in the federal urban renewal program, through the Medical Center project, did nothing to enhance citizen participation in Birmingham. By 1955, when the Workable Program began, serious, meaningful citizen participation by Birmingham's Black residents would be no closer than it was before the Medical Center project.

Birmingham was a city with an unbridgeable divide between the Whites who controlled the community and the 40 percent of the city's population who were Black. No Blacks sat on the city's three-man city commission, no Blacks served on the twelve-member Birmingham Planning Board, and no Blacks were board members of the Housing Authority of the Birmingham District (HABD), the city's housing and urban renewal authority.[9] Unlike other southern cities, Birmingham did not even have any Black police officers.[10]

The city's first major planning act, a zoning statute, passed in 1926, separated the city into areas to be occupied by Blacks and Whites. A second major planning initiative, the city's federally funded public housing program, begun in the 1930s, consisted of four racially segregated developments (two White and two Black), in which about 36 percent of the residents were Black.[11] Only through the Interracial Committee did Blacks and Whites officially come together, but this was not created until 1951 by the Jefferson County Coordinating Council of Social Forces. By 1956, with racial issues stirred by the 1954 *Brown* v. *Board of Education* decision outlawing school segregation, the Community Chest and Red Cross executive committees voted to dissolve the Interracial Committee, in part because it was seen as a "campaign hazard."[12]

Thus, when the city began planning its Medical Center urban renewal project in 1949, there were no formal avenues of communication between White and Black residents of Birmingham. Nevertheless, Blacks and Whites were forced into contact by this urban renewal project, because from its inception, the Medical Center project called for the acquisition and demolition of a significant number of Black-occupied homes in what was then Birmingham's largest Black neighborhood, Southside.[13]

Planning for the Medical Center project began soon after the passage of the 1949 Housing Act created the urban renewal program.[14] The city's plan called for redeveloping a twelve-and-a-half-block area just south and west of the existing University of Alabama Medical School and included construction of new hospitals, doctors' offices, and clinics, as well as the expansion of the Medical School. This meant 615 families would have to be relocated from the area, 85 percent of whom were Black.[15]

Not surprisingly, the city's Black residents were not involved in planning the Medical Center project (figure 14.1). Only one Black, attorney Arthur D. Shores, who was vice chairman of the Interracial Committee, was identified by the HABD housing and urban renewal authority as participating in planning for the Medical Center project.[16] The urban renewal program only required one public hearing, and at that meeting, with several hundred persons in attendance, Blacks protested being uprooted from their neighborhood. Reverend John W. Goodgame Jr., a Southside Black minister, asked, "And where will we go, if you put us out? Finding housing in Birmingham is not easy for my race." Another Black minister,

FIGURE 14.1. Medical Center urban renewal site before redevelopment. This photo, taken in 1952, shows the existing Medical School in the vicinity of 20th Street and Sixth Avenue and the urban renewal area running south to 10th Avenue and west to 15th Street. From *Annual Report of the Housing Authority of the Birmingham District,* 30 June 1952. Courtesy: Birmingham Public Library, Department of Archives and Manuscripts.

Reverend J. C. Carlisle, said, "We don't want to stand in the way of progress. We just want a fair deal. We're not looking for social equality, whatever that is, we're just looking for a paved street, an electric light, adequate police protection."[17]

These concerns did not sway the city of Birmingham. The *Birmingham News,* one of the city's two White-controlled papers, editorialized that "there will be sufficient vacancies in both White and Negro housing projects to accommodate all the eligible relocated families."[18] Such was not the case, however. In its 1956

Workable Program recertification report, the city of Birmingham noted that a December 1954 survey projected that by the end of 1957, 2,744 non-White families eligible for public housing would be displaced by the city's urban renewal program and other activities, but only 1,135 of these families could be located in existing public housing. In contrast, only 561 White families eligible for public housing would be displaced, and all of them could be accommodated in the city's public housing units.[19]

With limited access to public housing, Southside Black families were at the mercy of a private housing market that gave them few choices. According to the 1950 U.S. Census, slightly less than 12 percent of metropolitan Birmingham's Black households lived in standard-quality housing.[20]

Faced with a substantial loss of Black housing in Southside, few decent housing opportunities outside of that neighborhood, and no influence on the urban renewal planning process, Birmingham Blacks had no avenue to influence public policy. Even the housing subcommittee of the Interracial Committee took no stand on the forced relocation of Blacks from Southside.[21] Consequently, Birmingham's Blacks took their case directly to the courts and to federal officials. Black property owners, including three Black churches, filed suit, arguing that the city's eminent domain powers could not be used to obtain private property because parts of the urban renewal project were planned for private development rather than for a public purpose.[22] Even if this suit succeeded in derailing Birmingham's urban renewal efforts (which it did not), it would not have affected the 90 percent of Black households slated for relocation who were renters.[23]

Consequently, in May 1953 the Birmingham branch of the National Association for the Advancement of Colored People (NAACP), through the NAACP Washington Bureau, wrote Albert M. Cole, administrator for the Housing and Home Finance Administration (HHFA) under the Eisenhower administration, urging no federal assistance unless Birmingham agreed to support equal access to any housing built on the urban renewal site.[24] The Birmingham NAACP also contended that Birmingham had not developed specific and adequate relocation plans.[25]

The NAACP met with limited success, however. Aside from apparently causing the HHFA to delay its decision until Cole had the opportunity to visit Birmingham in October 1953, the NAACP achieved relatively little. Birmingham removed a housing component from the Medical Center plan. In this way, both Birmingham and the HHFA could claim that federal funds were not being used to build segregated housing. James W. Follin, HHFA's director of slum clearance, warned Birmingham that if the HABD placed housing back into the urban renewal plan that excluded Blacks, Follin would not approve such an amendment. At the same time, Follin noted that the Hill-Burton Act, which provided federal assistance for hospital construction, permitted segregated hospital facilities as long as the facilities and services for Whites and Blacks were of "like quality."[26] The Eisenhower administration therefore required Birmingham to refrain from using the Medical Center site for segregated housing, while basically ignoring the issues of adequate relocation housing and racial discrimination faced by Black medical personnel and patients.

The NAACP followed up with a June 1954 suit in Federal District Court, which was summarily dismissed on 28 January 1955 as having no legal merit.[27] In May 1955 the Birmingham NAACP discarded any plans to appeal as most of the property owning plaintiffs had dropped out of the suit to obtain the money that had been paid for their properties.[28] By this time, relocation of residents was proceeding and the project would be completely closed out by 1959, with 10½ of the acres sold to the University of Alabama.[29] Nevertheless, at the same time that the NAACP lawsuit was being dismissed, Birmingham Mayor James W. Morgan was writing HHFA asking for 750 additional units of public housing, to be rented to Blacks relocated from the Medical Center and Avondale urban renewal projects. In a cover letter, the mayor wrote: "These data indicate a substantial deficit of units, primarily for Negro families."[30]

The Workable Program

Under the Workable Program of the Housing Act of 1954, communities using the federal urban renewal, public housing, or urban renewal–related mortgage insurance programs were required to refrain from engaging in ad hoc slum clearance without a comprehensive approach to slum prevention and rehabilitation.[31] Toward this end, the Workable Program amendment required cities using federal urban aid funds to achieve seven objectives: adequate codes and ordinances, a comprehensive community plan, detailed neighborhood analyses, adequate administrative organization, financing ability, housing for displaced families, and full-fledged citizen participation.[32] At the time the Workable Program was enacted, Birmingham had made only limited progress in meeting these objectives. Nevertheless, by the end of the Eisenhower administration in 1961, Birmingham had developed a greatly enhanced planning capacity as a result of the program.[33]

Birmingham's citizen participation still remained poor, however. The absence of progress became apparent when in 1961 the HHFA, under the Kennedy administration, required cities to establish a citizens' advisory committee that was "community-wide" and "representative in scope." Moreover, each city was to establish a subcommittee of the advisory committee on minority housing problems that included "representative members of the principal minority groups in the community."[34]

In late 1961, the HHFA informed Birmingham that its upcoming Workable Program application needed to address these issues; otherwise the city risked having its recertification application rejected.[35] Birmingham's planning director, John Steinichen III, reacted by calling the HHFA's warning "ominous."[36] Steinichen then wrote the HHFA stating that Birmingham had "a number of citizens advisory groups for many different purposes" and that another committee was "unwarranted."[37]

Birmingham representatives met with an HHFA official in December 1961 and afterward the city designated its planning commission as the city's Citizens' Advisory Committee and the HABD as the subcommittee on minority housing problems. No Blacks served on either of these boards.[38]

In response, the HHFA wrote Birmingham Mayor Arthur Hanes that Birmingham's Workable Program would not be recertified because the Birmingham Planning Commission membership lacked sufficient breadth and because there were no apparent Black members of the committee to study minority group-housing problems.[39] After Public Works Commissioner James Waggoner wrote a letter of complaint to Alabama Senator John Sparkman, apparently to no avail, Mayor Hanes wrote the HHFA to say that five Black Birmingham residents had been named by the Housing Authority to a minority group–housing committee. Nothing was said about expanding the representativeness of the Birmingham Planning Commission or redefining the Citizens' Advisory Committee to include a more diversified set of citizens.[40]

In its 1963 recertification of Birmingham's Workable Program, the HHFA stated it was glad that Blacks had been added to the citizen-participation process, but urged Birmingham to do more in this regard.[41] Within weeks of receiving this letter, however, the Alabama Supreme Court ruled that Mayor Hanes was no longer Birmingham's mayor, as he and his fellow commissioners had been voted out in Birmingham's legally contested election of 2 April 1963.

Birmingham's more progressive business and political leaders had reacted to the excesses of Birmingham's Public Safety Commissioner, Eugene (Bull) Connor, especially the failure of the city's police department, which he commanded, to protect the Freedom Riders from being beaten in their 1961 visit to Birmingham. In 1962 these leaders persuaded the city's electorate to charter a new mayor-council form of government, which it was hoped would result in the defeat of Connor and his two fellow commissioners, Mayor Arthur Hanes and Public Works Commissioner James T. Waggoner. In the 2 April 1963 race for mayor, Albert Boutwell defeated Bull Connor.

Federal Urban Policy and Planning in Birmingham, Alabama

Until 23 May 1963, however, Birmingham was led by two governments, for the Hanes-Connor-Waggoner administration contended that the election of 2 April had illegally cut short their terms of office. It was during this interim period that Martin Luther King Jr. led demonstrations that culminated in Bull Connor's police and fire departments using dogs and fire hoses to attack demonstrators. Photographs and films of these scenes; printed and broadcast throughout the nation and world, helped to catapult the Civil Rights movement forward.[42]

Although the new mayor, Albert Boutwell, was by no means an integrationist, the new charter and Boutwell's election had represented a repudiation of the archsegregationist policies practiced by the previous administration. As a consequence, the new administration was no longer averse to including Blacks on the city's Citizens' Advisory Committee.

Immediately after Boutwell's election was certified, the newly elected City Council and mayor established the Community Affairs Committee to confront the city's economic and racial problems.[43] Although not immediately apparent, Birmingham designated the Community Affairs Committee the city's official Citizens' Advisory Committee under the Workable Program.[44] Of the approximately 212 people on the Community Affairs Committee, at least 27 were Black, including at least two individuals (attorneys Peter A. Hall and Orzell Billingsley) who had been involved in the NAACP-led protest against the Medical Center urban renewal project in 1953–54.[45] The nine-member Citizens' Advisory Committee on Relocation Housing (Birmingham's name for the HHFA-required Committee on Minority Housing) included three Blacks.[46]

By the spring of 1964, however, the Community Affairs Committee had been a disappointment to many because its efforts to encourage employers and the city's police department to hire Blacks had been squelched by an unresponsive Mayor Boutwell.[47] Birmingham had been able to at last create a structure for interracial citizen participation, but Boutwell's failure to respond to the committee's proposals demonstrated that the city still had not yet fully accepted Black participation in its affairs. As it became evident that the Community Affairs Committee was moribund, a new organization, Operation New Birmingham (ONB) was named to fill this role.[48]

Operation New Birmingham was descended from the Birmingham Downtown Improvement Association, formed in 1957 by the president of the *Birmingham News,* two downtown retailers, and a downtown realtor. Not surprisingly, the organization focused on downtown revitalization, and a 1963–65 downtown design project, titled Operation New Birmingham, became the organization's new name. By 1966 the organization boasted 220 members made up of leaders from business, labor, and government, including 23 leaders from the Black community. Operation New Birmingham was able to play a significant role in Birmingham affairs, effectively becoming a public-private partnership between business and government, with offices in City Hall and a full-time representative in Washington, D.C.[49]

By the late 1960s, therefore, Birmingham had established a modestly interracial forum for conducting citizen participation under the city's Workable Program. Although the city had not been pressed hard by the Eisenhower administration to implement the citizen-participation provisions of the Workable Program, the Kennedy administration had succeeded in pushing a stubborn city government to accept Blacks on a special committee for minority housing. And though Birmingham had finally come to accept biracial citizen participation, it still relied primarily on the city's business elite, whether Black or White, to advise it on city planning and urban renewal. Moreover, the Black leaders were selected by Birmingham's White business elite, not by other Blacks. Workable Program evaluations for the remainder of the 1960s accepted the citizen-participation structure developed by the Boutwell administration. Pressure for more grass-roots citizen participation would come from another federal source, the Johnson administration's War on Poverty.

The War on Poverty, Model Cities, and
Citizen Participation

The War on Poverty's Community Action Program was critical to the development of citizen participation and neighborhood planning in American cities.[50] Birmingham was among those cities.

In late 1964 Birmingham Mayor Boutwell applied for a project development grant under the Economic Opportunity Act of 1964. By June 1965 the city, in cooperation with Jefferson County, created a nonprofit community action agency, the Jefferson County Committee for Economic Opportunity (JCCEO), to implement programs under the Economic Opportunity Act.[51] OEO wanted to prevent Alabama Governor George Wallace from controlling JCCEO and delayed approval of funding for the committee until Birmingham and Jefferson County agreed to appoint at least six people living in low-income areas to the forty-one-member JCCEO board of directors. Candidates for these positions would be democratically nominated by Neighborhood Advisory Councils and appointed by the Birmingham and Jefferson County governments.[52]

In 1966 Congress amended the Economic Opportunity Act to require that at least one-third of the board members of community action agencies be directly elected by residents of the poor neighborhoods served by the agency. The new law required that sixteen of forty-eight JCCEO board members be elected directly by the public, with the remaining thirty-two members coming equally from public agencies and community groups. Previously, Birmingham and Jefferson County leaders had been able to name all of the JCCEO board members. As a result of OEO's interpretation of the new law, Birmingham and Jefferson County were required to accept both the democratic election of poor persons to the JCCEO board and the selection of public and community agencies by the JCCEO board.[53]

Several striking outcomes must be noted. First, OEO's citizen-participation demands met no resistance from Birmingham city government. Second, the push for increased participation by the poor in JCCEO did not come from Birmingham's poor and their representatives, but from the federal government.[54] Third, JCCEO's Black constituency confined its political activism to specific problems with the community action agency's job training program. In the 1960s and early 1970s Birmingham Blacks did not use the JCCEO forum as an opportunity to challenge the authority of Birmingham's White political establishment.[55]

In turn, Birmingham's political leaders essentially left JCCEO alone. Even when the 1967 Green Amendment presented cities with an opportunity to assume greater fiscal control over community action agencies, Birmingham elected not to do so, taking instead a position of "just keep us informed and pull no surprises."[56]

It was not just the cautious stance of Blacks but also the transition of Birmingham politics that explained the acceptance of poor Black participation in JCCEO governance. Birmingham's leaders in the post-Connor period of the 1960s and early 1970s were sufficiently liberal to favor programs such as the War on Poverty to address Black poverty, but were still sufficiently conservative to avoid strong association with social programs that served a Black constituency.[57]

That Birmingham's poor residents, particularly Black residents, did not initiate the movement for increased citizen participation in JCCEO, nor engage in broad-scale direct challenges to the existing White-dominated political system, can be attributed to the many obstacles Birmingham White politicians placed in the path of Black participation. But by the time the city of Birmingham submitted a Model Cities application in 1968, the Black community demanded direct control over the planning of its neighborhoods. The purpose of the Model Cities program was to enable cities to concentrate various federal resources in the most depressed urban neighborhoods. Perhaps reflecting its ambivalence toward social programs such as Model Cities, Birmingham skipped the first round of Model Cities funding in 1967 and decided less than two months before the next application's due date of 15 April 1968 to compete for funds.[58]

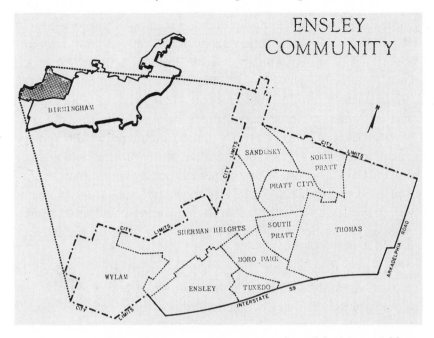

FIGURE 14.2. The Ensley Community proposed Model Cities neighbor-hoods. This map, prepared by the city of Birmingham for its Model Cities application, shows the location of the Ensley community and its neighbor-hoods. Courtesy: Birmingham Public Library, Department of Archives and Manuscripts.

The area designated for the Model Cities program was the Ensley community, which consisted of ten separate neighborhoods in northwest Birmingham (figure 14.2). According to a report prepared by Yale Rabin, a planning consultant brought in by neighborhood residents, the Ensley community population was more than two-thirds Black, up from the 1960 U.S. Census estimate of 54 percent Black reported in the city's Model Cities application.[59]

Perhaps because of its mixed racial composition, the city government took greater interest in retaining control of the Model Cities application than it had shown with its laissez-faire approach to JCCEO. Greater city government authority was possible since the Model Cities program, in contrast to the Community Action Program, placed local authority for decision making in city government rather than community action agencies.[60] Birmingham did not anticipate significant citizen participation and when pressure for such participation came from Ensley's Black residents, the city resisted a shift of power from City Hall to the neighborhood. Instead, it relied on a thirty-two-member mayor's task force, which originally consisted of six community agency heads, including JCCEO's Black executive director and a representative of the Birmingham chapter of the NAACP, two Black newspaper editors, and more than twenty local government officials. The city then undertook three meetings with citizen groups. At the last of these meetings, held on 21 March 1968, residents elected thirty persons to also serve on the mayor's task force.[61]

Despite these efforts, the city's citizen-participation procedure received sharp criticism. Marie Jemison wrote Mayor George Seibels urging him to make the neighborhood representatives elected at the 21 March neighborhood meeting the representatives for the Model Cities area. She regarded the city's chief planner, James Wright, as unsympathetic to the needs of Ensley's residents.[62] On 5 April 1968, the mayor's task force met for the last time to approve the "planning approach" for the Model Cities application. Although task force members adopted the general approach favored by the city, they appeared "uncertain" and expressed concern that the city's planner had spent insufficient time in the neighborhood. As one Black member of the task force observed: "Negroes are tired of coming to City Hall and okaying what you've already done. Some of the people from the neighborhood should have been included in the groundwork. If we're going to be a part of this task force, we want to be part of it all the way."[63]

Several weeks after the city's submission of its Model Cities application to HUD, disgruntled Black members of the mayor's task force, represented by attorney Harvey M. Burg, obtained a copy of the Model Cities application from the city; this was the first opportunity the citizens of the task force had to review the application. The NAACP Legal Defense Fund, at Burg's request, provided the

Black citizens with the services of planning consultant Rabin, who noted a number of flaws in the application, including the employment of a methodology that was alleged to have underestimated the Black population of the Ensley proposed Model Cities area.[64]

Rabin and the Black task force members complained that the city's application made no commitments concerning the responsibilities, resources, and powers of the proposed Model Cities Neighborhood Board, and failed to provide for selection of a majority of the board members by the residents of the Model Cities neighborhood. As an alternative, Rabin and the Black residents proposed that a citizens board be set up consisting of three individuals elected from each of the ten neighborhoods in Ensley and that the citizens board receive technical assistance from a full-time planner hired by the board and responsible to it. The citizens from the board, along with the citizens board planner, would have the right to sit on the City Development Agency (the designated decision-making body under Model Cities) and to make policy recommendations to the City Development Agency.[65]

After several rounds of proposals and counterproposals, the city refused to concede responsibility to the neighborhood residents for electing their own representatives to the neighborhood board, preferring to keep this power in the hands of the mayor.[66] Consequently, as promised, the Black task force neighborhood representatives took their case to HUD Secretary Robert Weaver.[67]

Finally, in November 1968 HUD informed Mayor Seibels that Birmingham had not been approved for the Model Cities planning grant.[68] Although reasons were given, it is clear that the Model Cities application represented an important transition point in the development of citizen participation in Birmingham. In contrast to the JCCEO experience in 1965 and 1966, Birmingham Blacks by 1968 pushed hard for self-determination in citizen participation; they were not content with the appointment by Whites of Black representatives. Further evidence of increased Black support for self-determination came in 1969, when Black leaders in Birmingham reacted to continuing problems with police brutality and employment discrimination. Responding to their concerns, the White business leaders of Operation New Birmingham proposed the creation of a biracial committee, the Community Affairs Committee, consisting of ten Blacks and ten Whites.[69] In response to selection of both the Blacks and Whites on the committee by White business leaders, Black leaders told the White business leaders that "we were going to appoint our own leaders."[70] The incident, according to one historian, "graphically depicted the rise in a new kind of Black leadership in Birmingham, not radical in the traditional sense of the word, but insistent that the Black community determine its own direction."[71]

For its part, the Model Cities case indicates that the White political community in Birmingham had not moved as far on citizen participation as the rise of Black citizen participation in JCCEO might indicate. By permitting "too much" Black self-determination, Birmingham city government appeared to fear that it would alienate the White residents and business leaders in the proposed Model Cities neighborhood. Evidence shows that the city was in danger of losing White support for the Model Cities application if the program appeared "too Black." Residents of the primarily White Wylam neighborhood asked to be taken out of the Model Cities program application and Mayor Seibels and the city council agreed to do so if the planning grant application was funded.[72] According to the citizen complaint filed with HUD, the city canceled a planned 23 May 1968 meeting with attorney Harvey Burg, representing the Black task force neighborhood representatives, because of a petition that had been reportedly signed by White Wylam residents opposing the Model Cities program.[73] The Ensley Chamber of Commerce, which had no Black members, voted to oppose the Model Cities application.[74]

Consequently, by the late 1960s, while the Black community moved toward self-determination in citizen participation, the White power structure still feared that such participation, especially in programs involving Whites as well as Blacks, would alienate the White community. Wherever possible, therefore, White political leaders continued to support citizen-participation programs that

TABLE 14.1. Racial Composition of
Birmingham, 1900–1980

Year	Number Black	Percentage Black
1900	16,575	43.1
1910	52,305	39.4
1920	70,230	39.3
1930	99,077	38.2
1940	108,938	40.7
1950	130,025	39.1
1960	135,113	39.7
1970	126,388	42.0
1980	158,217	55.6

SOURCE: U.S. Bureau of the Census, *Census of Population and Housing*, 1900–1980.

kept the mayor and the city council in control. Clearly, however, in a city where Black political consciousness was rising, as was the Black share of Birmingham's population, the White perspective on citizen participation would continue to be challenged (see table 14.1).

Birmingham's Citizen-Participation Program

To comply with the citizen-participation requirements of the Workable Program, Birmingham continued to employ the business-oriented Operation New Birmingham through the early 1970s. But in late 1972 a group of city residents objected to the designation of Operation New Birmingham as the city's Citizens' Advisory Committee under the Workable Program, complaining that ONB did not represent all community groups.[75] Aware of citizen concern with ONB, HUD's Birmingham area office wrote a letter to Mayor Seibels indicating that recertification of the city's Workable Program required significant changes in the city's citizen-participation procedures.[76] Most important, HUD required that no later than 1 January

1974, "the City will have developed, *under city control*, the functional capacity to involve its citizens *directly* in the community development process" (emphasis added), to "provide *direct* access of citizen representatives to the Office of the Mayor," and to "represent the ethnic, age, economic and business characteristics of the community at large." To accomplish these and other related tasks required a modification of the existing contract for citizen participation the city held with ONB.[77]

The city's Community Development Department staff then set out to develop a revised citizen-participation plan.[78] In January 1974, Mayor Seibels announced the "New, Comprehensive Citizen Participation Plan," which was to be enacted by administrative order.[79] The plan called for a three-tier organizational structure. The first tier consisted of Neighborhood Citizens' Committees, open to residents of the city's ninety-one neighborhoods delineated by the Community Development Department. Each neighborhood selected three individuals to represent the neighborhood on the Community Citizens' Committee (the middle tier). Finally, the Birmingham Citizens' Advisory Board consisted of sixteen members, one from each of the city's communities, along with nine at-large members appointed by the mayor. Under the proposal, Operation New Birmingham had "primary field responsibility for developing, organizing, and maintaining viable citizen participation groups in the neighborhoods and communities throughout Birmingham". and served as the conduit between the three-tiered citizen structure and city government.[80]

Vocal, active criticism of the plan was quick to form. As in the 1968 Model Cities application, Black residents in particular were firm in their opposition to Mayor Seibels's proposed citizen-participation plan. In contrast to 1968, however, opposition to the mayor's approach to citizen participation also came from the City Council. David Vann, elected to the council in 1971, played a key role in 1962 and 1963 by helping to reform Birmingham's government and mediate between the city's White business leadership and civil rights demonstrators.[81] In 1974, he chaired the City Council committee responsible for overseeing the adoption of a citizen-participation plan.[82]

In early 1974, Vann responded to Mayor Seibels's citizen-participation plan by pushing an alternative proposal, but it was defeated in a 5 to 3 City Council vote.[83] By March 1974, however, the city's Community Development Department staff took Mayor Seibels's plan to two Black neighborhoods, Fountain Heights and Collegeville, and encountered a high level of opposition.[84] An ecumenical church-based organization, Greater Birmingham Ministries, which engaged in community organizing in North Birmingham, had worked with neighborhood leaders to organize opposition to the city's citizen-participation plan.[85]

Faced with significant citizen criticism, Mayor Seibels and the City Council called for a public hearing on the citizen-participation plan.[86] Chaired by David Vann, the 1 April 1974 meeting was attended by 500 people, and 30 persons, mostly Black, spoke. Each opposed the Seibels plan. The plan's criticism boiled down to six key issues:

1. Citizens were upset that the city had attempted to develop a citizen-participation plan without consulting them.
2. Representatives of civic leagues, the traditional community organizations in Black Birmingham neighborhoods, objected to the idea of the city coming to organize their neighborhoods, when organizations were already in place.
3. Citizens were suspicious of ONB and its ties to the business community. Some argued that the plan was designed to permit City Hall and ONB to "handpick leaders for the Black community." Benjamin Greene, president of the Harriman Park Civic League, said: "We don't want an extension of City Hall into our neighborhoods."
4. Citizens objected to the layers of hierarchy placed by the plan between citizens and city government.
5. Citizens objected to the mayor's authority to appoint nine of the twenty-five members of the Citizens' Advisory Committee.

6. Citizens complained that the neighborhood boundaries delineated by the city did not correspond to actual neighborhood boundaries as their residents knew them.[87]

Under the leadership of Charles Lewis, a Community Development Department planner and former Peace Corps volunteer, the city followed up the 1 April meeting by holding a workshop for citizens to articulate what they wanted in the citizen-participation plan.[88] Out of the workshop came ideas that addressed the six major concerns and that the citizens wanted incorporated in the revised plan. The new responsiveness of the city to citizen concerns was noted in a *Birmingham News* column, which stated: "Ruffling breezes that bear new ways of thinking and new ways of doing are stirring in City Hall these days."[89]

The city revised its citizen-participation plan over the summer of 1974 and presented it to the citizens in the fall of that year. Citizens were granted nearly all of their demands. ONB was no longer part of the citizen-participation package; instead, employees of the Community Development Department would provide the staff work for the citizen-participation plan. The new plan kept the three-tier concept, but made it clear that going through channels was unnecessary if citizens or neighborhoods wanted to go straight to City Hall. Existing organizations, such as the civic leagues, were given special encouragement to participate in the citizen-participation program. The mayoral appointments were eliminated from the top-tier Citizens' Advisory Board. Neighborhood boundaries would be determined in consultation with residents. Moreover, the citizen-participation program would be used to inform people about zoning changes and city budgets. Finally, with the passage of the federal Community Development Block Grant program in mid-1974, Birmingham's citizen-participation program became the vehicle for receiving citizen opinion on how CDBG funds should be spent.[90]

At a public hearing on 1 October 1974, the revised plan was well received. Ironically, criticism came from the Birmingham Chamber of Commerce, whose representative objected to the fact that persons who owned businesses in a neighborhood, but did not live there, could not take part in the neighborhood committees. In response to the chamber's proposal, which was rejected, Mrs. William Pompey said: "You'll find we have sense enough—common sense—to determine our own needs." Finally, W. C. Patton, who in 1953 had led the local NAACP in its unsuccessful fight against the Medical Center Urban Renewal project, and who had opposed Mayor Seibels's original citizen-participation plan, stated that he supported the revised citizen-participation program.[91]

Conclusion

The evidence presented here confirms the important role played by federal urban policy in stimulating the development of citizen participation in Birmingham (figure 14.3). But it suggests, as well, that the federal impact was expressed in ways that distinguish the Birmingham experience, and perhaps more generally, the southern urban experience, from the general understanding of how these programs influenced the development of citizen participation.

The implementation of Birmingham's first urban renewal project, the Medical Center expansion, was consistent with urban renewal programs in other cities in its impact on the relocation of low-income, and particularly Black, residents.[92] This episode's importance lies in demonstrating the absence of any citizen participation involving Black residents prior to the establishment of the Workable Program in 1954. At the same time, it demonstrates that Birmingham's Black community was sufficiently organized to challenge the city's urban renewal plans and sufficiently savvy to make use of outside resources from NAACP national offices to appeal directly to the federal government. The development of organizing and political skills enabled Birmingham's Black community eventually to achieve a substantial role in influencing planning in Birmingham.

The roles played by the Community Action and Model Cities programs contrast with the roles customarily attributed to these

FIGURE 14.3. Birmingham neighborhood leaders attending the 1992 Birmingham Neighborhood Conference. Courtesy: City of Birmingham, Department of Community Development, Community Resources Divisions.

programs in fostering citizen participation. In contrast to the role played by the Community Action Program in northern cities, Birmingham's program did not focus on the stimulation of political conflict between Blacks and the White political establishment, but on the simple recognition of Blacks, particularly Blacks elected by the residents of Black neighborhoods, as equal participants in planning for social services.[93] The stimulus for Black grass-roots participation in the local community action agency came from the federal Office of Economic Opportunity.[94] Birmingham Blacks involved in JCCEO made no broad efforts to challenge the White political establishment, but instead focused their actions on improving the quality of JCCEO's services and employment opportunities.[95] Similarly, the White political establishment in Birmingham elected not to engage JCCEO in political conflict, but instead adopted a laissez-faire policy toward the agency.[96]

The Model Cities influence on citizen participation was two-fold. First, through the process of protesting the city's approach to citizen participation, Birmingham Blacks, as they had in the Medical Center protest, worked with the national NAACP offices to develop a plan for direct representation and election of the Model Cities Neighborhood Board. The plan called for the same type of democratic election-based citizen participation that was first introduced in Birmingham by the Community Action Program. This time, however, the demand for such direct representation came from Birmingham's Black community, not from the federal government.

The Model Cities episode also demonstrated the continued resistance by Birmingham's White political establishment to the concept of Black self-determination in citizen participation where such participation threatened White political support for city government's policies.

In contrast to the Community Action and Model Cities programs, the influence of the Workable Program seems less important, but is nevertheless significant. Under the Eisenhower administration, while the Workable Program influenced the development of a general planning capacity, the same cannot be said for its influence on citizen participation.

In the 1960s and 1970s, however, the Workable Program had a significant impact on citizen participation in Birmingham. In the early 1960s, the Workable Program administrators successfully pushed Birmingham to include Blacks on a special committee for minority housing at a time when archsegregationists such as Bull Connor still governed the city.

By the 1970s, HUD's Workable Program monitors responded to local concerns that the city's reliance on Operation New Birmingham failed to include a cross section of Birmingham's residents in the citizen-participation process. Consequently, the HUD area office in Birmingham in 1973 informed the city that a more inclusive citizen-participation program with direct access to city government must be implemented.

Despite the influence of the Workable Program, however, its role in stimulating the development of the city's citizen-participation program should not be overestimated. The HUD area office's interpretation of Workable Program requirements did not require the citizen-participation program that was finally adopted by Birmingham. Instead, at least four local factors seem to account for Birmingham's adoption of its citizen-participation program.

First, in contrast to the 1968 Model Cities application, Mayor Seibels assumed an apparent laissez-faire approach to the development of a neighborhood-based citizen-participation program. He acquiesced in the program's angry rejection by Birmingham citizens, most of whom were Black.

Second, in contrast to 1968, the Birmingham City Council in 1974 had an advocate of neighborhood-based citizen participation in David Vann. Using his position as chair of the committee responsible for a new citizen-participation plan, Vann pushed for a new plan throughout the spring and fall of 1974.[97]

Third, in contrast to 1968, the city's planners were genuinely interested in promoting grass-roots citizen participation. In 1968, the chief city planner was accused of being unsympathetic to the needs of the Model Cities neighborhood's Black constituency. By 1974, responsibility for citizen participation had been given to a planner, Charles Lewis, with a strong commitment to grass-roots citizen participation.[98] Despite the somewhat awkward and undemocratic features of the department's original citizen-participation plan, sponsored by Mayor Seibels in January 1974, the proposed plan set an important precedent for Birmingham government by calling for direct election by neighborhoods of their citizen representatives. This feature remained at the heart of what was to become Birmingham's citizen-participation program. It forced the city to take the plan to the neighborhoods. By developing a neighborhood-based citizen-participation program, the Community Development Department effectively gave citizens of the city's

TABLE 14.2.   Significant Dates and Events in the Development of
Birmingham's Citizen-Participation Program

Year	Event
1949	Passage of the Housing Act of 1949.
1953	Federal approval of Birmingham's Medical Center Urban Renewal Project.
1954	Passage of the Housing Act of 1954, including the Workable Program requirement.
1961	Increased enforcement of the citizen-participation requirements under the Workable Program.
1963	Birmingham's 1962 referendum changing the form of government leads to electoral defeat of Bull Connor and other archsegregationists. Albert Boutwell elected mayor.
1963	Newly elected Mayor Albert Boutwell Appoints Community Affairs Committee to serve as citizens advisory committee under Workable Program's citizen-participation requirement.
1965–66	Creation of Jefferson County Council for Economic Opportunity, a community action agency, with one-third of its board members elected from low-income neighborhoods.
1966	Designation of racially mixed Operation New Birmingham as Birmingham's Citizens' Advisory Committee.
1967	George Seibels elected mayor.
1968	Black citizens protest the lack of citizen participation in Birmingham's Model Cities Application and propose a neighborhood-elected model cities neighborhood board.
1971	George Seibels reelected mayor.
1973	HUD Area Office in Workable Program recertification requires Birmingham to replace Operation New Birmingham with a citizen-participation program that is under City Council control and directly involves a cross section of citizens in the community development process.
1974	Birmingham, after much debate, adopts a neighborhood-based, citywide citizen-participation program.

neighborhoods an important new source of leverage in the debate over citizen participation. Moreover, when citizens demanded that the plan be changed, the Community Development Department listened carefully and revised the plan in accordance with the citizens' concerns (table 14.2).

Finally, Birmingham's residents, particularly its Black community, proved ready to take advantage of the citizen-participation opportunity handed to them by HUD's Workable Program and Birmingham's city government. At public hearings held throughout 1974, Birmingham's Black citizen activists made clear that they wanted a citizen-participation program they controlled. Having done battle with the city government for twenty-one years over citizen participation in planning efforts, Birmingham's Black community learned that meaningful political power required direct community control over the planning process. They were finally in a position to implement this knowledge, as well as extend it to a broader political arena five years later in 1979 when Birmingham elected Richard Arrington its first Black mayor.

BROADENING THE PLANNING AGENDA

CHAPTER 15

Savannah's Changing Past

Historic Preservation Planning and the Social Construction of a Historic Landscape, 1955 to 1985

ROBERT HODDER

Savannah, Georgia, has long been renowned for its original town plan of 1733 by James Oglethorpe and for its historic building fabric. During the 1960s and 1970s, the city also garnered considerable national attention because Savannah's citizens were grappling with the consequences of gentrification and some of the other difficult social issues that accompanied the employment of historic preservation as a central strategy for urban redevelopment. Robert Hodder analyzes the evolution of preservation planning in Savannah in this chapter and discusses the impact of the city's changing preservation practice on Savannah's physical and social environments. He bases his analysis on reports of the Chatham County–Savannah Metropolitan Planning Commission, reports of the Historic Savannah Foundation and Savannah Landmarks Rehabilitation Project, and contemporary newspaper reports spanning three decades.

Hodder chronicles Savannah's embrace of preservation and rehabilitation of the city's historic resources as an alternative strategy to mainstream redevelopment plans for urban renewal. He reconstructs and analyzes three distinct phases of this history and shows how each phase developed logically from the previous rehabilitation efforts and their consequences. During Phase I, from 1955 to 1973, preservationists associated with the Historic Savannah Foundation "firmly established historic resource protection planning as a model for urban development." Their success in restoring historic housing, however, displaced many residents as these homes were sold or refurbished to command higher rents. During the second phase, from 1974 to 1979, the Savannah Landmark Rehabilitation Project reshaped preservation planning to include an explicitly social agenda; their effort focused on the restoration of Savannah's Victorian District while "preserving the neighborhood's racial and economic mix." During Phase III, from 1980 to 1985, African Americans working through the Beach Institute Historic Neighborhood Association developed their own preservation program to revitalize, preserve, and interpret Savannah's historic Black community.

Hodder argues that through this succession of interrelated efforts, Savannah citizens significantly bridged the "disjunction between historic preservation and race and housing issues." The Savannah experience is a forceful reminder that preservation planning has a social as well as an environmental dimension. Hodder illustrates the ways in which the Savannah landscape has been socially constructed by different populations in the city at different times for their own purposes. His analysis also demonstrates how "concerns about historic resource protection have been integrated into community political life," consequently broadening both discourses. The Savannah story is remarkable both because of the strong grass-roots nature of the city's preservation practice and for the alternatives those efforts provided to modernist schemes of urban redevelopment.

The standard histories of the historic preservation movement in the United States are Charles Hosmer's two volumes, Presence of the Past *(New York: Putnam, 1965) and* Preservation Comes of Age *(Charlottesville: Preservation Press, 1981). For coverage of the post–World War II years, see James Marston Fitch,* Historic Preservation *(New York:*

McGraw-Hill, 1982). Several important articles treat the tensions and social issues inherent in neighborhood revitalization and historic preservation efforts. Readers should consult Eugenie Ladner Birch and Douglass Roby, *"The Planner and the Preservationist,"* Journal of the American Planning Association *50 (1984): 194–207; Christopher Silver, "Revitalizing the Urban South,"* Journal of the American Planning Association *57 (1990): 69–84; Mary Corbin Sies, "The Politics and Ethics of Studying the Vernacular Environment of Others,"* Vernacular Architecture Newsletter *57 (Fall 1993): 14–17; and Catherine W. Bishir, "Yuppies, Bubbas, and the Politics of Culture," in Thomas Carter and Bernard L. Herman, eds.,* Perspectives in Vernacular Architecture *3 (Columbia: University of Missouri Press, 1989), pp. 8–15. An entire issue of the* CRM Bulletin *(15 [1992]), edited by Antoinette Lee, was devoted to discussions of the topic "Cultural Diversity and Historic Preservation."* EDITORS

The practice of historic preservation has expanded notably over the last generation, and concerns about historic resource protection have been integrated into community political life. Consequently, preservation policies that direct the character of urban change have occasioned intense debate. Although many preservationists remain intent solely on protecting individual buildings and significant historic districts, others have focused on the distributive effects of their practice on local populations.[1] One intriguing set of experiences, which demonstrates the maturation of historic preservation planning into a community-building and urban revitalization strategy, is found in Savannah, Georgia.

The Savannah landscape is well known in the annals of planning, urban design, architecture, and historic preservation.[2] Considered by many to be a model town layout, the system of wards and squares designed in the eighteenth century by James Oglethorpe uses open space to limit urban density (see figure 15.1). But the renowned grid—first established in 1733 and an icon for planning historians—has not always been highly treasured. In the early post–World War II era, the historic downtown core was in disarray. Like

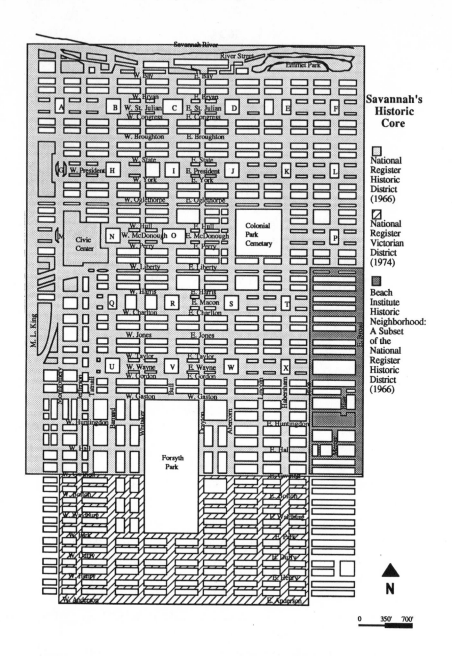

FIGURE 15.1. Savannah's historic grid is punctuated by open spaces. As historic preservation awareness expanded in Savannah, citizens sought public regulations to protect landmarks and secure neighborhoods. This map depicts the spread of local district designation. Map: Robert Hodder.

many American cities, Savannah was undergoing substantial demolition of residential and commercial properties for "higher and better uses." Exemplifying the faith in wholesale clearances that then drove urban renewal, pro-growth interests eagerly anticipated the construction of a "modern" downtown.[3]

During the same time, however, an alternative perspective on urban redevelopment arose in Savannah. Historic preservationists championed a strategy, based on rehabilitation and tourism, to counter mainstream rebuilding plans.[4] The preservationists, bolstered by support from a diverse array of public and private interest groups, worked assiduously to draw massive capital investment to Savannah's core—not for clearance, but for the rehabilitation and protection of historic downtown properties. Thus began a nationally recognized urban preservation campaign that would be continually broadened and refined.

The full scope of preservation planning in this southern city can be understood only through attention to the evolutionary process that marked it. Since preservation practice has had significant effects on the physical form and social geography of contemporary Savannah, the story of how that perspective was first instilled and subsequently developed is a substantive element of local history. This essay treats preservation in three distinct phases, which include the development of a citywide preservation movement, a successful attempt to counter the effects of displacement owing to gentrification of historic areas, and, more recently, the emergence of an indigenous African American preservation effort that has helped to bring the benefits of preservation to Savannah's Black community. Savannah's experiences are instructive because they reveal how preservation efforts have a social as well as a physical history, the intangible social effects intertwined with the visible changes. The process of creating and celebrating the "past" in Savannah has been highly selective and, at times, divisive; the story of the choices made along the way reflects the character of the community within the historic grid.

Broadening the Planning Agenda

Phase One: The Growth of an Ethic, 1955–1973

Urban redevelopment in Savannah came under increased scrutiny in 1955. Demolition of the Old City Market and the proposed destruction of the Factor's Walk–Factor's Row complex for a new commercial center prompted a diverse group of citizens to review the standard development process in the city's historic core and adjacent areas.[5] Alarmed by the piecemeal destruction of the architectural fabric, this group organized to plan for historic resource protection, envisioning an urban landscape of restored buildings and historic sites.[6] They turned for guidance to national experts in historic preservation and planning and worked to put preservation on the public agenda in Savannah. While these nascent preservationists believed intuitively in the inherent value of historic buildings and sites, they recognized that such a cultural rationale would not suffice; they would need sophisticated methods and a more pragmatic justification to establish preservation as a legitimate public policy.

When the proposed demolition of the Davenport House became known in 1955, community members rallied to protect the historic building. They established the Historic Savannah Foundation (HSF), which then quickly approached the owner about purchasing the Davenport House; rather than see another historic structure demolished to make room for surface parking, HSF sought an alternative use (see figure 15.2). Their initial inquiries met with a favorable response, and the new organization was able to shape hitherto informal concerns into a discrete preservation project.[7] Among those lending support was Irving Metz, spokesman for the Savannah Chamber of Commerce, who argued that preservation could protect the city's "prestige and distinctive personality."[8]

From its inception, HSF understood the importance of planning not only to save individual buildings, but for area preservation as well. While the preservation of a single property had been the original impetus for HSF, its mission quickly broadened to include "a long-range program for the protection and preservation of sites and

FIGURE 15.2. The Historic Savannah Foundation purchased the Davenport House and promptly began an extensive rehabilitation. The building's refurbished profile (on left) stands in stark contrast to its appearance shortly after the sale (on right). Courtesy: Historic Savannah Foundation.

structures of historic or architectural importance in Savannah," which the organization asserted was an essential component of urban development.[9] HSF's far-reaching program for managing change opposed the prevailing concept of growth, which derived from a notion of "progress and modern living" that many saw as misguided.[10] The principal HSF strategy was to control development through an enlightened private sector. At the same time, HSF leadership saw the usefulness of courting the increasingly powerful public sector.

HSF argued that restoration projects such as the Davenport House would reinvigorate the housing market and develop tourist trade. This point was essential to the HSF case, since the bulldozers that made way for industrial and commercial developers in what had been deteriorated neighborhoods were applauded as heralding economic growth. The HSF program, in staving off the bulldozers from the historic downtown core, had to counter the belief that without widespread clearance there could be no urban economic renewal. HSF gradually overcame the political allegiance to slum clearance by redefining historic preservation as a feasible alternative route to economic growth, by means of rehabilitation, attracting middle-class homebuyers, and boosting tourism and trade.

Thus HSF deliberately developed a strategy of reaching out to the growth coalition and speaking to them in their own terms. Arguing that more private capital should be invested in existing properties, John Rauers, president of HSF and a prominent real estate broker, stated:

> I have discovered . . . virtually no true opposition to Historic Savannah. Even those who are not active members and who may never be are in sympathy with us. They believe that the assets of any community cannot with any intelligence be destroyed. . . . [T]here is no real cleavage between the so-called progressive groups and the historic groups. Any thinking businessman must realize that something that can never be rebuilt must not be destroyed without grave consideration.[11]

Mayor W. Lee Mingledorff Jr. took another tack by emphasizing the return on investment in the physical plant of the city. He observed that "a terrific investment in the downtown residential areas, in the way of sewer lines, water lines, etc. . . . ha[s] practically been written off the books for city taxation purposes."[12] The argument was that allowing costly infrastructure to deteriorate was simply not good economic sense, and that reinfusing capital into a devalued area of the city increased the potential for economic growth. Thus historic preservation was presented both as a methodology for targeting areas for investment, and as a stimulus to economic growth through the development of tourist and convention trade. Mayor Mingledorff stressed that the HSF program represented not mere aesthetics, but "cold business opportunity."[13]

The foundation's activities succeeded in raising awareness of the value of historic landmarks. The newly formed Metropolitan Planning Commission (MPC) turned its attention toward historic resources in a report entitled *Savannah's Golden Heritage,* and Frederick Nichols produced a pictorial survey of Georgia architecture with

Savannah prominently featured.[14] HSF produced a guide to local historic points, and received publicity in the *New York Times;* meanwhile, it sought more stays of demolition. "History pays dividends" became a community mantra.[15]

Allegiance to that belief spoke as action in 1960, when four Savannah residents got together to purchase Marshall Row, not for profit but to protect it; they asserted, "we cannot ever expect to fully develop tourist-trade potential if we persist in destroying the very sites and atmosphere the tourist wishes to see."[16] Notwithstanding this prominent single initiative, private efforts to protect Savannah's architectural fabric still lacked an institutionalized base. In the early 1960s an array of ordinances for zoning and tax relief in the historic area came before the city council and administration, and before the state legislature as well, but the extended community gave them only limited support.[17] Voices arose to question constraining private development. The Home Builders Association contended historic zoning "would infringe on an individual's right to decide what he wants to do with his property."[18] It would be many years before such protections gained a formal, "public" character.

In 1966 the National Park Service placed an extensive area in Savannah's downtown on the newly formed National Register of Historic Places (see figure 15.1).[19] Although HSF officials characterized this recognition as public validation of their decade-long initiative, the largely ceremonial designation did little to protect the district's physical integrity. As in other American communities, local preservation regulations afforded historic properties the greatest measure of protection. Despite the efficacy of such zoning in other cities, the merits of public controls for preservation purposes continued to be vigorously contested well after the 1968 session of the Georgia assembly passed state enabling legislation for historic district zoning.[20]

The sole—but substantial—inroad on "privatism" was the entry of the federal government into the preservation field. Urban renewal as federally funded historic preservation, which had already occurred in other cities, came to Savannah in the early

1960s.[21] A pilot project by HSF in Troup Ward, a highly visible effort, shifted the redevelopment focus from demolition and construction to rehabilitation. The project showed the economic value of large-scale rehabilitation. As Walter Hartridge commented, Troup Ward showed "what can be done in a small area to revitalize a slum. The alternative is to have the government . . . tear down everything and erect slum clearance housing. There is a big difference economically."[22] Troup Ward drew national attention. A distinguished entourage of planners, preservationists, and architects including Carl Feiss, Charles Peterson, Lachlan Blair, Edmund Bacon, William Slayton, and Thomas McCaskey stopped in Savannah both to endorse and to shape the rehabilitation approach to urban renewal.[23] The Troup Ward project generated other private rehabilitation projects in the downtown area. Among the many individual and group projects of this era was the Pulaski Square–Jones Street Redevelopment Project.[24] This HSF initiative stressed private redevelopment, and financed protection of select historic buildings and streetscapes using a revolving fund.[25]

But these efforts were not without troubling ramifications. The Troup Ward renewal area was, literally, walled off, a concrete reinforcement (in all senses of the term) of the racial segregation in downtown neighborhoods.[26] When Savannah's school board ruled that Black children should attend Barnard Street School—a public facility in the historic core—prominent preservationists assailed the decision as "communistic," and a member of HSF railed that "every time we try to preserve some part of old Savannah . . . along comes someone to attack us."[27] One local architect likened Savannah's historic core to the Watts area of Los Angeles, and propounded the insight that "people not conditions make slums."[28]

Clearly the preservation effort was entangled in attitudes on race and raised fundamental social issues. Prominent among the latter was the loss in restored neighborhoods of the current residents' homes as rental properties were sold or commanded higher rents. In 1972 City Manager Don Mendosa put that issue succinctly: "Although this historic housing has been a great help in encouraging people to move back to the city . . . another problem is presented. These families moving out of historic areas have to find new places to live, and Savannah does not have a good supply of low-cost housing."[29]

As the preservation ethos succeeded in shaping urban neighborhoods, the full ramifications of the changes for the incumbent residents became clear. During the early 1970s, the recognition grew that the consequences of preservation programs differed for households according to their circumstances, race, and economic position. From being simply the story of an initially undervalued viewpoint whose insights then were triumphantly borne out, the preservation movement in Savannah came to represent as well the story of how the viewpoint of a well-placed group with the best of intentions can unthinkingly swamp the legitimate vital interests of other groups. The tensions that arise from such realizations are familiar. What distinguished Savannah, and may be the most interesting part of the story there, was the energy turned to confronting the problem and trying to solve it.

Despite the difficulties, the protection of historic sites and structures continued to garner accolades as a progressive form of revitalization. Columnist Tom Wicker proclaimed that "Savannah is living evidence that a city need neither decay nor accept ugliness and destruction as the price of progress."[30] The *Christian Science Monitor* hailed Savannah as "a national . . . leader in historic preservation and central-city reclamation."[31]

However, debate continued over the course of preservation in Savannah, focusing on an assortment of development issues. A local entrepreneur who proposed a bay-front complex met with vehement opposition from HSF and other preservation interests.[32] A blunt public dialogue ensued about the wisdom of public policies favoring preservation. Historic district zoning could control the height, bulk, and details of such projects in the downtown core, but the Savannah Real Estate Board and most city council members opposed any legislative language with that aim as being overly "dictatorial and restrictive." The MPC asserted that Savannah "has survived, but without legal protection it has been vulnerable."[33]

Historic zoning, although not public ownership, was the best means of control. Finally, in 1973, the city council approved a historic district zoning ordinance. The ordinance was a compromise, but it was nonetheless a crucial step in the institutionalization of the preservation ethic.[34] While preservation conflicts among various groups persisted, a public forum now existed for resolving them. Still, the debate about the appropriate value base of preservation was far from over.

Phase Two: A Revised Mission for Historic Preservation, 1974–1979

The rehabilitation effort in the 1950s and 1960s had been directly linked to substantial displacement of Black and low-income people. The denials of many in the preservation community aside, it was generally recognized that widespread rehabilitation displaced people, a consequence inequitable in terms not only of race but also of economic class. James Marston Fitch, for example, asserted that "rehabilitation programs inevitably created 'antagonism' between the various classes."[35]

A graphic example of this tension was revealed in 1974, when the National Park Service assigned another large portion of Savannah's core to the National Register of Historic Places (see figure 15.1).[36] Contiguous to the 1966 National Register district, federal designation of the "Victorian District" presaged the southward movement of market interest in historic properties, rehabilitation activity, and dramatic demographic change. That awkward realization fed a growing disenchantment with mainstream preservation practice.

Determined to forestall any more unplanned-for and profoundly disruptive consequences for people in rehabilitated neighborhoods, one of the prime movers in HSF's early efforts, Leopold

Adler, now urged the foundation to develop a program for the Victorian District that would both restore houses and keep residents in their homes. When his pleas met no response, he left HSF and with others founded the Savannah Landmark Rehabilitation Project (SLRP) in 1975, adopting the rallying cry, "Preservation is for people." Adler described the SLRP goal: "preserving the neighborhood's racial and economic mix, its social fabric. . . . The benefits of preservation can be shared by the rich and the poor."[37]

Indeed, the original claim of HSF had been that rehabilitation activities would benefit all segments of the city. But the establishment of SLRP confronted, head-on, the shortcomings of that supply-side version of preservation as economic development.[38] SLRP asserted that the market could no longer be given free rein, now that the consequences had become evident; private-market rehabilitation efforts—like clearance for development, before them—should be controlled to preserve essential social values.[39] Accordingly, SLRP set up a model program using federal, state, and local funds to maintain a neighborhood mixed by class *and* race.

As early as 1968, one Savannah banker, Mills B. Lane, had urged that Black ownership be promoted to stem the deterioration in historic neighborhoods; he had met with Black leaders and had set up a $10 million mortgage loan fund for low-income residents of historic neighborhoods. At that time, however, Lane had stood alone among preservationists in his overt support for low-income housing stabilization. Now, in the mid-1970s, the newly founded SLRP made a strong push for homeownership by the Victorian District's residents, but as Adler recounted, "we quickly found that ownership meant such pressing financing obligation, [we] just couldn't do it."[40] The SLRP program remained one of upgrading properties and rental assistance. In 1973 Mills Lane bought twenty-six rowhouses in another downtown area, financed their rehabilitation, and rented to the original tenants at below-market rates.

A few years later, more private rehabilitation projects were encouraged in the Victorian District by the city's $1.5 million loan subsidy for investors there. SLRP accepted this spur to private investment, which could undergird its own strategy of "seeding" rehabilitated rental housing across the district to prevent wholesale gentrification. The SLRP "seeding" policy agitated enthusiasts of free-market forces; the subsidy of private investment, on the other hand, agitated Black leaders and the city manager, Don Mendosa, who warned it might well open the floodgates to a tide of gentrifiers that would sweep low-income residents from their homes.[41]

In the 1970s an increased federal commitment to neighborhood preservation funded a range of programs to facilitate housing rehabilitation, and the SLRP drew on many of these.[42] With the assistance of local and regional banks—among them Savannah's major Black bank, Carver Bank—the board pieced together a funding network to support a rehabilitation project that allowed Victorian District tenants to remain in their renovated homes.[43] As Robert James, the president of Carver Bank observed, "This is no slum. . . . People have pride here. We want to stay the way we are, only we want to rehabilitate all these houses too."[44] Despite accusations of "double-dipping," Adler and the racially mixed board continued to draw on as many funding streams as possible to carry the SLRP program forward.[45]

Deplored by many as "socialism," the SLRP program was a courageous planned response to problems of equity. In attempting to radically reshape the mission of historic preservation, however, SLRP faced no small task. The program aroused vigorous debate among preservationists on some of the thorniest political questions: the disposition of private property, the role of government, the moral worth of unfettered market forces, and the ideal distribution of social classes. But the bedrock justification for SLRP was voiced by Adler: "We don't think it's fair, decent, or anything else to shove a whole bunch of people out. . . . Black people built a lot of this town. Some have lived in that neighborhood for 30 years."[46] Thus in the mid-1970s the effect of historic preservation on the social geography of Savannah received serious attention. The care of historic landmarks had to accommodate another concern, care for the people who lived in the buildings.

The SLRP program got national media attention, all laudatory. In 1978 First Lady Rosalyn Carter proclaimed the Savannah experiment "a model for the whole country."[47] The project, begun in an era of extensive federal funding for community development programs, continued on in the 1980s, albeit with some serious administrative and financial difficulties.[48] It was serving an important purpose. It alerted the African American community to the potential benefits of historic preservation and also proved it was possible to translate history into dollars without inflicting a painful cost on neighborhood residents. This demonstration was accomplished in the context of a new recognition of Black history.

Throughout the 1970s awareness of the long history of African Americans was rising. While historian Eric Foner contended that "many Americans still believe that Blacks are a people without a past," in Savannah that assumption was rapidly fading.[49] In 1973 the NAACP, led by its president, W. W. Law, began walking tours of Savannah that identified those historic resources relevant to African Americans, who in examining the historic fabric of Savannah were dealing with a "rather painful experience."[50]

An experienced civil rights activist of the 1950s and 1960s, W. W. Law served as the president of the NAACP for over twenty years, until 1976. He was a trenchant critic of Savannah's Housing Authority for remaining oblivious to the needs of tenants, and in connection with the plans to develop the riverfront he assailed HSF in 1971 for tailoring preservation projects to benefit Whites exclusively.[51] During the early 1970s, Law worked energetically to educate the public about the contributions made by African Americans to Savannah's development. In 1977 he was instrumental in establishing the local chapter of the Association for the Study of Afro-American Life and History (ASAALH).[52]

In 1975, planning moved forward for a federally supported housing project that exemplified the mainstream clearance and construction paradigm, the Wheaton Street Urban Renewal Project. The city's discovery that the project area contained several structures significant to Black heritage brought state and federal guidelines to bear. Although the Advisory Council on Historic Preservation had deemed the buildings eligible for inclusion in the National Register, both the city and HSF contended there was nothing "worth saving." Speaking for the NAACP, Law characterized this stance as "highly ironic." Though supporting the federal project, he stressed that "we are opposed to anyone going into a Negro area and recklessly wiping out everything standing as if Black people have nothing of value."[53]

Worried that six Victorian cottages could jeopardize a massive federal grant, Savannah leaders applied for demolition permits; the Black community quickly moved to bar the demolition legally. Eventually, one of the more significant houses, the King-Tisdell Cottage, was relocated to the Beach Institute Historic neighborhood—a traditionally Black enclave in the downtown historic core—after W. W. Law and the local chapter of the ASAALH arranged the financing.

After the battle over the endangered cottages, W. W. Law resigned as president of the NAACP and devoted himself to historic preservation issues, development in the Black community, and research into Black history. That shift in focus by a prominent Black leader foretold a new version of the preservation mission in Savannah.

Phase Three: The Beach Institute Historic Neighborhood, 1980–1985

When the relocated King-Tisdell Cottage opened in the Beach Institute neighborhood as headquarters of the local branch of ASAALH in 1981, the event symbolized the claim by local Black residents to both their past and their future (see figure 15.3).

The preservation of the building and its location also reflected new attention to the African American community by the city, HSF, the governor of Georgia, and the federal government. All of these actors, together with SLRP, had joined to finance the cottage's rescue and new use.[54] The dedication of the King-Tisdell Cottage

FIGURE 15.3. Serving as the headquarters of the Association for the Study of Afro-American Life and History, the King-Tisdell Cottage became closely aligned with an African American perspective on Savannah's past. Photograph: Robert Hodder.

hailed "the beginning of an achievement . . . to revitalize the black community, and to preserve vital links between the past and the present."[55] As well as presenting their own interpretive history on the Negro Heritage Trail, Blacks now had a cultural center.[56]

The King-Tisdell Cottage also was a place to organize the community and housed an organization that could document living conditions in the historic Black neighborhood. Sparked by the interest in protecting and interpreting historic resources significant for Savannah's Black heritage, the Beach Institute Historic Neighborhood Association (BIHNA) formed to promote community development there.

Although the neighborhood lay on the fringe of the historic core, the National Park Service had identified it as a significant part of the 1966 National Register district (see figure 15.1). The community was within the boundaries of the historic grid, but had never been targeted for meaningful public or private reinvestment.

The BIHNA worked diligently to protect the neighborhood's existing tenants. Employing an approach similar to that of HSF and SLRP, the BIHNA board successfully attracted federal and local funds for physical improvements in the housing stock through Section 8 and CDBG financial support. When the rental units on Price Street owned by Mills Lane were put on the market, the newly formed BIHNA saved them, using nearly $700,000 in CDBG funds. Law called the rescue "one of the finest hours of this city. Negroes in this city have been pulled from one end to another. We of the BIHNA say in 1980 this ought to come to an end."[57] Under the aegis of historic preservation, the Black community had shown it could mitigate market pressures and prevent the exploitation of its residents.

Another BIHNA effort was the publicity emphasizing investment opportunities for Blacks in the downtown area. Jesse Wiles, a Black organizer and realtor, said the push to have Blacks buy and rehabilitate properties in the district was not designed to "exclud[e] . . . whites from living in the area, but . . . to make black investors aware that they can have property and investments in the downtown area."[58] Setting a new precedent in this case, historic preservation spurred neighborhood revitalization but with Blacks benefiting along with Whites, rather than finding themselves only victims.

The development of a comprehensive historic preservation ethic was now complete. All three of the principal groups in Savannah—HSF, SLRP, and BIHNA—had contributed their own versions. In 1983 these organizations cosponsored a national housing conference on connections between preservation, housing, and community development.[59] Michael Ainslie, president of the National Trust, recognized the trend of "ethnic and low-income groups" using preservation as a strategy to improve neighborhoods.[60] Planner Edmund Bacon honored "low-income people . . . as the true preservationists because they held the community together."[61] Black citizens of Savannah had indeed done so; in their search for low-rent dwellings, they had safeguarded the historic housing stock at minimum levels long before the preservation process got under way. That stock had later been expropriated in a process of reverse filtering; but by the 1980s, the claims of low-income and Black residents had found respect.

The BIHNA launched a new vision by interpreting historic resources from a Black perspective, transforming preservation into a tool for development of the existing community. As a logical extension of the Civil Rights movement, the recognition of Black history united the neighborhood in a common purpose.

Historic Preservation and Social Change in Savannah, 1955–1985

Between 1955 and 1985, a broad coalition of interests revised the nature of urban redevelopment in Savannah's historic core. Although not successful in every endeavor, preservationists and their supporters countered demolition-and-construction schemes with rehabilitation techniques, in a rebellion against modernist urban planning. Preservationists, who included members of Savannah's establishment, forcefully brought their cultural program of historic preservation and design into the political arena. The coalition, in trafficking in history, aimed at improving the city's physical and social fabric, but its alternative agenda for physical change channeled the economic benefits of preservation only into certain social and racial terrains. Forced to recognize this problem, the preservation coalition then came to terms with it and to a creditable degree modified goals and techniques. Thus, beneath the descriptive history of preservation planning as a naïve cultural practice lies a story about the social construction of a historic landscape.

The history of preservation planning in Savannah as developed here reveals an evolution of attitudes toward the protection and interpretation of historic resources. Having been introduced to the merits of rehabilitation, a diverse array of individuals, groups, and institutions embraced preservation; but each one tailored the approach according to individual priorities. The history has three distinct phases: between 1955 and 1973, preservationists firmly established historic resource protection planning as a model for urban redevelopment; in the second phase, between 1974 and 1979, concern over the negative social effects of traditional preservation practice reshaped the rehabilitation program to include an explicit social agenda; and in the third phase, between 1980 and 1985, African Americans developed a distinctive version of the preservation paradigm to serve the goals of their community. Tracing the evolution of Savannah's preservation practice, one discerns in each of the three phases clear connections between the changing character of social and racial relations, and historic rehabilitation and interpretation programs.

In each phase, historic preservation effected a measure of social reform. As preservation coalitions followed their agendas, they encountered vexing community problems; social conflicts constrained all three coalitions. Yet, importantly, the historic preservation process in Savannah not only generated social friction, it also helped to relieve the problems it had revealed. Despite radically different social, economic, and political environments, what grassroots organizers in all three periods had in common was the attempt to further social goals by protecting historic resources.

The three phases were linked not only in chronological and spatial sequence, but as cause and effect: the initial rehabilitation effort created the problem of residential displacement, which the SLRP's Victorian District experiment countered; participation in SLRP galvanized Law and other Black activists to take up preservation as a tool for improving the neighborhood of a historically Black enclave (see figure 15.1).

With housing rehabilitation and infrastructure improvements, the work of BIHNA turned historic preservation into a tool to help the groups it had originally harmed. In Savannah the disjunction between historic preservation and race and housing issues, originally so profound, was to a significant extent bridged.

Over the course of a generation, diverse coalitions planning for different visions of the public good established preservation as an accepted local custom. Preservationists helped to define Savannah politics as they routinely sought advice and support from city officials and institutions. The introduction of rehabilitation values into public policy debates necessarily broadened the discourse and actions of preservationists.

By the end of the study period, three separate streams of thought fed historic preservation in Savannah. It is important to note that the evolutionary process was not a simple succession of paradigms, but rather an incremental enrichment of public priorities and social values. Sometimes complementing and sometimes competing with each other, the preservation methodologies eventually developed unified, accepted community criteria for responding to problems. Although multiple alliances created divisions in the community and made a uniform development program virtually impossible, the broadened base of preservation action ensured more equity in the allocation of public funds.

Each of the coalitions contributed a unique tradition to the culture of Savannah. Whites, in the first phase, relied on the free market to develop historic resources, thus accommodating the accumulation needs of local capitalists. White and Black preservationists in the second phase reoriented the agenda around broader public goals, viewing the market from a liberal perspective to correct previous injustices. Finally, as Blacks came to recognize the value of preservation as a tool for community development, they directed a separatist program of rehabilitation and infrastructure improvements to serve African Americans in the Beach Institute neighborhood. These somewhat idiosyncratic visions of historic preservation planning all valued grass-roots participation and respected the significance of social symbolism.

The transmission of the values and methods of preservation planning in Savannah is an intriguing story that points to one crucial insight: Savannah's historic landscape has been socially constructed. It is the product, not of a uniform historical process, but of an uneven social process in which community groups vied with one another under unequal political and economic conditions. Each coalition sought historic symbols to substantiate its social goal; all, however, sought both to reform community life and to affirm their place in the historical canon.

In Savannah, planning for historic resource protection avoided declining into a tyranny of history. Rather, moving from a politics of exclusion to one of inclusion, preservationists gave voice to the community development possibilities inherent in such planning. The record of historic resource protection shows Savannah to be a city with competing "pasts," which yet can all be converted into hard currency for community development. The spirit of the practice has benefited the quality of life for many in the historic core.

Exemplifying the built environment as social symbol, Savannah's present urban fabric reveals how historic preservation there has reflected and contributed to evolving social relations. The three waves of preservation practice that washed over the landscape have left a legacy now integral to the history of this southern city. Each program embodied attitudes toward race, markets, politics, social class, and history. Integrating historic resource protection into community political life and reshaping the economic and social order of Savannah, preservationists in each of the three phases were community rebuilders of the highest order.

CHAPTER 16

Seeking a Finer Detroit

The Design and Planning
Agenda of the 1960s

JUNE MANNING THOMAS

*A remarkable change in professional philosophy occurred during the
1960s and early 1970s as urban planners steered away from their traditional emphasis on design and civic beautification to address the social improvement of urban life. June Manning Thomas examines the decline of
the "grand civic design and planning agenda" in Detroit, Michigan, and
analyzes the factors that caused Planning Director Charles Blessing's ambitious plans for urban improvement to seem superfluous in the face of growing racial conflict and intractable socioeconomic problems. Thomas begins
by reviewing Blessing's sweeping vision for a "beautiful, healthful, and
safe" inner city and the steps he and his staff took to realize his grand
plan. Her account draws upon a rich body of primary sources: the Detroit
City Plan Commission records, Blessing's talks and published writings,*

contemporary newspaper reports, and the city of Detroit Master Plan *and urban renewal documents. From these documents, Thomas concludes that some of Blessing's schemes worked brilliantly for discrete redevelopments like Lafayette Park and the Detroit Medical Center, but as a comprehensive plan for inner-city redevelopment, Blessing's design agenda failed.*

Thomas compares Blessing's efforts with those of his planning counterpart in Philadelphia, Edmund Bacon, and argues that the implementation of urban design initiatives stalled in Detroit for several discernible reasons. Unlike Philadelphia, Detroit lacked both a central redevelopment agency and a strong pro-growth coalition. Although a brilliant designer, Blessing did not possess the public relations skills needed to sell his vision to the public or the political skills to push his ideas through the city bureaucracy. Bacon, in contrast, conveyed his design ideas through widely read publications, including The Design of Cities *(1967). Most important, Thomas suggests, were flaws in the city's urban renewal program. A plan for an expanded cultural center, for example, would have displaced nearly three thousand families and cleared a historic Black neighborhood. Blessing's physical design agenda was ultimately brought down by a lack of political support "made acute by the rise of neighborhood planning and the growing political consciousness of African American citizens."*

"Seeking a Finer Detroit" underscores the importance of political skills rather than design brilliance for successful urban planning. One of the lessons Blessing and his staff learned from their contests with other city officials was that their professional expertise did not provide them with sufficient clout to carry out their plans. More to the point, though, design solutions could not counteract the considerable social and economic forces tearing at Detroit and other cities in the 1960s and 1970s. But neither could the short-lived community-based planning that found expression in the Model Cities programs that followed. In this regard, the Detroit case study forms an instructive comparison with the previous selection by Robert Hodder on Savannah, where community-based preservation planning has scored modest victories in the smaller city's efforts to address entrenched social problems.

For two other strongly contrasting treatments of the contemporary inner city, readers should consult William Julius Wilson's controversial The Truly Disadvantaged *(Chicago: University of Chicago Press, 1987) and Mike Davis's* City of Quartz *(1992). On the impact of federal monies on urban redevelopment, see Mark Gelfand,* A Nation of Cities *(New York: Oxford University Press, 1975). For an overview of downtown revitalization efforts after World War II, see John R. Bauman, "The Paradox of Post-War Urban Planning," in Daniel Schaffer, ed.,* Two Centuries of American Planning *(1988), pp. 231–64. Two thoughtful commentaries on the backlash against planning are Robert Fishman's "The Anti-planners," in Gordon Cherry, ed.,* Shaping an Urban World *(New York: St. Martin's Press, 1980), pp. 243–52, and Howell S. Baum's "Problems of Governance and the Professions of Planners," in Daniel Schaffer, ed.,* Two Centuries of American Planning *(1988), pp. 279–302.* EDITORS

The grand civic design and planning agenda is scarcely still alive in U.S. cities. Although some cities, such as New York, have been able to carry out design agendas, these have tended to focus on the microscale, on items like civic plazas and building setbacks. In cities like San Francisco, the effort has been to protect the distinctive scale of buildings and to avoid the sensory overload that comes with an overconcentration of large, imposing office buildings. The promoters with grand civic vision, who were quite common during the City Beautiful movement in the early part of the century, are now seldom encountered, although one still sees the results of their tradition in cities large and small.

Actually, urban design captured considerable attention in the 1960s through the federal urban renewal program. Planners in many cities assembled teams of architects, landscape architects, and urban designers to create magnificent pockets of well-designed inner-city areas. Although some urban renewal projects imposed unworkable grand plazas or dysfunctional housing developments upon the populace, some revealed great possibilities for good urban design.

Even the "good" projects and city design initiatives faced incredible odds, however. This chapter examines some of these odds by focusing on the experience of one city, Detroit. Now often maligned as an archetypal city in distress, Detroit in the 1960s was one of the nation's best examples of planning for urban design. For two decades, Planning Director Charles Blessing added much to the character and beauty of specific sections of the city. At the same time, he visualized a substantial design agenda for reconstructing sections of the inner city into areas attractive for middle- and upper-class citizens.

Many of Blessing's design efforts did indeed improve the city. Their implementation stalled neither because of a lack of vision or faulty technical expertise among the city's planners, nor simply because of social upheaval. Rather, the planners' design vision was difficult to implement for inherent reasons. The planners' incomplete marketing skills played a part, as did flaws in the city's urban renewal program. Perhaps even more important was the lack of public and political support, made acute by the rise of neighborhood planning and the growing political consciousness of African American citizens. The Detroit design experience offers an example of the importance of political rather than professional variables in planning success. This experience suggests, as well, why urban design has not remained a driving force in contemporary big city planning.

A Design and Planning Agenda

Detroit's design and planning agenda in the 1950s and 1960s was largely the brainchild of the city's planning director, Charles Blessing, an extremely talented director with impeccable planning credentials. He earned an undergraduate degree in engineering from the University of Colorado and master's degrees in both planning and architecture from the Massachusetts Institute of Technology (MIT). Before coming to Detroit in 1953, he worked as state plan engineer for New Hampshire, as a regional plan director for the Greater Boston Development Committee, and as head of the master plan division for the city of Chicago. Blessing's educational and practical experience in planning was therefore well grounded. When he and forty-five applicants took a civil service examination for the planning directorship of Detroit in 1952, his score was the highest.[1]

Before Blessing took office, Detroit's planning staff of twenty-seven "presided over a good collection of statistics and demographic data, but had developed a zoning ordinance before they even had a city plan." Blessing sought to upgrade the quality and variety of staff planners. He hired a few planners trained in economics and sociology, but made a special effort to attract individuals trained in urban design. Of the four planners he brought from Chicago's planning office, three men had architecture degrees and one young woman had training in landscape architecture. In the 1950s, the number of professional planning schools was modest, and a large number of urban planners had architectural backgrounds.[2]

Blessing had strong professional ties in the areas of architecture and urban design, subjects that dominated the bulk of his correspondence from 1953 to the early 1970s. These letters went to or came from such notables as Baltimore's James Rouse, asking for advice on that city's riverfront; Norman Williams, seeking advice on planning Venezuela's Ciudad Guayana; Kevin Lynch, famed observer of urban design and human response, asked by Blessing to help recruit student designers and planners to Detroit; and Robert Weaver of the federal Housing and Home Finance Agency, who appointed Blessing to a community design awards committee. He also received numerous invitations to discuss urban design with audiences ranging from students at Harvard's Graduate School of Design, Princeton, and Notre Dame, to conferees at a Kansas City Conference on Design.[3] In 1963 the American Institute of Architects bestowed on Blessing their esteemed fellow status, in recognition of his distinguished service as chairman of their Urban Design Committee. In 1959 his fellow planners selected him to serve as president of the American Institute of Planners.[4]

Blessing's attachment to urban design was no mere professional association. His dogged pursuit of design activities led him one year to use his vacation time to work on an urban design project for Columbus, Ohio, donating his consultant fee back to the city of Columbus. He used other vacations to visit the world's cities, taking photographs and drawing sketches. He was a gifted sketcher and a keen observer of ancient and modern cities and their design elements. Only a fraction of his voluminous personal drawings of cities around the world were published. Examples are available in the February 1964 issue of the *Journal of the American Institute of Architects,* which published sketches made during a two-month journey through Crete, Greece, and the Middle East. During this trip, Blessing took more than three thousand slides and visited famed urbanist Constantinos Doxiadis. But the trip was best remembered for his drawings. His beautiful renderings of buildings, plazas, and urban forms such as the Acropolis in Athens, the palace city of Phaestos in Crete, and the temples of Egypt, clearly reflect the heart of a man enamored with city design.[5]

Designing Detroit

Blessing tried to apply to Detroit the design principles he learned through his travels and professional associations. He carefully monitored the design of routine redevelopment projects such as Gratiot-Lafayette and the Medical Center, but he also initiated a major effort to redesign Detroit.[6]

A 1956 *Detroit News* series, appropriately entitled "Detroit's 'City of Tomorrow,'" included an early statement of Blessing's design goal: to reconstruct 30 square miles of Detroit's inner city according to good planning and design concepts. The series included Blessing's bird's-eye sketch of a redesigned central core area and Woodward Avenue corridor. His initial focus was on the inner city, but the eventual goal was to "make our city beautiful, healthful and safe from one [city] limit to the other." Such an agenda would, Blessing hoped, restore the inner city "to the beauty and dignity it had fifty years ago."

Blessing calculated that a total of nine redevelopment projects would be needed to create a "pilot city." The Civic Center, constructed downtown in the early 1950s with city funding and private donations, formed the core of that city. A series of related redevelopment projects—including the central business district, Gratiot residential area, Corktown industrial area, a new Detroit Medical Center, and a Cultural Center—completed the picture. Blessing argued that "the task before us is to make certain that each of the new developments becomes part of a co-ordinated pattern." Each residential development, furthermore, should be made "safe, opened to light and air and greenery, made more humane." Drawing on the neighborhood unit concept, he argued that residential areas should be planned so as to protect pedestrians from automobile traffic.[7]

The design of modern cities, Blessing believed, should receive as much attention and reveal as much technological sophistication as car design. What he had in mind was a design center where research into building and redevelopment concepts could be carried out with the financial backing of local automobile manufacturers. Blessing suggested that the incentive for corporations to enter into the venture would be to beautify the city and thus help it advance economically. With such support, he promised, Detroit could "lead the world in city design and planning."[8]

His idea for a privately funded laboratory soon died. To expect automobile manufacturers to finance a technical center for improving urban design and redevelopment was wishful thinking. Support for a pilot city was even less likely. The most consistent financial support that Blessing and planners all over the United States had was the federal urban renewal program. In the 1950s Blessing used that support and his staff to apply good planning and design principles to redevelopment projects. In the 1960s, however, he became more intent on redesigning the inner city. He would, if necessary, create his own laboratory.

Blessing had already built up a "third-dimension plan," an architectural model of land uses for Detroit's central city. This model let Blessing show city plans in the "third dimension" as well as on flat two-dimensional maps. "To some," he remarked, "the third dimension has no part in city planning. That's for architects, they say. But two-dimensional plans are as flat as the paper they are drawn on. We have to be concerned with architectural form from the outset. We need grandeur on a civic scale."[9]

Blessing then moved beyond model-building toward an even bolder design agenda. First, he directed his staff to inventory the city's design resources, "ranging from the central business district, with its skyscrapers, to the many individual churches in the center city." Then he planned a survey of the attitudes, perceptions, and opinions of the general public and of local design professionals. Finally, with these two surveys in hand, the urban design staff would prepare an overall program for improvement, one that would "identify and rate significant urban design sources, establish reasonable priorities, and develop procedures for implementing better design through . . . realistic controls."[10]

Next, Blessing proceeded to carry out what was, he said in 1963, a "simple task": "recording everything of design worth in the city." This undertaking, he thought, would "very possibly [be] the most extensive center city redesign assignment currently under study in the nation. We are projecting what we call a new city of a third of a million people in the thirty square miles of contiguous blight, generally identified as the area within the Grand Boulevard in Detroit."[11]

The most visible result of the surveys is a series of impressive pamphlets and brochures that show the design potential of the city. Some of these focus on projects such as the Cultural Center, others on existing features such as architecturally significant churches. One lays out a design agenda for the city. Although these publications reflect the careful design standards used by Detroit's planners, their practical results are fairly negligible, except in the redevelopment projects the designers helped supervise.

It was really in selected redevelopment projects that the city's design agenda shone brightest. Gratiot-Lafayette Park was based on clustered neighborhood units designed to encourage pedestrian traffic. The city's planners worked closely with the first architect, Mies van der Rohe, to help plan an exceptional residential design. One contemporary proclaimed that "Gratiot joins Radburn, that other incomplete monument, as one of the few triumphs of American urban design." Another critic suggested that "the essence of what one is searching for is missing from all large-scale developments all over the world, but it can be smelt in Lafayette Park."[12] Another attractively designed project was the city's Medical Center. Blessing had recruited Gerald Crane to design the complex, and the planning commission provided office space for Crane, hired by the hospitals. Based on the institutional neighborhood unit concept, the center deftly mixed hospitals, medical buildings, and other community and residential uses. Blessing's bold initiative to redesign Detroit's inner city reaped great bounties for redevelopment project areas. As a comprehensive scheme for inner-city development, however, it was almost doomed to failure from the start.

Design Shortcomings

The problem was not that Blessing lost sight of more traditionally defined good planning or the human dimension in his aesthetic design. The bulk of the planning staff's efforts were devoted to more mundane activities related to zoning, master plan revisions, and planning and regulation of redevelopment areas. From all indications, this planning work was indeed carried out professionally.

In addition, Blessing paid close attention to the human component in his planning. At first he made only vague references to it, but by 1966, when the city had already been through warning tremors of civil disquiet, Blessing was talking openly about the need to understand that "physical renewal has only one purpose—a more human and humane environment for living." "If," he suggested, "we in cities glorify the form-making and form-giving role of physical design at the expense of meeting the real underlying emotional and social needs of all of the people of the city—the poor, the disadvantaged, the uneducated, the comfortable middle class—then, in a real sense, we court disaster."[13]

By then he had gone through a tumultuous experience with redevelopment and received less than universal support for his "city of tomorrow" idea. Concern for good design had overridden more practical considerations. Blessing had ambitious dreams for making Detroit a finer city. The trouble was, he had difficulty marketing his agenda, and at the same time had to work in the context of a flawed redevelopment program. The political and bureaucratic opposition was part of a rising tide of resentment against planning among the community residents in general.

Marketing and Implementing Design

A brief look at Philadelphia, where planners tried to do many of the things Blessing did, offers instructive insight into Detroit's deficiencies in marketing and implementation. Philadelphia's planning director Edmund Bacon gained widespread support for his vision of a rebuilt central city through the Better Philadelphia Exhibition. Open to the public in 1947, this exhibition featured Bacon's architectural model of the central business district. First presented in a department store and later in a museum, this multimedia exhibit attracted 400,000 Philadelphians in the first year alone. It was a show in the true sense of the word, offering viewers a graphic, mobile model of the city's future. The three-dimensional model displayed both the present state of the downtown and, on the flip-side, a new plan for each section of that downtown.

Bacon urged other planners in other cities to follow his lead. Hire staff with strong design credentials, he urged, select developers with good design plans, and promote a well-designed city. Blessing had of course already undertaken these steps in Detroit.[14] Yet Bacon was both more visible and apparently more successful than Blessing in promulgating his urban model. The different experiences had something to do with the two planning directors, and something with the cities and their redevelopment organizations.

Both Blessing and Bacon were widely respected by their peers for their plans. A 1961 survey of thirty-one recognized leaders in the field of planning of the United States showed that Detroit's comprehensive planning program was the most widely cited, having been mentioned by twenty-nine of the respondents, compared with twenty-five references to Philadelphia. Although agreement on the best individual planning directors was not as clear-cut, Bacon and Blessing received almost an equal number of votes: Bacon received nineteen and Blessing eighteen.[15]

That seemed to be where the similarity ended. Bacon had an outgoing personality and a particular flair for publicity and promotion. One former Detroit planner, who watched what he called a "friendly rivalry" between Blessing and Bacon, called Bacon "more of a showman than Blessing." The Philadelphia planner was also more influential with the public. In 1988, long after his retirement, Bacon caused a stir in Philadelphia by publicly attacking a new comprehensive plan that he regarded as too vague, insufficiently visual, and too divergent from his 1963 plan. Soon the public debate centered not on the new 1988 plan, but on Bacon's perception of it. Bacon had this kind of clout throughout his tenure. In contrast, Blessing valued the persuasiveness of the plan itself, rather than political skills. He was much less aggressive than Bacon about using the press to air his opinions, especially after retirement. The two men also differed in their publication styles. Whereas Blessing published short commentaries and sketches of Greece to illustrate his design inspirations, Bacon crafted promotional journal articles on Philadelphia, and eventually, released a textbook on urban design.[16]

Bacon also had a considerable advantage in operating in a city that was apparently more susceptible to renewal success than Detroit. Unlike Detroit, Philadelphia had a strong redevelopment agency, and a strong pro-growth coalition. In 1960, a special issue of the *Journal of the American Institute of Planners* highlighted the great achievements of Philadelphia's urban renewal program. A 1964 edition of *Architectural Forum* stated that "Philadelphia has what is generally accepted as the most rounded, well-coordinated renewal program in the U.S." In a 1964 cover story on urban renewal, *Time* magazine featured Philadelphia, New York, and San Francisco as three large cities that appeared to be "succeeding" in reshaping their central core areas. In 1966 Robert Weaver, secretary of the new U.S. Department of Housing and Urban Development, called Philadelphia "a trailblazer in planning, in renewal, and indeed, in most of our federal urban aid programs," a place "where planning has worked."[17]

Philadelphia gained national attention in part because of Bacon's overall design strategy, which built upon the original city plan by William Penn. Also impressive were visible project successes within that design strategy, such as garden concourses next to subway stations; Penn Center, a nine-building complex on Kennedy Boulevard; and the Market East project, which creatively combined retail operations with train, subway, and bus stations. Philadelphia constructed major new apartment buildings and townhouses designed by architect I. M. Pei and renewed the University City district, which contained several educational institutions and hospitals.

Detroit's redevelopment also had considerable success. Much of the city's Civic Center had been constructed in the 1950s. By the early 1970s, Detroit had completed the exemplary Gratiot-Lafayette Park and extended its impact with the nearby Elmwood Park project. These projects rejuvenated the eastern flank of the central business district, and the Corktown industrial project rebuilt the downtown's western flank. The Detroit Medical Center was also a fine example of institutional design. The city's 1951 Master Plan had provided an effective comprehensive strategy for much of this work.

At the same time, Detroit experienced persistent problems with its redevelopment agenda. It did not have one strong redevelopment agency, since the housing and planning commissions shared powers. This slowed down local action considerably. The city's weak pro-growth coalition also created problems since it tended to focus on specific projects. Furthermore, the automobile manufacturers who controlled the city's economy participated only a little in its redevelopment. Spatial problems, too, hampered the redevelopment effort. An unusually effective highway system and an overreliance on automobiles encouraged decentralization. Even within the central city that Blessing dreamed of rejuvenating first, dispersion was an important factor; the Cultural Center was located almost 2 miles from the central business district and its Civic Center. An even more serious challenge for Detroit's design agenda was the incomplete political and public support it received.

Political and Public Support

During Mayor Albert Cobo's administration (1950–57), Blessing's three-dimensional model of replanned Detroit caused constituents to complain that their neighborhood or church had been replaced with cardboard buildings or blank spaces representing some other land use. As Blessing noted in 1966, "This model poses some problems. . . . Subjecting such a presentation to citizen or neighborhood groups . . . , might disclose valid planning ideas at variance with the more limited but relevant ideas of the citizens' group." The "variance" that arose was summed up by a planner who later went to work for the school board. Calling Blessing "an impossible dreamer," the school board employee described a particular meeting with neighborhood residents and school board staff. The planners who came to the meeting brought beautiful sketches but little understanding of how those sketches affected the residents whose homes would have to be cleared out. As the school board employee noted, the sketches "showed the whole area within the [Grand] Boulevard with trees and lakes and God knows what all." Explaining the negative reaction to such schemes, the employee charged: "This was the kind of problem that Charlie Blessing created by holding up visions which could put anything else in a bad light. Is this only the beginnings of driving us all out of the city, or what is it?"[18]

During Jerome Cavanagh's administration, Blessing and his planners waged a prolonged battle over the city's changed plans for the Civic Center. They risked good relations with other city departments in the process. The Civic Center was the key to the city's central business district strategy. The 1947 plan drawn up by Eliel and Eero Saarinen, and revised by Eero in 1955, guided construction in the mid-1950s. But Eliel died in 1950, and Eero, the son, passed away in 1960. Then changes became necessary in the Saarinen plan, because of a donation for a $2 million fountain by the Dodge family and the need for additional parking facilities.[19]

The planning commission staff remained strongly committed to the original plan, which they had nurtured for years. Planners wanted the city to retain the most recent Saarinen plan instead of awarding a contract to Smith, Hinchman & Grylls, a firm with a design plan Blessing and several planners considered inferior to Saarinen's. Voluminous letters and memos indicate that the planners invested much time and emotion into this issue. Senior planner Charles McCafferty, of the Design Division, wrote: "I believe the Saarinen scheme is the best design that we could hope to get and I do not believe the chance of getting something better is worth the risk of getting [something] inferior." He warned that "our City Plan Commission staff position is being eroded by the direction of events in the last several weeks," an indication that the city was moving away from the Saarinen plan. "I believe this is the result of not returning to the original strong commitment and endorsement of the Saarinen scheme which has been our most valuable strategic resource." Blessing, McCafferty, and other planners met with representatives from several other city departments, but the planners complained that the department heads knew little about architectural design, and therefore "do not see any distinctions in the designs." Consequently McCafferty suggested, "they must be told that we don't accept anything but the detailed Saarinen plan."[20]

It is true that the other bureaucrats knew little about architectural design, but they did know what their departments needed, beginning with updated working drawings for new additions to the

Civic Center, whether or not these followed the original Saarinen plan. Their perspective prevailed, and the planners lost the battle when the city retained Smith, Hinchman, & Grylls to develop new Civic Center plans. The basis on which planners attempted to wield clout, their design expertise, was an insufficient basis for a political "victory."

The planners fought this battle just a few years before a major shakeup in city government. Heavily involved in the Civic Center debates was City Controller Richard Strichartz, one of Cavanagh's favored aides. After the 1967 civil disorders, Strichartz led a team that helped reorganize city government. That reorganization significantly reduced the power of planning in the city.

The battle over the Cultural Center offers an example of the growing community-based dissatisfaction over the planning commission's preoccupation with design. The Cultural Center contains the major branch of the Detroit Public Library and the Detroit Institute of Arts, two handsome, white marble structures. In late 1964 Mayor Cavanagh negotiated an agreement to expand the art institute and library and to encourage allied development within a larger redevelopment project. Cavanagh needed an updated area plan and directed Blessing to produce one. The urban design section's resulting plan was a marvel in design, but proposed a scheme that devastated the nearby neighborhood (figure 16.1).[21]

The concept of an expanded cultural center was not new. The city had long planned to enlarge existing facilities and add compatible museums and cultural buildings. But the new Cultural Center brochure, issued around 1965, graphically dramatized how large the project area would be. Few existing houses and neighborhood-based buildings remained. In their place were clustered apartment towers and townhouses, a beautifully sketched park with gardens, two huge connected reflecting pools, bricked plazas, and sculpture courts.[22]

The text of the brochure reveals the model that Blessing used to revamp the center. "This brochure," it began, "is a graphic presentation of a complete cultural center . . . , which if developed

Broadening the Planning Agenda

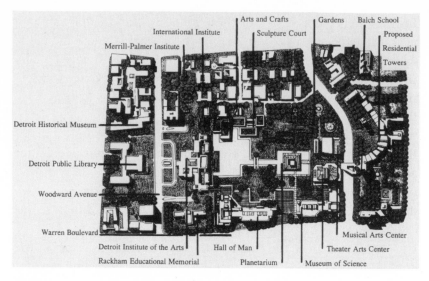

FIGURE 16.1. Detroit Cultural Center, from 1965 proposed project master plan. Drawn by Cheryl Coop; reproduced with permission from Detroit Planning and Development Department.

according to this plan will be comparable to the great cultural centers of the world, such as St. Mark's Square in Venice, with its panorama of life within a magnificently unified architectural composition, and Salzburg and Edinburgh, with their world famous music festivals." The Institute of Arts "would be the focus of the grand composition, with the reflecting pool lying at its base, merging into the sweeps of lawn, mirroring the shadowed trees." Equally flowery language described the park, gardens, and each major proposed cultural building, with appropriate references to European antecedents.[23]

If this had been developed as envisioned it would have gone a long way toward creating the totally redeveloped, beautifully designed inner city that Blessing dreamed of. The Cultural Center would make the city the focal point of art, drama, music, history, and science in the region, and help bring "the best of the world into Detroit." In a letter to federal urban renewal administrators, Blessing called the Cultural Center "a central feature in the new inner city of a third of a million people."[24]

But, politically, the mid-1960s were not the time to replace neighborhood buildings and housing with gardens and reflecting pools. The plan would have uprooted close to three thousand families at a time when tension over redevelopment projects was growing. Some charged that the city should be building low-income housing instead of encouraging deterioration by announcing such a project.[25] Critics pointed out that the proposed Cultural Center would tear down buildings of great historical significance to the African American community.

Public hearings in late 1967 revealed sharply drawn battle lines. On one side were the mayor, planning director, "civic leaders," and representatives of cultural institutions, including the president of the Detroit Science Museum Society and vice president of Wayne State University. On the other side a state representative, the assistant director of the Model Cities program, several church leaders and residents, and a group of Black architects, engineers, and planners represented the citizens' perspective.[26] This new group demonstrated that a major transformation had begun. The traditionally White and male planners had expanded their numbers to include women and racial minorities. These planners often had entirely different perspectives than their White colleagues.

An example is Hilanius Phillips, the planner assigned to the Cultural Center in the early 1970s. When Phillips began work for the planning commission in 1969, he was a junior clerk, later elevated to planner. He soon transferred from the planning commission to the city's community development department.

Phillips discovered that his grandmother, Bertha Hansbury, had founded an important music school for local children in the 1920s and that this building was scheduled to be razed. Phillips saw the Cultural Center plan as a glaring example of planners' insensitivity to inner-city residents and obeisance to dominant economic interests. As he put it: "It was basically who are the big shots and what do the big shots want, what do the big institutions want. Let's accommodate their needs, who cares about the adjacent property owners. And what really incensed me was the fact that in the Cultural Center I'd answer to the big wheels, the Founder's Society of the Art Institute, the Center for Creative Study, and the proposed science museum people. All of those were Farmington Hill folk, people with money."

The planning commission's emphasis on urban design over community needs only made matters worse. Design put a beautiful facade on what to this planner and his neighborhood was oppression. The designers themselves, chosen because of "how well they could render," tended to seek little input from users. Phillips notes that "it was easy to see why the orientation was that way simply by talking with those people. They had very introverted personalities and, yes, they were talented in drawing, but you could see that their designs didn't take into account how other people might view them and use them."[27]

The Cultural Center never was developed as Blessing envisioned it. In spite of constant promotion by Blessing, the city council cautiously chose not to adopt the 1965 design scheme. Efforts to improve the art center and build a science center did proceed, but the outdoor courts and reflecting pools went nowhere. Years of uncertainty about the area's future, however, steadily drove housing down. In time some area multifamily housing was built, but much of the original project site remained undeveloped.

The Cultural Center incident was symbolic not only of the political nonviability of the design agenda, but also of an entirely new direction in urban planning. This new direction had something to do with race, with the rise of planners of color and other social advocates who identified more closely with inner-city residents than had their predecessors. But it also had something to do with the coming of age of inner-city neighborhoods, and the rise of community-based urban planning. Model Cities played a part in bringing about this new perspective. In the old days the centrist redevelopment agenda of the postwar growth coalitions fostered top-down redevelopment and design schemes. In the 1960s and 1970s, such an orientation became much less viable politically.

The rise of urban disorders heightened these tendencies, and certainly played a part in cooling Detroit leaders' enthusiasm for urban aesthetics. Detroit—and this must have been true for Philadelphia as well—faced many more difficult problems than poor design. Poverty, racism, depopulation, and economic decline all clamored for attention. Neighborhoods fought for survival in the face of redevelopment and population loss. In this context, inner-city residents could not be expected to be enthusiastic about design agendas.

Things changed somewhat in the 1970s, with the demise of Model Cities and the rise of development-oriented Urban Development Action Grants and Community Development Block Grants. Also a significant factor for change in Detroit was the ascendancy of Mayor Coleman Young, who strongly supported riverfront and downtown development. The community-based orientation did not survive, even though social and economic conditions continued to worsen. The city turned once again to beautification as a development scheme. But this time the beautification focused on single buildings, such as the privately developed Renaissance Center, or on upper-middle-income complexes on the riverfront. Although the east riverfront evolved fairly cohesively, market forces and continued abandonment tended to isolate the city's other redevelopment projects like so many oases. The city functioned without an updated master plan, much less an overall design scheme.

As for the planners, they never again benefited from the single-minded vision Blessing had promoted. Mayor Roman Gribbs edged Blessing out with a meaningless office job in the early 1970s. With a new city charter, implemented in 1974, the planning director became a political appointee. Blessing retired gracefully, taught occasionally at Wayne State University, and died in September 1992.

Conclusion

Blessing had a magnificent vision for the city during years when
many people found it difficult to be optimistic. His professional skills
led some to call him "a planners' planner." His reputation and
expertise were nationally recognized, comparable in scope and
quality to Philadelphia's Edmund Bacon. But Bacon was better able
to use his design agenda as a springboard for major initiatives,
supported by popular mandate, and a strong redevelopment operation. Blessing's initiatives brought forth several successes, but neither his political position nor his redevelopment support system
were as strong as Bacon's.

Blessing's experience also showed that professional skills were
not sufficient to wield influence in Detroit. Blessing was a consummate professional with a well-qualified staff. As several incidents
showed, however, political viability was just as important as professional expertise. The planners had to fight for design principles
within a city government that gave such principles no particular
edge over administrative expediency. They also had to learn that,
when design initiatives appeared detrimental to existing residents,
skepticism manifested itself as opposition.

Detroit's urban designers helped produce several beautiful residential areas, in particular the Gratiot-Lafayette Park project site.
They also helped make institutional uses more cohesive and attractive, as in the Detroit Medical Center. Taken as a whole, the legacy
of the Blessing era was a set of tangible benefits for today's city. But
as an overall theme for inner-city revitalization, the design agenda
proved deficient. Design solutions could not rebuild the city, particularly when they ignored existing residents or failed to address their
community needs. These solutions could not, in themselves,
counteract substantial social forces leading to the abandonment of
the inner city by the very private market forces that would have
helped to rebuild that city.

In this context, it is entirely appropriate that the time came to
refocus planning. New federal policies helped urban communities

initiate self-improvement efforts. A new generation of planners—more diversified, more neighborhood based—took over from the urban designers.

But the full potential of this community-based initiative was also lost in the centrist development orientation of the 1980s. Occasionally some national planning leaders call for a return to the days of land-use planning and physical design, when professional skills were clearly focused and highly valued. This tale suggests caution, however. A modern, design-based agenda would need strong marketing, an aggressive redevelopment program, and a cooperative private sector—rare commodities in some cities. It would not only need a visionary urban designer on the order of Bacon or Blessing. It would also have to deal with a more inherent problem: without some provision for the social and economic transformation of America's central cities, design improvements provide only a pleasant facade. True revitalization has only a little to do with urban design.

CHAPTER 17

Five Strategies for Downtown

Policy Discourse and Planning since 1943

CARL ABBOTT

Scholars, planners, and citizens usually think of "downtown" as an entity too obvious to require careful definition. But as Carl Abbott argues in this chapter, "Americans have planned for their downtowns within a continually changing framework of images and assumptions about the nature of central business districts." During each decade since World War II, a different set of assumptions has dominated the discussion of downtown problems, shaped research, influenced federal policy, and favored certain planning solutions. Abbott delineates these changing ideas about "downtown" by examining the contents and analyzing the assumptions present in three types of formal and informal "texts": academic and professional

Reprinted from *Journal of Policy History* 5 (1993), pp. 5–27. Copyright © 1993 by Pennsylvania State University Press.

analyses of downtowns, implementation efforts and programs, and "formal downtown plans and planning processes that have tried to link theory and practice."

Abbott categorizes the changing images and assumptions that he distills from these sources into five sets of ideas about the nature of downtowns; he then outlines each set, explaining how the prevailing ideas conditioned the urban planning and policy solutions offered for each decade. Between 1945 and 1955, the central business district in major American cities was thought of as a "unitary center." From 1955 to 1965, downtowns were routinely described as "failing real estate markets." During 1965–75, scholars and planners characterized downtowns as a "federation of subdistricts." In the next decade, this image gave way to thinking about the downtown as a "set of individual experiences." After 1985, the central business district was viewed as "a command post in the global economy" requiring investment in office towers and supporting commercial services. The shift from one paradigm to the next has caused sharp discontinuities in the way people conceptualize the city and promoted the "repeated implementation of policies at right angles to those of the previous decade."

Abbott's analysis suggests that planners and scholars must understand that "downtown" is a constructed concept whose meaning has changed in accordance with broader trends in political thought, social circumstances, and cultural expression. People think differently now about cities than they used to, he contends, and those changes have inscribed contradictions in their planning policies and in the physical fabric of downtowns themselves. Planners, policy makers, and citizen participants can enhance long-range planning by becoming more aware of these operating assumptions and their history of changing with something approaching the speed of fashion. Readers who desire to become more familiar with some of the texts that Abbott argues have influenced the conception of the city during a particular decade will find abundant suggestions for further reading in the notes to this chapter. For two insightful critiques of the assumptions that scholars often employ in their thinking about the city, see Seymour J. Mandelbaum's "Historians and Planners," Journal of the American Planning Association *52 (Spring 1985): 185–88, and "Read-*

Broadening the Planning Agenda

ing Plans," Journal of the American Planning Association *56 (Summer 1990): 350–56. For case studies of the changes that have influenced planning in one post–World War II city, see Carl Abbott, "Urban Design in Portland, Oregon, as Policy and Process, 1960–1989,"* Planning Perspectives *6 (Jan. 1991): 1–18, and Howard Gillette Jr., "A National Workshop for Urban Policy,"* Public Historian *7 (Winter 1985): 7–27. For contrasting overviews of twentieth-century policy and planning, readers should consult Peter Hall's* Cities of Tomorrow *(London: Basil Blackwell, 1988) and Jon Teaford's* The Rough Road to Renaissance *(Baltimore: The Johns Hopkins University Press, 1990).* EDITORS

Americans have planned for their downtowns within a continually changing framework of images and assumptions about the nature of central business districts. During each decade since World War II, discussion of downtown problems and possibilities has been dominated by a distinct set of assumptions that have conditioned academic research, federal policy, and local planning. From decade to decade, experts on downtowns have chosen different themes on which to pin their interpretation of downtown growth, change, and policy needs. As the understanding of the situation has changed, so have the preferred planning solutions and public interventions.

This argument about the importance of understanding the history of "downtown" as an intellectual construct can be contrasted with three approaches that have dominated the analysis of downtown planning and policy in the United States over the past half century. A number of writers have analyzed downtown policy as an expression of interest-group or class politics. In this interpretation, downtown is one of several arenas in which different groups vie for the control of urban land patterns. Most commonly, the battle for downtown is seen as a one-sided contest between the city's large corporations, banks, and landowners on one side and small businesses and low-income residents on the other.[1]

Other analysts have adopted a structure-driven model in which downtown development and redevelopment programs are seen as rational responses to specific socioeconomic circumstances and problems. A pure structural model is organized around a dynamic of challenge and response. Changes external to the policy system such as new technologies, immigration, or the regional readjustment of economic activity create problems that call forth policy solutions. In turn, altered circumstances may give rise to new problems that call forth new solutions. This model assumes that policies are logically situated between problems and programs, although policies may have unintended as well as intended consequences.[2]

A third approach follows a teleological model that traces the roots of present successes. For example, Bernard Frieden and Lynne Sagalyn in *Downtown, Inc.: How America Rebuilds Its Cities* present a structural model written as the story of progress. A single clear problem is identified in the 1940s and 1950s. Politicians and planners then work through trial and error toward an increasingly effective solution, moving from urban renewal to festival markets and downtown malls.[3]

Without rejecting these three approaches to the history of downtown policy, this essay offers a supplementary perspective. I believe that many scholars and planners have shared an underlying assumption that "downtown" is a singular knowable entity— a basic category of urban analysis. In this common conception, academic and applied research presumably illuminate more and more aspects of this knowable entity, allowing the fine-tuning of plans and policies. My emphasis, in contrast, is on "downtown" as a constructed concept whose meaning or understanding has undergone surprisingly rapid changes. As the structural model suggests, these mutable understandings have certainly been rooted in the changing social and economic structure of American cities, and they have certainly proved of varying use to different groups and interests. However, they have also had lives of their own as intellectual constructs, with the thematic understanding of one decade defined in part as a reaction against earlier ideas. In turn, these ideas about downtowns can be seen as filtered reflections of broader trends in political thought or cultural expression.

Broadening the Planning Agenda

This essay explores these changing ideas by examining the contents and assumptions of a variety of formal and informal texts. One obvious set of sources is academic and professional analysis of downtowns by geographers, planners, and real estate specialists. The discussion is also based on my understanding of implementation efforts and programs, from urban renewal to the pursuit of amenity projects. Situated between the analysis and the programs have been formal downtown plans and planning processes that have tried to link theory and practice. Chronologically parallel shifts in content and emphasis among the three sorts of texts help to substantiate the assumption that public action about central business districts has been rooted in a partly autonomous realm of changing ideas.

The shift from one thematic understanding to another has not been unidirectional. Downtown policy has been characterized by sharp discontinuities and the repeated implementation of policies at right angles to those of the previous decade. The changing themes and recommended solutions can be summarized as a set of ideal types. No single city has exactly matched the sequence, and thematic elements from one policy era have carried over into the following decades. Nevertheless, the historian can define five successive themes and related policies:

1945–55: The downtown as the *unitary center* of the American metropolis required improved access through highway improvements and downtown ring roads.

1955–65: Downtown understood as a *failing real estate market* appeared to require the land assembly and clearance associated with the urban renewal program.

1965–75: Downtown as a *federation of subdistricts* called for community conservation, historic preservation, and "human-scale" planning.

1975–85: Downtown as a *set of individual experiences* required regulation of private design and public assistance for cultural facilities, retail markets, open space, and other amenities.

1985 to the present: Viewed as a *command post* in the global economy, downtown has required planning for expanded office districts and supporting facilities.

1945–1955: Downtown as the Unitary Center of the Metropolitan Area

During the first half of the twentieth century American downtowns were thought of as the hub of a unified metropolitan community. Although the metropolitan area concept was developed in the early twentieth century, it gained broad popularity with the definition of the easily grasped Standard Metropolitan Area for the 1950 census. The idea assumed the existence of a dominant central city, which was itself structured around a downtown core.

Building on work from the 1920s and 1930s, experts in the postwar decade analyzed land values to identify the precise center of central business districts (CBDs) and the gradient of real estate values away from that center. John Rannells examined central Philadelphia land uses to define the degree of dispersion of CBD activities.[4] Other researchers tried to distinguish "downtown" from its surrounding blocks of deteriorated or transitional uses. Raymond Murphy, James Vance, and Bart Epstein epitomized the research effort with an elaborate analytical definition of the downtown based on building heights and the percentage of total floor space on each block that was devoted to a carefully limited list of "central business uses." Their standardized definition was intended to allow easy comparisons among downtown areas taken as units.[5]

Related studies of commuting and shopping patterns found that the golden age of the 1920s, when downtowns were *the* place to go, was alive and well after World War II. Gerald Breese and Donald Foley found little substance to the notion that suburban dispersion was undermining central business districts.[6] Most planning projections of downtown land-use needs assumed a straight-line continuation of past relationships between metropolitan growth and the role and size of the central business district.[7]

Business and marketing literature agreed on the strength of downtown as an office and retail center. C. T. Jonassen's analyses of shopper preferences in Columbus, Seattle, and Houston found that downtowns held a significant edge over struggling suburban shopping centers. "The advantages now enjoyed by the central business district," he concluded, "are not easily alterable, for they are rooted in the ecological structure of American cities and in their cultural and social system." Downtowns, said J. D. Carroll, were the "only focus" and the "only sites" for essential urban activities. The sole requirement was successful treatment of traffic congestion and parking. Whatever the changes in metropolitan areas, concluded the Central Business District Council of the Urban Land Institute in 1954, "downtown continues to hold its position as the gathering place of America—the center of business and finance, the center of shopping on its most lavish scale, the center for theaters and for culture."[8]

The assumption that everyone still wanted to get downtown defined the logical focus of planning activity as the improvement of access and circulation. Downtown itself was taken as a given—as a unique and essential element within a metropolitan structure. The postwar development plans that dozens of cities prepared in 1943, 1944, and 1945 offered broadly inclusive programs for capital investment with little special targeting for downtown.[9] Prominent in the last generation of classic master plans during the 1940s were proposals for civic centers as metropolitan foci, a recycling of a key idea from the City Beautiful era that assumed the natural centering of the metropolis.[10]

Two points stand out in the major comprehensive plans prepared in the middle and late 1940s for Washington, Richmond, Dallas, and Cincinnati.[11] The first is that few of the planners considered the CBD to be seriously at risk. The plans tended to give greatest attention to housing, neighborhood identity, and neighborhood conservation. In turn, neighborhoods were to be linked together into a single metropolitan community by transportation improvements and by their common relation to the downtown. For example, Cincinnati's *Metropolitan Master Plan* of 1948 acknowledged the "close relationship between the Central Business District and each community" but did not see the CBD itself as requiring attention. The Dallas plan ran to fourteen volumes, none focused specifically on downtown.

When downtown did need attention, the solution was improved access through peripheral freeways. Harland Bartholomew wanted to use the 1946 *Master Plan for Richmond* to promote the vision of a tightly centralized city, in part by expanding the central business district and tying it to neighborhoods by a set of highways and widened boulevards. The new or improved roads would define the boundaries for an expanded business core. The result, said the document, would be "continued stability and protection of values within the central business district." The National Capital Park and Planning Commission offered a similar prescription in its 1950 plan for the Washington region. Its proposal for an inner highway loop drawing a 1-mile circle around the White House and the retail-office core was the work of Harland Bartholomew in his role as chief consultant to the NCPPC. The idea was seconded by the influential Washington architect Louis Justement, who had made a similar proposal in a 1946 book, *New Cities for Old.*[12]

Victor Gruen's highly publicized plan for downtown Fort Worth is a climax of thinking about a unitary downtown. An architect with experience in designing shopping centers, Gruen proposed a grand scheme to isolate the core of Fort Worth within a ring of six grand parking garages served by a highway loop. With its streets freed from automobiles, downtown Fort Worth could recapitulate the suburban shopping mall. Had Fort Worth acted on the plan, it would have given physical expression to Gruen's valuation of freeway loops and ring roads as "defense lines" and "fortification systems" around the downtown. It would also have expressed his understanding of the "metropolitan core" as the "heart of the city."[13]

1955–1965: Downtown as a Failing Business Center

In January 1955, J. Ross McKeever summarized the real estate trends of the past year for the readers of *Urban Land,* the trade journal of the real estate development industry. He left no doubt that downtown was "the functional heart of a metropolitan area" and the "focal point of community life." Two years later, Baltimore developer James Rouse told the same readership that downtowns were in serious trouble. They were physically obsolete and could not effectively reach the growing suburban market. Planners so far had dealt only with symptoms rather than sources of downtown problems. Only drastic action could ensure the *rebirth* of the central business district.[14]

The contrast between the two views demonstrates the rapid emergence during the middle 1950s of a new understanding of downtown as a declining activity center and failing real estate market. By the early 1960s, most Americans understood downtown as a district in crisis because of the relative or absolute decline of its attractiveness to shoppers, theatergoers, and service businesses. The 1958 Census of Business played an important role by documenting the shift of retailing and personal services to suburban locations. The 1960 Census of Population administered an additional shock by showing that many central cities had fallen far short of their expected populations. Scholars responded with a cluster of studies that examined 1948–58 data as evidence of decline. As in the previous decade, however, most of these studies continued to treat downtowns as economic units, comparing aggregated data on sales and employment.[15]

One local response was to organize a business group devoted specifically to upgrading the competitiveness of downtown. Unlike areawide chambers of commerce or the ubiquitous postwar planning committees of the 1940s, these downtown groups battled for a share of the retail and service market rather than working for aggregate economic development. The later 1950s and early 1960s

FIGURE 17.1.   The tower in the parking lot was typical of efforts to rescue downtown as a failing business center. Cleveland City Planning Commission (1959).

also brought a round of focused downtown plans that worried explicitly about the future of the central business district (figures 17.1 and 17.2). City planners now expressed the new understanding that downtown could easily lose its logical and organic predominance. Minneapolis and Cleveland planners worried that

FIGURE 17.2. The visual rhetoric of planning in the 1950s emphasized sweeping treatments of the entire downtown. Cleveland City Planning Commission (1959).

the future vitality of their downtowns was threatened by suburbanization and blight, as well as traffic. A series of downtown plans for Cincinnati in 1958, 1961, and 1964 noted the shortfall of new private investment, proposed new zoning, and called for redevelopment of blighted land.[16]

Five Strategies for Downtown

The most obvious policy response to downtown business decline was urban renewal. Amendments in 1954 and 1959 transformed the Housing Act of 1949 into a downtown renewal program. Urban renewal advocates assumed that downtown could be made competitive by underwriting the real estate market and adding in public projects as attractors. The preferred target was underutilized or "blighted" land just beyond the retail and office core. The nearly universal results were peripheral clearance projects and construction of public facilities. Academic research in the later 1950s supported the renewal strategy by emphasizing the distinction between an intensively used downtown core and a less intensively used "frame." Downtown frames were hodge-podge zones of warehouses, light industry, cheap housing, transportation terminals, auto dealers, and public institutions such as hospitals. The idea evolved in applied work in Seattle and Cincinnati and was elaborated in detail by Edgar Horwood and Ronald Boyce in 1959. Ernest Jurkat presented a similar concept with different terminology when he defined a "belt" zone in cities like St. Louis that roughly matched the functions of the frame.[17] The analysis justified land clearance in downtown fringe areas to protect and enhance the core.

Plans in Oakland and Baltimore were good summaries of the new views. A reviewer for the *Journal of the American Institute of Planners* called Baltimore's *Plan for the Central Business District* the "prototype of the comprehensive CBD plan." Increases in private and public offices partly balanced the projected declines in retail, wholesale, and industrial uses. Downtown not only needed new facilities such as parking garages but also required much broader replanning of land uses to support a selected set of region-serving functions. The centerpiece for implementation in Baltimore was the Charles Center redevelopment project to remake the downtown core. Oakland's *Central District Plan* in 1966 distinguished among a core, inner ring, and peripheral ring, each of which called for a different set of public interventions.[18]

1965–1975: Downtown as a Federation of Everyday Environments

The massive land clearances of the 1950s fueled a reaction against urban renewal in the early 1960s from both the conservative and liberal sides of the political spectrum. The former emphasized the economic failures of urban renewal and its inability to improve on the private market in land and housing. The latter described its unwanted social impacts and the destruction of viable lower-income communities. One of the perhaps unexpected side effects was the redefinition of downtown as a set of distinct functional subdistricts, each of which appeared to foster a different sort of activity and each of which needed particularized treatment.

This new vision or image drew on the work of Herbert Gans, Jane Jacobs, and Kevin Lynch, all of whom suggested that downtowns had to be experienced on the relatively small scale of individual buildings, blocks, and districts.[19] The contrast between older and newer views can be read in a comparison of Gruen's 1955 plan for Fort Worth and his plan for Boston from the early 1960s. In the latter he identified a dozen and a half "pedestrian nuclei, each devoted to a variety of land uses, with an emphasis, however, on those which have developed historically." Seven of the nuclei were in the so called "CBD" and eleven just outside.[20] The transition can also be seen in a comparison of 1961 statements by Jacobs and Charles Abrams. Drawing their sense of the American city from New York, both Jacobs and Abrams hoped to achieve vibrant, active downtown districts. Abrams also reaffirmed the idea of downtown as a single unit, asserting that "a downtown area is a cohesive unit which lives or dies as a whole." Jacobs, in contrast, treated downtown as a set of intertwined activity centers. In the best-selling *Death and Life of Great American Cities,* she wrote about diversity, subdistricts, and concentrated "pools of use."[21]

Academics participated in the new understanding of downtowns as multiple centers with behavioral studies of user subareas and efforts to define the social and economic geography of downtowns. Common products of the 1960s were studies of retail clustering and the mapping of functional subdistricts.[22] University of Washington researchers found that downtown Seattle was composed of "user subsystems" and activity nodes that should be delineated before the city undertook any new plans and projects.[23] Historical geographers such as David Ward and Martyn Bowden supplemented the current mapping efforts by studying the historical coalescence of downtown out of a variety of functional subareas.[24]

It is clear that subarea analysis was in the air by the later 1960s. In 1963 consultant Donald Monson had responded to the concerns of the Central Association of Seattle with a *Comprehensive Plan for the Central Business District*. Monson's proposal was Gruenesque, ignoring the constraints of the city's steep hills to propose a ring highway defining a unitary downtown, fringe parking garages, and pedestrianized shopping streets. Seven years later, the Central Association's own annual report stated that downtown Seattle was best understood in terms of a "system of functional zones, each with a distinct character that, when integrated into the whole, make[s] up the central nervous system of our metropolitan community."[25]

Omaha's formal plans also displayed the changing policy orientations of the three postwar decades. As Janet Daly-Bednarek has shown, the "Omaha Plan" of 1956 scarcely recognized downtown as a problem and emphasized infrastructure investment. Ten years later, the *Central Omaha Plan* (1966) recognized special downtown needs but placed its faith in interstate highways and urban renewal. The next seven years, however, brought a generational transition in civic leadership and a willingness to focus on the multiple experiences that downtown had to offer. A new central business district plan in 1973 divided downtown Omaha into eight "neighborhoods," or functional areas. Planners hoped that a variety of functions and attractions would pull residents back downtown, and that each identifiable district would strengthen the others.[26]

The story was the same in Portland. Urban renewal planners in 1957–60 envisioned a compact downtown defined by a freeway

Broadening the Planning Agenda

FIGURE 17.3. By the 1970s planners were thinking in terms of downtown subdistricts and depicting downtowns from the perspective of the street. From *Portland Downtown Plan* (1972). Courtesy: Portland State University Library.

loop and peripheral parking lots. A decade later, a new generation of business leaders, politicians, and citizens redefined downtown Portland around the theme of variety. The citizen advisory committee that wrote the planning guidelines for the new Downtown Plan of 1972 divided the core into twenty-one districts on the basis of current uses, opportunities for redevelopment, and visual coherence. Previous plans for downtown Portland had offered bird's-eye views in which tiny automobiles coursed along looping highways between toy houses and skyscrapers. The 1972 plan depicted downtown Portland as a sequence of sidewalk scenes. Retired men played chess in the park, students munched junk food near Portland State University, shoppers strolled a transit mall, and children played around a new fountain (figure 17.3).[27]

By the early 1970s, the subdistricted downtown was as much a staple of planning documents as the unitary downtown had been in 1950. Indeed, subarea analysis remained a standard for downtown description into the 1990s. After 1975, however, it became accepted background rather than an exciting discovery. A sampling of downtown plans from 1976–86 shows that Dallas and Atlanta each identified three districts. Dayton identified seven, Washington seven (or perhaps ten), Richmond eight, and Oakland eleven. Denver found six districts in its core and four more in a surrounding transition zone. Seattle built its downtown plan on eleven "areas of varied character."[28]

1975–1985: Downtown as a Set of Individual Experiences

As American cities recovered from the severe real estate recession of 1973–74, planners and policy makers reevaluated their discovery of the multiple downtown. Subdistrict analysis identified a wider range of development opportunities than had a unitary analysis. At the same time, its recognition of residential groups and secondary business clusters built in a bias in favor of conservation and enhancement rather than redevelopment.

The desire to stimulate downtown business and investment brought a renewed interest in downtowns as consciously manipulated artifacts. In this newest understanding, downtown was less a set of distinct social environments than a collection of opportunities for individual experiences. Downtown areas were increasingly seen as environments to be consciously designed in the interest of enjoyment and tourism. This conception of downtown as a theme park accepted its loss of primacy within the metropolitan community. It was to be reconstructed to serve tourists, conventioneers, and occasional visitors on safari from the suburbs. It also accepted that suburban "outer cities" were emerging as coequals to downtown and then borrowed some of the ideas of the consciously designed suburban environment. If direct retail competition with suburban malls was a failure, planners asked, why not emphasize specialized entertainment and shopping. The results were downtowns conceived as museums, cultural centers, amenity districts, and amusement parks.[29]

An obvious reflection of the new understanding was the flood of interest in the academic and professional literature on the economic role of the arts and on the recovery of physical amenities, especially along waterfronts. Books and articles on the arts as contributors to urban development policy peaked in the early 1980s.[30] Beginning in the early 1970s, William H. Whyte examined the environmental determinants of individual responses to parks, plazas, sidewalks, and other downtown public spaces. He helped to popularize a view of downtown as a series of personal experiences and choices.[31] A number of educational programs and public interest lobbying groups with an interest in the promotion of enjoyable downtowns also emerged or expanded during the late 1970s and early 1980s. Examples include the Main Street program of the National Trust for Historic Preservation, the Waterfront Center, and Partners for Livable Places.

Although usually read as cultural criticism rather than policy analysis, Robert Venturi, Denise Scott Brown, and Stephen Izenour's manifesto *Learning from Las Vegas* (1972) documents the same emerging understanding of downtowns. The book defined Las Vegas as the populist alternative to the carefully ordered and centered city. The city's "downtown" is its commercial strip, a new main street of activity nodes that are connected by automobiles and announced by huge signs. The purpose of commercial Las Vegas is to present a series of surfaces. It is a city whose business district is explicitly designed as a sequence of fragmented and individualized experiences.[32]

In rejecting the necessity and value of a unitary downtown, *Learning from Las Vegas* was an early example of the postmodern turn in Western culture. Postmodernism emerged in art, architecture, and literature as a reaction against the austerity, universalism, or formalism of mid-twentieth-century culture. Given its name in the early 1970s, its emergence as a set of linked ideas or artistic preferences has been dated variously to the early 1960s and to the 1970s.[33] The elevation of downtown as a stage set in the mid-1970s fit with a new postmodern emphasis on the inherent value of the unexpected. The self-consciously theatrical design of the show-off buildings that characterized postmodernism by the later 1970s depended on juxtaposition of styles, jumbling of spaces, and playful use of historical allusion. City centers themselves were increasingly presented as open theaters of individualism. Jonathan Raban's *Soft City* (1974), offered by David Harvey as one of the first postmodern treatments of the city, depicted London as an "encyclopedia" or "emporium of styles." In Raban's version, living in the city was an art in itself, making the physical setting a stage or canvas for its inhabitants.[34] In practical application, the new aesthetic meant downtown plans that emphasized design values and aimed for special attractions to appeal to the maturing baby boomers who would soon find themselves caricatured as "yuppies."

Boston and Baltimore are easily identified as pioneers of the American downtown as artifact. Baltimore's Inner Harbor redevelopment program and Boston's Faneuil Hall/Waterfront project, begun in the late 1960s, bore fruit between 1976 and 1981 with attractive new open space and spectacularly successful retail complexes that were quickly dubbed "festival markets." The Boston and Baltimore examples and dozens of imitative projects are open to David Harvey's critical description of "an architecture of spectacle, with its sense of surface glitter and transitory participatory pleasure."[35] A climax product of the species is Horton Plaza in San Diego, planned in the 1970s and opened in 1987. The "Plaza" is a contrived environment that draws visitors into a mildly but deliberately confusing shopping mall. The interior spaces offer multiple levels, bridges, passageways, and curving corridors, programmed with safely interesting activities and decked out in painful pseudo-Mediterranean pastels. They are explicitly presented as a "fun" alternative to the "gray" office towers of downtown San Diego.

Festival markets were part of a long shopping list of amenity projects for the 1980s. Exhibition space in major convention cities doubled between 1975 and 1990. Cities added performing arts centers, arts districts, waterfront redevelopments, downtown open spaces, historic districts, rehabilitated hotels, and museum/aquarium complexes.[36] San Antonio's roster of projects for the 1980s included the River Center festival market, an expanded convention center, a domed stadium, a restored theater, a new art museum in an adapted historic building, a luxury hotel, and a transit mall. Most of the projects on the standard list aimed at the creation of low-end service jobs to replace the manufacturing and warehousing jobs that were no longer located on the downtown fringe.

In formal planning, the emphasis shifted significantly to design control, preservation planning, fine-tuning of floor-area ratios, amenities bonuses, and similar approaches that treated downtowns as visual experiences. Federal allowance of accelerated depreciation for historic buildings in 1976 and investment tax credits after 1981 encouraged a boom in the designation of buildings and downtown districts. The interest built on the earlier thematic understanding of downtown as set of subareas. It took off when the designation of historic districts also appeared to meet the newly perceived need to turn downtown into a collection of stage sets.

Downtown planners by the early 1980s tended to see their task as promoting and linking groups of experiences from which visitors could pick and choose.[37] New Orleans's Growth Management Program (1975) used historic districts and incentive zoning for pedestrian amenities. The innovative *Time for Springfield* (Massachusetts) plan of 1978 emphasized recycling historical structures, open space, cultural facilities, reclamation of the Connecticut riverfront, and aggressive programming of public festivals. Milwaukee's *Downtown Goals and Policies* (1985) stressed pedestrian linkages among hotels, convention center, retailers, and cultural attractions; it placed design review and improved lakefront access near the top of implementation measures. Richmond's *Downtown Plan* (1984) emphasized the need to maintain an attractive environment, to cluster amenities, to expand cultural activities, and to tie together the downtown subdistricts. It placed marketing, public relations, advertising, and special events on the same level with financial assistance and transportation in the implementation program. "A more alive Downtown," said the plan, "means more culture and leisure time offerings, special shopping opportunities and other uniquely urban qualities which add to the quality of life in Richmond. Bit by bit it all results in an improved national image, a better local identity, and an increased sense of pride in one's city."[38] The new directions of aesthetic planning reached a climax in the San Francisco *Downtown Plan* of 1985. Although the document aimed at maintaining San Francisco's predominance as a world commercial city, it gave nearly half its space to issues such as protecting solar access; increasing open space; requiring the preservation of 271 historic buildings; and promoting an interesting skyline through the design review of new buildings by a panel of experts.[39]

1985 to the Present: Downtown as Command Post

Since the late nineteenth century, skyscrapers filled with executives and typists have been the essential symbol for downtowns. After spending the 1970s arm in arm with pedestrians, experts rediscovered downtown's continuing importance as a transaction center in the mid-1980s. The recognition was triggered by the continued downtown building boom that ran from the mid-1970s to the end of the 1980s. In the thirty largest metropolitan areas, office construction in the first half of the 1980s ran at twice the rate of the 1970s, which had in turn outpaced the 1960s by 50 percent.[40] The boom hit more than New York, Boston, and Los Angeles. Less glamorous cities like Louisville added three million square feet of office space and Cleveland added six million.[41]

The office boom held out the hope that downtowns could tap into the global service economy at the high end of managerial, professional, finance, and consulting jobs as well as at the low end of entertainment and personal services. It substantially re-created an understanding of downtowns as unique centers. In this case, however, they were seen less as the unitary center of an individual metropolis than as centralized nodes of activity within national and global networks. In this newest understanding, general retailing for the metropolitan market is no longer viewed as an important downtown function. Landscape critic J. B. Jackson agrees that the urban center has lost its role in daily life, transformed instead into "an impressive symbol of remote power and unattainable wealth." The downtown as command post is "dedicated to power and money and technology, not to traditional human activities or institutions."[42] One academic response has been a large literature on the restructuring of economic space within the globalized economy, presenting downtowns as the most visible expressions of the structure of economic power. As John Friedmann and Goetz Wolff have put it, world cities are increasingly divided between worker "ghettoes" and capitalists in their office tower "citadels."[43] Traditional geographers and economists explain the emergence of the high-rise downtown in terms of the continuing value of central locations for face-to-face contact and the quick exchange of sensitive or specialized information—what Gail Garfield Schwartz calls "off-the-record information [which] cannot be transmitted in any way except in person.[44]

A second academic and professional response has been a new interest in the politics of real estate development and deal making. Paul Peterson's *City Limits* set a theme for the 1980s by arguing that economic development is the primary and proper role for local government.[45] Urban policy specialists have zeroed in on cases such as the North Loop project in Chicago as examples of the political complexities of contemporary development.[46] The 1980s saw a new academic interest in real estate development curricula that span the interests of planning programs and business schools. Traditional regulatory planning is now matched by the newer subdiscipline of development planning, whose practitioners mobilize public resources to encourage growth on a project-by-project basis.

In formal planning, the 1980s brought a renewed attention to accommodating the perceived needs for downtown *growth,* at least in the form of office space. Philadelphia's extensively analyzed downtown plan of 1988 is characterized as an "economic development plan" whose first goal is to "achieve significant economic growth" by developing the "enormous potential" of the "office-based information and service economy."[47] New plans for Denver (1986) and Cleveland (1988) aim to reinforce downtowns as financial and administrative centers. The emphasis on the networked downtown suggests the continued strength of the generalizing forces of modernization. The current idea of downtown as command post affirms the essential characteristics of modernism: abstraction, deracination, universalism. It calls for architecture and planning in which the function of information exchange overrides complexities and variations in form. The rise of this newest interpretation implies that the postmodern themes of the 1970s and 1980s are ordinary turns in an ongoing discourse. Postmodernism as seen from downtown is part of a continuing dialogue rather than an epochal rewriting of a century-old understanding of urban development.

Conclusion

The primary texts of downtown policy show that we think differently about cities now than we did in earlier decades. Not only do we know more and different things, but we fit this knowledge together around different understandings and assumptions that seem too obvious to articulate. We already know that we must be careful in projecting economic and demographic trends. We need to exercise the same caution about intellectual trends, for accepted preferences in planning ideas can change with nearly the speed of artistic or architectural fashion. New understandings are as likely to reject or ignore the recent past as to amplify its particular themes. Only by taking the historian's backward step can we see how far and how quickly those understandings have moved.

An obvious lesson for policy makers is that our mutable understanding of downtown has built contradictions into its planning goals and physical fabric. Downtowns show an unresolved tension between the goals of the current and previous decades. At the street level, for example, they are structured as a grab bag of individual choices. Above the street they are utilized intensely by the corporate sector. The contemporary mixed-use development, with its lower-floor shops, restaurants, and theaters and upper-level offices, is a tangible manifestation of the tension. At the same time, the office-expansion agenda can clash directly with the earlier understanding of downtown as a coalition of subareas. Office-development planning offers little place to districts that do not contribute to the explicit corporate-center strategy. Given these contradictions, policy makers should not be surprised that the legitimation of subdistricts and the promotion of amenities created constituencies that may challenge the plans of the 1990s. Seattle is a case in point of popular resistance to plans with a tight focus on control functions. Many residents in the later 1980s came to view downtown development and the preservation of a downtown usable by average citizens as competing goals. In 1989 they voted a symbolic limit on downtown development when it appeared that the new *Land Use and Transportation Plan for Downtown Seattle* (1985) failed to protect either the appearance of downtown or the livability of close-in neighborhoods.

The challenge in Seattle and other cities such as San Francisco suggests that planners and policy makers need to turn their attention to the characteristics that make downtown different from other nodes in the transactional grid. Whether we call them outer cities or outtowns or edge cities, peripheral office clusters can house many transactional functions as effectively as established downtowns. Nevertheless, downtown continues to offer the urban advantages of variety and intensity in ways not possible on the edge. Indeed, the one advantage of core over periphery is its social inclusiveness. Downtown is certainly a natural home for plugged-in executives, but it can also be an effective setting for integrating old minorities, new minorities, and majority society. It remains the one part of the metropolis that most effectively generates new ideas by bringing together the greatest range of groups and individuals. The idea of a socially inclusive downtown could logically recombine the old idea of a unitary center with the mid-1960s vision of downtown as the home to distinct groups and communities. Such a reconstructed understanding of downtown as everybody's neighborhood would also reaffirm the belief in cities as single metropolitan systems that offer comparable sets of opportunities to all of their citizens.

CHAPTER 18

The Impact of Ideology on American Town Planning

From the Garden City to Battery Park City

TONY SCHUMAN

ELLIOTT SCLAR

Tony Schuman and Elliott Sclar maintain that Americans are losing two important social battles—for the quality of everyday life and for economic prosperity—because of their long-term reluctance to intervene in market operations. In this final chapter, the authors analyze the key assumptions underlying the historic debates concerning planning and housing that have occurred over the course of the twentieth century. They focus in particular on the question of what the public role should be in undertaking urban and regional planning, and they investigate that question by comparing the development of two new planned communities in New York City—Roosevelt Island and Battery Park City. These two projects offer competing paradigms of urban development and exemplify long-term ideological struggles over the government's role in supporting and regulating metropolitan development.

Sclar and Schuman frame their analysis of the two "new towns" with an overview of the "contradictory pulls" that ideology and specific historic circumstances have exerted upon American town planning from 1909 to the present. They focus on several examples of successful public interventions in planning—the Emergency Fleet housing of the World War I era and the federal greenbelt towns, for example—but note that only national emergencies like wars or depressions inspire Americans to abandon their normal antipathy to government intervention in regional and urban development. They go on to compare and contrast Roosevelt Island—a publicly funded project with a mandated heterogeneous community of residents—with Battery Park City—originally a public project, but later privatized and rapidly transformed into an exclusive upper-income enclave. For their accounts of the principal planning features and the contrasting paths of development and socioeconomic composition for the two planned communities, the authors draw upon reports from the Department of Housing and Urban Development, Regional Planning Association reports, plans of New York City, contemporary newspaper and magazine coverage, and official reports for both housing projects.

Using the course of development at Roosevelt Island to substantiate their argument, Schuman and Sclar contend that planning for equity can only succeed when a public authority exercises its will over the private market. The example of Battery Park City, on the other hand, suggests the vulnerability of comprehensive physical and social planning to distortion in the face of speculative market pressures and an ideology of privatism. The dilemma posed by these two examples is "how to give free reign to private investment to solve as many problems as possible while simultaneously superseding the market to solve problems beyond its capacity." The lesson to be learned, the authors argue, is that Americans must overcome the common wisdom that holds that equity and efficiency are mutually incompatible. They must realize that the ideology of privatism has long-term negative social consequences.

For the classic urban history analysis of privatism, readers should consult Sam Bass Warner's The Private City *(Philadelphia: University of*

Pennsylvania Press, 1987). An excellent recent study on the interaction between private and public forces in planning in New York City is Joel Schwartz's The New York Approach *(Columbus: Ohio State University Press, 1993). For an analysis of the few notable examples of successful public interventions in this century, see Michael Lang's article on Yorkship Garden Village in this collection, Joseph Arnold's* The New Deal in the Suburbs *(Columbus: Ohio State University Press, 1971), Clarence Stein's* Toward New Towns for America *(Cambridge: MIT Press, 1978), and Arnold R. Alanen and Joseph A. Eden's Main Street Ready-Made (Madison: State Historical Society of Wisconsin, 1987). For a pointed overview of the broader economic forces and policies widening the gap between rich and poor, see Kevin Phillips,* The Politics of Rich and Poor *(New York: Random House, 1990).* EDITORS

Democracy's Challenge

City and Region in Disequilibrium   The social and economic imbalance between central cities and their surrounding regions is today reaching crisis proportions. The inhabitants of both feel, in strikingly different ways, as though the market responses to the ideals of a privatized society have brought them face-to-face with a brick wall. America's central cities are in severe trouble. It matters little how we define that trouble. Their economic bases are shrinking as their rates of poverty, homelessness, and crime are rising. An ominous recent development is that these center city trends are becoming increasingly typical in some of the older suburbs adjacent to their borders. At the same time, increasing numbers of people are finding that the ownership of a single-family detached dwelling accessed by private automobiles and situated in self-governing communities located at safe, and hence ever lengthening, distances from the economic and social woes of the center city is no longer within economic reach. The New Jersey Supreme Court's ruling that municipalities everywhere in the state must provide a "fair share" of regional affordable housing (the Mount Laurel decisions) calls into question even the notion that distant suburbs should any longer be socially insulated. In a similar vein, the city manager of Hartford, Connecticut, proposed the dispersal of inner city public housing residents to surrounding suburban communities.[1] In 1991, when the mayor of Bridgeport, Connecticut, filed for municipal bankruptcy, she declared, "The system isn't working."[2]

This systemic disequilibrium between city and suburb is due in part to the restructuring of American society from a manufacturing-based economy to a service-based one. More important, it represents the geographical consequence of a decade of conservative fiscal policies that have widened the gap between rich and poor.[3] While the wealthy have been able socially to insulate themselves from the distressed and tense urban centers—"the secession of the successful"—the suburban enclaves to which they have moved are not immune from the ecological consequences of unplanned development.[4] The impact of environmental destruction, pollution, congestion, and chaotically dispersed land use has raised the cost of doing business and diminished the quality of daily life for them as well.

The renewed interest in more tightly planned communities among developers, design professionals, and the public at large attests to a widespread dissatisfaction with suburban sprawl.[5] More and more attention is being focused on the traditional neighborhood development advocated by architects Elizabeth Plater-Zyberk and Andres Duany and the pedestrian pocket concept developed by Peter Calthorpe.[6] Although this growing regional discontent may provide a window of opportunity for comprehensive planning efforts, any optimism must be guarded. The historical record suggests that only a commonly perceived national emergency can induce Americans to challenge their deep-rooted ideological antipathy to government intervention in urban and regional development.

Planning and Ideology Development in the United States continues to be guided by the assumption that only private investment creates economic value. What many people fail to recognize, however, is that the private sector does not have the ability to plan comprehensively, whereas the public sector does. This failing has thwarted comprehensive planning efforts for some time now. Although planning cannot, by itself, guarantee the creation of vital and viable human settlements, research suggests that it provides a greater range of benefits than the haphazard outcomes of speculative construction. This is especially true when the planning goals simultaneously promote equitable social development and rational and efficient physical growth.

To achieve this goal, however, planners must overcome the temptation to separate equity from efficiency in formulating their agendas for action. In economics, efficiency is defined as the parsimonious use of scarce resources in the creation of wealth; equity refers to fairness in the distribution of wealth. Conventional wisdom suggests that only the private market creates wealth efficiently. Since distribution cannot occur unless there is something of value to divide, equity concerns are always subservient to the market's drive for efficiency. Equity is viewed as "merely" a matter of politics and social values.

The weight given to efficiency over equity in the making of policy and investment decisions is most problematic when the commodity at issue is land. Since everyone and everything must exist in space as well as time, land must continually satisfy equity and efficiency concerns simultaneously. As a result, even if the market were as efficient in practice as it is in theory, it would still be necessary to impinge upon the freedom of the market to ensure space is available for socially necessary activities that the market cannot reward.

Because the dominant economic ideology holds that the market is the most efficient creator of wealth, society is faced with a continuing dilemma: how to give free reign to private investment to solve as many problems as possible, while simultaneously superseding the market to solve problems beyond its capacity. These problems are most urgently apparent in the process of metropolitan spatial development. When issues are initially deferred as matters of equity, they turn into crises of long-term urban and regional economic efficiency.

Planning, in essence, is the process of superseding market forces in creating the built environment. To be effective in this vocation, planners must be public authorities with the political will to exercise the necessary restraint on the private market. The willingness to do so depends ultimately on the social ideology of those who would guide society's planning efforts. Competing notions about how best to promote health, prosperity, productivity, attractiveness, and the like, derive ultimately from substantive differences in views about relationships among social classes and the ways in which the social product is distributed.

This chapter examines the impact of these competing ideas on American town planning from the 1909 National Conference on City Planning, where the terms of debate were first articulated, to two New York City projects: Roosevelt Island and Battery Park City. These two developments offer competing paradigms for future urban development and exemplify a century-long ideological struggle over the role of government in guiding metropolitan growth.

Framing the Debate   By the time the first National Conference on City Planning was held in Washington, D.C., the central issues of the debate were already well established. Although the forty-three conference participants were united in their enthusiasm for the developing "science" of city planning, their views on the appropriate goals and mechanisms for this new field were diverse. Despite general agreement that the planning function ought to shift from private civic and commercial organizations to public commissions, there was considerable disagreement about what this public role ought to be.

The debate centered on two main themes. On one hand, participants asked whether the discipline of planning should focus on improving the physical appearance of cities or on improving the conditions of daily life for its inhabitants; and thus whether the goal of planning was a more beautiful city or, in the words of English planner T. C. Horsfall, "a more beautiful life."[7] On the other hand, they asked whether the problems of urban life were due primarily to the systemic failings of a political economy based on private investment or to the individual moral failings of the population. Those who subscribed to the latter view sought relief through building codes and zoning regulations to control the physical fabric of the city, and municipal reform to curb the political power of clubhouse machines. Those concerned with identifying and dealing with the underlying systemic causes of congestion sought more drastic measures. Benjamin C. Marsh, executive secretary of the Committee on Congestion of Population, blamed congestion on land speculation and exploitation and insisted that these evils "must be checked by the only competent power—the government."[8] For him, planning was nothing less than "democracy's challenge to the American city."

Planning in Time of Crisis

Industrial Housing for War Workers   Although even conservative housing reformers believed that some degree of government intervention in urban development was necessary, they argued that this should go no further than modest regulation of market activity. In their view, only a national emergency—such as the threat to industrial production because of inadequate housing conditions during the first World War—would permit a brief opportunity to expand the acceptable boundaries of government control over development.

Even then it took a series of dramatic appeals by representatives of private industry—shipbuilders and munitions manufacturers —to persuade the government to enter into the direct provision of housing. It was not until leaders like Homer L. Ferguson, president of the Newport News Shipbuilding and Drydock Company, testified before the Senate that housing conditions were impeding wartime production efforts, that the government responded.[9] On 13 June

1918, the secretary of labor announced the wartime production measure: "The Government will build, own, control and rent the houses *until after the war*" (emphasis added).[10] Reflecting the prevailing opposition to permanent government involvement, the enabling legislation gave explicit instructions that "such property shall be sold as soon after the conclusion of the war as it can be advantageously done."[11] With this mandate, the U.S. Housing Corporation (USHC) was created in July 1918 to implement the construction program.

The magnitude of the task was impressive: housing was needed for almost 293,000 workers in seventy-one cities or districts.[12] In assuming responsibility for this undertaking, the government had no long-term vision for the future of these communities beyond recouping as much of their investment as possible after the war. The planners, on the other hand, under the leadership of Town Planning Division director F. L. Olmsted Jr., saw the program not only as an emergency measure but as a demonstration of the potential of comprehensive town planning. They envisioned the developments as "model communities in the sense that they are being studied and will inevitably be copied by the architects and builders of the future."[13]

In the planning stages this dichotomy between the planners' expansive goals and the government's more restricted ones posed no problem. On the contrary, the government's overriding concern with recouping its investment and salvaging materials after the armistice led to the decision to build permanent housing of good quality rather than quick temporary shelters.

Since the appropriations did not come through until August 1918, only a small part of the construction program was implemented. After the armistice on 11 November 1918, only twenty-two of the initially projected eighty-three projects were carried through to completion, with fifteen more built on a curtailed basis. The quality of these projects, however, did not escape notice. A contemporary review in *Architectural Forum* grasped the significance of this commitment of government funds to community development: "The opportunity for the individual to live in surroundings of

Broadening the Planning Agenda

FIGURE 18.1. Union Park Gardens, Wilmington, Delaware. Housing for World War I industrial workers. Photograph: Tony Schuman.

decency and amenity, so often denied to the man without financial backing, becomes now a matter of national policy."[14] Communities such as Fairview (in Camden, New Jersey) and Hilton (in Newport News, Virginia) along with residential districts such as those in Bridgeport (Connecticut), New Brunswick (New Jersey), and Wilmington (Delaware) (figure 18.1) remain socially and economically viable neighborhoods, often in the face of grave deterioration in surrounding areas.

The Depression Era Greenbelt Towns Despite continuing opposition to government intervention in the housing market, the depression afforded progressive town planners a second opportunity to implement their broader vision of balanced regional growth. This time, the economic crisis was so severe—a fourth of the work force was unemployed in 1932—that they were able to go far beyond the scope of the World War I housing projects.

Funded under the Emergency Relief Appropriation Act, the program was intended first and foremost to provide construction jobs for relief workers. Between twenty and thirty thousand workers participated in the construction of the three new towns built under the program.[15] Greenbelt, Maryland, alone employed more than thirteen thousand. As in the war-worker housing effort, the planners involved in the Greenbelt program were interested in pursuing a broad agenda. Guiding the operation was Resettlement Administration chief Rexford Guy Tugwell, whose intellectual affinity with the Garden City ideals of Ebenezer Howard included a belief in planning as a device to implement a broader social and economic restructuring of society.

Tugwell's version of the Garden City did not propose fully independent cities but rather a network of suburbs located near major cities on which they depended for employment. Other features of Howard's "social invention" survived intact: single ownership of land, controlled land values through government ownership and leasing, the establishment of the city as an independent legal and political entity, and the greenbelt itself. In the greenbelt towns, housing was seen as only one aspect of a broader problem. By building independent self-governing *cities* for the poor, the Resettlement Administration confronted the more basic problem of disenfranchisement.

The original greenbelt program called for construction of nineteen satellite towns close to major cities. As in the earlier case of industrial housing, conservative pressure imposed limits on the scope of development. Just three of the towns were actually built— Greenbelt, Maryland, Greenhills, Ohio (outside Cincinnati), and Greendale, Wisconsin (outside Milwaukee). The administration retained ownership until Congress ordered divestiture following World War II, with sale preference given to existing residents and returning veterans.

The greenbelt towns are frequently cited as the high point of comprehensive planning in the United States.[16] Ironically, although this successful government-led effort failed to launch a serious regional planning movement in the United States, the lessons were not lost on the British. The Greenbelt program provided the blue-print for the English postwar New Town effort.[17]

Planned Failure: The Federal New Towns

The prosperity of the decade following World War II seemed to make the planning debate a moot issue. For the first time, homeowner-ship appeared within reach of every working family. A suburban boom fueled by cheap oil, industrial jobs, and government-backed mortgages transformed a nation of renters into a solid homeowning majority. By the mid-1960s, however, a combination of social, political, and environmental problems forced another look at the need for planning. Central cities were becoming enclaves of lower-income minorities; suburbs were frustrated by the proliferation of jurisdictions; and there was growing concern about the environmental consequences of suburban sprawl.

A legislative response to these concerns emerged in 1970 as Title VII of the Urban Growth and New Community Development Act. Part A of the legislation directed the president to prepare a national growth report to assist in formulating a national growth policy; part B expanded the program of loan guarantees and grant assistance for new communities, making this aid available to public as well as private developers. In 1970 President Richard Nixon, in his State of the Union message to Congress, asserted that "the Federal government must be in a position to assist in the building of new cities and the rebuilding of old ones."[18] On the surface it appeared that the Title VII program represented the culmination of a sixty-year campaign for regional planning under government leadership. Here was a program to channel national growth explicitly based on the English New Towns model. Yet by 1975 the program was in shambles and a moratorium was placed on Title VII contract approvals. The Department of Housing and Urban Development (HUD) had funded thirteen separate projects with loan guarantees up to $50 million. Of the eight projects started under

Title VII and at least partly occupied by December 1976, HUD was obliged to acquire five. One was phased out as a conventional subdivision, another blocked by a lawsuit. Only the Woodlands, outside of Houston, Texas, was surviving.

HUD's own internal evaluation revealed that the program staff was thin on management, finance, construction, and marketing.[19] As a result, HUD relied on the developers and their consultants to produce estimates of regional growth rates, market share, and land valuations. Moreover, neither HUD nor the administration had formulated any national growth policy to guide the staff's work in selecting developers for Title VII new communities.

Ironies abound in this story of a new initiative gone awry. As long as the government built new communities for purposes other than planning (such as emergency war-worker housing, depression work relief) it employed the finest planning minds in the nation, who did careful research before committing federal funds. When at last the government sponsored a planning program as such, it turned over effective control of the process to the developers themselves. In the end, despite the good intentions of the bill's sponsors to encourage innovative and balanced development, Title VII was a pipeline of federal funds to private real estate companies whose motives were often no different from those of conventional land speculators. In the process, the reputation of government-assisted planning was given a black eye.

One arena in which the federal regulations did make a notable impact was in the racial and economic integration of the federally funded new communities. Although not all projects embraced the concept with equal enthusiasm, the results, especially with respect to income mix, were significant. A survey that compared HUD new towns with thirteen nonfederal communities found only 2,000 subsidized units out of 222,000 in the nonfederal communities, compared with 27 percent of all housing units in the Title VII projects. Moreover, the satisfaction of residents in subsidized housing in the new communities was found to be substantially higher than it was among residents in subsidized housing elsewhere.[20]

Contemporary Planning Strategies: Two Models

The *Plan for New York City*, published in 1969, described two new communities planned for Manhattan: Roosevelt Island and Battery Park City. The projects shared several important characteristics. Both involved innovative site assembly, the recycling of a derelict island in one case and the creation of landfill in the other. Both projects contained a mix of uses. The residential populations of both projects were described as a roughly even mix of upper- and low-middle-income residents.[21] As built, however, the two projects could not be more different. Whereas Roosevelt Island has held to the original intentions as a heterogeneous community, Battery Park City has become an exclusive upper-income enclave.

This shift represents more than a dramatic retreat from the democratic premise of the initial proposal. Battery Park City is emblematic of the privatization of planning activity that attended the ideological shifts of the 1980s. The public authority abdicates control over land-use decisions in favor of deal making and negotiation.[22] The process is justified by the economic efficiency of the marketplace. In the face of these same pressures, however, Roosevelt Island continues to pursue its original mandate. At stake are two competing views of urban life and social structure.

Roosevelt Island   Occupying a narrow 147-acre strip of land in the East River between Manhattan and Queens, Roosevelt Island is a remarkable community in many respects. Much of the credit is due to the accomplishments of its physical plan. It is accessed by the only commercial mass transit aerial tramway in the country. Vehicular traffic has been substantially curtailed. It is the only large-scale residential project in the country with an underground garbage collection system. The island is barrier-free and provides a substantial number of units for the handicapped. The landscaping includes 41 acres of parks and a 4½-mile pedestrian promenade at the water's edge (figure 18.2).

FIGURE 18.2. Roosevelt Island, New York. View from aerial tramway. Photograph: Tony Schuman.

The provision of such recreational facilities and generous open space is not uncommon in upper-income suburbs or luxury condominiums. What is distinctive about Roosevelt Island is its ability to deliver on its original commitment to a "diverse community." The General Development Plan (GDP) written in 1969 established a precise unit breakdown by income, with specific provision for the elderly and handicapped: 30 percent low-income; 25 percent moderate-income; 20 percent middle-income; and 25 percent market-rate units.[23] In addition to this income mix, Roosevelt Island has maintained an integrated racial composition, with a 23 percent minority population. Significantly, the median income for Black households on the island is higher than for White ones, suggesting that the island is a residence of choice for middle-income Blacks.[24]

In Northtown I, the first phase of development, completed in 1977, all 2,142 units received some form of public subsidy. The low-income units were dispersed throughout a large (1,000 units) apartment complex so that only management knows which tenants require the deeper subsidy. In 1984, however, when development resumed after an interruption caused by New York's fiscal crisis and

Urban Development Corporation's near bankruptcy, the flow of federal funds for housing subsidies had virtually dried up. The developer for the second construction phase, Northtown II, was designated because it had access to enough Section 8 rent-subsidy certificates to make 20 percent of the project affordable to low-income households. Although this permitted the new development to maintain its mixed-income character, conventional market wisdom concentrated all the subsidized units in a single, detached building, with four other new towers devoted to luxury rental units. For the first time, low-income households were segregated by place of residence, which led to some stereotyping of "the Section 8 kids." In response to this experience, the Roosevelt Island Operation Corporation is exploring ways to disperse the subsidized units throughout Southtown, the final phase of development.[25] In the absence of federal funds, and with only modest assistance available from city and state sources, Southtown will depend on an internal cross-subsidy of low- and moderate-income units by fees from developers of luxury apartments. Because the housing market is still mired in a deep recession, no contracts have been signed for Southtown. The present stalemate illustrates an inherent dilemma in linking the supply of "affordable" housing to the demand for luxury units.

Battery Park City   Battery Park City is a mixed residential and commercial development on 92 acres of landfill in the Hudson River stretching north from Battery Park at the southern tip of Manhattan. The current development plan is actually the fifth proposal for the site, and the only one whose residential component is entirely based on market-rate housing. Although earlier proposals for the site also emphasized luxury housing, by the time the *Plan for New York City* was published in 1969, the housing mix had become equal thirds of upper- and low-middle-income units.[26]

Battery Park City got off to a slow start. The landfill was not complete until 1977, and by then the city was mired in a recession. In 1979, Richard Kahan, the newly appointed head of the Battery Park City Authority (BPCA), hired architects/urban designers Alexander Cooper and Stanton Eckstut to produce a new master plan. To persuade the New York State Legislature to continue its support, this plan had to reconfigure the development not only in its physical dimension but also in its legal framework and financing strategy. The new legal approach was to have the New York State Urban Development Corporation condemn the site and convey the title to BPCA. By transferring ownership to an independent public benefit agency, this maneuver exempted the project from New York City's planning and zoning regulations, as well as public scrutiny.

The economic strategy was to attract private financing by eliminating all subsidized housing, offering tax abatements, and relocating the commercial buildings to the center of the project opposite the World Trade Center. Thus the much-praised physical character of the Cooper/Eckstut site plan—the reintegration of the landfill into the Manhattan grid—was as much a rediscovery of New York's history of incremental private development of small land parcels as it was a romantic invocation of its most livable neighborhoods.

The physical aspects of the plan have received a great deal of critical acclaim. The *New York Times* hailed it as a "triumph of urban design."[27] Writers wax enthusiastic over its public parks and promenades (figure 18.3).[28] But if the exterior spaces are indeed handsomely designed and inviting, the residential construction is less convincing in both physical and social terms. Despite the street and avenue organization of the master plan, Battery Park City lacks the heterogeneity of Manhattan's culturally diverse neighborhoods like Chelsea or the Upper West Side. It has no side streets to speak of and lacks the row houses to leaven the scale of the large apartment buildings. The apartments themselves are relatively small, both in the number and size of rooms, leaving the exterior styling an empty gesture to New York's grand old apartment buildings.

Demographically, the development reflects the flat profile of the narrow stratum that benefited from the 1980s surge in the financial services sector: the new households are young, wealthy, and childless. According to a 1988 tenant survey, 85 percent of the residents had incomes over $50,000 and 37 percent over $100,000.

FIGURE 18.3. Battery Park City, New York. View from South Cove park.
Photograph: Tony Schuman.

Less than 12 percent of the population was under nineteen years of
age or over sixty-five, and more than 88 percent of the units
contained only one or two people. Seventy-three percent are studio
and one-bedroom apartments.[29] Curiously, in two tenant surveys
the BPCA has not collected data on the racial composition of the
residential population. There are few neighborhood services, and
families with children had to organize to get a playground built.

The social justification for all this private luxury in a publicly
aided project is that Battery Park City spins off profits that the city
uses to rehabilitate low-income housing in poor neighborhoods like
the South Bronx and Harlem. Revenues from Battery Park City
ground rents are used to guarantee New York housing bonds issued
by the New York State Legislature. Proceeds from the first $210 mil-
lion in bonds have already been applied to rehabilitate 1,850 units
in the South Bronx and Harlem.[30] As the realization that the present
real estate market downturn is going to be a long-term phenome-

non has spread among Battery Park City residents, so has their active political opposition to housing subsidy programs.[31] It is thus difficult to understand how such an approach could ever work outside the context of the narrow window of hyperspeculation of the real estate market of the 1980s.

The public-private partnership that generates funds for housing subsidies through market development reinforces uneven spatial development in the process. The mostly uncritical praise that Battery Park City has received for the excellence of its "public" spaces masks both the exclusion of the public from the decision-making process and the ways in which different groups are affected by the broader development process involved.

Conclusion

The transfer of funds from Battery Park City to the South Bronx parallels the Regional Contribution Agreements (RCAs) that compromise the New Jersey Mt. Laurel decision.[32] The RCAs permit municipalities to buy their way out of 50 percent of their obligation to provide their "fair share" of low- and moderate-income housing. The result benefits willing receiver cities like Newark, Camden, and New Brunswick, but in the process reinforces the very economic and racial spatial stratification they were meant to redress.

Whether manifest in the bankruptcy of Bridgeport, Connecticut, or the explosion of pent-up racial rage in Brooklyn, New York, and Los Angeles, California, the spatial segregation of American society is an economic and social sinkhole. The failure to develop a strong and systematic approach to town planning and hence orderly regional growth has left Americans with a regional development pattern in which speculators erect scattered subdivisions for individuals who must seek personal solutions to the crises of urban life by fleeing cities and segregating themselves in small, homogeneous enclaves.

The ideological basis of this regional settlement pattern is what historian Sam Bass Warner Jr. has identified as "privatism."[33] Privatism is the view that society is organized around the individual pursuit of wealth. Happiness derives from the independence wealth creates. Society itself consists of the concentric circles formed around the individual first by family and second by association with like-minded families of similar wealth. The role of government is limited to peacekeeping among individual wealth seekers and, if possible, to ensuring a setting where all citizens can pursue wealth accumulation.

The times when a socially cooperative ideology of town planning broke through privatist policy prescriptions were characterized by a perceived grave external threat such as war or depression. In those extraordinary instances planners and architects were permitted to design communities whose purpose was to foster social cohesion. Thus the sequence of events behind the rise and demise of the U.S. Housing Corporation of the World War I era is powerfully and succinctly understood in Warren Harding's 1920 campaign slogan, "a return to normalcy."

The present dilemma of Americans is that although the social threats from urban and regional disintegration are arguably as serious as war and depression, they are sufficiently chronic that they are ordinarily invisible to the majority. As a result, the expedient of crisis cannot be mobilized to overcome the laissez-faire inertia of privatist ideology. Instead, the opposite occurs. The urban crisis is viewed as proof that there is too much intervention. The solutions that flow from this viewpoint call for privatization of public services, the rolling back of zoning restrictions, and curbing of environmental constraints. The justification that ties such proposals together is the conviction that unfettered market forces are the only hope for creating sufficient wealth with which to solve these problems.

Even when social segregation succeeds as a privilege of wealth, it becomes an ever more temporary and expensive expedient. As global economic competition intensifies, the ability of human beings to afford the high economic and environmental costs required by social segregation via suburban and exurban sprawl will be severely compromised. Instead, the social decay defined as the urban crisis will quickly become suburban, too.

Although a consensus is emerging among planners and civic-minded business people that more compact socially and economically mixed communities are necessary, it is not clear that this consensus extends to underlying social problems. Projects such as Seaside, Florida, offer scenographic and tightly concentrated plans that exploit the social appeal of the town center. In the main, however, these new (or borrowed) town-planning models do not address issues of equity. Their seductive appeal only fosters the illusion of solving problems by avoiding them.

The second obstacle is the contradiction between the short-term needs of investors, even civic-minded ones, to attain profits and the needs of society for a longer-term perspective on wealth creation. The situation of Gary Wendt, chairman and chief executive officer of GE Capital Corporation, is typical of this dilemma. In his civic capacity, Mr. Wendt chairs one of the most farsighted contemporary private planning organizations: the Regional Plan Association (RPA). The RPA recently launched its third plan for the New York region. It is called an effort at "reconcentration." The plan is visually and spatially appealing. It identifies the correct scale of operation: the region. It calls for the creation of a regional network of small, spatially compact, mixed-use settlements connected by rail, as well as highway. Pedestrian travel is emphasized for internal circulation. The plan is also notable for its specific concern with promoting "the equitable region" as a solution to "today's racial, economic and social polarization."[34]

Since Wendt is a chief executive officer of an investment corporation, his social concern can conflict with the imperatives of marketplace success. A front-page story in the *New York Times* carried the headline "Housing Earmarked for the Poor Enriching Big Investors Instead."[35] The article explained how the Bush administration subverted a legal mandate to make a large portion of the housing obtained though savings and loan defaults available to low-income families at low prices. Instead, the Resolution Trust

Corporation permitted cash-rich investors to buy this housing at bargain prices. The principal beneficiary was Wendt's GE Capital Corporation, which reportedly agreed to buy twenty-eight complexes containing almost six thousand units in ten cities at a price estimated at nearly half of market value. Our point is not to lambaste Mr. Wendt, but merely to point out the inherent difficulty of maintaining equity concerns when they conflict with market imperatives in the context of an ideology dominated by privatism.

Owing in no small measure to a reluctance to intervene in the operation of markets, the United States is losing two important social battles: one for the quality of everyday life and the other for economic prosperity. What is noteworthy about this social erosion in comparison to the situation among America's economic rivals in Western Europe and Japan is that they do not have the same ideological aversion toward social interventions intended to improve their market-oriented societies. In that context, the importance of this discussion lies in demonstrating that the United States has its own history of successfully planning superior alternatives. If we should choose to correct this situation, we do not have to turn to international examples but merely to draw upon our own past experience. But that will not happen until we reorient our ideology around an understanding that equity and efficiency are not antithetical; rather, they are two sides of a single coin.

Planning History and the New American Metropolis

MARY CORBIN SIES
CHRISTOPHER SILVER

In her 1991 presidential address to the Society for American City and Regional Planning History, Eugenie L. Birch challenged scholars to develop a planning history that would serve present-day planning practice. Contemporary planning suffers, she argued, when planners lack perspective on the historic contexts of their work. The most challenging such questions that planners encounter—concerning the why, where, how, and when certain actions have occurred—are the kinds of questions urban historians handle as a matter of course. Grounding planning history in the methodology of urban history will make our scholarship more useful, Birch contended.[1]

Planners in the United States today confront a relatively new and little-understood built environment—a hybrid urban form that combines features of city and suburb but conforms to neither of these traditional models as conceptualized by generations of urban theorists. It is possible to expand upon Birch's suggestions for the improvement of planning history by recommending four avenues of research that scholars might explore to provide planners and others with the historical perspective that will enable them to comprehend and plan more effectively the new American metropolis. First, as many of the contributions to this volume have demonstrated, scholars can produce insights of great practical value by employing interdisciplinary approaches to study specific episodes of plan development and implementation in something approaching their full complexity. Second, equally helpful for understanding past and present decision making is scholarship that uncovers and analyzes the assumptions that have driven planners and policy makers over the course of the twentieth century. Third, perhaps the costliest oversight in recent planning history is the lack of attention to the impact of planning and development initiatives on urban dwellers themselves, particularly those groups routinely excluded from local decision-making processes. Fourth, planning historians, like archaeologists, can mine prodigious amounts of information by studying the built environment itself for perspective on the costs, benefits, and logic of the decisions that produced the late-twentieth-century metropolis. Scholars can best pursue these four lines of inquiry by subjecting the "new city" and the actions that created it to tough-minded, constructive scrutiny. By infusing urban research with a critical spirit, scholars are more likely to produce an instrumental planning history, one that can help planners and citizens alike come to terms with the new American metropolis.

Multicentered Metropolis

The American metropolis in the 1990s is in the throes of a fundamental spatial transformation, one every bit as profound as the change induced by the advent of mass transit in the mid-nineteenth century and the automobile since the 1920s. Although scholars have anticipated this transformation for decades, only in the 1980s did analysts from a wide array of disciplines officially announce the arrival of a new urban form. In his history of suburbanization published in 1985, for example, Kenneth T. Jackson argued that the period from 1950 to 1980 witnessed the emergence of the "centerless city." This "deconcentration of post–World War II American cities was not simply a matter of the proliferation of split-level homes and neighborhood schools," he wrote; "it involved almost every facet of national life, from manufacturing to shopping to professional services."[2] In 1987 Robert Fishman coined the term "technoburb" to characterize the "new city"; he described it as a place lacking "any definable borders, a center or a periphery, or a clear distinction between residential, industrial, and commercial zones. Instead, shopping malls, research and production facilities, and corporate headquarters all seem scattered amid a chaos of subdivisions, apartment complexes, and condominiums."[3] Another more descriptive bit of jargon that identified the changing metropolis is "multinucleated metropolitan regions," a phrase used in 1991 by Mark Gottdeiner and George Kephart to capture the scope of the new city's "fully urbanized and independent spaces that are not dominated by any central city."[4] But the best-known term for this unfolding urban phenomenon is "Edge City," a name that journalist Joel Garreau has promulgated to signify what he claims is "the biggest change in a hundred years in how we build cities."[5]

Few urban and planning historians would dispute the assertion that deconcentration has been a central trait of American urban development since the mid-nineteenth century. What is it, then, about the current process that diverges from the long-term evolutionary trend? What seems new about Edge City is the dominance of an increasingly independent outer city, a new growth center that has usurped many of the resources and all of the functions, if not the civilities, of the traditional center city. The "centerless city" is considered a new phenomenon because it does not conform to the tidy geospatial models developed to describe cities in the post–World War I era. These models were conceived by sociologists, geographers, and economists to explain the form and spatial distribution of functions in the American industrial city at a time when it was already in a process of dissolution. Nonetheless, urban and planning historians have continued to employ two industrial-city models—the Burgess concentric-ring model and the Hoyt sectoral model—to explain urban morphology and the layering and stratification of the city by status and land use.[6] Both models are based on the assumption that the center city predominates over the periphery, even though each acknowledges some decentralization as more affluent residents move to the suburbs to escape the denser living conditions at the core.

The emergence of multiple centers of urban dominance rather than a single multiuse urban core dates back to the 1940s, however, as Greg Hise demonstrates in chapter 10. As early as the 1940s, Harris and Ullman recognized the inaptness of industrial-city models; their multinuclear model of metropolitan development more accurately depicted how the "edges" replaced the urban center as the locus of metropolitan life in the post–World War II era.[7] Some analysts in the 1970s argued that migration from the core to the edges was slowing since some families were opting for nonmetropolitan areas entirely. This "counterurbanization" process is now viewed, however, as a brief aberration in an otherwise consistent pattern of decentralization.[8] As more recent research attests, the leapfrogging of urban residents to nonmetropolitan locations established the outer reaches of a more expansive metropolis that by the 1990s was pushing the edges of some metropolitan areas more than 50 miles in all directions from the original urban core.[9]

Few planning historians have attempted to apply the Harris-Ullman model to recent metropolitan development even though the multinuclear concept describes more accurately than the industrial-city models the sort of metropolis that planners and developers have desired and to a great extent achieved in the twentieth century. For if the "edges" have now supplanted the "center," that "new" built environment is not just the product of an immutable process of evolution, but something Americans have carefully constructed over the past hundred years. A growing body of research substantiates that the separation of suburbs from the city center has been a consistent policy and planning objective. The "evolving metropolis," as urban designers Michael Southworth and Peter Owens refer to it, has seen the "preoccupation with the urban core" give way to greater activity on the "urban fringe." Suburban communities have grown from a few pockets of homes for wealthy families into the dominant form of American urbanism, a form that seems destined to determine geospatial, social, and economic patterns of the metropolis in the twenty-first century.[10] And as this has occurred, the function of the urban fringe has changed from urban frontier dependent upon a healthy core to urban competitor in its own right.

Edge City, then, may involve a wholesale restructuring from centralized city to multicentered metropolis, but it is a restructuring that has been planned for and anticipated and is, in turn, the product of several historical factors. The evolving suburban community model of the 1990s "is not a completely new invention but has roots in early models for ideal suburban communities." Those roots reach back to the ideas of nineteenth-century landscape architects Andrew Jackson Downing and Frederick Law Olmsted, continue through the turn-of-the-century planned, exclusive suburbs, through the era of the garden suburb and neighborhood unit plan of Clarence Perry, to the ambitious suburban community builders of the 1920s.[11] The rules that governed the development of the urban fringe were established by planners but also by large real estate interests. These two groups articulated and implemented standards for subdivisions, zoning, and urban infrastructure in the vast tracts that enlarged metropolitan areas in the interwar years and after World War II.[12]

Also central to the shaping of the new American metropolis was the suburban ideal—a deeply internalized set of beliefs and assumptions that promoted single-family housing, homeownership, homogeneous subdivisions, and suburban location. Codified and disseminated by a growing urban upper-middle class at the turn of the century, the suburban ideal delimits the very essence of the good life and the minimum expectations for middle-class respectability. This twentieth-century standard for modern middle-class living has, in turn, been encouraged and subsidized by the public and private sectors in countless ways: by cheap land, relatively few and loose land-use controls, transportation infrastructure, homeownership subsidies, educational campaigns, low gasoline taxes, and the achievement of economies of scale in residential and commercial construction.[13] In other words, the separation of suburbs from center cities has been a consistently evolving planning and development objective. The built environment of the new American metropolis encodes and embodies many qualities that many individuals support and hold dear: private property rights, choices in services, homogeneous neighborhoods, certain lifestyle subsidies, real estate speculation, convenient shopping, and local political autonomy.

Policy Considerations

If "every single American city that is growing is growing in the fashion of Los Angeles, with multiple urban cores," as Joel Garreau maintains, then it behooves planning historians to work out a conceptual framework better suited to understanding the new metropolis. Now that "postsuburban regions have become the most common form of metropolitan development in this country," how can we best confront their political, social, economic, and planning implications?[14] At the least, the spatial reconfiguration of the urban landscape occurring in edge cities will force planners and historians alike to reexamine their conventional, center-city focused approaches to the study of urban development. Beyond that, however, planners and planning historians must accept an array of new challenges posed by this cultural landscape, especially in the areas of transportation, provision of services, housing, equity issues, environmental concerns, and the many quality-of-life issues that have fueled a nationwide movement to manage urban growth.

While preliminary efforts to grapple with the new city have already begun, both scholars and policy makers have been hampered by a lack of consensus and inadequate historical perspective. Some urbanists, like geographer Michael Conzen, believe the edge city phenomenon affords an opportunity to introduce a new regionalist approach to managing metropolitan growth. Urban historian Richard C. Wade concurs but notes that the separation between suburb and city inherent in the new urban configuration has intensified longstanding urban social and economic problems that beg a metropolitan solution. Rather than advocating the sort of regional government proposed by Conzen—which Wade considers politically infeasible—he calls for the "consolidation of effort by function . . . in housing, education, transportation, water, pollution, and police." This solution would enable the new American metropolis to manage its critical needs without compromising cherished local autonomy.[15]

Others, like historian Eric Monkkonen, seem less prone to treat the political fragmentation of the spread city as a deficiency to be corrected through reconsolidation. He argues that the "woe of municipal fragmentation can also be thought of as the promise of variety." Although he concedes that municipal fragmentation can perpetuate wrongs such as racial or economic exclusion, Monkkonen contends that we would err "to throw out the good with the bad, losing the benefits of small governmental units and local options to combat serious social wrongs." To Monkkonen's reminder that "numerous multiple and small governments" have been part of the American city for two hundred years now,[16] William Sharpe and Leonard Wallock counter that "unregulated and exclusionary suburban expansion has led to the impoverishment of the inner city and the despoiling of outlying areas." They join Conzen in calling for "true regional thinking" that would ameliorate the present conflict in which cities and suburbs bid against one another for "federal dollars, wealthy residents, and employment opportunities." The refusal "to see the necessary connection between the suburbs and their surroundings," Sharpe and Wallock argue, "has prevented Americans from achieving an integrated metropolis that is equitable for all."[17]

The lack of consensus regarding the planning and governmental organization appropriate to the multicentered American metropolis is a function, at least in part, of an inability (or disinclination) to understand metropolitan change apart from its spatial characteristics. Garreau, Fishman, and geographer Peter Muller, for example, conceptualize Edge City as a minicity, a suburban-located variation of the traditional center city; it features "intricate and compact orchestrations of mixed land uses, including shopping, employment, offices, wholesaling, entertainment, hotels, restaurants, and personal services such as medical facilities." The new urban configuration has some promising qualities that redeem it from critics of suburbanization. It offers an urbanism that combines the benefits of the suburban residential lifestyle with centralized employment, cultural, and shopping facilities, at a scale that is more humane than what could be found in the traditional industrial metropolis.[18]

Yet many vocal critics deny that Edge City warrants the status of an urban place and stress that it is a geographical hybrid fraught with fundamental problems. According to Oliver Byrum, director of Planning for the City of Minneapolis, the spread city challenges the planning profession's dominant paradigm and threatens the very existence of the center city. "I absolutely know," Byrum continues, "that saving the city is the highest public purpose, that anything that threatens achievement of that purpose is unsound, that edge cities do threaten central cities and are, therefore, not good."[19] Sharpe and Wallock also challenge the assumption that Edge City has supplanted the center city or should do so. These outlying suburban clusters, they point out, "are being engulfed by larger urbanized areas that have come out to meet them." There is no convincing evidence that the ultimate course of metropolitan development will be toward further deconcentration.[20]

Carl Abbott's *The Metropolitan Frontier: Cities in the Modern American West* muddies the waters further about what exactly distinguishes the new cities, at least spatially. Whereas Garreau used the examples of Los Angeles and Dallas to argue that newer western cities sprawled more than cities elsewhere, Abbott came to a different conclusion. After analyzing data on population density, automobile usage, and commuting patterns, he concluded that cities—even edge cities—in the western region were no more spread out than metropolitan areas in the Midwest. The emerging western metropolis, he argued, differed instead in its design, in its adaptation to environmental factors, and in its land-use configuration. The traditional pattern of American cities involved a gradual decrease in the intensity of land use from the downtown to the periphery. The typical new metropolis, on the other hand, exhibited a land-use pattern that "plunge[d] abruptly from a glimmering set of new high-rises to a low-rise, usually one-story, city that stretches away to the horizon." The new American city, then, was not just an open city but an unbounded city, one that "is capable of indefinite extension by adding easily reproducible units pulled from the box of urban tinkertoys."[21] The western metropolis and the newer cities of the Sunbelt exhibited built environments shaped by twentieth-century urban planning processes, whereas cities of the East and Midwest grafted modern planning approaches onto the landscapes of the industrial/commercial city of the nineteenth century.

If, upon closer analysis, edge cities are not as spatially distinguishable from "traditional" metropolitan areas, neither do they offer a resolution to the social problems endemic to late-twentieth-century center cities. Proponents of the new urban form contend that any undesired spatial, environmental, or social "outcomes" of the edge city represent the normal glitches and discontinuities that have accompanied the continuous improvement in the quality of urban life in the United States throughout the century. The "cost-of-improvement" line of reasoning that planners employed to counter criticism of the vast tracts of suburban subdivisions developed in the 1950s and 1960s supplies a useful rationale for the edge cities of the 1980s and 1990s. With all their faults, the 1950s argument went, these suburbs were uniformly desired by America's working and middle classes as a relief from the turmoil, congestion, and squalor of the industrial city. Likewise, settlements at the urban edges are the popular choice of middle-class urbanites in the 1980s and 1990s. These fringe settlements have won, quite handily, the competition with revitalized inner city neighborhoods for the allegiance of new residents. Garreau contends, moreover, that in these edge cities the diversity and vitality previously associated only with the traditional city have been reintroduced within a decentralized urban model.[22]

Despite the seemingly relentless centrifugal movement of the recent metropolis, there has been since the 1970s a discernible countertrend in what has been termed the "Back-to-the-City movement." The focus of urban policy since the 1970s has been to revitalize cities by upgrading older neighborhoods in order to lure back the fleeing middle class (or, more accurately, to recapture the baby boomers whose parents had already departed), to sustain the population and tax base of declining center cities. As Laska and Spain noted in 1980, "It is a small but growing phenomenon in the majority of large cities . . . [and] has increased the tax base, preserved buildings, and suggested a trust in the viability of American cities as homes for Americans wealthy enough to choose their places of residence." Yet, as Laska and Spain were quick to point out, "these positive aspects of renovation have not occurred without the accompanying negative effects of displacement of the poor, increasing demands on city services, and the emergence of 'gilded ghettos' of affluence in still-poor cities."[23]

Although concern about gentrification and the displacement of the poor has persisted, most cities have embraced the notion that encouraging the revitalization of inner city neighborhoods is in their best interests, invoking the rationale that "an increase in relatively high-income households tends to aid the community, both economically and socially."[24] The experience of a few cities, like Savannah—as Robert Hodder suggests in chapter 15—

demonstrates that neighborhood revitalization need not serve the affluent exclusively. The steady upgrading of urban neighborhoods, when conducted cooperatively with residents living there, can redound to the benefit of those less well-off and form a catalyst for reestablishing a social structure in the center city "where residents are indeed socially, racially, and economically diverse."[25]

While neighborhood revitalization has been the predominant strategy for resurrecting the social and economic vitality of center cities, growth management has increasingly become the favored means of planners and officials seeking to put the brakes on developers' seemingly insatiable quest to expand metropolitan boundaries. The states of Florida, New Jersey, Maine, Vermont, Rhode Island, Georgia, Oregon, California, and Washington have all established growth management systems. These require, at minimum, that local infrastructure be in place prior to the approval of new development, and they discourage urban sprawl by encouraging compact development, urban infill, and revitalization of older areas. Growth management programs also call for affordable housing, especially in locations outside the center city, and they promote economic development by encouraging job creation. In addition, they endeavor to implement a system of protection for natural resources, particularly environmentally sensitive areas, farmland, open spaces, and forests. Programs promoting "urban growth boundaries" represent a more aggressive effort to define the spatial limits of metropolitan development.[26] In general, however, growth management initiatives—like urban revitalization programs—have only been partly successful in achieving their objectives. As a consequence, many communities at the edges as well as near the cores of cities are experiencing a "metropolitan crisis" in the 1980s and 1990s that seems disturbingly similar to the "urban crisis" of the 1960s.

According to David Rusk, the author of *Cities without Suburbs*, however, the metropolitan crisis of the 1980s and 1990s is not a universal phenomenon, but one experienced most acutely in cities that have not achieved some sort of political integration. Cities that have retained "elasticity"—the capacity to grow through annexation, consolidation, or, more rarely, by adopting a metropolitan government structure, as in Nashville and Indianapolis—have succeeded best in confronting the problems of poverty, dependency, and crime. They offer their citizens a far better quality of life. "Inelastic cities"—those that have failed to expand the corporate body—usually possess proportionately larger concentrations of the poorest residents and suffer from race and class segregation and a declining fiscal base. To substantiate his argument, Rusk identified twenty-three cities in which the social division between center and periphery was insignificant. In those places, the center cities possessed at least 50 percent of the metropolitan population, and the average per capita income of those living in the core was 90 percent or greater of the average income of suburban residents. Although he conceded that no cities today "are exempt from the social problems of modern-day America," Rusk observed that residents of "elastic" cities tended to have higher average incomes, and the cities had higher bond ratings and a lower incidence of racial segregation. "The severity of the social chaos in many inner-city neighborhoods—unemployment, poverty, dependency, illegitimacy, drugs, crime—is a function of the intense concentration and isolation of the poor."[27]

The future of the American metropolis, Rusk suggests, will depend on whether its citizens can manage growth more effectively and address fundamental social and economic problems that are intensifying rather than dissipating as growth corridor replaces neighborhood and social space gets measured in thousands of square miles rather than acres. It is important to conceptualize both past and future planning and development as more than geospatial or even economic processes and the relationship between traditional metropolis and edge city as one of continuity as well as change. Historians can contribute meaningfully to this restructuring of ideas and to future policy discussions by determining to what extent the new city replicates or repudiates the social structure of the traditional centralized metropolis. Sharpe and Wallock, for example, find considerable replication in patterns of racial and class segregation, exclusionary housing policies, defensive zoning measures, suburban gender role expectations, wasteful environmental practices, pastoral mythology, and what they call a characteristic "compartmentalization" of suburban life.[28]

On the other hand, urban geographer Brian Berry believes that urbanites were, indeed, constructing a new social structure—"a society with a number of parallel and distinctively different lifestyles." Urbanites were increasingly in a position to choose where they lived on the basis of life cycle, lifestyle, or occupation. The result may have been a new city, but its "mosaic of homogeneous communities [with] different lifestyles that are internally cohesive and exclusive" recapitulated many of the features of traditional suburban settlement. Berry properly observed that the mechanism driving this mosaic pattern was privatism; the "American style of planning" has supported privatism and the mosaic culture rather than envisioning or promoting alternative urban configurations.[29]

The American Style of Planning

The American style of planning in the twentieth century has certainly helped to generate the decentralization and social fragmentation that Sharpe and Wallock, Berry, and other scholars have observed in our cities. Indeed, the basic ingredients of our modern-day Edge City derive directly from the principal sources of planning theory and development practice established during the late nineteenth and early twentieth centuries. These include the expansion of the railway and roadway networks to facilitate access to decentralized development, the location of manufacturing plants and working-class residences in self-contained communities along the periphery, separate exclusive enclaves for the affluent and the middle class, the creation of multiple centers of commercial activity, and the development of a more expansive urban form through the

Conclusion

provision of abundant open spaces and reduction of overall residential densities.

These and other similar principles were formally enunciated at the First National Conference on City Planning in Washington, D.C., in 1909 during presentations by the leading planners of the day. For example, Robert Anderson Pope, a landscape architect from New York City, argued that one of the major purposes of planning was to "relieve congestion by aiding in the decentralizing and more equitable distribution of land values." Citing the German experience, Pope urged city planners in the United States to build circumferential highways that would enable "traffic to go from point to point in the suburbs without first going to the center of the city." In this way, "factories of all kinds can be attracted to the outskirts," encouraging a "wider disbursal of the laboring class."[30]

Pope's vision of the new American city in 1909 was modeled after Swedish and German cities that had already removed slums from their centers and directed new development to the periphery. There, both settlement and commercial development proceeded according to carefully conceived plans rather than the unregulated urban sprawl that was the norm in American cities of the same era. While American municipalities planned "showy civic centers of gigantic cost," European cities supported public planning to "relieve congestion through the establishment of more radial thoroughfares, [and] through widening of streets where congestion is greatest." Pope concluded that the new city based upon a suburban form "reduces the cost of living . . . , makes possible the beautiful city, [and] in providing a solution to the social and economic problem, it makes possible a more beautiful life."[31]

Pope's vision was realized to a significant extent, but not through a carefully orchestrated public planning process. The building blocks of the new American metropolis were privately financed and were used to develop self-contained communities that began to proliferate on the urban edge as early as the 1920s. To be sure, these new settlements drew on a series of planning and housing precedents that reached back to semiautonomous mid- to late-nineteenth-century commuter suburbs like Cambridge, Massachusetts, and Chestnut Hill, Philadelphia; and they refined the development techniques pioneered in infrastructure-rich, large-scale, mass-produced tract subdivisions like those created by Samuel E. Gross in Cook County, Illinois.[32] What made suburban community building distinctive in the twentieth century, however, was the uniformly massive scale of development. Beginning in the 1920s, a substantial contingent of private land developers in several cities across the nation took "very large tracts of land and slowly improved them, section by section, for lot sales and home construction."[33]

Even more important, these community builders routinely provided a whole system of land-use regulations and community amenities borrowed from the turn-of-the-century planned, exclusive suburbs of the urban elite. To direct growth and safeguard homeowners' (as well as their own) investments, developers used deed restrictions establishing uniform building lines, lot coverage, side and front yard setbacks, building size, and building cost. In many subdivisions, the deeds bore clauses barring non-Caucasians, perpetuating a convention of racial exclusion characteristic of affluent suburbs. Developers also provided their new communities with a full complement of amenities, including landscaping, public thoroughfares, special areas for retail establishments, schools, recreational areas, and utility services comparable to those available in the cities. Thus, it was the private subdivider of land, not the public planner, who proved to be "the actual city planner in practice" from the 1920s to the 1940s. The community builder helped to shape profoundly the residential infrastructure of the new American metropolis.[34]

During the 1920s, Clarence Perry combined and packaged many of these planning features in the form of a "neighborhood unit plan," a conceptual model that he prepared as a part of the Regional Plan for New York City. One of the core beliefs that Perry, a nonplanner, expressed in his land-use model, following the ideals of contemporary social reformers, was that a homogeneous residential environment provided a crucial counterpoint to the overwhelming diversity of modern urban life. To the greatest degree possible, the neighborhood could allow the virtues of the village to flourish within the metropolis. Perry's neighborhood plan was highly adaptable. It could be employed for areas already partly developed as well as for new suburbs; it was entirely suited to bringing both city and suburban neighborhoods into the automobile age.[35]

The widespread influence of the neighborhood unit plan on both urban and suburban community planning cannot be overstated, although Perry himself played little part in promoting his conceptual model after the mid-1930s. Private community builders reproduced the basic tenets of the neighborhood unit plan, as did the architects of America's public housing programs in the 1930s. Harland Bartholomew, who helped to shape the federally financed urban redevelopment program, promoted the neighborhood as the "Key to Urban Redemption," as he put it.

There was a fundamental social difference between the original scheme that Perry advanced to redeem urban neighborhoods and the kinds of developments actually built in the 1940s and 1950s, however. Drawing upon his experience of New York City during the 1920s, where high-rise apartments proliferated to serve the wealthy, Perry devised what he called the "Five Block Plan." It included the standard ingredients of the suburban version of the neighborhood unit plan—housing to accommodate 1,000 families, recreational space, neighborhood services that included retail space, a school and gymnasium, and paths to separate pedestrian from vehicular traffic—but it was designed to replace areas considered to be slums. Perry acknowledged that the kind of upper-class development he envisioned "would probably displace many of the present inhabitants," but he argued that rising land costs, not his neighborhood plan, made displacement inevitable.[36] To his credit, Perry envisioned that the retention of middle- and upper-income neighborhoods within the center city would "residentialize" the metropolis and slow down the widening gulf between affluent and poorer neighborhoods. One of the key failures of New York's regional plan makers, as historian Robert Fishman has noted, however, was their "belief that most residents would be content to live in high-density neighborhoods close to work. . . . Despite [the plan makers'] elaborate surveys, they completely failed to appreciate the breadth of the appeal of the single family suburban home."[37]

Beginning in 1933, the Public Works Administration did create a series of low-income communities based on the neighborhood unit plan in a direct effort to provide the working poor vastly improved housing at affordable rents. These public housing programs still reflected the race and class concerns of both their local and federal promoters, however, with the result that they were simultaneously used to upgrade deteriorated communities and to segregate poor minority families from the rest of the city. Although there was a certain logic to locating new housing on sites cleared of dilapidation, the policies of siting low-income housing only in the center city and of systematically removing the sort of social mixing that had occurred naturally in city neighborhoods established an insidious pattern of isolating the urban poor.[38] No public housing projects were built outside center cities anywhere in the United States until the 1970s.

Thus, over a fifty-year period, segregated public housing combined with a whole congeries of other factors and policies to produce a socially bifurcated urban structure. These factors included disinvestment in neighborhoods adjacent to low-rent projects, the incursion of commercial land uses in previously stable neighborhoods, the exclusion of working-class housing from the edges of the city, and the destruction of neighborhoods by massive public works projects in the center city, particularly freeway construction. Sociologist William J. Wilson contends that the resulting exodus of middle-class Blacks from the center city left behind the "truly disadvantaged," who were cut off socially, politically, and, most important, economically from the prosperity of the edges. Robert Fishman observes that these patterns have "resegregated American society into an affluent outer city and an indigent inner city, while erecting ever higher barriers that prevent the poor from sharing in the jobs and housing of the technoburbs."[39]

Conclusion

One other deliberate policy has contributed to the social fragmentation of the traditional American city. The separation of residential from nonresidential functions through zoning—a key principle of twentieth-century planning—eventually drove most residential uses from the urban core, with the exception of housing for the disadvantaged and a few stalwart clusters of affluent households in restored neighborhoods. The voracious spatial appetite of an expanding central business district after World War II and the availability of federal redevelopment funds to acquire and clear downtown neighborhoods for commercial uses undermined the central city's residential function. As early as 1954, only five years after urban renewal began, there were eighty-five such projects in the United States, and only ten of them involved rehousing for displaced residents. In rezoning urban residential neighborhoods in anticipation of the desired commercial and industrial renaissance after World War II, city planners made a costly miscalculation, particularly since the demand for this space never kept up with the supply.[40]

At the same time, developers were building new residential areas at the edges of the cities and in small towns, but most of these planned communities employed racial and income criteria to screen prospective neighbors, further increasing the social divide between core and periphery. After World War II, planners and realtors refined the exclusionary zoning and development standards created in turn-of-the-century elite suburbs and espoused in Perry's neighborhood unit plan. The exclusion of public housing from the edges of the city was easily accomplished because the program was a local option that suburbanites could choose not to exercise. Neighborhoods could also ensure social homogeneity by setting zoning standards that prohibited multifamily housing and set minimum lot or house sizes that would effectively preclude low-income ownership. Together with informal real estate practices that "steered" undesirables away from fashionable neighborhoods, these systematic mechanisms shaped urban development patterns across the nation. Only when federal civil rights legislation passed in the 1960s, culminating in the Fair Housing Act of 1968, did these planning conventions confront a serious challenge. Even so, African Americans still made up only 6 percent of suburban residents nationwide in 1980; a substantial portion of those families settled in race- or class-segregated suburban enclaves.[41]

Nearly a century of planning strategies and conventions has produced the two-nation phenomenon that Peter Hall refers to as a "city of the permanent underclass" coexisting uneasily with the "city of enterprise." During the years following 1970, cities throughout the United States successfully implemented large-scale downtown revitalization projects that replaced lost manufacturing and reoriented urban commerce to a service-based economy. These downtown revitalization efforts are "unashamedly tourist-based" and have "involved the deliberate creation of the city-as-stage," Hall charges. "Like theatre [the city] resembles real life, but it is not urban life as it ever actually was: the model is the Main Street America exhibit which greets entering visitors at the California Disneyland, sanitized for your protection . . . , wholesome, undangerous, and seven-eighths real size."[42] Offstage, beyond these festival marketplaces and tourist attractions, impoverished neighborhoods have also expanded, commensurate with the rate of revitalization. As the population of U.S. cities fell during the 1970s and 1980s, the numbers of urban residents in poverty increased. "What we have," according to historian David Goldfield, "is the anomalous metropolis in terms of social equity. Gleaming downtowns . . . vie with peripheral office parks, while decaying neighborhoods and hope-lost people crouch in the shadows.[43] In the meantime, and despite apparently herculean planning efforts to achieve genuine revitalization, the American center city faces a troubling and precarious future.

Redefining the Planning Agenda

The resolution of America's metropolitan crisis necessitates, at the very least, confronting planning's past. "New concepts for new cities are desperately needed," observes urban designer Jean-François Lejeune, but we can only discern these concepts when we acknowledge, through historical analysis, "the generations of planners and architects who transformed this ideal land [Florida] into the national laboratory of physical fragmentation, social isolation, and urban de-construction" that it has become. Lejeune also envisions, however, ways in which planning's past can serve as a constructive source for design ideas. He points to the neotraditional town plan of Seaside, Florida, conceived by Andres Duany and Elizabeth Plater-Zyberk, as evidence that new urban solutions can draw judiciously from past theories. In form, Lejeune imagines, the new city will not nostalgically embrace a singular past model, but "will be made out of a series of distinct and diverse parts, . . . offering the coexistence of the urban grid, of the skyscrapers, of the 'urban streets,' of the 'garden streets,' of the system of parks." The new urban form will combine growth management with a reintensification of urban space that draws upon multiple traditions.[44]

Not only in its form but in its social construction, planning the new metropolis requires balancing a wide range of interests. The social inequities evident in the division between the periphery and the center city are only the most recent manifestation of an urban social challenge that has been shadowing urban planning and policy since the nineteenth century. The survival of center cities depends not only on economic revitalization but on the development of effective strategies to reduce social inequities. Those strategies must facilitate a redistribution of wealth to the needy as well as improvements in education, housing, health care, and social services. Mel Levin's recent assessment of what makes planning successful underscores the shortsightedness of conceptualizing the urban poor as a spatial problem—that is, of individuals trapped in slums—or as an isolated social problem—the "truly disadvantaged." "The solution lies in creating reform programs that have clear immediate as well as long-term benefits for a broad spectrum of the electorate," and to remove discriminatory barriers that adversely affect any portion of the population.[45]

Yet, as has become all too clear in a series of past policy and planning failures, process and policy must be formulated together if we are going to address equity concerns effectively. "There is no physical planning without people planning," as Norman Krumholz and John Forester point out. Planners must not concentrate on "site-focused" planning without attending to the "organizational processes through which planners can make a difference." The more comprehensive approaches of neighborhood planning, advocacy planning, and policies planning have brought varying degrees of success in Cleveland and in many other cities over the past two decades. The goal in Cleveland, according to Rohe and Gates, has been to give priority to "promoting a wider range of choices for those Cleveland residents who have few."[46]

The Contributions of Planning History

Planning history can play a significant role in understanding past policy failures and illuminating promising future planning processes. Conventional planning history has too frequently defined its purpose narrowly—as narration of the story of plan making or celebration and understanding of the achievements of important planners. The literature of planning history explores in rich detail individual components of the planning process, such as highway planning, zoning, the construction of public housing or planned communities, urban renewal projects, landscape beautification efforts, and historic preservation initiatives. But few planning historians have tried to analyze the process as a whole, in its larger context, especially from the multiple perspectives of the agencies and individuals directly involved. Too often, they have been dazzled by the artistic genius or the social idealism of planning proposals and have overlooked the social inequities that have been fostered and perpetuated by the actual implementation of plans and planning policies.

Planning historians can contribute most constructively to contemporary planning discussions with research that analyzes the emergence of the new American metropolis and explains comprehensively the decisions and processes that have produced its distinctive environment. Such an instrumental planning history might profitably contain at least four interrelated, interdisciplinary lines of inquiry. Drawing upon the themes, insights, and methodological approaches of the disciplines that shape the field, scholars need to perform more basic case study research that studies the complex processes by which plans are developed and implemented in the local setting. It is especially important to understand the circumstances and considerations that mold a plan as proposed into a set of objectives that municipalities employ to guide actual development. It is equally crucial to discover the ways in which localities deviate from agreed-upon recommendations and to discern their reasons for doing so.

Several planning historians have already made significant contributions to this line of research, including Eric Sandweiss, Robert Fairbanks, John Hancock, and June Manning Thomas, through their analyses in this volume. Those examples of scholarship, in particular, have made clearer some of the political and popular dimensions of plan development and implementation in a few of the nation's largest twentieth-century cities. Scholars need to attend just as closely to the commercial and social dimensions of twentieth-century planning, and to study the planning process in a broader range of cities in terms of size, age, and regional location. Their largest challenge will lie in synthesizing the information they uncover, an enterprise that may call for collaborative scholarship and whose successful execution will determine the value of their insights for contemporary planners.

Throughout the twentieth century, planning—both in the abstract and in situ—has been guided by (sometimes conflicting) sets of assumptions that (various) participants in the process hold dear. These assumptions may, for example, determine an individual's conviction that only private investment can create economic value; thus, they can undermine support for public planning initiatives, as Schuman and Sclar argue in chapter 18 has happened in the United

States in recent history. Planners' changing conceptions of downtowns—from "unitary center" to "federation of subdistricts" to "command post in the global economy"—exemplify a second category of assumptions that, as Carl Abbott has demonstrated in chapter 17, can influence our planning goals and the urban physical fabric. The professional perspectives that different contributors bring to the planning process—whether architects, planners, landscape architects, or engineers—account for a third set of assumptions that shape both how practitioners perceive urban problems and what solutions they conceive, as Cliff Ellis has shown in chapter 11. Additional research is required to understand these and other acknowledged and unacknowledged assumptions that have affected how historical actors define the planning process, how citizens react to it, and what kinds of solutions to urban dilemmas citizens and planners will be able to imagine. Planning history can become a most useful analytical tool by revealing and challenging the assumptions of past and contemporary planning practice.

For too long, too little attention has been paid to the human implications and consequences of various plans, projects, and policies that have helped create the new American metropolis. A third line of inquiry planning historians should undertake is an investigation of the impact, particularly the social impact, of planning initiatives on urban populations. Four of the contributions to this anthology have already begun that process and suggest the kinds of inquiries scholars might profitably engage in. In chapter 9 Patricia Burgess explained that zoning actions had a differential impact on wealthy areas and low-income urban neighborhoods in metropolitan Columbus; her research questions both the efficacy and the fairness of zoning in actual planning practice. In his study of urban freeway design during the 1950s and 1960s, Cliff Ellis noted the disastrous human consequences of planning conducted with little regard for social and aesthetic considerations (see chapter 11). And both Robert Hodder and June Manning Thomas explore, from different directions, the potential of design solutions to ameliorate entrenched urban social problems; their preliminary research, discussed in chapters 15 and 16, respectively, seems to indicate that only planning initiatives that include targeted groups in the planning process, on their own terms, are likely to yield positive social outcomes. Much more research is needed, however, to reveal precisely how specific planning and development efforts have affected different racial, gender, age, and class groupings. In light of the increasing class and ethnic divisions incised onto the landscape of the new American metropolis, social impact studies may be the most urgently needed and potentially significant research problematic.

Planning historians should not overlook the built environment itself as a source of information for reconstructing and thinking about twentieth-century urban planning and development processes. The extant physical environment, together with its historical documentation and the patterns of usage inscribed onto it, comprise a remarkably articulate body of evidence. Many methodologies have been developed by historical geographers, landscape historians, architectural historians, and material culture studies specialists to "interrogate" the built environment for evidence that explains why it has taken its particular form.[47] A body of community or ethnographic studies focusing on how individuals or groups interact with the new American metropolis could produce tremendous information, for example, about the social impact of specific planning initiatives. Similar studies could show the kind of urban place metropolitan residents desire, especially those seldom asked for their opinions. Patterns of class or racial discrimination hard to pinpoint in written records and concerning which both past and contemporary informants may remain silent can be investigated and documented directly in the physical fabric of cities and suburbs. Research that focuses on the twentieth-century metropolis itself—that "indisputable artifact, a measure of human action"—is a fourth line of inquiry that can enable scholars to produce an instrumental planning history.

Recently, James Farmer, the founder of the Congress of Racial Equality (CORE) in the 1960s and currently a visiting professor at Mary Washington College in Virginia, delivered an extremely bleak assessment of the nation's urban-centered racial and class divisions: "I think we are headed for violence. Los Angeles is just the beginning." From the two-nation syndrome decried in the Kerner Commission Report in 1968, we are now "moving toward two separate souls, two separate spirits." If we are a nation in which our predominant metropolitan landscape formalizes housing, employment, and social opportunities segregated by race and income, then we must enlarge our understanding of how these circumstances have come to be. We must comprehend why, over the past fifty years, African American communities have consistently opposed many of urban planners' most celebrated efforts, even those explicitly promoted as beneficial to Black Americans. We must do more to uncover how a broader range of metropolitan residents interpret their problems and how they imagine workable solutions. Planning historians can provide the knowledge and the insight that will assist planners and policy makers to create a more civilized metropolitan environment. To do so, they must acknowledge that an urban place is more than the sum of its formal components; it is also the sum of the lives lived there.

Notes

Introduction

1. Scott 1969, pp. 2, 163–64.
2. Lippmann 1914. Zueblin and Simkhovitch are discussed in chapters 4 and 2 of this volume, respectively.
3. Churchill 1960; Hancock 1960.
4. Creese 1964; Buder 1969.
5. Goist 1972, 1974; Johnston 1973; Johnson 1974; Kantor 1974; Myhra 1974; Ross 1975; Grabow 1975.
6. Birch 1983.
7. Birch 1987, p. 136.
8. Krueckeberg 1983a, p. 3.
9. Brooks 1988.
10. Krueckeberg 1983a, p. 4.
11. Ibid., p. 1.
12. Scott 1969, p. xvii.

13. Ibid., p. xix.
14. Gillette 1983; Silver 1985, 1991; Weiss 1987; Haar and Kayden 1989; Banerjee and Baer 1984.
15. Haar and Kayden 1989.
16. K. Jackson 1980; Hirsch 1983; Silver 1984b; Bauman 1987; Bayor 1988; Mohl 1990; Lukas 1985.
17. Johnson and Schaffer 1985, pp. 131–32.
18. Ibid., p. 132.
19. Warner 1962; Edel, Sclar, and Luria 1984; Jackson 1985; Weiss 1987; Keating 1988.
20. Miller 1981; O'Connor 1983; Binford 1985; Fishman 1987; Sies 1987a; Ebner 1988; Worley 1990.
21. Sies 1987b, pp. 109–10, n. 18.
22. Muller and Bauman 1993.
23. Sies 1987a, 1987b; Weiss 1987; Keating 1988.
24. Mandelbaum 1985, p. 186.
25. Wilson 1988.
26. Schaffer 1988, pp. 4–5.
27. Ibid., pp. 6–7.
28. Schuyler 1986, p. 6; Hammack 1988, p. 156.
29. Peterson 1983. Quote from Krueckeberg 1983a, p. 4.
30. Schultz 1989, p. xiv.
31. Gillette and Miller 1987.
32. Marsh 1988; Weiss 1989; Konvitz, Rose, and Tarr 1990.
33. Gillette 1990.
34. Abbott 1983; Silver 1984b; Sies 1987a, 1987b, 1991.
35. Wallock 1988; Sharpe and Wallock 1983, 1994a.
36. Schuyler 1984; Sloane 1991.
37. Schuyler 1986, pp. 35, 59, 75.
38. Fisher 1986, p. 174.
39. Scott 1969, p. 80.
40. Wilson 1989, pp. 2–4.
41. Wilson 1989, pp. 2–3; Bluestone 1991, pp. 2, 195–98.
42. Duany and Plater-Zyberk 1991; Hancock 1991a.
43. Hall 1988, pp. 3, 87, 94.
44. Buder 1990, p. viii.
45. Hardy 1991; Ward 1992.
46. Boyer 1983, p. 292, n. 1. Words in brackets are those of the authors.
47. Boyer 1983, p. 7.
48. Buder 1967; Garner 1987; Wolfe 1987.

49. Foglesong 1986, pp. 11, 26–27.
50. Brownell 1977.
51. Kahn 1979.
52. Silver 1984b; Abbott 1983.
53. Goldfield 1980; Hammack 1982; Birch 1987, p. 143.
54. Rosen 1986, pp. 331–35.
55. Schwartz 1993, p. xxi.
56. Mandelbaum 1985, p. 185.
57. Schuyler 1986; Schultz 1989; Sies 1987a.
58. Mandelbaum 1985, pp. 186–87.

Chapter One

1. Tunnard 1970, pp. 178–207, 303–29; Schuyler 1986.
2. Fein 1972a, pp. 3, 27; Fisher 1986, pp. 1–5; Schuyler 1986, pp. 2, 176, 179; J. Peterson 1991, pp. 101–15.
3. See note 2. William H. Wilson also emphasizes Olmsted's preparatory role vis-à-vis the City Beautiful, in Wilson 1989, pp. 9–34.
4. The major biographies of Olmsted are Roper 1973; Stevenson 1977; and Kalfus 1990.
5. For biographical information about Frederick Law Olmsted Jr., see Klaus 1991, 1988. Also see Whiting and Phillips 1958; "Biographical Notes, FLO, Jr." in Olmsted Associates Collection. Hereafter, all note references to the younger Olmsted will be to Olmsted Jr.; publications not so designated will refer to Olmsted senior. The junior Olmsted dropped the "Jr." from his name about September 1908.
6. Roper 1973, p. 338.
7. Klaus 1991, p. 457; Klaus 1988, pp. 25–33.
8. Klaus 1988, pp. 38, 57.
9. "Biographical Notes, FLO, Jr."
10. Peterson 1985, pp. 144–45.
11. Caparn 1901, pp. 20–23; Klaus 1988, pp. 63–68.
12. Wilson 1987, pp. 397–99.
13. Hines 1974, pp. 174–96, 312–45; Wrigley 1983, pp. 58–72.
14. Kalfus 1990, pp. 277–96.
15. For the senior Olmsted as a planner, see Schuyler 1986. Also consult Fein 1968; Fisher 1986, pp. 113–49; Wilson 1989, pp. 9–34; and Zaitzevsky 1982, pp. 51–150.

16. Roper 1973, pp. xiv, 254–57, 272, 280, 318, 425, 450; Schuyler 1986, pp. 184–85; and Beveridge 1981. Schuyler uses the phrase "more openly built urban environment" repeatedly in Schuyler 1986, pp. 2, 3, 23.
17. Olmsted, Vaux, and Company 1869; Olmsted 1870.
18. J. Peterson 1991, pp. 103–5.
19. See, for example, Olmsted, Vaux, and Company 1869, p. 12.
20. Schuyler 1986, pp. 167–79; Olmsted et al. 1871, p. 253; and Olmsted and Olmsted 1888, pp. 9, 16, 20.
21. A notable exception is Copeland 1982. For another view of comprehensive planning in the nineteenth century, see Hammack 1988, pp. 139–65.
22. Olmsted 1870, pp. 12–13. See also Cleveland 1873, pp. 49–50.
23. For the programmatic sweep of Progressive Era reform, see Zueblin 1916. For an overview of the environmental agenda of Progressive urban reform, see Boyer 1978, pp. 220–83.
24. J. Peterson 1991, 1985.
25. For examples of early general-improvement plans, see Robinson 1906; Burnham and Bennett 1905; Civic League of St. Louis 1907; and Nolen 1907. For historical analysis of City Beautiful advisory planning in practice, see Wilson 1989, pp. 126–278.
26. See Olmsted [Jr.] 1908, 1910a, 1911b, 1913b; and Arnold, Freeman, and Olmsted [Jr.] 1910. Also see Klaus 1991.
27. Olmsted [Jr.] 1913b, pp. 305–9.
28. For the conventional approach to city planning as it evolved prior to World War I, see Ford 1917, pp. 1–3.
29. Letter from Olmsted Jr. to Ihlder 1908, File Folder: "Grand Rapids." In Olmsted Associates Collection.
30. Letter from Olmsted Jr. to Crawford 1909, File Folder: "Philadelphia City Plan." In Olmsted Associates Collection.
31. Olmsted Jr., address to American Civic League, quoted in "City Planning in Practice," 1911a, pp. 124–25.
32. Olmsted [Jr.] 1908, p. 5.
33. Arnold, Freeman, and Olmsted [Jr.] 1910, pp. 8–9.
34. Olmsted [Jr.] 1911b; Pittsburgh Civic Commission, "Purpose and Progress of City Planning in Pittsburgh," in Arnold, Freeman, and Olmsted [Jr.] 1910, p. 6.
35. Brunner, Olmsted [Jr.], and Arnold 1911.
36. Letter from Olmsted Jr. to Brunner 1911, File Folder: "City of Rochester, Civic Improvement Association." In Olmsted Associates Collection.

37. Olmsted [Jr.] 1913a.
38. For the intellectual background against which Olmsted Jr. rebelled, see Wiebe 1967, pp. 140–49; Hofstadter 1979, pp. 183–86; and Perry 1984, pp. 263–76.
39. In addition to Olmsted [Jr.] 1913a, see Olmsted [Jr.] 1916, pp. 1–18; and address, Olmsted [Jr.] 1911a, pp. 124–25.
40. Olmsted [Jr.] 1913a, pp. 306–7.
41. Ibid.
42. Walker [1941] 1950, pp. xv, 329–70.
43. Olmsted [Jr.] 1913a, pp. 305–6.
44. Letter from Olmsted Jr. to Kellogg 1920, File Folder: "Miscellaneous Correspondence, 1904–1924, R-Z." In Olmsted Associates Collection.
45. Shurtleff 1915, pp. 143–44; Shurtleff and Olmsted [Jr.] 1914; Olmsted [Jr.] et al. 1916, pp. 22–26; Olmsted [Jr.] 1910b, pp. 1–8.

Chapter Two

1. Gittel and Shtob 1981, p. 67. See also Hayden 1984, p. 31.
2. Coke 1968, p. 21.
3. Simkhovitch 1943b, p. 175.
4. Simkhovitch 1944b, p. 3.
5. Simkhovitch 1949, p. 132.
6. Marsh 1953, p. 17.
7. Simkhovitch 1938, p. 160.
8. Simkhovitch 1949, p. 124.
9. Cook 1979, p. 13. See also Sklar 1985, pp. 658–77.
10. Goldmark 1953, p. v.
11. Sklar 1985, p. 658.
12. "Twenty-five Years and After" 1907, p. 1124.
13. Davis 1967, p. 70.
14. "To Picture Congestion" 1908, p. 1639.
15. "Congestion of Population" 1908, p. 1740.
16. Kantor 1974, p. 423.
17. Marsh 1953, p. 17.
18. "Exhibit of Congestion" 1908, p. 1399.
19. Simkhovitch 1949, p. 124.
20. Marsh 1953, p. 19.
21. Simkhovitch 1949, p. 175.
22. "National Conference on City Planning" 1909, p. 299.

23. Coke 1968, p. 21.
24. Foglesong 1986, pp. 202–3.
25. Scott 1969, p. 95.
26. Kantor 1974, p. 427.
27. Simkhovitch 1910 [1909], p. 104.
28. Davis 1967, p. 72.
29. Simkhovitch 1910 [1909], p. 102.
30. Ibid., p. 103.
31. Ibid.
32. Davis 1967, p. 73.
33. Simkhovitch 1910 [1909], p. 104.
34. Simkhovitch 1943a, p. 4.
35. Simkhovitch 1949, p. 126.
36. Simkhovitch 1944a, pp. 1, 2.
37. Simkhovitch 1949, p. 126.
38. Weiss 1987, p. 56. See also Marcuse 1980, pp. 154–73.
39. "National Conference on City Planning" 1909, pp. 299–300.

Chapter Three

For their generous support at various stages in the research and writing of this material, the author wishes to acknowledge the University of California, Berkeley; the American Historical Association; and the Buell Center for the Study of American Architecture, Columbia University.

1. *Missouri Republican,* 21 Mar. 1910, p. 7, col. 1; 22 Mar. 1910, p. 3, col. 3.
2. See, for example, Scott 1969; Boyer 1983; Ciucci et al. 1979.
3. On St. Louis planning, see Martinson 1990; Rafferty 1991.
4. Teaford 1984; Schultz 1989.
5. Peterson 1993, pp. 6–23; Arena 1974; Richardson 1956; McDermott 1952; *The Acts of the Assembly* 1828, pp. 86–88, 96; "An Act to Authorize the Sale of the St. Louis Commons" 1856; St. Louis Common Claims Book 1835–1838; *Scheme for the Separation and Re-organization* 1877; Barclay 1962; Teaford 1984, pp. 112–17.
6. Richardson 1956, p. 279; Peterson 1993, p. 15; Alvord 1920, p. 220; Primm 1832, p. 115.
7. *Missouri Republican,* 16 July 1823, p. 2, col. 4; St. Louis Common Claims Book 1835–1838, 26 Jan. 1837, 11 July 1837, 15 May 1838, n.p.; "Report of the Board of Public Improvements" 1878, p. 199.
8. Sandweiss 1991, chap. 4.

9. *Labor,* 29 Apr. 1893, p. 1, col. 6.

10. *St. Louis Post-Dispatch,* 6 Nov. 1898, p. 12, col. 3.

11. For an earlier use of such rhetoric, see St. Louis Common Claims Book 1835–1838, 22 Aug. 1837, n.p. On the 1890s political scene, see Muraskin 1968.

12. *Missouri Republican,* 25 Jan. 1911, p. 8, col. 2; 27 Jan. 1911, p. 6, col. 2.

13. *St. Louis Post-Dispatch,* 1 Feb. 1911, p. 9, col. 1.

14. Civic Improvement League of St. Louis 1903, p. 11; Civic Improvement League Papers 1902–1920, 23 May 1902.

15. Civic League of St. Louis 1907, p. 9.

16. Ibid., pp. 49, 37. See also Crawford 1917; and Dreiser 1922, pp. 219–20.

17. McConachie 1976, pp. 200, 60 ff.

18. Wright 1911, p. 3.

19. Civic League of St. Louis 1911, p. 18; Kessler 1913; *Civic Bulletin* 1911, n.p.

20. City Plan Commission of St. Louis 1917c, pp. xxii, xv (original emphasis).

21. Fesler to Gundlach, 9 Mar. 1915, Gundlach Papers. Compare to the discussion of the shifting "dynamic of support and opposition between planners and businessmen" in Foglesong 1986, p. 231.

22. St. Louis Municipal Ordinances 1821–, no. 30199, 28 June 1918.

23. City Plan Commission of St. Louis 1919, pp. 4, 63.

24. Ibid., pp. 11, 30 (emphasis added).

25. Sandweiss 1991, chap. 3.

26. City Plan Commission of St. Louis 1917c, p. xv.

27. City Plan Commission of St. Louis 1919, pp. 34, 28, 11.

28. Bartholomew 1983, p. 3.

29. "Annual Report of the Park Commissioner" 1913, p. 13.

30. City Plan Commission of St. Louis 1917b, p. 8.

31. City Plan Commission of St. Louis 1917a, n.p.; City Plan Commission of St. Louis 1917c, p. 9.

32. "The Courthouse Site" 1924, n.p.; "Reasons for Keeping Courthouse on Broadway" 1924, n.p., Gundlach Papers.

33. Boyer 1983, p. 9.

Chapter Four

1. Taylor 1907b, p. 3.

2. For a sociologist's analysis of the small parks, see Cranz 1982.

3. See Draper 1982.
4. See Wilson 1989, pp. 53–74; Hines 1974.
5. Bluestone 1991, pp. 20–44; Ranney 1972.
6. Nash 1928, p. 65.
7. "Chicago Parks" 1908, p. 26. See also Draper 1989, pp. xi–xiii.
8. Burnham and Bennett 1909, p. 58, plate cxxx.
9. Olmsted to Foreman, 1 Dec. 1903, Olmsted Associates Collection.
10. Drawings in Chicago Park District, Special Collections.
11. Foreman 1905, pp. 610–20.
12. Davis 1908, p. 1505.
13. Head 1893, p. 526.
14. Olmsted to Foreman, 7 Dec. 1903, Olmsted Associates Collection.
15. Burnham and Bennett 1905; Civic League of St. Louis 1907.
16. Mero 1908–9, pp. 212 ff.
17. Leland and Leland 1913.
18. See, for example, McNutt 1904, pp. 612–17; O'Neill 1904, pp. 798–99; Foreman 1905, pp. 610–20; Taylor 1906, pp. 54–64; "Field Houses of Chicago" 1907, p. 49; "Chicago Parks" 1908, p. 26.
19. Brownell 1980.
20. Stormann 1991, pp. 142–43; Cavallo 1980, pp. 42–43; Cranz 1982, p. 122; Jacobs 1961, p. 82.
21. Lee 1903; Hardy 1980; Zaitzevsky 1982, pp. 96–99; Leland and Leland 1913, pp. 59–66.
22. The secondary and primary literatures on the Playground movement are immense. See especially Cavallo 1980; Boyer 1978; Rainwater 1921; Cranz 1971; Dickason 1979; Weyeneth 1984; Finfer 1974; Knapp 1971; Marsden 1961, pp. 48–58.
23. See, for example, Gems 1989; McArthur 1975; McCarthy 1972; Halsey 1940; Taylor 1910; Zueblin 1907.
24. Wilson 1927; unknown Chicago newspaper, Sept. 1901, Lincoln Park Commission Newspaper Clippings volumes, Chicago Park District, Special Collections; *Chicago Record-Herald,* 6 June 1899.
25. Olmsted to Foreman, 1 Dec. 1903, Olmsted Associates collection.
26. Osborn 1928; Rainwater 1921; Halsey 1940.
27. Woods and Kennedy 1909, pp. 66, 69.
28. Diner 1975, pp. 525–26; Diner 1980, p. 48; Wilson 1989, p. 45; Deegan 1988, pp. 19, 59, 89–92, 177–78.
29. *Hull-House Maps and Papers* 1895; Zueblin 1903, 1905.
30. Beilfuss 1908, pp. 259, 261.
31. Zueblin 1898.

32. Diner 1980, pp. 30–32; Deegan 1988, pp. 62–65.
33. Matthews 1977, p. 93.
34. Henderson 1894.
35. *Hull-House Maps and Papers* 1895; Kellogg 1912, pp. 1–2. Kellogg ran the famous Pittsburgh Survey published in 1909–14. Young 1956; Chambers 1971; Fish 1985; Deegan 1988, pp. 34–37, 62–67.
36. City Homes Association 1901.
37. See, for example, Bushnell 1901; Gillette 1901.
38. Only three of the six typescripts are to be found in the Special Park Commission Collection, Chicago Historical Society. These are "Report on Conditions to the Honorable the Commissioners of Lincoln Park, Chicago," 27 Jan. 1903; "Report on Sites and Needs to the Honorable the South Park Commissioners, Chicago," 25 Oct. 1902; and ["Report on Conditions to the Honorable the South Park Commissioners"], no date, first page missing. They are all stamped "George Hooker Library." Hooker was the secretary of the Chicago City Club and a close follower of planning issues internationally. His papers are now in Regenstein Library, University of Chicago, but the three missing reports are not there. Two maps are in the Chicago Park District, Special Collections.
39. The reports and maps indicate an earlier connection between Chicago sociologists and planners than that suggested by Fairfield 1992.
40. Nash 1928; Ford 1928.
41. Olmsted and Nolen 1906.
42. Hubbard 1914; Olmsted [Jr.] 1927.
43. See Breen 1989; Chicago Real Estate Board 1903.
44. Breen 1989, pp. 301–2, 326–27.
45. Chicago Real Estate Board 1905b, p. 15; 1905a, p. 8; 1907, p. 11.
46. Chicago Real Estate Board 1904. See also Perkins 1908.
47. Davis 1989, *passim.*
48. Peterson 1976; Wilson 1980, 1988.
49. Fairfield 1985.

Chapter Five

1. Whittick 1974, p. 437.
2. U.S. Deptartment of Commerce 1988; Lazare 1991.
3. Lubove 1960.
4. Schaffer 1982, p. 38; Lubove 1960; Bredemeier 1980, chap. 11; Colean 1940.

5. Lubove 1960; Kirschner 1986; Scott 1969, pp. 170–74; Hollomby 1991; Morton 1984.
6. Watkin 1982; Pevsner 1944.
7. Darley 1978.
8. Fein 1968, p. 39; Litchfield 1922; Childs 1918; May 1918; Olmsted [Jr.] 1919.
9. Beattie 1980.
10. Swenarton 1981; Beattie 1980.
11. Beaufoy 1950, p. 260.
12. Swenarton 1981.
13. Whitaker et al. 1918.
14. Ackerman 1917, 1918a, 1918b, 1918c, 1922; Lubove 1963, pp. 42–43.
15. Ackerman 1918a, p. 86.
16. Litchfield 1919, p. 599.
17. Jacobs 1961.
18. Lubove 1960; Dahir 1950, pp. 192–98; Wright 1920.
19. Lubove 1960, p. 478; Veiller 1918.
20. Davis 1967.
21. Scott 1969, p. 72.
22. Perry 1910.
23. Regional Planning Federation of Philadelphia 1932; Dahir 1950, pp. 192–98; Schuldiner 1981.
24. Ackerman 1917, 1922.
25. Litchfield 1939; Regional Planning Federation 1932; Schuldiner 1981.
26. Whitaker 1920; Lubove 1960; Bredemeier 1980, chap. 11; *Evening Bulletin*, 11 Dec. 1921.
27. Lubove 1963.
28. Litchfield 1919, pp. 599–600.
29. Moulton 1918.
30. Colean 1940.

Chapter Six

1. Moore and Odum 1938, p. 2.
2. Ireland 1991, pp. 125–57.
3. Rose and Seely 1979, p. 6.
4. Jolley 1969.
5. Pinchot 1947, pp. 45–48.

6. Kolko 1963. It may also be argued that organizations such as those presided over by Pratt were more typical of the scientific specialist, as found in Samuel P. Hays's treatment of the Progressive Era. Hays 1959.
7. Pratt 1922.
8. Penick 1968, p. 22.
9. Penick 1974, p. 120.
10. Adelstein 1991, p. 168.
11. Weaver 1984, p. 57.
12. Tindall 1958, p. 293.
13. Clapp 1955; Friedmann 1955; Kyle 1958.
14. Lepawsky 1949, p. 8.

Chapter Seven

1. Banfield and Wilson 1963, p. 18.
2. Warner 1890; McGrew 1922; Miller 1940; Davis 1953.
3. Holmes and Pendleton 1918, vol. 1, pp. 5–14; Pryde 1992, pp. 1–12, *passim.*
4. Starr 1986, p. 48.
5. Carrico 1986; Trafzer and Carrico 1992, pp. 51–67; Crane 1991, pp. 104–27; Davis 1953, pp. 1–33; Pourade 1960–67; Starr 1986, pp. 1–29; Reps 1979, pp. 42, 87–89, 95, 177.
6. Nolen 1937–38; Nolen Papers, Marston folder, Project no. 52, pp. 1–2.
7. Starr 1986, p. 52; U.S. Department of Commerce 1890.
8. Mott 1932, pp. 53–85, 159–208; Starr 1986, pp. 30–113; Pourade 1964, pp. 34–42; Crane 1991, pp. 110–27; Reps 1979, pp. 108–9; Quastler 1992, pp. 171–74; Ford 1992, pp. 188–96.
9. Starr 1986, pp. 82–113; Mott 1932, p. 72; Reps 1979, pp. 239–84, 688; Pourade 1964–67.
10. Hancock 1964, pp. 487–559; Polos 1984; Hennessey 1986; *San Diego Union,* 7 Sept. 1907, quotation from p. 1.
11. Nolen 1908, pp. 2–5, 89–91, quotations from pp. 91 and iii.
12. Mott 1932, pp. 49, 72–75, 81–82, 126–27, 144–46, 160, *passim.*
13. *San Diego Union,* 28 Oct. 1910 to 28 Mar. 1914, *passim;* San Diego 1908, Resolution nos. 2642, 3821, 4070, 4518; Ford 1917, pp. 163–64; Marston 1956, vol. 2, pp. 57–58; Nolen Diary, 19 Oct. 1908, 4 Dec. 1909, 13–17 Oct. 1911; Nolen Papers, Marston folder, Project nos. 52 and 299, and Marston to Nolen, 18 May 1920, 19 Jan. 1923; Hancock 1964, pp. 489–532; Pourade 1965, pp. 112–222.

14. *San Diego Union,* 15 Oct. 1911.
15. Mott 1932, pp. 47–92, quotation from p. 73; Nolen Diary, 13–17 Oct. 1911; *San Diego Union,* 16 Feb., 15 Nov. 1911, 16 Apr., 5 May 1912, 2 Feb. 1913, 6–7 Apr. 1915; *San Diego City and County Directory* 1915, pp. 196, 298, 722, 1193; McGrew 1922 vol. 2, pp. 189–93, 227–33, 309–15, 393–96; Stone, Stone, and Price 1940, pp. 134–52; Pourade 1965, pp. 112–36, 179–200; Castanien 1993, pp. 27–39; King and Frederick 1916, pp. 11–14, fn. 12, quotation from p. 3.
16. See, for example, Hays 1957; Wiebe 1967; Warner 1972; Schiesl 1977; Link and McCormick 1983.
17. Stone, Stone, and Price 1940, pp. 141–52; San Diego 1915, Resolution no. 5817, and Charter Amendments 1915; Mott 1932, pp. 75–76; Ford 1917, p. 164; Scott 1969, p. 150; Weiss 1987, pp. 9–10, 110–14, *passim.*
18. San Diego 1913, Book 33, 4 Nov. 1912 to 23 Apr. 1913, p. 461; *San Diego Union,* 8 Mar., 9 Apr., 2 (quotation) and 4 Nov. 1913.
19. Kettner 1923, pp. 52–59, 61 ff.; Pourade 1965, quoting Marston to Ed Fletcher 1912; Lotchin 1979b; Gordon 1981.
20. *San Diego Union,* 4–27 Apr. 1917; Marston 1956, vol. 2, pp. 57–108, quotation from p. 63; Pourade 1965, pp. 223–25; Showley 1988, p. F-1, quoting campaign song.
21. Marston 1956, vol. 2, quotation from p. 67; Polos 1984; Hennessey 1986, pp. 230–53, quotation from p. 242.
22. Pourade 1965, p. 231.
23. Hancock 1991b; Kettner 1923; Gordon 1981; Lotchin 1992, pp. 23–41 ff.
24. U.S. Department of Commerce, Bureau of the Census 1920, 1930; Stone, Stone, and Price 1940, p. 146, 157; Pourade 1967; M. L. Scott 1991, pp. 27–55, 94–127; Starr 1986, pp. 142–63.
25. Stone, Stone, and Price 1940, pp. 141–43; Nolen 1937–38; Nolen Papers, Marston folder, Project no. 299.
26. Nolen 1937–38; Nolen Papers, Marston folder, Project no. 299, pp. 2–3.
27. Nolen Papers, Marston folder, Project no. 299, pp. 2–8; Pourade 1967, pp. 27–29, 38–45.
28. Nolen 1926, pp. 8–9.
29. Ibid., pp. 12, 25–31.
30. Ibid., Nolen quoted p. 28; Pourade 1967, pp. 49–72, 199–218; M. L. Scott 1991, pp. 57–91, 151–59; Young 1990.
31. Nolen 1937–38; Nolen Papers, Marston folder, Project no. 299, pp. 6–8, Gardner to Nolen, 27 Feb. and 19 Dec. 1929, and Reports 1927–31;

folder no. 299; Pourade 1967, pp. 82–89, 122; Stone, Stone, and Price 1940, pp. 139–40; Weiss 1987, pp. 122–35.

32. San Diego 1931, sections 24, 29, 54; cf. San Diego 1958, section 42; Stone, Stone, and Price 1940, pp. 152–206; Mott 1932, pp. 71–118.

33. Pourade 1967, pp. 139–40, 226–35; Castanien 1993, pp. 66–69; Stone, Stone, and Price 1940, pp. 175–96; Nolen 1937–38; Nolen Papers, Marston folder, Project no. 299.

34. Nolen Papers, Project folder no. 209, Rick report, pp. 13–14, and Rick to Nolen, 29 Jan. 1936; Marston folder, Marston to Nolen, 7 Jan. 1936, and to Charlotte Parsons, 1 May 1939; *San Diego Union*, 2 Jan. 1936 (Rick), 24 Apr., 5, 6, 11 Dec. 1937; Scott 1969, pp. 352–53, quotation from p. 353; Nolen quotation from Nolen Papers, Marston folder, Nolen to Marston, 15 Jan. 1936.

35. *San Diego Union*, 19 Feb. 1937.

36. U.S. Department of Commerce, Bureau of the Census 1900–1990; Pryde 1992, *passim*.

37. See, for example, Ford 1917; Scott 1969; Boyer 1983; Silver 1984b; Foglesong 1986; Schultz 1989; Weiss 1987; Wilson 1989; Cullingworth 1993.

38. Cullingworth 1993, p. 19.

39. Stone, Stone, and Price 1940, p. 144.

40. San Diego 1979; Corso 1983; Lotchin 1992, pp. 297–318.

41. Starr 1986, p. 85; Pourade 1977, pp. 167, 249–50; Showley 1988, p. F-1; Showley 1992, p. F-10.

Chapter Eight

1. Sharp 1955, p. 237; "Trinity River Flood Control—One of Greatest American Projects," *Dallas* (Oct. 1929), pp. 13–14.

2. For more on this changing approach to the city and to planning see Fairbanks 1988, pp. 39–57.

3. Wilson 1989, pp. 257–60; Head, n.d., p. 3; "Remarks at the Civic Luncheon" 1928, p. 235.

4. Kessler 1912, pp. 9–12.

5. Wilson 1983, p. 253.

6. *Dallas Morning News*, 14 July 1915, 6 Apr. 1916; Black 1982, p. 142.

7. Head 1925, p. 3; Wood et al. 1920, pp. 13–16; *Dallas Morning News*, 28 May 1919.

8. Wilson 1990, p. 27.

9. Head 1925, p. 3; City Plan Commission, Minutes, 10 Feb. 1919; Black 1982, p. 81.

10. *Dallas Morning News*, 1 Jan. 1923.

11. Ibid., 15 May 1933.

12. Dealey Papers, Memo, John E. Surratt to George Dealey, Charles Sanger et al., 7 Mar. 1924, Box 3.

13. Dealey 1929, pp. 180–84.

14. Dealey Papers, Report, Committee for County and City-Wide Association, to Dallas Property Owners Association, 11 Apr. 1924, Box 3; *Dallas Morning News*, 2 Jan. 1925.

15. "The Ulrickson Committee Report," *Dallas* (Nov. 1927), p. 7; Ulrickson Committee 1927.

16. Ulrickson Committee 1927, p. 17.

17. The Committee on Supervision of Expenditures was made up of two delegates from the City Plan Commission, the Kessler Plan Association, the Dallas Clearing House, the Chamber of Commerce, the Ulrickson Committee, and one delegate from the Presidents Club, the Technical Club, the School Board, the Oak Cliff-Dallas Commercial Association, and the Park Board. *Dallas Morning News*, 16 Dec. 1927.

18. Ulrickson Committee 1927, pp. 14–15.

19. *Dallas Morning News*, 5 Nov. 1927, 6 Dec. 1927, 17 Dec. 1927.

20. City Plan Commission, Minutes, 5 Jan. 1928, 17 July 1928, 2 Aug. 1928, 16 Aug. 1928.

21. City and County of Dallas Levee Improvement District, n.d., pp. 3, 8. *Dallas Morning News*, 28 Dec. 1928.

22. Head, n.d.

23. *Dallas Morning News*, 11 May 1933, 26 Mar. 1933.

24. Dealey Papers, W. T. Davis to Simon Linz, 12 June 1929.

25. Dealey Papers, Petition of Dallas Drainage Association to City Council, n.d.; Industrial Properties Corporation 1931; *Dallas Morning News*, 20 Feb. 1928, 1 Oct. 1935.

26. *Dallas Morning News*, 2 Apr. 1929.

27. *Dallas Times Herald*, 6 June 1938.

28. *Dallas Times Herald*, 8 June 1930.

29. *Dallas Times Herald*, 28 Sept. 1933.

30. *Dallas Morning News*, 10 June 1930.

31. Sharp 1955, p. 252; *Dallas Morning News*, 24 May 1933.

32. *Dallas Times Herald*, 11, 12 June 1930; *Dallas Morning News*, 12 June 1930.

33. *Dallas Morning News*, 15 June 1930.

34. *Dallas Morning News,* 30 Oct. 1930, 3 Dec. 1930.
35. Sharp 1955, pp. 251–52.
36. Ibid., p. 252.
37. *Dallas Morning News,* 19 Dec. 1930.
38. Dealey Papers, L. A. Stemmons to L. S. Stemmons, 18 Mar. 1938; L. A. Stemmons to John E. Owens, 24 Apr. 1933.
39. Stone et al. 1939, pp. 30–34; *Dallas Morning News,* 16 Apr. 1931.
40. *Dallas Morning News,* 2 May 1931, 1 July 1931, 21 Sept. 1931.
41. *Dallas Morning News,* 21 Sept. 1931.
42. *Dallas Times Herald,* 23 Sept. 1931.
43. *Dallas Times Herald,* 24 Sept. 1931, 1 Aug. 1932; Dealey Papers, JCM to Leslie A. Stemmons, 26 May 1933; Louis Head to King, 29 Nov. 1932.
44. Dealey Papers, E. D. Hurt's statement, 2 Mar. 1932.
45. City and County of Dallas Levee Improvement District 1951, p. 3.
46. *Dallas Morning News,* 15 Aug. 1933.
47. *Dallas Morning News,* 3 Jan. 1936.
48. Barta 1970, pp. 43–49.
49. *Dallas Morning News,* 8 Sept. 1946.
50. Dealey Papers, Memo, from George Dealey, undated [1930?], Box 3.
51. See Fairbanks 1990, pp. 125–50.

Chapter Nine

1. Burgess 1994.
2. NCCP 1909 (U.S. Senate, Doc. 422, 61st Cong., 2d sess.).
3. NCCP 1909, 1915, 1916, 1921, 1926; Lubove 1962; Makielski 1966; Toll 1969.
4. Schultz 1989, pt. 2; Bettman 1926, p. 30; Gerckens 1983; James 1926, pp. 84–86; Toll 1969, p. 117.
5. *Village of Euclid* v. *Ambler Realty Co.,* 272 U.S. 365, 47 Sup. Ct. 114, 71 L. Ed. 303 (1926).
6. U.S. Department of Commerce 1933.
7. Scott 1969, chap. 3; James 1926; Hubbard and Hubbard 1929; Bassett 1940; Burgess 1994, chap. 3.
8. Hubbard and Hubbard 1929, pp. 176–89, 138–39; Delafons 1969, p. 93.
9. Lubove 1962, pp. 237–44.
10. Weiss 1987; Hubbard and Hubbard 1929, p. 154; NCCP 1915, pp. 75–78; NCCP 1916, pp. 99–104.

11. Jackson 1985.
12. *Planning* 1960, pp. 172–86.
13. Green 1955; Feiss 1961.
14. *Planning* 1954, pp. 133–59; 1960, pp. 196–202.
15. *Planning* 1963, pp. 4–14, 62–67.
16. Jacobs 1961; *Planning* 1964, pp. 56–67.
17. Teaford 1979; Jackson 1985; Keating 1988.
18. The discussion that follows is based on empirical research on the application of public and private land-use controls in Columbus, Ohio, and seven of its suburbs. This essay uses only part of a larger body of data on more than 300 subdivisions platted between 1880 and 1970 and more than 3,700 zoning actions taken between 1922 and 1970.
19. The larger body of research from which this work is drawn examined residential development and zoning activity in six corridors or "strips" of the metropolitan area, which included all or part of seven suburbs. These corridors include areas in which development occurred earliest and continued longest.
20. Columbus City Ordinance 34010, 6 Aug. 1923; Columbus City Ordinance 966–54, 13 Sept. 1954; Columbus City Planning Commission 1957; author's interview with Harmon Merwin (retired, Mid-Ohio Regional Planning Commission), 19 July 1990.
21. Monchow 1928; Sies 1987a; Worley 1990; Stach 1988.
22. NCCP 1916, pp. 93–100.
23. Jackson 1985; Checkoway 1984.
24. This discussion is based on an examination of 115 recorded subdivision plats, 76 of which were restricted. There were no plats filed on either the north side or Riverlea. The two filed in Bexley and Marble Cliff (one each) as well as the seven in Grandview were all subject to fairly restrictive zoning and their developers imposed no further restrictions. The developer of the lone west side subdivision, which was very small and subject to Columbus zoning, also imposed no restrictions.
25. The density, construction-cost, and floor-area minimums for each area indicated in table 9.3 are means calculated on the entire twenty-five-year time span this essay addresses. Because of the irregular shape and varying size of lots in many subdivisions, density for all has been calculated by dividing the total number of platted lots by the total acreage. The actual lots developed are smaller than the resulting figure would indicate because the amount of land area given over to dedicated streets and utility easements (a figure not recorded in subdivision plats) has not been subtracted from the total acreage.

26. *Shelley* v. *Kramer* 344 U.S. 1 (1948).
27. Jackson 1985, pp. 234–38.
28. Stach 1989.
29. NCCP 1921, pp. 26–29; Bassett 1940, p. 68.
30. Flint 1977; Silver 1991.
31. Jackson 1985, chap. 11.
32. NCCP 1927, p. 10; NCCP 1941, pp. 294–97.
33. *Planning* 1953, pp. 119–31; 1955, pp. 96–102; 1954, pp. 133–59; 1960, pp. 196–202.

Chapter Ten

1. See "Contest wins future for American couple and aid to Europeans," n.d., *Los Angeles Examiner Files,* Regional History Center, Department of Special Collections, University of Southern California Library; and Kaiser Homes Press Department, "Contest winner starts 'new future' in Southern California," n.d., Henry J. Kaiser Papers, Bancroft Library, University of California, Berkeley, Carton 312, Folder Panorama City. Hereafter cited as Kaiser Papers.
2. U.S. Department of Commerce 1940, vol. 1, pt. 2, table 5; vol. 2, pt. 1, table 6.
3. Kaiser Community Homes marketed their projects through newspaper advertisements and sales brochures. See the *Los Angeles Evening Herald-Express, Los Angeles Examiner,* and *Van Nuys News.* Brochures are archived in the Eugene Trefethen Papers, Bancroft Library, Carton 11, Folder 8. (Trefethen was vice president of Kaiser Community Homes.) Hereafter cited as Trefethen Papers. The spatial proximity of community development and employment is called out in everything from the Bank of America's preliminary appraisal, 28 Apr. 1946, to the final phase of commercial development in 1959. See Bank of America Appraisal and Research Department, "Distance to Employment," and "Panorama City Shopping Center: The Center of the San Fernando Valley," both in the Trefethen Papers.
4. There is an important distinction between the working-class housing and pattern of homeownership examined in this chapter and corporate-sponsored company towns and philanthropic housing. The case studies presented here are self-contained neighborhoods planned and constructed by speculative builders. Community building hinges on several factors; speed and scale are critical. The control of a contiguous

parcel that can be site-planned for residences, retail, and community services is fundamental. Speed was achieved through standardization of parts and product. See Doucet and Weaver 1991; Harris 1990; Hise 1992; Weiss 1987.

5. Taylor 1915; Supplementary Report of the Urbanism Committee 1939, vol. 2, pt. 1.

6. Park, Burgess, and McKenzie 1925; Hoyt 1939, 1943b.

7. Vance 1964.

8. East 1941; Fogelson 1967; Bottles 1987.

9. Viehe 1981; Soja 1986; Scott 1988; Vance 1966. The sources for descriptive terminology are Fishman 1987; Kling, Olin, and Poster 1991; New York Regional Plan Association 1962; and Garreau 1991.

10. "Home Ownership Drive," *Commercial Standards Monthly*, Nov. 1930, p. 149.

11. U.S. Department of Commerce 1939, pp. 94, 540–52; North American Aviation 1945; Cunningham 1951; Maynard 1962; Rae 1968.

12. Bloch 1987; A. Scott 1991.

13. Security First National Bank, *Monthly Summary of Business Conditions*, June 1941, p. 3. Hereafter cited as *Monthly Summary*. U.S. Department of Commerce 1944. Although nationally most sectors of the economy slumped following the mild recovery of 1935–36, Los Angeles aircraft manufacturers were recruiting employees from outside the region. See, for example, *Newsweek*, Feb. 1936.

14. *Monthly Summary*, Oct. 1937, Aug. 1940, Sept. 1940. In July 1940 the Big Six prime contractors projected a 51 percent increase from 3.56 million square feet to 5.4 million. This proved to be a 14.5 million-square-foot underestimate; by 1944 there were 19.9 million square feet of floor space in the Los Angeles region. See *Monthly Summary*, June 1940; Cunningham 1951.

15. For unit output and employment see U.S. Department of Commerce 1946. For floor space see North American Aviation 1945, pp. 8, 11, 95.

16. The landscape of industry is revealed in contemporary photographs. See Maynard 1962. Also U.S. Department of Commerce 1940, table 20; U.S. Department of Labor 1944 (May).

17. North American Aviation 1945; Rae 1968.

18. Los Angeles Chamber of Commerce, Apr. 1939 to Dec. 1941.

19. U.S. Federal Housing Administration, *Annual Report* 1936–41, tables: "Mortgages accepted for insurance in States."

20. Jacobs 1982.

21. By 1940 the southern California total of 18,849 new FHA homes was first in the nation, and the 384 new subdivisions containing 23,775 lots filed between May 1940 and May 1941 not only led the nation, but were 103 units higher than the San Francisco Bay Area total of 281 subdivisions, which was second. U.S. Federal Housing Administration, *Annual Report,* 1940. The 1940 housing and subdivision numbers were published in "California Subdivision Activity Reaches Peak: Number of Tracts Placed on Market in Year Just Ended Sets All-time Record with 854," *Los Angeles Times,* 25 May 1941, p. 1.

22. "Southland Leads the Entire Nation in FHA Insured Housing: Early 1941 Volume Indicates Total Will Exceed All-time Peak Recorded Last Year," *Los Angeles Times,* 9 Mar. 1941, p. 13.

23. *Monthly Summary,* Dec. 1942, p. 2.

24. U.S. Federal Housing Administration, *Annual Report* 1940, p. 146.

25. Weiss 1987; U.S. Department of Labor 1954; Security Bank 1939.

26. California Labor Statistics 15 July 1940, tables 3 and 5; U.S. Federal Housing Administration, "Homes in Metropolitan Areas: Los Angeles Metropolitan District," table 1, p. 203; idem, "Monthly Amortization Payment Computing Chart," in *Insured Mortgage Portfolio,* Aug. 1939, p. 8.

27. Author's interview with Fred Marlow, 25 Feb. 1991, and William H. Hannon, a salesman with the Burns organization and now chairman of the Fritz B. Burns Charitable Foundation, 29 July 1991. See also Marlow 1981 and an unpublished biography of Fritz Burns written by Jack Tobin and Associates, Inc. in the possession of William Hannon. U.S. Bureau of Labor Statistics, Sept. 1940, p. 738.

28. Kaiser Photo Collection: 1983.50.4:1–49.

29. U.S. Federal Housing Administration, July 1936 and May 1936 are the best sources for the agency's recommendations concerning site planning and neighborhood design. The Westside Village site plan is in the Kaiser Papers, Carton 311, Folder Housing-Development Standards.

30. Author's interview with Kenneth Skinner, a Burns associate and member of the Kaiser Community Homes staff now with the Burns Foundation, 25 Feb. 1991.

31. Author's interview with Hannon.

32. See Hise 1992 for a detailed discussion of this revolution in building practice.

33. Toluca Wood sales brochure, n.d. Kaiser Papers, Carton 369, Folder Housing.

34. Robbins and Tilton, 1941. U.S. Department of Commerce 1940, vol. 3; Los Angeles City Planning Commission 1949.

35. U.S. Federal Housing Administration 1942; *California Real Estate Magazine*, June 1947, p. 287.

36. Quotation is from Federal Reserve Bank of San Francisco, *Monthly Review of Business Conditions*, 1 Nov. 1941, p. 56. U.S. Department of Labor, Bureau of Labor Statistics, 14 May 1945. "The Builders' House 1949," *Architectural Forum*, April 1949.

37. Regional Planning Commission, "Dwelling Units and Population," 16 July 1945.

38. Author's interviews with Marlow and Hannon. The John Anson Ford Papers, Huntington Library, San Marino, Calif., contain a complete set of National Housing Agency referral forms from the War Housing Center, Box 65 Housing.

39. Author's interview with Fred W. Marlow. *Monthly Summary*, 2 Aug. 1942, p. 1.

40. On the development of the business center see the *Los Angeles Down Town Shopping News*, 15 Aug. 1942, p. 12. Marlow-Burns site-planned schools and religious institutions into their developments; dedications and purchases were noted on property maps. See Trefethen Papers, Carton 11, Folder 9: Kaiser Community Homes Property Maps, Tract 13711.

41. Spence and Fairchild Aerial Photo Collections, UCLA Department of Geography, contain low-altitude oblique images of Westchester. For "Homes at Wholesale" see the *Los Angeles Evening Herald-Express*, 28 Mar., 25 Apr. 1942, 2 Jan. 1943; *Los Angeles Daily News*, 25 Dec. 1942; and *Los Angeles Examiner*, 12 Apr. 1942.

42. Warner 1962; Jackson 1985; Stilgoe 1988.

43. See, for example, Southern California Telesis, "And Now We Plan," n.d., an exhibition catalog for the Los Angeles Museum of Natural History.

44. In the projects under discussion, lot coverage ranged from 4 to 6.5 units per acre.

45. U.S. Department of Commerce 1940; 1950.

46. *Los Angeles Herald-Express*, 28 Mar. 1942, p. A-6.

47. The Fontana case study is drawn from material in the Kaiser Papers, Carton 369, Folder War Housing, and oversized volume "War Housing"; and California State Reconstruction and Reemployment Commission 1944.

48. U.S. Federal Housing Administration 1936b.

49. Inter-Office Memorandum, 20 Feb. 1947, Kaiser Papers, Carton 180. Quotation in "Henry J. Kaiser-Fritz B. Burns Announce the Organiza-

tion of Kaiser Community Homes: A National Home and Community Building Enterprise," 1945, Kaiser Papers, Carton 311, Folder Housing.

50. For the Kaiser Company's contribution, see Carton 848, Folder Kaiser Community Homes. Quotations from "Henry J. Kaiser-Fritz B. Burns Announce," and State Housing Committee, 18 Feb. 1947, Carton 180, Kaiser Papers.

51. "Statistical Areas and Jurisdictions: Dwelling Units and Populations" 46, Oct. 1954. The data on decentralization were taken from the 1953 Special Census. From the 1950 census to the end of 1952, the San Fernando Valley accounted for just over 90 percent of the population growth recorded in the city. See Los Angeles County Regional Planning Commission, "Statistical Areas," 39, May 1953.

52. Manuscript in the Fletcher Bowron Papers, Huntington Library, Box 57, Folder City Planning Progress, p. 6. On the San Fernando Valley plan see Los Angeles City Planning Commission, *Accomplishments,* pp. 5–12.

53. City Planning Manuscript in the Bowron Papers; Bennett and Breivogel 1945.

54. See note 4.

55. U.S. Department of Commerce 1950.

56. California State Reconstruction and Reemployment Commission 1945b, p. 38; Marlow 1981.

57. Multisite production planning for projects in Los Angeles and Santa Clara County required a degree of coordination beyond the scope of Burns and his associates. The Kaiser staff trained Burns's colleagues in standard corporate practice, including flowcharts and ledgers to track work in progress. At the same time, they were exhorting land purchasers to speed up their property search to allow the Kaiser engineering division time for processing and subdividing properties at the rate their production quotas mandated. Trefethen Papers, Carton 11, Folders 2–5.

58. Fishman 1987, p. 156.

Chapter Eleven

1. Ellis 1990.
2. Rose 1979; Gifford 1983; Jones 1989.
3. Webber 1992.
4. Kemp 1986.

5. Berger and Luckmann 1966; Larson 1977; Sayer 1984.
6. Foster 1981; McShane 1988.
7. Barrett 1983.
8. Willis 1986; Frampton 1992.
9. Caro 1975; Krieg 1989; Wallock 1991.
10. "Pattern for the Future" 1943.
11. Caro 1975, pp. 522–25.
12. Kellett 1969; Gifford 1983.
13. Whitten 1930.
14. Foster 1981.
15. Meikle 1979, pp. 200–210; Geddes 1940.
16. U.S. Bureau of Public Roads 1939; National Interregional Highway Committee 1944.
17. Seely 1987, p. 181.
18. National Interregional Highway Committee 1944, pp. 51–52.
19. National Interregional Highway Committee 1944, p. 53.
20. Groth 1989, 1994.
21. National Interregional Highway Committee 1944, p. 56.
22. U.S. Bureau of Public Roads 1955; Schwartz 1976.
23. Rose 1979.
24. American Institute of Planners 1947; Rose 1979, chap 5.
25. Jones 1989, pp. 1–2.
26. Blucher 1950; Tunnard 1951.
27. Moses 1943, p. 53.
28. Kemp 1986.
29. St. Clair 1986, pp. 151–55.
30. American Association of State Highway Officials 1957.
31. Weiss 1987.
32. Lynch 1981.
33. Tyrwhitt, Sert, and Rogers 1952.
34. Montgomery 1969; Gutman 1988; Ellis and Cuff 1989; Cuff 1991.
35. Larson 1983.
36. Newton 1971; Fein 1972b.
37. Downs 1970, pp. 192–227; Sevilla 1971; Silver 1984b; Mohl 1993.
38. Lathrop 1971.
39. Jacobs 1961.
40. Mumford 1961.
41. Mumford 1958.
42. Miller 1959.
43. Smith 1962.

44. Kemp 1986.
45. Lynch 1960.
46. Pushkarev 1963.
47. "Team Concepts for Urban Highways and Urban Design" 1968.
48. California Department of Public Works 1964; Halprin 1966.
49. Kemp 1986, p. 797; Levin and Abend 1971.
50. Mashaw 1973.
51. Armstrong 1972; Kelly 1970.
52. Rose and Seely 1990.
53. Seely 1987, p. 251.
54. Winner 1977.
55. Wills 1987, p. 372.
56. Bauman 1987.
57. Sorkin 1992; Mollenkopf and Castells 1991.
58. Peattie 1987, p. 111.
59. Krumholz and Forester 1990; "Architecture vs. Planning" 1990.
60. Lynch 1981; Kreditor 1990; Fishman 1987.
61. Logan and Molotch 1987.

Chapter Twelve

1. Blucher 1945, p. 268.
2. Blucher 1946, pp. 254–56; 1947, p. 235.
3. Abbott 1981a, p. 114; Abbott 1984, pp. 163–90; Huggins 1967, p. 116; Silver 1984b, pp. 159, 321–28; Silver 1984a, pp. 122–25; Bauman 1983, pp. 170–89; Scott 1969, pp. 369–462.
4. Scott 1969, p. 397.
5. Scott 1969, pp. 386–98; Abbott 1984 and 1981a, pp. 104–11; Schiesl 1980, p. 129; Funigiello 1978; Daniel 1990, pp. 899–911; McKelvey 1968, pp. 118–24.
6. Scott 1969, p. 398; Funigiello 1978, pp. 124–26; Schiesl 1980, p. 128.
7. Abbott 1981a, chap. 5, esp. 145; Silver 1984b, pp. 159, 326.
8. Scott 1969, pp. 407–11, 415, 429; Funigiello 1978, pp. 217–58; Graham 1976, p. 69; Eisner, Gallion, and Eisner 1993, pp. 177–79. While accepting the idea that Washington overtly did little to advance planning in the 1940s, Schiesl argues that city administrators stepped up planning in part because they foresaw that federal urban redevelopment programs would eventually be enacted. Schiesl 1980, pp. 126–43.

9. Though federal involvement in urban planning in the 1940s has been almost unanimously downplayed by historians and planning scholars, political scientists who specialize in the field of "intergovernment relations" identify the 1940s as the start of the modern "grants economy," characterized by "the use of intergovernmental grants-in-aid by one government (especially the federal government) to stimulate, support or otherwise influence the policy decisions of another government." Wright 1990, p. 62; 1988, pp. 71–77.

10. Federal Works Agency 1941, p. 53. On the 1940 act, see pp. 29–54; also Funigiello 1978, p. 45.

11. Federal Works Agency 1946, p. 149; 1948, p. 34.

12. Federal Works Agency 1946, pp. 2, 154–57.

13. Ibid., p. 1.

14. The planning loans came under Title V of the Reconversion Act. Federal Works Agency 1947, p. 4.

15. Ibid.

16. National Housing Agency 1945, p. 6.

17. National Housing Agency 1944, p. 43; Funigiello 1978, p. 110.

18. National Housing Agency 1945, p. 13.

19. National Housing Agency 1946, p. 69.

20. Federal Works Agency 1945, p. 2. On the history of federal highway funding, see Federal Works Agency 1940, pp. 93–130; and Foster 1981. On the 1956 Highway Act, see Gelfand 1975, p. 183.

21. Federal Works Agency 1945, p. 2.

22. Federal Works Agency 1944, pp. 24–25.

23. Federal Works Agency 1948, p. 19.

24. Highway plans were drawn up for Atlanta; Baltimore; Baton Rouge; Bay Area, California; Boston; Charlotte; Charleston, South Carolina; Chattanooga; Cincinnati; Clinton, Iowa; Columbus, Georgia; Denver; Fort Wayne, Indiana; Greenville, South Carolina; Harrisburg, Pennsylvania; Indianapolis; Jacksonville, Florida; Johnson City, Tennessee; Kalamazoo; Kansas City, Missouri; Lincoln, Nebraska; Little Rock; Macon, Georgia; Mason City, Iowa; Memphis; Milwaukee; Muskegon, Michigan; Nashville; Newark; New Orleans; Oklahoma City; Omaha; Ottumwa, Iowa; Port Huron; Portland, Oregon; Providence, Rhode Island; Richmond, Virginia; St. Joseph, Missouri; St. Louis; Salt Lake City; Savannah; Seattle; Shreveport; South Bend, Indiana; Spokane; Spartanburg, South Carolina; Springfield, Missouri; Tampa; Tulsa; Waycross, Georgia. Federal Works Agency 1946, p. 66.

25. Caves 1962, pp. 193–204; Barrett 1987, pp. 112–37; Martin 1970, pp. 83–108; Keyes 1951, pp. 72–104; Morgan 1981, pp. 13–24.
26. *Charlotte Observer,* 29 Apr. 1944.
27. Weiss 1987; Scott 1969, pp. 455–58; Checkoway 1980, pp. 21–45; K. Jackson 1980, pp. 419–52, and 1985, chap. 11; Fish 1979, pp. 188–94, 200–207; Wright 1981, pp. 240–43.
28. Quoted in K. Jackson 1980, p. 435.
29. Federal Housing Administration 1938, p. 8. For background on the concept of municipal subdivision regulations, see Burnham 1991.
30. Federal Housing Administration 1938, p. 3; Weiss 1987, p. 150.
31. Wheaton 1953, p. 338; Weiss 1987, p. 154.
32. Wheaton 1953, p. 376; Jackson 1985, pp. 204–5; Wright 1981, pp. 242–43.
33. A small farm community from its founding in the 1750s until the rail era of the 1850s, Charlotte grew rapidly after the Civil War and surpassed the old colonial port of Charleston to become the Carolinas' population leader in 1930. Hanchett 1985a, pp. 68–76.
34. Hanchett 1993, chaps. 6 and 7; Kratt and Hanchett 1986; Hanchett 1985b.
35. John Nolen Papers, Folders 4 and 5, box 98. See especially Nolen to Black, 29 Sept. 1917. The sole extant copy of the 1917 "Civic Survey for Charlotte" is in the Nolen Papers. Charlotte's reluctance seems to have been part of a regional pattern. Brownell notes that Southerners were less enthusiastic about urban plans than were non-Southerners during the profession's boom years of the 1910s and 1920s. Brownell 1975a, pp. 343–44. On planning in the South, see also Silver 1987, pp. 371–83; Chapin 1954, pp. 268–82; Brownell 1975b, pp. 172–89.
36. *Charlotte News,* 5 Sept. 1930; Social Science Research Council 1939, p. 7. No copies of Swan's plan have been located.
37. *Charlotte News,* 7–12, 14 Feb., 11 Mar., 10 June, 22 Aug. 1937; Charlotte Housing Authority 1944; Harold Dillehay to Charles R. Brockmann, 4 Mar. 1959, letter in the Charlotte Housing Authority file. On the importance of women's clubs in the New Deal public housing effort, see Birch 1983, pp. 149–75.
38. The study counted some 4,500 dwellings that urgently needed plumbing, heat, or other major basic improvements. Charlotte City Council Minutes, 23 Sept. and 30 Nov. 1938; *Charlotte Observer,* 15 Feb. 1945. By comparison, the city's total housing stock was 25,402 units in 1940. *Charlotte News,* 9 Feb. 1945.

39. Charlotte City Council Minutes, 7 May 1941; Blythe and Brockmann 1961, p. 450; *Charlotte Observer,* 7 May 1944; 14 Mar. 1945.

40. A Committee on Congested Production Areas, established by FDR in 1943, aided those cities that were particularly hard-pressed, a total of eighteen across the United States. Charlotte was not among them. Daniel 1990, pp. 899–911.

41. Blythe and Brockmann 1961, pp. 412–14; *Charlotte Observer,* 19 Aug. 1945.

42. *Charlotte News,* 26 Oct. 1967. See also *Charlotte Observer,* 27 Oct. 1967.

43. *Charlotte Observer,* 7 May 1944; Herbert H. Baxter Papers.

44. *Charlotte Observer,* 21 Apr., 1 June 1944. Earlier the city won allocation of rationed materials to rebuild Villa Heights School, which had burned early in the war. *Charlotte Observer,* 7 May 1944.

45. *Charlotte Observer,* 20 June 1947. For a sketchy history of early public works in Charlotte, consult Pace and Green 1949.

46. On the library study see *Charlotte Observer,* 4 Mar., 18 Apr., 5 Aug. 1944. On the recreation study see *Charlotte Observer,* 7 May, 25 June, 5 Aug., 15 Nov. 1944; Funigiello 1978, pp. 151–57.

47. *Charlotte Observer,* 27 July 1944; 17 Mar., 5 Aug. 1945.

48. *Charlotte Observer,* 7, 26, 27, 29 Apr., 2 May 1944; 23 Aug. 1945. An example of a brief is Lassister 1946.

49. *Charlotte News,* 6 Feb. 1945; *Charlotte Observer,* 6 Feb. 1945.

50. *Charlotte Observer,* 26 Feb. 1946.

51. Roberts 1944a.

52. *Charlotte Observer,* 20 Dec. 1944.

53. Roberts 1944a, p. 29.

54. Abbott 1981a, p. 114; Brownell 1975b, pp. 172–89.

55. Charlotte City Council Minutes, 20 Dec. 1944; *Charlotte Observer,* 20, 21 Dec. 1944.

56. *Charlotte Observer,* 4 Feb. 1945. See also *Charlotte News,* 5 Feb. 1945.

57. *Charlotte Observer,* 4 Feb. 1945.

58. *Charlotte Observer,* 11 Jan. 1945; 1 Feb. 1946.

59. "City Council Adopts Realtors' Definition of Standard House," headlined the *Charlotte News,* 1 Mar. 1945; Charlotte City Council Minutes, 11 Dec. 1945. In 1948, after all FHA requirements had been met, the planning commission finally got around to extending the "standard house" ordinance to existing dwellings, and the city hired its first building inspector. The National Association of Real Estate Boards spotlighted Charlotte's code-enforcement initiative in a booklet that

urged cities to consider alternatives to public housing. National Association of Real Estate Boards 1952; Nash 1959, pp. 86–96, 106.
60. Charlotte City Council Minutes, 29 Jan. 1946.
61. Charlotte City Council Minutes, 14 Jan. 1947; *Charlotte Observer,* 5 Feb. 1947.
62. Pease 1949.
63. Schellie 1945.
64. Blucher 1942.
65. Kent 1948.
66. Bettman et al. 1944.
67. Ibid.
68. Ibid.
69. Black 1948.
70. Walker 1941, p. 348.
71. Kent 1948.
72. Blucher 1949, pp. 261–62.
73. *ASPO Newsletter* 15 (10): 85.
74. Walker 1941, p. 186; Blucher 1942, 1949.
75. Computed from data in Blucher 1942 and 1949.
76. Funigiello 1978, pp. 215–16, 241, 249–50; Scott 1969, pp. 403–4.
77. Abbott 1981a, pp. 114–15.
78. *Charlotte News,* 9 Feb. 1945.
79. See chapter 14 of this volume.

Chapter Thirteen

1. Nef 1952.
2. McNeill 1982; Merrill 1948, p. 2.
3. Nash 1977, pp. 1–7, and 1990, 1985a; Johnson 1990, p. 44; Verge 1988, pp. 209–19; Wollenberg 1985, p. 239, and 1990, pp. 1–5; Bean and Rawls 1983, p. 364.
4. Nash 1985b, pp. 99–112; Schiesl 1980, pp. 127–41; M. Johnson 1991, pp. 283–308.
5. U.S. Bureau of the Census 1947, pp. 71–83.
6. U.S. Bureau of the Census 1952, pp. 5-9 through 5-11; California State Planning Board [L. Deming Tilton] 1942, pp. 1–8.
7. Schiesl 1980, p. 134.
8. California State Reconstruction and Reemployment Commission 1945a, p. 7.

9. California Housing and Planning Association 1942, p. 4.
10. California State Reconstruction and Reemployment Commission 1945c, pp. 1–5.
11. Scott 1959, p. 249; California State Planning Board 1941, p. 35.
12. Los Angeles County Regional Planning Commission 1945a, p. 6.
13. Jamison 1948, pp. 50–54.
14. Long Beach City Planning Commission 1946, pp. 3–5, 8.
15. Long 1991.
16. Schiesl 1980, p. 130.
17. Vallejo 1945, p. I-3.
18. Los Angeles County Regional Planning Commission 1945c, p. 7.
19. Vallejo 1945, p. I-3.
20. Hanchett chapter in this volume.
21. Scott 1959, p. 253; Wollenberg 1990, pp. 86–97.
22. "Shopping Center: Linda Vista, California. . ." 1944, pp. 81–93; "Valencia Gardens" 1944, pp. 26–35; "Cabrillo Homes Community Building" 1944, pp. 36–43.
23. Nolen 1912, pp. 33–53.
24. John Hancock has correctly observed that the navy plans did not invariably fit into the city's plans. Fortunately, on this occasion they seem to have meshed. For Nolen's work in San Diego, see Hancock 1991a,b.
25. California State Reconstruction and Reemployment Commission 1945b, pp. 1–5.
26. Vallejo 1945, pt. 7, p. 1; Tilton 1943c, p. 15; Tilton 1943a, p. 40; Tilton 1943b, p. 40; Los Angeles County Regional Planning Commission, 1945a, pp. 9–10.
27. California State Chamber of Commerce 1944, pp. 1–4.
28. I have argued elsewhere that cities have at least partly transformed military assets into civilian ones—warfare into welfare. See Lotchin 1992. The Presidio is a case in point. Even before being recycled into civilian hands, the Presidio served urban as well as military needs. City streets ran through it, people jogged in it, those adjacent to it enjoyed the "lungs of the city," grande dames walked their dogs in it, the Julius Kahn Playground actually sits on a part of it, and the greenery broke up the urban mass for everyone in Pacific Heights.
29. Kinnaird 1966, pt. 2, pp. 613–27.
30. Freeman 1991, pp. 22–28.
31. *San Francisco Chronicle,* 27 May 1991, p. A-11.

32. Scott 1969, pp. 397–406.
33. Abbott 1981a, pp. 113–19, and 1981b, pp. 12–24; Bauman 1983; Biles 1985, pp. 267–84; Fairbanks 1990; Funigiello 1978; Hirsch 1983, pp. 101–34; Nash 1985b, pp. 99–112; Silver 1983, pp. 33–60.
34. U.S. Congress 1943, pp. 70–71, 85–88.
35. City and County of San Francisco, Citizens' Post War Planning Committee 1945, pp. 32, 23.
36. *The Downtowner,* 13 June 1945, pp. 1–2. John Mollenkopf's contention that a "growth coalition" was formed in San Francisco only after the Second World War underestimates the longevity of this alliance. Mollenkopf 1983, pp. 139–79. Urban rivalry had always been important there and a growth coalition existed at least as early as 1896 and continued thereafter. See Lotchin 1979a, pp. 357–81; McDonald 1986; Issel and Cherny 1986.
37. Oakland Postwar Planning Committee 1945, p. 55.
38. San Diego Chamber of Commerce, Temporary Postwar Plans Committee 1942, pp. 1–16. See also statement of Albert G. Reader, Chairman, Post-War Planning Committee, San Diego Chamber of Commerce, in San Diego Committee for Economic Development 1944, pp. 17–24.
39. California State Reconstruction and Reemployment Commission 1944, p. 6.
40. California State Reconstruction and Reemployment Commission 1945b, p. 25.
41. Vallejo 1945, p. I-3.
42. Ibid., p. II-1.
43. Ibid., p. I-2.
44. Ibid.
45. The Oakland Plan was especially diversified. See Oakland Postwar Planning Committee 1945, pp. 1–69.
46. Los Angeles County Regional Planning Commission 1945a, pp. 1–10.
47. Abbott 1981b, pp. 12–24.
48. California State Reconstruction and Reemployment Commission 1945b, p. 27.
49. San Francisco, City and County of San Francisco Post War Planning Committee, Subcommittee on Revenue and Taxation 1945, p. 7.
50. San Francisco Post War Planning Committee 1945, pp. 8–10.
51. Scott 1959, p. 267; Jamison 1948, pp. 1–54.

52. San Francisco Citizens Postwar Planning Committee, Subcommittee on Revenue and Taxation 1945, p. 305.
53. Johnson forthcoming.
54. For Catherine Bauer, see below.
55. The California Housing and Planning Association publications conferences cited above indicate the kind of thought popular during the war.
56. For a different view, see Nash 1985b.
57. California Housing and Planning Association 1943, p. 1.
58. Bauer 1944b, pp. 66–70.
59. Bauer 1944a, p. 78.
60. "Doherty Assails 'Planners' Using War to Destroy Free Enterprise" 1943, pp. 1, 4; "Postwar Planning Versus Mobility" 1943, pp. 1–3; Schiesl 1980, pp. 127–41.
61. California Housing and Planning Association 1943, p. 2.
62. Long Beach City Planning Commission 1946, pp. 3–5; Los Angeles City Planning Commission 1946, p. 5.
63. Oakland Postwar Planning Committee 1945, pp. 45, 50.
64. San Francisco Planning and Housing Association 1943, pp. 1–2.
65. Ibid.
66. Scott 1959, p. 258.
67. Tilton 1943c, p. 15.
68. Bauer 1944a, pp. 74–75.
69. California Housing and Planning Association 1942, p. 1.
70. Jacobs 1980.
71. For eastern planning thought, see Bettman 1944, pp. 3–8, and 1945, pp. 5–11; Howard 1944, pp. 18–23; Weinberg 1944, pp. 23–28; McHugh 1946, pp. 17–29; Adams 1945, pp. 11–15; Ludlow 1945, pp. 5–10; Kincaid 1945, pp. 23–28. Other journals stressed many other matters, however. See especially the *American City*, 1942–45, which considered everything from playground swings to preservation to housing to sewers to recreation as postwar planning. That journal ran a very useful scorecard of postwar planning in its wartime issues. Yet it seemed to define postwar planning as every administrative task that administrators were thinking ahead about!
72. Gerald Nash has argued that the West became the pacesetter for the nation during the twentieth century. See Nash 1977, 1985a, 1985b, 1990.

Chapter Fourteen

1. U.S. Department of Housing and Urban Development 1977, p. 10.
2. Berry, Portney, and Thomson 1993, pp. 301–3.
3. Goldfield 1987, pp. 104–5.
4. See Branch 1988 for a more complete discussion.
5. With adoption of the Community Development Block Grant Program in 1974, the Workable Program was discontinued.
6. Gelfand 1975, pp. 214, 425.
7. Rohe and Gates 1985, p. 34.
8. Connerly and Wilson 1992, p. 13. Birmingham was the last city to have racial zoning.
9. *Birmingham News*, 23 July 1953.
10. Corley 1982, p. 176.
11. *Birmingham Post-Herald*, 8 June 1954.
12. Corley 1982, pp. 174–79.
13. Jefferson County Board of Health 1950, p. 8; Birmingfind n.d., p. 5.
14. *Birmingham Age-Herald*, 25 Dec. 1949.
15. Housing and Home Finance Agency, 25 Nov. 1953, in James W. Morgan Papers, File 25.21.
16. Housing Authority of the Birmingham District, 28 July 1953, in Morgan Papers, File 25.19.
17. *Birmingham Post-Herald*, 31 Mar. 1953.
18. *Birmingham News*, 31 Mar. 1953.
19. Birmingham 1956.
20. Thompson, Lewis, and McEntire 1960, p. 55.
21. Corley 1979, pp. 70–72.
22. *Birmingham News*, 16 May 1953.
23. *Birmingham News*, 16 May 1953.
24. *Birmingham World*, 5 June 1953.
25. *Birmingham World*, 9 Oct. 1953.
26. James W. Follin to Col. Harold Harper, HABD, 25 Nov. 1953, in Morgan Papers, File 25.21; *Birmingham News*, 25 Nov. 1953.
27. Complaint Filed in Clerk's Office, Northern District of Alabama, 7 June 1954; U.S. District Court for the Northern District of Alabama, Southern Division, *Rosa Watts, et al.,* v. *Housing Authority of the Birmingham District*, 28 Jan. 1955.
28. *Birmingham World*, 5 May 1955. One of the homeowners was quoted as "tearfully pleading 'I am in dire need of the money. I am not young

anymore. I must have my money in the morning. I am facing an embarrassing situation.'" *Birmingham World,* 10 May 1955.

29. Housing Authority of the Birmingham District 1962.

30. James W. Morgan to A. R. Hanson, HHFA, Morgan Papers, File 25.9.

31. Sections 220 and 221 were also enacted in the Housing Act of 1954. Section 220 insured mortgages for rental housing located in urban renewal areas and Section 221 insured mortgages for families displaced by urban renewal and other low- and moderate-income households.

32. U.S. Housing and Home Finance Agency 1954, pp. 1–4.

33. Birmingham 1956, pp. 2–3; Birmingham Planning Commission 1961a, 1961b, 1962; City of Birmingham, Annual Review of Progress for Recertification of the City's Workable Program for Community Improvement, Birmingham, Alabama, 31 Mar. 1964, in Albert Boutwell Papers, File 25.16.

34. U.S. Housing and Home Finance Agency 1962, pp. 38–39.

35. Walter E. Keyes, HHFA, to Honorable Arthur Hanes, 6 Nov. 1961, in Planning and Zoning Papers, uncataloged, Birmingham Public Library, Birmingham, Ala.

36. John Steinichen III to Urban Renewal Committee, 14 Nov. 1961, James T. Waggoner Papers, File 6.7.

37. John Steinichen III to Walter E. Keyes, HHFA, 15 Nov. 1961, Waggoner Papers, File 6.7.

38. City of Birmingham, A Review of Progress Under the Program for Community Improvement, 9 Jan. 1962, in Planning and Zoning Papers.

39. Walter E. Keyes, HHFA, to Honorable Arthur J. Hanes, 21 Feb. 1962, Arthur J. Hanes Papers, File 3.38.

40. J. T. Waggoner to Honorable John Sparkman, 6 Mar. 1962, Waggoner papers, File 6.10; Hanes to Walter E. Keyes, HHFA, 14 Mar. 1962, Hanes Papers, File 3.38.

41. McClellan Ratchford, HHFA, to Honorable Arthur J. Hanes, 9 May 1963, Hanes Papers, File 3.39.

42. A more detailed account of Birmingham's change in government and its relation to the Civil Rights movement can be obtained from LaMonte 1976; Vann 1978; and Branch 1988.

43. City of Birmingham Annual Review of Progress for Recertification of the City's Workable Program for Community Improvement, 31 Mar. 1964, pp. 1–6, in Boutwell Papers, File 25.16.

44. Albert Boutwell to Edward Baxter, HHFA, 15 Jan. 1965, Boutwell Papers, File 25.19.

45. LaMonte 1976, p. 326; City of Birmingham Annual Review of Progress for Recertification of the City's Workable Program for Community Improvement, 31 Mar. 1964, p. 23b, in Boutwell Papers, File 25.16.
46. City of Birmingham Resolution on Citizens Advisory Committee on Relocation Housing, 22 Dec. 1964, in Boutwell Papers, File 25.18.
47. LaMonte 1976, pp. 326–29.
48. City of Birmingham Annual Review of Progress for Recertification of the City's Workable Program for Community Improvement, 1 Feb. 1966, pp. 6–7, in Boutwell Papers, File 25.21.
49. LaMonte 1976, pp. 330–33; City of Birmingham Annual Review of Progress for Recertification of the City's Workable Program for Community Improvement, 1 Feb. 1966, in Boutwell Papers, File 25.21.
50. Rohe and Gates 1985, pp. 32–50.
51. LaMonte 1976, pp. 351–56.
52. LaMonte 1976, pp. 357–59.
53. LaMonte 1976, pp. 362–64.
54. LaMonte 1976, pp. 359, 364, 376–82.
55. LaMonte 1976, pp. 367–75.
56. LaMonte 1976, pp. 376–78, 397.
57. LaMonte 1976, pp. 376–82, 395–97.
58. George Seibels to Earl H. Metzer, Jr., HUD, 4 Mar. 1968, George Seibels Papers, File 32.6.
59. Rabin 1968.
60. Frieden and Kaplan 1975, pp. 69–72.
61. Judson P. Hodges, City of Birmingham, to John Page, HUD, 5 Apr. 1968, Seibels Papers, File 32.7.
62. Marie Jemison to George Seibels, 22 Mar. 1968, Seibels Papers, File 32.6.
63. *Birmingham News*, 6 Apr. 1968.
64. Harvey Burg to Robert Weaver, HUD, 14 June 1968, Seibels Papers, File 32.8; Rabin 1968.
65. Position Paper of Citizen's Group, Birmingham Model Cities Plan, 20 May 1968, Seibels Papers, File 32.7.
66. J. M. Breckenridge, City Attorney, to Alan T. Drennen, Jr., City Council Member, 24 May 1968, Birmingham City Council Papers, File 13.16; Clarification of the City of Birmingham's Application for Model Cities Planning Grant, 29 May 1968, Seibels Papers, File 32.7; Citizen's Proposal to Consolidate Its Position with the City's "Clarification" Proposal of 29 May 1968, 31 May 1968, Seibels Papers, File 32.8.
67. Harvey Burg to Robert Weaver, HUD, 14 June 1968, Seibels Papers, File 32.8.

68. Edward Baxter, HUD, to George Seibels, 22 Nov. 1968, Seibels Papers, File 32.8.
69. The CAC should not be confused with the short-lived committee of the same name founded in 1963 during the Boutwell administration.
70. Franklin 1989, p. 61.
71. Franklin 1989, p. 61.
72. *Birmingham News,* 30 May 1968.
73. Harvey Burg to Robert Weaver, HUD, 14 June 1968, Seibels Papers, File 32.8.
74. *Birmingham World,* 23 Mar., 6 Apr. 1968.
75. LaMonte 1976, p. 403.
76. The Nixon administration had reorganized HUD so that each state would be served by an Area Office. These Area Offices report to HUD Regional Offices, such as the Southeast Regional Office in Atlanta.
77. *Birmingham News,* 8 Nov. 1972; LaMonte 1976, p. 403; Jon Will Pitts to George Seibels, 6 July 1973, Seibels Papers, File 49.34.
78. The city's Community Development Department was created in 1972. *Birmingham News,* 1 May 1972; Birmingham Department of Community Development 1988.
79. LaMonte 1976, p. 404.
80. City of Birmingham *Proposed Citizen Participation Plan,* Nov. 1973, Seibels Papers, File 18.53.
81. Branch 1988, pp. 768, 772.
82. *Birmingham News,* 30 June 1974.
83. *Birmingham News,* 5 Feb. 1974.
84. *Birmingham News,* 10 Mar. 1974.
85. Author's interview with Charles Lewis, former citizen participation planner, Birmingham Department of Community Development, 23 Mar. 1992; author's telephone interview with Rev. George Quiggle, former director, Greater Birmingham Ministries, 7 June 1993; author's interview with Benjamin Greene, president, Harriman Park Neighborhood Association, Birmingham, Alabama, 24 Mar. 1992.
86. *Birmingham News,* 12 Mar. 1974.
87. *Birmingham News,* 10, 12 Mar., and 2, 24 Apr. 1974.
88. *Birmingham News,* 24 Apr. 1974.
89. *Birmingham News,* 26 May 1974.
90. Birmingham 1974; Seibels Papers, File 18.53; Birmingham 1988.
91. *Birmingham News,* 2 Oct. 1974.
92. Sanders 1977, pp. 321–63.

93. Levine 1970, p. 65; Frieden and Kaplan 1975, p. 83.
94. LaMonte 1976, pp. 359, 364.
95. LaMonte 1976, pp. 367–75.
96. LaMonte 1976, pp. 376–82.
97. *Birmingham News*, 3, 10, 13 Sept., and 1, 8 Oct. 1974.
98. Author's interview with Charles Lewis, former citizen participation planner, Birmingham Department of Community Development, Birmingham, Alabama, 23 Mar. 1992; telephone interview with Rev. George Quiggle, former director, Greater Birmingham Ministries, 7 June 1993; author's interview with Benjamin Greene, president, Harriman Park Neighborhood Association, Birmingham, Alabama, 24 Mar. 1992.

Chapter Fifteen

1. Thurber 1985; Smith and Williams 1986; Stipe and Lee 1987.
2. Tunnard and Pushkarev 1963; Nairn 1965; Bacon 1967; Reps 1980; Fitch 1982; Kostof 1987.
3. Mollenkopf 1983; Gillette and Miller 1987.
4. Rouzie 1954; Feiss 1956; Codman 1956.
5. Adler 1969, p. 14.
6. Adler 1967, p. 331.
7. *Savannah Evening Press* [*SEP*], 25 June 1955, p. 16.
8. *SEP*, 23 June 1955, p. 28.
9. *Savannah Morning News* [*SMN*], 18 June 1955, p. 16.
10. *SMN*, 11 Mar. 1956, op. ed., p. 6.
11. *SMN*, 16 Nov. 1955, p. 18.
12. *SEP*, 23 Mar. 1955, p. 24.
13. *SMN*, 15 May 1956, p. 22.
14. *Savannah's Golden Heritage* 1958; Nichols 1957.
15. *SMN*, 7 Jan. 1958, p. 6.
16. *SMN*, 18 Jan. 1960, p. 5B.
17. *SMN*, 6 July 1960, p. 6B; 12 Feb. 1961, p. 1B.
18. *SMN*, 20 Jan. 1962, p. 8B.
19. Rogers 1969.
20. *SMN*, 8 Feb. 1968, p. 6D.
21. Carroll 1963.
22. *Atlanta Journal & Constitution Magazine*, 4 June 1961, p. 14.
23. *SMN*, 26 Apr. 1962, p. 10D; 16 Aug. 1962, p. 5C; 10 Apr. 1965, p. 10B.

24. *SMN*, 11 Nov. 1965, p. 5D.

25. Ziegler et al. 1975.

26. O. Johnson 1990.

27. *SMN*, 19 Apr. 1962, p. 10D.

28. *SMN*, 27 Sept. 1965, p. 8B.

29. *SMN*, 30 Mar. 1972, p. 9B.

30. *New York Times*, 9 Dec. 1971, p. 47.

31. *Christian Science Monitor*, 1 Dec. 1971, p. 20.

32. *SMN*, 13 Oct. 1967, p. 10B; 6 Oct. 1969, p. 10B; 4 Feb. 1970, p. 1D.

33. *SMN*, 10 June 1972, p. 14B.

34. *SMN*, 12 Jan. 1973, p. 1D; 16 Feb. 1973, p. 1A.

35. Fitch 1982, pp. 65–66.

36. Stavrolakis and Lattimore 1974.

37. Warner 1989, p. 21.

38. Reiter et al. 1983.

39. Black et al. 1977; Zeitz 1979.

40. *Atlanta Journal & Constitution*, 24 July 1978, p. 1B.

41. *SMN*, 10 June 1979, p. 1C.

42. Chabli and Hussey 1975.

43. Matlack 1979, p. 16.

44. *Washington Post*, 22 Mar. 1979, p. A27.

45. Adler 1990.

46. *Atlanta Journal & Constitution*, 4 Sept. 1977, p. 20B.

47. *Atlanta Journal & Constitution*, 9 Dec. 1978, p. 7A.

48. Apgar and Daniels 1983.

49. Foner 1970.

50. *SMN-SEP*, 14 Jan. 1973, p. 1C; *SMN*, 30 Apr. 1973, p. 1B.

51. *SMN-SEP*, 2 Dec. 1971, p. 1D.

52. *SMN*, 26 Jan. 1972, p. 8D, and 3 Feb. 1975, p. 1B; *SMN-SEP*, 14 Jan. 1973, p. 1C.

53. *SMN*, 16 Feb. 1975, p. 1B.

54. *SMN*, 24 Feb. 1979, p. 1B.

55. *SMN*, 15 June 1981, p. 1B.

56. *SMN*, 24 Feb. 1979, p. 1B.

57. *SMN*, 7 Mar. 1980, p. 1B.

58. *SMN*, 1 Feb. 1983, p. 1B.

59. *Georgia Gazette*, 1 Dec. 1983, p. 6.

60. *SMN*, 5 Dec. 1983, p. 1C.

61. *SMN*, 6 Dec. 1983, p. 1B.

Chapter Sixteen

1. Minutes, Detroit City Plan Commission (DCPC), 8 May 1952; Blessing information in *Detroit News*, 6 June 1956, p. 76; author's interview with Charles Blessing, 18 July 1986.
2. Author's interview with Blessing, 18 July 1986. This and 9 Sept. 1986 interview used for several subsequent facts. Blessing 1959, p. ii; Krueckeburg 1985.
3. James Rouse, letter to Blessing, 1 Mar. 1961, DCPC Collection, Box 2, "Blessing Correspondence 1952–1961" Folder; Blessing, letter to Norman Williams, 14 Aug. 1962, ibid., "August to October 1962" Folder; Blessing, letter to Kevin Lynch, 14 Feb. 1964, ibid., "Nov. 1963–Feb. 1964" Folder; and Robert Weaver, letter to Blessing, 9 July 1964, ibid., Box 6, "May–December, 1964" Folder; invitations in DCPC Collection, Box 2.
4. Blessing 1959, p. ii; minutes, DCPC, 17 Mar. 1963.
5. Blessing 1964, pp. 39–44. Greek trip described in Blessing, letter to Morris Ketchum, 27 Sept. 1963, DCPC Collection, Box 2, "August 1963–October 1963" Folder.
6. DCPC 1965, p. 5. Originally submitted in May 1964 for the AIP Honors Award in Comprehensive Planning.
7. *Detroit News*, 6 June 1956, p. 76.
8. *Detroit News*, 7 June 1956, p. 72 (quote); and 8 June 1956, p. 1; AIP statement in Blessing 1959, p. ii.
9. Harry Golden, "Detroit's Charles Blessing," *Detroit Free Press Magazine*, 14 Aug. 1966, p. 20 (quotes); Blessing, letter to Jack Kent, 29 Jan. 1961, DCPC Collection, Box 2, "Blessing Correspondence," "September 1952 to April 1961" Folder.
10. Blessing, comments at the 1962 National Association of Housing and Redevelopment Officials Conference, DCPC Collection, Box 6, "July–December 1966" Folder.
11. Charles Blessing, letter to Joe Waterson, 6 June 1963, DCPC Collection, Box 2, "Blessing Correspondence June–July 1963" Folder; Charles Blessing, letter of recommendation to Harvard Graduate School of Design, 27 Jan. 1965, DCPC Collection, Box 6, "January–April 1965" Folder.
12. Montgomery 1965, p. 11.
13. *Detroit News*, 6 June 1956, p. 76; 1966 quote in Golden, "Detroit's Charles Blessing," p. 20.
14. Cohen 1990; Bacon 1960.

15. Connolly 1961.
16. Anonymous interviews, 26 Aug. 1986 and 1 Mar. 1988; Cohen 1990; Bacon 1967.
17. Herrera 1964, p. 181; "Boston" 1964; "Planning and Development in Philadelphia" 1960; "Under the Knife" 1964, pp. 69–75; Weaver 1966, p. 6.
18. Blessing 1966; quotation from anonymous interview, 9 Mar. 1987.
19. Material on Civic Center in DCPC Collection, Box 3, "Civic Center Plaza 1955–65" Folder.
20. Charles McCafferty, memo to Charles Blessing, 1 Sept. 1965, DCPC Collection, Box 3, "Civic Center Plaza 1955–65" Folder.
21. Cavanagh account to Blessing, author's interview, 18 July 1996; minutes, DCPC, 21 Apr. 1965.
22. Detroit 1951; DCPC 1962, p. 42.
23. City of Detroit, *Detroit Cultural Center*, n.d. (c. 1965). See original text and letters in DCPC Collection, Box 4, "Cultural Center" Folder.
24. Charles Blessing, letter to William Slayton, 24 Nov. 1965, DCPC Collection, Box 4, "Cultural Center" Folder; *Detroit Free Press*, 22 Apr. 1965, p. 1-A.
25. *Detroit Free Press*, 30 Sept. 1966, p. 1-A; 10 Mar. 1971, p. A-6 (uprooting).
26. City of Detroit press release, 13 Apr. 1967, Hilanius Phillips personal files; minutes, DCPC, 7 Dec. 1967.
27. Author's interview with Hilanius Phillips, 18 Feb. 1987.

Chapter Seventeen

1. Stone 1976; Hirsch 1983; Hartman 1984; Silver 1984b; Suttles 1990; Krumholz and Keating 1991.
2. Teaford 1990.
3. Frieden and Sagalyn 1989.
4. Hurd 1924; Schmid 1941; Rannells 1956.
5. Murphy and Vance 1954; Murphy, Vance, and Epstein 1955; Hartman 1950.
6. Breese 1949; Foley 1952.
7. Weiss 1957, pp. 27–36.
8. Jonassen 1955; Carroll 1953; Burton 1954, pp. 208, 257–60.
9. Abbott 1981a, pp. 113–22; Nash 1985b; Teaford 1990, pp. 36–42.
10. Thomas 1990; Hoover 1990.

11. Gillette 1985; Fairbanks 1987; Fairbanks and Miller 1984; Silver 1984b.
12. Silver 1984b, p. 84; Gillette 1985; Justement 1946, pp. 95–144.
13. Gruen 1964, pp. 47, 218–29, 225, 305.
14. McKeever 1955, p. 4; Rouse 1957, pp. 1, 3–5.
15. Boyce and Clark 1963; Sternlieb 1963; Russwurm 1964.
16. Cleveland City Planning Commission 1959; Merkel 1990; Fairbanks 1987; Altshuler 1965.
17. Horwood and Boyce 1959; Browning 1961; Smith 1961. Jurkat's work described in Rannells 1961, p. 23.
18. Oakland 1966; Browning 1961; Weiss and Thabit 1961.
19. Jacobs 1961; Gans 1962; Lynch 1960.
20. Gruen 1964, pp. 321–25.
21. Abrams 1961, p. 6; Jacobs 1961, p. 168.
22. Getis and Getis 1960; Berry 1967; Conway et al. 1976; Lewis 1976.
23. Grey et al. 1978.
24. Bowden 1971, 1975; Ward 1966.
25. Central Association of Seattle 1963, 1970.
26. Daly-Bednarek 1992.
27. Abbott 1983, 1991.
28. Dallas Department of Planning and Development 1982; Central Atlanta Progress 1988; Dayton Department of Planning 1976; District of Columbia 1981, 1982; Richmond City Planning Commission 1984; JA/WRT Associates 1984; Denver Partnership, Inc., and Denver Planning Office 1986; Seattle 1985.
29. Zukin 1982; Boyer 1992.
30. Hendon and Shaw 1987; Whitt 1987; Snedcof 1985.
31. Whyte 1980, 1988.
32. Venturi, Brown, and Izenour 1972.
33. Jameson 1984; Jencks 1987; Harvey 1989.
34. Raban 1974; Harvey 1989, pp. 3–6.
35. Harvey 1989, p. 91.
36. Wrenn 1983; McNulty 1985.
37. Falk 1986; Hall 1988; Fondersmith 1988; Attoe and Logan 1989.
38. Brooks and Young 1991; O'Connell 1991; Milwaukee Department of City Development 1985; Richmond City Planning Commission 1984, pp. 131, 135.
39. San Francisco Department of City Planning 1985; Krumholz and Keating 1991; Jencks 1987, pp. 247–49.
40. Frieden and Sagalyn 1989, p. 265.

41. Levitt 1987, p. 67; Campbell 1990, p. 131.
42. J. Jackson 1980b, pp. 32–33.
43. Cohen 1979; Friedmann and Wolff 1982; Sassen 1991.
44. Schwartz 1984; Pred 1977; Black 1980; Friedrichs and Goodman 1987.
45. Peterson 1981; Squires 1989; Lassar 1990; Frieden 1990.
46. Bennett 1986; Suttles 1990.
47. Philadelphia City Planning Commission 1988; Cohen 1990; Mandelbaum 1990; Krumholz and Keating 1991, pp. 146–47.

Chapter Eighteen

1. K. Johnson 1991.
2. Mayor Mory Moran interview, broadcast on National Public Radio, 23 Aug. 1991.
3. Phillips 1990.
4. Reich 1991.
5. I. Peterson 1991.
6. Langdon 1988; Boles 1989; Kelbaugh 1989.
7. National Conference on City Planning 1909, p. 77.
8. Ibid., p. 105.
9. Chambers 1967, p. 10.
10. U.S. Housing Corporation 1920, p. 22.
11. Ibid., p. 1.
12. Ibid., p. 7.
13. Ibid., p. 44.
14. May 1918, p. 210.
15. Christensen 1986, p. 72.
16. Arnold 1971; Stein 1978; Christensen 1986.
17. Hall 1988, pp. 164–65.
18. U.S. Department of Housing and Urban Development 1976, app. A, p. 23.
19. Ibid., p. 34.
20. U.S. Department of Housing and Urban Development 1971, app. D.
21. New York City Planning Commission (NYCPC) 1969.
22. Fainstein 1991.
23. Allee, King, Rosen, and Fleming, Inc. 1990, p. II.C-1.
24. Ibid., p. II.C-10.

25. T. Schuman interview with Alyce M. Russo, planner, Roosevelt Island Operating Corporation, 26 Aug. 1991.
26. Deutsche 1991; NYCPC 1969, p. 26.
27. Goldberger 1988.
28. Gill 1990; Hiss 1990.
29. Battery Park City Authority 1988.
30. Battery Park City Authority 1987.
31. Golway 1993.
32. Lamar et al. 1989.
33. Warner 1987.
34. Regional Plan Association 1990.
35. *New York Times,* 27 June 1991.

Conclusion

1. Birch 1991, pp. 1268–69.
2. Jackson 1985, pp. 265–67.
3. Fishman 1987, p. 184; 1990, p. 38.
4. Gottdiener and Kephart 1991, p. 34.
5. Garreau 1988, p. 3. For a pointed listing of all the appellations thus far applied to the "new city," see Sharpe and Wallock 1994a, pp. 4–6.
6. Harris and Ullman 1945; Chapin 1965, pp. 19–21; Berry and Horton 1970, pp. 306–11.
7. Harris and Ullman 1945.
8. Berry and Gillard 1977; Conzen 1983.
9. Garreau 1988.
10. Southworth and Owens 1993, pp. 271–72.
11. Ibid.
12. Weiss 1987.
13. Sies 1987a; Jackson 1985.
14. Garreau 1988, p. 3; Kling, Olin, and Poster, 1991, p. 10.
15. Wade 1988, pp. 272, 275.
16. Monkkonen 1988, pp. 242–44.
17. Sharpe and Wallock 1994b, p. 60.
18. Muller 1981, pp. 162–75; Fishman 1987, p. 184.
19. Byrum 1992, p. 395.
20. Sharpe and Wallock 1992, pp. 394–95.
21. Abbott 1993, pp. 131, 138.
22. Garreau 1994.

23. Laska and Spain 1980, p. xiii.
24. Schill and Nathan 1983, p. 138.
25. Palen and London 1983, p. 265.
26. Easley 1992.
27. Rusk 1993, p. 128.
28. Sharpe and Wallock 1994a.
29. Berry and Gillard 1977, pp. 64–66.
30. NCCP 1909, p. 76.
31. Ibid., p. 77.
32. Binford 1985; Sies 1987b; Keating 1988.
33. Bassett 1925.
34. Weiss 1987, p. 45; Sies 1990.
35. Perry 1929.
36. Gillette 1983, pp. 421–44; Silver 1985, pp. 161–74.
37. Fishman 1992, pp. 121–22.
38. Bauman 1987; Fairbanks 1988, pp. 147–49.
39. W. J. Wilson 1987; Thomas 1991, pp. 218–31; Fishman 1987, p. 198.
40. Abrams 1965, pp. 82–85.
41. Babcock and Bosselman 1973; Sharpe and Wallock 1994a, p. 7.
42. Hall 1988, pp. 350–51.
43. Goldfield 1993, p. 318.
44. Lejeune 1991, p. 4.
45. Levin 1987, pp. 226–30.
46. Krumholz and Forester 1990; Rohe and Gates 1985.
47. Lewis 1985; Meinig 1979; Chappell 1986; Sies 1991; K. Jackson 1980; Herman 1992; Upton 1985.

Bibliography

Abbott, Carl. 1981a [1987]. *The New Urban America: Growth and Politics in Sunbelt Cities.* Chapel Hill: University of North Carolina Press.

————. 1981b. "Portland in the Pacific War: Planning from 1940 to 1945." *Urbanism Past and Present* 6 (Spring/Winter): 12–24.

————. 1983. *Portland: Planning, Politics, and Growth in a Twentieth Century City.* Lincoln: University of Nebraska Press.

————. 1984. "Planning for the Home Front in Seattle and Portland, 1940–45." In *The Martial Metropolis: U.S. Cities in War and Peace,* edited by Roger W. Lotchin, 163–90. New York: Praeger.

————. 1991. "Urban Design in Portland, Oregon, as Policy and Process, 1960–1989." *Planning Perspectives* 6 (Jan.): 1–18.

————. 1993. *The Metropolitan Frontier: Cities in the Modern American West.* Tucson, Ariz.: University of Arizona Press.

Abrams, Charles. 1961. "Downtown Decay and Revival." *Journal of the American Institute of Planners* 27 (Feb.): 3–9.

————. 1965. *The City Is the Frontier.* New York: Harper and Row.

Bibliography

Ackerman, Frederick L. 1917. "The Significance of England's Program of Building Workman's Homes." *Journal of the American Institute of Architects* 5: 538–40.

———. 1918a. "Houses and Ships." *American City* 19: 85–86.

———. 1918b. "War-Time Housing—England's Most Urgent Civic Lesson for America." *American City* 18: 97–100.

———. 1918c. "The Government, the Architect, and the Artisan in Relation to Government Housing." *Journal of the American Institute of Architects* 6: 86–89.

———. 1922. "Cooperative Housing." *Journal of the American Institute of Architects* 10 (12): 388.

"An Act to Authorize the Sale of the St. Louis Commons." 1856. In *The Ordinances of the City of St. Louis*. St. Louis, Mo.: George Knapp.

The Acts of the Assembly Incorporating the City of St. Louis and the Ordinances of the City Which are Now in Force. 1828. St. Louis, Mo.: Orr and Keemle.

Adams, Frederick Johnstone. 1945. "Rehousing vs. Rehabilitation." *Journal of the American Institute of Planners* 11 (Summer): 11–15.

Adelstein, Richard P. 1991. "The Nation as an Economic Unit: Keynes, Roosevelt, and the Managerial Ideal." *Journal of American History* 78 (1): 160–87.

Adler, Emma. 1967. "Trustee's Garden Village." *Antiques* 91 (3): 331.

Adler, Leopold II. 1969. "The Savannah Story." *Historic Preservation* 21 (1): 8–21.

———. 1990. Presentation to Armstrong State College Class. Scarbrough House, 15 June, Savannah, Ga.

Alanen, Arnold R., and Joseph A. Eden. 1987. *Main Street Ready-Made: The New Deal Community of Greendale, Wisconsin.* Madison: State Historical Society of Wisconsin.

Allee, King, Rosen, and Fleming, Inc. (AKRF). 1990. *Roosevelt Island Southtown: Final Environmental Impact Statement.* New York: Roosevelt Island Operating Corp.

Altschuler, Alan. 1965. *The City Planning Process.* Ithaca, N.Y.: Cornell University Press.

Alvord, Clarence Walworth. 1920. *The Illinois Country, 1673–1818.* Vol. 1 of *The Centennial History of Illinois.* Springfield: Illinois Centennial Commission.

American Association of State Highway Officials. 1957. *A Policy on Arterial Highways in Urban Areas.* Washington, D.C.

American Institute of Planners, Committee on Urban Transportation. 1947. *Urban Freeways.* New York: American Transit Association.

Bibliography

"Annual Report of the Park Commissioner." 1913. In *The Mayor's Message, with Accompanying Documents, to the City Council of the City of St. Louis.* St. Louis, Mo.

Apgar, William, and Belden Daniels. 1983. *Savannah Landmark Rehabilitation Project.* Cambridge, Mass.: Kennedy School of Government.

"Architecture vs. Planning: Collision and Collaboration in the Design of American Cities." 1990. *Center: A Journal for Architecture in America* 6: 1–110.

Arena, Richard C. 1974. "Land Settlement Practices in Spanish Louisiana." In *The Spanish in the Mississippi Valley, 1762–1804,* edited by John Francis McDermott. Urbana: University of Illinois Press.

Armstrong, Kathleen. 1972. "Litigating the Freeway Revolt: Keith v. Volpe." *Ecology Law Quarterly* 2 (Winter): 761–99.

Arnold, Bion J., John R. Freeman, and Frederick Law Olmsted [Jr.]. 1910. *City Planning for Pittsburgh: Outline and Procedures.* Pittsburgh, Pa.: Pittsburgh Civic Commission.

Arnold, Joseph. 1971. *The New Deal in the Suburbs: A History of the Greenbelt Towns Program, 1935–1954.* Columbus: Ohio State University Press.

Attoe, Wayne, and Donn Logan. 1989. *American Urban Architecture: Catalysts in the Development of Cities.* Berkeley: University of California Press.

Babcock, Richard F., and Fred P. Bosselman. 1973. *Exclusionary Zoning: Land Use Regulation and Housing in the 1970s.* New York: Praeger.

Bacon, Edmund N. 1960. "A Case Study in Urban Design." *Journal of the American Institute of Planners* 26 (Aug.): 224–35.

———. 1967. *The Design of Cities.* New York: Penguin Books.

Banerjee, Tridib, and William C. Baer. 1984. *Beyond the Neighborhood Unit: Residential Environments and Public Policy.* New York: Plenum.

Banfield, Edward C., and James Q. Wilson. 1963. *City Politics.* New York: Vintage Books.

Barclay, Thomas S. 1962. *The St. Louis Home Rule Charter of 1876, Its Framing and Adoption.* Columbia: University of Missouri Press.

Barrett, Paul. 1983. *The Automobile and Urban Transit: The Formation of Public Policy in Chicago, 1900–1930.* Philadelphia: Temple University Press.

———. 1987. "Cities and Their Airports: Policy Formation, 1926–52." *Journal of Urban History* 14 (1): 112–37.

Barta, Carolyn Jenkins. 1970. "The Dallas News and Council-Manager Government." Master's thesis, University of Texas.

Bartholomew, Harland. 1983. Interview by Mary Seematter, 14 July. Missouri Historical Society Community Program Division Files. Missouri Historical Society, St. Louis.

Bartholomew, Harland, and Associates. 1957a. "Existing Zoning—1954." *A Report upon Economic Base, Population, and General Land Uses.* Columbus, Ohio.

———. 1957b. "Existing General Land Use." In *A Summary Report: The Master Plan: Columbus Urban Area.* Columbus, Ohio.

Bassett, Edward M. 1925. *Planning of Unbuilt Areas in the New York Region.* New York: Regional Plan of New York and Its Environs.

———. 1940. *Zoning: The Laws, Administration, and Court Decisions during the First Twenty Years.* New York: Russell Sage Foundation.

Battery Park City Authority (BPCA). 1987. *Annual Report.* New York.

———. 1988. Internal memorandum. 6 April. New York.

Bauer, Catherine. 1944a. "Cities in Flux: A Challenge to the Postwar Planners." *American Scholar* 13: 70–85.

———. 1944b. "Planning Is Politics . . . but . . . Are Planners Politicians?" *Pencil Points: The Magazine of Architecture* 25 (Mar.): 66–70.

Bauman, John F. 1983. "Visions of a Post-War City: A Perspective on Urban Planning, Philadelphia and the Nation, 1942–1945." In *Introduction to Planning History in the United States,* edited by Donald A. Krueckeberg, 170–89. New Brunswick, N.J.: Rutgers University Center for Urban Policy Research.

———. 1987. *Public Housing, Race, and Renewal: Urban Planning in Philadelphia, 1920–1974.* Philadelphia: Temple University Press.

Baxter, Herbert H. Papers. Manuscripts Department, Atkins Library, University of North Carolina at Charlotte.

Bayor, Ronald H. 1988. "Expressways, Urban Renewal, and the Relocation of the Black Community in Atlanta." Unpublished paper. Organization of American Historians Annual Conference, Reno, Nevada.

Bean, Walton, and James J. Rawls. 1983. *California: An Interpretive History.* New York: McGraw-Hill.

Beattie, Susan. 1980. *A Revolution in London Housing: LCC Architects and Their Work, 1893–1914.* London: Architectural Press.

Beaufoy, S. G. L. 1950. "Well Hall Estate, Eltham." *Town Planning Review* (Oct.): 259–71.

Beauregard, Robert, ed. 1989. *Atop the Urban Hierarchy.* Totowa, N.J.: Rowman and Littlefield.

Beilfuss, A. W. 1908. "Municipal Playgrounds in Chicago." *Playgrounds* 2: 259, 261.

Bennett, Charles, and Milton Breivogel. 1945. "The Plan for the San Fernando Valley." *Pencil Points* 26 (6): 93–98.

Bennett, Larry. 1986. "Beyond Urban Renewal: Chicago's North Loop Redevelopment Project." *Urban Affairs Quarterly* 22 (Dec.): 242–57.

Bibliography

Berger, Peter L., and Thomas Luckmann. 1966. *The Social Construction of Reality.* Garden City, N.Y.: Doubleday, Anchor Books.

Berry, Brian J. L. 1967. *The Geography of Market Centers and Retail Distribution.* Englewood Cliffs, N.J.: Prentice-Hall.

Berry, Brian J. L., and Quentin Gillard. 1977. *The Changing Shape of Metropolitan America.* Cambridge, Mass.: Ballinger.

Berry, Brian J. L., and Frank E. Horton. 1970. *Geographic Perspectives on Urban Systems.* Englewood Cliffs, N.J.: Prentice-Hall.

Berry, Jeffrey M., Kent E. Portney, and Ken Thomson. 1993. *The Rebirth of Urban Democracy.* Washington, D.C.: Brookings Institution.

Bettman, Alfred. 1926. "The Present State of Court Decisions on Zoning." *City Planning* 2 (1): 24–35.

———. 1944. "Problems of Planning and Democracy in Urban Redevelopment Legislation." *Journal of the American Institute of Planners* 10 (Autumn): 3–8.

———. 1945. "Statement to the Sub-Committee on Housing and Urban Redevelopment." *Journal of the American Institute of Planners* 11 (Spring): 5–11.

Bettman, Alfred, et al. 1944. "How Cities are Preparing for the Post-War Period." In *Planning 1944: Proceedings of the Annual Meeting,* 31–116. Chicago: American Society of Planning Officials.

Beveridge, Charles Eliot. 1981. "Frederick Law Olmsted and the 'More Openly Built City.'" Paper prepared for Columbia University Seminar on the City. New York City, Oct.

Biles, Roger. 1985. "Epitaph for Downtown: The Failure of City Planning in Post-World War Memphis." *Tennessee Historical Quarterly* 54 (Fall): 267–84.

Binford, Henry C. 1985. *The First Suburbs: Residential Communities on the Boston Periphery, 1815–1860.* Chicago: University of Chicago Press.

Birch, Eugenie Ladner. 1983. "Woman-Made America: The Case of Early Public Housing Policy." In *The American Planner: Biographies and Recollections,* edited by Donald A. Krueckeberg, 149–75. New York: Methuen.

———. 1987. "Design, Process, and Institutions: Planning in Urban History." In *American Urbanism: A Historiographical Review,* edited by Howard Gillette Jr. and Zane L. Miller. New York: Greenwood.

———. 1991. "Presidential Address." *Proceedings of the Fourth Conference in American Planning History.* Hilliard, Ohio: Society for American City and Regional Planning History.

Birch, Eugenie Ladner, and Douglass Roby. 1984. "The Planner and the Preservationist: An Uneasy Alliance." *Journal of the American Planning Association* 50 (2): 194–207.

Birmingfind. n.d. *The Other Side: The Story of Birmingham's Black Community.* Birmingham, Ala.

Birmingham, City of. 1956. Application for Recertification, Workable Program for Urban Renewal (5 July), p. 16. Planning and Zoning papers, uncataloged, Birmingham Public Library, Birmingham, Ala.

———. 1974–1988. *Citizen Participation Plan.* Birmingham, Ala.

———. City Council Papers. Birmingham Public Library, Birmingham, Ala.

———. Planning and Zoning Papers, uncataloged. Birmingham Public Library, Birmingham, Ala.

Birmingham Department of Community Development. 1988. *A Brief History of Citizen Participation in Birmingham, 1972–1988.* Birmingham, Ala.

Birmingham Planning Commission. 1961a. *Annual Report: 1961.* Birmingham, Ala. In Planning and Zoning Papers, uncataloged. Birmingham Public Library, Birmingham, Ala.

———. 1961b. *The Comprehensive Plan.* Birmingham, Ala.

———. 1962. Annual Report: 1961–62. Birmingham, Ala. In Planning and Zoning Papers, uncataloged, Birmingham Public Library, Birmingham, Ala.

Bishir, Catherine W. 1989. "Yuppies, Bubbas, and the Politics of Culture." In *Perspectives in Vernacular Architecture* 3, edited by Thomas Carter and Bernard L. Herman, 8–15. Columbia: University of Missouri Press.

Black, J. Thomas. 1980. "The Changing Economic Role of Central City and Suburbs." In *The Prospective City,* edited by Arthur Solomon, 80–123. Cambridge, Mass.: MIT Press.

Black, J. Thomas, Allan Borut, and Robert Dubinsky. 1977. *Private Market Housing Renovation in Older Urban Areas.* ULI Research Report 26. Washington D.C.: Urban Land Institute.

Black, Russell VanNest. 1948. "Land Planning in New Jersey." *American Planning and Civic Annual, 1948.* 29–33.

Black, William Neil. 1982. "Empire of Consensus: City Planning, Zoning, and Annexation in Dallas, 1900–1960." Ph.D. diss., Columbia University.

Blessing, Charles. 1959. "Challenge and Response." *Journal of the American Institute of Planners* 25 (May): ii.

———. 1964. "Sketches." *Journal of the American Institute of Architects* 41 (Feb.): 39–44.

———. 1966. "The Planner's Role in Creating Beauty in Urban America." Paper presented at the Conference on Urban Design, Kansas City, Missouri, March 30–31. In DCPC Collection, Box 8, "Miscellaneous Speeches" Folder.

Bloch, Robin. 1987. *Studies in the Development of the United States Aerospace Industry.* GSAUP Discussion Paper D875. University of California at Los Angeles.

Blucher, Walter H. 1942. "Planning and Zoning Developments in 1941." In *The Municipal Yearbook,* edited by Clarence Ridley and Orin Nolting, 359–83. Chicago: International City Managers' Association.

Bibliography

———. 1945. "Planning Developments in 1944." In *The Municipal Yearbook, 1945*, edited by Clarence Ridley and Orin Nolting, 265–93. Chicago: International City Managers' Association.

———. 1946. "Planning Developments in 1945." In *The Municipal Yearbook, 1946*, edited by Clarence Ridley and Orin Nolting, 251–66. Chicago: International City Managers' Association.

———. 1947. "Planning Developments in 1945." In *The Municipal Yearbook, 1947*, edited by Clarence Ridley and Orin Nolting, 233–50. Chicago: International City Managers' Association.

———. 1949. "Planning and Zoning Developments in 1948." In *The Municipal Yearbook, 1949*, edited by Clarence Ridley and Orin Nolting, 253–79. Chicago: International City Managers' Association.

———. 1950. "Moving People." *Virginia Law Review* 36: 849.

Bluestone, Daniel. 1991. *Constructing Chicago*. New Haven, Conn.: Yale University Press.

Blythe, LeGette, and Charles Brockmann. 1961. *Hornets' Nest: The Story of Charlotte and Mecklenburg County*. Charlotte, N.C.: McNally of Charlotte.

Boles, Daralice D. 1989. "Reordering the Suburbs." *Progressive Architecture* 70 (5): 78–91.

"Boston" (special issue). 1964. *Architectural Forum* 120 (6).

Bottles, Scott L. 1987. *Los Angeles and the Automobile: The Making of the Modern City*. Berkeley: University of California Press.

Boutwell, Albert. Papers. Department of Manuscripts and Archives, Birmingham Public Library, Birmingham, Alabama.

Bowden, Martyn J. 1971. "Downtown through Time: Delineation, Expansion, and Internal Growth." *Economic Geography* 47 (Apr.): 121–35.

———. 1975. "Growth of Central Districts in Large Cities." In *The New Urban History*, edited by Leo Schnore, 75–109. Princeton, N.J.: Princeton University Press.

Boyce, Ronald R., and W. A. V. Clark. 1963. "Selected Spatial Variables and Central Business District Retail Sales." *Papers of the Regional Science Association* 11: 167–94.

Boyer, M. Christine. 1983. *Dreaming the Rational City: The Myth of American City Planning*. Cambridge Mass.: MIT Press.

———. 1992. "Cities for Sale: Merchandising History at South Street Seaport." In *Variations on a Theme Park: The New American City and the End of Public Space*, edited by Michael Sorkin, 181–204. New York: Hill and Wang.

Boyer, Paul. 1978. *Urban Masses and Moral Order in America, 1820–1920*. Cambridge, Mass.: Harvard University Press.

Branch, Taylor. 1988. *Parting the Waters: America in the King Years, 1954–63*. New York: Simon and Schuster.

Bibliography

A Breath of Fresh Air: Chicago's Neighborhood Parks of the Progressive Reform Era, 1900–1925. 1989. Chicago: Chicago Public Library, Special Collections Department.

Bredemeier, Harry. 1980. *The Federal Public Housing Movement.* New York: Arno Press.

Breen, Daniel, ed. 1941. "Historical Register of the Twenty Two Superseded Park Districts." Typescript, WPA project, Chicago.

Breese, Gerald. 1949. *The Daytime Population of the Central Business District of Chicago.* Chicago: University of Chicago Press.

Brooks, Jane S., and Alma Young. 1991. "Revitalizing the Central Business District in the Face of Decline: The Case of New Orleans, 1970–1990." Working Paper 5. Division of Urban Research and Policy Studies, University of New Orleans.

Brooks, Michael P. 1988. "Four Critical Junctures in the History of the Urban Planning Profession: An Exercise in Hindsight." *Journal of the American Planning Association* 54 (Spring): 241–48.

Brownell, Blaine A. 1975a. "The Commercial-Civic Elite and City Planning in Atlanta, Memphis, and New Orleans in the 1920s." *Journal of Southern History* 41 (Aug.): 339–68.

———. 1975b. *The Urban Ethos in the South, 1920–1930.* Baton Rouge: Louisiana State University Press.

———. 1977. "The Urban South Comes of Age, 1900–1940." In *The City in Southern History,* edited by Blaine A. Brownell and David R. Goldfield. Port Washington, N.Y.: Kennikat.

———. 1980. "Urban Planning, the Planning Profession, and the Motor Vehicle in Early Twentieth Century America." In *Shaping an Urban World,* edited by Gordon Cherry, 59–74. New York: St. Martin's Press.

Browning, Clyde. 1961. "Recent Studies of Central Business Districts." *Journal of the American Institute of Planners* 27 (Feb.): 82–86.

Brunner, Arnold W., Frederick Law Olmsted [Jr.], and J. Bion Arnold. 1911. *A City Plan for Rochester: A Report Prepared for the Rochester Civic Improvement Committee.* New York: Cheltenham Press.

Buder, Stanley. 1967. *Pullman.* New York: Oxford University Press.

———. 1969. "Ebenezer Howard: The Genesis of a Town Planning Movement." *Journal of the American Institute of Planners* 35 (Nov.): 390–98.

———. 1990. *Visionaries and Planners: The Garden City Movement and the Modern Community.* New York: Oxford University Press.

Burgess, Patricia. 1994. *Planning for the Private Interest: Land Use Controls and Residential Patterns in Columbus, Ohio, 1900–1970.* Columbus: Ohio State University Press.

Bibliography

Burnham, Daniel H., and Edward H. Bennett. 1905. *Report on a Plan for San Francisco,* edited by Edward F. O'Day. San Francisco: City of San Francisco.

———. 1909. *Plan of Chicago,* edited by Charles Moore. Chicago: Commercial Club.

Burnham, Robert A. 1991. "The Divided Metropolis: Subdivision Control and the Demise of Comprehensive Metropolitan Planning in Hamilton County, Ohio, 1929–53." *Planning Perspectives* 6 (1): 47–67.

Burton, Hal. 1954. *The City Fights Back.* New York: Citadel Press.

Bushnell, Charles J. 1901. "Some Social Aspects of the Chicago Stock Yards, Part 2." *American Journal of Sociology* 7 (Nov.): 289–330.

Byrum, Oliver. 1992. "Edge Cities: A Pragmatic Perspective." *Journal of the American Planning Association* 58 (Summer): 395–96.

"Cabrillo Homes Community Building: Community Facilities for War Housing [Long Beach]." 1944. *Pencil Points* 25 (2): 36–43.

California. Department of Public Works. Division of Highways. 1964. *San Francisco Panhandle Parkway and Crosstown Tunnel: Technical Report.* San Francisco.

California Housing and Planning Association. 1942. "California Must Plan Now." San Francisco.

———. 1943. "California Must Look Ahead." San Francisco.

California State Chamber of Commerce. 1944. "Disposal of Surplus Government-Owned War Property." *California Magazine of the Pacific* (Nov.): 1–4.

California State Planning Board. 1941. "Hearing on the Establishment of a San Francisco Bay Regional Planning District." Sacramento.

——— [L. Deming Tilton]. 1942. "Sausalito Housing and Transportation Problems." Sacramento.

California State Reconstruction and Reemployment Commission. 1944. "The First Step and the Unfinished Task: Summary of a Report on Postwar Planning—San Bernardino County." Sacramento.

———. 1945a. "A City Earns a Purple Heart." Sacramento.

———. 1945b. *Postwar Housing in California.* Sacramento.

Campbell, Thomas. 1990. "Cleveland: The Struggle for Stability." In *Snowbelt Cities: Metropolitan Politics in the Northeast and Midwest since World War II,* edited by Richard Bernard, 109–36. Bloomington: Indiana University Press.

Candee, Richard. 1985. *Atlantic Heights: A World War I Shipbuilder's Community.* Portsmouth: P. E. Randall.

Caparn, Harold A. 1901. "The Founding of the American Society of Landscape Architects." *American Landscape Architect* 4 (Jan.): 20–23.

Caro, Robert. 1975. *The Power Broker: Robert Moses and the Fall of New York.* New York: Vintage.

Bibliography

Carrico, Richard. 1986. *Stranger in a Stolen Land: American Indians in San Diego, 1850–1880.* San Diego: San Diego State University Press.

Carroll, J. D. Jr. 1953. "The Future of the Central Business District." *Public Management* 35 (July): 150–53.

Carroll, Margaret. 1963. *Historic Preservation through Urban Renewal.* Washington D.C.: Urban Renewal Administration.

Castanien, Pliny. 1993. *To Protect and Serve: A History of the San Diego Police Department and Its Chiefs.* San Diego: San Diego Historical Society.

Castells, Manuel. 1983. *The City and the Grassroots: A Cross-cultural Theory of Urban Social Movements.* Berkeley: University of California Press.

Cavallo, Dominick. 1980. *Muscles and Morals: Organized Playgrounds and Urban Reform, 1880–1920.* Philadelphia: University of Pennsylvania Press.

Caves, Richard E. 1962. *Air Transport and Its Regulators: An Industry Study.* Cambridge, Mass.: Harvard University Press.

Central Association of Seattle. 1963. "Discussion Guide: Seattle Central Business District Plan." In Downtown Seattle Development Association Papers, Box 8. University of Washington, Manuscripts Department, Seattle, Washington.

———. 1970. "The Emerging Downtown: 1970." In Downtown Seattle Development Association Papers, Box 8. University of Washington, Manuscripts Department, Seattle, Washington.

Central Atlanta Progress. 1988. *Central Area Study II.*

Chabli, Margery, and Pamela B. Hussey. 1975. *HUD's New Catalog of Neighborhood Preservation Programs.* Washington D.C.: U.S. Department of Housing and Urban Development.

Chambers, Clarke. 1971. *Paul U. Kellogg and the Survey: Voices for Social Welfare Justice.* Minneapolis: University of Minnesota Press.

Chambers, Ruth Hanners. 1967. *Hilton Village, 1918–1968.* Booklet published by Woman's Club of Hilton Village, Virginia.

Chapin, F. Stuart Jr. 1954. "City Planning: Adjusting People and Place." In *The Urban South,* edited by Rupert B. Vance and Nicholas J. Demerath, 268–82. Chapel Hill: University of North Carolina Press.

———. 1965. *Urban Land Use Planning.* 2d ed. Urbana: University of Illinois Press.

Chappell, Edward. 1986. "Architectural Recording and the Open-Air Museum: A View from the Field." In *Perspectives in Vernacular Architecture 2,* edited by Camille Wells, 24–36. Columbia: University of Missouri Press.

Charlotte [N.C.] City Council Minutes, 1938–48.

Charlotte [N.C.] Housing Authority. 1944. *Public Housing in Charlotte: Better Homes for Better Citizens and a Better City: Report of the Housing Authority of the City of Charlotte.* Charlotte.

Bibliography

Checkoway, Barry. 1977. "Preservation Is a Verb." In *Historic Preservation: Setting, Legislation, and Techniques: Proceedings of the Second Annual Winter Conference of Planning,* edited by L. Blair and J. Quinn. Urbana, Ill.: University of Illinois at Urbana-Champaign.

———. 1980. "Large Builders, Federal Housing Programs, and Postwar Suburbanization." *International Journal of Urban and Regional Research* 4 (1): 21–45.

———. 1984. "Large Builders, Federal Housing Programs, and Postwar Suburbanization." In *Marxism and the Metropolis: New Perspectives in Urban Political Economy.* 2d ed., edited by William K. Tabb and Larry Sawers. New York: Oxford University Press.

Cherry, Gordon, ed. 1980. *Shaping an Urban World.* New York: St. Martin's Press.

Chicago Park District. Special Collections. Drawings and Maps.

"Chicago Parks and Their Landscape Architecture." 1908. *Architectural Record* 24 (July): 26.

Chicago Real Estate Board. 1903, 1905a, 1907. *Report of the South Park Commissioners to the Board of County Commissioners of Cook County.* Chicago.

———. 1904. *Report of the Special Park Commission . . . on the Subject of a Metropolitan Park System.* Compiled by D. H. Perkins. Chicago: Special Park Commission.

———. 1905b. *Report of Special Committee Appointed to Procure Information in Reference to the Expenditures . . . by the South Park Commission.* Chicago.

Childs, Richard S. 1918. "The First Emergency Government Towns for Shipyard Workers, Yorkship Village at Camden N.J." *Journal of the American Institute of Architects* 6: 237–44, 249–51.

Christensen, Carol A. 1986. *The American Garden City and the New Towns Movement.* Ann Arbor, Mich.: UMI Research Press.

Churchill, Henry. 1960. "Henry Wright: 1878–1936." *Journal of the American Institute of Planners* 25 (Nov.): 293–301.

City and County of Dallas Levee Improvement District. Dallas, Texas. 1951. Dallas: First Southwest Co.

———. n.d. *Trinity Improvement District.* Dallas: City and County of Dallas Improvement District.

City and County of San Francisco, Citizens' Post War Planning Committee. 1945. "Report to Mayor Roger D. Lapham, August 20, 1945." San Francisco.

City Homes Association [Chicago]. 1901. *Tenement Conditions in Chicago.* Chicago.

City Plan Commission of St. Louis (Harland Bartholomew, engineer). 1917a. *Annual Report, 1916–1917.* St. Louis, Mo.

———. 1917b. *A Major Street Plan for St. Louis.* St. Louis, Mo.: Nixon-Jones.

———. 1917c. *Problems of St. Louis.* St. Louis, Mo.: Nixon-Jones.

————. 1919. *The Zone Plan*. St. Louis, Mo.: Nixon-Jones.

Ciucci, Giorgio, Francesco Dal Co, and Mario Manieri-Elia. 1979. *The American City: From the Civil War to the New Deal*. Cambridge, Mass.: MIT Press.

Civic Bulletin. 1911. 1 (Mar.).

Civic Improvement League of St. Louis. 1903. *First Annual Report*. St. Louis, Mo.

Civic Improvement League Papers. 1902–1920. Missouri Historical Society Archives, St. Louis, Mo.

Civic League of St. Louis. 1907. *A City Plan for St. Louis*. St. Louis, Mo.

————. 1911. *Year Book*. St. Louis, Mo.

Clapp, Gordon. 1951. "The Tennessee Valley Authority." In *Regionalism in America*, edited by Merrill Jensen, 317–29. Madison: University of Wisconsin Press.

————. 1955. *The T.V.A.: An Approach to the Development of a Region*. Chicago: University of Chicago Press.

Cleveland, H. W. S. 1873. *Landscape Architecture as Applied to the Wants of the West*. Chicago: Jansen, McClurg.

Cleveland City Planning Commission. 1959. *Downtown Cleveland, 1975. The Downtown General Plan*.

Codman, John. 1956. *Preservation of Historic Districts by Architectural Control*. Chicago, Ill.: American Society of Planning Officials.

Cohen, Madeline L. 1990. "The 1963 and the 1988 Plans for Philadelphia's Center City: A Problem of Differing Philosophies." Working Paper 202. Society for American City and Regional Planning History.

Cohen, Robert. 1979. "The Changing Transactional Economy and Its Spatial Implications." *Ekistics* 46 (Jan.-Feb.): 7–14.

Coke, James G. 1968. "Antecedents of Local Planning." In *Principles and Practice of Urban Planning*, edited by William I. Goodman and Eric C. Freund. Washington, D.C.: International City Managers' Association.

Colean, Miles. 1940. *Housing for Defense: A Review of the Role of Housing . . . and a Program for Action*. New York: Twentieth Century Fund.

Columbus [Ohio] City Planning Commission. 1957. *Annual Report*. Columbus.

Committee for County and City Wide Association. Report to Dallas Property Owners Association, 11 Apr. 1924. Dealey Papers, Box 3, Dallas Historical Society (DHS).

"Congestion of Population." 1908. *Charities and the Commons* 19 (Mar.): 1739–40.

Connerly, Charles E., and Bobby M. Wilson. 1992. "Planning, Jim Crow, and the Civil Rights Movement: The Rebirth and Demise of Racial Zoning in Birmingham. Paper presented at the Annual Conference of

Bibliography

the Association of Collegiate Schools of Planning, Columbus, Ohio, Oct. 31.

Connolly, Julia. 1961. "An Identification of Communities in the U.S. Making the Greatest Progress in Comprehensive Planning and Development." Report, Urban Studies Program, University of North Carolina (May). In vertical file, "DCPC" folder, Detroit Municipal Reference Library, Detroit.

Conway, Dennis, et al. 1976. "The Dallas-Fort Worth Region." In *Contemporary Metropolitan America*. Vol. 4, edited by John S. Adams. Cambridge, Mass.: Ballinger.

Conzen, Michael. 1983. "American Cities in Profound Transition: The New City Geography of the 1980s." In *The Making of Urban America*, edited by Raymond A. Mohl, 277–92. Wilmington: Scholarly Resources.

Cook, Blanche Wiesen. 1979. *Women and Support Networks*. Brooklyn, New York: Out & Out Books.

Copeland, Robert Morris. 1982. *Essay and Plan for the Improvement of the City of Boston*. Boston: Lee & Shepard.

Corley, Robert G. 1979. "The Quest for Racial Harmony: Race Relations in Birmingham, Alabama, 1947–1963." Ph.D. diss., University of Virginia, Charlottesville.

———. 1982. "In Search of Racial Harmony: Birmingham Business Leaders and Desegregation, 1950–1963." In *Southern Businessmen and Desegregation*, edited by Elizabeth Jacoway and David R. Colburn. Baton Rouge: Louisiana State University Press.

Corso, Anthony. 1983. "San Diego: The Anti-City." In *Sunbelt Cities: Politics and Growth since World War II*, edited by Richard Bernard and Bradley Rice, pp. 328–44. Austin: University of Texas Press.

Crane, Clare. 1991. "The Pueblo Lands: San Diego's Hispanic Heritage." *Journal of San Diego History* 37 (2):104–27.

Cranz, Galen. 1971. "Models for Park Usage: Ideology and Development of Chicago's Public Parks." Ph.D. diss., University of Chicago.

———. 1982. *The Politics of Park Design. A History of Urban Parks in America*. Cambridge, Mass.: MIT Press.

Crawford, Ruth. 1917. *The Immigrant in St. Louis*. St. Louis, Mo.: Studies in Social Economics.

Creese, Walter. 1964. "The Planning Theories of Sir Raymond Unwin, 1863–1948." *Journal of the American Institute of Planners* 30 (Nov.): 295–304.

Crowe, Charles Thaddeus. 1987. *Savannah's Victorian District: A Ten Year Analysis of Neighborhood Revitalization*. Master's thesis, Georgia Institute of Technology.

Cuff, Dana. 1991. *Architecture: The Story of Practice*. Cambridge, Mass.: MIT Press.

Cullingworth, Barry. 1993. *The Political Culture of Planning: American Land Use Planning in Cultural Perspective*. New York: Routledge.

Cunningham, William Glenn. 1951. *The Aircraft Industry: A Study in Industrial Location*. Los Angeles: L. L. Morrison.

Dahir, James. 1950. *Communities for Better Living*. New York: Harper.

Dallas Department of Planning and Development. 1982. *Central Business District: Past Planning and Current Issues*.

Daly-Bednarek, Janet. 1992. *The Changing Image of the City: Planning for Downtown Omaha, 1945–1973*. Lincoln: University of Nebraska Press.

Daniel, Pete. 1990. "Going among Strangers: Southern Reactions to World War II." *Journal of American History* 77 (3): 886–911.

Darley, Gillian. 1975. *Villages of Vision*. New York: Architectural Press.

Davis, Allen F. 1967. *Spearheads for Reform: The Social Settlements and the Progressive Movement, 1890–1914*. New York: Oxford University Press.

Davis, Dwight F. 1908. "The Neighborhood Center—A Moral and Educational Factor." *Charities and the Commons* 19: 1505.

Davis, Edward J. P. 1953. *Historical San Diego, the Birthplace of California*. San Diego: Davis.

Davis, Eric Emmett. 1989. *Dwight Heald Perkins. Social Consciousness and Prairie School Architecture*. Chicago: University of Illinois at Chicago, Gallery 400.

Davis, Mike. 1992. *City of Quartz*. New York: Vintage.

Dayton Department of Planning. 1976. *Downtown Dayton*.

Dealey, George B. Papers. Dallas Historical Society, Dallas, Texas.

———. 1929. "Dallas Is Realizing the Kessler Plan." In *American Civic Annual*, edited by Harlean James, 180–84. Washington: American Civic Association.

Dean, Andrea Oppenheimer. 1995. "Savannah's Law." *Historic Preservation* 47 (1): 28–35.

Deegan, Mary Jo. 1988. *Jane Addams and the Men of the Chicago School, 1892–1918*. New Brunswick, N.J.: Transaction Books.

Delafons, John. 1969. *Land-Use Controls in the United States*. 2d ed. Cambridge, Mass.: MIT Press.

Denver Partnership, Inc., and Denver Planning Office. 1986. *Downtown Area Plan*.

Detroit, City of. 1951. *Master Plan*. Detroit: City Plan Commission.

Detroit City Plan Commission. 1962. *Renewal and Revenue: An Evaluation of the Urban Renewal Program in Detroit*. Detroit: City Plan Commission.

———. 1965. *Detroit: Achievement Through Planning*. Detroit: City Plan Commission.

Detroit City Plan Commission Collection. Burton Historical Collections, Detroit Public Library, Detroit.

Deutsche, Rosalyn. 1991. "Uneven Development: Public Art in New York City." In *Out of Site: A Social Criticism of Architecture,* edited by Diane Ghirardo. Seattle, Wash.: Bay Press.

Dickason, Jerry. 1979. "The Development of the Playground Movement in the United States: A Historical Study." Ph.D. diss., New York University.

Diner, Steven J. 1975. "Department and Discipline: The Department of Sociology at the University of Chicago, 1892–1920." *Minerva* 13 (Winter): 525–26.

————. 1980. *A City and Its Universities: Public Policy in Chicago, 1892–1919.* Chapel Hill: University of North Carolina Press.

District of Columbia. 1981. *A Living Downtown for Washington, D.C.: Planning Concepts.*

District of Columbia, Mayor's Downtown Plan Committee. 1982. *Downtown D.C.: Recommendations for the Downtown Plan.*

"Doherty Assails 'Planners' Using War to Destroy Free Enterprise." 1943. *Southern California Business* 5 (5): 1, 4.

Doucet, Michael, and John Weaver. 1991. *Housing the North American City.* Montreal: McGill University Press.

Downs, Anthony. 1970. *Urban Problems and Prospects.* Chicago: Markham.

Draper, Joan E. 1982. *Edward H. Bennett: Architect and City Planner, 1874–1954.* Chicago: Art Institute of Chicago.

————. 1989. "Introduction." *The Final Official Report of the Director of Works of the World's Columbian Exposition,* by Daniel H. Burnham, xi–xiii. New York: Garland Publishing, Inc.

Dreiser, Theodore. 1922. *A Book About Myself.* New York: Boni and Liveright.

Duany, Andres, and Elizabeth Plater-Zyberk. 1991. *Towns and Town-Making Principles.* New York: Rizzoli.

Easley, Gail. 1992. *Staying Inside the Lines: Urban Growth Boundaries.* Chicago: American Planning Association.

East, E. E. 1941. "Streets: The Circulatory System." In *Los Angeles: Preface to a Master Plan,* edited by George W. Robbins and L. Deming Tilton, 91–100. Los Angeles: Pacific Southwest Academy.

Ebner, Michael H. 1988. *Creating Chicago's North Shore: A Suburban History.* Chicago: University of Chicago Press.

Edel, Matthew, Elliott Sclar, and Daniel Luria. 1984. *Shaky Palaces: Homeownership and Social Mobility in Boston's Suburbanization.* New York: Columbia University Press.

Eisner, Simon, Arthur Gallion, and Stanley Eisner. 1993. *The Urban Pattern.* 6th ed. New York: Van Nostrand Reinhold.

Bibliography

Ellis, Cliff. 1990. "Visions of Urban Freeways, 1930–1970." Ph.D. diss., University of California, Berkeley.

Ellis, Russell, and Dana Cuff, eds. 1989. *Architects' People*. New York: Oxford University Press.

"Exhibit of Congestion." 1908. *Charities and the Commons* 19 (18 Jan.): 1399.

Fainstein, Susan S. 1991. "Promoting Economic Development: Urban Planning in the United States and Great Britain." *Journal of the American Planning Association* 57 (1): 22–33.

Fainstein, Susan S., Norman I. Fainstein, Richard Child Hill, Dennis Judd, and Michael Peter Smith, eds. 1983. *Restructuring the City: The Political Economy of Urban Redevelopment*. New York: Longman.

Fairbanks, Robert B. 1987. "Metropolitan Planning and Downtown Redevelopment: The Cincinnati and Dallas Experiences." *Planning Perspectives* 2 (Sept.): 237–53.

———. 1988. *Making Better Citizens: Housing Reform and the Community Development Strategy in Cincinnati, 1890–1960*. Urbana: University of Illinois Press.

———. 1990. "The Good Government Machine: The Citizens' Charter Association and Dallas Politics, 1930–1960." In *Essays on Sunbelt Cities and Recent Urban America*, edited by Robert B. Fairbanks and Kathleen Underwood. College Station, Tex.: Texas A&M University Press.

Fairbanks, Robert B., and Zane Miller. 1984. "The Martial Metropolis: Housing, Planning, and Race in Cincinnati, 1940–1955." In *The Martial Metropolis*, edited by Roger Lotchin, 191–222. New York: Praeger.

Fairfield, John D. 1985. "Neighborhood and Metropolis: The Origins of Modern Urban Planning, 1877–1935." Ph.D. diss., University of Rochester.

———. 1992. "Alienation and Social Control: The Chicago Sociologists and the Origins of Urban Planning." *Planning Perspectives* 7 (Oct.): 418–34.

Falk, Nicholas. 1986. "Baltimore and Lowell: Two American Approaches." *Built Environment* 12: 145–52.

Federal Housing Administration. 1938. *Circular No. 5: SUBDIVISION STANDARDS for the Insurance of Mortgages on Properties Located in Undeveloped Subdivisions*. Washington, D.C.: Government Printing Office.

Federal Works Agency. 1940. *First Annual Report: Federal Works Agency, 1940*. Washington, D.C.: Government Printing Office.

———. 1941. *Second Annual Report: Federal Works Agency, 1941*. Washington, D.C.: Government Printing Office.

———. 1945. *Sixth Annual Report: Federal Works Agency, 1945*. Washington, D.C.: Government Printing Office.

———. 1946. *Seventh Annual Report: Federal Works Agency, 1946*. Washington, D.C.: Government Printing Office.

Bibliography

————. 1947. *Eighth Annual Report: Federal Works Agency, 1947.* Washington, D.C.: Government Printing Office.

————. 1948. *Ninth Annual Report: Federal Works Agency, 1948.* Washington, D.C.: Government Printing Office.

Fein, Albert, ed. 1968. *Landscape into Cityscape: Frederick Law Olmsted's Plans for a Greater New York City.* Ithaca: Cornell University Press.

————. 1972a. *Frederick Law Olmsted and the American Environmental Tradition.* New York: George Braziller.

————. 1972b. *A Study of the Profession of Landscape Architecture: Technical Report.* Washington, D.C.: American Society of Landscape Architects.

Feiss, Carl. 1956. "Historic Town Keeping." *Journal of the Society of Architectural Historians* 15 (4): 2–6.

————. 1961. "Planning Absorbs Zoning." *Journal of the American Institute of Planners* 27: 121–26.

"Field Houses of Chicago." 1907. *Playground* 1: 49.

Finfer, L. A. 1974. "Leisure as Social Work in the Urban Community: The Progressive Recreation Movement, 1890–1920." Ph.D. diss., Michigan State University.

Fish, Gertrude Sipperly, ed. 1979. *The Story of Housing.* New York: Macmillan.

Fish, Virginia Kemp. 1985. "Hull House: Pioneer Research during its Creative Years." *Journal of the History of Sociology* 6: 33–54.

Fisher, Irving D. 1986. *Frederick Law Olmsted and the City Planning Movement in the United States.* Ann Arbor, Mich.: UMI Research Press.

Fishman, Robert. 1987. *Bourgeois Utopias: The Rise and Fall of Suburbia.* New York: Basic Books.

————. 1990. "America's New City: Megalopolis Unbound." *Wilson Quarterly* 14 (Winter): 25–45.

————. 1992. "The Regional Plan Transformation of the Industrial Metropolis." In *The Landscape of Modernity: Essays on New York City,* edited by David Ward and Olivier Zunz. New York: Russell Sage Foundation.

Fitch, James Marston. 1982. *Historic Preservation: Curatorial Management of the Built Environment.* New York: McGraw-Hill.

Flint, Barbara J. 1977. "Zoning and Residential Segregation: A Social and Physical History, 1910–1940." Ph.D. diss., University of Chicago.

Fogelson, Robert M. [1967] 1993. *The Fragmented Metropolis: Los Angeles, 1850–1930.* Berkeley: University of California Press.

Foglesong, Richard E. 1986. *Planning the Capitalist City: The Colonial Era to the 1920s.* Princeton, N.J.: Princeton University Press.

Foley, Donald L. 1952. "The Daily Movement of Population into Central Business Districts." *American Sociological Review* 17 (Oct.): 538–43.

Fondersmith, John. 1988. "Downtown 2040." *Futurist* 22 (Mar.–Apr.): 9–17.

Foner, Eric. 1970. *America's Black Past: A Reader in Afro-American History.* New York: Harper and Row.

Ford, George B. 1928. "Parks and Playfields. A Mathematical Method of Determining Their Location, Size, and Urgency." *American City* 38 (Apr.): 115–88.

————, ed. 1917. *City Planning Progress, 1917.* Washington, D.C.: American Institute of Architects.

Ford, Lawrence. 1992. "The Visions of the Builders: The Historic Evolution of the San Diego Cityscape." In *San Diego: An Introduction to the Region . . . of San Diego County.* 3d ed., edited by Philip Pryde, 185–203. Dubuque: Kendall/Hunt.

Foreman, Henry G. 1905. "Chicago's New Park Service." *Century* 69 (Feb.): 610–20.

Foster, Mark S. 1981. *From Streetcar to Superhighway: American City Planners and Urban Transportation, 1900–1940.* Philadelphia: Temple University Press.

Frampton, Kenneth. 1992. *Modern Architecture: A Critical History.* 3d ed. rev. and enl. London: Thames and Hudson.

Franklin, Jimmie Lewis. 1989. *Back to Birmingham: Richard Arrington, Jr. and His Times.* Tuscaloosa: University of Alabama Press.

Freeman, Allen. 1991. "Changing of the Guard." *Historic Preservation* (July/Aug.): 22–28.

Frieden, Bernard J. 1990. "Center City Transformed: Planners as Developers." *Journal of the American Planning Association* 56 (Autumn): 423–38.

Frieden, Bernard J., and Marshall Kaplan. 1975. *The Politics of Neglect: Urban Aid from Model Cities to Revenue Sharing.* Cambridge, Mass.: MIT Press.

Frieden, Bernard J., and Lynne Sagalyn. 1989. *Downtown, Inc.: How America Rebuilds Its Cities.* Cambridge, Mass.: MIT Press.

Friedmann, John R. P. 1955. *The Spatial Structure of Economic Development in the Tennessee Valley: A Study in Regional Planning.* Department of Geography Research Paper 39. Chicago: University of Chicago.

Friedmann, John, and Goetz Wolff. 1982. "World City Formation: An Agenda for Research and Action." *International Journal of Urban and Regional Research* 6 (Sept.): 309–43.

Friedrichs, Jurgen, and Allen Goodman. 1987. *The Changing Downtown: A Comparative Study of Baltimore and Hamburg.* New York: Walter de Gruyter.

Bibliography

Funigiello, Philip. 1978. *The Challenge to Urban Liberalism: Federal-City Relations during World War II.* Knoxville: University of Tennessee Press.

Gans, Herbert. 1962. *The Urban Villagers.* Glencoe, Ill.: The Free Press.

Garner, John, ed. 1987. *The Company Town: Architecture and Society in the Early Industrial Age.* Lexington: University Press of Kentucky.

————. 1991. "S. S. Beman and the Building of Pullman." In *The Midwest in American Architecture,* edited by John Garner, 230–49. Urbana: University of Illinois Press.

Garreau, Joel. [1988] 1991. *Edge City: Life on the New Frontier.* New York: Doubleday.

————. 1994. "Edge Cities in the '90s." Paper presented at "Americans in Motion: Virginia, the South, Mobility, and the American Dream," a symposium sponsored by the Virginia Historical Society, Richmond, Virginia.

Geddes, Norman Bel. 1940. *Magic Motorways.* New York: Random House.

Gelfand, Mark I. 1975. *A Nation of Cities: The Federal Government and Urban America, 1933–1965.* New York: Oxford University Press.

Gems, Gerald R. 1989. "Not Only a Game." *Chicago History* 18 (Summer): 4–21.

Gerckens, Laurence C. 1983. "Bettman of Cincinnati." In *The American Planner: Biographies and Recollections,* edited by Donald A. Krueckeberg. New York: Methuen.

Getis, Arthur, and Judith M. Getis. 1960. "Retail Store Spatial Affinities." *Urban Studies* 5: 317–32.

Gifford, Jonathan. 1983. "An Analysis of the Federal Role in the Planning, Design, and Deployment of Rural Roads, Toll Roads, and Urban Freeways." Ph.D. diss., University of California, Berkeley.

Gill, Brendan. 1990. "The Skyline: Battery Park City." *New Yorker* (20 Aug.).

Gillette, Howard Jr. 1983. "The Evolution of Neighborhood Planning: From the Progressive Era to the 1949 Housing Act." *Journal of Urban History* 9 (Aug.): 421–44.

————. 1985. "A National Workshop for Urban Policy: The Metropolitanization of Washington, 1946–1968." *Public Historian* 7 (Winter): 7–27.

————. 1990. "Rethinking American Urban History: New Directions for the Posturban Era." *Social Science History* 14 (Summer): 203–21.

Gillette, Howard Jr., and Zane L. Miller, eds. 1987. *American Urbanism: A Historiographical Review.* New York: Greenwood Press.

Gillette, John M. 1901. "The Culture Agencies of a Typical Manufacturing Group: South Chicago. Part 1." *American Journal of Sociology* 7 (July): 91–121.

Gittell, Marilyn, and Teresa Shtob. 1981. "Changing Women's Roles in Political Volunteerism and Reform of the City." In *Women and the*

Bibliography

American City, edited by Catharine R. Stimpson et al. Chicago: University of Chicago Press.

Goist, Park D. 1972. "Seeing Things Whole: A Consideration of Lewis Mumford." *Journal of the American Institute of Planners* 38 (Nov.): 379–91.

———. 1974. "Patrick Geddes and the City." *Journal of the American Institute of Planners* 40 (Jan.): 31–37.

Goldberger, Paul. 1988. "Public Space Gets a New Cachet in New York." *New York Times* (22 May), sec. H, p. 35.

Goldfield, David. 1980. "Urban Growth in the Old South." In *Rise of Modern Urban Planning, 1800–1914,* edited by Anthony Sutcliffe, 11–30. New York: St. Martin's Press.

———. 1987. *Promised Land: The South since 1945.* Arlington Heights, Ill.: Harlan Davidson.

———. 1993. "Black Political Power and Public Policy in the Urban South." In *Urban Policy in Twentieth-Century America,* edited by Arnold R. Hirsch and Raymond Mohl. New Brunswick, N.J.: Rutgers University Press.

Goldfield, David, and Blaine Brownell. 1979. *Urban America: From Downtown to No Town.* Boston, Mass.: Houghton Mifflin.

Goldmark, Josephine. 1953. *Impatient Crusader: Florence Kelley's Life Story.* Urbana: University of Illinois Press.

Golway, Terry. 1993. "Irked in Battery Park by 'Affordable Housing.'" *New York Observer* (3 Mar.), p. 1.

Gordon, Martin. 1981. "The Marines Have Landed and San Diego Is Well in Hand: Local Politics and Naval Base Development." *Journal of the West* 20 (Oct.): 43–50.

Gottdiener, Mark, and George Kephart. 1991. "The Multinucleated Metropolitan Region: A Comparative Analysis." In *Postsuburban California: The Transformation of Orange County since World War II,* edited by Rob Kling, Spencer Olin, and Mark Poster. Berkeley, Calif.: University of California Press.

Gould, Lewis, ed. 1974. *The Progressive Era.* Syracuse: Syracuse University Press.

Grabow, Stephen. 1975. "The Outsider in Retrospect: E. A. Gutkind." *Journal of the American Institute of Planners* 41 (May): 200–212.

Graham, Otis L. Jr. 1976. *Toward a Planned Society: From Roosevelt to Nixon.* New York: Oxford University Press.

Green, Philip P. Jr. 1955. "Is Zoning by Men Replacing Zoning by Law?" *Journal of the American Institute of Planners* 21: 82–87.

Greer, Scott. 1965. *Urban Renewal and American Cities: The Dilemma of Democratic Intervention.* New York: Bobbs-Merrill.

Bibliography

Grey, Arthur L., David L. Bonsteel, Gary H. Winkel, and Roger A. Parker. 1978. "People and Downtowns: Use, Attitudes, Settings." *Downtown Mall Annual and Urban Design Report* 4: 55–72.

Groth, Paul E. 1983. "Forbidden Housing: The Evolution and Exclusion of Hotels, Boarding Houses, Rooming Houses, and Lodging Houses in American Cities, 1880–1930." Ph.D. diss., University of California, Berkeley.

———. 1989. "Nonpeople: A Case Study of Public Architects and Impaired Social Vision." In *Architects' People,* edited by Russell Ellis and Dana Cuff, 213–38. New York: Oxford University Press.

———. 1994. *Living Downtown: The History of Residential Hotels in the United States.* Berkeley, Calif.: University of California Press.

Gruen, Victor. 1964. *The Heart of Our Cities.* New York: Simon and Schuster.

Gundlach, John H. Papers. 1888–1926. Missouri Historical Society Archives, St. Louis.

Gutman, Robert. 1988. *Architectural Practice: A Critical View.* Princeton: Princeton Architectural Press.

Haar, Charles. 1975. *Between the Idea and the Reality: A Short Study in the Origin, Fate, and Legacy of the Model Cities Program.* Boston: Little, Brown.

Haar, Charles M., and Jerold S. Kayden, eds. 1989. *Zoning and the American Dream: Promises Still to Keep.* Washington, D.C.: American Planning Association Press.

Hall, Peter. 1988. *Cities of Tomorrow: An Intellectual History of Urban Planning and Design in the Twentieth Century.* London: Basil Blackwell.

Halprin, Lawrence. 1966. *Freeways.* New York: Reinhold.

Halsey, Elizabeth. 1940. *Development of Public Recreation in Metropolitan Chicago.* Chicago: Chicago Recreation Commission.

Hammack, David C. 1982. *Power and Society: Greater New York at the Turn of the Century.* New York: Russell Sage Foundation.

———. 1988. "Comprehensive Planning before the Comprehensive Plan: A New Look at the Nineteenth-Century American City." In *Two Centuries of American Planning,* edited by Daniel Schaffer, 139–65. Baltimore: The Johns Hopkins University Press.

Hanchett, Thomas W. 1985a. "Charlotte: Suburban Development in the Textile and Trade Center of the Carolinas." In *Early Twentieth-Century Suburbs in North Carolina: Essays on History, Architecture, and Planning,* edited by Catherine Bishir and Lawrence Earley, 68–76. Raleigh: Division of Archives and History, North Carolina Department of Cultural Resources.

———. 1985b. "Earle Sumner Draper, City Planner of the New South." In *Early Twentieth-Century Suburbs in North Carolina: Essays on History, Archi-*

tecture, and Planning, edited by Catherine Bishir and Lawrence Earley, 78–79. Raleigh: Division of Archives and History, North Carolina Department of Cultural Resources.

———. 1993. "Sorting Out the New South City: Charlotte and Its Neighborhoods." Ph.D. diss., University of North Carolina.

Hancock, John. 1960. "John Nolen: The Background of a Pioneer Planner." *Journal of the American Institute of Planners* 26 (Nov.): 302–12.

———. 1964. "John Nolen and the American City Planning Movement: A History of Culture Change and Community Response, 1900–1940." Ph.D. diss., University of Pennsylvania.

———. 1991a. "John Nolan: New Towns in Florida." *New City* 1 (Fall): 68–87.

———. 1991b. "'And a Few Marines': Military Bases, City Growth, and Planning in San Diego." ACSP/AESOP International Congress, Oxford, United Kingdom.

Hanes, Arthur J. Papers. Manuscripts and Archives Division, Birmingham Public Library, Birmingham, Alabama.

Hardy, Dennis. 1991. *From Garden Cities to New Towns: Campaigning for Town and Country Planning, 1899–1946.* London: E. & F. N. Spons.

Hardy, Stephen. 1980. "Parks for the People: Reforming the Boston Park System, 1870–1915." *Journal of Sport History* 7 (Winter): 5–24.

Hargrove, Edwin C., and Paul K. Conkin, eds. 1983. *TVA: Fifty Years of Grass-Roots Bureaucracy.* Urbana: University of Illinois.

Harris, Chauncey D., and Edward L. Ullman. 1945. "The Nature of Cities." *Annals American Academy* 242 (Nov.): 7–17.

Harris, Richard. 1990. "Working-Class Home Ownership in the American Metropolis." *Journal of Urban History* 17/1 (Nov.): 46–69.

Hartman, Chester. 1979. Comment on "Neighborhood Revitalization and Displacement: A Review of the Evidence." *Journal of the American Planning Association* 45 (4): 488–91.

———. 1984. *The Transformation of San Francisco.* Totowa, N.J.: Rowman and Allenheld.

Hartman, George W. 1950. "The Central Business District: A Study in Urban Geography." *Economic Geography* 26 (Oct.): 237–44.

Harvey, David. 1989. *The Condition of Postmodernity: An Enquiry into the Origins of Cultural Change.* London: Basil Blackwell.

Hayden, Dolores. 1981. *The Grand Domestic Revolution: A History of Feminist Designs for American Homes, Neighborhoods, and Cities.* Cambridge, Mass.: MIT Press.

———. 1984. *Redesigning the American Dream: The Future of Housing, Work, and Family Life.* New York: W. W. Norton.

———. 1995. *The Power of Place*. Cambridge, Mass.: MIT Press.

Hays, Samuel. 1957. *The Response to Industrialism, 1885–1914*. Chicago: University of Chicago Press.

———. 1959. *Conservation and the Gospel of Efficiency: The Progressive Conservation Movement, 1890–1920*. Cambridge, Mass.: Harvard University Press.

Head, Franklin. 1893. "The Fair's Results to the City of Chicago." *Forum* 16: 526.

Head, Louis. 1925. *The Kessler City Plan for Dallas: A Review of the Plan and Progress of Its Accomplishments*. Dallas: Dallas Morning News.

———. n.d. "Shall Dallas Continue to 'Just Grow' As Topsy Did or Will You as a Citizen Have It Grow by Plan?" Undated Kessler Plan Association pamphlet.

Henderson, Charles. 1894. *A Catechism for Social Observation*. Chicago: University of Chicago.

Hendon, William, and Douglas Shaw. 1987. "The Arts and Urban Development." In *The Future of Winter Cities*, edited by Gary Gappert, 209–17. Beverly Hills, Calif.: Sage Publications.

Hennessey, Gregg. 1986. "George White Marston and Conservative Reform in San Diego." *Journal of San Diego History* 32 (4): 230–53.

Herman, Bernard L. 1992. *The Stolen House*. Charlottesville: University Press of Virginia.

Herrera, Philip. 1964. "Philadelphia: How Far Can Renewal Go?" *Architectural Forum* 121 (Aug.-Sept.): 181–92.

Hines, Thomas S. 1974. *Burnham of Chicago: Architect and Planner*. New York: Oxford University Press.

Hirsch, Arnold. 1983. *Making the Second Ghetto: Race and Housing in Chicago, 1940–1960*. New York: Cambridge University Press.

Hise, Greg. 1992. "The Roots of the Postwar Urban Region: Mass-Housing and Community Planning in California, 1920–1950." Ph.D. diss., University of California, Berkeley.

Hiss, Tony. 1990. "At Land's Edge, a Contentment of Light and Shape." *New York Times* (19 Oct.), sec. C, p. 1.

Hofstadter, Richard. 1979. *The Progressive Historians: Turner, Beard, Parrington*. Chicago: University of Chicago Press.

Hollomby, Edward. 1991. *Red House, Bexleyheath, 1859*. London: Architectural Design and Technical Press.

Holmes, L. C., and R. L. Pendleton. 1918. *Reconnaissance Soil Survey of the San Diego Region, California*. 2 vols. Washington, D.C.: U.S. Department of Agriculture.

Bibliography

Hoover, Dwight. 1990. "City Planning in Middletown, U.S.A.: Muncie, Indiana, 1920–1990." in *Proceedings of the Third National Conference on American Planning History,* 198–218. Hilliard, Ohio: Society for American City and Regional Planning History.

Horwood, Edgar, and Ronald R. Boyce. 1959. *Studies of the Central Business District and Urban Freeway Development.* Seattle: University of Washington Press.

Hosmer, Charles. 1965. *Presence of the Past.* New York: Putnam.

———. 1981. *Preservation Comes of Age.* Charlottesville, Va.: Preservation Press.

Housing Authority of the Birmingham District. 1962. *Annual Report for 1962.* Birmingham, Alabama.

Howard, John T. 1944. "An Urban Rehabilitation Program for Cleveland." *Journal of the American Institute of Planners* 10 (Autumn): 18–23.

Hoyt, Homer. 1939. *The Structure and Growth of Residential Neighborhoods in American Cities.* Washington, D.C.: Government Printing Office.

———. 1943a. "Preparing for Post-War Competition Among Cities." *American City* 59 (3): 85.

———. 1943b. "The Structure of American Cities in the Post-War Era." *American Journal of Sociology* 48 (Jan.): 475–81.

Hubbard, Henry V. 1914. "The Size and Distribution of Playgrounds." *Proceedings, National Conference on City Planning,* 265–305. Toronto.

Hubbard, Theodora Kimball, and Henry Vincent Hubbard. 1929. *Our Cities To-day and Tomorrow: A Survey of Planning and Zoning Progress in the United States.* Cambridge, Mass.: Harvard University Press.

Huggins, Koleen Alice Haire. 1967. "The Evolution of City and Regional Planning in North Carolina, 1900–1950." Ph.D. diss., Duke University.

Hull-House Maps and Papers. 1895. New York: T. Y. Crowell.

Hurd, Richard M. 1924. *Principles of City Land Values.* New York: Record and Guide.

Industrial Properties Corporation. 1931. "Under the Skyline of Dallas." In *Trinity Industrial District.* Dallas, Tex.

Ireland, Robert E. 1991. "Prison Reform, Road Building, and Southern Progressivism: Joseph Hyde Pratt and the Campaign for 'Good Roads and Good Men.'" *North Carolina Historical Review* 68 (2): 125–57.

Issel, William, and Robert W. Cherny. 1986. *San Francisco, 1865–1932: Politics, Power, and Urban Development.* Berkeley: University of California Press.

———. 1991. "Urban Arsenals: War Housing and Social Change in Richmond and Oakland, California, 1941–1945." *Pacific Historical Review* 60 (Aug.): 283–308.

Bibliography

JA/WRT Associates. 1984. *Oakland Central District Development Program: Initial Planning and Management Concepts.* Oakland.

Jackson, Anthony. 1976. *A Place Called Home: A History of Low Income Housing in America.* Cambridge, Mass.: MIT Press.

Jackson, John Brinckerhoff. 1980a. "By Way of Conclusion: How to Study the Landscape." In *The Necessity for Ruins,* edited by J. B. Jackson. Amherst: University of Massachusetts Press.

———. 1980b. "The Sunbelt City: The Modern City, the Strip, and the Civic Center." In *The Southern Landscape Tradition in Texas,* edited by J. B. Jackson, 25–35. Fort Worth: Amon Carter Museum.

Jackson, Kenneth T. 1980. "Race, Ethnicity, and Real Estate Appraisal: The Home Owners Loan Corporation and the Federal Housing Administration." *Journal of Urban History* 6 (4): 419–52.

———. 1985. *Crabgrass Frontier: The Suburbanization of the United States.* New York: Oxford University Press.

Jacobs, Allan B. 1980. *Making City Planning Work.* Washington, D.C.: American Planning Association.

Jacobs, Barry G. 1982. *Guide to Federal Housing Programs.* Washington, D.C.: Bureau of National Affairs.

Jacobs, Jane. 1961. *The Death and Life of Great American Cities.* New York: Random House.

James, Harlean. 1926. *Land Planning in the United States for the City, State, and Nation.* New York: Macmillan.

Jameson, Frederick. 1984. "Postmodernism, or the Cultural Logic of Late Capitalism." *New Left Review* 146 (July–Aug.): 53–92.

Jamison, Judith N. 1948. *Coordinated Public Planning in the Los Angeles Region: A Bibliography.* Los Angeles: University of Los Angeles, Bureau of Governmental Research Studies in Local Government.

Jefferson County Board of Health. 1950. *Health as an Indication of Housing Needs in Birmingham, Alabama.* Birmingham, Alabama.

Jencks, Charles. 1987. *Post-Modernism: The New Classicism in Art and Architecture.* New York: Rizzoli.

Johnson, David A. 1988. "Regional Planning for the Great American Metropolis: New York between the World Wars." In *Two Centuries of American Planning,* edited by Daniel Schaffer, 167–96. Baltimore: The Johns Hopkins University Press.

Johnson, David A., and Daniel Schaffer. 1985. "Learning from the Past—The History of Planning: Introduction." *Journal of the American Planning Association* 51 (Spring): 131–33.

Johnson, Donald Leslie. 1974. "Walter Burley Griffin: An Expatriate Planner at Canberra." *Journal of the American Institute of Planners* 39 (Sept.): 326–36.

Johnson, Kirk. 1991. "Take our Poor, Angry Hartford Tells Suburbs." *New York Times* (12 Feb.), pp. 1, 85.

Johnson, Marilynn S. 1990. "The Western Front: World War II and the Transformation of the West Coast Urban Life." Ph.D. diss., New York University.

———. 1991. "Urban Arsenals: War Housing and Social Change in Richmond and Oakland, California, 1941–1945." *Pacific Historical Review* 60: 283–308.

———. Forthcoming. "Mobilizing the Home Front: Labor and Politics in Oakland, 1943–1951." *Journal of Urban History.*

Johnson, Otis. 1990. Presentation to Armstrong State College Class. Scarbrough House, June 19, Savannah, Ga.

Johnston, Norman J. 1973. "Harland Bartholomew: Precedent for the Profession." *Journal of the American Institute of Planners* 40 (Mar.): 115–24.

Jolley, Harley. 1969. *The Blueridge Parkway.* Knoxville: University of Tennessee Press.

Jonassen, Christen T. 1955. *The Shopping Center versus Downtown: A Motivation Research on Shopping Habits and Attitudes in Three Cities.* Columbus: Ohio State University, Bureau of Business Research.

Jones, D. G. 1954. "Some Early Works of the L.C.C. Architects Department." *The Architectural Association Journal* 70 (786): 95–105.

Jones, David W. Jr. 1989. "California's Freeway System in Historical Perspective." Ms., Institute of Transportation Studies, University of California at Berkeley.

Judd, Dennis R. 1988. *The Politics of American Cities: Private Power and Public Policy.* 2d ed. Glenview, Ill.: Scott, Foresman.

Justement, Louis. 1946. *New Cities for Old: City Building in Terms of Space, Time, and Money.* New York: McGraw-Hill.

Kahn, Judd. 1979. *Imperial San Francisco: Politics and Planning in an American City, 1897–1906.* Lincoln: University of Nebraska Press.

Kalfus, Melvin. 1990. *Frederick Law Olmsted: The Passion of a Public Artist.* New York: New York University Press.

Kantor, Harvey A. 1974. "Benjamin C. Marsh and the Fight over Population Congestion." *Journal of the American Institute of Planners* 40 (Nov.): 422–29.

Keating, Ann Durkin. 1988. *Building Chicago: Suburban Developers and the Creation of a Divided Metropolis.* Columbus: Ohio State University Press.

Kelbaugh, Douglas, ed. 1989. *The Pedestrian Pocket Book: A New Suburban Design Strategy.* Princeton: Princeton Architectural Press.

Kellett, John R. 1969. *The Impact of Railways on Victorian Cities.* London: Routledge and Kegan Paul.

Bibliography

Kellogg, Paul U. 1912. "The Spread of the Survey Idea." *Proceedings of the Academy of Political Science* 2 (July): 1–2.

Kelly, John Barry II. 1970. "Challenging Highways: Widening the Access to Judicial Review." *Catholic University Law Review* 20 (1): 143–56.

Kemp, Louis Ward. 1986. "Aesthetes and Engineers: The Occupational Ideology of Highway Design." *Technology and Culture* 27 (Oct.): 759–97.

Kent, T. L. Jr. 1948. "Planning Renaissance in San Francisco." *Journal of the American Institute of Planners* 14 (1): 29–32.

Kessler, George. 1912. *A City Plan for Dallas.* Dallas: Dallas Park Board.

———. 1913. Unidentified ms. (26 March). In Kessler Papers, 1893–1923. Missouri Historical Society Archives, St. Louis.

Kettner, William. 1923. *Why It Was Done and How.* San Diego: Frye and Smith.

Keyes, Lucille Sheppard. 1951. *Federal Control of Entry into Air Transportation.* Cambridge, Mass.: Harvard University Press.

Kincaid, H. Evert. 1945. "The Chicago Comprehensive City Plan." *Journal of the American Institute of Planners* 11 (Autumn): 23–28.

King, Edith S., and Frederick A. King. 1916. *Pathfinder Social Survey of San Diego: Report of Limited Investigation of Social Conditions in San Diego, California.* San Diego: Women's Club.

Kinnaird, Lawrence. 1966. *History of the Greater San Francisco Bay Region.* Vol. 2. New York: Lewis Historical Publishing Company.

Kirschner, Don S. 1986. *The Paradox of Professionalism: Reform and Public Service in Urban America, 1900–1940.* New York: Greenwood.

Klaus, Susan. 1988. "'Intelligent and Comprehensive Planning of a Common Sense Kind': Frederick Law Olmsted, Junior, and the Emergence of Comprehensive Planning in America, 1900–1920." Master's thesis, The George Washington University.

———. 1991. "Efficiency, Economy, Beauty: The City Planning Reports of Frederick Law Olmsted, Jr., 1905–1915." *Journal of the American Planning Association* 57 (Autumn): 456–70.

Kling, Rob, Spencer Olin, and Mark Poster, eds. 1991. *Postsuburban California: The Transformation of Orange County since World War II.* Berkeley: University of California Press.

Knapp, Richard. 1971. "Play for America: The National Recreation Association, 1906–1950." Ph.D. diss., Duke University.

Kolko, Gabriel, 1963. *The Triumph of Conservatism: A Reinterpretation of American History, 1900–1916.* New York: Free Press.

Konvitz, Josef W., Mark H. Rose, and Joel A. Tarr. 1990. "Technology and the City." *Technology and Culture* 31: 284–94.

Kostof, Spiro. 1987. *America by Design.* New York: Oxford University Press.

Kratt, Mary Norton, and Thomas W. Hanchett. 1986. *Legacy: The Myers Park Story.* Charlotte, N.C.: Myers Park Foundation.

Kreditor, Alan. 1990. "The Neglect of Urban Design in the American Academic Succession." *Journal of Planning Education and Research* 9 (3): 155–63.

Krieg, Joann P., ed. 1989. *Robert Moses: Single-Minded Genius.* Interlaken, N.Y.: Heart of the Lakes.

Krueckeberg, Donald, ed. 1983a. *The American Planner: Biographies and Recollections.* New York: Methuen.

———, ed. 1983b. *Introduction to Planning History in the United States.* New Brunswick, N.J.: Rutgers University Center for Urban Policy Research.

———. 1985. "The Tuition of American Planning: From Dependence Toward Self-Reliance." *Town Planning Review* 56 (4): 421–44.

Krumholz, Norman, and John Forester. 1990. *Making Equity Planning Work: Leadership in the Public Sector.* Philadelphia: Temple University Press.

Krumholz, Norman, and W. Dennis Keating. 1991. "Downtown Plans of the 1980s: The Case for More Equity in the 1990s." *Journal of the American Planning Association* 57 (Spring): 136–52.

Kyle, John H. 1958. *The Building of the T.V.A.: An Illustrated History.* Baton Rouge: Louisiana State University.

Lamar, Martha, Alan Mallach, and John N. Payne. 1989. Mount Laurel at Work: Affordable Housing in New Jersey, 1983–1988." *Rutgers Law Review* 41 (4): 1197–1277.

LaMonte, Edward S. 1976. "Politics and Welfare in Birmingham, 1900–1974." Ph.D. diss., University of Chicago.

Langdon, Philip. 1988. "A Good Place to Live." *Atlantic Monthly* (March): 38–60.

Larson, Magali S. 1977. *The Rise of Professionalism: A Sociological Analysis.* Berkeley: University of California Press.

———. 1983. "Emblem and Exception: The Historical Definition of the Architect's Professional Role." In *Professionals and Urban Form,* edited by Judith R. Blau, Mark La Gory, and John S. Pipkin, 49–86. Albany: State University of New York Press.

Laska, Shirley B., and Daphne Spain. 1980. *Back to the City: Issues in Neighborhood Renovation.* New York: Pergamon Press.

Lassar, Terry Jill, ed. 1990. *City Deal Making.* Washington: Urban Land Institute.

Lassister, Robert Jr. 1946. "Before the Civil Aeronautics Board, in the Matter of Boston-New York-Atlanta-New Orleans Case, Docket No. 730 et. al.: Brief of the City of Charlotte, North Carolina, Before the

Examiners." Charlotte: Cochran, McCleghan and Lassister, attorneys. Bound pamphlet in "Douglas Airport" file of the Carolina Room of the Public Library of Charlotte and Mechlenburg County.

Lathrop, William H. Jr. 1971. "The San Francisco Freeway Revolt." *Transportation Engineering Journal of the American Society of Civil Engineers* 97 (TE1): 133–44.

Lazare, Daniel. 1991. "Collapse of a City: Growth and Decay in Camden, New Jersey." *Dissent* 38 (Spring): 267–75.

Lee, Antoinette. 1992. "Cultural Diversity and Historic Preservation." *CRM Bulletin* 15 (7): 1–3.

Lee, Joseph. 1903. "Boston's Playground System." *New England Magazine* 27: 521–36.

Lejeune, Jean-François. 1991. "The Airplane Indicts." *New City* 1:4–5.

Leland, Arthur, and Lorna Higbee Leland. 1913. *Playground Technique and Playcraft*. Vol. 1. 2d ed. New York: Doubleday Page.

Lepawsky, Albert. 1949. *State Planning and Economic Development in the South.* Kingsport, Tenn.: Committee of the South, National Planning Association.

Levin, Melvin R. 1987. *Planning in Government.* Chicago: Planner's Press.

Levin, Melvin R., and Norman A. Abend. 1971. *Bureaucrats in Collision: Case Studies in Area Transportation Planning.* Cambridge, Mass.: MIT Press.

Levine, Robert G. 1970. *The Poor Ye Need Not Have With You: Lessons from the War on Poverty.* Cambridge, Mass.: MIT Press.

Levitt, Rachelle, ed. 1987. *Cities Reborn.* Washington, D.C.: Urban Land Institute.

Lewis, Peirce. 1976. "New Orleans—The Making of an Urban Landscape." In *Contemporary Metropolitan America.* Vol. 2, edited by John S. Adams. Cambridge, Mass.: Ballinger.

———. 1985. "Axioms for Reading the Landscape." In *Material Culture Studies in America,* edited by Thomas J. Schlereth, 174–82. Nashville: American Association for State and Local History.

Link, Arthur S., and Richard L. McCormick. 1983. *Progressivism.* Arlington Heights, Ill.: Harlan Davidson.

Lippmann, Walter. 1914. *Drift and Mastery.* London: T. F. Unwin.

Litchfield, Electus D. 1919. "Yorkship Village." *American Review of Reviews* 6: 599–602.

———. 1922. "Model Village That Is: The Story of Yorkship Village, Planned and Completed in Less than Two Years." *House Beautiful* 51: 533–36.

———. 1939. "Yorkship Village in 1917 and 1939." *American City* 54: 42–43.

Logan, John R., and Harvey L. Molotch. 1987. *Urban Fortunes: The Political Economy of Place.* Berkeley: University of California Press.

Long, David. 1991. "Participatory Planning in the San Francisco Bay Area." Paper presented to the Fourth National Conference on American Planning History/Fifth International Conference of the Planning History Group, Richmond, Virginia, Nov. 8.

Long Beach City Planning Commission. 1946. *Planning Progress, 1944–46.* Long Beach, Calif.

Los Angeles Chamber of Commerce. 1941. *Southern California Business,* n.s. 1.

Los Angeles City Planning Commission. 1944–50. *Accomplishments.* Los Angeles.

Los Angeles County Regional Planning Commission. 1945a. *Annual Report, 1944–45.* Los Angeles.

———. 1945b. *Population and Dwelling Units in the North County Area of Los Angeles County.* 16. Los Angeles: Population Research Section.

———. 1945c. *Master Plan.* Los Angeles.

Lotchin, Roger W. 1979a. "The Darwinian City: The Politics of Urbanization in San Francisco between the World Wars." *Pacific Historical Review* 58 (Aug.): 357–81.

———. 1979b. "The Metropolitan Military Complex in Comparative Perspective: San Francisco, Los Angeles, and San Diego." *Journal of the West* 18 (July): 19–30.

———, ed. 1984. *The Martial Metropolis: U.S. Cities in War and Peace.* New York: Praeger.

———. 1992. *Fortress California, 1910–1961: From Warfare to Welfare.* New York: Oxford University Press.

Lowenthal, David. 1985. *The Past Is a Foreign Country.* Cambridge: Cambridge University Press.

Lubove, Roy. 1960. "Homes and 'A Few Well Placed Fruit Trees': An Object Lesson in Federal Housing." *Social Research* 27: 468–86.

———. 1962. *The Progressives and the Slums: Tenement House Reform in New York City, 1890–1917.* Pittsburgh: University of Pittsburgh Press.

———. 1963. *Community Planning in the 1920's.* Pittsburgh: University of Pittsburgh Press.

Ludlow, William H. 1945. "Land Values and Density Standards in Urban Redevelopment." *Journal of the American Institute of Planners* 11 (Autumn): 5–10.

Lukas, J. Anthony. 1985. *Common Ground: A Turbulent Decade in the Lives of Three American Families.* New York: Knopf.

Lynch, Kevin. 1960. *The Image of the City.* Cambridge, Mass.: MIT Press.

———. 1981. *Good City Form.* Cambridge, Mass.: MIT Press.

Makielski, S. J. Jr. 1966. *The Politics of Zoning.* New York: Columbia University Press.

Bibliography

Mandelbaum, Seymour J. 1985. "Historians and Planners: The Construction of Pasts and Futures." *Journal of the American Planning Association* 52 (Spring): 185–88.

———. 1990. "Reading Plans." *Journal of the American Planning Association* 56 (Summer): 350–56.

Marcuse, Peter. 1980. "Housing in Early City Planning." *Journal of Urban History* 6 (2): 153–76.

Marlow, Fred. 1981. "Memoirs and Perceptions." Unpublished memoir in possession of the Marlow family, Los Angeles.

Marris, Peter. 1975. *Loss and Change.* London: Routledge and Kegan Paul.

Marsden, Gerald. 1961. "Philanthropy and the Boston Playground Movement, 1885–1907." *Social Service Review* 35 (Mar.): 48–58.

Marsh, Benjamin C. 1953. *Lobbyist for the People: A Record of Fifty Years.* Washington, D.C.: Public Affairs Press.

Marsh, Margaret S. 1988. "Reconsidering the Suburbs: An Exploration of Suburban Historiography." *Pennsylvania Magazine of History and Biography* 112 (Oct.): 579–605.

Marston, Mary, ed. 1956. *George White Marston: A Family Chronicle.* 2 vols. Los Angeles: Ward Ritchie Press.

Martin, Roscoe C. 1970. *The Cities and the Federal System.* New York: Atherton Press.

Martinson, Tom. 1990. "The Persistence of Vision: A Century of Civic Progress in St. Louis." *Places* 6 (4): 22–33.

Mashaw, Jerry L. 1973. "The Legal Structure of Frustration: Alternative Strategies for Public Choice Concerning Federally Aided Highway Construction." *University of Pennsylvania Law Review* 122 (1): 1–29.

Matlack, Carol. 1979. "Savannah Landmark: A New Type of Landlord." *American Preservation* 2 (3): 16.

Matthews, Fred H. 1977. *Quest for an American Sociology: Robert E. Park and the Chicago School of Sociology.* Montreal: McGill-Queens University Press.

May, Charles C. 1918. "Yorkship Village; a Development for the New York Shipbuilding Corporation, Camden, N.J.; Electus Litchfield, Architect." *Architectural Forum* 28 (June): 205–10.

Maynard, Crosby, ed. 1962. *Flight Plan for Tomorrow: The Douglas Story—A Condensed History.* Santa Monica: Douglas Aircraft.

McArthur, Benjamin. 1975. "The Chicago Playground Movement: A Neglected Feature of Social Justice." *Social Service Review* 4 (Sept.): 376–95.

McCarthy, Michael P. 1972. "Politics and the Parks. Chicago Businessmen and the Recreation Movement." *Journal of the Illinois State Historical Society* 65: 158–72.

Bibliography

McCaskey, Thomas G. 1965. *The McCaskey Report: Savannah, Georgia, as a Travel Destination.* Savannah, Ga: Historic Savannah Foundation, and Savannah Area Chamber of Commerce.

McConachie, Scot. 1976. "The Big Cinch: A Business Elite in the Life of a City, St. Louis, 1895–1915." Ph.D. diss., Washington University.

McDermott, John Francis, ed. 1952. *The Early Histories of St. Louis.* St. Louis, Mo.: St. Louis Historical Documents Foundation.

McDonald, Terrence J. 1986. *The Parameters of Urban Fiscal Policy: Socioeconomic Change and Political Culture in San Francisco, 1860–1906.* Berkeley: University of California Press.

McDonogh, Gary. 1988. "Ethnicity, Urbanization, and Historical Consciousness in Savannah." In *Shades of the Sunbelt,* edited by Randall Miller and George Pozzetta. New York: Greenwood Press.

McGrew, Clarence A. 1922. *City of San Diego and San Diego County; Birthplace of California.* 2 vols. Chicago: American Historical Society.

McHugh, F. Dodd. 1946. "Broad Specifications for Urban Redevelopment." *Journal of the American Institute of Planners* 12 (Winter): 17–29.

McKeever, J. Ross. 1955. "A View of the Year." *Urban Land* 14 (Jan.): 1–5.

McKelvey, Blake. 1968. *The Emergence of Metropolitan America, 1915–66.* New Brunswick, N.J.: Rutgers University Press.

McNeill, William. 1982. *The Pursuit of Power: Technology, Armed Force, and Society since* A.D. 1000. Chicago: University of Chicago Press.

McNulty, Robert. 1985. *The Economics of Amenity: Community Futures and Qualify of Life: A Policy Guide to Urban Economic Development.* Washington, D.C.: Partners for Livable Places.

McNutt, George L. 1904. "Chicago's Ten Million Dollar Experiment in Social Redemption." *Independent* 57 (Sept.): 612–17.

McShane, Clay. 1988. "Urban Pathways: The Street and Highway, 1900–1940." In *Technology and the Rise of the Networked City in Europe and America,* edited by Joel A. Tarr and Gabriel Dupuy, 67–97. Philadelphia: Temple University Press.

Meikle, Jeffrey L. 1979. *Twentieth Century Limited: Industrial Design in America, 1925–1930.* Philadelphia: Temple University Press.

Meinig, Donald William. 1979. "The Beholding Eye: Ten Versions of the Same Scene." In *The Interpretation of Ordinary Landscapes: Geographical Essays,* edited by Donald W. Meinig, 33–48. New York: Oxford University Press.

Merkel, Jayne. 1990. "Mid-Century Planning in Cincinnati: The 1948 Cincinnati Metropolitan Master Plan and the 1964 Plan for Downtown Cincinnati." In *Proceedings of the Third National Conference on American*

Planning History, 452–78. Hilliard, Ohio: Society for American City and Regional Planning History.

Mero, Everett B., ed. 1908–9. *American Playgrounds: Their Construction, Equipment, Maintenance, and Utility.* New York: Baker and Taylor.

Merrill, Francis E. 1948. *Social Problems on the Home Front: A Study of War-time Influences.* New York: Harper.

Miller, Max. 1940. *Harbor of the Sun.* New York: Doubleday, Doran.

Miller, Randall M., and George E. Pozzetta, eds. 1988. *Shades of the Sunbelt: Essays in Ethnicity, Race, and the Urban South.* New York: Greenwood Press.

Miller, Richard A. 1959. "Expressway Blight." *Architectural Forum* 111 (Oct.): 159–63.

Miller, Zane L. 1981. *Suburb: Neighborhood and Community in Forest Park, Ohio, 1935–1976.* Knoxville: University of Tennessee Press.

Milwaukee Department of City Development. 1985. *Downtown Goals and Policies.* Milwaukee.

Mohl, Raymond A. 1990. "On the Edge: Blacks and Hispanics in Metropolitan Miami since 1959." *Florida Historical Quarterly* 69 (July): 37–56.

———. 1993. "Race and Space in the Modern City: Interstate-95 and the Black Community in Miami." In *Urban Policy in Twentieth-Century America,* edited by Arnold R. Hirsch and Raymond A. Mohl, 100–158. New Brunswick, N.J.: Rutgers University Press.

Mollenkopf, John N. 1983. *The Contested City.* Princeton: Princeton University Press.

Mollenkopf, John N., and Manuel Castells, eds. 1991. *Dual City: Restructuring New York.* New York: Russell Sage Foundation.

Monchow, Helen. 1928. *The Use of Deed Restrictions in Subdivision Development.* Chicago: Institute for Research in Land Economics and Public Utilities.

Monkkonen, Eric. 1988. *America Becomes Urban: The Development of U.S. Cities and Towns, 1780–1980.* Berkeley: University of California Press.

Montgomery, Roger. 1965. "Improving the Design Process in Urban Renewal." *Journal of the American Institute of Planners* 31 (Feb.): 11.

———. 1969. "Spoons in the Morning, Cities in the Afternoon." *Landscape* 18 (2): 32–38.

Moore, Harry E., and Howard W. Odum. 1938. *American Regionalism: A Cultural-Historical Approach to National Integration.* New York: H. Holt.

Morgan, Ivor P. 1981. "Government and the Industry's Early Development." In *Airline Deregulation: The Early Experience,* edited by John R. Meyer and Clinton V. Oster Jr., 13–24. Boston: Auburn House.

Morgan, James W. Papers. Department of Archives and Manuscripts, Birmingham Public Library, Birmingham, Ala.

Bibliography

Morris, William. [1890] 1962. *News from Nowhere.* New York: Penguin.

Morton, Arthur L. 1984. *The Political Writings of William Morris.* London: Lawrence and Wishart.

Moses, Robert. 1943. "Parks, Parkways, Express Arteries, and Related Plans for New York City after the War." *American City* 58 (Dec.).

Mott, George F. Jr. 1932. *San Diego—Politically Speaking.* San Diego: Mott.

Moulton, Robert H. 1918. "Overnight Towns for War Workers." *Bellman* 25: 403–7.

Muller, Edward K., and John F. Bauman. 1993. "The Olmsteds in Pittsburgh (Part I): Landscaping the Private City." *Pittsburgh History* 76 (Fall): 122–40.

Muller, Peter. 1981. *Contemporary Suburban America.* Englewood Cliffs, N.J.: Prentice-Hall.

Mumford, Lewis. 1958. "The Highway and the City." *Architectural Record* 123 (4): 179–86.

———. 1961. *The City in History.* New York: Harcourt, Brace, & World.

Muncy, Robyn. 1991. *Creating a Female Dominion in American Reform, 1890–1935.* New York: Oxford University Press.

Muraskin, Jack. 1968. "St. Louis Municipal Reform in the 1890s: A Study in Failure." *Bulletin of the Missouri Historical Society* 25: 38–49.

Murphy, Raymond, and James E. Vance Jr. 1954. "Delimiting the CBD." *Economic Geography* 30 (July): 189–222.

Murphy, Raymond, James E. Vance Jr., and Bart Epstein. 1955. "Internal Structure of the CBD." *Economic Geography* 31 (Jan.): 18–46.

Myhra, David. 1974. "Rexford Guy Tugwell: Initiator of America's Greenbelt New Towns, 1935 to 1936." *Journal of the American Institute of Planners* 40 (May): 176–88.

Nairn, Ian. 1965. *The American Landscape: A Critical View.* New York: Random House.

Nash, Gerald D. 1977. *The American West in the Twentieth Century: A Short History of an Urban Oasis.* Albuquerque: University of New Mexico Press.

———. 1985a. *The American West Transformed: The Impact of the Second World War.* Bloomington: Indiana University Press.

———. 1985b. "Planning for the Postwar City: The Urban West in World War II." *Arizona and the West* 27 (Summer): 99–111.

———. 1990. *World War II and the West: Reshaping the Economy.* Lincoln: University of Nebraska Press.

Nash, Jay N. 1928. *The Organization and Administration of Playgrounds and Recreation.* New York: A. S. Barnes.

Bibliography

Nash, William W. 1959. *Residential Rehabilitation: Private Profits and Public Purposes.* New York: McGraw-Hill.

National Association of Real Estate Boards. 1952. *A Primer of Rehabilitation under Local Law Enforcement.* Washington, D.C.: National Association of Real Estate Boards, Committee on Rehabilitation.

"National Conference on City Planning." 1909. *Charities and the Commons* 22 (9): 299–301.

National Conference on City Planning (NCCP). 1909, 1915, 1916, 1921, 1926, 1927, 1941. *Proceedings.* Washington, D.C.

———. 1909. *Proceedings of the First National Conference on City Planning.* Facsimile edition. Chicago, Ill.: American Society of Planning Officials.

National Conference on Planning. 1953, 1954, 1955, 1960, 1963, 1964. *Proceedings of the National Planning Conference.* Chicago: American Society of Planning Officials.

National Housing Agency. 1944. *Second Annual Report of the National Housing Agency: January 1 to December 31, 1943.* Washington, D.C.: Government Printing Office.

———. 1945. *Third Annual Report of the National Housing Agency: January 1 to December 31, 1944.* Washington, D.C.: Government Printing Office.

———. 1946. *Fourth Annual Report of the National Housing Agency: January 1 to December 31, 1945.* Washington, D.C.: Government Printing Office.

National Interregional Highway Committee. 1944. *Interregional Highways.* 78th Cong., 2d sess., H. Doc. 379. Washington, D.C.: Government Printing Office.

National Resources Committee, Research Committee on Urbanism. 1939. *Urban Planning and Land Policies.* Vol. 2. Washington, D.C.: Government Printing Office.

Needleman, Martin, and Carolyn Needleman. 1974. *Guerrillas in the Bureaucracy: The Community Planning Experiment in the United States.* New York: Wiley.

Nef, John U. 1952. *War and Human Progress: An Essay on the Rise of Industrial Civilization.* Cambridge, Mass.: Harvard University Press.

The New City: Foundations. 1991. Miami: University of Miami School of Architecture.

New York City Planning Commission. 1969. *The Plan for New York City.* New York: Department of City Planning.

Newton, Norman. 1971. *Design on the Land: The Development of Landscape Architecture.* Cambridge, Mass.: Harvard University Press, Belknap Press.

Nichols, Frederick Doveton. 1957. *The Early Architecture of Georgia.* Chapel Hill: University of North Carolina Press.

Nolen, John. 1905–37. Diary. Annual volumes in possession of Nolen family.

———. 1907. *Remodeling Roanoke: Report to the Committee on Civic Improvement.* Roanoke: Stone Printing and Manufacturing.

———. 1908. *San Diego: A Comprehensive Plan for Its Improvement.* Boston: Geo. H. Ellis.

———. 1912. *Replanning Small Cities: Six Typical Studies.* New York: B. W. Huebsch.

———. 1926. *City Plan for San Diego, California.* San Diego: City of San Diego.

———. 1927. *New Towns for Old.* Boston: Marshall Jones.

———. 1937–38. "A Selected List of Office Projects." In Nolen Papers, Olin Library, Cornell University, Ithaca, New York.

———. n.d. Marston folder, Project folders 52 and 299 (San Diego). In Nolen Papers, Olin Library, Cornell University, Ithaca, New York.

———. Papers. Department of Manuscripts and Archives, Olin Library, Cornell University, Ithaca, New York.

North American Aviation. 1945. "A Brief History of Operations Immediately Prior to and during WWII." Los Angeles.

Oakland, City of. 1966. *Central District Plan.* Oakland.

Oakland Postwar Planning Committee. 1945. "Oakland's Formula for the Future." Oakland.

O'Connell, James C. 1991. "The Role of Marketing in Urban Plans: The Case of Springfield, Massachusetts." Paper presented at Fourth National Conference on American Planning History, Richmond, Va.

O'Connor, Carol. 1983. *A Sort of Utopia: Scarsdale, 1891–1981.* Albany: State University of New York Press.

Odum, Howard. 1936. *Southern Regions of the United States.* Chapel Hill, N.C.: University of North Carolina Press.

Olmsted, Frederick Law. [1870] 1970. *Public Parks and the Enlargement of Towns.* New York: Arno Press.

Olmsted, Frederick Law, et al. [1871] 1967. "Report to the Staten Island Improvement Commission of a Preliminary Scheme of Improvements." In *Landscape into Cityscape: Frederick Law Olmsted's Plans for a Greater New York City,* edited by Albert Fein. Ithaca: Cornell University Press.

Olmsted, Frederick Law, and John Charles Olmsted. 1888. *The Projected Park and Parkway of the South Side of Buffalo.* Buffalo.

Olmsted, Frederick Law [Jr.]. 1908. *Report of the Committee on Improving and Beautifying Utica.* Utica: Utica Chamber of Commerce.

———. 1910a. *The Improvement of Boulder, Colorado.* Boulder: Boulder City Improvement Association.

———. 1910b. "Street-Traffic Studies." *Landscape Architecture* 1 (Oct.): 1–8.

Bibliography

————. 1911a. "Address to American Civic League." In "City Planning in Practice." *Municipal Journal and Engineer* 30 (Jan.): 124–25.

————. 1911b. *Pittsburgh: Main Thoroughfares and the Down Town District.* Pittsburgh: Pittsburgh Civic Commission.

————. 1913a. "How to Organize a City Planning Campaign." *American City* 9 (Oct.): 305–9.

————. 1913b. *Proposed Improvements for Newport.* Newport: Newport Improvement Association.

————. 1916. "Introduction." In *City Planning: A Series of Papers Presenting the Essential Elements of a City Plan,* edited by John Nolen. New York: D. Appleton.

————. 1919."Lessons from Housing Developments of the United States Housing Corporation." *Monthly Labor Review* 8: 1253–61.

————. 1927. "The Importance of Community Recreation Centers in Connection with Park Development." *Proceedings,* Nineteenth National Conference on City Planning, 9–11 May, Philadelphia, 230–39.

Olmsted, Frederick Law [Jr.], et al. 1916. "Building Lines." Reprinted from "Report of the Planning Board of Brookline, Mass., 1915." *Landscape Architecture* 7 (Oct.): 22–26.

Olmsted, Frederick Law [Jr.], and John Nolen. 1906. "The Normal Requirements of American Towns and Cities in Respect to the Public Open Spaces." *Charities* 16 (July): 411–26.

Olmsted Associates Collection. Manuscripts Division, Library of Congress, Washington, D.C.

Olmsted, Vaux, and Company. 1869. *Preliminary Report Respecting a Public Park in Buffalo, and a Copy of the Act of the Legislature Authorizing its Establishment.* Buffalo.

O'Neill, A. W. 1904. "Chicago Playgrounds and Park Extension." *Charities* 12 (6): 798–99.

Osborn, Marian Lorena. 1928. "The Development of Recreation in the South Park System of Chicago." Ph.D. diss., University of Chicago.

Owens, Allynne Tosca. 1986. "Can Historic Preservation Succeed in Minority Communities? A Look at the Beach Institute Historic Neighborhood in Savannah, Ga." Master's thesis, University of Florida.

Pace, Clifford, and Phillip Green Jr. 1949. *Public Water Supply and Sewerage Disposal in Charlotte and Mecklenburg County: Consolidation Possibilities.* Chapel Hill: University of North Carolina, Institute of Government.

Palen, J. John, and Bruce London, eds. 1983. *Gentrification, Displacement, and Neighborhood Revitalization.* Albany: State University of New York Press.

Park, Robert E., Ernest W. Burgess, and Roderick D. McKenzie. 1925. *The City.* Chicago: University of Chicago Press.

"Pattern for the Future." 1943. *Architectural Forum* 78 (May): 4.

Pease, J. N. 1949. *A Master Plan Outline for Charlotte, 1949.* Charlotte: City of Charlotte.

Peattie, Lisa. 1987. *Planning: Rethinking Ciudad Guayana.* Ann Arbor: University of Michigan Press.

Penick, James Jr. 1968. *Progressive Politics and Conservation: The Ballinger-Pinchot Affair.* Chicago: University of Chicago Press.

———. 1974. "The Progressive and the Environment." In *The Progressive Era,* edited by Lewis Gould. Syracuse: Syracuse University Press.

Perkins, Dwight Heald. 1908. "A Metropolitan Park System for Chicago." *World Today* 8 (Nov.): 268–74.

Perry, Clarence Arthur. 1910. "The Wider Use of the School Plant." New York: Russell Sage Foundation.

———. 1929. *The Neighborhood and Community Plan of New York and its Environs.* New York: Committee of the Regional Plan of New York.

Perry, Lewis. 1984. *Intellectual Life in America: A History.* Chicago: University of Chicago Press.

Peterson, Charles E. 1993. *Colonial St. Louis: Building a Creole Capital.* 2d ed. Tucson: Patrice Press.

Peterson, Iver. 1991. "Planned Communities are Multiplying." *New York Times* (21 Apr.), sec. 10, pp. 1, 11.

Peterson, Jon A. 1976. "The City Beautiful Movement: Forgotten Origins and Lost Meanings." *Journal of Urban History* 2 (Aug.): 415–34.

———. 1983. "The Impact of Sanitary Reform upon American Urban Planning, 1840–1890." In *Introduction to Planning History in the United States,* edited by Donald A. Krueckeberg. New Brunswick, N.J.: Rutgers University Center for Urban Policy Research.

———. 1985. "The Nation's First Comprehensive City Plan: A Political Analysis of the McMillan Plan for Washington, D.C., 1900–1902." *Journal of the American Planning Association* 51 (Spring): 144–45.

———. 1991. "The Mall, the McMillan Plan, and the Origins of American City Planning." In *The Mall in Washington, 1791–1991,* edited by Richard Longstreth. Washington, D.C.: National Gallery of Art.

Peterson, Paul E. 1981. *City Limits.* Chicago: University of Chicago Press.

Pevsner, Nikolaus. 1944. "Price on Picturesque Planning." *Architectural Review* 95: 47.

Philadelphia City Planning Commission. 1988. *Plan for Center City.* Philadelphia.

Bibliography

Phillips, Kevin. 1990. *The Politics of Rich and Poor: Wealth and the American Electorate in the Reagan Aftermath.* New York: Random House.

Pinchot, Gifford. 1947. *Breaking New Ground.* New York: Harcourt, Brace.

"Planning and Development in Philadelphia" (special issue). 1960. *Journal of the American Institute of Planners* 26 (3): 155–241.

Polos, Nicholas. 1984. "George White Marston: The Merchant Prince of San Diego." *Journal of San Diego History* 30 (4): 252–78.

Portland Downtown Plan. 1972. Portland, Ore.: City Council.

"Postwar Planning versus Mobility." 1943. *Southern California Business* (16 Aug.): 1–3.

Pourade, Richard. 1960–77. *History of San Diego. The Explorers,* vol. 1 (1960); *Time of the Bells,* vol. 2 (1961); *The Silver Dons,* vol. 3 (1963); *The Glory Years,* vol. 4 (1964); *Gold in the Sun,* vol. 5 (1965); *The Rising Tide,* vol. 6 (1967); *City of the Dream,* vol. 7 (1977). San Diego: Union Tribune Publishing Co.

Pratt, Joseph H. 1922. "Forestry Problems of the Southern Appalachian and Southeastern States." *North Carolina Geological and Economic Survey* circular 3.

Pred, Alan. 1977. *City-Systems in Advanced Economies.* New York: John Wiley.

Primm, Wilson. [1832] 1952. "History of St. Louis." In *The Early Histories of St. Louis,* edited by John Francis McDermott. St. Louis, Mo.: St. Louis Historical Documents Foundation.

Pryde, Philip, ed. 1992. *San Diego: An Introduction to the Region, An Historical Geography of the Natural Environments and Human Development of San Diego County.* 3d ed. Dubuque: Kendall/Hunt.

Pushkarev, Boris. 1963. "Highway Location as a Problem of Urban and Landscape Design." *Highway Research Record* 23: 7–18.

Quastler, I. E. 1992. "San Diegans on the Move: Transportation in the County." In *San Diego: An Introduction to the Region, An Historical Geography of the Natural Environments and Human Development of San Diego County.* 3d ed., edited by Philip Pryde, 165–84. Dubuque: Kendall/Hunt.

Raban, Jonathan. 1974. *Soft City.* London: Hamilton.

Rabin, Yale. 1968. "Evaluation of the Application to the Department of Housing and Urban Development by the City of Birmingham, Alabama, for a Grant to Plan a Comprehensive City Demonstration Program." Unpub. rpt., National Archives, Model Cities Reports 1966–73, Box 3, NC3-207-84-2, RG 207.

Rae, John B. 1968. *Climb to Greatness: The American Aircraft Industry, 1920–1960.* Cambridge, Mass.: MIT Press.

Bibliography

Rafferty, Edward C. 1991. "Orderly City, Orderly Lives: The City Beautiful Movement in St. Louis." *Gateway Heritage* 11 (4): 40–62.

Rainwater, Clarence E. 1921. *The Play Movement in the United States.* Chicago: University of Chicago Press.

Rannells, John. 1956. *The Core of the City: A Pilot Study of Changing Land Uses in Central Business Districts.* New York: Columbia University Press.

———. 1961. "Approaches to Analysis." *Journal of the American Institute of Planners* 27 (Feb.): 17–25.

Ranney, Victoria Post. 1972. *Olmsted in Chicago.* Chicago: R. R. Donnelley.

Regional Plan Association. 1962. *Spread City: Projections of Development Trends and the Issues They Pose.* New York.

———. 1990. *Visions for the Region Tomorrow: Towards a New Regional Plan.* New York.

Regional Planning Federation of the Philadelphia Tri-State District. 1932. "The Subdivision of Land." In *The Regional Plan of the Philadelphia Tri-State District.* Philadelphia.

Reich, Robert B. 1991. "Secession of the Successful." *New York Times Magazine* (20 Jan.).

Reiter, Beth, Rita S. Jones, Lee Adler II, and Catherine Swan Adler. 1983. *Preservation for People in Savannah.* Savannah, Ga.: Savannah Landmark Rehabilitation Project.

"Remarks at the Civic Luncheon." 1928. *Proceedings of the National Conference on City Planning, 1928.* Philadelphia: NCCP.

"Report of the Board of Public Improvements." 1878. In *The Mayor's Message, with Accompanying Documents, to the City Council of the City of St. Louis.* St. Louis, Mo.: Times Printing House.

Reps, John. 1979. *Cities of the American West: A History of Frontier Urban Planning.* Princeton: Princeton University Press.

———. 1980. *Town Planning in Frontier America.* Columbia, Mo.: University of Missouri Press.

Richardson, Lemont K. 1956. "Private Land Claims in Missouri." *Missouri Historical Review* 50: 132–44, 271–86, 387–99.

Richmond City Planning Commission. 1984. *Downtown Plan.* Richmond: City Planning Commission.

Robbins, George W., and L. Deming Tilton, eds. 1941. *Los Angeles: Preface to a Master Plan.* Los Angeles.

Roberts, Coleman W. 1944a. *A Pattern for Charlotte.* Charlotte: Chamber of Commerce.

———. 1944b. *A Pattern for Charlotte.* rev. ed. Charlotte: Chamber of Commerce.

Robinson, Charles Mulford. 1906. *Proposed Plans for the Improvement of the City of Denver.* Denver, Colo.: Denver Art Commission.

Rogers, Jerry. 1969. *National Register of Historic Places Inventory Nomination Form: Savannah Historic District.* Washington, D.C.: National Park Service.

Rohe, William M., and Lauren B. Gates. 1985. *Planning with Neighborhoods.* Chapel Hill: University of North Carolina Press.

Roper, Laura Wood. 1973. *FLO: A Biography of Frederick Law Olmsted.* Baltimore: The Johns Hopkins University Press.

Rose, Mark H. 1979. *Interstate: Express Highway Politics, 1941–1956.* Lawrence: Regents Press of Kansas.

———. 1990. *Interstate: Express Highway Politics, 1939–1989.* Knoxville, Tenn.: University of Tennessee Press.

Rose, Mark H., and Bruce E. Seeley. 1990. "Getting the Interstate System Built: Road Engineers and the Implementation of Public Policy, 1955–1985." *Journal of Policy History* 2(1): 23–55.

Rosen, Christine Meisner. 1986. *The Limits of Power: Great Fires and the Process of City Growth in America.* New York: Cambridge University Press.

Ross, John R. 1975. "Benton MacKaye: The Appalachian Trail." *Journal of the American Institute of Planners* 41 (Mar.): 110–114.

Rouse, James W. 1957. "Will Downtown Face Up to Its Future?" *Urban Land* 16 (Feb.): 1–5.

Rouzie, J. Ben. 1954. Planning for Preservation of Historical Areas. In *Planning 1954, Proceedings of The Annual National Planning Conference, Philadelphia, Pennsylvania.* Chicago, Ill.: American Society Planning Officials.

Rusk, David. 1993. *Cities without Suburbs.* Washington, D.C.: Woodrow Wilson Center Press.

Ruskin, John. [1907] 1968. *Unto This Last: And Other Essays on Art and Political Economy.* London: J. M. Dent.

Russwurm, Lorne. 1964. "The Central Business District Retail Sales Mix, 1948–58." *Annals of the Association of American Geographers* 54 (Dec.): 524–36.

St. Clair, David J. 1986. *The Motorization of American Cities.* New York: Praeger.

St. Louis Common Claims Book. 1835–1838. Mesker Collection, Missouri Historical Society Archives.

St. Louis Municipal Ordinances. 1821– . St. Louis City Law Library.

San Diego, City of. 1908–15. *Resolution* [Ordinance] *Book*[s].

———. 1913. *Record of Common Council.* Bk. 33, 4 Nov. 1912 to 23 Apr. 1913.

———. 1931. *Charter of the City of San Diego, California.* San Diego: Dougherty.

———. 1958. *Charter . . . as Amended.* San Diego.

————. 1967. *A General Plan for the City of San Diego.* San Diego.

————. 1979. *Progress Guide and General Plan.* San Diego.

San Diego Chamber of Commerce, Temporary Postwar Plans Committee. 1942. "Post War San Diego." San Diego.

San Diego City and County Directory. 1915. San Diego: Directory Co.

San Diego Committee for Economic Development: The Postwar Planning Committee of the San Diego Chamber of Commerce. 1944. "San Diego." 7 July. San Diego.

San Francisco, City and County of San Francisco, Postwar Planning Committee. 1945. "Report of the Citizens Postwar Planning Committee to Mayor R. D. Lapham." San Francisco.

San Francisco, City and County of San Francisco, Postwar Planning Committee. Subcommittee on Revenue and Taxation. 1945. "Report to Chairman Adrien J. Falk of the Citizens Post War Planning Committee." San Francisco.

San Francisco Department of City Planning. 1985. *Downtown Plan.* San Francisco: Office of the Clerk, Board of Supervisors.

San Francisco Planning and Housing Association. Special Committee. 1943. "A Report on the Japanese Section." San Francisco.

Sanders, Heywood T. 1977. "The Politics of City Redevelopment." Ph.D. diss., Harvard University.

Sandweiss, Eric. 1991. "Construction and Community in South St. Louis, 1850–1910." Ph.D. diss., University of California, Berkeley.

Sassen, Saskia. 1991. *The Global City: New York, London, Tokyo.* Princeton, N.J.: Princeton University Press.

Savannah's Golden Heritage. 1958. Savannah, Ga.: Chatham County-Savannah Metropolitan Planning Commission.

Sayer, Andrew. 1984. *Method in Social Science: A Realist Approach.* London: Hutchinson.

Schaffer, Daniel. 1982. *Garden Cities for America: The Radburn Experience.* Philadelphia: Temple University Press.

————, ed. 1988. *Two Centuries of American Planning.* Baltimore: The Johns Hopkins University Press.

Schellie, Kenneth L. 1945. "Indiana's Planning Program." *American Planning and Civic Annual, 1945.* 75–80.

Scheme for the Separation and Re-organization of the Governments of St. Louis City and County and Charter for the City of St. Louis. 1877. St. Louis, Mo.: Woodward, Tiernan, and Hale.

Schiesl, Martin. 1977. *The Politics of Efficiency: Municipal Administration and Reform in America, 1880–1920.* Berkeley: University of California Press.

————. 1980. "City Planning and the Federal Government in World War II: The Los Angeles Experience." *California History* 59 (Summer): 127–43.

Schill, Michael H., and Richard P. Nathan. 1983. *Revitalizing America's Cities: Neighborhood Reinvestment and Displacement.* New York: State University of New York Press.

Schmid, Calvin F. 1941. "Land Values as an Ecological Index." *Research Studies of the State College of Washington* 9 (Mar.): 16–36.

Schuldiner, Lori H. 1981. "Fairview, Camden's Best Kept Secret." Unpublished paper, Camden County Historical Society, Camden, New Jersey.

Schultz, Stanley K. 1989. *Constructing Urban Culture: American Cities and City Planning, 1800–1920.* Philadelphia: Temple University Press.

Schuyler, David. 1984. "Evolution of the Anglo-American Rural Cemetery: Landscape Architecture as Social and Cultural History." *Journal of Garden History* 4 (July): 291–304.

————. 1986. *The New Urban Landscape: The Redefinition of City Form in Nineteenth-Century America.* Baltimore: The Johns Hopkins University Press.

Schwartz, Gail Garfield. 1984. *Where's Main Street, U.S.A?* Westport, Conn.: Eno Foundation for Transportation.

Schwartz, Gary T. 1976. "Urban Freeways and the Interstate System." *Southern California Law Review* 49 (Mar.): 406–513.

Schwartz, Joel. 1993. *The New York Approach: Robert Moses, Urban Liberals, and Redevelopment of the Inner City.* Columbus: Ohio State University Press.

Scott, Allen J. 1988. *Metropolis: From the Division of Labor to Urban Form.* Berkeley: University of California Press.

————. 1991. "The Aerospace-Electronics Industrial Complex of Southern California: The Formative Years, 1940–1960." *Research Policy* 20: 439–56.

Scott, Mary L. 1991. *San Diego: Air Capital of the West.* Virginia Beach: Donning Co. for San Diego Aerospace Museum.

Scott, Mel. 1959. *The San Francisco Bay Area: A Metropolis in Perspective.* Berkeley: Institute of Governmental Studies, University of California.

————. 1969. *American City Planning since 1890.* Berkeley: University of California Press.

Seattle, City of. 1985. *Land Use and Transportation Plan for Downtown Seattle.* Seattle.

Seely, Bruce. 1987. *Building the American Highway System: Engineers as Policy Makers.* Philadelphia: Temple University Press.

Seibels, George. Papers. Manuscripts and Archives Division, Birmingham Public Library, Birmingham, Alabama.

Sevilla, Charles Martin. 1971. "Asphalt through the Model Cities: A Study of Highways and the Urban Poor." *Journal of Urban Law* 49 (2): 297–322.

Sharp, Ernest G. B. 1955. *Dealey of The Dallas News.* New York: Henry Holt.

Sharpe, William, and Leonard Wallock. 1992. "The Edge of a New Frontier?" *Journal of the American Planning Association* 58(3): 393–95.

———. 1994a. "Bold New City or Built-Up 'Burb? Redefining Contemporary Suburbia." *American Quarterly* 46 (Mar.): 1–30.

———. 1994b. "Contextualizing Suburbia." *American Quarterly* 46 (Mar.): 55–61.

———, eds., 1983. *Visions of the Modern City: Essays in History, Art, and Literature.* New York: Columbia University Press.

"Shopping Center: Linda Vista, California. . . ." 1944. *Architectural Forum* (Sept.): 81–93.

Showley, Roger. 1988. "Growth Issues Have been Sprouting since 1917." *San Diego Union,* 7 Feb.

———. 1992. "Visionary Plans for San Diego Have Gone Largely Unfulfilled." *San Diego Union-Tribune,* 26 July, p. F-10.

Shurtleff, Flavel. 1915. "The Landscape Architect in City Planning." *Landscape Architecture* 5 (Apr.): 143–44.

Shurtleff, Flavel, and Frederick Law Olmsted [Jr.]. 1914. *Carrying Out the City Plan: The Practical Application of American Law in the Execution of City Plans.* New York: Survey Associates.

Sies, Mary Corbin. 1987a. "American Country House Architecture in Context: The Suburban Ideal in the East and Midwest, 1877–1917." Ph.D. diss., University of Michigan.

———. 1987b. "The City Transformed: Nature, Technology, and the Suburban Ideal, 1877–1917." *Journal of Urban History* 14: 81–111.

———. 1990. "Paradise Retained: An Analysis of Persistence in Planned, Exclusive Suburbs, 1880–1980." *Proceedings of the Third Conference in American Planning History.* Hilliard, Ohio: Society for American City and Regional Planning History.

———. 1991. "Toward a Performance Theory of the Suburban Ideal." In *Perspectives in Vernacular Architecture* 4, edited by Thomas Carter and Bernard Herman. Columbia: University of Missouri Press.

———. 1993. " The Politics and Ethics of Studying the Vernacular Environment of Others." *Vernacular Architecture Newsletter* 57 (Fall): 14–17.

Silver, Christopher. 1983. "The Ordeal of City Planning in Postwar Richmond, Virginia: A Quest for Greatness." *Journal of Urban History* 10 (Nov.): 33–60.

———. 1984a. "Norfolk and the Navy: The Evolution of City-Federal Relations, 1917–46." In *The Martial Metropolis: U.S. Cities in War and Peace,* edited by Roger W. Lotchin, 109–34. New York: Praeger.

————. 1984b. *Twentieth-Century Richmond: Planning, Politics, and Race.* Knoxville: University of Tennessee Press.

————. 1985. "Neighborhood Planning in Historical Perspective." *Journal of the American Planning Association* 51 (2): 161–74.

————. 1987. "Urban Planning in the New South." *Journal of Planning Literature* 2 (Autumn): 371–83.

————. 1990. "Revitalizing the Urban South: Neighborhood Preservation and Planning since the 1920s." *Journal of the American Planning Association* 57 (1): 69–84.

————. 1991. "The Racial Origins of Zoning: Southern Cities from 1910 to 1940." *Planning Perspectives* 6: 189–205.

Simkhovitch, Mary K. 1910. "Address by Mrs. V. G. Simkhovitch, of Greenwich House, New York City, at City Planning Banquet, Saturday Evening, May 22, 1909." U.S. Congress. Senate. Committee on the District of Columbia. *Hearing on the Subject of City Planning*, 61st Cong., 2d sess., S. Doc. 422.

————. 1938. *Neighborhood: My Story of Greenwich House.* New York: W. W. Norton.

————. 1943a. "Neighborhoods and Planning." Simkhovitch Papers. Schlesinger Library, Radcliffe College, Cambridge, Mass.

————. 1943b. "Neighborhood Planning and the Settlements." *Survey Midmonthly* (June): 174–75.

————. 1944a. "Neighborhood and Nation." National Federation of Settlements and Neighborhood Centers, New York. Papers, 1891–1961.

————. 1944b. "The Neighborhood Looks at Planning." Simkhovitch Papers. Schlesinger Library, Radcliffe College, Cambridge, Mass.

————. 1949. *Here Is God's Plenty: Reflections on American Social Advance.* New York: Harper and Brothers.

Sitte, Camillo. [1889] 1909. *City Building According to Artistic Principles.* Vienna: Graeser and Co.

Sklar, Kathryn Kish. 1985. "Hull House in the 1890s: A Community of Women Reformers." *Signs: Journal of Women in Culture and Society* 10 (4): 658–77.

————, ed. 1986. *The Autobiography of Florence Kelley: Notes on Sixty Years.* Chicago: Charles H. Kerr.

Sloane, David. 1991. "The American Cemetery: Private Enterprise in the Public City, 1830–1990." *Proceedings of the Fourth National Conference on American Planning History.* Hilliard, Ohio: Society for American City and Regional Planning History.

Smith, Chloethiel Woodard. 1962. "Esthetic Lion-Taming in the City." *Journal of the American Institute of Architects* 38 (Nov.): 37.

Smith, Larry. 1961. "Space for the CBD's Functions." *Journal of the American Institute of Planners* 27 (Feb.): 35–42.

Smith, Neil, and Peter Williams, eds. 1986. *Gentrification of the City.* Boston, Mass.: Unwin Hyman.

Snedcof, Harold. 1985. *Cultural Facilities in Mixed-Use Development.* Washington, D.C.: Urban Land Institute.

Social Science Research Council. 1939. *City Manager Government in Charlotte.* New York: Social Science Research Council.

Soja, Edward W. 1986. "Taking Los Angeles Apart: Some Fragments of a Critical Human Geography." *Environment and Planning D: Society and Space* (Feb.): 255–72.

Sorkin, Michael, ed. 1992. *Variations on a Theme Park: The New American City and the End of Public Space.* New York: Hill and Wang.

Southworth, Michael, and Peter M. Owens. 1993. "Evolving Metropolis: Studies of Community, Neighborhood, and Street Form at the Urban Edge." *Journal of the American Planning Association* 59 (3): 217–87.

Squires, Gregory, ed. 1989. *Unequal Partnerships: The Political Economy of Urban Redevelopment in Postwar America.* New Brunswick, N.J.: Rutgers University Press.

Stach, Patricia Burgess. 1988. "Deed Restrictions and Subdivision Development in Columbus, Ohio, 1900–1970." *Journal of Urban History* 15 (1): 42–68.

———. 1989. "Real Estate Development and Urban Form: Roadblocks in the Path to Residential Exclusivity." *Business History Review* 63: 356–83.

Starr, Raymond. 1986. *San Diego: A Pictorial History.* Norfolk: Donning Co.

Stavrolakis, Kristina, and Beth Lattimore. 1974. National Register of Historic Places Inventory Nomination Form: Savannah Victorian Historic District. Atlanta: Georgia Department of Natural Resources.

Steel and Garnet. 1936. Cover portrait of John Nolen (June). Philadelphia, Pa.: Girard College.

Stein, Clarence S. 1978. *Toward New Towns for America.* Cambridge, Mass.: MIT Press.

Sternlieb, George. 1963. "The Future of Retailing in the Downtown Core." *Journal of the American Institute of Planners* 29 (May): 102–11.

Stevenson, Elizabeth. 1977. *Park Maker: A Life of Frederick Law Olmsted.* New York: Macmillan.

Stilgoe, John. 1988. *Borderland: Origins of the American Suburb, 1820–1939.* New Haven: Yale University Press.

Bibliography

Stipe, Robert E., and Antoinette J. Lee, eds. 1987. *The American Mosaic: Preserving A Nation's Heritage.* Washington, D.C.: US/ICOMOS.

Stone, Clarence N. 1976. *Economic Growth and Neighborhood Discontent: System Bias in the Urban Renewal Program of Atlanta.* Chapel Hill: University of North Carolina Press.

Stone, Harold A., Don K. Price, and Kathryn H. Stone. 1939. *City Manager Government in Dallas.* Chicago: Public Administration Service.

Stone, Harold A., Kathryn H. Stone, and Don K. Price. 1940. *City Manager Government in Nine Cities.* Chicago: Public Administration Service.

Stormann, Wayne F. 1991. "The Ideology of the American Urban Parks and Recreation Movement: Past and Future." *Leisure Sciences* 13 (Apr.–June): 142–43.

Supplementary Report of the Urbanism Committee to the National Resources Committee. 1939. *Urban Planning and Land Policies.* 2 vols. Washington, D.C.: Government Printing Office.

Suttles, Gerald. 1990. *The Man-Made City: The Land Use Confidence Game in Chicago.* Chicago: University of Chicago Press.

Swenarton, Mark. 1981. *Homes Fit for Heroes: The Politics and Architecture of Early State Housing in Britain.* London: Heinemann.

Taylor, Graham Romeyn. 1906. "The Recreation Centers of Chicago." *17th and 18th Annual Reports of the City Parks Association of Philadelphia,* 54–64. Philadelphia.

———. 1907a. "Field Houses of Chicago." *The Playground* 1: 49.

———. 1907b. "How They Played in Chicago." *The Playground* 1: 1–10.

———. 1908. "Chicago Parks and Their Landscape Architecture." *Architectural Record* 24 (July).

———. 1910. "Recreation Developments in Chicago Parks." *Annals of the American Academy of Political and Social Science* 35 (Mar.): 88–105.

———. [1915] 1970. *Satellite Cities: A Study of Industrial Suburbs.* New York: D. Appleton.

Teaford, Jon C. 1979. *City and Suburb: The Political Fragmentation of Metropolitan America, 1850–1970.* Baltimore: The Johns Hopkins University Press.

———. 1984. *The Unheralded Triumph: City Government in America, 1870–1900.* Baltimore: The Johns Hopkins University Press.

———. 1990. *The Rough Road to Renaissance: Urban Revitalization in America, 1940–1985.* Baltimore: The Johns Hopkins University Press.

"Team Concepts for Urban Highways and Urban Design." 1968. *Highway Research Record* 220.

Thomas, June Manning. 1990. "Attacking Urban Blight in Postwar Detroit." In *Proceedings of the Third National Conference on American Planning*

History, 165–84. Hilliard, Ohio: Society for American City and Regional Planning History.

———. 1991. "The Cities Left Behind." *Built Environment* 17 (3/4): 218–31.

Thompson, Robert A., Hyland Lewis, and Davis McEntire. 1960. "Atlanta and Birmingham: A Comparative Study in Negro Housing." In *Studies in Housing and Minority Groups,* edited by Nathan Glazer and Davis McEntire. Berkeley: University of California Press.

Thurber, Pamela, ed. 1985. *Controversies in Historic Preservation: Understanding the Movement Today.* Washington, D.C.: National Trust for Historic Preservation.

Tilton, L. Deming. 1943a. "A County Plans Its Post-War Public Works." *American City* (Jan.): 40.

———. 1943b. "Post-War City and Regional Planning." *American City* (Feb.): 40.

———. 1943c. "San Francisco Plans Its Future." *California Magazine of the Pacific* 43 (Dec.): 15.

Tindall, George. 1958. "The Significance of Howard W. Odum to Southern History: A Preliminary Estimate." *Journal of Southern History* 24 (Aug.): 290–307.

"To Picture Congestion." 1908. *Charities and the Commons* 19 (Feb.): 1639.

Toll, Seymour I. 1969. *Zoned American.* New York: Grossman Publishers.

Trafzer, Clifford, and Richard Carrico. 1992. "American Indians: The Country's First Residents." In *San Diego: An Introduction to the Region, An Historical Geography of the Natural Environments and Human Development of San Diego County.* 3d ed., edited by Philip Pryde, 51–67. Dubuque: Kendall/Hunt.

Tunnard, Christopher. 1951. "Cities by Design." *Journal of the American Institute of Planners* 17 (3): 142–50.

———. 1970. *The City of Man: A New Approach to the Recovery of Beauty in American Cities.* 2d ed. New York: Charles Scribner's Sons.

Tunnard, Christopher, and Boris Pushkarev. 1963. *Man-Made America: Chaos or Control?* New Haven, Conn.: Yale University Press.

"Twenty-five Years and After: The Anniversary Conference Last Week of the New York Charity Organization Society." 1907. *Charities and the Commons* 19 (Nov.): 1113–46.

Tyrwhitt, Jaqueline, Jose L. Sert, and E. N. Rogers. 1952. *The Heart of the City: Towards the Humanisation of Urban Life.* New York: Pellegrini and Cudahy.

Ulrickson Committee. 1927. *Forward, Dallas: A Program of Public Improvements.* Dallas.

Bibliography

"Under the Knife, or All For Their Own Good." 1964. *Time* (Nov.): 60–75.

U.S. Bureau of Public Roads. 1939. *Toll Roads and Free Roads.* 76th Cong., 1st sess., H. Doc. 272. Washington, D.C.: Government Printing Office.

———. 1955. *General Location of National System of Interstate Highways.* Washington, D.C.: Government Printing Office.

United States Conference on Mayors. Special Committee on Historic Preservation. 1966. *With Heritage So Rich.* New York: Random House.

U.S. Congress. 1943. Senate. Special Committee on Post-War Economic Policy and Planning. *Post-War Economic Policy and Planning, Hearings before a Subcommittee of the Special Committee on Post-War Economic Policy and Planning, Pursuant to S. Res. 102,* 78th Cong., 1st sess.

U.S. Department of Commerce. 1988. *County and City Data Book.* Washington, D.C.: Government Printing Office.

U.S. Department of Commerce. Bureau of the Census. 1850–1990. Decennial *U.S. Census* reports. Washington, D.C.: Government Printing Office.

———. 1944. *Wartime Changes in Population and Family Characteristics: Los Angeles Congested Production Area, April, 1944.* Series CA-2, No. 5. Washington, D.C.: Government Printing Office.

———. 1947. *County Data Book 1947.* Washington, D.C.: Government Printing Office.

———. 1952. *A Report of the Seventeenth Decennial Census of the United States Population, II: Characteristics of the Population, Pt. 5, California.* Washington, D.C.: Government Printing Office.

U.S. Department of Commerce. Bureau of Standards. 1933. *Zoned Municipalities in the United States.* Letter Circular LC-374, May 5. Washington, D.C.: Government Printing Office.

U.S. Department of Commerce. Civil Aeronautics Administration. 1946. *United States Military Aircraft Acceptances, 1940–45: Aircraft, Engine, and Propeller Production.* Washington, D.C.: Government Printing Office.

U.S. Department of Housing and Urban Development (HUD). 1976. *New Communities: Problems and Potentials.* Washington, D.C.: Government Printing Office.

———. 1977. *Citizen Participation: Experience and Trends in Community Development Block Grant Entitlement Communities.* Washington, D.C.: Government Printing Office.

U.S. Department of Labor. Bureau of Labor Statistics. 1940. "Building Operations: Builders of 1-Family Houses in 72 Cities." *Monthly Labor Review.* Washington, D.C.: Government Printing Office.

———. 1944. "Average Hourly Earnings in the Airframe Industry, 1943." Bulletin no. 790. Reprinted in *Monthly Labor Review.* Washington, D.C.: Government Printing Office.

———. 1945. "Probable Volume of Postwar Construction." Bulletin no. 825. Washington, D.C.: Government Printing Office.

———. 1954. "Structure of the Residential Building Industry in 1949." Bulletin no. 1170. Washington, D.C.: Government Printing Office.

U.S. Federal Housing Administration. 1936–42. *Annual Report.* Washington, D.C.: Government Printing Office.

———. 1936a. *Principles of Planning Small Houses.* Technical Bulletin 4. Washington, D.C.: Government Printing Office.

———. 1936b. *Planning Neighborhoods for Small Homes.* Technical Bulletin 5. Washington, D.C.: Government Printing Office.

———. 1939. "Monthly Amortization Payment Computing Chart." *Insured Mortgage Portfolio* (Aug.).

U.S. Housing Corporation. 1920. *Report of the United States Housing Corporation.* Vol. 1, edited by James Ford. Washington, D.C.: Government Printing Office.

U.S. Housing and Home Finance Agency. 1954. *How Localities Can Develop a Workable Program for Urban Renewal.* Washington, D.C.: Government Printing Office.

———. 1962. *Workable Program for Community Improvement.* Washington, D.C.: Government Printing Office.

U.S. Shipping Board Emergency Fleet Corporation. 1920. "Housing the Shipbuilders." Philadelphia: Government Printing Office.

Unwin, Raymond. [1909] 1919. *Town Planning in Practice: An Introduction to the Art of Designing Cities and Suburbs.* New York: Charles Scribner's Sons.

Upton, Dell. 1985. *Holy Things and Profane: Anglican Parish Churches in Colonial Virginia.* Cambridge, Mass.: MIT Press.

"Valencia Gardens: USHA War Housing in San Francisco." 1944. *Pencil Points* 25 (Jan.): 26–35.

Vallejo, City of. Board of Planning Commissioners. 1945. "Master Plan." San Francisco: Builders of the West.

Vance, James E. 1964. *Geography and Urban Evolution in the San Francisco Bay Area.* Berkeley: Institute of Governmental Studies, University of California.

———. 1966. "Housing the Worker: The Employment Linkage as a Force in Urban Structure." *Economic Geography* 42: 294–325.

Vance, Rupert. 1935. *Human Geography of the South: A Study of Regional Resources and Human Adequacy.* Chapel Hill, N.C.: University of North Carolina Press.

Vann, David. 1978. "Events Leading to the 1963 Change from the Commission to the Mayor-Council form of Government in Birmingham, Alabama." Birmingham, Alabama: Center for Urban Affairs, University of Alabama in Birmingham.

Veiller, Lawrence. 1918. "The Government's Standards for War Housing." *Architectural Record* 43: 344–59.

Venturi, Robert, Denise Scott Brown, and Stephen Izenour. 1972. *Learning from Las Vegas.* Cambridge, Mass.: MIT Press.

Verge, Arthur C. 1988. "The Impact of the Second World War on Los Angeles, 1939–1945." Ph.D. diss., University of Southern California.

Viehe, Fred W. 1981. "Black Gold Suburbs: The Influence of the Extractive Industry on the Suburbanization of Los Angeles, 1890–1930." *Journal of Urban History* 8 (Nov.): 3–26.

Wade, Richard. 1988. "America's Cities Are (Mostly) Better Than Ever." In *The Making of Urban America,* edited by Raymond A. Mohl, 268–76. Wilmington, Del.: Scholarly Resources.

Waggoner, James T. Papers. Manuscripts and Archives Division, Birmingham Public Library, Birmingham, Alabama.

Walker, Robert Averill. [1941] 1950. *The Planning Function in Urban Government.* 2d ed. Chicago: University of Chicago Press.

Wallock, Leonard. 1991. "The Myth of the Master Builder: Robert Moses, New York, and the Dynamics of Metropolitan Development since World War II." *Journal of Urban History* 17 (Aug.): 339–62.

———, ed. 1988. *New York: Culture Capital of the World, 1940–1965.* New York: Rizzoli.

Ward, David. 1966. "The Industrial Revolution and the Emergence of Boston's Central Business District." *Economic Geography* 42 (Apr.): 152–71.

Ward, Stephen V., ed. 1992. *The Garden City: Past, Present, and Future.* London: E. & F. N. Spons.

Warner, Charles Dudley. 1890. *Our Italy.* New York: Harper's Magazine.

Warner, Chris. 1989. "Attractive Housing for Savannah's Poor." *Urban Land* 48 (2): 21–23.

Warner, Sam Bass Jr. 1972. *The Urban Wilderness: A History of the American City.* New York: Harper and Row.

———. [1962] 1978. *Streetcar Suburbs: The Process of Growth in Boston, 1870–1900.* Cambridge, Mass.: Harvard University Press.

———. 1987. *The Private City: Philadelphia in Three Periods of Its Growth.* 2d ed. Philadelphia: University of Pennsylvania Press.

Watkin, David. 1982. *The English Vision: The Picturesque in Architecture, Landscape, and Garden Design.* New York: Harper and Row.

Weaver, Clyde. 1984. *Regional Development and the Local Community: Planning, Politics, and Social Context.* New York: Wiley.

Bibliography

Weaver, Robert C. 1966. "Planning in the Great Society: A Crisis of Involvement." *Planning 1966.* Chicago: American Society of Planning Officials.

Webber, Melvin M. 1992. "The Joys of Automobility." In *The Car and the City: The Automobile, the Built Environment, and Daily Urban Life,* edited by Martin Wachs and Margaret Crawford, 274–84. Ann Arbor: University of Michigan Press.

Weinberg, Nathan. 1979. *Preservation in American Towns and Cities.* Boulder, Colo.: Westview Press.

Weinberg, Robert C. 1944. "A Technique for Urban Rehabilitation." *Journal of the American Institute of Planners* 10 (Autumn): 23–28.

Weiss, Marc A. 1987. *The Rise of the Community Builders: The American Real Estate Industry and Urban Land Planning.* New York: Columbia University Press.

———. 1989. "Real Estate History: An Overview and Research Agenda." *Business History Review* 63 (Summer): 241–82.

Weiss, Shirley. 1957. *The Central Business District in Transition.* Chapel Hill: Department of City and Regional Planning, University of North Carolina.

Weiss, Shirley, and Walter Thabit. 1961. "The Central Business District Plan for Downtown Baltimore." *Journal of the American Institute of Planners* 27 (Feb.): 88–91.

Weyeneth, Robert Richard. 1984. "Moral Spaces: Reforming the Landscape of Leisure in Urban America, 1850–1920." Ph.D. diss., University of California, Berkeley.

Wheaton, William Linous Cody. 1953. "The Evolution of Federal Housing Programs." Ph.D. diss., University of Chicago.

Whitaker, Charles H. 1919. "How Shall We Provide Good Houses for All?" In *Homes for Workmen.* New Orleans: Southern Pines Association.

———. 1920. "The Senate and the United States Housing Corporation." *Journal of the American Institute of Architects* 8: 103–4.

Whitaker, Charles H., et al. 1918. *The Housing Problem in War and Peace.* Washington, D.C.: The Octagon.

Whiting, Edward Clark, and William Lyman Phillips. 1958. "Frederick Law Olmsted, 1870–1957: An Appreciation of the Man and His Achievements." *Landscape Architecture* 48 (Apr.): 145–57.

Whitt, J. Allen. 1987. "Mozart in the Metropolis: The Arts Coalition and the Urban Growth Machine." *Urban Affairs Quarterly* 23 (Sept.):15–36.

Whitten, Robert. 1930. *Report on a Thoroughfare Plan for Boston.* Boston: Boston City Planning Board.

Whittick, Arnold, ed. 1974. *Encyclopedia of Urban Planning*. New York: McGraw-Hill.

Whyte, William H. 1980. *The Social Life of Small Urban Spaces*. Washington, D.C.: Conservation Foundation.

———. 1988. *City: Rediscovering the Center*. New York: Doubleday.

Wiebe, Robert H. 1967. *The Search for Order, 1877–1920*. New York: Hill and Wang.

Willis, Carol. 1986. "Skyscraper Utopias: Visionary Urbanism in the 1920s." In *Imagining Tomorrow: History, Technology, and the American Future*, edited by Joseph J. Corn, 164–87. Cambridge, Mass.: MIT Press.

Wills, Garry. 1987. *Reagan's America: Innocents at Home*. Garden City, N.Y.: Doubleday.

Wilson, Howard Eugene. 1927. "Mary R. McDowell and Her Work as Head Resident of the University of Chicago Settlement House, 1894–1904." Ph.D. diss., University of Chicago.

Wilson, William H. 1980. "The Ideology, Aesthetics, and Politics of the City Beautiful Movement." In *The Rise of Modern Urban Planning, 1800–1914*, edited by Anthony Sutcliffe, 165–98. London: Mansell.

———. 1983. "Adapting to Growth: Dallas, Texas, and the Kessler Plan." *Arizona and the West* 25 (Aug.): 245–60.

———. 1987. "The Billboard: Bane of the City Beautiful." *Journal of Urban History* 13 (Aug.): 397–99.

———. 1988. "The Seattle Park System and the Ideal of the City Beautiful." In *Two Centuries of American Planning*, edited by Daniel Schaffer, 113–37. Baltimore: The Johns Hopkins University Press.

———. 1989. *The City Beautiful Movement*. Baltimore: The Johns Hopkins University Press.

———. 1990. "Merely Unpractical Dreams: Removing the Texas & Pacific Tracks from Pacific Avenue." *Legacies: A History Journal for Dallas and North Central Texas* 2 (Fall): 26–34.

Wilson, William Julius. 1987. *The Truly Disadvantaged: The Inner City, the Underclass, and Public Policy*. Chicago: University of Chicago Press.

Winner, Langdon. 1977. *Autonomous Technology: Technics-out-of-Control as a Theme in Political Thought*. Cambridge, Mass.: MIT Press.

Wolfe, Margaret Ripley. 1987. *Kingsport, Tennessee: A Planned American City*. Lexington: University Press of Kentucky.

Wollenberg, Charles. 1985. *Golden Gate Metropolis: Perspectives on Bay Area History*. Berkeley: Institute of Governmental Studies, University of California.

———. 1990. *Marinship at War: Shipbuilding and Social Change in Wartime Sausalito*. Berkeley: Western Heritage Press.

Wood, E. A., L. V. Sheridan, and K. K. Hooper. 1920. "City Planning in Dallas, Texas." Proceedings of the National Conference on City Planning, 13–16. Philadelphia: NCCP.

Wood, Edith Elmer. 1919. *The Housing of the Unskilled Wage Worker.* New York: Macmillan.

Woods, Robert A., and Albert J. Kennedy. 1909. *Handbook of Settlements.* New York: Charities Publication Committee.

Worley, William S. 1990. *J. C. Nichols and the Shaping of Kansas City: Innovation in Planned Residential Communities.* Columbia: University of Missouri Press.

Wrenn, Douglas M. 1983. *Urban Waterfront Development.* Washington, D.C.: Urban Land Institute.

Wright, Deil S. 1988. *Understanding Intergovernmental Relations.* 3d ed. Pacific Grove, Calif.: Brooks/Cole.

————. 1990. "Policy Shifts in the Politics and Administration of Intergovernmental Relations, 1930s–1990s." *Annals of the American Academy of Political and Social Science* 509: 60–72.

Wright, Gwendolyn. 1981. *Building the Dream: A Social History of Housing in America.* Cambridge, Mass.: MIT Press.

Wright, Henry. 1920. "Platting City Areas for Small Homes." *Journal of the American Institute of Architects* 8: Suppl. 1–16.

————, ed. 1911. *City Plan Association Report.* St. Louis, Mo.

Wrigley, Robert L. Jr. 1983. "The Plan of Chicago." In *Introduction to Planning History in the United States,* edited by Donald A. Krueckeberg. New Brunswick, N.J.: Rutgers University Center for Urban Policy Research.

Young, Pauline V. 1956. *Scientific Social Surveys and Research.* 3d ed. Englewood Cliffs, N.J.: Prentice-Hall.

Young, Robert V. 1990. "A Pilot's-Eye View of Lindbergh Field." *San Diego Magazine* 42 (6): 98–103, 200–206.

Zaitzevsky, Cynthia. 1982. *Frederick Law Olmsted and the Boston Park System.* Cambridge, Mass.: Belknap Press.

Zeitz, Eileen. 1979. *Private Urban Renewal: A Differential Residential Trend.* Lexington, Mass.: Lexington Books.

Ziegler, Arthur P. Jr., Leopold Adler II, and Walter C. Kidney. 1975. *Revolving Funds for Historic Preservation: A Manual of Practice.* Pittsburgh: Ober Park Associates.

Zueblin, Charles. 1898. "Municipal Playgrounds in Chicago." *American Journal of Sociology* 4 (Sept.): 145–58.

————. 1903. *American Municipal Progress: Chapters in Municipal Sociology.* New York: Macmillan.

———. 1905. *A Decade of Civic Development.* Chicago: University of Chicago Press.

———. 1916. *American Municipal Progress.* New York: Macmillan.

Zueblin, Rho Fisk. 1907. "Playground Movement in Chicago." *The Playground* 1 (4): 3–13.

Zukin, Sharon. 1982. *Loft Living: Culture and Capital in Urban Change.* Baltimore: The Johns Hopkins University Press.

Contributors

CARL ABBOTT is professor of urban studies and planning at Portland State University. His recent publications on urban growth and planning in the United States in the twentieth century include *Metropolitan Frontier: Cities in the Modern American West* (University of Arizona Press, 1993) and *Planning the Oregon Way: A Twenty Year Evaluation* (Oregon State University Press, 1994).

PATRICIA BURGESS conducts historical research on housing and residential development, land-use controls, and the planning profession. Her book, *Planning for the Private Interest: Land Use Controls and Residential Patterns in Columbus, Ohio, 1900–1970,* was published by Ohio State University Press in 1994, and she is the coauthor of a forthcoming history of American zoning.

Contributors

CHARLES E. CONNERLY is an associate professor of urban and regional planning at Florida State University. He is coeditor of the *Journal of Planning Education and Research,* and his research interests include planning history and housing policy.

JOAN E. DRAPER is associate professor in the College of Architecture and Planning, University of Colorado, Boulder and Denver. She is author of *Edward H. Bennett: Architect and City Planner, 1874–1954* (Art Institute of Chicago, 1982) and recently published an essay on planning and riverfront development in Chicago in *Streets* (University of California Press, 1994).

CLIFF ELLIS is assistant professor in the Department of Geography and Planning at the State University of New York at Albany. His research interests include urban-form history and theory, planning history, land use and transportation, growth management, and urban design.

ROBERT B. FAIRBANKS is associate professor in the Department of History at the University of Texas, Arlington. He is author of *Making Better Citizens: Housing Reform and the Community Development Strategy in Cincinnati, 1890–1960* (University of Illinois Press, 1988) and coeditor with Kathleen Underwood of *Essays on Sunbelt Cities and Recent Urban America* (Texas A&M University Press, 1990).

THOMAS W. HANCHETT is a historian of the built environment who teaches at Youngstown State University. His University of North Carolina Ph.D. dissertation, "Sorting Out the New South City: Charlotte and Its Neighborhoods," was named 1993's "Best Dissertation in Southern Studies" by the St. George Tucker Society and "Best Dissertation in Urban History" by the Urban History Association.

JOHN HANCOCK is professor of urban design and planning, University of Washington, Seattle. He has published extensively on the career of planner John Nolen and is currently engaged in a book-length study of Nolen's contributions to modern urban and regional planning in the United States.

GREG HISE is an urban historian and assistant professor in the School of Urban and Regional Planning, University of Southern California. His research and writing focus on modern community planning, industrial location, and the twentieth-century expansion of American cities. In a forthcoming study (The Johns Hopkins University Press), the author examines these themes in detail.

ROBERT HODDER is the managing editor of the *Journal of the American Planning Association*. He holds a Ph.D. in city and regional planning from Cornell University and focuses in his research on historic preservation planning and its role in shaping urban community life.

ROBERT E. IRELAND holds a doctorate in social and intellectual history from the University of Maine and is the author of *Entering the Auto Age: The Early Automobile in North Carolina* (Division of Archives and History, North Carolina Department of Cultural Resources, 1990). He lives in Hillsborough, North Carolina, and teaches the history of technology at Wake Technical Community College in Raleigh.

MICHAEL H. LANG is associate professor and chairman of the Department of Urban Studies and Community Planning at the College of Arts and Sciences, Rutgers University, Camden, New Jersey. Author of several books and numerous articles and monographs dealing with housing and urban planning, he is currently studying the influence of John Ruskin on the Anglo-American town planning movement with the assistance of a grant from the National Endowment for the Arts.

ROGER W. LOTCHIN, professor of history at the University of North Carolina, is author of *Fortress California, 1910–1961: From Warfare to*

Contributors

Welfare (Oxford University Press, 1992); editor of *The Martial Metropolis: U.S. Cities in War and Peace* (Praeger, 1984); and editor of and contributor to *Fortress California at War: San Francisco, Los Angeles, Oakland, and San Diego, 1941–1945,* a special edition of the *Pacific Historical Review* (August, 1994). His chapter in this volume is drawn from the research for a book he is currently writing on the impact of World War II on California cities.

JON A. PETERSON is associate professor of history at Queens College of the City University of New York. He has written on the City Beautiful, mid-nineteenth-century sanitary reform, the McMillan Plan for Washington, D.C., the origins of American city planning and the Borough of Queens. He is currently completing a national study entitled *The Birth of American City Planning, 1840–1917.*

ERIC SANDWEISS is director of the Research Center at the Missouri Historical Society in St. Louis. He received his Ph.D. in architectural history from the University of California, Berkeley, and coauthored with David Harris *Eadweard Muybridge and the Photographic Panorama of San Francisco* (MIT Press, 1993).

TONY SCHUMAN is associate professor at the New Jersey Institute of Technology. Active with advocacy organizations including Planners Network and Architects/Designers/Planners for Social Responsibility, he has written on design and policy issues in numerous professional journals and edited anthologies. The research for his contribution to this volume was supported by an Independent Project grant from the New York State Council on the Arts.

ELLIOTT SCLAR is professor of urban planning at the Graduate School of Architecture, Planning and Preservation, Columbia University. An economist, he writes extensively on issues of urban economic development and public services.

Contributors

MARY CORBIN SIES is associate professor in the Department of American Studies at the University of Maryland, College Park; associate editor of *American Quarterly;* and past president of the Society for American City and Regional Planning History. A cultural historian and specialist in material culture studies, she writes on the history of suburbanization and the built environment.

CHRISTOPHER SILVER is professor of urban studies and planning, Virginia Commonwealth University. He is coauthor of the recently published book, *The Separate City: The Black Community in the Urban South, 1940–1968* (University Press of Kentucky, 1995) and is completing a book on the history of planning in the urban South since 1890. He is coeditor of the *Journal of the American Planning Association* and past president of the Society for American City and Regional Planning History.

JUNE MANNING THOMAS is professor in the Urban and Regional Planning Program at Michigan State University. She is a coauthor of *Detroit: Race and Uneven Development* (Temple University Press, 1987), author of *Planning a Finer City: Redevelopment, Urban Planning, and Race in Postwar Detroit* (The Johns Hopkins University Press, 1996), and coeditor of *U.S. Planning History and Race: Shadows in Black and White* (Sage Publications, 1996).

SUSAN MARIE WIRKA holds a master's degree in urban planning from the Graduate School of Architecture and Urban Planning at the University of California, Los Angeles. She is currently a doctoral candidate in the women's history program at the University of Wisconsin–Madison, where she is researching women's planning history.

Index

Index

Index